A Feminist Companion to Shakespeare

Blackwell Companions to Literature and Culture

This series offers comprehensive, newly written surveys of key periods and movements and certain major authors, in English literary culture and history. Extensive volumes provide new perspectives and positions on contexts and on canonical and post-canonical texts, orientating the beginning student in new fields of study and providing the experienced undergraduate and new graduate with current and new directions, as pioneered and developed by leading scholars in the field.

A FEMINIST COMPANION TO

SHAKESPEARE

EDITED BY **DYMPNA CALLAGHAN**

BLACKWELL
Publishers

Copyright © Blackwell Publishers Ltd 2000, 2001
Editorial matter, selection and organization copyright © Dympna Callaghan 2000, 2001

First published 2000
Reprinted 2001
First published in paperback 2001

Blackwell Publishers Inc.
350 Main Street
Malden, Massachusetts 02148
USA

Blackwell Publishers Ltd
108 Cowley Road
Oxford OX4 1JF
UK

Library of Congress Cataloging-in-Publication Data

A feminist companion to Shakespeare / edited by Dympna Callaghan.
p.   cm. – (Blackwell companions to literature and culture)
Includes bibliographical references (p.) and index.
ISBN 0-631-20806-2 (hbk: acid-free paper) ISBN 0631-20807-0 (pbk: acid-free paper)
1. Shakespeare, William, 1564–1616 – Characters – Women. 2. Shakespeare, William, 1564–1616 – Political and social views.   3. Feminism and literature – England – History – 16th century.   4. Feminism and literature – England – History – 17th century.   5. Women and literature – England – History – 16th century.   6. Women and literature – England – History – 17th century.   7. Sex role in literature.   8. Women in literature.   I. Title: Shakespeare. II. Callaghan, Dympna.   III. Series.

PR2991.F45   2000
822.3'3 – dc21   99-056237

British Library Cataloguing in Publication Data

A CIP catalogue record for this book is available from the British Library.

Typeset in 11 on 13pt Garamond 3
By Best-set Typesetter Ltd., Hong Kong
Printed in Great Britain by T. J. International, Padstow, Cornwall
This book is printed on acid-free paper.

Contents

PART THREE Social Economies

PART FOUR Race and Colonialism

PART FIVE Performing Sexuality

PART SIX　Religion

Contributors

Denise Albanese is Associate Professor of English and Cultural Studies at George Mason University. She is author of *New Science, New World* (Duke University Press, 1996), and has published on Francis Bacon, historicity and the early modern period, and recent Shakespeare films as global commodities. She is currently working on early modern mathematics instruction, and on Kenneth Branagh, Anglophilia, and the Americanization of Shakespeare.

Philippa Berry is Fellow and Director of Studies in English at King's College, Cambridge. She is the author of *Of Chastity and Power: Elizabethan Literature and the Unmarried Queen* (Routledge, 1989) and of *Shakespeare's Feminine Endings: Disfiguring Death in the Tragedies* (Routledge, 1999), and co-editor of *Shadow of Spirit: Postmodernism and Religion* (with Andrew Wernick, Routledge, 1993) and *The Texture of Renaissance Knowledge* (with Margaret Tudeau-Clayton, forthcoming).

Dympna Callaghan is William P. Tolley Distinguished Professor in the Humanities at Syracuse University. Her latest books are *Shakespeare Without Women: Representing Gender and Race on the Renaissance Stage* (Routledge, 1999) and an edited collection, *The Duchess of Malfi Casebook* (Macmillan, 2000). Earlier books include *Woman and Gender in Renaissance Tragedy* (Harvester, 1989), the co-authored volume, *The Weyward Sisters: Shakespeare and Feminist Politics* (Blackwell, 1994), and the co-edited *Feminist in Early Modern Culture* (Cambridge, 1995).

Juliet Dusinberre is the author of the pioneering work in feminist criticism, *Shakespeare and the Nature of Women* (Macmillan, 1975, 1996). She has written two books on Virginia Woolf: *Alice to the Lighthouse* (Macmillan, 1987, 1999) and *Virginia Woolf's Renaissance* (Macmillan, 1997), and is currently editing *As You Like It* for Arden 3. She is M.C. Bradbrook Fellow in English at Girton College, Cambridge.

Juliet Fleming is a University Lecturer in the Faculty of Cambridge, and a Fellow of Trinity Hall. She is writing a book on writing practices in early modern England, which will be published by Reaktion Press.

Margo Hendricks is Associate Professor in the Department of Literature at the University of California at Santa Cruz. She is the co-editor of *Women, Race, and Writing in the Early Modern Period*. Her current projects are *Forms of Passing: Race and Genres in the Making of Aphra Behn*; *Shaping Fantasies: William Shakespeare's Concept of Race*; and *The Philology of Race*.

Theodora A. Jankowski is the author of *Women in Power in the Early Modern Drama* (University of Illinois Press, 1992) and *Pure Resistance: Queer Virginity in Early Modern English Drama* (University of Pennsylvania Press, 2000). She is also the author of a number of articles on Shakespeare, John Lyly, John Webster, and Thomas Heywood. She is currently involved in a project which argues for the use of "class" as a legitimate modality of analysis within early modern English literary texts and also explores the development, in Thomas Heywood's plays, of a "middle-class" identity that is clearly set in contrast to gentry identity.

M. Lindsay Kaplan is an Associate Professor of English at Georgetown University. She authored *The Culture of Slander in Early Modern England* (Cambridge University Press, 1997) and co-edited, with Valerie Traub and Dympna Callaghan, *Feminist Readings of Early Modern Culture* (Cambridge University Press, 1996). She is editing *The Merchant of Venice* for Bedford/St. Martin's and writing a book on the intersections of gender and Judaism in early modern England.

Ania Loomba is Professor of English at the University of Illinois at Urbana-Champaign. She is the author of *Gender, Race, Renaissance Drama* (1989) and *Colonialism/Postcolonialism* (1998), and co-editor (with Martin Orkin) of *Postcolonial Shakespeares* (1998). She is currently writing a book on Shakespeare and race, and researching early modern English representations of the East Indies.

Joyce Green MacDonald is Associate Professor of English at the University of Kentucky, where she teaches courses in Shakespeare and Renaissance non-dramatic literature. The author of several articles on women, race, and gender in early modern drama, she has also edited Thomas Southerne's *Oroonoko* for the forthcoming *Broadview Anthology of Restoration Drama*.

Laurie E. Maguire is University Lecturer and Tutorial Fellow at Magdalen College, Oxford. She is the author of *Shakespearean Suspect Texts* (Cambridge University Press, 1996), co-editor of *Textual Formations and Reformations* (University of Delaware Press, 1998), and has written many articles on feminist, textual, and theatrical issues.

Carol Thomas Neely, Professor of English and Women's Studies at the University of Illinois, Urbana-Champaign, is co-editor of *The Woman's Part: Feminist Criticism of Shakespeare*; author of *Broken Nuptials in Shakespeare's Plays*; and has written articles on Shakespeare, sonnet sequences, feminist theory, and, recently, on Margaret Cavendish's feminist utopia. Her essay in this collection is from chapter 4 of her book manuscript, *Distracted Subjects: Madness, Gender, and Confinement in Shakespeare and Early Modern Culture*.

Phyllis Rackin, Professor of English in General Honors at the University of Pennsylvania, is a past president of the Shakespeare Association of America. Her books include *Stages of History: Shakespeare's English Chronicles* and (with Jean E. Howard) *Engendering a Nation: A Feminist Account of Shakespeare's English Histories*. "Misogyny is Everywhere" comes from her current project, a revisionist study of the roles of women in Shakespeare's world and in his plays.

Katherine M. Romack is a doctoral candidate in English at Syracuse University specializing in women's cultural pursuits in seventeenth-century England. Her dissertation explores women's changing relationship to representation between the outbreak of Civil War and the Restoration of the monarchy, and she is currently compiling an anthology of mid-century works by Englishwomen.

Rachana Sachdev is an Assistant Professor of English at Susquehanna University. She continues to work on medical and travel literature from the early modern era, and is currently completing a book entitled *Exotic Private Parts: Literature and Cultural Gynecology in Early Modern England*.

Jyotsna G. Singh is an Associate Professor of English at Michigan State University. She is the author of *Colonial Narratives, Cultural Dialogues: "Discoveries" of India in the Language of Colonialism* (Routledge, 1996) and the co-author of *The Weyward Sisters: Shakespeare and Feminist Politics* (Blackwell, 1994). She is currently co-editing (with Ivo Kamps) *Travel Knowledge: European "Discoveries" in the Early Modern Period* (St. Martin's Press, forthcoming).

Molly Smith teaches at the University of Aberdeen. She is the author of *The Darker World Within: Evil in the Tragedies of Shakespeare and his Successors* (1991) and *Breaking Boundaries: Politics and Play in the Drama of Shakespeare and his Contemporaries* (1998). She is currently completing a book, tentatively titled *Shifting Centers and Expanding Margins: Literature and Culture in Early Modern England*.

Kay Stanton, Shakespeare specialist and Professor of English at California State University, Fullerton, has published sixteen articles, including work on Marlowe, Milton, and Arthur Miller, as well as on Shakespeare. In the course of presenting over sixty professional conference papers, she has spoken in six countries and eighteen American states. She is currently completing her book, *Shakespeare's "Whores": Spirited Erotics, Politics, and Poetics*.

Mihoko Suzuki is Associate Professor of English at the University of Miami. She is the author of *Metamorphoses of Helen: Authority, Difference, and the Epic* (1989) and editor of *Critical Essays on Edmund Spenser* (1995). She has published articles on Shakespeare, Spenser, Nashe, and Deloney, and on early modern women writers such as Marguerite de Navarre, Margaret Cavendish, and Mary Carleton. She recently completed a book on gender and the national popular and literary form in seventeenth-century England.

Susan Zimmerman is Associate Professor of English at Queens College, City University of New York, and Book Review Editor for *Shakespeare Studies*. She is editor of *Urban Life in the Renaissance* (1985), *Erotic Politics: Desire on the Renaissance Stage* (1992), and *Shakespeare's Tragedies* (1999). She is currently working on a book which examines representations of the corpse on the Jacobean stage.

Introduction

Dympna Callaghan

To read . . . texts against themselves is to concede that the performativity of the text is not under sovereign control. On the contrary, if the text acts once, it can act again, and possibly against its prior act. This raises the possibility of resignification as an alternative reading of performativity and of politics.

Butler (1997: 69)

In my more distrustful moments, I sometimes feel that feminist Shakespeareans are a persecuted minority, vulnerable to attack from all sides. More reactionary non- (if not anti-)feminists claim that feminism has "gone too far" and is only outlandishly brought into juxtaposition with the venerable activities of Shakespearean scholarship. Rather than dismissing concerns about gender and sexuality (as "pelvic studies" in one particularly retrograde instance I came across recently), a more progressive school of thought claims that these issues are already assimilated into the mainstream of a post-feminist, post-gender world. Nor is there much comfort to be had within the feminist community, where there is an insistent critique of abstruse intellectualism in general, and the energy spent on elite literary culture in particular. For feminists in other spheres of life and academic discipline often regard Shakespeare as at worst irrelevant and at best marginal to the core of its concern: the status of women.

Feminist Shakespeareans must tackle the onslaught, then, from both outside the perimeters of feminist concern and, more significantly, within them. For if the essentialist view of identity has been dispatched in terms of gender, race, class, and a host of other categories, so that we no longer consider, for example, people to be wholly or primarily defined by their biology, skin color, or socio-economic status, it remains in relation to the feminist Shakespeare scholar. Under the mantle of this identity, it is unfairly assumed that one reads Shakespeare but none of his contemporaries, no early modern women writers, no non-canonical writers. Allegedly insulated in the bowels of the library from the toils and troubles of life in general, at the start of the millennium feminist Shakespeareans are even thought, however unwittingly, to contribute and compound social ills by failing to engage in practical politics.

I will admit that such perceptions, though not wholly unwarranted, may unreasonably amplify the dilemmas facing people of a feminist persuasion who study Shakespeare. I must further concede – however reluctantly – that such criticism, paradoxically, is itself an integral part of feminist Shakespeare scholarship. For questions about both scholarly and political relevance are of course also questions that feminist Shakespeareans ask themselves all the time because we necessarily also belong to broader intellectual and political communities, whose critiques not only pressure but also shape feminist studies of Shakespeare. Even, or perhaps especially, blunt, uncomfortable questions like "What's the point?" – often posed not by "experts," but by students, those most vigorous representatives of a feminist future – have an invaluable place here. A scholarly example of this phenomenon is to be found in a recent commentary by feminist cultural historian Margaret King, who argues against canonicity in all its forms, and whose argument has crucial implications for the study of Shakespeare as literature's most venerated and studied canonical object:

> The scholar must turn away from the grand monuments: the palaces, cathedrals, fortifications, and most of the painted and sculpted works of art. To understand women, it is necessary to look at the objects most associated with them, above all, spun, woven, sewn, embroidered by female hands; their boxes, books, and toys; the beds, chairs, stools and buckets associated with cooking, laundering, and giving birth; the rooms in which they sat to spin, sew, weave, embroider, cook, and talk. (King 1997: 22)

For if the object of feminist inquiry is "women" of the late sixteenth and early seventeenth centuries, then Shakespeare, undoubtedly the grand monument of literary studies, would seem to offer only a very oblique bearing on the subject. While, indeed, there must be something to be gleaned about women's diurnal domestic activities in Shakespeare's plays, these are heavily mediated by male representation and the constraints of literary convention.

Of course, the importance of juxtaposing canonical information with all kinds of new knowledge about women in Shakespeare's time cannot be underestimated. However, feminist Shakespeareans are also interested in how the plays may reflect real women as well as how they help produce and reproduce ideas about women that then shape, perpetuate, or even disturb prevailing conditions of femininity. For "woman" is never an already accomplished, cold, hard, self-evident fact or category, but always a malleable cultural idea as well as a lived reality that, to use a Derridean formulation, *always already has a history*. An example framed within the theoretical terms of Judith Butler's important book, *Excitable Speech*, may make this clearer. In misogynist diatribe, for instance, the word "whore" (examined in detail by one of the contributors to this volume, Kay Stanton) does not secure its injurious effect because women are powerless victims who wilt at its very utterance. Rather, the word is injurious because in the long history of its usage it has become freighted with systemic patriarchal violence. (Notably, this remains true whether enunciated by males or females – women regularly slandered and defamed one another in early modern England – because women, no less than men, inhabit and implement the social and conceptual structures of the patriarchal order.) A staggering, old man who drinks to allay the poverty and misery of his life and calls a woman a "whore" before he passes out cold on the stone floor of a tavern is not a powerful representative of patriarchy, but his words nonetheless may have the power to wound. "Whore" is probably the worst name you can call a woman in Shakespeare's England and its capacity to "wound" means not only the power to hurt someone's feelings but potentially also to deprive women (who might be disowned by their kin as the result of allegations of unchastity) of all means of social and economic support. This word has accrued patriarchal power and its attendant material effects by means of its insistent reiteration in the culture. That is, there is no such thing as an isolated instance of the denigration of women – were it isolated, it would be devoid of cultural power. However the way that history is always inextricably woven into the materiality of discourse applies not just to particular words relating to women, but to the entire edifice of gender organization itself. Thus, femininity is continually produced and reproduced in ways that may subvert conventional understandings or, more commonly, in ways that may further subjugate women, and the operation of this reiteration has to be carefully unraveled and examined in any given historical and/or discursive instance. If language in general is crucial to any understanding of gender organization, then canonical representations of women – that is preeminent cultural re-presentations, reiterations, self-conscious reenactments and rearticulations of the condition of femininity – hold a hugely important place. However, they do so only in relation to all manner of non-canonical knowledges and texts. That is, we can only tell what Shakespeare means about gender, sexuality, race, or social relations by reading his texts in the context of the culture in which he wrote them.

What answers there are, then, to the critiques of feminist Shakespeare studies it must be emphasized are historically complex and intellectually demanding. Indeed, this volume aims to push ahead with uncomfortable questions rather than to offer reassuring answers. For only by doing so can feminism thrive both in its intellectual agenda and as a vibrant social politics. Crucially, all work that conceives itself as feminist necessarily situates itself within a wider political purpose. That purpose, however, is not necessarily, of course, a practical or pragmatic one. Thus, none of the contributors to this volume believes that her essay will diminish patriarchal violence, the number of women on the welfare rolls, or demolish the ubiquitous glass ceiling. Of course, attention to Shakespeare does not prohibit feminist scholars from vigorous participation in the social issues so central to the feminist agenda, and, more to the point, it does not magically extricate Shakespearean feminists from the world of gender trouble, or more specifically, the institutional issues which daily concern feminist educators and students. The point is that no single feminist intervention is an isolated act. Contributors to this volume are part of an ever-growing body of scholarship that has set out to discover what the world, and in this instance, quite specifically what a hugely influential body of canonical literature, might look like from the perspective of women, from the margins of hitherto patriarchal knowledge.

While the objection to feminist pragmatism can be fairly readily dispatched, perhaps a more difficult critique of the intellectual project of feminist Shakespeare scholarship is one I have only touched on so far, namely, that it further marginalizes already neglected non-canonical women writers. Feminist Shakespeareans no longer consider themselves as purely literary scholars but as cultural historians who are especially interested in women's own representations of themselves, which range from poetry to embroidery. Indeed, the interest in women's writing in particular has been a vital part of redrawing the map of Renaissance literature in general. As Maureen Quilligan points out in making the case for reading non-canonical women writers in relation to canonical men, the effect is not merely "sticking a heretofore unnoticed feature onto the map but by seeing how that new feature changes the relationship among all other features" (Quilligan 1997: 42).

The kind of intervention feminist Shakespeare scholarship understands itself to be making is gestured to in another context by Judith Butler in the epigraph to this introduction. What is at stake for Butler is how to do things differently, how to understand differently. Interestingly, what she says is something Shakespeare scholars have known all along, namely, that performance altered Shakespeare's playtexts and continues to do so – that is, that changes in understanding and interpretation of the variety that feminist scholarship seeks to effect are already written into the cultural transactions of theater.

Other forms of reiteration have, however, also proved necessary: feminists have had to repeat themselves in order to be understood. But now, at least in the realms of Renaissance literary criticism, feminism is so much a part of the common currency of the discourse, that, as Carol Neely pointed out at the 1997 meeting of the Modern Language Association in San Francisco, feminism barely needs announce itself. Thus, feminist Shakespeare is caught in the position of being, depending on how you look at it, completely integrated or completely invisible. On the one hand, it is in an important sense a measure of the work done by feminist Shakespeareans over the last twenty years that our project is likely, as we have noted, to be subject to far more rigorous scrutiny and interrogation from within the feminist ranks than outside them. No class or conference worth its salt, after all, fails to include some reference to the gender hierarchy which so fundamentally informs the culture of Shakespeare's England. On the other hand, the questionable progress of feminism may be measured by Stephen Orgel's infamous declaration that "Everyone in this [Renaissance] culture was in some respects a woman" (Orgel 1996: 124). Orgel writes from the position of an anti-essentialism so radical that it is impossible to posit the real historical existence of women, let alone women's oppression. He argues, in other words, that back then everybody – male and female – was victimized anyway. However, the difference between men being subordinate within the social hierarchy, to which Orgel alludes, and the position of women is not just a relative but rather an absolute distinction. This distinction is, in fact, foundational to the feminist enterprise and constitutive of the very core of feminist politics, which concerns itself with the historical, structural, and systemic facts of women's subjugation. (There was, for instance, no notion in the period of releasing women from traditional social roles.) Even where the oppression of women overlaps with certain other instances of difference – such as race and class – it is never wholly coincident with them. Furthermore, despite backlash rumors to the contrary, feminism has no investment in identifying the complex subjugation of women in patriarchy with mere victimization. Nor can the position of women be reduced to or elided with all other forms of social hierarchy. In short, feminism, while in some sense more prominent than ever, has not quite escaped the danger of being swept under the carpet, and has certainly not escaped the necessity of repeating itself in order to be properly understood.

The aim of this volume is to demonstrate feminist visibility – even to the point of conspicuousness – *and* its integration into the broader field of Shakespeare studies via a series of overlapping categories: the history of feminist Shakespeare criticism, text and language, social economies, sexuality, race, and religion. Beginning with an account of the origins of feminist readings of Shakespeare and their contribution to the political project of feminism, the essays included here cover historical and theoretical contexts and perspectives as well as readings of Shakespeare's texts within a feminist problematic. In particular, the essays in this volume demonstrate that feminism, because it commands a view from the margins, is especially well placed to access the eccentric categories of Renaissance knowledge – those aspects of thought in the period ranging from female circumcision to early modern ideas about the blood – that sit uneasily with our own but are nonetheless central to the period's core concerns – in these instances, religion and national identity.

Feminism is about creating the future differently by looking at history differently. And, of course, we cannot tell what the future, what that world beyond patriarchy might be. Here our project might be seen to parallel that of our Renaissance humanist forbears who ushered in the era of modernity only by looking back and examining afresh a world long past.

The volume begins with two essays that address the origins of Shakespeare criticism. **Juliet Fleming** historicizes the project of Shakespearean feminism or feminist Shakespeare by addressing its late nineteenth- and early twentieth-century precursor, "The Ladies' Shakespeare." The concept of such an enterprise was proposed, tongue in cheek, by J. M. Barrie in a speech to the Stationer's Company. Fleming explores the need of all Shakespeareans – male, female, feminist, and otherwise – "to identify Shakespeare's interests with our own." Fleming takes the parodic proposition of the Ladies' Shakespeare to its logical conclusion. She looks also at those notoriously eccentric projects of editing and interpretation (a high proportion of them, notably, undertaken by women) in order to show that, like Freud's patients, far from being so aberrant that they are irredeemably distinct and separated from the norm, rather they are but exaggerated versions of it. Thus, Henrietta Bowdler, for example, in purging Shakespeare of "indelicacy," merely enacted with a self-consciously ideological clarity nowhere available until the Oxford Shakespeare the standard principles of textual editing. Delia Bacon too, whose intellectual labor seems at first far beyond the margins of sanity, believed that Shakespeare was written by a consortium of playwrights of the Baconian persuasion. Textual studies now demonstrates, of course, that she may have been right – or at least less off the mark than those critics who support the model that Shakespeare's plays were a product of his isolated genius.

Katherine M. Romack, in "Margaret Cavendish, Shakespeare Critic," argues that though the Duchess of Newcastle may have been the first Shakespeare critic, she was far from being the feminist late twentieth-century scholars have sought to make her. In fact, Cavendish's retrograde political views are deeply enmeshed in her cultural theory, which argues that women can only exercise their rational capacities under the strict supervision of their husbands. Furthermore, she asserts, they have no business in the commonwealth. It is odd, then, that she regards Shakespeare as a writer able to metamorphose himself into a woman. However, as Romack explains, feminizing Shakespeare is vital to Cavendish's attempt to depoliticize the realm of letters. The latter project is particularly charged in a period in which women are beginning to assert not only their rights to cultural representation but also to political representation. Cavendish is careful to distance herself from the women who petitioned Parliament in this period. While the standard critical line on Cavendish is the contradictory and complex nature of her thought, Romack's placement of it in its historical context of other women's arguments for representation serves to lay bare the reactionary ideological thrust of her views in ways that not only place Cavendish beyond the confines of protofeminism, but place her vividly in the anti-feminist camp. There were, however, many radical women who were active in this period, and Romack asserts it is no accident that their political representation became possible in the period during which neither Shakespeare, the boy actress, nor the woman actress were anywhere on the scene.

Phyllis Rackin, in "Misogyny is Everywhere," asks about critics' own investments in their readings of Shakespeare. She interrogates the standard feminist assumption that in early modern culture men were anxious in the face of female power and that women were invariably disempowered, and that misogyny was rampant and pervasive. Rather, Rackin suggests, reports of women's victimization in an unrelentingly misogynist culture are everywhere not so much in Shakespeare's England as in late twentieth-century cultural criticism: "Reminders that women were expected to be chaste, silent, and obedient probably occur more frequently in recent scholarship than they did in the literature of Shakespeare's time." Why, she asks, are critics so deeply invested in this view of history, and who benefits from the investment? Rackin argues that "The problem is that the conceptual categories that shape contemporary scholarly discourse, no less than the historical records of the past, are often man-made and shaped by men's anxieties, desires, and interests. As such, they constitute instruments of women's exclusion, and often women's oppression." Interest in gender is now, at least in the American academy, an accepted conceptual tool which has become detached from feminism's earlier and explicitly political agenda.

Like Juliet Fleming's opening essay, **Laurie E. Maguire** argues that the processes of textual and therefore ideological selection have always been with us. Maguire adds, so has feminism, though neither feminism nor textual editing were formalized until the early years of the twentieth century. While Christabel Pankhurst was being imprisoned for suffragist activities in Manchester, W. W. Greg and R. B. McKerrow were founding the Malone Society. Though these contemporaneous movements appeared completely alien to one another at the start of the century, there is now an emergent phenomenon which promises to merge their disparate agendas. That phenomenon is feminist editing, and Maguire goes on to develop its practical and epistemological implications in relation to the infamous textual crux in *As You Like It* on the pairing of Rosalind and Orlando, which troublingly (for many editors at least) implies a male marriage: "That thou mightst ioyne his hand with his." However, as Maguire points out, textual cruces are not the only, or even the primary, space in which feminism can insert itself in the grand and hitherto wholly white male enterprise of textual studies. A feminist editor must confront head-on the way that Renaissance texts abound in the politically incorrect and, in doing so, confront the history that has made feminist politics necessary in the present.

Kay Stanton's "Made to write 'whore' upon" begins by exploring the sometimes startling results of feminist pedagogy in the Shakespeare classroom, and, like Maguire, argues that historicizing Shakespeare's words (and thus our own) is a fundamental political act of empowerment. "Whore," she argues, that word by which Desdemona is so tragically defamed, is unique in the lexicon of debasement. For whereas homophobic slurs and racist epithets have been reappropriated by the groups they were used to denigrate, feminism has been unable to rehabilitate the stubborn misogynist insistence inherent in the word "whore." Further, while "callet," "drab," "stale," "strumpet," "harlot," and "minion" have fallen out of everyday usage, "whore" has had an appalling longevity. Because, rather remarkably, neither the sonnets nor Shakespeare's long poems use the word at all, Stanton argues that we should be cautious about asserting that the word's usage provides evidence that Shakespeare is "the patriarchal bard." In marked contrast to the poems, in *Troilus and Cressida* Thersites uses the word ten times, and the play with the most usages is *Othello*, in which, Stanton argues, Othello commits the "verbal rape" of Desdemona. Furthermore, as readers and audiences we are complicit in this violation if we continue to believe that Desdemona is not a whore because Bianca really is one: "[W]e continue to give cultural sanction to the abusive use of the term for women of any status who are not professional sex workers, like Doll Tearsheet, who owns the term by applying it to herself."

Margo Hendricks, in "'A word, sweet Lucrece': Confession, Feminism, and *The Rape of Lucrece*," takes up Lucrece as a rape-suicide text that seems inherently problematic for, and perhaps even actively resistant to, feminist readings. The problem Hendricks extrapolates is one that extends far beyond the historical and textual limits of Shakespeare's poem, namely that female agency may manifest itself in ways that do not accord with feminist prescriptions. In order to unravel these issues in fresh though still feminist ways, Hendricks approaches the play via the discourses of the confessional (newly troubled by the Reformation) as a primary way of constructing subjectivity and the issue of race, both as lineage and of ethnicity. Far from being two discrete concerns, however, race and confession are linked as features of the narrative representation of Lucrece's psychologically complex subjectivity, which "highlight the relationship between speech and a gendered notion of 'self' as part of the process of identity-making." Rape engenders Lucrece's lengthy pre-suicide confession, much of which is concerned with evading the consequences of her violation understood as Tarquin's pollution of Collatine's "stock."

Mihoko Suzuki's "Gender, Class, and the Ideology of Comic Form: *Much Ado About Nothing* and *Twelfth Night*" claims that even Elizabeth I felt the couplings at the end of Shakespeare's comedies were a reproach to her own unmarried state. This, Suzuki argues, is an indication of the degree to which people in early modern England possessed a consciousness of the social politics of drama. Suzuki claims that contemporary anxiety about social mobility and unrest – changes for which the culture had inherited no ready-made conceptual or rhetorical framework – is articulated as anxiety about the behavior of women. There is in this period a historically new and explosive convergence between anxieties about gender and anxieties about class. In her exploration of these social tensions, Suzuki juxtaposes instances from Shakespearean comedy with two domestic tragedies, *Arden of Faversham* and *A Warning for Fair Women*. While the latter explicitly connect transgressive femininity with issues of social mobility, the former represses "anxieties about unruly women to displace them onto male scapegoats," a phenomenon which points to the nature of the cultural work Shakespearean comedy performs. Ironically, as Suzuki points out, we always assume, largely because it is so profoundly punitive, that tragedy is the expression of the reality principle that enacts a male fantasy of assigning to women the blame for social disorder. In fact, comic denouement foregrounds its displacement of the problematics of gender and class as its plots unravel the tropes of cross-dressing and cross-class marriage.

Jyotsna G. Singh offers a feminist reading of *The Merchant of Venice*. Singh's feminism is particularly attuned to the economic system which underlies the early modern gender hierarchy and which she addresses via an analysis of the cultural practices of gift exchange as they appear in the play. The gift marks the cusp both between the strictly economic and the socio-cultural mechanism of communication and reciprocity as well as between symbolic exchange in a feudal/agrarian economy and the libidinally charged exchange of commodities characteristic of emerging capitalism. While such exchanges are clearly evident in the play's traffic in women, far from being a romantic version of the circulations of global trade, romantic alliances are complicated by their inextricable implication in the bloody transaction of Shylock's bond. This, Singh argues, is the play's ingenious demystification of economic violence as literal rather than symbolic. Obligations are variously discharged in the play as gifts and commodities in a way that anticipates the ideological occlusions capitalism needs to obscure the coercion inherent in its transactions.

Ania Loomba's "The Great Indian Vanishing Trick – Colonialism, Property, and the Family in *A Midsummer Night's Dream*" examines the play's ideological investments in the discourses of travel, trade, and colonialism even though it was produced five years before the setting up of the East India Company in 1600. Loomba addresses the way criticism has habitually segregated gender issues from questions of race and colonialism, and like Joyce MacDonald, suggests ways in which the ostensible focus on discourses about gender and the family can actually work to amplify their historic interrelation with matters of race and exoticism. Loomba reads the dynamics of Titania and Oberon's tussle over the Indian boy in terms of a contest about colonial goods set in the context of familial strife. She argues that there is an important sense in which "India" – as both place and concept – might have contributed to the emergence of the normative ideals of companionate marriage and the nuclear family. The Amazon, for example, is not only a figure of potentially or formerly unruly femininity within the play, but simultaneously a category of the exotic, of racial difference, and of colonial conquest. Like Rachana Sachdev in a later essay, Loomba analyzes the envy with which English travelers comment on barbaric practices used by alien peoples to discipline women. Drowning as a punishment for adultery and the immolation of widows are remarked upon with frank admiration by English commentators. All women, these writers charge, are like those foreign women who will in their wantonness even abuse a cucumber if it is not given to them sliced and drug their husbands so that they can cavort at their leisure. This is, of course, the reverse of the situation in *Dream* where Oberon has his wife drugged. The nuclear family of Western culture, Loomba argues, "was established by othering, but also appropriating and transforming *both* the dynastic marriages and family structures of a feudal past, and the domestic institutions of the non-Western world."

Joyce Green MacDonald's "Black Ram, White Ewe: Shakespeare, Race, and Women" offers an exploration of the entanglements of racial and gender identity in the complex process of vindicating social authority in early modern England. That the connections between race and gender are solidly historical rather than purely metaphorical becomes vividly apparent in the fact that in 1619, approximately sixteen years after the first production of *Othello*, the first Africans and the first white women landed in Virginia, where a white woman could be bought for 120 pounds of tobacco. In 1662, in a reversal of English common law, white men who fathered children on black women were excused of any legal or moral responsibility for them. Race, MacDonald insists, is constituted by a complex interaction of social, familial, and economic interests. Because the languages of racial identity are heavily dependent on gender and sexuality, when Cassio calls the onomastically white Bianca a "monkey" he links her with those black women in the period who were believed to copulate with apes. When Lucrece stabs herself, she bleeds corrupted black blood as well as red, as emblems of both her violation and her virtue. Lucrece is the "white hind" to Tarquin's "rough beast" so that "his crime takes on some of that aura of cross-species impropriety Brabantio sees in his daughter's union with Othello." Less ideologically adept than either of these texts, *Titus Andronicus* demonstrates that the race and gender

hierarchies which purport to constitute social order are demonstrated as raw power –
a license to kill. The demonization of Tamora and Aaron provides vital support for
the play's restored patriarchal order.

Rachana Sachdev's essay demonstrates the flexibility of feminist reading practices
in a postcolonial approach to Sycorax, the fugitive female "other" of *The Tempest*, by
utilizing early modern medical discourse. Sycorax, Sachdev argues, represents both
the threat and promise male European travelers found in the foreign procedure of
female circumcision with which Algiers, Sycorax's birthplace, was particularly identified. On the one hand, female circumcision could serve as the standard of the unciv-
ilized, the irrefutable mark of the difference between England and its African others,
and on the other it presented a novel and hitherto unrealized prospect of disciplining
English women once and for all, controlling their unmanageable sexual desires. Albeit
that this discipline was deployed at the level of ideological prescription rather than
practice, it served to render womanhood itself as racialized and unEnglish, alienated
from the normative conceptualization of nationhood that the concept of female circumcision helped construct. But even the idea of female circumcision at the level of
ideology could never quite allay the problem of sexual difference, especially the
fear/belief that, as one sixteenth-century commentator claimed, the clitoris "gradually increases in bulk and finally rises up into a penis that is fully formed in every
respect." As a consequence, careful directions for undertaking the procedure were
included in English medical treatises such as the popular *Directory for Midwives* by
Nicholas Culpeper and Jane Sharp's widely circulated *The Midwives Book*. Sachdev uses
this information to construct a cultural history of Sycorax as the play's enigmatic, disembodied other. Although banished from Algiers, we are told "for *one thing* she
did / They would not take her life." It is Sycorax who provides the ideological underpinning of Miranda's much prized virginity on which, after all, the future of
Prospero's line depends.

Denise Albanese's "Black and White, and Dread All Over" analyzes ideological
issues constellating the 1997 "photonegative" production of *Othello* in Washington,
DC in which Patrick Stewart (a.k.a. Captain Picard of the starship *Enterprise*) played
the lead while black actors comprised the majority of the rest of the cast. The production, Albanese argues, demonstrates the one-sidedness of the purportedly utopian
notion that race does not "matter." The production's director, Jude Kelly, sought to
emphasize the problematic relationship between signs and referents in the instance of
race. However, white and black, it transpires, are not interchangeable because they
are profoundly unequal elements of the racial equation in American society: "[T]he
staging of Othello's anger against Desdemona before he murders her introduces a
hauntingly inapposite juxtaposition of white male body against black female that
makes it especially difficult to view Stewart as the racially beleaguered subject of the
play." A further aspect of the production is that it comports rather disturbingly with
white America's belief that it is being attacked by affirmative action policies, which
attempt to make some compensation for the historical prejudice against African-
Americans in hiring practices. That is, the reverse of the photo image – the

photonegative – nicely coincides with the judicially supported belief in reverse discrimination. Albanese makes clear, however, that the point isn't to condemn the bold experiment of Kelly's production, but rather to explore the unintended resonances of racially innovative casting practices.

In "Women and Boys Playing Shakespeare," **Juliet Dusinberre**, like Albanese, considers the issue of casting. While much critical ink has been spilt on the matter of the female impersonation required by the boy actor playing Rosalind, and even a few drops on Celia, the impersonation of Phoebe and Audrey has received no comment at all. "Phoebe must be all woman" in order to convince the audience about the plausibility of Rosalind's disguise, while Audrey appears to be "all body," to have a physical solidity to her which might appear to negate any sense of problematic gender identity. Not so, argues Dusinberre, even though the play's plot does not highlight these instances of gender identity to the degree that it does for Rosalind and Celia. The fictionality of gender in relation to both Phoebe and Audrey, furthermore, resides not only in the extra-diegetic nature of male bodies of the actors who play them, but also in the discursive context of pastoral. Gender impersonation does indeed change the play – in a recent all-male Cheek by Jowl production, Audrey rose to new levels of hilarity, while audiences used to women – all legs – in tights in the forest of Arden found Celia and Rosalind less charming and palatable when played by grown men. The problem of cross-dressing is not just the politics of gender but in our literal-mindedness about dramatic representation, which is always, preeminently, a matter of fiction.

Molly Smith's "Mutant Scenes and 'Minor' Conflicts in *Richard II*" begins, like Joyce MacDonald's essay, with a contemporary reference to Shakespeare in a scene of intense feminist moment, namely the Clarence Thomas–Anita Hill hearings. Shakespeare was brought to weigh in for Thomas, while the opposition could only come up with a quotation from Congreve, which leads Smith to meditate on the issue of "minor," relatively marginalized and feminized texts as a specifically feminist issue, taking as her focus the allegedly minor scenes and characters from a relatively marginalized play in the Shakespearean canon, *Richard II*. Borrowing Deleuze and Guattari's concept of "minor language," Smith suggests that Shakespeare endows the language of women in the play with revolutionary force.

Carol Thomas Neely, in "Lovesickness, Gender, and Subjectivity: *Twelfth Night* and *As You Like It*," examines the ways in which comedy can serve to license wayward desires, while lovesickness offers a means by which early modern subjects acted through and against the actual and ideological constrictions their social structure imposed upon them. Desire, even though it is ubiquitously constructed as a pathology – lovesickness – is, argues Neely, a potentially powerful locus of agency. Although initially men, not women, were understood to be subject to lovesickness, in the course of the English Renaissance there was increasing interest in women's vulnerability to the disease. Precisely because eroticism was recognized as inherently perverse and unpredictable, the comedies do not neatly reproduce patriarchal hegemony. Furthermore, not all marriages are the same. In *Twelfth Night*, the relation between gender and desire is completely unhinged, unleashing women's erotic potential and social power. Olivia, for example, meets no resistance from Sebastian when she declares, reversing the traditional gender hierarchy, "Would thou'dst be ruled by me!" Although in *As You Like It* Neely discovers desire to be more deeply embedded in the dichotomy of gender, she nonetheless finds Rosalind's insatiable desires ("My affection hath an unknown bottom") an expression of her improperly feminine subjectivity.

Theodora Jankowski's ". . . in the Lesbian Void: Woman–Woman Eroticism in Shakespeare's Plays" addresses, via an irreverent interrogation of standard critical protocols, the resurrection of Hermione in *The Winter's Tale*, an event that is unique in the canon, because unlike other revivified characters, Shakespeare's audience, and not just certain of the characters on stage, believes her to be dead. Where, precisely, asks Jankowski, was Hermione for the sixteen years she has feigned death? Perhaps, muses Jankowski, she was in the closet behind the bedchamber, or in the withdrawing room or lodge associated with a post-banquet phenomenon known as the void. These speculations are deliberately outside the perimeters of typical literary criticism and are so in order to address the specifically gynocentric spaces of woman–woman eroticism. Jankowski wrestles with the problem of making visible those aspects of women's eroticism occluded by generations of heterocentric critical commentary, a problem that can only be addressed by a reading practice that refuses the typical limits of scholarly inquiry. There are, however, as Jankowski discovers, traces of an eroticism which jars with patriarchal and critical precept in several of Shakespeare's plays. The point is not so much that this space can be "proved" (that is, verified in the terms of masculinist criticism) to be the exact equivalent of late twentieth-century lesbian encounters, but rather that this space can be marked by the feminist critic as "lesbian" precisely because it is shrouded in the indecipherability of relations between women that have hitherto not been subject to the kind of cultural attention that could produce them as "fact." The void she addresses, Jankowski claims, can only ever be, to use Terry Castle's terminology, an apparitional production because historically women's love for women, in whatever form it takes, has never been granted the solid facticity of heterosexual love.

Susan Zimmerman's "Duncan's Corpse" turns our attention to the uncategorizable, the twilight zone between life and death, which in *Macbeth* is intimately related to androgyny and the indecipherability inherent in the nature of sexual difference. Zimmerman's essay marks the way in which feminist criticism is now able to extend itself so far from "women" fictional and real, in this instance focusing especially on death and the body of the slain king. His corpse emblematizes the violent and generative power of nature which simultaneously murders and reproduces, and whose vertiginous indeterminacy was newly charged by the Protestant insistence on the distinction between flesh and spirit. *Macbeth*, then, dramatizes the horrors of a world without, or rather, beyond difference. The terrifying liminality of human remains suspended, at least in pre-Reformation thought, between life and death shifted in

Protestantism and with the advent of anatomical dissection, which now suggested that the deceased was definitively an object rather than a partially animated subject. Popular belief was tenacious, however, and still held that anatomical practice constituted the desecration of the corpse. In *Macbeth*, Zimmerman argues, Macbeth and Lady Macbeth "seek Duncan's power as a king, but discover instead Duncan's power as a corpse." Lady Macbeth, who rationalizes the murder by objectifying Duncan as a mere representation not to be feared, "The sleeping, and the dead / Are but as pictures," now becomes haunted by his blood. The corpse, finally, serves to articulate the possibilities but also the limits of theatrical representation itself.

M. Lindsay Kaplan's essay on *The Merchant of Venice* takes as its starting point Emmanuel Levinas's work on alterity in *Totality and Infinity* in order to explore the tension between the same and the other in relation to Jews and married women in Shakespeare's play. Issues of difference, especially around matters of religion, reached their peak in the Renaissance when Protestantism's separation from the Church replayed a much earlier crisis of difference, namely the Christian deviation from Judaism, whereby the former posits that it supersedes the latter. Christians hoped that Jews would disappear by conversion, while women, in an analogous manner, vanished, at least in legal discourse, under the law of coverture. While Elizabeth I might seem to be rather too conspicuous a figure to leave the ideology of female invisibility undisturbed, some contemporary commentators in their extrapolation of this doctrine signally never troubled themselves with the anomaly she constituted to theories of female subjection. Kaplan goes on to theorize this subsumption and suppression of women and Jews in relation to Levinas's philosophical interrogation of a concept of difference which cannot be assimilated or subordinated into another entity. Kaplan argues that Bassanio's marriage to Portia, Antonio's debt to Shylock, Launcelot's relation to his old master, and Jessica's to her father involve structurally analogous abrogations of contract, complex negotiations of the relation between the other and the same.

Philippa Berry's essay touches upon a key new element of Shakespeare criticism in general, namely Shakespeare's Catholicism. While Berry is not concerned to establish Shakespeare's own religious identity, there are, she demonstrates, many Catholic resonances in *Romeo and Juliet*, in particular many references to the pre-Reformation calendar of saints. Numerous saints and saints' days appear in the play in a way that suggests a religious temporality not yet erased by either a Protestant or a secular understanding of time. However, this temporality marks not just the persistence of residual Catholicism, but also the pagan and astrological temporality whereby the fate of the lovers is always already written in the stars. The volume concludes with this essay, which is subtly informed by Julia Kristeva's work on monumental time, because it demonstrates feminism's conceptual and critical reach by undoing linear notions of temporality and more locally, squabbles about Shakespeare's own religious affiliation. Notably, Juliet and her relation to July, and the bawdy "Jule," is a significant figure in Berry's analysis, but not the sole focus of the piece. A feminist epistemology can thus address itself to fundamental questions of historicism by unraveling the logic of patriarchal history, and even of time itself. Such an investigation suggests the distance feminism has traveled from "images of women."

REFERENCES

Butler, J. 1997: *Excitable Speech: A Politics of the Performative*. New York: Routledge.

King, M. L. 1997: "Women's Voices, the Early Modern, and the Civilization of the West." In Leeds Barroll (ed.), *Shakespeare Studies*, XXV, 21–31.

Orgel, S. 1996: *Impersonations*. Cambridge: Cambridge University Press.

Quilligan, M. 1997: "Completing the Conversation." In Leeds Barroll (ed.), *Shakespeare Studies*, XXV, 40–99.

PART ONE
The History of Feminist Shakespeare Criticism

1

The Ladies' Shakespeare

Juliet Fleming

On July 3, 1925, together with Lord Balfour and Rudyard Kipling, James Barrie was granted the freedom of the Stationer's Company. The text of Barrie's acceptance speech was printed the following morning in the London *Times* (and subsequently by Clement Shorter in a private edition of twenty-five copies). The speech, which posited the existence of an edition of Shakespeare newly sensitive to the needs of women, is here quoted at length:

> The other sex – if so they may still be called – have long complained that his women, however glorious, are too subservient to the old enemy for these later days, as if he did not know what times were coming for women. Gentlemen, he knew, but he had to write with the knowledge that if he was too advanced about Woman his plays would be publicly burned in the garden of Stationer's Hall. So he left a cipher, not in the text, where everybody has been looking for them, but in the cunning omission of all stage directions, and women, as he had hoped, have had the wit to read it aright, with the result that there is to be another edition, called appropriately "The Ladies' Shakespeare." For the first time on any stage, some fortunate actress, without uttering one word, but by the use of silent illuminating "business," is to show us the Shrew that Shakespeare drew. Katherine was really fooling Petruchio all the time. The reason he carried her off before the marriage feast, though he didn't know it, was that her father was really a poor man, and there was *no* marriage feast. So Katherine got herself carried off to save that considerable expense. On that first night in Petruchio's house, when he was out in the wind and rain distending his chest in the belief that he was taming her, do you really think with him that she went supperless to bed? No, she had a little bag with her. In it a wing of chicken and some other delicacies, a half bottle of the famous Paduan wine, and such a pretty corkscrew. I must tell you no more; go and book your seats, you will see, without even Sir Israel Gollancz being able to find one word missed out or added, that it is no longer Katherine who is tamed.

Barrie is mimicking many of the various resources that women (or at least, those women who have wished to retain the poet as an object of affection and veneration) have repeatedly brought to the problem of Shakespeare. These include resources of editing, reading (both individually and in societies), and the development of character criticism; the adaptation of Shakespeare's stories for specialized (usually juvenile or school) audiences; the performance activities of producing, acting, and directing; and women's promotion of Shakespeare, within the heritage industry, as a man who loved women (it was, for example, with the crucial support of the Shakespeare Ladies Club that in 1741 a monument was erected to Shakespeare in Westminster Abbey, copies of which were subsequently placed in Stratford, and in Leicester Square).

Women have also been interested, as "The Ladies' Shakespeare" suggests, to "re-read," "re-write," "re-figure," "re-vision," or "de-center" Shakespeare – that is, to criticize the poet from a woman's point of view while continuing to appropriate the cultural capital that accrues to his name. In this essay, I use the term "The Ladies' Shakespeare" to describe both the imaginary text that is the object of Barrie's joke, *and* the set of gestures whereby some critics have asserted a particularist, woman-centered interest in Shakespeare – and whereby other critics, taking such assertions at face-value, have understood them to represent errors of judgment within Shakespeare criticism. Both as an essay and as a concept, "The Ladies' Shakespeare" is intended to demonstrate that the "woman-question" within Shakespeare criticism is a reflex whereby such criticism recognizes and castigates itself: neither as essay nor concept does it therefore attempt to account for the differences of class, nationality, and ethnicity as these have recently become visible within feminist criticism, and as they continue to make their difference to the ways in which Shakespeare may be read, viewed, and valued.

As Barrie's admixture of suffragist gender politics to Shakespeare criticism and performance suggests, women have regularly taken pleasure in, and understood the contemporary material benefits of, the enterprise of arguing the case for women's special relation to England's national poet. While women's labor has contributed to the development of Shakespeare studies, the study and performance of Shakespeare may have helped to articulate the interests of (and hence offer benefits to) women as a group. In "Shakspere Talks with Uncritical People" (1879–91), Constance O'Brien imagined women gathering in small, informal groups to talk over characters "whose life seems as vivid as our own." Through such meetings, as well as through more organized Shakespeare study clubs and the distribution of what Elizabeth Latimer (herself a speaker on the study-club circuit) called their "fugitive Shakspearian Criticism," women articulated social and intellectual communities that intersected, but were not entirely coincident with, those of their male counterparts. So the study of Shakespeare cemented the friendship of critic Anna Jameson and actor Fanny Kemble; Mary Cowden Clarke learned her love for Shakespeare from her tutor Mary Lamb, and conceived the idea for her *Shakespeare Concordance* (1845) at the Lambs' breakfast table; Mary Lamb was encouraged to write *Tales from Shakespear* (1807) with her brother Charles by the publisher Mary Jane Godwin; the actress Helen Faucit wrote her volume *On Some of Shakespeare's Female Characters: By One Who Has Personated Them* (1885) in the form of personal letters to her female friends; and Elizabeth

Griffith was "stirred" to write *The Morality of Shakespeare's Drama Illustrated* (1775) by her desire to emulate Elizabeth Montagu's *Essay on the Writings and Genius of Shakespear* (1769).

Less clear, within Barrie's parody, is the fact that self-directed humor has also been characteristic of women's approaches to Shakespeare. In 1896 Emily Bissell [Priscilla Leonard] published an anti-suffragist article in the conservative *Century Magazine* which has obvious affinities with Barrie's speech. Claiming to be an account of a lecture given in a Twentieth-Century Women's Club, "The Mistaken Vocation of Shakespeare's Heroines" charges Shakespeare with having put his female characters in the wrong plays ("in a word, ladies, with these heroines in their appropriate places, there would have been no tragedies at all among Shakespeare's works!"). To prolonged applause, and cries of "Down with Shakespeare!" the speaker reassigns the female roles of an author she considers "well-meaning, but inadequate – blind to the true powers of Woman and the illimitable wideness of her sphere." Mrs. Launch Macluarin also anticipated the tone of Barrie's address in a paper delivered to the Dallas Shakespeare Club in 1897. Beginning from the premise that "Shakespeare has told us everything, about everything, that is, and was, and is to come," Macluarin pretends to search for the figure of the business woman in his plays, before finally forgiving Shakespeare for his omission of the character. For "how could he anticipate her, great man that he was, any more than he could the typewriter and the phonograph and other pleasant and surprising things we have?" Bissell and Macluarin republished their essays in the *American Shakespeare Magazine*, the journal of the largely female-staffed Fortnightly Shakespeare Club of New York. Mocking themselves as lady Shakespeareans, Bissell, Macluarin, and the women who laughed with them explored what was not in Shakespeare primarily in order to demonstrate and enjoy their familiarity with what *was* there. Even as this strategy stakes its claim to some part of the cultural territory that is Shakespeare studies in the late nineteenth century, however, it hints at the pleasures of a criticism that, departing from strict textual considerations, is free to ask not what women can do for Shakespeare, but what Shakespeare can do for women.

The essays of Bissell, Macluarin, and Barrie are written from a culturally conservative position which uses the specter of a ludicrous and anachronistic feminist criticism to deflect attention, both from a serious consideration of women's rights, and from a critical analysis of the premises of Shakespearean criticism itself. It is the argument of this essay that if the extravagancies that Barrie attributes to "The Ladies' Shakespeare" have been legible within woman-centered criticism of Shakespeare, they have been equally legible within a more general appreciation of Shakespeare as that has been developed both within and beyond the academy. I am suggesting that in "The Ladies' Shakespeare," and in subsequent attacks on feminist approaches to the plays, scholars and others attempt to distance themselves from the undesired consequences of some of their *own* readings of Shakespeare by projecting them onto women. Conducted by men or by women, such readings begin from the unexceptionable premise that literary criticism necessarily responds, in however mediated a form, to current political concerns. The criticism that follows is itself what Marx called "ideological" to the extent that it attributes to acts of intellection (such as Shakespeare's, or its own) the power to change the circumstances of men's and women's lives. The fantasy that is "The Ladies' Shakespeare" is not the fantasy of women alone – it is the productive and necessary fantasy of all those who have allowed themselves to read Shakespeare as if it mattered to do so. I am proposing, then, that the specificities of woman-centered criticism as mocked by its detractors are almost always standing in for the specificities of Shakespeare criticism in general as these are recognized and disavowed by its own practitioners – laugh at "The Ladies' Shakespeare," and "The Ladies' Shakespeare" laughs at you. But my argument is twofold, for if there is nothing particularly unusual, subjective, or particularist about the grounds on which woman-centered criticism of Shakespeare proceeds, then such criticism cannot be distinguished, for good or ill, from that which surrounds it. That is to say, there *is* no feminist criticism of Shakespeare, but thinking makes it so.

I

Women's deployment of the critical resources of editing, character criticism, performance, adaptation, and the promotion of Shakespeare has been largely and variously governed by the assumption (questioned by Macluarin, and mischievously dramatized by Barrie when he pretends to read Shakespeare as a suffragist *avant la lettre*) that Shakespeare's plays can and should be made to speak to present concerns. According to "The Ladies' Shakespeare," the plays anticipate the affective needs of future generations, and to find those needs met is consequently to read Shakespeare "aright":

> Shakespeare has heard that he is to be understood at last. . . . They say that a look of expectancy has come over the face of the statue in Leicester Square. If the actress who is to play the real Katherine has the courage to climb the railings, while the rest of London sleeps, she may find him waiting for her at the foot of his pedestal to honour her by walking her once round that garden, talking to her in the language not of Petruchio, but of Romeo.

After three centuries of immobilization, Shakespeare is to be "understood at last," his intentions reanimated by a feminist sympathy that is here imagined as the product of a complex process of identification between Shakespeare and the women who love him. The term "identification" indicates the psychological process whereby a subject assimilates an attribute of another person, and is transformed, wholly or partially, after the model the other provides. But identification operates in two directions: the subject can identify her own self with the other, or the other with herself. In practice these tendencies are mutually involved and together they comprise a complex mode of identification that can be used to account for the constitution of a "we." In Freud's work, identification describes the various operations of imitation, assimilation, and indifference to difference that constitute, more or less favorably, the human subject. In more general terms, a reader or spectator may be said to identify herself with a particular character, and thereby to "enrich" and pleasurably reencounter her own personality. To identify with a character or writer is to read with confidence in our ability to understand, and with a feeling of companionship that comes from a sense of being understood. "The Ladies' Shakespeare" invokes this complex, reciprocal mode of identification, which it imagines to be present in both Shakespeare and the women who love him. The actress (who is standing in for the female reader) identifies Shakespeare as a feminist, like herself, and identifies herself with what she sees as Shakespeare's feminism; while Shakespeare identifies the actress as a feminist like *him*self, and consequently falls in love with her.

Barrie intends such identifications – which originate in the mind of the female reader, where their logic may be summarized as the claim that "Shakespeare loves me *because I am a feminist*" – to raise a smile in his audience. He underlines the solipsistic nature of the fantasy he is attributing to women (a fantasy whose inverted form constitutes the pleasure of entertaining Shakespeare's thoughts *as if they were our own*) by borrowing its motifs of reciprocated love from *Romeo and Juliet*, and from *The Winter's Tale*. In the first case, the female reader identifies with the character of Juliet, with whom she has in common the wish to be loved. The plot being what it is, the reader is then able to feel loved herself – first by Romeo, and then by Shakespeare, who talks "to her in the language . . . of Romeo." In the second case, Shakespeare himself is saved, by the courageous action of a woman, from the pedestal on which he has been fixed. Standing in the place of Hermione, and now the grateful object of an heroic female rescue, the revivified Shakespeare briefly figures the love between women that underpins women's identification with female characters and the man who made them. For Shakespeare loves the actress both as Romeo loved Juliet, and as Hermione loved Perdita. The composite figure of Romeo–Hermione – which is really the figure for the position of sympathy toward women out of which Shakespeare is supposed to write – responds with maternal love and with sexual interest to the actress who scales the railings to save her; while the actress embodies the gallant femininity that has always rendered Shakespeare's heroines the object of erotic approbation. Directed, as here, toward the imaginary object that is Romeo–Hermione (an object we may call *the woman in Shakespeare*), such gallantry marks the presence both of a complex mode of identification, and of a sexuality whose object is neither male, nor female, but both at once.

The joke that is "The Ladies' Shakespeare" derives in part from Barrie's intuitive recognition of the complexity of patterns of identification as these operate within theatrical performance – a complexity that other forms of criticism have been comparatively slow to recognize. Recent discussion of the fact that, before the Restoration, women did not appear on the public stage in England, where female parts were taken by boys (or, possibly, by adult men), has centered on the male homoeroticism of the spectacle of boys dressed as women (a spectacle that is held to be intensified when female characters are then "disguised," as Shakespeare's heroines often are, as men). For critics such as Lisa Jardine, there are *no* women on Shakespeare's stage, and few of any account in his audience: "'playing the woman's part' – male effeminacy – is an act for a male audience's appreciation." Jardine's argument operates as a timely warning against the historical error of imputing "peculiarly female insights" to characters who are merely theatrical ciphers. But other critics have objected that Shakespeare's plays are not most usefully read as if they were historical documents *tout court*, and that critical concentration on the body of the boy actor beneath the female character's clothes, however historically accurate, "erases" women from the spheres of representation and discussion. Countering Jardine on her own ground, Jean Howard has worked to demonstrate the importance of women as spectators, paying customers, and "desiring subjects" in the early modern theater; while Jardine's work has also been extended, and its heterosexist bias corrected, by Stephen Orgel, Laura Levine, and Jonathan Goldberg, who argue for the constructedness of sexuality, as well as of gender, on the English Renaissance stage. The amalgamation of these critical insights – of Howard's desiring women ("stimulated to want what was on display at the theatre"), with the labile sexuality of Goldberg's transvestite boy, and the "unmooring of desire" from gender that Stephen Greenblatt has suggested is "the special pleasure of Shakespearean fiction" – culminates in the work of Valerie Traub, who argues that erotic desire circulates through and across "'masculine' and 'feminine' sites" in Shakespeare's drama, where it elicits and expresses heterosexual and homoerotic fantasies and fears. Of course it does so not because of Shakespeare's unusual empathy with marginalized sexualities, or oppressed genders, but because gender identities in early modern England appear, with hindsight, to have been more fluid than they have since become. But Traub's work allows us to imagine Shakespeare's theater as a site of identification between women who can desire each other, differently but equally well, through identification with male, with female, or with transvestite characters. In this it can be said to have arrived back at Barrie's vision of a woman who loves herself as a woman through loving the woman in Shakespeare.

II

Of course, not all women have chosen to read Shakespeare from an overtly sexed or gendered position. In the first decade of the New Shakespere Society, which was founded by F. J. Furnivall in 1874 for the purposes of encouraging "the widest study of Shakespeare" in "every English-speaking land," and admitted women on an equal footing with men, women gave papers on the First and Second Quartos of *Hamlet* (T. Rochfort-Smith, who was preparing to edit the play); the medieval source of the bond story in *The Merchant of Venice* (T. Rochfort-Smith again); the authorship of *Henry VI* Parts 2 and 3 (Jane Lee, editor of the Society's parallel text of that play); natural history similes in *Henry VI* (Emma Phipson); a reading of *Julius Caesar* (E. H. Hickey); "Shakespeare's Old Men" (Constance O'Brien); and the construction of Shakespeare's verse

(Grace Latham). Some also gave more woman-centered papers (for example, Latham's defense of Ophelia), but this was an enterprise in which they were encouraged and joined by their male colleagues, and within which both women and men employed strategies to distance themselves quite markedly from the identificatory practices with which they engaged.

So, according to the *Transactions* of the Society, in 1881 Hickey gave a paper on *Romeo and Juliet* that noted an "element of cunning" in Juliet's character (who had "arranged" for Romeo to overhear her declaration of love, just as Barrie's Kate "arranged" to have herself carried off before the wedding feast). The paper sparked a brisk debate between Furnivall, Peter Bayne, and the Rev. W. A. Harrison concerning the cunning propensities of Shakespeare's women in love – a discussion which was closed, for the time being, by Emma Phipson's observing in all Shakespeare's characters "an indifference to truth" characteristic of his era. This debate, and one of 1882 in which Peter Bayne led a discussion comparing Shakespeare and George Eliot in terms of what each knew about women (eliciting from Joseph Knight the opinion "that there never had been in the world any man at any time who knew anything at all about women"), demonstrate two things. First, that a concern with what Shakespeare understood "of a woman's heart" was shared among the female and male members of the New Shakespere Society (as it was by nineteenth-century Anglo-American middle-class culture more generally). Second, that the question elicited a marked degree of self-irony from its participants, who used it to explore the potential for anachronism, special pleading, and self-interest in Shakespeare criticism at large. Leaving the "sound basis" of textual studies to take passionately interested sides on the well-worn topic of woman's nature, the men and women of the New Shakespere Society showed themselves more interested in quarrelling with and courting each other than in accounting for the poet under whose aegis they had gathered. Embracing the misogynist assumption that women's interests are "sectional" rather than general or objective, and proceeding with the topic nevertheless, members at once celebrated, and remonstrated with themselves for, the realization that their criticism of Shakespeare was the product of contemporary desires.

If woman-centered readings are often made to function as the scapegoat for the tendency to read Shakespeare's plays as political commentaries on present moments, that is in part because the articulation of women's concerns is only too readily understood as the special pleading of a "minority" interest. But it is also because women have themselves been prepared to frankly disavow attempts to produce generally valid readings of the plays. Mary Cowden Clarke understood her notorious book, *The Girlhood of Shakespeare's Heroines in a Series of Fifteen Tales* (1850), as few have understood it since – as a work of fiction. "It was believed that such a design would combine much matter of interesting speculation, afford scope for pleasant fancy, and be productive of entertainment." The work of Anna Jameson now known as *Shakespeare's Heroines* was originally entitled *Characteristics of Women, Moral, Political, and Historical* (1832), and was designed as a treatise on the nature of women, illustrated with examples from Shakespeare's plays. Although Clarke and Jameson each undertook a

deliberately instrumental reading of Shakespeare, they were subsequently vilified
for lack of an "objectivity" to which they had never aspired. "The Ladies' Shakespeare"
may be understood as the name for the critical impulse that impelled Clarke
and Jameson, as it impels others, to acknowledge their own situatedness *vis-à-vis*
Shakespeare.

A list of those who have read Shakespeare from a woman's point of view would
necessarily include the names of some men – Barrie himself, for example, who played
the woman's part after dinner in Stationer's Hall in order to charm and disarm his
colleagues; John Fletcher, whose play *The Woman's Prize, or the Tamer Tam'd* was performed ca. 1611 as a sequel to *The Taming of the Shrew*, and was subsequently dedicated to the "Ladies . . . in whose defence and right / Fletchers brave Muse prepar'd
herself to fight"; and more recently, Peter Erickson (whose *Rewriting Shakespeare,
Rewriting Ourselves* is a useful study of the ways in which a feminist interest such as
his own may appropriate and rearticulate the legacy of Shakespeare). In fact, the majority of those writing as women have perhaps *been* women. But if the body of criticism
that they have produced is largely conformable with that parodied by Barrie, this is
true because, good and bad, the presumptions and techniques of "The Ladies' Shakespeare" are characteristic of those of Shakespeare criticism as a whole.

III

The typicality of "The Ladies' Shakespeare" may be demonstrated, in the first instance,
if it is considered as an acting script – one that alters the inherited text in order to
"restore" on stage what it takes to be Shakespeare's original intention. In *The Shakespeare Key* (1879), Charles and Mary Cowden Clarke remarked with interest "the mea-
greness of the stage-directions" in the "earliest printed copies" of the plays (which
they took to be an index of Shakespeare's intent). As well as describing the modern
practice of altering, elaborating, or adding stage directions ("the needful particulars
being either deduced from the dialogue text, from the situation, or from known historical details"), the Cowden Clarkes also noted "a few stage situations . . . which have
no accompanying stage direction either in the ancient or modern editions of his works;
yet which require bearing in mind duly to comprehend the passages where they
occur." To "bear in mind" the actions implied by Shakespeare's text is the first principle of dramatic exegesis. But it is also the principle whereby "The Ladies' Shakespeare" is able to invert the received meaning of Shakespeare's text "without one word
missed out or added." As a performance script, "The Ladies' Shakespeare" authorizes
an actress to countervail the action of (and therefore to preserve within the canon) a
play that Bernard Shaw notoriously found "altogether disgusting to modern sensibilities." Refusing to equate the perspective of the male characters with authorial intention, the "restored" performance demonstrates what many have argued before and
since – that Katherine knows more about Petruchio than he knows about himself,
and that her taming is nothing more than his own mistaken fantasy.

Attending to Shakespeare as a writer for the stage, *The Shakespeare Key* identifies other moments in which the author's intention has to be *added back in* in the course of performance. So there are "several passages in Shakespeare's plays where a word must be emphasised in order to develop the full meaning of the sentence" – as if without emphasis, or with the wrong emphasis, the original meaning would be missed. Then there are points left "for filling up as occasion served, or as the ingenuity of the actor entrusted with the part . . . might suggest," such as songs ("the choice of which was left to the singer or to the theatrical manager or for improvisation"), and certain of the clown's routines ("some of the scraps of quoted ballad, or impromptu levity, which he had to utter, being left to the memory or extempore wit of the performer to supply"). Like Barrie, the Cowden Clarkes also note the theatrical opportunities posed by Shakespeare's "admirable power in indicating silence in certain of his characters"; as well as by his "potent art in conveying perfect impression of a speaker's meaning, through imperfectly expressed speech"; and his skill "in introducing upon occasion an unfinished sentence," as when a character is interrupted, or distracted by his own thoughts. In this last case, however, it is conceivable that the actor occasionally works to dramatize not Shakespeare's intention, but a textual corruption:

> In the Folio, these unfinished sentences are generally indicated by a dash (that is, by a long line or a line composed of short hyphen-marks, thus - - -); but, in several cases, are so imperfectly indicated (by a full stop, by a comma, by no stop at all, or even by a blank space) that it is difficult to decide whether an interrupted sentence is really intended by the dramatist, or whether the printer may not have made a blunder, and even (in the last-mentioned case) have left the passage incompletely given.

Here the "unfinished sentence" becomes one more "point for improvisation" on the part of the actor or editor. Exacerbated as it is by the complex materiality of the surviving texts, the identification of significant absences or silences in Shakespeare's plays starts a series of questions that finally make nonsense, even on the pragmatic level, of our will to know and stabilize the author's "intention." Where is improvisation intended, and where not? How can we know when silence "speaks," how long it lasts, and when it is just silence? To ponder such questions is to realize that Shakespeare's work is not an object of the type that could ever be restored or "completed." It thus replicates, in a material register, the capacity of texts to release new interpretations on being read. And it is these two indeterminacies – the material and the textual – that have allowed to each generation the impression that Shakespeare is still waiting to be understood.

It is as a practitioner of techniques exemplified in "The Ladies' Shakespeare" that, in "The Shakespearean Editor as Shrew-Tamer" (1995), Leah Marcus discusses the causes and consequences of the differences between the 1594 Quarto and the 1623 Folio versions of *The Taming of the Shrew* – differences so marked that the two are considered sometimes as earlier and later drafts, and sometimes as discrete plays. Where textual criticism has tended to concern itself with the question of which text or textual part bears the imprint of the "true" Shakespeare, Marcus argues that this critical enterprise can itself be seen as an act of taming: one which reduces textual indeterminacy by invocation of what Foucault calls the author function. After arguing a case for the "bad quarto" as the record of a performance with its "own logic and artistic merits" (and with less pernicious gender politics), Marcus finally advocates an editorial practice that would think of the different versions of the play "intertextually – as a cluster of related texts which can be fruitfully read together and against each other as 'Shakespeare.'" Marcus speaks from her moment when she proposes to disestablish the texts that eighteenth- and nineteenth-century editors worked to establish; for modern critics have increasingly come to recognize and value the non-uniformity of early modern printed books, and the consequent provisionality of any single-text edition. But the instability of the Shakespearean text is something that editors in the tradition of "The Ladies' Shakespeare" have long known, and sometimes admitted. Preparing multiple-text editions of Shakespeare's works for the New Shakespere Society in the late nineteenth century, Teena Rochfort-Smith (who worked on a four-text *Hamlet*) and Jane Lee (a parallel text of *Henry VI*) were already working deep within the consequences of the fact that to edit a play is to *produce* variant readings.

In the preface to their edition of *The Works of William Shakespeare* (1864), the Cowden Clarkes remarked the impossibility of isolating "the genuine Shakespearian reading in disputed passages," and went on to imagine a reading practice that has since become possible through the medium of hypertext:

> The time may come, when every reader of Shakespeare will be, to a certain extent, his own editor; and the difficulties arising out of the early and original copies almost demand this: meantime, the best thing that an appointed Editor can do, is honestly and conscientiously to set forth the text according to his own belief of what it is, as gathered from such (in many cases imperfect) materials as exist to found it upon. These anxious deliberations, these conscientious cares on the part of Editors in selecting what they conceive to be the genuine Shakespearian reading in disputed passages, – leading to occasional variance even in *their own individual opinions*, and to differing actually *with themselves*, – ought surely to teach diffidence in maintaining their own decision.

While the Cowden Clarkes remain visibly anxious at their inability to fix "the genuine Shakespearian reading," they are able to take pleasure, both in the lesson in humility that is Shakespeare's special gift to his editors, and in imagining a text that is so multiple that the question of Shakespeare's original intention is dissolved by the proposition that no single variant need be cut off, and no possible meaning denied.

Of course, the impossibility of fixing the text correctly can also justify a different editorial practice, one based on the conclusion that Shakespeare's texts are the result of a collaborative process so extensive, and so various, that there *is* no originating intention to recover. Since Shakespeare's plays were adapted by actors, changed by other writers, and altered by theatrical scriveners, censors, compositors, and proofreaders – since, beyond this, the texts varied from themselves at the moment of their first publication – the editor is free to modernize them in her turn. Women editors of Shakespeare have implicitly followed this line in their production of editions to meet particular educational or other needs: Henrietta Bowdler cut passages and entire plays in order to produce *The Family Shakespeare* (1807), a work fit to be "placed in the hands of young persons of both sexes." Bowdler's work is notorious; her name is now used as a verb to describe the expurgation of indelicate passages in texts; and her edition of Shakespeare is regarded as the mistaken product of an overly nice pre-Victorian sensibility. But, as more recent critical practice has been forced to admit, every new edition addresses itself to a particular audience, and every edition is, to that extent, an "adaptation." In their article "The Materiality of the Shakespearean Text" (1993), Margreta de Grazia and Peter Stallybrass argue that "there is no intrinsic reason *not* to have a modernized, translated, rewritten 'Shakespeare'" – indeed, because even the material signs of the original printed texts are reinterpreted as their meaning is apprehended by modern sensibilities, "in an important sense, that is all we *can* have." In other words, however energetically we work to develop an active historical imagination, and a "context" within which to read Shakespeare outside the ambit of our own concerns, in the end we will still have some version of "The Ladies' Shakespeare."

IV

In order to elaborate and remotivate Katherine's part, "The Ladies' Shakespeare" has recourse to a critical practice that is sometimes held to be women's special contribution to Shakespeare studies (though it was begun by Alexander Pope and continued by A. C. Bradley, among others). Character criticism concentrates its energies on the dramatic personae of a play, and works, according to a logic of realism derived from the novel, to supply their actions with psychological motivation, and consequently to explain them as resulting from a combination of in-born traits, early life experience, and current circumstances. So, according to "The Ladies' Shakespeare," Kate has herself carried off before the marriage feast because she "knows" what no critic has thought to assert before – that "her father was really a poor man and there was *no* marriage feast." A strong form of such criticism, and its most famous example, is Cowden Clarke's *The Girlhood of Shakespeare's Heroines*, which aimed "to trace the probable antecedents in the history of some of Shakespeare's women . . . to invent such adventures as might be supposed to colour their future lives" and "to place the heroines in such situations as should naturally lead up to, and account for, the known conclusion of their subsequent confirmed character and after-fate."

Cowden Clarke's "prequels" to Shakespeare's plays are now discounted as exemplifying the naivety of a criticism that, blind to the historical and textual integrity of his works, *adds itself* to Shakespeare. But Cowden Clarke's "speculations" are structured by a self-deprecating wit that has already taken account of the problem that to write about Shakespeare may be seen as an act of presumption. Beginning both before and after Shakespeare's plays, and working to motivate something that has already occurred there, they function to propose that (at least in the curious genealogy that is literary criticism) the cause of events can come after their happening. The logic of time's inversion, whereby we see the trace of an object's vanishing before we see the object itself, has occupied philosophers (it is used, for example, by Lacan when he describes the symptom as something that returns *from the future*). Here it is being used to suggest the proper relation of subsequent writers to Shakespeare, for if his plays represent the vanishing of the (subsequent) girlhood of his heroines, they also represent the vanishing of Cowden Clarke's work back into his. In this aspect – the aspect of time's inversion – *The Girlhood of Shakespeare's Heroines* represents a filial model of criticism that, loving its object, seeks first to "restore" and then to be erased by Shakespeare's prior truth. But to come, however tactfully, to the aid of a parental text – to suggest that it now needs support – is to begin to supplant it; and Cowden Clarke's work has consequently been read as the type of a criticism that holds Shakespeare to be an object whose origin and utility are discontinuous, so that the plays constantly need to be redirected by some power superior to them. This is the premise on which most criticism of Shakespeare continues to proceed. As represented by its detractors, however, it is governed by the figure of the inappropriately masterful daughter – for example, of Cowden Clarke herself, or of Barrie's suffragist, who makes common cause with Shakespeare's Shrew.

Character criticism can extend its reach after, as well as before, the action of a play. In *Shakespeare's Garden of Girls* (1885) (a series of talks originally given to the New Shakespere Society), M. Leigh-Noel speculated (as many have done since) on how the married life of Katherine and Petruchio "turned out." Leigh's portrait includes that inversion of apparent power relations that "The Ladies' Shakespeare" also read into *The Taming of the Shrew*: "we should think it was a very happy [marriage], and that in time Katherine . . . having learned the secret of making her lord imagine that he was the master, while she was really directing everything he did . . . would prove to have tamed Petruchio, rather than he to have subdued her" (a fable that, in another register, functions as an allegory for the kind of "bad" feminist criticism that would "tame" Shakespeare). Helen Faucit identified (and allowed herself to be identified) so closely with Shakespeare's heroines that she acquired the power to "interpret" their subsequent actions. As she explained in her widely admired writing on the roles she had played, "I could never leave my characters when the curtain fell and the audience departed. As I had lived with them through their early lives, so I also lived into their future." Faucit based her claims to be Shakespeare's "interpreter" on her own considerable acting skill: a power that she felt Shakespeare had been counting on when he left to sympathetic actors such as herself the task of "filling up his outlines, and giving full and vivid life to the creatures of his brain." A character is necessarily what an actor does with the script before her – the special extravagance of Faucit's claims to "read Shakespeare aright" resides in her belief that such "doing" returned Shakespeare to himself.

V

For Faucit, as for others, Shakespeare was an author who wrote for the future. In Faucit's case he wrote in anticipation of the coming of the actress to the English public stage:

> Without this belief, could he have written as he did, when boys and beardless youths were the only representatives of his women on the stage? Yes, he must have looked beyond "the ignorant present", and known that a time would come when women, true and worthy, should find it a glory to throw the best part of their natures into these ideal types which he has left to testify to his faith in womanhood. . . . How could any youth, however gifted and specially trained, even faintly suggest these fair and noble women to an audience? Woman's words coming from a man's lips, and man's heart – it is monstrous to think of! One quite pities Shakespeare, who had to put up with seeing his brightest creations thus marred, misrepresented, spoiled.

Erasing the material practices that constitute the actor's art, Faucit was able to understand her stage career as a form of moral philosophy. Her aim was to make Shakespeare's "ideal types" into "living realities for thousands to whom they would else have been unknown." The decision to read Shakespeare's plays as works of moral philosophy found its license in Pope's much-repeated assertion that the dramatist provided a model for, rather than a copy of, nature. Elizabeth Montagu subsequently undertook to prove that Shakespeare's works "answer the noblest end of fable, moral instruction"; while Elizabeth Griffith read each play not only for its "general moral," but also for local ethical maxims, and situations illustrative of the truths and dilemmas of "general life." Anna Jameson gave a strong gender inflection to this tradition when she used the plays, more instrumentally still, as evidence of what women could become if they were freed from the oppressive conditions and mistaken educational system of nineteenth-century Britain; while M. Leigh-Noel quoted Charles Cowden Clarke to the effect that Shakespeare's writings had, by their influence, changed the conditions of existence for early modern women: "Shakespeare is the writer of all others whom the women of England should most take to their hearts; for I believe it to be mainly through his intellectual influence that their claims in the scale of society were acknowledged in England, when throughout the civilised world, their position was not greatly elevated above that of the drudges in modern low life."

Shakespeare's moral efficacy is usually derived from his capacity, as Montagu put it, to "throw his soul into the body of another man." Or, of course, of another woman. "How Shakespeare attained to such familiarity with the feminine nature it is impossible to say" (M. Leigh-Noel), but Shakespeare's reputation as the man who understood women has been established – though contested – since Margaret Cavendish remarked his capacity to "Metamorphose from a Man to a Woman" in the first critical essay to be published on his work (in her *Sociable Letters* (1664)). To those women who have loved him, Shakespeare's great gift has usually been said to be his ability to draw women "from life": "of all the male writers that ever lived, he has seen most deeply into the female heart; he has most vividly depicted it in its strength, and in its weakness" (M. Cowden Clarke). Such critics have tended to stress the strengths rather than the weaknesses of Shakespeare's women; working to find good things to say about Ophelia, Volumnia, and Lady Macbeth, and praising more obvious heroines as ideal types. The tension in such criticism between finding Shakespeare's women to be at once thoroughly sympathetic *and* thoroughly realistic is resolved by the assumption that Shakespeare was able to understand women as they really are, rather than as they have been made to appear and act by prevailing social conditions. If Shakespeare's heroines appear to be idealized, that is because woman's nature – the nature she will be free to express only once she has been liberated from the distorting influence of her current constraints – *is* ideal. It is in this sense that Shakespeare can be said to understand the women of the future while – this happens in "The Ladies' Shakespeare" – the women of the future will be able to recognize themselves in Shakespeare's heroines.

Mary Cowden Clarke built rather differently on Shakespeare's reputation as a moral instructor in "Shakespeare as the Girl's Friend" (1887), an essay which describes Shakespeare's heroines offering themselves as ego ideals to young women:

> To the young girl, emerging from childhood and taking her first step into the more active and self-dependent career of woman-life, Shakespeare's vital precepts and models render him essentially a helping friend. . . . Through his feminine portraits she may see, as in a faithful glass, vivid pictures of what she has to evitate, or what she has to imitate . . . in accordance with what she feels and learns to be the supremest harmonious effect in self-amelioration of character. She can take her own disposition in hand, as it were, and endeavour to mould and form it into the best perfection of which it is capable, by carefully observing the women drawn by Shakespeare.

While Cowden Clarke leaves unspecified the principle according to which the young woman knows what to "evitate" and what to "imitate" in Shakespeare, she implies that it originates with feeling, and is subsequently ratified by the reader's own experience of "self-amelioration of character." Through their identification with the different aspects of Shakespeare's heroines, Cowden Clarke expects readers to "gain lessons in artlessness, guilelessness, modesty, sweetness, and the most winning candour . . . moral courage, meekness, magnanimity, firmness, devoted tenderness, high principle, noble conduct, loftiest speech and sentiment." According to Cowden Clarke, Shakespeare works his effects by requiring readers to give themselves up, through identification with one of his characters, to his own ethical intelligence, and, by rehearsing the ethical position so offered, to gain knowledge both of themselves and of an ideal to which they might aspire. This introduces a prosthetic element into the circular logic of an ethical education whereby, without it, only the good would be moved to identify with the good. Shakespeare, it seems, is morally efficacious not because his portraits are uniformly good, but because of his ability to effect a logic of identification whose object is finally himself.

The operation of this logic can be seen within "The Ladies' Shakespeare" in the fantasy whereby a woman's unique capacity to understand Shakespeare renders her heroic to herself and others. That the fantasy exists outside Barrie's joke is demonstrated in the reception of Elizabeth Montagu's *Essay*, which defends Shakespeare against the criticism of Voltaire, and was commended by Garrick in a poem that represents Montagu as an armed Pallas, rushing to "protect the Bard" from the malice of the Gallic Giant; and by the case of Elizabeth Griffith, who modeled herself on Montagu as a "Lady . . . champion in [Shakespeare's] cause." In 1736 the Shakespeare Ladies Club, which was established to petition theater managers to stage Shakespeare's plays, was praised in similar terms by Mary Cowper, in a poem that attributes Shakespeare's revival in the eighteenth century to women alone: "the softer Sex redeems the Land / And Shakespear lives again by their Command"; while in 1833 Fanny Kemble wrote to Anna Jameson: "A lady assured me the other day, that when you went to heaven, which you certainly would, Shakespeare would meet you and kiss you for having understood, and made others understand, him so well."

The tone of these tributes is mock-heroic and raises the important question of what it means for women to read and defend a poet whom everyone is reading, and who needs no defending. In 1726 Lewis Theobald underlined the "universal" popularity of Shakespeare by noting there were very few English poets "more the Subject of the Ladies Reading" – a statement which should not be taken as an index of women's serious involvement with Shakespeare, for Theobald seems to have found it remarkable not that *only* women read Shakespeare, but that *even* women did. To value a poet and believe him in need of defending – perhaps especially if others agree with you – may act as an ethical tonic on an individual's life; while the role of Shakespeare's champion may have resulted in real, if incalculable, cultural benefits, individually and as a group, to the women who have accepted it. But Barrie's essay suggests, rather, that where women and their interests are included in the study of Shakespeare, there that study is liable to derogation. For Barrie's talk erects a structure of exclusion *within* the Stationer's Company dinner – on the one side Lord Balfour, Kipling (the most manly of writers, as Virginia Woolf called him), and the Company members; on the other Barrie (who represented himself the least serious of the new members), the women who, not being Company members, could not be there, and Shakespeare. And here Shakespeare has become, in jest, the figurehead for that coalition between women and literature that has – in earnest – rarely translated into increased cultural authority for either one of them.

VI

Barrie ended his speech at Stationer's Hall by invoking its ghost, at once "the glory and the terror" of the Company. This specter is the ghost not of Hamlet's father (in which guise the poet has revisited Shakespeareans since Rowe), but of his mother:

> As I understand, all of you who are members have seen it. It is what gives you that look that is to be found on no other faces. . . . The ghost is a scrap of paper which proves that Bacon did not write the plays, and so far so good, but – I get this from "the Ladies' Shakespeare" – but Bacon was not the only author in that household. The document is signed by Shakespeare and is in these words: "Received of Lady Bacon for fathering her play of *Hamlet* – five pounds."

The proposition that Shakespeare was a woman was repeated – with a difference – in 1985 by Maya Angelou, who in an address to the National Assembly of Local Arts Agencies in Washington, DC famously remarked "William Shakespeare was a black woman," for he had marvelously understood and written about her "outcast state." Angelou produced this witty formulation by extending two assumptions that she expected her audience to share: that Shakespeare's empathy reached into every subject position, and that his work can properly be appropriated in order to give voice to such positions. Barrie puts the same assumption, in what he considers to be a ludicrous form, on display in "The Ladies' Shakespeare" when he also claims that Shakespeare was a woman. In either form, the claim is only a strong registration of that need to identify Shakespeare's interests with our own which is the premise of historicist as well as feminist criticism.

Barrie's identification of Shakespeare's signature as being that of Lady Bacon is also designed to invoke the Baconian controversy; an argument which first emerged within Shakespeare criticism with the suggestion, in the eighteenth century, that "the Shakespearian works" had been written by Sir Francis Bacon. The theory received important impetus from the work of Delia Bacon, whose *Philosophy of the Plays of Shakspere Unfolded* (1859) argued that "Shakspere" was the name of a consortium of writers, who wrote the plays in order to promote (in "carefully hidden, yet not less carefully indicated" form) Bacon's new system of philosophy, and to prepare the populace for the social revolution that was to follow. According to Delia Bacon, Bacon and his associates were writing both for and to bring about the future age that would understand them, and they had recourse to literature in the first instance "for the purpose of instituting a gradual encroachment on popular opinions." But they were also living in dangerous times, when the new absolutism of the Tudors was sitting athwart an intellectual renaissance, and they consequently deployed a "rhetoric of secrecy" that hid their purposes from the authorities of the State, while at the same time provoking the "philosophic curiosity" of those fit to learn them. Explaining that the language of literature uniquely met these conflicting needs of communication and disguise, education and discretion, Delia Bacon argues that literature, and drama in particular, provided the radical "Few" with a register into which they could "translate their doctrine," as well as with a philosophical style which could address quotidian circumstances – "That is the reason why the development of that age comes to us as *Literature*. . . . The leadership of the modern ages, when it was already here in the persons of its chief interpreters and prophets, could as yet get no recognition of its right to teach and rule – . . . it could only wave, in mute gesticulation, its signals to the future."

Subsequent Baconians, such as Constance Pott, elaborated this argument, tying it ever more tightly to the person of Francis Bacon and his known interest in cryptic wisdom. According to Pott's bathetic account, Bacon (who was the illegitimate son of Elizabeth I) decided at a young age to "set to work and endeavour to bring about a universal Revival or Renaissance." After traveling in France (where he wrote the first draft of Montaigne's essays), Bacon founded a secret intellectual society, wrote "the Shakspeare plays" and other works (which he gave "to be fathered and adopted by anyone who gave promise of . . . sending them out into the world to do their destined work for the good of humanity"), and lived beyond 1626, revising and enlarging former works, and writing "a mess of new books, historical, scientific, religious." Believing that Bacon "left his fingerprints" – both his signature and his true message – in the works he did not dare acknowledge as his own, Pott and others searched "Bacon's" works for cryptograms; and secret signs that had been seeded in them as signals to posterity were subsequently found, not only in the writings themselves, but in title pages, chapter headings, page numbers, printer's marks, textual discrepancies, and, in the case of the Shakespeare plays, in the differences between the Quartos and the Folios.

For those outside it, as for Barrie himself, the Baconian theory has come to embody the madness of unregulated scholarship; a spectacle instructive only as a demonstration of the way in which historical naivety may elaborate itself on the margins of an academic field. But Delia Bacon's proposition that "Shakspeare" was the name not of an author but of a book produced by multiple hands and collaborative intellectual practices is no longer scandalous within a discipline that is currently itself working to think outside the author function. Similarly, her argument that Shakespeare's plays code a criticism of the prevailing order that dare not speak its name, her belief that there are "heroic intellects" who are not simply "blind historical agents" but can see beyond the circumstances of their moment, and her conclusion that works of literature have political meanings that can become legible only under certain historical circumstances, are also familiar suppositions within Shakespeare criticism, and may be summed up in the line from *Coriolanus* which Bacon used as the epigraph to her work: "One time will owe another." In Bacon's work, this line functions to propose that the present both owns and remains in debt to the past, while the past both owns and remains in debt to the present for its realization. It is this proposition (startling only because it usually lies unnoticed behind the various critical practices for which it is the final motive) that is given full parodic form in "The Ladies' Shakespeare" – a text that, deriving its being from Shakespeare, manages nevertheless to put him in debt to itself. The critical practice that is being mocked here is both intelligent and historically naive, ethically strenuous and narcissistic, loving and unfilial: for Shakespeareans, it is both "The Ladies' Shakespeare" and the only form of criticism we have.

REFERENCES AND FURTHER READING

Auerbach, N. 1982: *Woman and the Demon.* Cambridge, MA: Harvard University Press.

Callaghan, D., Helms, L., and Singh, J. 1994: *The Weyward Sisters: Shakespeare and Feminist Politics.* Oxford: Blackwell.

Carlisle, C. 1979: "The Critics Discover Shakespeare's Women." In A. L. DeNeef and M. T. Hester (eds.), *Renaissance Papers 1979.* Southern Renaissance Conference, 59–73.

Dobson, M. 1992: *The Making of the National Poet: Shakespeare, Adaptation, and Authorship, 1660–1769.* Oxford: Clarendon Press.

Erickson, P. 1991: *Rewriting Shakespeare, Rewriting Ourselves.* Los Angeles: University of California Press.

Goldberg, J. 1992: *Sodometries: Renaissance Texts, Modern Sexualities.* Stanford: Stanford University Press.

de Grazia, M. 1992: *Shakespeare Verbatim.* Oxford: Clarendon Press.

——and Stallybrass, P. 1993: "The Materiality of the Shakespearean Text." *Shakespeare Quarterly,* 44, 255–83.

Greenblatt, S. 1988: *Shakespearean Negotiations: The Circulation of Social Energy in Renaissance England.* Berkeley and Los Angeles: University of California Press.

Howard, J. 1989a: "Scripts and/versus Playhouses: Ideological Production and the Renaissance Public Stage." *Renaissance Drama,* 20, 31–49.

——1989b: "Crossdressing, the Theatre, and Gender Struggle in Early Modern England." *Shakespeare Quarterly,* 39, 418–40.

Jardine, L. 1989: *Still Harping on Daughters.* London: Harvester Wheatsheaf, and New York: Columbia University Press.

Lenz, C. R. S., Greene, G., and Neely, C. T. (eds.)

1980: *The Womans Part: Feminist Criticism of Shakespeare.* Chicago: Chicago University Press.

Levine, L. 1986: "Men in Women's Clothing: Anti-Theatricality and Effeminization from 1579 to 1642." *Criticism,* 28, 121–43.

McLuskie, K. 1985: "The Patriarchal Bard: Feminist Criticism and Shakespeare: *King Lear* and *Measure for Measure.*" In J. Dollimore and A. Sinfield (eds.), *Political Shakespeare.* Manchester: Manchester University Press, 88–108.

Marcus, L. 1995: "The Shakespearean Editor as Shrew-Tamer." In D. Barker and I. Kamps (eds.), *Shakespeare and Gender: A History.* London: Verso, 214–34.

Marsden, J. (ed.) 1991: *The Appropriation of Shakespeare.* London: Harvester Wheatsheaf.

Novy, M. (ed.) 1990: *Women's Re-Visions of Shakespeare: On the Responses of Dickenson, Woolf, Rich, H.D., George Eliot and Others.* Urbana: University of Illinois Press.

——(ed.) 1993: *Cross-Cultural Performances: Differences in Women's Revisions of Shakespeare.* Urbana: University of Illinois Press.

——(ed.) 1994: *Engaging with Shakespeare: Responses of George Eliot and Other Women Novelists.* Athens: University of Georgia Press.

Taylor, G. 1989: *Reinventing Shakespeare: A Cultural History from the Restoration to the Present.* New York: Weidenfeld and Nicolson.

Thompson, A. 1996: "Pre-feminism or Proto-feminism? Early Women Readers of Shakespeare." *Elizabethan Theatre,* 14, 195–211.

——and Roberts, S. 1997: *Women Reading Shakespeare, 1660–1900: An Anthology of Criticism.* Manchester: Manchester University Press.

Traub, V. 1992: *Desire and Anxiety: Circulations of Sexuality in Shakespearean Drama.* London: Routledge.

2

Margaret Cavendish, Shakespeare Critic

Katherine M. Romack

Introduction

In 1896, anti-suffragist Emily Perkins Bissell ridiculed the women's movement in an article entitled "The Mistaken Vocation of Shakespeare's Heroines." It is an elaborate fantasy depicting an outspoken advocate of "progressive Womanhood" delivering a lecture to a "Twentieth-Century Women's Club" on "Shakespeare's attitude with respect to his heroines" (233). Published first in *The Century Magazine*, and a year later in the *American Shakespeare Magazine* (1897), her satire includes a transcript of the fictional "lecture" complete with invented audience response. The exuberant speaker, in Bissell's parody of feminism, decries "the whole structure of Shakespeare's dramas" which rest "upon the disenfranchisement of those heroines whom he is falsely supposed to idealize" (233). She opens her lecture with a brief critique of Shakespeare's reception:

> Doubtless you have been taught in youth, as I was, to consider him as an unsurpassed delineator of female character; doubtless Rosalind and Juliet, Portia and Cordelia, Ophelia and Imogen, Viola and Beatrice, have been held up to you as the ideals of a perfect Womanhood. Doubtless, also, you have believed it all, and never stopped to think that Shakespeare himself was but a man, and that his commentators have been men without being Shakespeares. The masculine conception of female character has thus been forced upon us. Shall we submit? (Cries of "No!" "No!"). (233)

Furthermore, the imagined speaker asserts, Shakespeare's plots are motivated not by the actions of male characters but by the deliberate misplacement of his heroines. Hamlet "would have killed the king half an hour after Lady Macbeth came to court," she claims; Macbeth was a "weak" man who needed the strong hand of Portia to guide him, and Beatrice would have quickly dispelled Othello's "jealousies like a summer cloud, laughed away his suspicions, and teased him out of his authority" (234). "In view of these plain facts, my sisters," she asks, "can we longer accept William Shakespeare as an authority?" (235). Her audience enthusiastically replies, " 'No!' 'No!' " (235).

Bissell's demeaning portrait of feminism deploys the quintessential figure of Western literary culture – Shakespeare – to suggest that an aspiration for women's political rights is self-evidently ludicrous. Women's political entitlement is here rendered synonymous with the epitome of cultural corruption: cries of " 'Down with Shakespeare!' " (235). Her fiction indicates that an imagined "feminist aversion to Shakespeare" was, by the nineteenth century, if not commonplace, at least conceivable as she posits a close affinity between women claiming political right and courting cultural depravity. The central role Shakespeare plays in Bissell's figuration of women's's calls for political right raises important questions at the conjuncture of feminist historiography and Shakespeare studies about the historical relationship between feminism and bardolatry. Her satiric assertion of a nineteenth-century animosity between feminists and Shakespeare is prescient; explicitly feminist critiques of Shakespeare are really a product of the century to follow. Historically, the feminist tradition is, instead, one of *identification with* the Bard. As Marianne Novy points out, it is only in "the early twentieth century, a time of self-conscious belief in new possibilities for women" that "several women writers begin to see limitations in Shakespeare's characters" (1990: 7–8). The recognition of Shakespeare's limitations by a handful of female critics "emerged fairly recently out of a tradition that more often appropriated Shakespeare for women" (1990: 2). Even today, feminist readings of Shakespeare remain predominantly affirmative. In 1990, Novy introduced the long-standing tradition of women's identification with Shakespeare to literary studies in her ground-breaking anthology, *Women's Re-Visions of Shakespeare*. Since its publication, a number of works have begun to fill in the gaps of this history, substantiating, through example, Novy's original assertion of a largely affirmative women's tradition and making it, at long last, impossible to write a compelling history of Shakespeare criticism without first considering women's role in its development.

I began this essay with a nineteenth-century anti-feminist phantasm because it points to a direct, though not necessarily causal, relationship between antagonism toward women's calls for political entitlement and identification with Shakespeare. Bissell's satire, in short, unintentionally suggests a structural tension between women's access to political and cultural representation. In hinting at an adversarial relationship between the canon – with Shakespeare as its representative – and women's attempts to achieve political enfranchisement, Bissell's satire indicates that women's relationship to representation cannot be understood exclusively in cultural terms. A different type of explanation, a different history of women and Shakespeare, is needed. Such a history requires a careful consideration of *both* women's literary and political endeavors – endeavors playing a constitutive role in the creation of "the Bard" – and can reveal not only the political grounds of women's exclusion from culture, but also, as I hope to demonstrate here, the cultural grounds of women's political exclusion as well.

This essay turns back to the seventeenth century in order to chart the emergence of the tradition of women's identification with Shakespeare, taking up the cultural politics of the work of Margaret Cavendish, Duchess of Newcastle, in order to evaluate her fraught contributions to early modern "bardolatry" and "feminism." Here, I will examine the first appraisal of Shakespeare by a woman writer in an attempt to account for the remarkable historical endurance of the anti-feminist bardolatry so scathingly advanced 200 years later in Bissell's lampoon.

Taken up as early as the Restoration by such women writers as Katherine Philips, Dorothy Osborne, Mary Evelyn, Bathsua Makin, and Mary Astell, Cavendish has occupied a prominent, if troublesome, place in women's literary history for over three centuries. Historically characterized as neurotic, eclectic, narcissistic, foolish, dull, mad, eccentric, singular, irregular, and contradictory, Cavendish's writing has, in spite of – or rather, because of – these epithets, retained a degree of currency, remarkable for a woman, in political, scientific, and literary history. Cavendish has come to signal early modern women's literary conventions, conventions situated "off the map" of the male tradition. At the same time, her work can be read as marking a turning point in the history of women's efforts to achieve cultural "inclusion." In taking up Shakespeare as a model for her own writerly authority, Cavendish inaugurated the tradition of female identification with Shakespeare, a tradition that has come to dominate feminist Shakespeare criticism today. Her appropriation of Shakespeare is significant, not least because it demonstrates that women, marginalized by the literary tradition, could and did transform Shakespeare in ways that affirmed, and rendered authoritative, *the very exteriority of their own writerly engagements*.

The persistence and pervasiveness of the Bard as an icon linking the English-speaking world to early modern culture, and as an emblem of culture more broadly, gives feminists good cause to ask, what relation, historically and today, do women have to the Shakespearean ethos and, by extension, to the signposts of high culture more generally? Just as women's relationship to Shakespeare was historically one of identification, today this literary icon continues to offer many feminists a fruitful ground for the elucidation of women's relationship to culture. The strength and duration of the Bard's reputation, his power as cultural currency, and the sheer magnitude of the "Shakespeare industry," appear to compel feminists to lay claim to him. It would seem that feminists will be required to take Shakespeare up as long as the power relations of culture remain a central feminist concern – he is today, after all, commonly cast as synonymous with "culture" itself.

Yet, if Bissell's nineteenth-century anti-feminist fantasy (however unwittingly) signals anything, it is that there is an implicitly adversarial dimension of the relationship between women and Shakespeare that feminists would do well to attend to. Although it would be specious to argue that there is something endemic to the works of Shakespeare themselves that contributes to the continued political and cultural disenfranchisement of women, like any "document[s] of civilization" surviving the progress of history, Shakespeare's works carry with them a kind of historical baggage, a historical trace or residue which, in the words of Walter Benjamin, one "cannot contemplate without horror" (1969: 256). Our elation at Gwyneth Paltrow's success on the boards in the blockbuster *Shakespeare in Love* (1999) swiftly fades when we recall the specter of Woolf's "Judith Shakespeare" lying dead, misplaced, under a bus-stop, or when we visualize the stark contrast between the numerous national monuments erected in honor of Shakespeare and Aphra Behn's worn-out marker sitting at the foot of a ramp in Westminster Abbey.

Foreshadowing the twentieth-century recognition of the limitations of Shakespeare for women, Constance O'Brien, in 1879, cautiously mentions in passing that "[t]he intercourse of mother and daughter is not one of Shakespeare's favourite subjects; he only touches it twice, as if he was not quite sure of the ways of women together" (O'Brien 1997: 143). Almost 120 years later, Hillary Hinds – revealing full-blown irritation and quite justified frustration with the continued neglect of women's early modern cultural production – more pointedly asks,

> Why should Shakespeare's history plays, with their overt concern to construct a fitting genealogy for the glories of the reign of Elizabeth I, or his Roman plays, with their direct and unmistakable political commentaries, be accepted as being at the heart of English literature, whilst [women's] sectarian texts are excluded on the basis of their political character? (1996: 5)

Such a question attests to the Janus-faced nature of Shakespeare's relationship to feminism. On the one hand, women have historically appropriated Shakespeare to authorize their own cultural engagements – an approach to Shakespeare that remains dominant today; on the other, Shakespeare stands as a monument to the historical exclusion of women from culture – a side of Shakespeare that feminists have been far more reluctant to address.

To elucidate Cavendish's cultural theory, and the role that bardolatry plays within it, requires a foregrounding of the fundamental alterity of early modern women's cultural production. This involves a careful mapping of women's relationship to both cultural and political economies of representation, a map which does not conform well to dominant generic modes and formal conventions, to conventional periodization or political categories. In as far as Shakespeare has come to embody the canon, women's cultural production always stands in a somewhat ambivalent relationship to him, even if the relationship between women and Shakespeare has been largely construed as a "positive" one. Cavendish's use of the Bard to produce a theory of and justification for women's cultural production is troublesome for feminism in as far as her appropriation of Shakespeare as a symbol of women's literary inclusion necessarily contributed to the production of the very forms of authorship and standards of literary value that would subsequently be used to exclude women's cultural production. Shakespeare stands at the center of the literary tradition but Cavendish, resisting this masculinist tradition, works to situate him outside of its institutions and their conventions. Cavendish, in short, figures Shakespeare as a "natural wit" who stands next to the woman writer at the margins of the literary tradition. For many feminists today,

Shakespeare continues to represent this type of exteriority. However, in taking up Shakespeare, Cavendish inaugurated a tradition in which women from the Restoration on would – by taking up the works and words of Shakespeare to justify women's ever-increasing participation in the cultural arena – paradoxically participate in the construction of the very masculinist paradigms of literary value associated with the elevation of Shakespeare to the apex of British culture.

My aim here is to investigate the political implications of women's identification with the Bard. Exploring the first known example of a woman's published engagement with Shakespeare, I will suggest that there is a necessary affinity between bardolatry and anti-feminism, an affinity hypervisible in Bissell's parody of feminism and endemic to the very origins of the tradition of identification itself. In the sections that follow, I first outline the contours of Cavendish's bardolatry, situating it within the fraught political arena of mid-seventeenth-century England. I then move on to draw explicit connections between Cavendish's bardolatry and the ambivalence of her relationship to feminism, for Cavendish's praise of Shakespeare is intricately bound up with the politics of her "Tory feminism," a concept, I will contend, in need of substantial rethinking. The conjunction of bardolatry with Tory feminism appears in Cavendish's work at a decisive moment in the rearticulation of authorship and political authority. Writing between two economies of authorship, Cavendish imagines not only a new kind of author but a new subject of patriarchy. Each qualify and temper the other. If the revolutionary mid-century collapse of established cultural and political institutions provided an opportunity for subjects to negotiate their own representational status, this also opened spaces for women to contest their subordinate place in representation. Unlike a number of her mid-century counterparts, Cavendish strictly divorces culture and politics using women's exclusion from the political arena as a justification for their writerly engagement in a now depoliticized, ungendered cultural arena. If the decline of absolutism offered women the opportunity to reconfigure their relationship to representation, for the "rude sort," this opportunity would be a fleeting one. The renegotiation of privileged women's relationship to representation – filtering out, as it did, the "rude sort," and transforming, by devulgarizing, Shakespeare into a universalized representative of high culture – would prove to be much more enduring.

Margaret Cavendish, Shakespeare Critic

Cavendish's defense of Shakespeare against a detractor who characterized Shakespeare's plays as "made up onely with Clowns, Fools, Watchmen and the like," in her *Sociable Letters*, published in 1664, has been used to bestow upon her the title of first Shakespeare critic (1997: 130). According to the Riverside Shakespeare, Cavendish "anticipates Dryden in being the first to give a general prose assessment of Shakespeare as dramatist" (Evans 1974: 1847). Following the Riverside, Ann Thompson and Sasha Roberts assert that Cavendish penned "the first critical essay ever to be published on Shakespeare" (1997: 2). Shakespeare, for Cavendish, is a self-motivated natural wit: "indeed Shakespear had a Clear Judgement, a Quick Wit, a Spreading Fancy, a Subtil Observation, a Deep Apprehension, and a most Eloquent Elocution; truly, he was a Natural Orator, as well as a Natural Poet" (1997: 131). Here, as in all of Cavendish's commentaries on what it means to produce "true" poetry, conformity to the laws of nature is given priority over conformity to the laws of art. In her *Poems and Fancies* (1653), for example, Cavendish strictly divides art and nature, aligning art with "pedantry": "GIVE *Mee* the *Free*, and *Noble Stile*, / Which seems *uncurb'd*, though it be *wild* . . . Give me a *Stile* that *Nature* frames, not *Art*: / For *Art* doth seem to take the *Pedants* part" (110). Her entire oeuvre is consistent in aligning true wit with nature and art with artificial learning. The value of Shakespeare's works rests in their novelty, their breaking of literary convention, in their naturalness.

The deep commitment to literary originality that pervades her laudatory account of Shakespeare's skill as a dramatist has been frequently noted by critics. On numerous occasions, Cavendish charged a variety of playwrights with literary theft in order to accentuate, by contrast, both her esteem for originality and the very uniqueness of her own literary creations. Although Shakespeare numbered among those she derided for pilfering, it is clear that Cavendish finds in Shakespeare a type of authorial model preferable to that of other playwrights (especially the "learned" Jonson). Shakespeare, while not as original as Cavendish might have liked, is still characterized as the best model for her own formulation of a theory of criticism based on the ideals of originality and native genius. In Letter 123, for example, she excuses Shakespeare's borrowings in an elaborate apology:

> Shakespear's Wit and Eloquence was General, for, and upon all Subjects, he rather wanted Subjects for his Wit and Eloquence to Work on, for which he was Forced to take Some of his Plots out of History, where he only took the Bare Designs, the Wit and Language being all his Own; and so much he had above others, that those, who Writ after him, were Forced to Borrow of him, or rather to Steal from him (Cavendish 1997: 131).

Although Cavendish was the first to give a comprehensive assessment of Shakespeare's work, her attributions of native artistic genius, self-generated creativity, singularity, and originality to Shakespeare were not, in themselves, novel. The various collections of seventeenth-century allusions to Shakespeare, for example, attest to a pervasive association of these characteristics with the Bard. The attachment of natural wit, unpolished genius, and native poet to the "gentler shepheard" and his "hony-flowing Vaine" are part of tradition dating all the way back to the late sixteenth century and the writings of Edmund Spenser and Richard Barnfeild (quoted in Ingleby 1879: 1, 26).

Cavendish's innovation is instead that she depicts Shakespeare's "gentle wit" as one transcending gender, thereby clearing a space for women to lay claim to Shakespeare as a model for their own authorship. She even imagines Shakespeare himself as a woman: "one would think that he had been Metamorphosed from a Man to a Woman, for who could Describe Cleopatra Better than he hath done, and many other Females of his own Creating, as Nan Page, Mrs. Page, Mrs. Ford, the Doctors Maid, Bettrice, Mrs. Quickly, Doll Tearsheet, and others, too many to relate?" (Cavendish 1997: 130). Cavendish values Shakespeare for his protean ability to know the secrets of gender, to write as if he were a natural woman.

Cavendish's transformation of Shakespeare into an icon that could be used to legitimate women's literary production was to become a common feature of women's writings on Shakespeare from the Restoration on. Shakespeare, the unlearned native genius, for the female dramatist of the late seventeenth century, set literary precedent for, justified, and served as an authorial model of dramatic engagement that did not require admission into the formal and informal institutions of male culture and learning. In the seventeenth century, Aphra Behn, echoing Cavendish, writes, "plays have no room for that which is men's great advantage over women, that is learning; We all well know that the immortal Shakespeare's plays . . . have better pleas'd the world than Jonson's works" (Behn 1915: I, 224). In the eighteenth, nineteenth, and twentieth centuries, such writers as Elizabeth Montagu, Mary Lamb, and Sylvia Townsend Warner would similarly maintain that Shakespeare's untutored status set him on grounds equivalent to that of the woman writer.

Cavendish's derision of the artificial arbitration of literary/dramatic "taste" and her seemingly deep commitment to aristocratic aesthetics would each seem to be at odds with Shakespeare; Shakespeare was, after all, a professional hack himself, situated in opposition to the aristocratic culture she wished to defend. A Royalist woman attempting to justify her own literary production, Cavendish attempts to resurrect a Renaissance authorial paradigm of literary property which can lend authority to the woman of quality's cultural engagements. Cavendish, sympathetic to the old regime, engages in the Royalist process of cultural redefinition by taking up a figure traditionally located in opposition to dominant Renaissance cultural institutions as a way to reject the "learned" transformations of her male contemporaries. This, however, required her to take up a figure fundamentally opposed to court culture more generally. Cavendish neutralized the problems for Royalism this presented by attributing to Shakespeare an androgynous, abstracted, and decommercialized wit, a wit to which the aristocratic woman of quality could lay claim. Cavendish thus "purifies" Shakespeare. He is purged not only of all attachments to masculinist institutions of learning, but also of all associations with the professionalism of the commercial theater. The works of Shakespeare are carefully detached from the popular, vulgar, commercial, illicit history of the Renaissance theater. By strategically manufacturing precedent for her own literary production, Cavendish propels Shakespeare to the exalted heights of universal paragon of authorship. Through a profoundly complex and instrumental misreading, she then proceeds to restrict what is, ostensibly, a universal paradigm of authorship to a small group of "aristocratic" cultural arbiters. The process of wresting Shakespeare from the environment of the professional theater reflects not so much Cavendish's investment in restoring aristocratic culture as her investment (as a member of the dispossessed aristocracy) in an entirely new set of emergent cultural values. As we shall see, Shakespeare is, in short, transformed by Cavendish into a locus for the abstract cultural values of the privileged, a locus that is unmistakeably bourgeois – through and through.

It was Shakespeare's elevation to the status of universal cultural icon in the project of restoration that constitutes bardolatry's inauguration. As Shakespeare became increasingly associated with Royalist "high culture," he came to instantiate the modern myth of authorship. He begins to be regarded, as Jeffrey Masten so aptly puts it, "as *the* individual Author and the author of individuality," his works "as chronologies of personal/generic development, as material for authorial psychoanalysis, as the organic efflux of the singular mind of genius, as maps of a particularly individuated language and imagery" (1997: 10). Or, to use the words of Stephen Greenblatt, Shakespeare began to take on the character of a "great creating nature: the common bond of humankind, the principle of hope, the symbol of the imagination's power to transcend time-bound beliefs and assumptions, peculiar historical circumstances, and specific artistic conventions" (1997: 1).

Cavendish's Shakespeare criticism, in short, opened a space for women in culture, but her commitment to limiting this space to aristocratic women constantly tempers and logically contradicts the universality she ascribes to Shakespeare. She would certainly have been dismayed by the uses to which Shakespeare would be put by ever-increasing numbers of women – following her lead – in the centuries to come. Cavendish attempted to use Shakespeare to restrict cultural production to a female elite. However, the elevation of Shakespeare's originality and native genius over Royalist institutional insularity contradicts her commitment to defending aristocratic conceptions of literary culture as such, revealing, instead, a deeper commitment to limiting literary property to her own class. She carefully distinguishes between "noble amateurs and mercenary professionals," as she works to place culture into the hands of the aristocratic person of quality who possesses the natural ability to dabble in a variety of activities and be successful at each (Tomlinson 1992: 144). For Cavendish, the ideal person of quality possesses a general knowledge, an unbound fancy, and a natural wit, qualities suppressed by institutional learning, professional specialization, political interest, and necessity. Learning, careerism, polemic, and need each quelch the literary imagination. Shakespeare, in Cavendish's account, transcends gender, class, and the politics of each. He is abstracted into a universally androgynous, classless, and apolitical figure. Her attempts to appropriate and limit claims to Shakespeare reflect the emergence of a new conceptualization of authorship which emerges in the wake of absolutism's decline, an authorship characterized by an amorphously asexual yet profoundly individualized sense of literary property. The qualities Cavendish attributes to him – a "general" knowledge and a "natural" wit – were the same qualities that would ultimately become dominant ideals of subjective worth. Her figuration of the Bard – decontextualized, depoliticized, decommercialized, idealized, and de-gendered – in short, mirrors the parallel development of the abstract subject of liberal patriarchy.

Cavendish's cultural theory and the complicated role of Shakespeare within it need to be related to the seventeenth-century transformation of authorship and situated within this development's intimate attachment to long-standing political transformations of an absolutist model of government. By the mid-century, this political model (and its attendant configuration of corporate rights and representation) gave way to a proliferation of competing political theories which included the production of some of the most radically democratic theorizations of individual rights and political representation ever before seen in England. Absolutist authority – compromised by its overextension to subjects beyond the monarch – crumbled under the weight of the contradictions produced by the sheer bulk and multiplicity of social groups vying for representational enfranchisement. There was an increased awareness in the mid-century of the stakes of widening the terrain of political interpretation. If authorship is typically a "high" cultural issue, intimately bound up with the question of who possesses the power to represent, then by the mid-seventeenth century authorship as a concept was shaken to its very foundations by the widespread contest over who was to be granted the right to politically represent. Pressures on conventional modes of political representation were thus matched by a rapid reconfiguration of modes of cultural representation and their concepts, including "authorship," as Roundheads, Royalists, and independents scrambled to rearticulate the very grounds of representation itself.

What would ultimately emerge as "high culture" in the later part of the century was already well under construction by the mid-century as Royalists aggressively engaged in the task of "restoring" culture. This project of cultural restoration is characterized by the enclosure, privatization, and careful regulation of culture by small Royalist literary coteries. These circles were pervaded by a strong aristocratic ethos and effectively transferred the aesthetics of court-based culture into the homes of Royalists. Between 1642 and 1660, for example, there was an explosion of "closet drama": "some ninety closet plays were written, three times as many as in the four previous decades. The authors and publishers of these plays were without exception Royalists" (Straznicky 1995: 357). Shakespeare as an icon – if not an agent – would play a central role in this project of cultural restoration. Royalist women's approaches to authorship reflect the changing economy of culture as well as they struggled to situate their writing within this project of "restoration":

> In this process we find women writers developing a fantasy of a Royalist return to Renaissance values in which women figure the possibility of a "restored" economy of literary-social relations without the underpinning of a patriarchalist belief (in the divine "fatherhood" of sovereign power) as an exclusively masculine circuit of patronage and power. (Ballaster 1996: 274)

As much as Royalists framed their project as a restoration of the political and cultural ideals of aristocracy, it is clear that by the mid-century, the "aristocratic" culture which both male and female Royalists were ostensibly attempting to restore was no longer viable; "return" was an ideological obfuscation, a chimera. Political "restoration" was, by this time, a practical impossibility, as was the cultural ethos attached to it. Royalists' heated assertions of deep commitment to both political absolutism and aristocratic culture were, after the events of the mid-century, nothing more than the ideological mystification of an increasingly bourgeois class paying homage to the defunct regime which had granted it the historical privilege it had once enjoyed and fought to regain. Royalist culture would ultimately become synonymous with "high" culture, a culture which took up and transformed court culture, turning to classical models to buttress and legitimate an aristocratic regime in decline.

Cavendish's theory of writerly authority, and her figuration of Shakespeare within it – in as far as they constitute just such a fantasy of return by appropriating the Renaissance for women – were part and parcel of the larger project of restoring monarchy. Her depiction of women's relationship to culture reflects the complexity of this mystificatory project. Her writings on women and culture are riddled with logical inconsistency, strained by her attempts to restrict access to the universal model of cultural authority she paradoxically requires to authorize her own writings. For example, Cavendish often claims that poetry is women's province by virtue of their differently tempered "brains." Women are depicted as better suited for poetry than men because of their natural imaginative capacity. Her work, Cavendish claims, is *"free* from all *dishonesty"* if not from vanity: "for that is so *naturall* to our *Sex*, as it were unnatural, not to be so. Besides, *Poetry*, which is built upon *Fancy*, *Women* may claime, as a *worke* belonging most properly to themselves (1653: Sig. A3). Existing alongside such biologistic alignments of women with literary creativity and narcissism are statements which indicate a clear recognition of the historically contingent nature of women's domain:

> There will be many Heroick Women in some Ages, in others very Propheticall; in some ages very pious, and devout: for our Sex is wonderfully addicted to the spirits. But this Age has produced many effeminate [female] Writers, as well as Preachers, and many effeminate Rulers as well as Actors. And if it be an age when the effeminate spirits rule, as most visible they doe in every Kingdome, let us take advantage. . . .
> *That though our Bodies dye,*
> *Our Names may live to after memory.* (Sig. Aav)

Cavendish's assertion that various historical "ages" will configure women's role in them in manifold ways demonstrates that she was acutely aware of the conventional nature of women's historical exclusion from culture. Cavendish thus aligns women with poetic skill through a strategic double move by which women are, simultaneously, biologically and customarily affiliated with creativity. In other words, Cavendish's repeated argument that women have specific, gendered, natural capacities for certain kinds of writing and that these capacities are simultaneously "customary" (historically and socially contingent) is a necessary, if irrational, double position. Cavendish is required to justify women's engagement with culture. This requires both a recognition of the social nature of women's historical exclusion from literary production and a naturalized justification for women's inclusion. Cavendish uses the same tactic to set limits on women's cultural production, to ensure that cultural inclusion will not be used to grant women a political voice, but, rather, a cultural "name." For example, the possibility of women playing a role as political agents (female "rule") is entertained only to be dismissed through a complicated cultural sleight of hand. Through such maneuvering, Cavendish transforms women's increasing confinement to the domestic sphere from a condition to be contested into the very grounds of women's autonomy. Privileged women, who possess the luxury of idle time and privacy – supplied by their exclusion from public life – are granted the liberty to take to the realm of letters. However, in Cavendish's cultural theory, even this freedom is conditioned by their natural and customary status as privatized and leisured beings.

Women's writerly capacities are similarly constrained. In her preface to the *Blazing World* (1666), she maintains:

> The end of reason, is truth; the end of fancy, is fiction: but mistake me not, when I distinguish *fancy* from *reason* . . . both being effects, or rather actions of the rational parts of matter; of which, as that is a more profitable and useful study than this, so it is also more laborious and difficult, and requires sometimes the help of fancy, to recreate the mind, and withdraw it from its more serious contemplations. (Cavendish 1992: 123–4)

Cavendish's definition of "fancy" as a "voluntary creation or production of the mind" distinguished itself from earlier strategies of legitimating women's authorship by grounding all writerly authority in the "rational parts of matter" or in the natural workings of matter in the individual. However, at the same time as she insists upon the universality of these "rational parts of matter" (thereby suggesting that women are capable of rational thought), she posits a strict bifurcation between cultural and political thinking and aligns the former, "fancy," with women, recreation, and privatized experience, and the latter, "reason," with the more serious contemplation of public affairs, and institutional learning, undertaken by men. Despite her ostensible attempt to demonstrate that fancy and reason are derivative of the same "rational parts of matter," her argument finally works to solidify the alignment of women's intellectual capacity with frivolity, leisure, and domesticity. [T]*he truth is*," she argues in her *Worlds Olio* (1655),

> *Men have great Reason not to let us in to their Government. . . . Man is made to Govern Common-Wealths, and Women their privat Families. . . . Women can have no excuse, or complaints of being subjects, as a hinderance from thinking; for Thoughts are free, those can never be inslaved, for we are not hindered from studying, since we are allowed so much idle time that we know not how to pass it away, but may as well read in our Closets as Men in their Colleges.* (Sig. A4–A5)

If Cavendish uses such convoluted arguments to strategically justify women's engagement in high culture, the price paid is that women are divested of civic or political subjectivity; Cavendish anchors women to their closets even as she provides justification for their engagement in cultural pursuits. Cavendish's writing will cause no harm, especially when we compare her innocuous cultural pursuits to the potential dangers of more political ones, for which women deserve not only to be "cast out of all *Civill society*, but to be blotted out of the *Roll* of *Mankinde*" (Cavendish 1653: Sig. A4). For women to "deny the *Principles* of their *Religion*," "break the *Lawes* of a *well-governed Kingdome*," "disturbe *Peace*," "be unnaturall," "break the *Union* and *Amity* of *honest Friends*," and "be a *Whore*" is to transgress both their social and natural place in civil society (Sig. A4).

Cavendish's construction of a cultural economy in which women could participate through writing is thus, at its very foundation, *premised upon the detachment of politics and culture*. This detachment reflects the larger sea change in women's material relationship to the cultural arena that occurred between the Renaissance and Restoration. By the late century, women are regularly writing for the theater, they appear on the stage, serve as editors and even stage managers, their literary output increases dramatically as they begin to take up writing as a profession. It is widely accepted that these Restoration developments mark a profound change in women's relationship to culture. Crucially, as women became increasingly visible as cultural producers, they became increasingly invisible politically. For the first time in English history women are granted a role in culture, as the relationship between politics and culture is itself mystified. At the center of these two linked developments stands Cavendish, her theory of authorship, and her bardolatry.

Margaret Cavendish, First Feminist?

Perhaps the most troubling aspect of her work for feminists attempting to recover Cavendish as feminist foremother is the convergence of feminism and absolutism in her writings, a convergence, it is argued, that demands that feminists recognize that feminism emerged in close association with an "adoption of the patriarchal ethos of absolutism that monarchy, both male and female, mystifies and enshrines" (Trubowitz 1992: 241). To label Cavendish "first feminist" requires a recognition that feminism was born out of wealth, status, power, prestige, privilege, luxury, classism, racism, and imperial domination; for feminists to find their origins in what has been termed "Tory feminism" involves an admission of complicity, of guilt.

Conversely, there is disavowal. Margaret Ezell, for example, calls attempts to evaluate the " 'feminism' of earlier generations as it meets our standards" "lamentable":

> Some of the most widely known seventeenth-century women writers, such as Margaret Cavendish and Mary Astell, have extensive apologies offered up on their behalf for their "conservativism" or are dissected as not being sufficiently feminist [;] . . . [w]e worry whether our literary forbears were "good" feminists. (Ezell 1993: 27)

Ezell here calls into question the way in which women writers such as Cavendish are demonized for not living up to our expectations. While I would agree that we must be attentive to our own biases in studying the past, this does not mean that we cannot pass judgment on Cavendish's troublesome contribution to feminism. This, I suggest, requires a rethinking of Cavendish's relationship to feminism which situates her within a larger historical continuum of feminist activity. Such a reading necessarily asks: what counts as the line of demarcation between women's cultural production and political emancipation? Such a reading pressures narratives which depict Cavendish as a "first feminist."

In 1982 Hilda Smith made the ground-breaking assertion that women who were predominantly Tory and Anglican such as Cavendish "were the first group of modern 'feminists'" (1982: 4). For Smith, a presumed class privilege was the source of these women's recognition that gender was the primary reason for their exclusion from public life. In 1988, Catherine Gallagher augmented and strengthened Smith's assertion by pointing out that the logic of absolutism, as transformed through its encounter with women, was particularly conducive to the development of protofeminism. This association has come to dominate early modern feminist historiography as a gyno-critical common sense. "Protofeminism" is thus regarded as consisting of a type of subjective interiority which allowed women to make feminist claims as it qualified and subverted these claims by relegating them to the privatized and imaginative realm of the absolute self: "English Feminism, which has generally preferred to see its origins in various anti-authoritarian movements, remains indebted to the absolutist imagination. For in its historical context, that imagination paradoxically supplied the terms of 'emancipated' subjectivity" (Gallagher 1988: 38).

This is clearly discernible in Cavendish's commentary on the marriage contract's relationship to the imagination. Marriage, for Cavendish, is a contract conducive to leisure which allows certain (privileged) women to explore their fancies (if they are carefully tutored by husbands). Such a contract is the foundation upon which women's originality and genius are built. Too much leisure time is damaging to women; unregulated, women's flights of fancy can lead them to dangerous actions. For Cavendish, women's natural affinity with fancy renders them prone to folly. Writing is a useful corrective. Cavendish, appropriating the standard humanist rationale for women's education, asserts that to write makes women more honest, less gossipy, and less likely to "busie my selfe out of the *Sphear* of our *Sex*, as in *Politicks* of *State*, or to Preach *false Doctrine* in a Tub, or to entertaine my selfe in hearkening to *vaine Flatteries*, or to the *incitements* of eyill *perswasions*; where all these *Follies*, and many more may be cut off by such innocent worke as this" (1653: Sig. A5). Even writing itself requires careful regulation. In her *Worlds Olio*, Cavendish states,

> I found the World too difficult to be understood . . . till the time I was married, I could only read the letters, joyn the words, but understood nothing of the sense of the World, until my Lord . . . as my Master, instructed me. . . . Thus my minde is

become an absolute Monark, ruling alone, my thoughts as a peaceable Commonwealth, and my life an expert Souldier, which my Lord setled, composed, and instructed.
(1655: 46–7)

In Cavendish's absolutist and militaristic model for the government of the mind and
discipline of the "fancy," required to train the hand to write, women's ability to govern
is restricted to the privatized realm of the imagination, and even this governance of
the self is to be strictly regulated by husbands. The endorsement of patriarchy is here
voiced by a woman, proud to proclaim that her mind is under male control.

Smith maintains that "feminism," above all else, involves the identification of
"women as a sociological group whose social and political position linked them
together more surely than their physical or psychological natures" (1982: 4). By recognizing that their sociological position as women was what barred them from emancipation, she contends, these women began to identify "woman" as a sociological
category of exclusion; it was this recognition that laid the foundation for all subsequent feminist development. However, Cavendish's cultural theory was premised
upon the refusal of sociological categories. For example, Shakespeare was, as we have
seen, only useful to Cavendish as a figure abstracted from the sociological categories
of gender and class. In fact, her entire theory of women's literary capacity is premised
upon the detachment of gender and class from writing.

In both Smith and Gallagher, feminism springs from a commitment to absolutism,
whether this be its institutions or its ideology, and in each case Cavendish is given
an incipient place in the genesis of feminism. Feminists are asked to accept the historical imbrication of feminism and oppression and learn to live with it. Yet,
Cavendish's work defies the terms of "feminism," even as they are laid out by both
Smith and Gallagher, rendering the very term "Tory feminism" something of a contradiction in terms. A simple comparison between one instance of Cavendish's many
invectives against women's engagement in public affairs and one such engagement
shatters both the myth of Cavendish as feminist foremother – as "first feminist" – and
the related equation of "Tory feminism" with the "origins" of feminism. In her "True
Relation," when she is required to travel to London to petition for reparations for the
loss of her Husband's estate, Cavendish is careful to disassociate herself from other
women petitioners, stating, "I was never at the Parliament House . . . I am sure, not
as a petitioner" (n.d.: 167). Her multiple denials – "Neither did I haunt the committees," "I never was at any, as a petitioner" – ultimately lead to the abashed confession that she had petitioned once, where she received "only an absolute refusal, I
should have no share of my Lord's estate" (n.d.: 167). Upon this refusal, Cavendish
demurely asks her brother-in-law to "conduct me out of that ungentlemanly place,
so without speaking to them one word good or bad, I returned to my lodgings,
and as that committee was the first, so it was the last, I ever was at as a petitioner"
(n.d.: 167).

Cavendish disassociated herself from the bold inconstancy of women "pleaders,
attorneys, petitioners, and the like, running about with their several causes,

complaining of their several grievances, exclaiming against their several enemies, bragging of their several favors they receive from the powerful, thus trafficking with idle words bring in false reports and vain discourse" (n.d.: 168). For if these women were to "rationally ponder" they would recognize that "neither words nor place . . . can advance them, but worth and merit" (n.d.: 168). Cavendish is careful to remark that she has nothing against those "noble, virtuous, discreet, and worthy persons whom necessity did enforce to submit, comply, and follow their own suits" as she derides "such as had nothing to lose, but made it their trade to solicit" (n.d.: 168).

How are we to characterize Cavendish's "feminism" when we contrast her invective against female petitioners with the words of one such petition:

> [W]e have an equal share and interest with men in the Commonwealth . . . for our encouragement and example, God hath wrought many deliverances for severall Nations, from age to age by the weake hand of women . . . by the British women this land was delivered from the tyranny of the *Danes* . . . therefore we shal take the boldnesse to remember you; that our Husbands, selves and friends have done their parts for you, and thought nothing too dear and pretious in your behalf, our money, plate, jewels, rings, bodkins, &c. have bin offered at your feet . . . make good those promises of freedom and prosperity to the Nation. (Anon. 1649: 4–5)

This women's Leveller petition, composed at least five years before Cavendish began her publishing career, presented collectively, perhaps collectively composed, unlike Cavendish, explicitly claims for women – identified here as a specific sociological group – a share of rights in the commonwealth and, as a document, stands in stark opposition to Cavendish's cultural and political vision. These petitioners lay claim to the nation, while Cavendish lays claim to the imagination. Its style and content, its date and its claims render hypervisible Cavendish's investment in the unique, leisured, privileged, individual, asexual, autonomous Author. The desire to locate Cavendish and other "Tory feminists" at the inception of feminist history has resulted, to put it bluntly, in an inability to see such women for what they are: privileged anti-feminists.

To begin to view the work of Cavendish not as "feminist foremother" but as antifeminist is to begin to see that "the bond between the feminization of the absolute and the new absolutism of the private female" was related to feminism only as negation, only as a reaction *against feminism*, for the decline of absolutism, and the representational possibilities this decline rendered visible, was precisely what engendered the development of feminism itself (Gallagher 1988: 31). Civil war and the execution of Charles I constituted a blow to the logic and institutions of absolutism from which they would never recover. Absolutism, as a doctrine and ideology buttressing the subjugation of women, was dealt a similar blow. Presented with the opportunity to renegotiate their social position, women did lay claims to social enfranchisement that were largely contingent upon the explicit rejection of patriarchal absolutism. These claims were, I am suggesting, more in keeping with the "ends" of feminism than the simultaneous refigurations of women's duties and obligations within a paradigm of defunct absolutism that emerged in direct response to the dangers of women's increased social mobility – a defunct paradigm, yet one powerful enough to persist (as a superannuated language through which culture and politics were to be conceptualized) well into the century to follow.

Cavendish's discussion of women's relation to government, in *Sociable Letter* 14, is not only a far cry from the type of emancipatory project of the September '48 petition of the women Levellers; it is an expressly anti-feminist, anti-social reaction against it:

> And as for the matter of Governments, we Women understand them not, yet if we did, we are excluded from intermedling therewith, and almost from being subject thereto; we are not tied, nor bound to State or Crown; we are free, not Sworn to Allegiance, nor do we take the Oath of Supremacy; we are not made Citizens of the Commonwealth, we hold no Offices, nor bear we any Authority therein; we are accounted neither Useful in Peace, nor Serviceable in War; and if we be not Citizens in the Commonwealth, I know no reason we should be Subjects to the Commonwealth: And the truth is, we are no Subjects, unless it be to our Husbands, and not alwayes to them, for sometimes we usurp their Authority, or else by flattery we get their good wills to govern. (1997: 25)

In this passage, commonly used to depict the contours of "Tory feminism," Cavendish directly attacks the most radical ideals of the republican commonwealth and the potentially liberatory relationship of women to them. Women, unfettered from the shackles of social obligation, existing outside the confines of the political state, are at the same time imprisoned within the home, limited politically to privatized supplication, wheedling, seduction, and flattery. Interestingly enough, Cavendish's proclamation employs, to quite different ends, the same logical strategy Colonel Rainsborough did at Putney in 1647 during his poignant argument for universal male suffrage:

> for really I think that the poorest he that is in England has a life to live as the greatest he; and therefore truly, sir, I think it's clear, that every man that is to live under a government ought first by his own consent to put himself under that government; and I do think that the poorest man in England is not at all bound in a strict sense to that government that he has not had a voice to put himself under. (Wootton 1986: 286)

If Rainsborough used the contention that men without a voice in government should not be required to serve that government in order to argue that all men, regardless of property status, should be given a voice, Cavendish makes no such attempt to do so. Instead, she argues that because women have no voice in government they should not concern themselves with the business of politics. In providing women with a compensatory role in culture, Cavendish is indeed "first," but this does not constitute feminism, it is a reaction against it.

Although it is clear that no one ever argued explicitly for the right of women to the franchise, the events of the mid century – stretching, as they did, long-standing justifications for representational authority to their breaking point – could no longer effectively function to enforce women's exclusion from civic institutions. As women expressed increasing commitment to the ideal of spiritual equality in order to justify their increased participation in the political and cultural arenas, the possibility that women might begin to claim the political right to represent comes very close to surfacing. Women had long exercised (unofficially) rights of citizenship, including such things as subscribing to oaths, agrarian collective action, more visible collective demonstrations in the cities, contributing to the construction of public opinion by issuing pamphlets and petitioning – on occasion, they even voted. As demands for universal male suffrage became explicit, women's political writings become more explicitly organized around questions of equality, as Cavendish's emphatically did not. As Stevie Davies characterizes the increasingly explicit nature of women's political writings, "The word 'equal' recurs insistently, alongside 'the same' ('interest in Christ *equal* unto men,' '*equal* interest,' 'by *the same* rule' . . . '*the like* unjust cruelties,' [my italics]) in a political discourse which abstains from recognizing the unenfranchised and voiceless condition of women under the law" (1998: 86).

Again, though Cavendish commonly deploys absolutism as trope, she is, in fact, less absolutist than *nostalgic* for absolutism; she is less Royalist than she is anti-republican; her work is conciliatory and reactive. These characteristics are common to much of Royalist women's Restoration cultural production. It is important to remember that for all intents and purposes, by 1649, absolutism proper, as an ideology and as an institutional structure, was obsolete. Struggling for a language in which to express an alternative to the riotous disorder of the commonwealth, Cavendish, like Hobbes, is finally unable to turn to divine justifications for absolutism and women's place within this political economy. Her insistence on the unknowable nature of God's plan and the workings of Nature, conjoined with an acute awareness of the historically contingent nature of custom and tradition, forces her into many slippery propositions. In her *Worlds Olio*, for example, Cavendish states, "nothing pleaseth Divinity more than Obedience to Magistrates, and Nature loves Peace, although she hath made all things to War upon one another; so that Custome and the Law make the same thing Civil or Pious, Just or Unjust" (1655: 81). Cavendish consistently avoids the question of how monarchy is to be authorized without divine mandate. In fact, she regards any speculation about the nature or will of God to be extremely dangerous. The justification for aristocratic hierarchy, and the position of women of different ranks within it, cannot, in Cavendish's view, be explained, only asserted. There can be no appeal to God or Nature for such authority. The best that can be done is to work to maintain order, and the best way to do that is to privatize and contain ideological (and social) differences.

Cavendish's theory of culture thus reflects the emergence of a Restoration sea change in views toward writerly authority, to the body politic, and to the future, the generalization of which constitutes a backlash against previous engagements of women and commoners in the public sphere. If Cavendish's "feminism" is troubled by an inability to disassociate absolutism and patriarchy, this is because this was not her intent. Instead, her work is conciliatory, it deploys the terms of a defunct *"roi absolu"* in order to constitute, and mask, the *"moi absolu,"* the myth of individualized, autonomous subjectivity that would come to both ground modern paradigms of authorship and effectively subvert the articulation of a truly feminist praxis (Gallagher 1988: 25). Cavendish was complicit in this project for her primary political aim seems to have been the active disenfranchisement – the erasure – of women in political and, ultimately, in cultural terms, for her work in both political and cultural arenas contributed to the privatization of women's material domain in both fact and in idea.

The well-known work of Carole Pateman on the relationship of gender to the contractarian/patriarchal debate between Locke and Filmer has recently been complicated by a number of literary theorists and historians who emphasize the *silences* contained in the early modern debates over political and cultural representation. Smith has recently attempted to map the historical development of the "false universal" grounding both "women's exclusion from the state or civil society" and the "supposedly masculine or feminine qualities attached to men and women or male and female roles" that attend such exclusion (Smith 1998: 329). This logic helped to "define the independent, modern individual who was at the heart of the shift from subject to citizen associated with the English Civil War of the mid-seventeenth century" (Smith 1998: 329n). This logic "led contemporaries, and later scholars, to use words such as people, person, citizen, England, etc. in ways that excluded women without explicitly saying so" (1998: 329). The political turmoil that resulted directly from the contradictions of patriarchy and liberal individualism was not addressed as such. Instead, the social role of gender in these conflicts was stridently avoided. Gordon Schochet (1998) outlines this prevalent evasion and concludes:

> The deep danger of so-called "liberal" political neutrality in which the state evinces no interest in the outcome of the conflicts it mediates is that it becomes officially blind to *social* injustice and virtually prides itself on that fact by insisting upon this state/society (or public/private) separation . . . [I]t is precisely the questioning of the legitimacy of the differential distribution of benefits and burdens from the perspective of social-justice-denied that alerts us to presumptive injustices and ultimately undergirds their removal. (1998: 240)

Schochet suggests that it is not the contractual conception of rights *per se* but a political schema which strictly divides the state and society, rendering the inequities of the social invisible, that results in the continued disenfranchisement of women. Schochet maintains that the problem with the theorizations of Locke and Hobbes was that their formulation of civil society was "built on top of a set of not merely non- but determinedly *pre*-political arrangements that are sustained by and themselves sustain the resulting polity" (1998: 240). This "pre-political" polity includes a wide range of irrational assumptions about the nature of women, which have retained a remarkable degree of currency in modern political thought, precisely because modern thought depends upon the relegation of social difference to the unexaminable (because un-public) space of individual social life. The emphasis on the "unspoken" in the work of Smith and Schochet has wide-ranging implications for feminist historiography as it indicates that *silence* is perhaps a more important factor in the disenfranchise-ment of women than the explicit invectives against them. What is obscured through silence is the contradictory subject-constitution of women in the liberal-patriarchal common sense.

Since the beginning of the development of the modern nation-state women have been simultaneously constituted as abstract individuals and as "women." Dympna Callaghan marks the unreconcilability of the assumption that "the rights – and thence political representation – accorded to the privileged white male subject could be almost infinitely extended to include all social groups" to the discordant fact that "Man was accorded his privileged status by defining himself against those he excluded (those who were not 'like him') and who now question the political usefulness of claiming the right to be represented on the grounds of a sameness which can only corroborate his hegemony" (Callaghan 1996: 49, 50). This abstracted liberal subject of patriarchy bears a strong resemblance to Cavendish's Shakespeare and the woman writer he authorizes.

The history of bardolatry is also a history of women's cultural and political exclusion effected through gestures toward inclusion. Feminism's failure to have achieved the political as well as the cultural right to represent is one of the more "horrific" aspects of the Bard. We need therefore to approach Shakespeare, at least in part, as a symbol of loss for women, a reminder of feminism's failure to have effected the achieve-ment of political representation – feminism's end. The history of bardolatry is inti-mately related to women's claims not only to cultural representation but to political representation as well. Carried in the historical aura that surrounds the Bard is a history of cultural exclusions which cannot be extricated from political ones. Cavendish, in the final instance, is really not so different from her nineteenth-century counterpart, Bissell. For their fantasies demonstrate a remarkable continuity. The "dif-ferences" which constitute "women" are social and economic ones, the inequitable allocation of labor and resources engenders women and their oppression. It was pre-cisely these differences that Cavendish sought to render invisible – to silence – in her depoliticization of culture and in her privatization of social gender difference. If women have made remarkable gains in their access to cultural representation, they today remain notoriously underrepresented politically. What I am suggesting here is that a powerful tendency to silence social difference – a silence endemic to the seventeenth-century development of the abstract subject of the liberal state and its attendant paradigms of cultural authority – remains firmly entrenched today.

We must wonder, then, if the feminist anti-bardolatry alluded to by Bissell at the outset of this essay couldn't have silently existed at bardolatry's very inception. Is it all that remarkable that, without exception, sectarian women ignored Shakespeare completely? Is it so difficult to imagine that the continued attention to pre '42 and post '60 Shakespeares has blinded us to the revolutionary potential of "feminisms" – informed by conceptions of representation that do not posit bifurcated gendered capacity or make distinctions between the cultural and political and, further, that are not conditioned by the weight of institutional tradition or authority as much as they are directly responsive to the social inequity of the day? It is surely no accident that women's most radical seventeenth-century calls for equality took place *between* overtly and covertly homosocial authorial paradigms, *between* the decline of the boy actor and rise of the actress, and *without* Shakespeare.

REFERENCES AND FURTHER READING

Anon. 1649: To the Supreme authority of This Nation, the Commons assembled in PARLIAMENT: The humble PETITION Of divers wel-affected WOMEN, Inhabiting the Cities of London and *Westminster*, the Borough of *Southwark, Hamblets* and Places adjacent; *Affecters and Approvers of the late large Petition) of The Eleventh of September* 1648. London.

Ballaster, R. 1996: "The First Female Dramatists." In Helen Wilcox (ed.), *Women and Literature in Britain, 1500–1700*. Cambridge: Cambridge University Press, 267–90.

Behn, A. 1915: *The Works of Aphra Behn*. Ed. Montague Summers. 6 vols. London: William Heinemann.

Benjamin, W. 1969: "Theses on the Philosophy of History." In Hannah Arendt (ed.), *Illuminations: Essays and Reflections*. Trans. Harry Zohn. New York: Schocken Books, 253–64. (Original work published 1955.)

Bissell, E. P. [Priscilla Leonard] 1997: "The Mistaken Vocation of Shakespeare's Heroines." In Ann Thompson and Sasha Roberts (eds.), *Women Reading Shakespeare, 1660–1900: An Anthology of Criticism*. Manchester: Manchester University Press, 233–5. (Original work published 1896.)

Callaghan, D. 1996: "Representing Cleopatra in the Post-Colonial Moment." In Nigel Wood (ed.), *Antony and Cleopatra*. Philadelphia: Open University Press, 40–65.

Cavendish, M. L. 1653: *POEMS, and Fancies: Written by the Right HONOURABLE, the Lady MARGARET MARCHIONES NEWCASTLE*. London:

Printed by T. R. for I. Martin, and I. Allestrye at the Bell in Saint *Pauls* Church Yard.

——1655: *The Worlds Olio. Written by Right HONOURABLE, the Lady MARGARET NEWCASTLE*. London: Printed for I. Martin and I. Allestrye at the Bell in St. *Pauls* Church-Yard.

——1992: *The Description of a New World Called the Blazing World and Other Writings*. Ed. Kate Lilley. New York: New York University Press. (Original work published 1666.)

——1997: *Margaret Cavendish: Sociable Letters*. Ed. James Fitzmaurice. New York: Garland Publishing. (Original work published 1664.)

——n.d.: "A True Relation of My Birth, Breeding and Life." In C. H. Firth (ed.), *The Life of William Cavendish, Duke of Newcastle: To Which is Added The True Relation of My Birth Breeding and Life*. Second edition. London: Routledge, 155–78. (Original work published 1656.)

Davies, S. 1998: *Unbridled Spirits: Women of the English Revolution*. London: The Women's Press.

Evans, G. B. et al. (ed.) 1974: *The Riverside Shakespeare*. Boston: Houghton Mifflin Company.

Ezell, M. J. M. 1993: *Writing Women's Literary History*. Baltimore: Johns Hopkins University Press.

Gallagher, C. 1988: "Embracing the Absolute: The Politics of the Female Subject in Seventeenth-Century England." *Genders*, 1 (Spring), 24–39.

Greenblatt, S. et al. (eds.) 1997: *The Norton Shakespeare: Based on the Text of the Oxford Edition*. New York: W. W. Norton and Company.

Hinds, H. 1996: *God's Englishwomen: Seventeenth-Century Radical Sectarian Writing and Feminist Criticism*. Manchester: Manchester University Press.

Ingleby, C. M. 1879: *Shakespeare's Centurie of Prayse; Being Materials for a History of Opinion on Shakespeare and His Works, A.D. 1591–1693*. Second edition. Ed. Lucy Toulmin Smith. London: Alexander Moring Ltd.

Masten, J. 1997: *Textual Intercourse: Collaboration, Authorship, and Sexualities in Renaissance Drama*. Cambridge: Cambridge University Press.

Novy, M. (ed.) 1990: *Women's Re-Visions of Shakespeare: On the Responses of Dickenson, Woolf, Rich, H.D., George Eliot, and Others*. Urbana: University of Illinois Press.

O'Brien, C. 1997: "Romeo and Juliet." In Ann Thompson and Sasha Roberts (eds.), *Women Reading Shakespeare, 1660–1900: An Anthology of Criticism*. Manchester: Manchester University Press, 143–4. (Original work published 1879.)

Schochet, G. 1998: "The Significant Sounds of Silence: The Absence of Women from the Political Thought of Sir Robert Filmer and John Locke (or, 'Why can't a woman be more like a man?')." In Hilda Smith (ed.), *Women Writers and the Early Modern British Political Tradition*. Cambridge: Cambridge University Press, 220–42.

Smith, H. 1982: *Reason's Disciples: Seventeenth-Century English Feminists*. Urbana: University of Illinois Press.

——1998: "Women as Sextons and Electors: King's Bench and Precedents for Women's Citizenship." In Hilda Smith (ed.), *Women Writers and the Early Modern British Political Tradition*. Cambridge: Cambridge University Press, 324–42.

Straznicky, M. 1995: "Reading the Stage: Margaret Cavendish and Commonwealth Closet Drama." *Criticism*, 37, 3 (Summer), 355–90.

Thompson, A. and Roberts, S. (eds.) 1997: *Women Reading Shakespeare, 1660–1900: An Anthology of Criticism*. Manchester: Manchester University Press.

Tomlinson, S. 1992: "'My Brain the Stage': Margaret Cavendish and the Fantasy of Female Performance." In Clare Brant and Diane Purkiss (eds.), *Women, Texts and Histories, 1575–1760*. New York: Routledge, 134–63.

Trubowitz, R. 1992: "The Reenchantment of Utopia and the Female Monarchical Self: Margaret Cavendish's *Blazing World*." *Tulsa Studies in Women's Literature*, 11, 2 (Fall), 229–45.

Wootton, D. 1986: "The Putney Debates: The Debate on the Franchise (1647)." In David Wootton (ed.), *Divine Right and Democracy: An Anthology of Political Writing in Stuart England*. New York: Penguin, 285–319. (Original work published 1891.)

3
Misogyny is Everywhere
Phyllis Rackin

Misogyny presents an interpretive embarrassment of riches: it is everywhere, unabashed in its artic-
ulation and so overdetermined in its cultural roots that individual instances sometimes seem emo-
tionally underdetermined, rote and uninflected expressions of what would go without saying if it
weren't said so often.

Mullaney (1994: 141)

This description of late sixteenth-century English culture is likely to ring true
for readers of current feminist/historicist Shakespeare criticism. "In historical
research," as a wise old teacher once warned me, "you're likely to find what you
are looking for"; and what most of us have been looking for in recent years is a
history of men's anxiety in the face of female power, of women's disempowerment,
and of outright misogyny. I want to interrogate that history, not because it is
necessarily incorrect but because it is incomplete. It constitutes only one of many
stories that could be told about women's place in Shakespeare's world, and I think
we need to consider the implications of its current hegemony. Why does the evidence
for misogyny in Shakespeare's world strike the writer as "an interpretive embarrassment of riches"? Who is enriched by the many "rote and uninflected expressions
of what would go without saying if it weren't said so often" in recent feminist
criticism?

One reason the story of patriarchal oppression has become so influential is that it
has been disseminated in recent textbooks. The editor of a reader designed to illustrate *The Cultural Identity of Seventeenth-Century Woman*, for instance, states flatly that

Woman's place was within doors, her business domestic. . . . Women of evident intelligence themselves accepted this divorce between the private (feminine) and public (masculine) spheres and, despite the recent precedents of Mary Queen of Scots, Mary Tudor
and Elizabeth, they shared the age's "distaste . . . for the notion of women's involvement
in politics." (Keeble 1994: 186)

However, even the most sophisticated scholarship often includes similar claims. For example, in what is likely to become a standard history of gender in early modern England, Anthony Fletcher writes,

> It was conventional, as we have seen, to assume men and women had clearly defined gender roles indoors and out of doors. . . . Femininity, as we have seen, was presented as no more than a set of negatives. The requirement of chastity was, as we have seen, the overriding measure of female gender. Woman not only had to be chaste but had to be seen to be chaste: silence, humility and modesty were the signifiers that she was so. (1995: 120–2)

Some of the most important recent feminist/historicist literary scholarship includes reminders that "the period was fraught with anxiety about rebellious women and particularly their rebellion through language" (Newman 1991: 40); that "women's reading was policed and their writing prohibited or marked as transgressive even when they were not engaged in other criminal activities" (Dolan 1996: 159); and that "an obsessive energy was invested in exerting control over the unruly woman – the woman who was exercising either her sexuality or her tongue under her own control rather than under the rule of a man" (Boose 1991: 195). In a sense, of course, these quotations are misleading because they are taken out of context, and they belie the subtlety and complexity of the arguments from which they were taken. Nonetheless, I believe the excerpts are significant because they indicate how often even the best feminist scholarship feels the need to situate itself within a patriarchal master narrative.

Feminist scholars found a brilliant explication of that narrative in Peter Stallybrass's essay, "Patriarchal Territories: The Body Enclosed," which argued that women's bodies were assumed to be "*naturally* 'grotesque'" and that women were therefore "subjected to constant surveillance . . . because, as Bakhtin says of the grotesque body, it is 'unfinished, outgrows itself, transgresses its own limits.'" This constant surveillance, Stallybrass continued, focused on "three specific areas: the mouth, chastity, the threshold of the house," which "were frequently collapsed into each other." "Silence, the closed mouth, is made a sign of chastity. And silence and chastity are, in turn, homologous to woman's enclosure within the house" (Stallybrass 1986: 126–7). Published in 1986, "Patriarchal Territories" theorized the relationships between sexual loathing, the silencing of women's voices, and the constriction of women's activities in a beautifully articulated analysis that has proved to have remarkable influence and explanatory power in subsequent feminist criticism. It is significant, I believe, that the conclusion of Stallybrass's article, where he suggests that the figure of the unruly woman was also valorized as a rallying point for protest against social injustice, was often ignored.

The pervasive scholarly investment in Renaissance misogyny has led to a massive rereading of Shakespeare's plays. As Valerie Traub observes, "It is by now a commonplace that Shakespeare was preoccupied with the uncontrollability of women's sexuality; witness the many plots concerning the need to prove female chastity, the threat of adultery, and, even when female fidelity is not a major theme of the play, the many references to cuckoldry in songs, jokes, and passing remarks" (1995: 121). Reminders that women were expected to be chaste, silent, and obedient probably occur more frequently in recent scholarship than they did in the literature of Shakespeare's time; the connections between female speech and female sexual transgression are retraced and the anxieties evoked by the possibility of female power are discovered in play after play. "Female sexuality in Shakespeare's plays," we are told, "is invariably articulated as linguistic transgression – that is, a verbal replication of female obliquity" (Carroll 1995: 184). If speech is transgressive, reading and writing are even more dangerous. Lavinia's gruesome fate in *Titus Andronicus*, for instance, is "expressive of the anxieties she generates as an educated, and hence potentially unruly, woman" (Eaton, cited by Garner and Sprengnether 1996: 12–13).

Plays with overtly repressive and misogynist themes have proved increasingly popular, and the stories they tell are held up as historically accurate expressions of beliefs generally endorsed in Shakespeare's time. *The Taming of the Shrew*, for instance, is the subject of 105 listings for the years 1985–97 in the online *MLA Bibliography*, far more than any of the other early comedies (for those same years, the *Bibliography* lists twenty-eight for *Two Gentlemen of Verona*, forty-seven for *Comedy of Errors*, and sixty-one for *Love's Labour's Lost*). Other plays are reinterpreted. *The Merchant of Venice*, for example, "instructs its audience that daughters who submit, who know their place, will ultimately fare better than daughters who rebel" (Leventen 1991: 75). The heroines of Shakespeare's middle comedies were especially attractive to the feminist critics of the 1970s, when it seemed important to mobilize Shakespeare's authority in the service of our own political goals. In the 1980s, however, a more pessimistic picture emerged as scholars marshaled historical evidence to demonstrate the pervasiveness of patriarchal beliefs and practices and discredit the optimistic feminist readings of the 1970s as unhistorical.

One of the characteristics that traditionally made the heroines of Shakespeare's middle comedies attractive is their erotic appeal, but influential critics associated that attraction with the fact that they were portrayed by male actors. Stephen Greenblatt's widely cited article on "Fiction and Friction" used Thomas Laqueur's arguments about the conception of a single-sexed body in Renaissance anatomical theory to argue that "the open secret of identity – that within differentiated individuals is a single structure, identifiably male – is presented literally in the all-male cast." "Men," Greenblatt wrote, "love women precisely as *representations*, a love the original performances of these plays literalized in the person of the boy actor" (1988: 93). For Lisa Jardine, the heroines of these plays were "sexually enticing *qua* transvestied boys, and the plays encourage the audience to view them as such" (1991: 61). Moreover, at the same time that criticism like Greenblatt's and Jardine's taught us to recognize that cross-dressed boys may have been objects of desire for Shakespeare's original audience, we were also taught that sexualized women were not: female sexual desire, we are repeatedly told, was regarded as threatening. In *Antony and Cleopatra*, for instance, "Egypt's queen . . . resembles other Jacobean females who in desiring or being desired become a source of pollution" (Tennenhouse 1986: 144). In *II Henry VI*, depicting "Margaret as a figure of open and unrestrained sexual passion is one way of demonizing her and representing the dangers of a femininity not firmly under the control of a father or husband" (Howard and Rackin 1997: 74).

Sexual passion is not the only characteristic that makes women threatening in recent feminist Shakespeare criticism, where it seems that virtually any manifestation of female strength or ability, even if it is admired by other characters on stage, would have had to evoke anxiety in the original audiences. Helena in *All's Well That Ends Well* is a good example. In the playtext her virtues are celebrated and her aspirations endorsed by the King and the Countess. The Introduction to the play in the Riverside Shakespeare summed up the traditional view of the character: "Helena is prized by the older generation not only because they recognize her intrinsic worth, but because she is a living example of the attitudes of the past" (Evans et al. 1997: 535). She is also the center of dramatic interest, with the longest part in the play. According to the Spevack *Concordance* (1968), she speaks 15.858 percent of the words in the script; Bertram speaks only 9.042 percent, a total that is exceeded not only by Helena, but also by his mother, who has 9.618 percent. Nonetheless, according to a leading male feminist critic,

> Helena's gender makes impossible any one-sided identification with Helena against Bertram. . . . Reacting against Helena's triumph, Shakespeare remains in part sympathetically bound to the besieged male positions of both Bertram and the king; the play thereby gives voice not only to the two male characters' discomfiture but also to Shakespeare's. The authorial division that blocks a convincing resolution is significant because it dramatizes a much larger cultural quandary: the society's inability to accommodate, without deep disturbance, decisive female control. (Erickson 1991: 73–4)

The last two sentences are carefully worded, attributing ambivalence about Helena's achievement and anxiety about the spectacle of "decisive female control" to Shakespeare and to the culture in which he wrote, thus authorizing ambivalence and anxiety as the historically appropriate responses to Helena's triumph. But the first sentence I quoted – "Helena's gender makes impossible any one-sided identification with Helena against Bertram" – seems to claim even more. The present tense of the verb seems to universalize Erickson's reading and deny its historical specificity, implying that ambivalence and anxiety are the only possible responses to the character for any reader or viewer in any time or place.

It may be unfair to make too much of Erickson's use of the present tense, but it points to a larger problem for historicist literary criticism, which has pressing implications for feminist/historicist scholarship. The conventions of scholarly writing have been to write about literary texts in the present tense, thus expressing their imaginative presence, and about historical events in the past tense to mark their temporal distance from the writer who recounts them. This distinction is breaking down, both in popularized history, where the present tense is increasingly used to describe past events, and in postmodern historical theory, which is shaped by the recognition that history, no less than fiction, is constantly updated to fit the shapes of present interests and assumptions. The question of grammatical tense poses an especially pressing problem for new historicist literary criticism. The present tense effaces historical distance, the past denies literary presence, and the distinction between past tense for history and present tense for fiction implicitly denies the imbrication of the literary text in its historical context that animates the entire new historicist project. If the text and its historical context are components of a seamless discursive web, it is difficult to sustain the grammatical distinction between present and past tenses that marks the separation of literary text from its historical context. But if that distinction is elided, where does the new historicist scholar situate herself in relation to the literary/historical objects of her analysis? Using the present tense, as Erickson does in the passage I quoted, seems to claim universal validity for a historically situated response. At the same time, however, it implicitly acknowledges that the version of past experience being constructed is a projection of current interests and anxieties.

The present tense is also the conventional form for references to the work of other scholars, as if it too existed in a timeless, ahistorical space. As we all know, however, scholarly texts, no less than the texts scholars study, are imbricated in the historical contexts in which they were produced and shaped by the social locations and personal interests and desires of their writers, even though the conventions of academic civility make those factors difficult to discuss. Nonetheless, I believe it is important to note, not only that the feminist/historicist Shakespeare criticism of the 1980s often tended to privilege male experience, emphasizing masculine anxiety in the face of powerful women, but also that some of the most influential work of that period was, in fact, the work of male critics.

One of the most influential modern readings of *As You Like It*, for instance, Louis Adrian Montrose's 1981 article, "'The Place of a Brother,'" proposed to reverse the then prevailing view of the play by arguing that "what happens to Orlando at home is not Shakespeare's contrivance to get him into the forest; what happens to Orlando in the forest is Shakespeare's contrivance to remedy what has happened to him at home" (Montrose 1981: 29). Just as Oliver has displaced Orlando from his rightful place in the patriarchy, Montrose's reading displaces Rosalind from her place as the play's protagonist, focusing instead upon the relationships among brothers, fathers, and sons. Although Oliver appears only briefly on stage and the brothers' reconciliation is narrated, not shown, the main issue in the play is said to be Orlando's troubled relationship with his brother and consequent loss of his rightful place in society; Rosalind is reduced to a vehicle for its restoration: marrying her enables Orlando to become "heir apparent to the reinstated Duke" (Montrose 1981: 38). Montrose does not cite Gayle Rubin's 1975 article on "the traffic in women," but this is the paradigm that seems to lie behind his argument.[1] The power of Rubin's paradigm is so great that it supersedes the textual evidence that the marriage satisfies Rosalind's own long-standing desire (see, e.g., I.iii.9) and that it is she, not her father, who tells

Orlando "To you I give myself" (V.iv.106). In fact, none of the marriages in the play is arranged by a father. The only marriage that can be said to be arranged is that of Silvius and Phoebe, which Rosalind herself arranges. Rosalind dominates the action of the play (she has the longest part in the script, speaking, according to the Spevack *Concordance* (1968), 26.744 percent of the words in the playscript). Nonetheless, Montrose's argument that the play "is a structure for her containment" (1981: 52) has been widely influential in subsequent criticism.

With the turn to history in literary studies generally, and especially in the field of the Renaissance, feminist Shakespeare criticism has been almost completely shaped by the scholarly consensus about the pervasiveness of masculine anxiety and women's disempowerment in Shakespeare's world. Much of this criticism is sympathetic to women's plights, exposing women's oppression and describing the sociological, psychological, and ideological mechanisms that produced it, but it poses problems which are simultaneously intellectual and political. Feminist scholarship needs history, and it needs the analytic instruments the new historicism provides. The problem is that the conceptual categories that shape contemporary scholarly discourse, no less than the historical records of the past, are often man-made and shaped by men's anxieties, desires, and interests. As such, they constitute instruments of women's exclusion, and often of women's oppression. What Kathleen McLuskie wrote about *Measure for Measure* in 1985 seems increasingly applicable to the entire Shakespearean canon and to historical accounts of the world in which he wrote: "Feminist criticism," she argued, "is restricted to exposing its own exclusion from the text. It has no point of entry into it, for the dilemmas of the narrative and the sexuality under discussion are constructed in completely male terms" (McLuskie 1994: 97). How then can we enter the discourse of current feminist/historicist Shakespeare criticism without becoming so thoroughly inscribed within its categories that we are forced to imagine both the plays and the culture in which they were produced from a male point of view?

It is important to remember that feminist criticism began with a political agenda, although – especially in the United States – it has increasingly entered the mainstream of academic discourse. The current interest in issues of sex and gender has provided increased academic visibility for feminist concerns and increased professional visibility for academic feminists, but it has not come without costs. Adopted as a conceptual tool by women and men without a serious political commitment to feminist political agendas, criticism designated as "feminist" has provided arguments that can just as easily be used to naturalize women's oppression as to oppose it. Among the consequences of this selective history for feminist students of Shakespeare's plays is the fact that we are being taught to read from the subject position of a man, and a misogynist man at that. The cultural prestige of Shakespeare makes his plays a model for contemporary values and the privileged site where past history is reconstructed. Even academic historians often turn to Shakespeare for evidence of past practices and attitudes (the index to Anthony Fletcher's *Gender, Sex and Subordination in England 1500–1800*, for instance, lists fifty-four references to Shakespeare's plays). For the feminist political project, there are obvious dangers in contemplating our past from

the point of view of late twentieth-century academic men who may – consciously or
not – be anxious or ambivalent about the progress women have made in the wake of
the contemporary women's movement. The stories we tell about the past have consequences for the present and future, and if the story of misogyny and oppression is the
only story we tell about the past, we risk a dangerous complacency in the present.
Like the Virginia Slims ads that tell us, "You've come a long way, baby" because we
can now smoke openly rather than hiding our habits from our menfolk, an oversim-
plified history that emphasizes past oppression is likely to encourage an equally over-
simplified optimism about our present situation. As Lena Cowen Orlin observes, "if
we have enjoyed this construction of women, perhaps it is because it offers us the
comforting reassurance that history has made progress and that we have come a long
way (baby) from our early modern predecessors."[2]

This is not to deny that there is ample evidence for a history of misogyny and of
women's oppression in Shakespeare's world and that there are good reasons why it
needed to be told. All the statements I have cited are documented with quotations
from early modern texts and citations of early modern cultural practice; and, as Linda
Boose has eloquently written in her brilliant study of *The Taming of the Shrew*, it is
essential to "assert an intertextuality that binds the obscured records of a painful
women's history" to the Shakespearean text because "that history has paid for the right
to speak itself"; and "the impulse to rewrite the more oppressively patriarchal material in this play serves the very ideologies about gender that it makes less visible by
making less offensive" (1991: 181–2). However, as Boose also makes clear, although
the history of male misogyny is inextricably entangled with the history of women's
oppression, those histories had strikingly different consequences for women and men.
In considering the evidence for Renaissance misogyny and the oppressive practices
it produced, it is essential to remember an essential axiom of postmodern historical
study – the fact that, as Sandra Harding has wittily remarked, there is no such thing
as a "view from nowhere." We need to view the textual evidence for misogyny
and oppression more critically, considering both the social locations of the original
writers and those of the contemporary scholars who have put those texts back into
circulation.

As Deborah Payne has argued in another context, certain anecdotes, texts, and passages from texts are repeatedly cited and assumed "to represent dominant social views:
for positivists, a historical transparency; for poststructuralists, a sign within a culturally determined system of signification. This 'short-circuit fallacy' . . . can occur only
by ignoring [the writer of the text's or the recorder of the anecdote's] vexed position
within the social space" from which he writes (1995: 22). Payne adopts the phrase
"short-circuit fallacy" from Pierre Bourdieu, who defines it as ignoring "the crucial
mediation provided by . . . the field of cultural production . . . a social space with its
own logic, within which agents struggle over stakes of a particular kind." "The most
essential bias," he goes on to warn, is the " 'ethnocentrism of the scientist,' which con-
sists in ignoring everything that the analyst injects into his perception of the object
by virtue of the fact that he is placed outside of the object, that he observes it from

afar and from above" (Bourdieu and Wacquant 1992: 69–70). Carol Thomas Neely makes a similar point in a recent study of madness and gender in Shakespeare's tragedies and early modern culture:

> The complexities of reading the discourse of madness in Shakespeare and his culture reveal the difficulty and necessity of historicizing: examining one's own position and that of one's subject(s) in contemporary culture in relation to the construction of those subject(s) which emerged in early modern culture, working to tease out disjunctions and connections. This project reveals that the shape of gender difference cannot be assumed but must always be reformulated in specific historical contexts. (1996: 96)

The lesson, in the words of Jean E. Howard's famous essay on the new historicism, is that "there is no transcendent space from which one can perceive the past 'objectively.'" "Our view," she continues, "is always informed by our present position" (Howard 1986: 22). It follows from this that "objectivity is not in any pure form a possibility," that "interpretive and even descriptive acts" are inevitably political, and that "any move into history is [therefore] an intervention" (Howard 1986: 43).

One strategy for intervention adopted by feminist scholars in the 1980s and 1990s has been to look for places for female agency within patriarchal scripts. In 1981, for instance, Coppélia Kahn argued in *Man's Estate* that the power over women given to men by patriarchy made men paradoxically "vulnerable to women" because "a woman's subjugation to her husband's will was the measure of his patriarchal authority and thus of his manliness" (Kahn 1981: 15–17). In 1985, Catherine Belsey pointed out in *The Subject of Tragedy* that women convicted of witchcraft were empowered at the moment of their execution by the "requirement for confessions from the scaffold," which, "paradoxically . . . offered women a place from which to speak in public with a hitherto unimagined authority which was not diminished by the fact that it was demonic" (Belsey 1985: 190–1). In 1994, Frances E. Dolan focused in *Dangerous Familiars* on early modern representations of domestic crimes perpetrated by women in an effort "to uncover the possibilities, however contingent and circumscribed, for human agency in historical process" because "accounts of domestic violence" are "one set of scripts in which women could be cast as agents, albeit in problematic terms" (Dolan 1994: 5).

Increasingly, however, feminist scholars are challenging the patriarchal narrative itself, recovering the materials for alternative narratives and emphasizing that repressive prescriptions should not be regarded as descriptions of actual behavior. In her 1993 study of *Women and Property in Early Modern England*, Amy Louise Erickson points out that

> it is one thing to observe that early modern male writers invariably described women's place in the social hierarchy, the "great chain of being", entirely in terms of marriage. It is quite another to remember that they did so in a society in which most adult women in the population at any given time were not married – they were either widowed or they had never married. (Erickson 1993: 8–9)

Similarly, in a 1997 essay, Diana E. Henderson reminds us that

> Some aristocratic women, in fact, managed to avoid being confined to any of their numerous homes, much less "the" home; those at the other end of the social scale might have no home at all, and they could hardly afford to create gendered space. . . . Texts (especially literary ones) tend to preserve the voices and perspectives of those who dominated within society; we must supplement them with both historical data and our scholarly imaginations if we wish to hear more of the conversation. Female-headed households in *Gammer Gurton's Needle* may be only a schoolmaster's source of comedy or deflected anxiety, but it is also true that there were many female-headed households in town and city alike; historical study of Southwark, the theater district itself, reveals that at least 16 percent of households were headed by a woman. The type of historical evidence we bring to bear when interpreting plays undoubtedly informs what types of domesticity we see represented, what gaps we notice, how we value them. (Henderson 1997: 192)

Thus, while *As You Like It* is a fantasy, the female household that Rosalind and Celia establish in the forest had precedents in the very district where the theater was located. Moreover, Rosalind's role in arranging her own marriage and Phoebe's as well also had ample precedents in the real world. As Margaret Ezell has demonstrated, early modern women played central roles in arranging marriages, not only their own, but those of their daughters, nieces, and granddaughters as well. Far more fathers than mothers had died by the time their children reached marriageable age (Ezell 1987: 18). Moreover, even when both parents were alive, great numbers of women lived away from their parents' homes, often supporting themselves independently and negotiating their own marriages. Vivien Brodsky Elliott's study of single women in the London marriage market during the years 1598 to 1619 shows that women who had migrated from the country to work in London tended to marry later than London-born women and to marry men who were closer to their own age, statistics which, Elliott concludes, suggest "a greater freedom of choice of spouse and a more active role for women in the courtship and marriage process" (Elliott 1982: 89): "without the control or influence of their parents the marriage process for them was one in which they had an active role in initiating their own relationships, in finding suitable partners, and in conducting courtships" (Elliott 1982: 97). Among the upper levels of society where there was more property involved and parents were more likely to take an active role in arranging their children's marriages, Ezell's study of women's correspondence with other women reveals that mothers, grandmothers, and aunts played central roles in negotiating marriages for their children (Ezell 1987: 20–34).

Women's power and authority extended beyond the limits of their families. The example of the Tudor queens Mary and Elizabeth is well known, and the "anomaly" of Elizabeth's position has been endlessly noted; but they were not the only women who exercised political authority. Patricia Crawford's examination of voting registers reveals that in some parts of England, "women had been regularly voting in parliamentary elections during the seventeenth century into the 1650s at least" (Orgel

1996: 74). Women also possessed considerable economic power, not only through inheritance from fathers and husbands (and from mothers and other female relatives as well), but also by virtue of their own gainful employment. Widows were usually named executrix in their husband's wills, and when a husband died intestate, the widow was legally entitled to administer the estate (Erickson 1993: 19, 61–78, 175). Bess of Hardwick began with a marriage portion of forty marks, but ended, after inheriting the property of four successive husbands, as the Countess of Shrewsbury and one of the wealthiest women in England (Hogrefe 1977). Women lower on the social scale earned their livings, not only as servants, but also in a variety of trades that took them outside the household. Itinerant chapwomen peddled a variety of goods, and Amy Louise Erickson has noted that "prohibitions upon girls and women appearing in public places like markets and fairs are entirely absent from early modern ballads and broadsides" (Erickson 1993: 10). Women's prominence in the marketplace is also attested by the drawings of thirteen London food markets produced by Hugh Alley in 1598, which include numerous images of women, both alone and with other women or men, both buying and selling. These images are particularly significant, because Alley's text is not specifically concerned with the activities of women in the markets; the women are simply there, apparently as a matter of course.

Even the guilds, generally believed to be bastions of male privilege, included women. The Statute of Artificers referred to apprentices as "persons"; and individual acts mentioned girls as well as boys and mistresses as well as masters: women were legally entitled, not only to enter apprenticeship, but also to take on apprentices of their own (Snell 1985: 177). As Stephen Orgel points out,

> until late in the seventeenth century women in one place or another, were admitted into practically every English trade or guild. Women did not, moreover, limit their efforts to ladylike pursuits: in Chester, in 1575, there were five women blacksmiths. Elsewhere, women were armourers, bootmakers, printers, pewterers, goldsmiths, farriers, and so forth . . . and they pursued these trades not as wives, widows, or surrogates, but as fully independent, legally responsible craftspersons. This point needs especially to be stressed, since a common modern way of ignoring the presence of women in the Renaissance workforce is to claim that they were there only as emanations of absent or dead husbands: this is not the case. The *percentage* of female apprentices is especially notable, for a practice that Lawrence Stone and E. P. Thompson believe did not exist. In Southampton, for example, at the beginning of the seventeenth century, 48 percent – almost half – the apprentices were women. (Orgel 1996: 73; see also Clark 1992; Snell 1985)

The historical evidence I have sampled undermines the current scholarly consensus that respectable women were expected to stay at home, that they were economically dependent on fathers and husbands, and that they were subjected to constant surveillance by jealous men, obsessively anxious about their sexual fidelity. I found it because I was looking for it. Historical evidence, as my old teacher reminded me, is subject to selective citation and motivated interpretation. The same, of course, is true of literary texts. In a 1985 study of *King John*, I easily discovered that

Lady Faulconbridge's infidelity has created the nightmare situation that haunts the patriarchal imagination – a son not of her husband's getting destined to inherit her husband's lands and title. Like Shakespeare's ubiquitous cuckold jokes, the Faulconbridge episode bespeaks the anxiety that motivates the stridency of patriarchal claims and repressions. (Rackin 1985: 341)

That reading seemed valid to me because it confirmed the paradigmatic view of women's place in Shakespeare's world. Looking at it now, I realize that it elided a number of features of the text: the facts that the revelation of Lady Faulconbridge's adultery is depicted in humorous terms, that the Bastard it produced is a sympathetic character, that he welcomes the revelation of his bastardy, and that it results in his acceptance as the son of Richard Cordelion and consequent social elevation. Of course, the lady's husband, who might indeed have been jealous, is no longer alive when the revelation occurs.

Nonetheless, if we reexamine the representations of male sexual jealousy in Shakespeare's other plays, it is difficult to sustain the assumption that it expresses a normative view. Othello's jealousy of Desdemona is the source of tragedy, Leontes's jealousy of Hermione is the source of near-tragedy, Ford's jealousy of his wife is the subject of comic debunking. And all are mistaken. To be sure, Shakespeare does depict unfaithful wives. Goneril and Margaret are obvious examples. But it is worth noting that in neither case is the woman's infidelity her only, or even her chief, offense; and neither husband is wracked by jealousy. In other plays of the period, unfaithful wives are forgiven. Sometimes, in fact, their infidelity goes undetected. Consider, for instance, the case of Winnifride in *The Witch of Edmonton*, who is pregnant by another man when she marries Frank Thorney, who believes the baby is his. Never punished for her transgression, she is depicted throughout in sympathetic terms and, at the end of the play, is welcomed into the home of the supremely virtuous Carters. Sir Arthur Clarington, the coldhearted aristocrat who seduced Winnifride when she was his maidservant, is denounced as "the instrument that wrought all" the "misfortunes" of the other characters. According to Old Carter, he is "worthier to be hang'd" than Frank Thorney, who murdered Carter's daughter (V.ii).

In attempting to interpret plays historically, probably the best starting place for a feminist critic is Jean E. Howard's reminder that women were paying customers in early modern theaters (Howard 1988: 439–40; see also Gurr 1996: 61–5 and appendices 1 and 2; Levin 1989). According to the records of early English playgoers compiled by Andrew Gurr, these included respectable women, such as the wife of John Overall, who was Regius Professor of Theology at Cambridge from 1596 to 1607 and Dean of St. Paul's from 1602 to 1618 (Gurr 1996: 207). In fact, Gurr found far more references to citizens' wives and ladies than to whores (1996: 62), even though references to prostitutes seeking customers are more familiar to modern readers whose assumptions about the women in the playhouses have been shaped by scholarly citations of anti-theatrical literature. Those assumptions were not, apparently, shared by the players, who explicitly defer to female playgoers in prologues and epilogues and express the players' awareness that the women in the audience, as well as the men, had to be pleased. The Epilogue to *As You Like It* is a good case in point. Spoken by the actor who played Rosalind, it addresses female and male playgoers separately, beginning with the women, whom it charges "to like as much of this play as please you," thus suggesting that the "you" in the play's title refers primarily to them. The Epilogue to Shakespeare's *Henry VIII* expects to hear "good" about the play "only in / The merciful construction of good women, / For such a one we showed 'em," acknowledging that positive representations of female characters were likely to appeal to female playgoers. In *The Knight of the Burning Pestle*, a citizen and his wife repeatedly interrupt the players to demand changes in the represented action, and although both are the subjects of satire, there is no suggestion that her interruptions are more inappropriate than his because she is a woman or that her husband's wishes are more to be honored than hers. Ben Jonson, whom it would be difficult to accuse of excessive deference to women, dedicated *The Alchemist* to Lady Mary Wroth, and declared in the Prologue to *Epicoene* his intention to provide a dramatic feast "fit for ladies . . . lords, knights, squires, . . . your waiting-wench and city-wires [i.e., citizens' wives who wore fashionable ruffs supported by wires], . . . your men, and daughters of Whitefriars." Jonson's assumption that women's interests might be different from men's and that both needed to be pleased is supported by no less a personage than Queen Anne, who not only patronized two companies of players (The Children of the Queen's Revels and Queen Anne's Men), but also, according to the French ambassador, attended plays in which "the comedians of the metropolis bring [King James] upon the stage." The Queen, the ambassador reported, "attends these representations in order to enjoy the laugh against her husband" (Chambers 1951: I, 325).

It is generally assumed that private playhouse audiences were more homogeneous than those in the large public amphitheaters like Shakespeare's Globe, but even the private playhouses catered to women as well as men, and, as these examples show, those women came into the playhouses with tastes, interests, and allegiances which were not necessarily the same as men's. Moreover, it is difficult to imagine a totalizing master narrative that would account for the varied experience, tastes, interests, and allegiances of all the women who enjoyed playgoing in Shakespeare's England. They included applewives and fishwives, doxies and respectable citizens, queens and great ladies (Gurr 1996: 60–4). Because playing was a commercial enterprise, it was in the players' interests to please as many of the paying customers as they could, the women no less than the men. The female playgoers in Shakespeare's London brought their own perspectives to the action. Perhaps we should try harder to emulate their example. *Women* were everywhere in Shakespeare's England, but the variety of their roles in life and in the scripts of plays too often "goes without saying." If we wanted to look for it, I think we could find "an interpretive embarrassment of riches" for a revitalized feminist criticism.[3]

NOTES

1   "The Traffic in Women" is a core text for contemporary feminist/historicist criticism, but, as Stephen Orgel observes, this "brilliant, classic essay" illustrates how "even the most powerful feminist analyses are often in collusion with precisely the patriarchal

assumptions they undertake to displace." "To define Renaissance culture simply as a patriarchy," he explains, is "to limit one's view to the view the dominant culture took of itself; to assert that within it women were domestic creatures and a medium of exchange is to take Renaissance ideology at its word, and thereby to elide and suppress the large number of women who operated outside the family system, and the explicit social and legal structures that enabled them, in this patriarchy, to do so" (Orgel 1996: 125).

2 I am grateful to Lena Cowen Orlin for sharing with me her brilliant unpublished essay, "The Witness Who Spoke When the Cock Crowed," and allowing me to quote from it. Here is the context of her comment: "Here [in second-wave feminism], the female victim has been an object of our scholarly desires. Literary historians have so often repeated the mantra that women were enjoined to be chaste, silent, and obedient; have so often described the spatial restrictions on women; have so often 'explained' playtexts in terms taken from the most conservative literatures of their time, that the reigning orthodoxy of historiography has become that of patriarchal philosophy. I have myself been oppressed by the sheer weight of the homiletic record, by the sermons and conduct books that are so readily available, so generically familiar, so textually congenial. I and perhaps others have been seduced by the efforts of our own research into thinking these prescriptions were culturally operative in a way that they cannot have been in many women's daily lives. Even though we have reminded ourselves that such admonitions would not have been necessary had their strictures been more generally observed, we have nonetheless persisted in depicting women as victims of unrelenting misogyny, patriarchy, and oppression. If we have enjoyed this construction of women, perhaps it is because it offers us the comforting reassurance that history has made progress and that we have come a long way (baby) from our early modern predecessors" (Orlin 1998).

3 I wish to thank Rebecca Bushnell, Jean E. Howard, Lena Cowen Orlin, and Donald Rackin for helpful critical readings of drafts of this essay.

REFERENCES AND FURTHER READING

Archer, I., Barron, C., and Harding, V. (eds.) 1988: *Hugh Alley's Caveat: The Markets of London in 1598*. London: London Topographical Society Publication No. 137.

Belsey, C. 1985: *The Subject of Tragedy: Identity and Difference in Renaissance Drama*. London: Methuen.

Boose, L. E. 1991: "Scolding Brides and Bridling Scolds: Taming the Woman's Unruly Member." *Shakespeare Quarterly*, 42, 179–213.

Bourdieu, P. and Wacquant, L. J. D. 1992: *An Invitation to Reflexive Sociology*. Chicago: University of Chicago Press.

Carroll, W. C. 1995: "The Virgin Not: Language and Sexuality in Shakespeare." In Deborah E. Barker and Ivo Kamps (eds.), *Shakespeare and Gender: A History*. London and New York: Verso, 283–301.

Chambers, E. K. 1951: *The Elizabethan Stage*. Oxford: Clarendon Press. Reprinted with corrections. (Original work published 1923.)

Clark, A. 1992: *Working Life of Women in the Seventeenth Century*. Third edition. London and New York: Routledge.

Dolan, F. E. 1994: *Dangerous Familiars: Representations of Domestic Crime in England 1550–1700*. Ithaca and London: Cornell University Press.

——1996: "Reading, Writing, and Other Crimes." In Valerie Traub, M. Lindsay Kaplan, and Dympna Callaghan (eds.), *Feminist Readings of Early Modern Culture: Emerging Subjects*. Cambridge: Cambridge University Press, 142–67.

Eaton, S. 1996: "A Woman of Letters: Lavinia in *Titus Andronicus*." In Shirley Nelson Garner and Madelon Sprengnether (eds.), *Shakespearean Tragedy and Gender*. Bloomington: Indiana University Press, 54–74.

Elliott, V. B. 1982: "Single Women in the London Marriage Market: Age, Status and Mobility,

1598–1619." In R. B. Outhwaite (ed.), *Marriage and Society: Studies in the Social History of Marriage*. New York: St. Martin's Press, 81–100.

Erickson, A. L. 1993: *Women and Property in Early Modern England*. London and New York: Routledge.

Erickson, P. 1991: *Rewriting Shakespeare, Rewriting Ourselves*. Berkeley: University of California Press.

Evans, G. B. et al. 1997: *The Riverside Shakespeare*. Second edition. Boston and New York: Houghton Mifflin.

Ezell, M. 1987: *The Patriarch's Wife: Literary Evidence and the History of the Family*. Chapel Hill and London: University of North Carolina Press.

Fletcher, A. 1995: *Gender, Sex and Subordination in England 1500–1800*. New Haven and London: Yale University Press.

Garner, S. N. and Sprengnether, M. (eds.) 1996: *Shakespearean Tragedy and Gender*. Bloomington: Indiana University Press.

Greenblatt, S. 1988: "Fiction and Friction." In *Shakespearean Negotiations: The Circulation of Social Energy in Renaissance England*. Berkeley: University of California Press, 66–93.

Gurr, A. 1996: *Playgoing in Shakespeare's London*. Second edition. Cambridge: Cambridge University Press.

Henderson, D. E. 1997: "The Theater and Domestic Culture." In John D. Cox and David Scott Kastan (eds.), *A New History of Early English Drama*. New York: Columbia University Press, 173–94.

Hogrefe, P. 1977: *Women of Action in Tudor England*. Ames, IA: Iowa State University Press.

Howard, J. E. 1986: "The New Historicism in Renaissance Studies." *English Literary Renaissance*, 16, 13–43.

—— 1988: "Crossdressing, the Theatre, and Gender Struggle in Early Modern England." *Shakespeare Quarterly*, 39, 418–40.

—— and Rackin, P. 1997: *Engendering a Nation: A Feminist Account of Shakespeare's English Histories*. London and New York: Routledge.

Jardine, L. 1991: "Boy Actors, Female Roles, and Elizabethan Eroticism." In David Scott Kastan and Peter Stallybrass (eds.), *Staging the Renaissance: Reinterpretations of Elizabethan and Jacobean Drama*. New York and London: Routledge, 57–67.

Kahn, C. 1981: *Man's Estate: Masculine Identity in Shakespeare*. Berkeley: University of California Press.

Keeble, N. H. (ed.) 1994: *The Cultural Identity of Seventeenth-Century Woman: A Reader*. London: Routledge.

Leventen, C. 1991: "Patrimony and Patriarchy in *The Merchant of Venice*." In Valerie Wayne (ed.), *The Matter of Difference: Materialist Feminist Criticism of Shakespeare*. Ithaca: Cornell University Press, 59–79.

Levin, R. 1989: "Women in the Renaissance Theatre Audience." *Shakespeare Quarterly*, 40, 165–74.

McLuskie, K. 1994: "The Patriarchal Bard: Feminist Criticism and Shakespeare: *King Lear* and *Measure for Measure*." In Jonathan Dollimore and Alan Sinfield (eds.), *Political Shakespeare: Essays in Cultural Materialism*. Second edition. Ithaca: Cornell University Press, 88–108.

Montrose, L. A. 1981: "'The Place of a Brother' in *As You Like It*: Social Process and Comic Form." *Shakespeare Quarterly*, 32, 28–54.

Mullaney, S. 1994: "Mourning and Misogyny: *Hamlet*, *The Revenger's Tragedy*, and the Final Progress of Elizabeth I, 1600–1607." *Shakespeare Quarterly*, 45, 139–62.

Neely, C. T. 1996: "'Documents in Madness': Reading Madness and Gender in Shakespeare's Tragedies and Early Modern Culture." In Shirley Nelson Garner and Madelon Sprengnether (eds.), *Shakespearean Tragedy and Gender*. Bloomington: Indiana University Press, 75–104.

Newman, K. 1991: *Fashioning Femininity and English Renaissance Drama*. Chicago: University of Chicago Press.

Orgel, S. 1996: *Impersonations: The Performance of Gender in Shakespeare's England*. Cambridge: Cambridge University Press.

Orlin, L. C. 1998: "The Witness Who Spoke When the Cock Crowed." Unpublished essay.

Payne, D. C. 1995: "Reified Object or Emergent Professional? Retheorizing the Restoration Actress." In J. Douglas Canfield and Deborah C. Payne (eds.), *Cultural Readings of Restoration and Eighteenth-Century English Theater*. Athens and London: University of Georgia Press, 13–38.

Rackin, P. 1985: "Anti-Historians: Women's Roles in Shakespeare's Histories." *Theatre Journal*, 37, 329–44.

Rubin, G. 1975: "The Traffic in Women: Notes on the 'Political Economy' of Sex." In Reina Reiter (ed.), *Towards an Anthropology of Women*. New York: Monthly Review Press, 157–210.

Snell, K. D. M. 1985: "The Apprenticeship of Women." In *Annals of the Labouring Poor: Social Change and Agrarian England, 1660–1900*. Cambridge: Cambridge University Press, 270–319.

Spevack, M. 1968: *A Complete and Systematic Concordance to the Works of Shakespeare*. Hildesheim: Georg Olms.

Stallybrass, P. 1986: "Patriarchal Territories: The Body Enclosed." In Margaret W. Ferguson, Maureen Quilligan, and Nancy J. Vickers (eds.), *Rewriting the Renaissance: The Discourses of Sexual Difference in Early Modern Europe*. Chicago: University of Chicago Press, 123–42.

Tennenhouse, L. 1986: *Power on Display: The Politics of Shakespeare's Genres*. New York and London: Methuen.

Traub, V. 1995: "Jewels, Statues, and Corpses: Containment of Female Erotic Power." In Deborah E. Barker and Ivo Kamps (eds.), *Shakespeare and Gender: A History*. London and New York: Verso, 120–41.

PART TWO
Text and Language

4

Feminist Editing and the Body of the Text

Laurie E. Maguire

There is no avoiding edited Shakespeare; the question is only what kind of editing.

Gibbons (1994–: v)

In a period of heightened sensitivity to gender-determined cultural biases, when there are increased efforts by most women and many men to extirpate the endemic patterns of sexual discrimination, an editor of whichever sex, whether willing to do so or not, plays an active role in combatting gender biases or in maintaining them.

Reiman (1988: 358)

Editing has been with us for hundreds of years. Gary Taylor calls the process "mediation" (1987: 1), and mediation applies to ancient manuscripts (where scribes, deliberately or unwittingly, meddled with the text they were employed to copy) as well as to early modern printed editions like the First Folio of Shakespeare (1623), where Heminge and Condell, Shakespeare's fellow actors, made editorial decisions about canon formation (which Shakespeare plays to include) and text (which exemplars of multiple texts to reproduce). Despite a long tradition of Shakespeare editing by poets such as Pope and men of letters such as Malone and Johnson, the editing of Renaissance drama was not formalized until the early years of the twentieth century when, under the aegis of a formidable triumvirate of Oxbridge graduates, A. W. Pollard, R. B. McKerrow, and W. W. Greg, the Shakespeare text was subjected to the systematic "scientific" rules and principles spawned by analytical bibliography. The "New Bibliography," as it came to be known, joined the history of manuscript and book production to interpretive textual criticism. Together these areas led to rigorous taxonomic rules for editing, expressed first in guerilla-warfare fashion – local raids and attacks on negligent editors whose flawed editions Greg reviewed – and subsequently in two book-length studies: McKerrow's *Prolegomena for the Oxford Shakespeare* (1939) and Greg's *The Editorial Problem in Shakespeare* (1942).

Feminism has also been with us for centuries, as long as editing (see the women in Aristophanes' *Lysistrata*, for instance), although it too was not formalized until the early years of the twentieth century. John Stuart Mill may have included women's suf-frage in his election address of 1865; ladies' colleges may have been founded at Oxford, Cambridge, and London universities in the late 1800s; but it was the developments of 1905/6 onwards that organized and politicized campaigns for women's rights in a way that made them impossible for the public to ignore. In October 1905, Christa-bel Pankhurst and Annie Kenney were imprisoned in Manchester for disruptive activ-ities to promote women's suffrage; in 1906 the Women's Political and Social Union, founded by Emmeline and Christabel Pankhurst, staged a series of London demon-strations that led to much-publicized arrests; and in the same year the British press coined the label "suffragette."

In the same period McKerrow and Greg were occupied with a different political agenda, founding the Malone Society (1906), editing the works of Thomas Nashe according to New Bibliographical principles (1907), excavating manuscript plays and records, presenting editorial manifestos in pugnacious reviews and articles. The New Bibliographers never spoke of their project as political; to them New Bibliography, like its near-contemporary critical twin, New Criticism, aimed for a transcendental text. Just as New Criticism applied scientific positivism to literary criticism, focus-ing on the poem's autonomy and "public linguistic fact" (Makaryk 1993: 120), so New Bibliography aimed for factual, scientific objectivity and detachment. But objec-tivity, like truth, is never pure and rarely simple, and editing, we now realize, is sub-jective in part and political in total, from the choice of author (i.e., the definition of a "classic") and the works that represent that author (canon formation) through the choice of text to represent those works (first thoughts or last thoughts? revised the-atrical "play" or authorial literary "book"?), the layout of the *dramatis personae*, the presentation of the text on the page, and the content of the commentary notes and introduction (both of which are ideological, whether overtly or not).

Nowadays we tend to label our editions, as we label our criticism, as historicist, feminist, theatrical, etc., declaring at the outset our personal perspective, our parti-san allegiance. We no longer pretend that editions are a product of editorial neutral-ity – what the facts say; they are a product of interpretation: what the editor says the facts say.

In the past we bought Shakespeare's text (or thought we did); now we know we are buying the editor's. This explains the commercial success of all the competing Shakespeare series on the market today (so many that Ann Thompson compiled a con-sumer guide, *Which Shakespeare?*). When one buys one's first Shakespeare (whether individual volume or complete works), the editor's textual collation, glosses, and introduction, helpful and interesting though they may be, are ancillary to the text; in subsequent purchases of the same title they are the reason for buying the text.

In literary criticism, the term "feminism" has metamorphosed and evolved since its first introduction in the 1960s. We have experienced the deliberate merging of the political and the personal, the reinscription of women writers in history, the replace-ment of the historicized focus on the woman writer with the concept of the feminine in writing, and a Foucault-influenced intersection of literary and cultural history focusing on class and gender (Janet Todd). We have lesbian feminism, Marxist feminism, gynocriticism, classical feminism, Anglo-American feminism, French feminism, and so on.

Given the plurality of feminisms, "feminist editing" is clearly a slippery term. Most feminisms, however, are political in orientation and challenge the "hegemony of male subjectivity and phallogocentric discourse" (Dawson 1989: 440). In this essay I would like to consider feminist editing as a sociological agent for awareness and change that points out (and hence combats) misogyny in whatever form. With this as a working definition, it is clear that male editors can be feminists, and that feminist editing can be performed on works by male as well as female authors. Not all critics would agree with this inclusivity. However, it will serve for the initial stages of this essay in which I consider textual problems and editorial practices in selected plays by Shakespeare and his contemporaries.

Readers tend to think of the three main components of editorial activity as construction of the text, annotation/commentary, and introduction (I list these components in the order in which the editor tackles them, not the order in which the reader encounters them). I want to begin by considering these three key areas and a feminist editor's potential contribution to them. I start with a gender-relevant textual crux, move on to annotation (the editor's language and attitude in commentary notes), before considering the role of the introduction and other editorial ancillaries. I then reexamine what we mean by, and desire from, feminist editing.

Gender and Textual Crux

As You Like It is one of Shakespeare's most gender-sensitive comedies. Although Shakespeare heroines often don male disguise for self-protection or plot advancement (Julia in *Two Gentlemen of Verona*, Viola in *Twelfth Night*, Rosalind in *As You Like It*, Imogen in *Cymbeline*, Portia in *Merchant of Venice*), it is unusual to find the hero correspondingly feminized. In *As You Like It*, entry into the forest of Arden reverses the gendered characteristics of both Orlando and Rosalind (Rutter 1988: 97–9, 105). Orlando's first appearance in the forest is characterized in feminine fashion: he is a nurturing, maternal figure, caring for and feeding the helpless Adam; at one point he carries him in his arms; and the vocabulary depicts Orlando as a "doe" looking after a "fawn." Rosalind is, of course, in male attire, with a "swashing and a martial outside," and she adopts masculine behavior: she initiates conversations, negotiates finances, and arranges marriages. Furthermore, she enjoys her male attire and the freedom it affords her so much that she retains it long after it has served its practical protective purpose in facilitating the cousins' flight. In Act I Celia suggests that she and Rosalind go "to seek my uncle in the Forest of Arden" (I.iii.103). This goal is accomplished in Act III, as Rosalind reveals in an incidental remark to her cousin: "I met the Duke my father yesterday and had much chat with him. He asked me of what parentage I was; I told him of as good as he so he laughed and let me go" (III.iv.30).

Nonetheless, Rosalind retains her male disguise for a further two acts, giving up her masculine identity only because Orlando says he can "live no longer by thinking" (V.ii.50).

At the end of the play Duke Senior and his courtiers, Celia and Oliver, Rosalind and Orlando, plan to return to the court, but they have not yet done so: the last scene keeps us in the pastoral world of magic and make-believe, presided over by the ambiguous figure of Hymen (the god of marriage? or a rustic figure representing the god of marriage?). Hymen joins the couples and addresses Rosalind and Orlando in a line that most editors emend, believing that the compositor in the Folio of 1623 (our only early authority for the text) made an error. F reads as follows:

> That thou mightst ioyne his hand with his
> Whose heart within his bosome is
> (TLN 2689–90)

The bosom referred to in 2690 is, of course, Orlando's. The two hands indicated by the possessive pronoun in 2689 are the hands being joined in marriage, Orlando's and Rosalind's; so most editors from F3 on (1664) emend the first "his" to "her": "That thou mightst join [her] hand with his / Whose heart within his bosom is."

It was Nicholas Rowe, in 1709, who first supplemented the Folio stage direction that precedes this speech ("Enter Hymen, Rosalind and Celia") with the explanation "Rosalind in Woman's Cloths." In 1768 Edward Capell expanded the stage direction to include "Rosalind and Celia in their proper Dress." Thomas Caldecott, however, in 1832, queried Rowe's stage direction and retained the two "his" pronouns of 2690 (cited by J. W. Holme, Arden edition, 1914). Over a century later, Maura Slattery Kuhn argued in detail that the first "his" should stand, observing that Rosalind is still dressed as Ganymede. She points out that Orlando is never told that Rosalind was Ganymede and that, unlike Julia, Viola, Portia, and Imogen, Rosalind is never given an opportunity in dialogue to reveal to her future husband that *she* has in fact been a *he*. Kuhn suggests that costume here reveals what dialogue does not, Rosalind choosing to wear male costume for her marriage to Orlando.

In fact, the character Rosalind has a choice here, although the boy actor playing her may not: the intricacies of Elizabethan female costume, with its laces and layers, would be hard to negotiate successfully in the 75 lines (two to three minutes) the text allows for a costume change. Kuhn argues that a costume change for the last hundred lines of the play would be extravagant on the Elizabethan stage, and that the tradition of Rosalind appearing in her wedding finery began in the Restoration with the introduction of actresses who would have relished the opportunity for a feminine finale in bridal attire. The F3 emendation coincides with the change in stage tradition.

In *As You Like It* the appearance of Rosalind-as-Rosalind-but-dressed-as-Ganymede provides one more exuberant coup for the heroine, as well as adding to the play's multiple perspectives on gender: Phoebe won't marry a woman, but Orlando does marry a "man," or at least the appearance of one. It also links Orlando's hesitant, conditional reaction to Rosalind/Ganymede's appearance – "If there be truth in sight, you are my Rosalind" – to Touchstone's stress on "if" in the Seven Degrees of a Lie, to the litany of "ifs" that surrounds Hymen's appearance and the final pairing off of the couples, to the "if" of Rosalind's epilogue ("If I were a woman"), and to Sir Philip Sidney's defense of the poet's attempt to "reconcile poetic feigning and absolute truth" (Kuhn 1977: 48). The appearance of Rosalind/Ganymede, in other words, is a visual representation of the Lie Direct: "If the daughter's garb belies her sex, this is assuredly the Lie Direct, which is unavoidable except 'with an If'" (Kuhn 1977: 42).

If we think about the play in these ways, Hymen's statement that he has come to join "his hand with his" is perfectly intelligible. Greg wrote that an editor should never alter his copytext unless the text is demonstrably wrong. But definitions of "wrong" depend on literary interpretation as well as textual information. Textual information can tell us that misreading of "hir" as "his" and vice versa was an easy error for a compositor to make in the period, for a terminal "r" and "s" were very similar in Elizabethan secretary hand. Even when misreading is not the issue, the possessive pronoun can cause problems as we see in one manuscript and one other printed text. In the manuscript of Middleton's *The Witch*, the scribe initially wrote "his" at IV.iii.36, later "corrected" it to "her," but editors from Steevens onwards restore the original "his" which the sense requires. In the six quarto reprints of Edmund Tilney's *Flower of Friendship* (1568), the compositors inexplicably altered the first quarto's "hir" (which refers to Flora, goddess of spring), to "hys"/"his" (Tilney 1992: 95, 143). Thus it is possible that the "his" in *As You Like It* is an error requiring emendation. But emendation of the possessive pronoun seems only to follow from expansion of the stage direction, itself predicated on assumptions from a non-Elizabethan tradition of actresses, and a failure to consider the larger interrogation of appearance, ontology, and gender in the play. Analyzing this crux in the context of a reading of gender removes the crux.

It was, as I have mentioned, Caldecott – neither a woman nor a feminist, in a century not renowned for its gender sensitivity – who first queried Rowe's stage direction and the F3 emendation. Such textual analysis might be construed as "feminist" and a text based on such analysis might be a feminist text; however, such textual cruces are few and far between. Although Suzanne Gossett notes suggestive examples of variant textual choices in editions of *The Taming of the Shrew* edited by Brian Morris (1981) and Ann Thompson (1984), so-called feminist editions of Shakespeare do not differ notably, in the construction of their text, from non-feminist editions. Where feminist editions have more scope to indicate their feminism is annotation.

Gender and Annotation (1): Misogyny

Annotation was once the realm of the apolitical, the lexical, the philological, the neutral, the local, the straightforward identification of the proverbial. Annotation was a service industry, and, like all good servants, the notes did not call attention to themselves as they efficiently and unostentatiously performed their work. So reluctant were editors to allow notes to intrude that glosses were couched in a grammatical shorthand: phrasal, appositive, anti-narrative, non-discursive (Middleton 1990: 169–70).

This is still true, although to a lesser extent, for notes now also contain miniature essays, critical debates, editorial personality, expressions of distaste. Annotation has outgrown footnote status so that "Long Notes" now appear at the end of volumes.

The extent of, and detail in, annotation obviously depends on the intended audience. Any editor begins not by thinking about the text but about its audience. When an edition is to form part of a series, this audience has already been considered by the general editor and the editorial board. Most commercial editions are aimed at the high school and undergraduate markets – an impressionable audience by any standards, and often an enthusiastic one, eager to think about social values, critical methodology, and literary relevance; the editor has the opportunity therefore to function as teacher and social worker, both proselytizer and poser of provocative questions. We generally think of the introduction as providing the forum for such interrogative or partisan discussions, but the annotation provides a more effective and persistent conduit. Readers can ignore an introduction; few are those who do not glance at a gloss at some stage, if only to find that "an" means "if."

Given that Renaissance plays abound in sexual slang and politically incorrect aphorisms – often denigrating to women and to racial others – the question is how can an editor responsibly and sensitively indicate the meaning of the material for the sixteenth-century audience, and the unacceptability of this material to the twenty-first century?

The treatment of racism can provide an instructive analogue. A few generations ago, the British school paintbox contained a color called "nigger brown." The linguistically unaware schoolchild (i.e., all schoolchildren) had no concept that the adjective was not an inoffensive description like "chestnut brown." We have since become aware that such unthinking terminology has a history, a context, and causes pain. In the same way, the reader of a Renaissance text has to be alerted to the problems of gender-insensitive language. And just as one fights fire with fire, one fights language with language.

Let us look at examples of misogynist thinking in Renaissance plays, and see how commentary notes deal with it. The frequency and copiousness of women's tears (in comparison to those shed by men, who have been socialized not to weep) have long rendered suspect the sincerity of female distress expressed through weeping. A recent newspaper report noted that men who cry are more likely to be taken seriously by medical doctors than women who do so. In the Renaissance, women's tears were viewed as part of a complex and misunderstood system of female fluids (menstruation, lactation, urination; see Paster 1987), but the bottom line was that female lachrymosity was not to be trusted. When Othello strikes Desdemona, causing her to weep, he views her reaction as insincere:

> O devil, devil!
> If that the earth could teem with women's tears,
> Each drop she falls would prove a crocodile
> (IV.i.239–41)

Women's tears, then, were crocodile tears (to exchange a misogynist for a species-ist metaphor).

The stereotype associated with women's tears appears throughout Renaissance plays, expressed by both male and female characters. In *All's Well That Ends Well* the Countess says that neither joy nor grief "can woman me unto't" (III.ii.50). In *Knight of the Burning Pestle* the Merchant is dismissive: "Come, they are women's tears. I know your fashion" (IV.136). In *The Revenger's Tragedy* the Duchess's wicked sons discuss their stepbrother, whose death they had urged and whose supposed passing they had grieved; "did we make our tears women for thee?" they ask in frustration as they encounter their very alive stepbrother (III.vi.83). Bartholomew the page is instructed how to act convincingly as a woman in the Induction to *The Taming of the Shrew*. Among the characteristics he is advised to adopt – curtsies, low voice, modestly inclined head – are tears, and these tears can be prompted by an onion in a handkerchief if Bartholomew lacks "a woman's gift to rain a shower of commanded tears" (Ind.i.124–5). It is, it seems, such stereotypes of femininity that Bianca manipulates to her advantage and that her more vocal sister Katherine sees through and reacts against: "A pretty peat! It is best / Put finger in the eye, and she knew why," exclaims Katherine when Bianca has just received all the paternal sympathy in a scene in which Katherine, not her sister, was humiliated and hurt (I.i.78–9). And again in Act II it is Bianca's tears that garner her support from her father before he has evidence that she is wronged : "Poor girl, she weeps" (II.i.23).

How should an editor gloss such phrases? Not by accepting them without comment, as do Loughrey and Taylor in the Penguin edition of *Thomas Middleton: Five Plays*, where we read: "**make our tears women**] i.e. dissemble grief" (Middleton 1988: 130), or as H. J. Oliver and Brian Morris do in the Oxford and Arden editions respectively of *The Taming of the Shrew*. Even Ann Thompson, in the New Cambridge *Taming of the Shrew*, refrains from head-on confrontation. At Ind.i.120 she provides a cross-reference to I.i.78–9, thereby deferring the topic of women's "commanded tears," and she diverts the reader with a thespian consideration at Ind.i.122: "perhaps onions really were used by the less competent actors." In a more responsible gloss in the Revels edition (1984) of *Knight of the Burning Pestle*, Sheldon P. Zitner points out the speaker's misogyny: "**women's tears**] hence not to be taken seriously, *the Merchant thinks*" (p. 133; my emphasis). In the Oxford *All's Well* Susan Snyder calls attention to the stereotype (and hence untruth) invoked: "**woman me unto't**] make me break down under it in tears, *like the stereotypical woman*" (p. 148; my emphasis); and in a half-hearted rehabilitation of women, the Riverside *All's Well* qualifies the stereo-type: "**woman me unto't**]: make me respond like a *(weak)* woman, i.e. with tears" (p. 557; my emphasis). Zitner locates the misogyny in the speaker, Snyder in society (both sixteenth and twentieth centuries), whereas the Riverside partially accepts the stereotype. All three glosses, however, make an effort to confront the statement while explaining it, and that seems to me the hallmark of an ideologically respon-sible gloss.

Shakespeare's plays pose fewer such sexist dilemmas for editors than those of his contemporaries. The following phrase comes from Middleton's *A Trick to Catch the Old One*, and the gloss is Loughrey and Taylor's.

> You do so ravish me with kindness that I'm constrain'd to play the maid and take it! (III.i.447–8)
>
> **play the maid and take it**]: proverbial: "say 'no,' but accept the offer"

When anti-rape campaigns proclaim "No means No," and wryly expose the casuistry in male attempts to read subtext into a simple monosyllable ("What part of 'No' don't you understand?"), this gloss is reprehensible, particularly when one considers the sexual nature of the verb ("ravished") that introduces the phrase to be glossed. And "proverbial"? Given that *OED* 1a defines proverb as "a concise statement . . . which is held to express *some truth ascertained by experience or observation and familiar to all*" (my emphasis), to gloss any misogynist, racist, or similarly retrograde view as "proverbial" is unthinkable (or unthinking). Elizabeth Schafer suggests (in a personal communication) that "proverbial" should always be followed by a noun: "proverbial misogyny" or "proverbial male misogynist wisdom [*sic*]."

The early modern adhered to many ideas that are no longer part of current belief systems: that hysteria is caused by a wandering womb, that the liver is the seat of passion, that insane people make an amusing spectacle, that eggs are aphrodisiac and gold medicinal, that Venetian women are lascivious, Italians vengeful, and tailors effeminate. Editors regularly distance themselves from dietary superstition, medical folklore, and racial stereotypes, as in the following glosses (all emphases mine):

> eggs were *thought* to be an aphrodisiac
>
> (*Women Beware Women*, I.ii.119; Middleton 1988: 253)

> The mandrake . . . was *said* to shriek when pulled from the ground
>
> (*Duchess of Malfi*, II.v.1–2; ed. E. M. Brennan, third edition)

> *Popular superstition* had it that a vein or nerve ran from the third finger of the left hand to the heart
>
> (*A Chaste Maid*, III.i.21; ed. Alan Brissenden)

> liver] The *supposed* seat of the passions
>
> (*As You Like It*, III.ii.422; ed. G. B. Evans, Riverside II)

> Venetian women were *believed* lascivious and weak
>
> (*A Chaste Maid*, IV.xxii.38; ed. Alan Brissenden)

> in the *understanding of a seventeenth-century audience*, to become Italian was to become an expert in the art of revenge
>
> (Ford, *'Tis Pity*, V.iv.28; ed. Simon Barker)

> double chins were *considered* to be the distinguishing feature of the bawd
>
> (*A Chaste Maid in Cheapside*, II.ii.71; Middleton 1988: 185)

Should we not also distance ourselves from other outmoded beliefs?

This distancing language need not be overzealous; one is inclined to ignore nothing so much as egregious proselytizing. Loughrey and Taylor show how effective punctuation can be in emphasizing critical commentary. In Middleton's *A Chaste Maid*, the undergraduate Tim, embarrassed by the hectoring bluntness of his mother's hortatory exclamations, criticizes her for entreating "like a freshwoman." The noun is a Middleton neologism, formed by analogy with "freshman." The editors gloss as follows: "**freshwoman**: first-year female undergraduate (although at this period none existed!)" (Middleton 1988: 199). The editorial exclamation mark is instructive. An exclamation mark calls attention, and here it functions litotically as wry commentary on the sad social reality behind Middleton's deliberate solecism.

Recent literary criticism is more linguistically sensitive than is editorial annotation. Note Michael Neill's consistent care, in his article on *The Revenger's Tragedy*, to avoid complicity with the text and its characters' coercive strategies (all emphases mine):

> If men are coiners, it is women, *according to Vindice*, who are most "apt . . . to take false money." (Neill 1996: 404)

> "Virginity," *as Gratiana is made to say*, "is paradise, locked up." (Neill 1996: 407)

> Men are conceived as being "made close" (1.3.81) by their very gender, rendering them, *ideally* at least, self-contained and impenetrable (Neill 1996: 407)

Contrast the following glosses, also from Middleton plays (ed. Loughrey and Taylor):

> 1 *Women Beware Women*, IV.i.1 (Middleton 1988: 315)
> **How goes your watches, ladies?**] Watches were a relatively new invention and very unreliable. Therefore they were often compared to the sexual behaviour of women; in particular to "set a watch" was slang for having sex.

(The editors' gloss (unwittingly?) agrees with the causal logic of the equation: watches were unreliable; *therefore* they were like women.)

> 2 *Women Beware Women*, IV.ii.148 (Middleton 1988: 329)
> **Be but a woman so far**] be true to your sex in this respect (women were dissemblers)

(The editors do nothing to suggest that they do not identify with the statement.)

> 3 *A Trick to Catch the Old One*, IV.v.28–9 (Middleton 1988: 58)
> **The tavern bitch has bit him i'th' head**] i.e. he is drunk.

(Middleton's metaphor here assumes that women provide pleasure, but if they linger too long they cause the male to suffer; the editors do nothing to suggest that they do not concur with this view.)

A slight adjustment of phrasing can make a big difference, as in the following glosses, all of which serve the dual function of explanation and interpretive guidance, to varying degrees:

> 4   *All's Well*, ed. Susan Snyder (Shakespeare 1993: 136)
> kicksy wicksy downgrades even a loved woman as an irrelevant trifle

(The editor's verb makes clear her viewpoint.)

> 5   Ford, *'Tis Pity She's a Whore*, III.ii.11; ed. Simon Barker
> Giovanni refers to a stereotype of women as inconstant

(The simple reference to stereotype distances the editor from the view that women are fickle.)

> 6   *The Witch*, ed. Elizabeth J. Schafer (Middleton 1994: 40)
> An unchaste woman would be seen to be mutilated

(The conditional suggests historical distance.)

> 7   *The Witch*, ed. Elizabeth J. Schafer (Middleton 1994: 44)
> Almachildes would have been outraged if his bride (like the woman he has just had sex with) had lost her virginity

(The parenthesis points out the double standard.)

> 8   *The Shrew*, ed. Ann Thompson (Shakespeare 1984: 92)
> Petruchio is not the only Shakespeare hero to assume a woman with spirit must be unchaste

(The editor situates Petruchio among his fictional contemporaries with a tone of mild criticism and/or regret that Petruchio thinks this way.)

Language, as any book-burning dictator knows, is a powerful instrument for change. Today's editors have a duty to combat gender biases in their glosses. As Gary Taylor observes, "we see what we can say, and if we say things differently, we will see them differently" (Taylor 1988: 53). More important, so will the generation of male and female students we are teaching.

Gender and Annotation (2): Bawdy

If the early modern was conservative in its attitude toward gender relations, it was imaginative to a fault in its use of everyday vocabulary to describe sexual relations. Gordon Williams's three-volume *Dictionary of Sexual Language and Imagery in Shakespearean and Stuart Literature* (1994) is a tribute not just to Williams's diligence in documenting sexual subtexts, but to Renaissance versatility in devising them. How explicitly, and how colloquially, should an editor gloss bawdy? The question has received different answers at different stages of editorial history. Thus, early twentieth-century editorial policy was predictable: do in editing as you do in life. References to sex or the intimate body were avoided, if not through omission then through the safe refuge of Latin euphemism. Thus "pudenda" appears frequently in footnotes, and even Eric Partridge, compiler of the pioneering and explicit *Shakespeare's Bawdy*, uses Latin to civilize sexual activity. To "put the bridal-bit in her mouth" is explained as "penem in vaginam inmittere" (Partridge 1993: 71), and "on occasion Partridge seems even to have coined Latinisms for sexual activity: the word 'penilingism' (p. 73), apparently meaning 'tonguing the penis', is not recorded in the *Oxford English Dictionary* or its supplements" (foreword to Partridge 1993: vii). Whether editors sanitize sexual explanations to conceal their embarrassment at confronting such sexual topics, or whether it stems from a *noblesse oblige* which prevents them imposing these subjects on the unsuspecting audience, is not clear.

Gratiano's bawdy joke in the last two lines of *Merchant of Venice* ("Well, while I live I'll fear no other thing / So sore, as keeping safe Nerissa's ring") receives no gloss in the 1905 Arden edition of C. N. Pooler. In the 1955 New Arden edition, J. R. Brown tells us simply that it is "a bawdy pun," referring the reader to Eric Partridge, and in the New Cambridge Shakespeare of 1987 M. M. Mahood provides an explanation in anatomically formal language: "Gratiano's last bit of bawdy, since 'ring' could mean 'vulva'." "Vulva" certainly conveys the meaning, but whereas "ring" was harmless sexual slang in the Renaissance, "vulva," like "pudenda," is not a modern colloquialism.

The editor is, in many respects, on easier ground when faced with stronger sexual slang that has an exact modern equivalent or descendant: cut = cunt, foutre = fuck. Even so, editors have been reluctant to articulate such terms. Malvolio unwittingly treads on sexual territory when examining Olivia's alleged handwriting in II.v of *Twelfth Night*. "These be her very C's, her U's, and her T's," he says. "I am afraid some very coars and vulgar appellations are meant to be alluded to by these capital letters," wrote Blackstone. That was in 1793 (quoted by Lothian and Craik in New Arden *Twelfth Night*, 1975); here is John Dover Wilson less allusively but nonetheless euphemistically in the New Shakespeare of 1930: "Malvolio is unconsciously guilty of a bawdy jest, 'cut' meaning the female pudendum" (p. 139); and here are J. M. Lothian and T. W. Craik in the 1975 New Arden edition: "indecent joke . . ., 'cut' being the female genital organ" (p. 67). The editor as Desdemona? Cf. "I cannot say 'whore.' It does abhor me now I speak the word." The same reticence is found in glosses on Hamlet's bawdy "country matters" (III.ii.103), which the Riverside, edited by G. B. Evans (1997) tells us is an "indecency," the New Cambridge Shakespeare, edited by Philip Edwards (1985) tells us is a "sexual pun," and the Oxford edition, edited by G. R. Hibbard (1987) reveals means "sexual intercourse (quibbling indecently on the first syllable of country)." The "country" pun in *Hamlet* shares a syllable with its sexual subtext, and so it does not need to be spelled out. But "cut" does, for it is not "the female pudendum" but a slang word for the female pudendum, and we have an exact equivalent today: cunt.

Editors are less modestly self-censoring when dealing with Katherine of France's bawdy in *Henry V*: the three recent editors of *Henry V* (Taylor 1982; Gurr 1992; Craik 1995) unself-consciously use "cunt" and "fuck" when glossing "con" and "foutre," as do Holderness and Loughrey in their edition of Q1 *Henry V*. Even Partridge can use the terms in his discussion of Katherine of France (1993: 87), although he, like Alice, judges the vocabulary "bad, corrupt, gross, and indelicate." In the case of Katherine, editors may be protected by the foreign language, providing the sexual gloss as *translation*, not as explanation; or Katherine's embarrassment may provide a conduit for theirs; or the recent dates of the *Henry V* editions may indicate that editors are increasingly comfortable with dirty words.

However, we need to ask ourselves what purpose such liberality serves. The Loughrey and Taylor edition of *Middleton: Five Plays* is free to the point of indiscrimination in its use of sexual colloquialism: I count twenty-two appearances of "cunt" and fifteen of "fuck" in the glosses. Some of these coincide with Middleton's use of the equivalent early modern term, but most do not. Furthermore, the glosses are not consistent in their use of sexual slang, for having found "fuck" in many glosses where it seems unnecessary, we do not find it in places where it might be appropriate. Thus, Tim's rendering of the Welsh "fogginis" as "foggin" in *Chaste Maid*, IV.i.121 is glossed "bawdy sense," although "figging" in III.iii was glossed unambiguously as "fucking" (Middleton 1988: 202). In addition, the editors are content with "copulate," "sexual intercourse," "bawdy innuendo," and "sexual innuendo" on many occasions, so one wonders what are the criteria that necessitate "fuck" on others. There may be a reverse *noblesse oblige* operating here – "we'll show you how much we respect your openmindedness" – but overall these editors protest too much. As Ralph Hanna observes, glossing has always been a "socially sanctioned form of aggression" (unpublished paper, quoted by Middleton 1990: 169); the Loughrey/Taylor annotation, by sheer volume, borders on sexual harassment.

We can observe a different comfort level in feminist editions, which reject the euphemisms of Latin which characterized the early twentieth century, but eschew the gratuitous slang of Loughrey and Taylor. In the three examples below I cite sexual glosses from Ann Thompson and Elizabeth Schafer, comparing them with Loughrey and Taylor's glossing of the same vocabulary.

1   *Taming of the Shrew*, I.ii.109, ed. Thompson
"Partridge gives 'eye' as one of the many euphemisms for the vagina" (Shakespeare 1984: 73)

Women Beware Women, III.iii.66, and *The Changeling*, III.iii.69, ed. Loughrey and Taylor
eyes] punning on "eye" = cunt (Middleton 1988: 312)
eye] perception/cunt (Middleton 1988: 377)

2   *Taming of the Shrew*, II.i.73, ed. Thompson
doing] perhaps including the meaning "having sexual intercourse" (Shakespeare 1984: 83)

Revenger's Tragedy, I.i.4, ed. Taylor and Loughrey
do] fuck (p. 73)

3   *The Witch*, I.i.75, ed. Elizabeth Schafer
Since "riding" could mean sexual intercourse, there is an innuendo (Middleton 1994: 8)

The Changeling, IV.iii.75, ed. Loughrey and Taylor
ride] quibbles on "ride" = fuck were common (Middleton 1988: 401)

Suzanne Gossett notes that her "female delicacy" in glossing obscene phrases in Middleton's *A Fair Quarrel* was overruled by her general editor, Gary Taylor, who added "pun on fuck us" to her gloss on "fucus," and "pun on cunt" to her gloss on "callicut," where Gossett had "coyly written 'with obscene pun on cut as in *Twelfth Night*'" (Gossett 1996: 117). The explicitness is appropriate, indeed required, here, whereas my objection to much of the explicitness in Loughrey and Taylor is that it is otiose.

Ultimately, as these examples make clear, glossing bawdy is simply a question of taste. We need editions that are not coy nor brash but impudent. I am using impudent here in its etymological sense of "freedom from shame," as John Fletcher does in *The False One*, IV.iii: "Off my dejected looks, and welcome impudence. / My daring shall be deity, to save me." Impudence is not restricted to feminism (although it may sometimes be a by-product of it).

Gender, the Introduction, and the *Dramatis Personae*

The most identifiably feminist part of any edition, the introduction, requires little comment here. We can identify feminist criticism – criticism informed by the "attitudes, assumptions, and preconceptions" of a feminist politics (Barratt 1993: 48) – when we read it, and a feminist introduction is feminist criticism prefixed to an edition.

Introductions are not forums for the extremist (although they accommodate bias), or for the proselytizer. The extreme is inevitably ephemeral, and the proselytizer may find s/he is preaching to the converted. The aim of feminism, like most combative politics, is to make itself redundant. Thus, a defiant assertion of the 1970s becomes, one hopes, a statement of the obvious in the 1980s, a truth universally acknowledged in the 1990s, and a cliché in the twenty-first century. The degree of rhetorical vigor required in a feminist introduction depends on the date of the edition and the critical history of the play. In 1982 Ann Thompson felt that *The Taming of the Shrew* has been somewhat neglected by critics," and that the "relationship between Petruchio and Katherine is obviously the heart of the problem" (Shakespeare 1984: 225). Her introduction therefore concentrated on the dynamics of the main plot, concluding spiritedly that "the real problem lies outside the play in the fact that the subjection of women to men, although patently unfair and unjustifiable, is still virtually universal. It is the world which offends us, not Shakespeare" (1984: 41).

In the twenty-first century editors of *The Taming of the Shrew* cannot complain of the play's critical neglect. Consequently they no longer need to focus predominantly on the sexual politics of the Katherine–Petruchio relationship. The play's two most recent editors, Frances Dolan (in the Bedford *Texts and Contexts* volume, 1996) and Jean Howard (in the Norton Shakespeare, 1997), expand and complicate the critical debate by locating the gender issues in the larger area of class. Thus Dolan:

> When Petruchio yells at and strikes his servants, he abuses or exaggerates power that his culture gives him as a man: householder, master, and husband. . . . When Katherine lashes out, she seizes power not properly hers. . . . In the other instances of violence in the play, superiors lash out against inferiors . . . [T]he play suggests that persons with power over others often abuse that power, relying on violence to assert themselves. . . . When Katherine uses violence to dominate servants and other women rather than to resist her father or her husband, her conduct is presented as laudable (pp. 19–24)

Howard focuses on agricultural politics and land enclosures, concluding with a wry linking of class and gender: "there is always something lower than a beggar – a beggar's wife" (p. 139). Thus feminist editors are freeing *The Taming of the Shrew* from "the stultifying straitjacket of being interpreted as a one-issue play" (Mason 1995: 137).

Betty Bennett warns that "gender privileged over all other aspects of analysis often leads to a single focal point that limits rather than amplifies interpretation" (1993: 72–3); as if heeding this caveat, the critical introduction has become more expansive, more complicated, and consequently more exciting. As introductions become more expansive, their presentation and organization need to be rethought. The most thoughtful presentation is found in the Routledge English Texts series, where the introduction is divided into two parts. A short essay (called "Introduction") precedes the text, providing a helpful overview of author and text as well as specific information that is useful to read before one reads the play or poem: alchemy for Jonson's *Alchemist* (ed. Peter Bement), Chaucerian language and the position of medieval women in Chaucer's *Tales of the Clerk and the Wife of Bath* (ed. Marion Wynne-Davies), sources and Italian settings in Ford's *'Tis Pity She's a Whore* (ed. Simon Barker). The text is followed by a more extended "Critical Commentary," an essay-length and often original discussion of the text's critical issues. (Marion Wynne-Davies's commentary, for example, brilliantly links the moments in the two tales in which Alice and Griselda faint [pp. 140–2]; she shows that neither character abdicates narrative control at this moment of apparent weakness, and provocatively analyzes the implications of her observation.) These Routledge commentaries are unself-consciously aware of their partisan bias in the realm of cultural politics, and one would expect no less from a series whose general editor is John Drakakis. As Wynne-Davies explains, "whatever our critical allegiances, it is essential to recognize that they are social, cultural, political, and personal constructions" (p. 120).

The introduction is followed in all series by an area of the text that is unjustly neglected in editorial discussion: the *dramatis personae*. In most editions *dramatis personae* lists are arranged hierarchically: men on top. This practice began in the early modern period where *dramatis personae* lists are prefaced to some quarto texts, and are attached to selected plays in the Shakespeare Folio of 1623 (where they follow the playtext).

The six Folio Shakespeare plays that conclude with *dramatis personae* lists (*Measure for Measure, Tempest, Winter's Tale, II Henry IV, Timon of Athens*, and *Othello*) call the list "The Names of the Actors." In fact, the actors' names do not appear at all, the list containing simply the names of the characters in the play. However, the actors hover in the background of the lists in that the roles are generally arranged in descending order of thespian importance. The roles that were played by the lead serious actors are listed first, then those assumed by the comic actors, followed by the minor roles; the women's roles, played by boy apprentices, conclude the list. (The only list that places the women's roles in the middle is *Othello*; the list for *Timon*, curiously, omits the women's roles altogether.) Thus, it is the apprenticeship of the boy actor rather than the inferiority of the female character that is indicated by the low placing on the list.

There is no reason for modern editions to relegate female characters to the foot of the *dramatis personae*, or to place them below the male roles but above the minor, unnamed roles. When one considers the alternative taxonomic systems available (alphabetical; order of appearance; plot and subplot; familial and political allegiance), a classification based on gender and/or rank (and the two are linked) is nothing less than editorial apartheid. Even in its revised second edition of 1997, the Riverside Shakespeare still separates male from female roles by a line of white space – a system possibly of use to twenty-first-century acting companies anxious to calculate the number of male and female actors required, but confusing and misleading to the first-time reader.

A number of modern editions have abolished segregation, a commonsense practice not confined to feminist editions. Brian Gibbons divides the *Romeo and Juliet* characters into households – nobles, Montagues, Capulets, Franciscans – and then lists the few miscellaneous others who complete the cast. Andrew Gurr lists the *Henry V* characters in order of appearance. Ann Thompson orders the characters of *The Shrew* in three groups: "The Induction," "The Taming Plot," "The Sub-plot." In *All's Well* Susan Snyder mixes the women characters along with the men in a general order of dramatic importance. M. M. Mahood's *Merchant of Venice* seems to observe a class hierarchy, with the Duke at the top and servingmen at the bottom; Portia is in the middle, below the men of her rank, but above men of lower rank. The editorial guidelines for Arden 3 advise editors that "the practice of segregating female roles at the foot of the list should be abandoned" (p. 18); it seems that the assumptions and practice of editions such as Riverside 2 may soon be a thing of the past.

Along with the decision about where to place women comes a decision about what to call them, both in the *dramatis personae* list and in speech prefixes. In *The Shrew* Petruchio relabels the heroine "Kate," perhaps an attempt to give her a new identity, perhaps an attempt to diminish her with a diminutive, an onomastic form of taming. Katherine objects to the nomenclature, and instantly corrects her wooer: "They call me Katherine that do talk of me." Petruchio ignores this corrective; editors should not. The Signet editor labels Katherine "Kate" in speech prefixes and stage directions, an intimacy offered by only two other characters (Katherine's father and sister). No other twentieth-century editor adopts the diminutive (although editors occasionally refer – negligently rather than deliberately? – to "Kate" in critical introductions [see Shakespeare 1984: 22]). Editors do not call Helen of Troy "Nell" in the *dramatis personae* of *Troilus and Cressida*, although this is how Paris refers to her in III.i; nor do editors label Katherine of France "Kate" of France, although this is Henry V's most frequent address to her. Why should they adopt Petruchio's preference over Katherine's in *The Taming of the Shrew*?

The main female character in Middleton's *A Trick to Catch the Old One* is called "Courtezan" in all the early editions. The text makes clear that she is not paid for professional sexual services but has slept with only one man – the hero – to whom she has lost her virginity. As Valerie Wayne (1998) explains, the early modern had no category for such a woman other than courtezan/whore. But for an editor to label this character "courtezan" privileges fidelity to a seventeenth-century text at the expense of the twenty-first-century reader's cultural associations, for this noun sends the contemporary audience specific interpretive signals about sexual attitude and availability which are not appropriate to the heroine of the play.

Identification and interrogation of subject positions (particularly where they are complicated by disguise in its everyday form, sartorial fashion) is a recurrent theme in both Middleton and Shakespeare, and the point in *A Trick* is that the categories of courtezan/widow/wife, and the (dis)respectability attached to them, are constructs. Obviously these categories have no ontological basis since the men cannot distinguish between the "courtezan" and the (fake) "widow," who are one and the same. Wayne adopts the character's first name, Jane, for speech prefixes in her forthcoming edition – a sensible and sensitive choice. All other editors, all male, accept the quarto's label "courtezan."

We know from many studies that Shakespeare and his contemporaries were alert to onomastic resonance. Editors must be too. Naming, like editing, is a powerful and politically sensitive activity.

Feminist Editing

Editing in the early twenty-first century is full of paradoxes. The editor has a responsibility both to the politics of the dead author and the author's society, and to the politics of the contemporary audience; the editor is a parasite on the text, and also the reason for that text's continuing existence; s/he is both guardian of text and constructor of text, both guardian and maker of meaning. Such paradoxes are further complicated by feminist politics.

Having considered some specific examples of editorial activity in the areas of text, annotation, introduction, *dramatis personae*, and onomastics, I now want to return to the larger theoretical concept of feminist editing. Bookstores and publishers advertise Shakespeare texts edited by women and/or feminists (Mahood, Potter, Patterson, Ioppolo, Thompson, Snyder, Osborne), Shakespeare texts edited by men and women (del Vecchio and Hammond, Weil and Weil), and women authors edited by women and feminists. The criteria for considering some of these editions feminist have never been made clear.

Some critics assert that "male feminist" is an oxymoron, for men can be sympathetic to feminism but cannot be feminists; hence a feminist edition by a man is the editorial equivalent of *Haec Vir* and *Hic Mulier*. If that is true, then we have no feminist editions of Shakespeare, since most general editors are male. (The exceptions are few: Ann Thompson is one third of the general editors of Arden 3; Barbara Mowat is one half of the editorial team of the New Folger Shakespeare series.)

Some critics believe that truly feminist editors do not waste time on male authors, who are already heavily edited, but have as their editorial aim the excavation of neglected female authors. This act of literary rehabilitation is crucial, and its values have been pointed out by those engaged in it: "Now that I know some of its women writers, the male writers look different to me than they used to, and I have modified my ideas about women's 'place' in our period" (Hageman 1993: 105). Poststructuralism's expansion of what constitutes literature first enabled critics to avoid the exclusive focus on public, male writing (printed and performed plays, epics, lyrics, manuscript sonnet sequences circulated at court), and this facilitated the examination of women's private manuscript writings – letters, diaries, spiritual journals – as well as poetry and closet drama by women. Such literary excavation might be prompted by feminist impulses or it might be prompted by poststructuralist principles. However, feminism is certainly involved in the project's origin (an interest in women's history) and in its results, for as Elaine Crane observes, editing such texts can "contribute as much to the revision of women's history as the historian or literary scholar who uses the documentary material for the basis of a book" (Crane 1988: 381).

Does the involvement of feminism make the edition feminist? I suspect not. That some editions have feminist content is indisputable, but it is usually localized in the introduction (see Thompson, Dolan; Wynne-Davies's Chaucer is a notable exception). The only totally feminist editing that I have encountered to date is theater production. Productions are editions inasmuch as they mediate an author's text for an audience. Unlike editing, however, their aim has never been to represent the author in any neutral unbiased fashion but to represent the director's interpretation of that author. We talk of Trevor Nunn's *Macbeth*, Peter Brook's *Midsummer Night's Dream*, John Barton's or Michael Bogdanov's *Wars of the Roses*. If editors have to think in three dimensions – the past, the present, and the future – so that self-conscious vigorous tilting at sexual politics does not seem overstated or outdated to a future generation, the director operates under no such constraints. Productions are by definition ephemeral. They can therefore afford to be blatantly ideological.

Furthermore, productions have resources not available to editions (costume, gesture, specific verbal intonation, and knowledge of the specific time and place in which the audience is encountering the production), which help anchor ideological interpretations. Productions are also obliged to commit themselves to one interpretation of moments and characters: Hippolyta is a reluctant, conquered bride or she is not; Isabella rejects the Duke's offer of marriage, or she does not. Book editions, on the other hand, have the luxury of plurality. The textual collation shows the variant texts possible, and commentary notes regularly offer multiple options for interpretations (usually based on contrasting moments in stage history). Thus, while editors make choices, they also comment on those choices (however innocently) by listing or discussing the alternatives; directors make an interpretive choice, which locks them into subsequent choices, and an ideological through-line is created.

Adjectives cannot be attached comfortably to all nouns, as Robin Riddle points out (personal communication), and the adjective *feminist* is particularly problematic in this regard: a feminist carburettor or a course in feminist calculus would seem an anomaly. However, what is problematic about the term "feminist editing" is not the label but the concept itself. I cannot advocate something called "feminist editing" any more than I can endorse "masculinist editing" (which is the only editorial model we have had in the twentieth century).

What editors, male and female, are increasingly striving for, and what I have described in the working definition of feminist editing with which I began (gender awareness and linguistic sensitivity to combat misogyny), is something we might call a "humanist" edition: an edition that is conscious of and sensitive to inequality, marginalization, and victimization, of, and by, gender, class, race, or some other category not yet at the forefront of our social and critical consciousness, and which actively works to correct such anomalies. The second epigraph to this essay argues that "an editor of whichever sex, whether willing to do so or not, plays an active role in combatting gender biases or in maintaining them" (Reiman 1988: 358). In other words: if an editor is not part of the solution s/he is part of the problem. The minimum desideratum for all editors, male or female, must be the creation of an edition that is "gender equitable without being gender blind" (Reiman 1988: 353). This humanist aim does not seem a lot to ask.

The Editor as Teacher/The Future of Editing

Humanist editing, like the contemporary literary criticism which gives rise to it, is a supremely powerful tool, for in their roles as social workers and teachers, editors influence their audience and through them, the future. Note the pedagogical emphases in the following quotations, where humanist editing revises our reading of the past and consequently affects our practices in the future:

> [A]ll editors must take into consideration . . . the future. (Reiman 1988: 359)

> We believe in the power of language to help shape the attitudes of the future. (Reiman 1988: 359)

> The end of editing is to change literary history: to change our collective organization of the intertextual spaces of the past, and by doing so to change the kind of intertextual spaces that may be created by future readers, critics, writers. To change our reading of the past, in order to change the future of reading. (Taylor 1993: 143)

Changing the future of reading, however, requires that we make critical reading of editions – their apparatus and construction – as prominent a focus in the undergraduate and postgraduate curricula as the critical reading of other texts. I am not advocating bibliography classes but a basic critical awareness of how the act of editing "is a major determinant in what and how we read" (Bennett 1993: 89). This has become easier in the undergraduate classroom in recent years with the proliferation of rival Shakespeare editions, so that students encounter words, lines, and even names and scenes in one edition that are not present in another. The editor is a teacher, and, like all teachers, fallible. Our students need to be made aware of that.

Margaret Ferguson and Barry Weller explain that

> in the presentation of *Mariam . . .* we have *for pedagogical reasons* foregrounded the whole process of (re)constructing a seventeenth-century text for modern readers, and our annotations therefore give more prominence to textual choices and emendations than most editions designed for the classroom. It seems to us useful to emphasize to students, both in literature and in other disciplines, the process of historical recovery and inference through which the texts of the past reach a modern reader. (Carey 1994: 49; my emphasis)

This is the closest thing to a manifesto for teaching editorial awareness, and I cannot endorse it too strongly.

In 1998 I taught a third-year course in Stuart Drama as an exercise in feminist criticism and humanist editing. I scanned out-of-copyright Old Mermaids editions of the Renaissance plays on my syllabus, gave the students disks, and made each student responsible for editing one act in a gender-conscious manner (in the form of printed text or website). The edited act was due in the last weeks of the course; in the preceding months we considered problems and possible treatments in the unedited texts we were reading, beginning each class with an editorial Show and Tell to which the students brought dilemmas for our consideration. The discussions became increasingly informed and wide-ranging as the students began to note and analyze editorial practices in texts they were reading in other courses. Why, we wondered, do editors of the *Wife of Bath's Tale* refer to the male protagonist of the tale as a knight? Isn't a man who rapes a woman a rapist? Or does rank confer semantic as well as social privileges? The attempts of the Riverside editor to gloss the bawdy in *The Miller's Tale* prompted much discussion, as editorial coyness clashed with the unrestrained exuberance of the Miller; the scholarly footnotes use euphemism and Latin to conceal the body which the tale so unashamedly exposes. Why in editions of Ibsen's *A Doll's House* is the heroine always identified by her first name, Nora, and her husband by his surname, Tolmer? This may fit with Victorian politics, which accorded the man the "public" and legal identity, but it does not suit (except perhaps ironically) the politics of the play, which examines the construction of the little woman, and it perpetuates an inequality still seen in today's workplaces where (female) support staff (for example) are called by their first names and (male) managers by their full titles. Is there an edition that identifies the couple equitably as Nora and Helmer? (Yes: *one*.) What does it signify that Ibsen called the couple Mr. and Mrs. (Stenborg) in his first draft? In the classroom it signifies quite a lot, but only when the students realize that the text is a product of editorial choice and not authorial fiat. The future of humanist editing lies not just with editors but with consumers of editions.

REFERENCES AND FURTHER READING

Barratt, A. 1993: "Feminist Editing: Cooking the Books." *AUMLA (Journal of the Australasian Universities Language and Literature Association)*, 79, 45–57.

Bennett, B. T. 1993: "Feminism and Editing Mary Wollstonecroft Shelley: The Editor And?/Or? the Text." In George Bornstein and Ralph G. Williams (eds.), *Palimpsest: Editorial Theory in the Humanities*. Ann Arbor: University of Michigan Press, 67–96.

Carey, E. 1994: *The Tragedy of Mariam*. Ed. Barry Weller and Margaret Ferguson. Berkeley: University of California Press. (Original work published 1613.)

Crane, E. F. 1988: "Gender Consciousness in Editing: The Diary of Elizabeth Drinker." *TEXT*, 4, 375–83.

Dawson, A. B. 1989: "Making a Difference? Shakespeare, Feminism, Men." *English Studies in Canada*, 15, 427–40.

Gibbons, B. 1994–: General Editor's Foreword to New Cambridge Shakespeare Early Quartos.

Gossett, S. 1996: "Why Should a Woman Edit a Man?" *TEXT* 9, 111–18.

Hageman, E. H. 1993: "*Did* Shakespeare Have Any Sisters? Editing Texts by Englishwomen of the Renaissance and Reformation." In W. Speed Hill (ed.), *New Ways of Looking at Old Texts*. Binghampton, NY: Medieval and Renaissance Texts and Studies, and Renaissance English Text Society, 103–9.

King, K. 1989: "Bibliography and a Feminist Apparatus of Literary Production." *TEXT*, 5, 91–103.

Kuhn, M. S. 1977: "Much Virtue in If." *Shakespeare Quarterly*, 28, 40–50.

Makaryk, I. R. (ed.) 1993: *Encyclopedia of Contemporary Literary Theory*. Toronto: University of Toronto Press.

Mason, P. (ed.) 1995: *Shakespeare: Early Comedies. A Casebook*. London: Macmillan.

Middleton, A. 1990: "Life in the Margins, Or What's an Annotator to Do?" In Dave Oliphant and Robin Bradford (eds.), *New Directions in Textual Studies*. Austin TX: University of Texas, Harry Ransom Humanities Research Center, 167–83.

Middleton, T. 1988: *Five Plays*. Ed. Bryan Loughrey and Neil Taylor. Harmondsworth: Penguin.

——1994: *The Witch*. Ed. Elizabeth J. Schafer. London: A & C Black.

Neill, M. 1996: "Bastardy, Counterfeiting and Misogyny in *The Revenger's Tragedy*." *SEL*, 397–416.

Partridge, E. 1993: *Shakespeare's Bawdy*. London: Routledge.

Paster, G. K. 1987: "Leaky Vessels: The Incontinent Women of City Comedy." *Renaissance Drama*, 18, 43–65.

Reiman, D. H. 1988: "Gender and Documentary Editing: A Diachronic Perspective." *TEXT*, 4, 351–9.

Rutter, C. 1988: *Clamorous Voices*. Ed. Faith Evans. London: Women's Press.

Shakespeare, W. 1984: *The Taming of the Shrew*. Ed. Ann Thompson. Cambridge: Cambridge University Press.

—— 1993: *All's Well That Ends Well*. Ed. Susan Snyder. Oxford: Oxford University Press.

Taylor, G. 1988: "The Rhetoric of Textual Criticism." *TEXT*, 4, 39–57.

—— 1993: "The Renaissance and the End of Editing." In George Bornstein and Ralph G. Williams (eds.), *Palimpsest: Editorial Theory in the Humanities*. Ann Arbor: University of Michigan Press, 121–49.

—— et al. 1987: *William Shakespeare. A Textual Companion*. Clarendon: Oxford University Press.

Tilney, E. 1992: *The Flower of Friendship*. Ed. Valerie Wayne. Ithaca: Cornell University Press.

Wayne, V. 1998: "The Sexual Politics of Textual Transmission." In Laurie E. Maguire and Thomas L. Berger (eds.), *Textual Formations and Reformations*. Newark, DE: University of Delaware Press, 179–210.

White, P. S. 1989: "Black and White and Read All Over: A Meditation on Footnotes." *TEXT*, 5, 81–90.

5

"Made to write 'whore' upon?": Male and Female Use of the Word "Whore" in Shakespeare's Canon

Kay Stanton

Anita strode into the room smiling, attired in earrings, high heels, and a red dress. That did not seem anomalous to me: she always had a sunny disposition, and she was scheduled to present her research paper for my graduate seminar in Renaissance Drama that day; sometimes my students dress up a little more than usual to do their oral presentations. I was always particularly proud of Anita. She had transferred to my university, before completing her undergraduate work, from a small Bible college, where she had met and married her husband. The first of several courses that she had taken from me was my undergraduate Shakespeare course, in which she began as a good student and became the best, and on her course and instructor evaluation form, she had written what remains the most unconventional comment on my teaching that I have yet received: "Her Shakespeare course improved my sex life with my husband!" I remember reading it and wondering what the committees that would be evaluating my file for tenure consideration would make of that. Anita was definitely the one who had written it, because she had made the same remark directly to me, further explaining that after class she would go home and share with her husband the sexual implications of various passages that we had covered in class discussion, and apparently that had an effect similar to the one experienced by Dante's Francesca and Paolo as they read the tale of Lancelot and Guinevere.

As prelude to her presentation of her seminar paper on female sexuality in Renaissance Drama, Anita surprised me and stunned the other twelve women and two men in the course by asking the women to show by raising their hands if they had ever been called a "whore." Her hand and mine went up immediately, and about two-thirds of the other women then raised theirs; the other students simply dropped their collective jaws. Bright, sweet, mild-natured, religiously devout, and happily married Anita, mother of two daughters, then went on to say that the first of several times she had been called a "whore" was by an older male cousin, when she was five years old and happened to be wearing a red dress. She of course then had no understanding of the word's meaning, but recognized it to be a very bad insult.

The first time for me had come when I was a still quite sexually inexperienced and naive high school student. A friend of Jerry, a boy whom I had dated, very innocuously, one time, grinned lasciviously and showed me a five-dollar bill, asking, "You'll go down for five?" When I indicated my incomprehension, he declared, "You're a **whore**, right? Jerry said you'd go down for five!" Although my virginity was still intact, certainly part of my innocence died in that moment: female words of truth could mean nothing; male words could assert themselves as truth against fact and logic. It was not until several years and repetitions of the insult later, in diverse but similarly unwarranted circumstances, that I could understand, as Anita too at this point did, various political and social implications involved in the use of the word, not just for myself and Anita, but for all women, some of whom have suffered far more severe consequences from it – as does Shakespeare's Desdemona, with whom any female who has had this term unjustly flung her way can identify.

The word "**whore**" is not the only word in the Shakespeare canon used for denigration of female sexuality (see Rubinstein 1989; Williams 1994), but it is one of particular interest because, whereas "strumpet," "harlot," and "minion" are still recognized, they are considered old-fashioned, and terms like "callet," "drab," and "stale" are unknown among the general populace. **Whore** is the one that endures, and, even among the many near-synonyms found in Shakespeare's works, it is the term with the most abusive punch, the "dirtiest" word. It is probably also the one with the most slippery definition, as it can be used, by Shakespeare and currently, with any of the following primary meanings, and more: professional prostitute; promiscuous woman; woman who has had sexual relations with more than one man; woman who has had or seems to want sexual relations with a man other than the one laying claim to her; woman who has had, or is believed to have had, sexual relations with men, or even only one man, without marriage; woman who, consciously or unconsciously, provokes sexual desire in men; woman who has, or attempts to take or maintain, control over her own sexuality, integrity, or life; and woman who has gone, or has expressed a desire to go, into territories, geographical and/or professional, claimed exclusively for men. But each of these very different meanings slides into the overall connotation of professional prostitute. As Dusinberre notes, "To call a woman a **whore**, as Othello calls Desdemona . . . not only casts aspersions on her morals, but takes away her place in society," since "A **whore** is always lower-class, a rake always upper-class" (1996: 52). This sense is established by means of a process called by Schulz, in an article so titled, "The Semantic Derogation of Women," by which paired male/female roles and behaviors lose their parallelism to elevate the male and defame the female, usually through unsavory sexual connotations (Schulz 1975).

For women, then, the word "**whore**" functions in hegemonic use in a roughly similar way as the word "nigger" does for blacks and the word "queer" does for homosexuals: to keep troubling individuals grouped in their marginalized place and to insist that the place is a vulgar, degraded one from which they can never escape. Some

American blacks have tried to desensitize the word "nigger" by using it affectionately among themselves, and American homosexuals belonging to a group called Queer Nation chant, "We're here, we're queer, get used to it!" Any female, of any race or class, sexually expert or inexperienced, heterosexual or homosexual, old or young, rich or poor, alluringly or conservatively dressed, educated or not, feminist or not, can always be called a "**whore**" by a male who wishes to assert mastery over her by demeaning her. Some of us women have at different times called ourselves suffragists, feminists, womanists, etc., with some progress made, but not enough to obliterate this term of insult as a verbal weapon of cultural authority. Should we next form ourselves into a **Whore** Nation and chant, "We're here, we're **whores**, we want more!"? A question not to be asked?

As Kramarae and Treichler note, "Examination of the processes of cultural authorization has led feminists to the institution where language and authority most dramatically intersect: the dictionary" (1985: 10), so let us look at the reigning Patriarch of English Language Dictionaries. *The Oxford English Dictionary* (OED), after stating (in 1933, reprinted unchanged in 1977) that "*Whore* is now confined to coarse and abusive speech, except in occas. echoes of historical expressions, as *the whore of Babylon*," provides the following definitions of the noun **whore**:

> 1. A woman who prostitutes herself for hire; a prostitute, harlot [. . .] [The earliest given citation is from 1100, the latest from 1894; the citation for 1597 is from Shakespeare's *II Henry IV,* III.ii.338 (Qo.).]
> b. More generally: An unchaste or lewd woman; a fornicatress or adulteress. *To play the whore* (of a woman) to commit fornication or adultery. In early use often as a coarse term of abuse. Occas. (esp. with possessive) applied opprobriously to a concubine or kept mistress; also with distinguishing epithet to a catamite. [. . .] [The earliest citation comes from 1205, the latest from 1607; the citation for 1605 is from Shakespeare's *King Lear,* I.iv.137, and the citation for 1606 is from Shakespeare's *Troilus and Cressida,* V.i.20.]
> 2. *fig.; spec.* in biblical use, applied to a corrupt or idolatrous community [. . .] and hence in controversial use, esp. in phr. *the whore of Babylon,* to the Church of Rome (in allusion to Rev. xvii.I, 5, etc. (Murray et al. 1933: XII, 97–8)

The *OED* defines the verb **whore** as

> 1. *intr.* To have to do with a **whore** or **whores**; to commit **whoredom**, fornicate; (of a woman) to play the **whore**. [. . .]
> b. *trans.* To spend in **whoring**; (with adv.) to get or bring by **whoring**. [. . .]
> 2. *trans.* To make a **whore** of; to corrupt by illicit intercourse; to debauch (a woman). [. . .] [The earliest given citation, for 1602, is from Shakespeare's *Hamlet,* V.ii.64.]

Related entries, all extrapolated from these definitions, are provided for **whore-call, whor[e]cop, whoredom, whoredomer, whore-haunter, whore-house, whore-hunt, whore-hunter, whore-hunting, whore-keeper, whore-like, whoremaster** (with the 1596 citation from Shakespeare's *I Henry IV,* II.iv.516), **whoremasterly,** whoremastery (with the 1606 citation from Shakespeare's *Troilus and Cressida*, V.iv.7), whoremonger (with the 1603 citation from Shakespeare's *Measure for Measure*, III.ii.37), whoremonging, whore-play, whorer, whore's bird, whoreship, whoreson (for definition 1. the 1592 citation is from Shakespeare's *Romeo and Juliet*, IV.iv.20, and the 1613 citation is from Shakespeare's *Henry VIII*, I.iii.39; for definition b. the 1597 citation is from Shakespeare's *II Henry IV*, II.iv.225), whore-toll, whor[e]y, whoring (with the 1604 citation from Shakespeare's *Othello*, V.i.116), whorish (for definition b. the 1606 citation is from Shakespeare's *Troilus and Cressida*, IV.i.63), whorishly, whorishness, whorism, and whorester (Murray et al. 1933: XII, 97–100).

A Supplement to the Oxford English Dictionary, published in 1986, notes under the noun whore, "Add: 1. c. A male prostitute; any promiscuous or unprincipled person. (Esp. as a term of abuse.)." For the verb whore is the emendation "Add: 1. c. *intr.* fig. To pursue or seek *after* (something false or unworthy)." Also added are related extrapolated terms whoremistress, whore's egg, and whore-shop, and later examples are provided for whore-like, whore-hunt, whore-house, whoreson, whorish, whorishly, and whor[e]y. Minor revisions for some of these terms are also given, usually to amend "*Obs.*" to "Revived in recent use." Of the later citations provided for the whore extrapolations, the latest date is 1982 (IV, 1289–90). From these revisions in the *OED*'s *Supplement*, then, we may infer that in 1933 the compilers had underestimated the amount of continued usage of the word (and by 1986 they had still missed some of the usages that I noted above).

Rather than citing the *OED*'s etymological information on the word, I offer the passage below, which summarizes and interprets closely similar information, taken from the entry for whore (quoted from Dennis Baron by Kramarae and Treichler) in *A Feminist Dictionary*:

> The derivations of *whore* often reveal more about the attitudes of the etymologists than they do about the nature of the word. Twentieth-century etymologists are generally agreed that the word *whore* comes ultimately from an Indo-European root, *ka-* according to the *American Heritage Dictionary*, which means "like, desire," and which produces such cognates as *care*, *caress*, and *cherish* as well as *whore*. Proposed derivations by earlier etymologists, however, link *whore* to words that mean "to hire," "for sale," "venereal sport," "wife," "to conduct business," "excrement," "pregnant," "fornication," "filthy," and "to pour out, urinate." (Kramarae and Treichler 1985: 484)

Their extensive analysis of traditional dictionaries in preparation for their compilation of *A Feminist Dictionary* led Kramarae and Treichler to write that

> Women in their pages have been rendered invisible, reduced to stereotypes, ridiculed, trivialized, or demeaned. Whatever their intentions, then, dictionaries have functioned as linguistic legislators which perpetuate the stereotypes and prejudices of their writers and editors, who are almost exclusively male. (Kramarae and Treichler 1985: 8)

They also note that "Definitions for many dictionaries" are "constructed from usages found in works of the 'best authors'; though the equation has been challenged in recent years, this designation usually means 'male authors'" (Kramarae and Treichler 1985: 2). By the thirteen examples (all from the speech of male characters) of **whore** as word and root-word given from Shakespeare (many more, of course, than from any other one source), we may note how prominently the Bard's work figures in the *OED*'s interpretation of the word's meaning; thus its linguistic authority partially accrues from his literary authority as the best of the "best authors" of English, and the *OED* and Shakespeare's combined authority yield cultural authority to the word's continued use. But before leaping to the conclusion that Shakespeare is indeed, as Kathleen McLuskie (1985) has called him (in her article so titled), "The Patriarchal Bard," not only in cultural authority but also in deliberately reinscribing and thus proscribing patriarchal authority over women, we should examine his usages of the word more comprehensively.

The singular noun **whore** appears forty-five times in the Shakespeare canon, plural **whores** eight times, singular possessive **whore's** twice, adjective **whorish** once, gerund **whoring** once, verb forms **whored** once, and **bewhored** once, for a total of fifty-nine. These forms are found collectively in sixteen plays: *I Henry VI* (1), *Titus Andronicus* (1), *Romeo and Juliet* (1), *Macbeth* (1), *The Merry Wives of Windsor* (1), *Cymbeline* (1), *The Tempest* (1); *Henry V* (1), *Hamlet* (2); *II Henry IV* (3), *Measure for Measure* (3); *Antony and Cleopatra* (4); *King Lear* (5); *Timon of Athens* (9); *Troilus and Cressida* (11); and *Othello* (14). Thus a form of the word **whore** appears in all of the tragedies except for *Julius Caesar* and *Coriolanus*, three history plays, and five comedies, four of which are now otherwise classed (two as "romances" and two as "problem plays," unless *Troilus and Cressida* is classed as a tragedy).[1] No form of the word is found in either the narrative poems or the sonnets (in which, although he may not be unlocking the secrets of his private heart, Shakespeare at least uses a poetic persona that in some sense represents his voice). A form of **whore** appears in a total of fifty-one instances by twenty-one male characters and in a total of eight instances by five female characters. Below (with a minor adjustment in the order cited above to allow for unbroken discussion of characters continuing between plays) I provide citation of each instance with a brief discussion of its context and implications.

There is much smirking speculation in *I Henry VI* on the sexual behavior of Joan [of Arc] La Pucelle, but the word **whore** is only used once, and not in regard to her, but as part of the ranting of Gloucester, brother of the late King Henry V, at Cardinal Winchester (Henry Beaufort), who has denied him entrance to the Tower. Gloucester calls Winchester a

> manifest conspirator,
> Thou that contrivedst to murder our dead lord,
> Thou that giv'st **whores** indulgences to sin.
> I'll canvass thee in thy broad cardinal's hat
> If thou proceed in this thy insolence.
> (I.iii.33–7, Bevington 1992 edition,
> here and henceforward)

History documents that Winchester used his cardinalate authority to license brothels and thereby collect revenues from them; Cardinal's Cap Alley, still extant in London, was named for a brothel located there with a cardinal's cap sign (see Burford 1973 for more information). If French religious leader Joan tries to turn the slanderous suggestions of her illicit sexual behavior to her favor in an attempt to save her own life by pleading pregnancy, certainly English religious leader Winchester is more factually and fully employed in illicit sex – but who burns?

In IV.ii of *Titus Andronicus*, a Nurse comes from Tamora to Aaron to show him the fruit of the couple's adulterous affair:

> A joyless, dismal, black, and sorrowful issue!
> Here is the babe, as loathsome as a toad
> Amongst the fair-faced breeders of our clime.
> The Empress sends it thee, thy stamp, thy seal,
> And bids thee christen it with thy dagger's point.
>
> (IV.ii.67–71)

Aaron, however, prioritizes differently: "Zounds, ye **whore**! Is black so base a hue? / [*To the child.*] Sweet blowze, you are a beauteous blossom, sure" (IV.ii.72–3). If the Nurse has disparaged his and his son's color and regards it as needing extermination, he will revenge himself by disparaging her sexual status, and, after she has been reduced to being a **whore**, he saves the child and kills her. This dynamic of **whorishness**/blackness/murder will of course be reexamined with much more complexity in *Othello*.

Mercutio discusses Tybalt in *Romeo and Juliet* as the "courageous captain of compliments" (II.iv.20):

> The pox of such antic, lisping, affecting phantasimes, these new tuners of accent! "By Jesu, a very good blade! A very tall man! A very good **whore**!" Why, is not this a lamentable thing, grandsire, that we should be thus afflicted with these strange flies, these fashionmongers, these pardon-me's, who stand so much on the new form that they cannot sit at ease on the old bench? (II.iv.28–35)

The word **whore** here is a casually used epithet for a sexually objectified woman as part of a catalogue of objects of temporary and faddish interest to and use by a fashionmongering "captain," which status Ancient Pistol will aspire to have in *II Henry IV*, to be discussed below.

The one mention of the word **whore** in *Macbeth* is made by the bleeding captain, who, reporting on the progress of the battle, states that Macdonwald, "Worthy to be a rebel, for to that / The multiplying villainies of nature / Do swarm upon him" (I.ii.10–12), was also assisted by "Fortune," who, "on his damnèd quarrel smiling, / Showed like a rebel's **whore**" (I.ii.14–15). Yet he was vanquished by "brave Macbeth," who, "Disdaining Fortune, with his brandished steel, / Which smoked with bloody execution, / Like Valor's minion carved out his passage" (I.ii.16–19), not stopping "Till he unseamed him from the nave to th' chops, / And fixed his head upon our battlements" (I.ii.22–3). Thus Macdonwald's "rebel's **whore**" Fortune is matched against

Macbeth's "Valor's minion" sword, which is employed in "brave" masculine assertion against the feminine "multiplying villainies of nature" assisting Macdonwald. "Minion" is a parallel, but not exact synonym, for **whore**, as it suggests at least an affectionate relationship, thus more loyalty and devotion for the man in her favor, who here temporarily wins. Yet, from this frame of reference, the **whore** Fortune ultimately conquers Macbeth through the revolution of her wheel. If Macbeth untimely rips life from Macdonwald through the abdomen, his own life will be taken by one who was untimely ripped from his mother's abdomen; if he puts Macdonwald's head on public display, so will be the fortune of his own head. Score one for the **whore**.

In *Cymbeline*, Iachimo lays the foundation to convince Posthumous that he has seduced the latter's wife by providing details of Imogen's bedchamber, including a description of a tapestry showing "Proud Cleopatra when she met her Roman" (II.iv.71), surely to employ suggestive equation of himself as Antony and Imogen as Cleopatra in adulterous relations. When, just a few lines later, Iachimo produces the husband's parting gift to his wife of a bracelet, previously identified as a "manacle of love" (I.i.124), Posthumous is all too quickly convinced that Iachimo

> hath enjoyed her.
> The cognizance of her incontinency
> Is this. She hath bought the name of **whore** thus dearly.
> There, take thy hire, and all the fiends of hell
> Divide themselves between you!
>
> (II.vi.129–33)

It is of course rather the case that Posthumous has bought the name of **whore** for Imogen in his own imagination and paid for it with the bracelet and Imogen's diamond. Nevertheless, convinced of this idea, besides commanding his wife's murder, he will also later doubt his mother's fidelity to his father and wish that there were some other way for men to come into existence without women being "half-workers" in their breeding (see Stanton 1995).

The word **whores** appears in *The Tempest* only in response to Gonzalo's discussion of his ideal commonwealth, which would have "No occupation; all men idle, all, / And women too, but innocent and pure" (II.i.157–8). In answer to Sebastian's "No marrying 'mong his subjects?" (II.i.168), Antonio states, "None, man, all idle – **whores** and knaves" (II.i.169). Thus female **whores** are equated with male knaves, with both offered as the inevitable product of idleness – but, as their own idleness on the island gives rise to Antonio's knavery and shows Gonzalo's innocence and naivety, their comments speak more of their own respective natures than of the general condition of humanity.

It is noteworthy that in *Hamlet*, where Hamlet rails with verbal sexual abuse in accusations at both his mother and Ophelia, and, in a parallel with *Macbeth*, Fortune is extensively discussed as a "strumpet" (II.ii.236), the word **whore** is found only twice and is both times applied to behavior of male characters. The first instance is found in a list of three prostitution similes that Hamlet uses to describe himself:

> Why, what an ass am I! This is most brave,
> That I, the son of a dear father murdered,
> Prompted to my revenge by heaven and hell,
> Must like a **whore** unpack my heart with words
> And fall a-cursing, like a very drab,
> A scullion!
>
> (II.ii.583–8)

Curiously, Hamlet compares his *in*ability to kill his current king with behaving *like* a **whore**. In the second instance, in V.ii, he speaks of that king as one who did accomplish involvement in both activities. Hamlet describes Claudius as "He that hath killed my king and **whored** my mother" (V.ii.64) and asks Horatio, "is 't not perfect conscience / To quit him with this arm? And is 't not to be damned / To let this canker of our nature come / In further evil?" (V.ii.67–70). This instance is the only verb usage of a form of **whore** by a male speaker in Shakespeare's canon; both it and the only other verb usage (by Emilia in *Othello*, discussed below) identify and blame a specific man for sexual defilement of a particular woman. The parallelism of the two contexts of **whore** forms within *Hamlet* suggests, too, that Hamlet's own linkings of **whoredom** and murder, as "canker of *our* nature," lead to damnation: his own verbal "**whoring**" of his mother in III.iv was involved in his killing of Polonius, as his own "**whoring**" of Ophelia in III.i will be in his killing of Laertes, soon to come (see Stanton 1994). The conjunction of the two activities also harks back to Gloucester's combined complaints in *I Henry VI* against Cardinal Winchester's conspiring to kill his king and involvement with prostitution.

In *Measure for Measure*, Lucio, obviously a frequent patron of Mistress Overdone's brothel, taunts her tapster/bawd Pompey as he is being led to prison: "What, is there none of Pygmalion's images, newly made woman, to be had now, for putting the hand in the pocket and extracting it clutched?" (III.ii.45–8), providing an apt representation of the prostitute as substance upon which to inscribe male fantasies, both of eroticism and degradation. When, a few lines later, in response to Lucio's question about his "dear morsel" (III.ii.54), Mistress Overdone, Pompey informs Lucio that she "hath eaten up all her beef, and she is herself in the tub" (taking the cure for venereal disease), Lucio then comments, "Why, 'tis good. It is the right of it, it must be so. Ever your fresh **whore** and your powdered [pickled] bawd; an unshunned consequence, it must be so" (III.ii.56–60). Showing his hypocrisy and lack of a sense of his responsibility in the maintenance of prostitution, Lucio denies Pompey's request for bail, further implicating him to the officers as "bawd-born" (III.ii.68): consumable objects for satisfaction of appetite, sex workers are born to be punished; the solicitors of their services are not.

Pompey, in IV.ii now in prison and in training to become an executioner, says to his instructor, Abhorson,

> Painting, sir, I have heard say, is a mystery, and your **whores**, sir, being members of my occupation, using painting, do prove my occupation a mystery. But what mystery there should be in hanging, if I should be hanged, I cannot imagine. (IV.ii.36–40)

The lines suggest the bawd's attempt to usurp such status as the **whores** might have for make-up artistry, besides juxtaposing, as in *Hamlet* and *I Henry VI*, the activities of killing and **whoring**. A few lines earlier, the roles of "unlawful bawd" and "lawful hangman" (IV.ii.15–17) had been similarly paralleled and linked.

Duke Vincentio brings Lucio to account in V.i for his casual exploitative attitudes and behavior:

> If any woman wronged by this lewd fellow –
> As I have heard him swear himself there's one
> Whom he begot with child – let her appear,
> And he shall marry her. The nuptials finished,
> Let him be whipped and hanged.
>
> (V.i.520–4)

Lucio replies,

> I beseech Your Highness, do not marry me to a **whore**. Your Highness said even now I made you a duke; good my lord, do not recompense me in making me a cuckold. (V.i.525–7)

A few lines later, Lucio adds that "Marrying a punk [prostitute], my lord, is pressing to death, whipping, and hanging" (V.i.533–4). The social hypocrisy represented by Lucio is not thoroughly exposed and punished, however; on the contrary, it is precisely what "made" Vincentio "a duke," as, in the process of regaining his political authority, Vincentio has been a "lawful bawd," in facilitating the coupling of Angelo and Mariana, and an attempted "unlawful hangman," in trying to kill Barnardine before his scheduled time to save Claudio.

Although in *I Henry IV* Falstaff declares that Mistress Nell Quickly's tavern "is turned bawdy house" (III.iii.99–100) and he habitually regards her as a prostitute, there is no evidence of truth for either implication, whereas in *II Henry IV*, the tavern has indeed become one, with Quickly knowingly preparing Doll Tearsheet for a sexual assignation with Falstaff. In their pre-coital conversation of the sexual assignation scene, II.iv, Doll counters Falstaff's accusation that men catch diseases from women with her assertion that instead men catch from women "our chains and our jewels" (II.iv.47) – their valuables, as the play repeatedly shows Falstaff to do, particularly in regard to Mistress Quickly. Doll and Falstaff's rendezvous is interrupted a number of times, first by Pistol and then by Hal and Poins. In her furor over the disruptive behavior and "swaggering" (II.iv.70) of Pistol – which involves his intent to "discharge" his "bullets" upon both Doll and Mistress Quickly (II.iv.112), his "murder" of Doll's ruff (II.iv.132), and his attempt to pass himself off as a captain – Doll is provoked to unpack her heart with words: "You a captain? You slave, for what? For tearing a poor **whore's** ruff in a bawdy house?" (II.iv.142–3). This is the *only* instance in Shakespeare's canon of the word's use as spoken by a female character in her own chosen description of herself, with her non-euphemized self-designation contrasting Pistol's social pretensions. Having heard of Falstaff's appointed rendezvous with Doll, Hal and Poins, in disguise as drawers, spy on him with Doll later in this scene, with Poins suggesting to Hal the plan to "beat him before his **whore**" (II.iv.256; cf. *Measure*). Later, Falstaff, commenting about Justice Shallow as a young man, says that he was "lecherous as a monkey, and the **whores** called him mandrake" (III.ii.313–14). This instance at least shows Shakespeare doing what Kramarae and Treichler complain that lexicographers rarely do: crediting women for linguistic coinages (1985: 2) – and women at the lowest level of social regard at that.

In V.iv, although the word **whore** does not appear, the contexts of the play's three instances of it recombine. There Doll and Nell Quickly are in the custody of beadles; they, not Falstaff (whose name is invoked), are being whipped. The beadles' excuse is that Pistol's murderous swaggering has manifested itself in the killing of a man, and the women, simply by being known as involved in **whoredom**, are being used as convenient scapegoats. Pistol, named as the guilty one, is free, with no mention made of a planned arrest of him, and the women are threatened with even more whipping. When reference to her pregnancy is taken as a lie (cf. Joan La Pucelle), Doll launches into creative cursing and vows to give up wearing skirts if the beadle himself is not whipped for his treatment of them.

The Merry Wives of Windsor is the one comedy still classed as such (rather than as "problem play" or "romance") in which the word **whore** appears, and it differs too from the other comedies by its strange relationship to the Henriad: it shares some common characters and seems in some regards to cover the period between the action of Act IV of *II Henry IV* and *Henry V*, as Hal is mentioned as still a prince, and Pistol states his desire to marry Mistress Quickly, which he has done by Act I of *Henry V* – yet in *Merry Wives*, Falstaff seems for the first time to meet Quickly, who here functions as housekeeper to Dr. Caius. Since her duties for him parallel those performed by a tavern-keeper, and her actions as matchmaker for Anne Page and go-between for Mistresses Ford and Page and Falstaff parallel those of her previous role as bawd, I suspect that Shakespeare in this play has set up something like a "parallel universe," putting some of the Henriad's characters into a realm where women are more empowered to show how their lives and social regard would be affected. In presiding as Fairy Queen over the tormenting of Falstaff at the end, Quickly is given "revenge" for Falstaff's ill treatment of her in both parts of *Henry IV*.

The only mention of the word **whore** in *Merry Wives* is made by Quickly, in castigation. When Sir Hugh Evans questions William Page about his Latin – "What is your genitive case plural, William?" – and the boy answers, "*Genitivo – horum, harum, horum*," Quickly disapprovingly comments, "Vengeance of Jenny's case! Fie on her! Never name her, child, if she be a **whore**" (IV.i.53, 56–8). Quickly furthermore chastises Sir Hugh:

You do ill to teach the child such words: he teaches him to hick and to hack, which they'll do fast enough of themselves, and to call "whorum." Fie upon you! (IV.i.60–3)

As is habitually the case with Shakespeare's malaprop speakers, they speak more wisely than they are aware of: not only does Quickly point to puns otherwise missed by most, but she also intuitively understands and opposes how classical education contributes to the inscription and abuse of woman as **whore**.

In *Henry V*, the one mention of the word **whore** is again made by Quickly, here too in correction to a boy (perhaps to be understood as standing for future generations of men), as she describes Falstaff's death. When the boy says that Falstaff "said once the devil would have him about women" (II.iii.34–5), Quickly acknowledges that "'A did in some sort, indeed, handle women; but then he was rheumatic, and talked of the **Whore** of Babylon" (II.iii.36–8). Here too she puns (rheum/Rome) and seems to allows the concept of **whoredom** only as part of a patriarchal structure of propaganda (the Catholic Church as the **Whore** of Babylon).

Antony and Cleopatra contains many near-synonyms for **whore** applied to Cleopatra – who, as Anderson and Zinsser note, was for centuries in Roman writing called *regina meretrix*, the "prostitute queen" (1988: I, 56) – but forms of the word **whore** appear only four times. The first comes in the speech of Alexas after Iras and Charmian, consulting with the Soothsayer, playfully entreat Isis to send Alexas the fortune of an unfaithful wife. He states, "Lo now, if it lay in their hands to make me a cuckold, they would make themselves **whores** but they'd do 't" (I.ii.78–80), which, however, indicates that, contrary to the attitudes of the Romans, he does not believe them to be such now.

The second instance is found in Caesar's informing of Octavia on the whereabouts of her husband, Antony: "Cleopatra / Hath nodded him to her. He hath given his empire / Up to a **whore**" (III.vi.67–9). In IV.xii, Antony finally yields to this Roman characterization of her: understanding that "All is lost" in the sea battle (III.vi.9), he interprets that since "My fleet hath yielded to the foe" (III.vi.11), "This foul Egyptian hath betrayèd me" (III.vi.10), and he continues, "Triple-turned **whore**! 'Tis thou / Hast sold me to this novice, and my heart / Makes only wars on thee" (III.vi.13–15). His failure of belief in her, of course, is what leads him to his suicide.

Cleopatra, foreseeing her ultimate fortune in V.ii, tells Iras that "Thou an Egyptian puppet shall be shown / In Rome as well as I" (V.ii.208–9), providing another form of the "Pygmalion's images" idea, used in *Measure*, of objectified woman as site for male fantasy projection. She adds that "Saucy lictors [equivalent to beadles, cf. *II Henry IV* above and *King Lear* below] / Will catch at us like strumpets" and the "quick comedians / Extemporally will stage us" (V.ii.214–15), with Antony "brought drunken forth, and I shall see / Some squeaking Cleopatra boy my greatness / I' the posture of a **whore**" (V.ii.214–21). Her use of the word does not own it, as does that of Doll; Cleopatra regards male-performed female impersonation, even such as was at that very moment being staged by Shakespeare's boy actor, as a travesty not only of her sexuality (which she will continue to emphasize through her attire), but also of her personal and political range of identity.

The first usage of **whore** in *King Lear* comes as part of the "speech" that the Fool, in his first appearance in the play, offers to "teach" Lear (I.iv.113); its concluding lines are "Leave thy drink and thy **whore**, / And keep in a door, / And thou shalt have more, / Than two tens to a score" (I.iv.122–5). Lear's comment is "This is nothing, Fool" (I.iv.126), revealing that he has neither learned from the speech nor as yet understood the implications of "nothing." In II.iv, the Fool offers Lear another speech:

> Fathers that wear rags,
>   Do make their children blind,
> But fathers that bear bags,
>   Shall see their children kind.
> Fortune, that arrant **whore**,
> Ne'er turns the key to the poor.
>   (II.iv.47–52)

The connection, as in *Macbeth* and *Hamlet*, of the **whorishness** idea to Fortune seems to yield more meaning for Lear. This time he immediately afterward complains, "O, how this mother swells up toward my heart!" (II.iv.55), suggesting not only incipient madness signaled by "*Hysteria passio*" (II.iv.56), but also the initial stage of identification with the female.

The word **whore** appears for the third time directly after Kent has come to lead Lear to the hovel. After they have left and before heading there himself, the Fool says, "This is a brave night to cool a courtesan. I'll speak a prophecy ere I go" (III.ii.79–80). It concludes,

> When usurers tell their gold i' th' field [cf. *Timon* below],
> And bawds and **whores** do churches build,
> Then comes the time, who lives to see 't,
> That going shall be used with feet.
>   (III.ii.91–4)

He then states that "This prophecy shall Merlin make, for I live before his time" (III.ii.95–6). Possibly this strange passage, bordered with references to reversals in female **whorish** behavior, can be connected to historical information on Joan of Arc. In her first appearance before the Dauphin and French court, Joan "reminded them of Merlin's prophecy, revived by the peasant visionary Maxine Robine at the end of the fourteenth century, 'that France would be ruined through a woman and afterward restored by a virgin'" (Pernoud 1955: 77). Dishonored Cordelia, never far from the Fool's mind, is also associated with France, military leadership, and, in Lear's future, salvation.

The fourth instance of a form of **whore** is found just before Lear begins his imaginary arraignment of Goneril and Regan. The Fool states, "He's mad that trusts in the tameness of a wolf, a horse's health, a boy's love, or a **whore's** oath" (III.vi.18–19), with the word used as part of a seemingly casual list, like that of Mercutio, but here itemizing attributes of madness, Lear's current mental state. The final use of the word in the play, however, is made in IV.vi, by Lear, in his "behold the great image of authority" (IV.vi.158) speech, in which he exhibits the clarity of vision that he has found through madness:

> Thou rascal beadle, hold thy bloody hand!
> Why dost thou lash that **whore**? Strip thine own back;
> Thou hotly lusts to use her in that kind
> For which thou whipp'st her [. . .].
> Through tattered clothes small vices do appear;
> Robes and furred gowns hide all.
>
> (IV.vi.160–5)

The **whore**, like Cordelia, has moved from signifying "nothing" to becoming a means to teach Lear to become more humane. Patriarch Lear finally understands, and joins with Doll and Quickly in condemning, male scapegoating of the female.

All nine instances of **whore** in *Timon of Athens* are found in one scene, IV.iii, where Timon, in the depths of misanthropy, prays, "Earth, yield me roots!" (IV.iii.23). As he begins to dig, he finds gold, which is indeed the root of his loathing of humanity and of the world's ills that he then rails upon. He calls the gold "damnèd earth, / Thou common **whore** of mankind, that puts odds / Among the rout of nations" and vows to "make thee / Do thy right nature" (IV.iii.42–5). His opportunity to do so comes almost immediately, with the appearance of Alcibiades with Phyrnia and Timandra.

Seeing Alcibiades prepared for war, Timon says of Phyrnia, "This fell **whore** of thine / Hath in her more destruction than thy sword, / For all her cherubin look" (IV.iii.62–4; cf. *Macbeth*'s "Valor's minion" sword). To Timandra, he states, "Be a **whore** still. They love thee not that use thee; / Give them diseases, leaving with thee their lust" (IV.iii.84–5). Each woman curses him for his words to her, but when the two find that he has gold, their manner changes. Having learned that Alcibiades intends to war on his own home city of Athens, Timon gives him gold, counseling him to commit war atrocities, including on the elderly and infants. Alcibiades says, "I'll take the gold thou givest me, / Not all thy counsel" (IV.iii.132–3), and in response Timon curses him whether he takes the counsel or not.

When the women ask Timon for gold, if he has more, he claims to have "Enough to make a **whore** forswear her trade, / And to make **whores**, a bawd" (IV.iii.136–7). Paying them to increase their clientele (which of course makes him a bawd), Timon entreats them to "Be **whores** still; / And he whose pious breath seeks to convert you, / Be strong in **whore**, allure him, burn him up," and adds, "**Whore** still; / Paint till a horse may mire upon your face" (IV.iii.142–4, 149–50). When the women say, "What then? / Believe 't that we'll do anything for gold" (IV.iii.151–2), Timon urges them to spread venereal disease:

> Plague all,
> That your activity may defeat and quell
> The source of all erection. There's more gold.
> Do you damn others and let this damn you,
> And ditches grave you all!
>
> (IV.iii.164–8)

Unlike Alcibiades, who takes the money and rejects some of the counsel, they say, "More counsel with more money, bounteous Timon," but Timon, who disbelieves their oaths, wants to see results first: "More **whore**, more mischief first; I have given you earnest" (IV.iii.169–70).

In *Troilus and Cressida*, the first of the eleven usages of a form of **whore** comes from Thersites, after his lesson to Achilles and Patroclus on how Agamemnon, Achilles, himself, and Patroclus are all fools. In soliloquy just afterward, he speaks of the war: "All the argument is a **whore** and a cuckold, a good quarrel to draw emulous factions and bleed to death upon" (II.iii.71–3). The second and third instances come in Diomedes's speech to Paris in IV.i. Menelaus, he says,

> like a puling cuckold, would drink up
> The lees and dregs of a flat 'tamèd piece;
> You, like a lecher, out of **whorish** loins,
> Are pleased to breed out your inheritors.
> Both merits poised, each weighs nor less nor more;
> But he as he, the heavier for a **whore**.
>
> (IV.i.63–8)

This speech is made during the night when Troilus has sex with Cressida; by later having sex with Cressida himself, he will put himself into a role parallel to the one that he has characterized for Paris.

Thersites tells Patroclus in V.i, "I profit not by thy talk. Thou art thought to be Achilles' male varlet" (V.i.14–15). When Patroclus asks, "Male varlet, you rogue? What's that?," Thersites answers, "Why, his masculine **whore**" (V.i.16–17). This passage, being the only instance in which Shakespeare directly speaks of actualized male homosexual relations, has called forth much commentary. But it is also of interest as the only place where the insult word **whore** as noun is hurled at a specific male character. In addition to its homosexual implications, it perhaps also signals the masculinization of the concept of **whore** in the play.

Hesitating before giving herself to Diomedes, after she has already yielded him Troilus's love token to her of his sleeve, Cressida in V.ii makes her speech of farewell in apostrophe to Troilus, whom she mistakenly believes to be absent – "One eye yet looks on thee, / But with my heart the other eye doth see" (V.ii.110–11) – concluding that "Minds swayed by eyes are full of turpitude" (V.ii.115). These lines provoke the eavesdropping Thersites to comment that "A proof of strength she could not publish more, / Unless she said, 'My mind is now turned **whore**'" (V.ii.113–14). Ulysses and Troilus, also eavesdropping and spying, then discuss how Troilus's mind is in a sense being unfaithful to him, as he cannot reconcile the sight and spoken words to his "soul" (V.ii.119). Troilus would prefer not to believe that this was Cressida, because if it were, then all mothers and womanhood are tainted through her (cf. Posthumous). When Ulysses asks him, "May worthy Troilus be half attached / With that which here his passion doth express?," Troilus answers, "Ay, Greek; and that shall be divulgèd well / In characters as red as Mars his heart / Inflamed with Venus"

(V.ii.165–9), a male and violent version of the sexual inscription motif discussed above. After Troilus and Ulysses exit, Thersites states that "Patroclus will give me anything for the intelligence of this **whore**. The parrot will not do more for an almond than he for a commodious drab" (V.ii.196–8) – even a "masculine **whore**" will exploit a female "**whore**." He then proclaims what is essentially the play's theme: "Lechery, lechery, still wars and lechery; nothing else holds fashion" (V.ii.196–9).

During the next day's battle, in V.iv, Thersites, speaking of Troilus and Diomedes, says,

> I would fain see them meet, that same young Troyan ass, that loves the **whore** there, might send that Greekish **whoremasterly** villain with the sleeve back to the dissembling luxurious drab, of a sleeveless errand. (V.iv.4–8)

When Troilus and Diomedes do indeed enter and begin fighting a few lines later, Thersites cheers them on with "Hold thy **whore**, Grecian! – Now for thy **whore**, Troyan! Now the sleeve, now the sleeve!" (V.iv.24–5). In V.vii, Thersites similarly enjoys and encourages the fighting of "The cuckold and the cuckold maker" (V.vii.9), Menelaus and Paris. But when he himself is asked to fight, by Margareton, who identifies himself as "A bastard son of Priam," Thersites identifies himself as "a bastard too," continuing that "I love bastards. I am bastard begot, bastard instructed, bastard in mind, bastard in valor, in everything illegitimate" (V.vii.15–18). Bastards, he believes, should be in alliance, not at odds: "Take heed, the quarrel's most ominous to us. If the son of a **whore** fight for a **whore**, he tempts judgment" (V.vii.20–1). Although Margareton then curses Thersites, he departs without physically assaulting him. The play, which has repeatedly demonstrated that it is in male characters' military interests to employ the label of **whore** for women like Helen and Cressida, and thereby scapegoat such women for their own frailties, yet concludes by identifying Pandarus, the patriarchal trafficker of female sexuality, rather than Cressida, as the primary dispenser of venereal disease (cf. *Measure* and *II Henry IV*).

As indicated above, the highest number of uses of the word **whore** in a single work by Shakespeare, fourteen, is found in *Othello*. Empson comments that "The fifty-two uses of *honest* and *honesty* in *Othello* are a very queer business; there is no other play in which Shakespeare worries a word like that" (Empson 1971: 98); we may add, as he does not, that Shakespeare similarly "worries" the word **whore** in the play, and in deliberate juxtaposition with "honest." Although for Troilus belief that Cressida is a **whore** inflames his desire for war, in the lines just prior to the first use of the word in *Othello*, such a belief has an opposite effect. Already tainted but not yet thoroughly convinced by Iago's suggestions about Desdemona, Othello states, "I had been happy if the general camp, / Pioners and all, had tasted her sweet body, / So I had nothing known" (III.iii.361–3). But as he is beginning to believe otherwise in the case of Cassio, then, he reasons, he must bid farewell to "Pride, pomp, and circumstance of glorious war" (III.iii.370), since "Othello's occupation's gone" (III.iii.373). The negation of his occupation as sole lover of Desdemona by marriage somehow engulfs his occupation as military leader; apparently he cannot fathom how to command those who, he thinks, have shared his sexual place. What may be involved, if we recall Timon's saying that the **whore** commands more than the sword and Thersites's demonstration of that concept in self-preservation, is that Othello is jealous of Desdemona's presumed ability to command desire from men and believes it to be a more potent force than military ideals. Othello's next words to Iago (who has not yet planted the handkerchief but has it in his possession) are "Villain, be sure thou prove my love a **whore**! / Be sure of it. Give me the ocular proof" (III.iii.375–6). But a few lines later, still asking for such evidence, he displays a doubleness of attitude similar to that which Troilus exhibits *after* viewing the sleeve as *his* "ocular proof": "I think my wife be honest and think she is not; / I think that thou [Iago] art just and think thou art not" (III.iii.400–1). But, like Posthumous, Othello quickly inclines to belief in the male against the female, but then expresses an idea *opposite* to that of Aaron, who had put blackness in a superior position over **whorishness**: Desdemona's "name, that was as fresh / As Dian's visage, is now begrimed and black / As mine own face / . . . / I'll not endure it" (III.iii.385–7, 390).[2] He does not, apparently, hold Aaron's understanding of black as beautiful, and he begins his process of inscription from himself as "begrimed" black onto chaste Desdemona.

The next appearance of the word **whore** in *Othello* comes directly after Cassio's interlude with Bianca, in which she returns the handkerchief to him as "some minx's token" (IV.i.154), so she will not copy its needlework for him, with the incident being marketed by Iago to Othello as the requested "ocular proof." Iago comments, "And to see how he prizes the foolish woman your wife! She gave [the handkerchief to Cassio], and he hath given it his **whore**" (IV.i.175–6). This equation of Desdemona with Bianca is enough to convince Othello to kill his wife that night.

Unlike Posthumous in *Cymbeline*, who orders his servant Pisanio to kill Imogen simply on the basis of Iachimo's tale, Othello does try for more proof before his wife's murder by questioning Emilia. But when her answers do not fit his disposition to believe in the **whorishness** of his wife, Othello decides that Emilia is aligned with Desdemona in dishonesty as he is aligned with Iago on the side of honesty: Emilia is "a simple bawd / That cannot say as much," and Desdemona is "a subtle **whore** / A closet lock and key of villainous secrets" (IV.ii.21–3). When Emilia reenters with Desdemona, Othello requests of Emilia "Some of your function, mistress. Leave procreants alone and shut the door; / Cough or cry 'hem' if anybody come. / Your mystery, your mystery [cf. *Measure*]!" (IV.ii.27–30). When Desdemona, after some verbal abuse from Othello, asks, "Alas, what ignorant sin have I committed?," Othello exclaims, "Was this fair paper, this most goodly book, / Made to write '**whore**' upon?" (IV.ii.72–4), which I use in my title as the most concise instance of the several lines in Shakespeare's canon, as discussed above, that demonstrate the concept of **whore** as male-initiated inscription onto the female as scapegoat.

A few lines later Othello demands, "Are you not a strumpet?" (IV.ii.84). Desdemona answers, "No, as I am a Christian. / If to preserve this vessel for my lord / From any other foul unlawful touch / Be not to be a strumpet, I am none," but Othello persists, "What, not a **whore**?" (IV.ii.85–9). Although Desdemona had used the word "strumpet" in her first denial, she avoids saying "**whore**" in her second: "No, as I shall be saved" (IV.ii.90). Othello responds ironically (but with even more irony than he intends, as his replacement soulmate is Iago, as that of Posthumous is Iachimo): "I cry you mercy, then. / I took you for that cunning **whore** of Venice / That married with Othello" (IV.ii.92–4). He then calls for Emilia and says, "We have done our course; there's money for your pains. / I pray you, turn the key and keep our counsel" (IV.ii.97–8). As Emilia's line "Alas, what does the gentleman conceive?" (IV.ii.99) makes plain, neither woman has understood herself to be in the service of **whoredom**: the brothel has been the construction of Othello's mind, with him, not them, at home there. He is the only one to participate knowledgeably in a degraded sexual act, and he insists on paying for his ejaculatory defilement of Desdemona, which absolves him of guilt for his verbal rape and allows him a sense of superiority through economic mastery.

After Othello has exited and Iago entered later in this scene, Emilia tells Iago that Othello "hath so **bewhored**" Desdemona, "Thrown such despite and heavy terms upon her, / That true hearts cannot bear it" (IV.ii.121–3). When Desdemona asks him, "Am I that name, Iago?," and Iago, seeming to wish to force her articulation of the word, says, "What name, fair lady?," Desdemona still cannot speak it: "Such as she said my lord did say I was" (IV.ii.124–6). Emilia, however, clarifies: "He called her **whore**. A beggar in his drink / Could not have laid such terms upon his callet" (IV.ii.127–8). Iago seems somewhat disconcerted at Desdemona's tears – "Do not weep, do not weep. Alas the day!" – but Emilia justifies them: "Hath she forsook so many noble matches, / Her father and her country and her friends, / To be called **whore**? Would it not make one weep?" (IV.ii.131–4). Desdemona immediately afterward comments, "It is my wretched fortune" (IV.ii.135), unwittingly connecting herself to the traditional representation of Fortune as a **whore**, as employed in *Macbeth*, *Hamlet*, and *Lear*.

In further unperceived irony, Emilia correctly intuits that "some eternal villain, / Some busy and insinuating rogue, / Some cogging, cozening slave, to get some office, / . . . devised this slander" (IV.ii.137–40), without realizing his identity as her own husband. Again expressing incredulity at Othello's behavior, Emilia asks, "Why should he call her **whore**? Who keeps her company? / What place? What time? What form? What likelihood?" (IV.ii.144–5), emphasizing the ignored illogic of such an accusation. Returning to her conjecture of a male provocateur of the imputation, in the line "The Moor's abused by some most villainous knave" (IV.ii.146, with "knave" poised against **whore** as in *The Tempest*, as discussed above), Emilia continues by expressing her wish that "heaven" would "unfold" "such companions," "And put in every honest hand a whip / To lash the rascals naked through the world / Even from the east to th' west!" (IV.ii.148–50), which parallels Lear's and Doll's lines entreating that those who whip "**whores**" should themselves be whipped.

Soon afterward, Desdemona, on her knees to Iago, beseeching his help and swearing her innocence, finally says the word **whore** while simultaneously unsaying it:

> I cannot say "**whore**."
> It does abhor me now I speak the word;
> To do the act that might the addition earn
> Not the world's mass of vanity could make me
> (IV.ii.168–71),

with the further irony of her repeating the word as embedded homonym in "abhor." As the prefix "ab" means "to turn away from," however, even in that ironic articulation, she makes denial.

Shakespeare's only instance of the word **whore** in gerund form is found in V.i of *Othello*, employed when Iago attempts to scapegoat Bianca for Cassio's wounding: "This is the fruits of **whoring**" (V.i.118). As the audience well knows, though, the hurt is actually the fruits of Iago's own efforts, in the process of constructing others as **whores** (as in the verb usage in *Hamlet*). Thus the label of **whore** more properly belongs to Iago himself, as it does also to Othello, as discussed above, as being the denizen of a brothel. Yet Iago's mode of scapegoating the female is also employed by Emilia, who had earlier argued against the double sexual standard (IV.iii.96–106). When she encounters Bianca, a woman who actually does grant herself exactly the same sexual freedom that men allow themselves, shortly after this "fruits of **whoring**" line is spoken, Emilia accepts that male-defined double standard and says, "O, fie upon thee, strumpet!" (V.i.123). To Bianca's answer, "I am no strumpet, but of life as honest / As you that thus abuse me," Emilia responds, "As I? Faugh! Fie upon thee!" (V.i.124–6), refusing to see any connection between Bianca's and her own roles and status.[3]

Yet the socially approved role of wife is not in fact protected. Othello and Iago each use the word **whore** one more time in the play, each in reference to his own wife. Othello explains his murder of Desdemona to Emilia by saying, "She turned to folly, and she was a **whore**" (V.ii.136). When, after Iago has even once tried to stab her, Emilia confesses her unwitting involvement in Iago's plot – "O thou dull Moor! That handkerchief thou speak'st of / I found by fortune [cf. discussions of Fortune above] and did give my husband" (V.ii.232–3) – at this revelation Iago calls Emilia "Villainous **whore**" (V.ii.236). After she fills in a bit more of the story and denies his accusation that she lies, Iago stabs and thereby kills her. The only female character left alive at the end of the play is the non-married "**whore**," Bianca.

Othello and *Timon of Athens* are the only two plays by Shakespeare in which each given female character is specifically called a **whore**. In *Timon*, the accusation proves true for both of the women, but in that play, all who fawn on Timon for his money come to be regarded by him as **whores**, and that group also includes not only the militarist Alcibiades, but also a poet and a painter – so, by extension, all artists, including Shakespeare himself, as his function as a provider of pleasure and the theaters' proximity to the brothels must have daily reminded him. Besides, in *Timon*, gold rather than woman is called the "root" of **whoredom**, so all who must live in the material conditions of a market economy are in some sense **whores**. In *Othello*, the culturally prescribed sexual roles for women of virgin, wife, and **whore**, represented respectively by Desdemona, Emilia, and Bianca, are revealed to be a social artifice that easily collapses into belief in **whorishness** as all women's true and essential nature. That belief, however, is continually demonstrated by the accusations' contexts to be a perverse projection from diseased male imaginations, with nothing to do with either the realities of the women's attitudes about themselves or the facts of their behavior. Such is the case even of Bianca, who never herself manifests any behavior indicative of prostitution (such as receiving money or gifts for sex or having more than one partner). Simply by boldly asserting for herself the freedom to have sex outside of the confines of marriage, as Cassio as a matter of course grants himself, Bianca has been made the scapegoat for the attitudes of male characters in regard to **whorishness** in the play, as well as in the remarks of commentators on the play, both male and female, over the centuries. I believe that as long as we think that Desdemona is not a **whore** because the real **whore** is Bianca, we continue to give cultural sanction to the abusive use of the term for women of any status who are not professional sex workers like Doll Tearsheet, who "owns" the term by applying it to herself.

Although feminists have long understood that, as Stanley notes (1977: *passim*), the prostitute has been constructed as the paradigm for woman, with marriage simply the most "respectable" and seemingly protected of prostitution's forms under patriarchy's limited (and usually artificially offered) range of female sexual choices, we are still left with unresolved problems in regard to the actual professional prostitute: whether she ever actually chooses the role or is always the victim of patriarchal exploitation, how her continued existence reflects upon other women's freedom of sexual lifestyle choice, and how to incorporate her into a positive feminist-theorized model of heterosexual relations. Thus Bianca, Doll, and Shakespeare's other so-called "**whores**" lead me back to my introduction's question. Can we, at this point in feminist theory and criticism, come to any consensus about whether the word **whore** should be banned, or "owned" and thereby desensitized?

Shakespeare, I believe, in the entirety of his treatment of the term, can give us some help in dealing with this issue, which continues to be a daily-experienced cross-cultural social problem, in consequences of which some women even now are murdered and many others are otherwise still abused. As I hope to have established through my presentation of the range of Shakespeare's usage of the word in at least minimally instructive analyses, his contexts and associations for **whore** demonstrate him to be much more on the side of the solution than, as a cursory reading of his citations in the *OED* might suggest, on the side of maintaining the problem.

The high concentration of appearances of the word **whore** in the tragedies demonstrates that Shakespeare considered men's failure to accommodate themselves to the idea of female sexual choice and integrity to be particularly instrumental in war, violence, and, ultimately, societal suicide. As Phyllis Rackin notes, for Shakespeare and his contemporary dramatists, the theater was a forum "where changing gender definitions could be displayed, deplored, or enforced and where anxieties about them could be expressed by playwrights and incited or repressed among their audiences" (1987: 29), and his plays continue in that function, as anyone who teaches them knows. What Rackin continues on to say, about early modern dramatists' treatments of the marriages of "boy heroines," can, I believe, be extended into the realm of non-marital heterosexual relations in Shakespeare's canon: unions that incorporate the concept of androgyny show not only "their authors' and audiences' changing visions of what is desirable and undesirable in relationships between persons of different sex," but also "their changing gender definitions and changing visions of the relations between masculine and feminine gender attributes within an individual human psyche and within the culture that shapes it" (Rackin 1987: 30). The attribute of **whorishness**, as treated by Shakespeare, is androgynous; its societal construction as a primarily female condition is presented as mainly the product of patriarchal denial of women's status as co-equal members of humanity, with equal rights to enjoy our own sexuality as we deem appropriate.

I deliberately began this essay in the "personal as political" mode, as I intend to close it, because we are obviously in a time of transition in feminist criticism, and I wanted specifically to hark back to the anecdotal days of the second wave, when women were more penetratingly questioning the full range of our oppression and testing theory against contemporary female lived experience. In our present fixation on historicizing and situating ourselves theoretically, this contemporary and personal dimension seems to have been lost, and with it, the sense of feminist criticism as *Making a Difference*, as in the title of a collection of essays co-edited by Greene and Kahn (1985). Now, in an age that many call "post-feminist" (and mean in the sense of "been there, done that"), it seems unlikely that anyone would dare to use a title like that. Also at present, as noted by Whelehan (1995: 146–76, *passim*), though French feminism does deal with the issue of female sexual desire, Anglo-American academic feminist criticism is stalled on the theorizing of heterosexual women's expressions of sexuality. Although this charge is less comprehensively true in the case of Shakespeare criticism, as seen, for example, in the book recently co-authored by Callaghan, Helms, and Singh (1994), generally Anglo-American feminist criticism seems to be more focused on gender roles than on female heterosexuality, seeming to be content to keep the issue of sexuality as a Queer Theory matter, even though the majority of feminists are exclusively or primarily heterosexual (Whelehan 1995: 153–70, *passim*).

On behalf not only of myself, in personally and repeatedly experiencing the **whore** insult, but also of Anita and my other female students, and of all women of various races, cultures, and economic classes, then, I invite my readers, female and male, to join me in considering the question of whether, and if so, how, women should own the term **whore**. Varying treatments of the term by Shakespeare's five female characters who speak it provide us with a range of possible positions from which we can extrapolate others. Should we like Desdemona consider the word to be so foreign to our lived experience that we can barely speak it? Should we like Emilia not be intimidated from saying the word, but use it only when denying its relevance in some, but not all, women's cases? Should we own it outright, as does Doll, while we vent our anger at male abuse and pretensions of superiority? Should we like Nell Quickly use it naively, in ways that will provoke men's laughter against us, even when we are nevertheless making relevant points about its use? Should we like Cleopatra and Bianca deny a double standard by granting ourselves sexual freedom equal to that which men grant to themselves, regarding the concept of **whore** not as an accurate description of such freedom, but only as a stance of male-constructed female representation that travesties the majesty of our sexual power?

My position is that we women must make our individualized selections of models and be free to move from one to another as experience guides us, but my own choice as the best Shakespearean model upon which to theorize female heterosexuality is that of Cleopatra/Bianca. Though it could mean so much more as well, at the very least it endorses the liberty of a meritorious woman like Anita to dress in red not for others "to write '**whore**' upon" but as her own badge of triumphantly self-assured *jouissance*, and it has inspired and continues to embolden me to register the voices of Shakespeare's "**whores**."

NOTES

1 In order to keep length manageable, I do not here analyze Shakespeare's uses of **whore-master** (5 instances), **whoremasterly** (1), **whoreson** (40), and **whoresons** (1), which, although dependent on the notion of female as **whore**, are applied exclusively to male characters. Spevack (1970), my initial guide to locating the citations, lists one further instance of **whore** as noun, "to be his **whore** is witless," II.iv.5 of *The Two Noble Kinsmen*, a play not included in the Shakespeare folios, but that many modern scholars believe to have been co-authored by Shakespeare and John Fletcher. As I cannot be certain that Shakespeare rather than Fletcher wrote that line, I do not consider it here, although its implications do not contradict my overall argument. Interestingly, no form of the word **whore** appears in *The Comedy of Errors*, which includes a courtesan among its characters, nor is it found in *Pericles*, which features a brothel as one of its settings and three bawds among its characters. The near-absence of use of the word **whore** in Shakespeare's comedies, in contrast with the tragedies, is consistent with their more playful attitudes toward language and their increased acceptance of female

sexuality as part of the reproductive processes of nature. Bold type everywhere in this essay for forms of the word **whore** is my emphasis.

2 Although Bevington follows the folios in beginning this passage with "My [Othello's] name," many other editors prefer the quartos' "Her [Desdemona's] name," as do I. See the discussion by editors on the issue provided by Furness in the New Variorum edition of *Othello* (205, gloss number 445) and the account in its Appendix of the play's textual history (336–43). The choice of "My name," though, does not invalidate the sense of my argument here, as the name being blackened through masculine inscription is emblematic of feminine chastity through the metaphoric comparison to Diana.

3 Emilia's bold speeches to Desdemona about female sexual equality (among other positive attributes of her character) inspired Carol Thomas Neely, in a justly famous article on the play (1980), to break out from the pack of commentators on *Othello* whom she described as Othello, Iago, or Desdemona critics, in order to name herself an "Emilia critic." Yet, for all of her brave talk, Emilia is complicitous

in the male vilification of female sexuality in *Othello* in a way that Bianca is not, which led me to name myself a "Bianca critic" (Stanton 1984), as I still consider myself to be.

REFERENCES AND FURTHER READING

Anderson, B. S. and Zinsser, J. P. 1988: *A History of Their Own: Women in Europe from Prehistory to the Present*. Vol. 1. London and New York: Penguin.

Baron, D. 1982: *Grammar and Good Taste: Reforming the American Language*. New Haven: Yale University Press.

Burchfield, R. W. (ed.) 1986: *A Supplement to the Oxford English Dictionary*. 4 vols. Oxford: Clarendon Press.

Burford, E. J. 1973: *The Orrible Synne: A Look at London Lechery from Roman to Cromwellian Times*. London: Calder and Boyars.

Callaghan, D., Helms, L., and Singh, J. 1994: *The Weyward Sisters: Shakespeare and Feminist Politics*. Oxford, UK, and Cambridge, MA: Blackwell.

Dusinberre, J. 1996: *Shakespeare and the Nature of Women*. Second edition. London: Macmillan.

Empson, W. 1971: "Honest in *Othello*." In John Wain (ed.), *Othello: A Selection of Critical Essays*. London: Macmillan, 98–122. (Originally published 1951 in *The Structure of Complex Words*. London: Chatto and Windus.)

Greene, G. and Kahn, C. (eds.) 1985: *Making a Difference: Feminist Literary Criticism*. London: Methuen.

Kramarae, C. and Treichler, P. A., with assistance from Russo, A. 1985: *A Feminist Dictionary*. London: Pandora.

McLuskie, K. 1985: "The Patriarchal Bard: Feminist Criticism and Shakespeare: *King Lear* and *Measure for Measure*." In Jonathan Dollimore and Alan Sinfield (eds.), *Political Shakespeare: New Essays in Cultural Materialism*. Manchester: Manchester University Press, 88–108.

Murray, J. A. H., Bradley, H., Craigie, W. A., and Onions, C. T. 1933: *The Oxford English Dictionary*. 12 vols. Oxford: Clarendon Press. Reprinted 1977.

Neely, C. T. 1980: "Women and Men in *Othello*: 'What should such a fool / Do with so good a woman?'" In Carol Ruth Swift Lenz, Gayle Greene, and Carol Thomas Neely (eds.), *The Woman's Part: Feminist Criticism of Shake-*speare. Urbana: University of Illinois Press, 211–39.

Pernoud, R. 1955: *The Retrial of Joan of Arc*. Trans. J. M. Cohen. New York: Harcourt.

Rackin, P. 1987: "Androgyny, Mimesis, and the Marriage of the Boy Heroine on the English Renaissance Stage." *PMLA*, 102, 29–41.

Rubinstein, F. 1989: *A Dictionary of Shakespeare's Sexual Puns and their Significance*. Second edition. New York: St. Martin's Press.

Schulz, M. 1975: "The Semantic Derogation of Women." In Barrie Thorne and Nancy Henley (eds.), *Language and Sex Difference and Dominance*. Rowley, MA: Newberry House, 64–73.

Shakespeare, W. 1992: *The Complete Works of William Shakespeare*. Ed. David Bevington. Fourth edition. New York: Harper Collins.

—— 1963: *Othello*. New Variorum Edition. Ed. Horace Howard Furness (1886). New York: Dover.

Spevack, M. (comp.) 1970: *A Complete and Systematic Concordance to the Works of Shakespeare*. 9 vols. Hildesheim: Georg Olms.

Stanley, J. P. 1977: "Paradigmatic Woman: The Prostitute." In David L. Shores and Carol P. Hines (eds.), *Papers in Language Variation*. Birmingham, AL: University of Alabama Press, 303–21.

Stanton, K. 1984: "Iago: The Whore of Venice." Paper presented at the *Ohio Shakespeare Conference: Shakespeare and Gender*. University of Cincinnati, Cincinnati, Ohio, March 1–3, 1984. (Paper was revised, expanded, and presented under the title "Male Gender-Crossing in *Othello*," in the "Shakespearean Tragedy and Gender" seminar of the *Shakespeare Association of America Convention*. Seattle, Washington, April 9–11, 1987.)

—— 1994: "*Hamlet's* Whores." In Mark Thornton Burnett and John Manning (eds.), *New Essays on Hamlet*. New York: AMS, 167–88.

—— 1995: "Paying Tribute: Shakespeare's *Cymbeline*, the 'Woman's Part,' and Italy." In Michele Marrapodi (ed.), *Il Mondo Italiano del*

Teatro Inglese del Rinascimento: Relazioni Cultur-
ali e Intertestualità [*The Italian World of English*
Renaissance Drama: Cultural Exchange and Inter-
textuality]. Palermo: S. F. Flaccovio, 65–79.

Whelehan, I. 1995: *Modern Feminist Thought: From*
the Second Wave to "Post-Feminism." Edinburgh:
Edinburgh University Press.

Williams, G. 1994: *A Dictionary of Sexual Lan-*
guage and Imagery in Shakespearean and Stuart
Literature. Atlantic Highlands, NJ: Athlone.

6

"A word, sweet Lucrece": Confession, Feminism, and *The Rape of Lucrece*

Margo Hendricks

The story of Lucrece would have been well-known to Elizabethan audiences. Its passive/active linking of her rape/suicide was left largely unquestioned. The presumed choice presented in the poem between death or shame was a foregone conclusion. The theological position counseled choosing shame, of which one could be shriven, over suicide, a mortal sin. Preferring death implied that rape was necessarily, regardless of the purity of mind, a pollution of the body's chastity, an effect which could not be undone.

Carter (1995: 212)

Produced in a society that considered itself deeply Christian, William Shakespeare's *The Rape of Lucrece* poses an intriguing dilemma for those moralists who would evoke the Roman wife Lucretia as an emblem of feminine chastity.[1] As Stephen J. Carter's observation, noted above, illustrates, the audience "could imagine, and perhaps praise, a woman's choosing a public transformation of unchastity through death, over the private shame of bodily pollution, however technically virtuous of mind she remains" (Carter 1995: 212). The effect, according to Carter, is a deployment "of a secular discourse within the larger theological context. The former produces a reading of female space as that which needed to be kept enclosed, unseen, pure – within a larger, allegedly protective male space." The "theological context," Carter asserts, produces a reading that condemns Lucrece's actions as, in St. Augustine's view, a failure to see

> that while the sanctity of the soul remains even when the body is violated, the sanctity of the body is not lost; and that in like manner, the sanctity of the body is lost when the sanctity of the soul is violated, though the body itself remains intact. (Carter 1995: 212)

Shakespeare's "anticipation" and conflation of these two positions, Carter observes, seem to imply that "Lucrece's choice of suicide is not presented as the automatic secular choice it was assumed to be" (Carter 1995: 212). In the end, Carter contends, the narrative's Elizabethan audience becomes "aware of [the text's] emphatically split reading: that she courageously chose and acted on a theologically incorrect reading, for which she could not be held responsible given the Roman setting of the story" (Carter 1995: 212–13).

I begin with Carter's somewhat problematic commentary on the spatial and theological significance of Lucrece's suicide because, in many ways, her suicide has been a thorny issue for feminist criticism. Over the course of the narrative, Lucrece is transformed from a silent object of male gaze to an iconographic model of feminine subjectivity, the latter idealized in her death and the use of her lifeless body as a symbol of Roman unity against the Tarquins. For feminist critics seeking to find some definitive source of political power and agency in Lucrece, the narrative seems not to aid such an endeavor. The problem that faces any feminist reader of *Lucrece* is that any analysis must find a way to come to terms with the contradictory representations Shakespeare's retelling of the myth of Lucretia engenders. Thus feminist readings appear caught in a theoretical position of having to "stress the extent to which the idea of woman which it [*Lucrece*] represents is one overdetermined by patriarchal ideology, and [have] typically interpreted. Lucrece herself as a sign is used to mediate and define men's relationships to men" (Berry 1991: 33). To illustrate this point, I want to summarize a few of the recent feminist positions on *Lucrece*.[2]

In a cogent and insightful essay, Katharine Eiasman Maus explores the relationship between the "use and abuse of tropes" by both Lucrece and Tarquin as part of a "literalizing" tendency in the narrative. "Shakespeare's poem," Maus argues, "is essentially an account, punctuated by terrible violence, of two people making important decisions" (Maus 1986: 67). For both characters "their decision-making process becomes not the activity of a moment but a continuously repeated process." As a result, the "difficult process of decision-making is, for both characters, inseparable from their employment of a few crucial metaphors" (Maus 1986: 67). Ultimately, Maus suggests, the use of tropes, by both Lucrece and Tarquin, becomes intricately linked to the moral choices the characters make and occasional critical frustration with Shakespeare's excessive and elaborate rhetorical technique.

Like Maus, Joyce Green MacDonald is interested in Shakespeare's "poetic technique" and its relation to Lucrece's "voice," but with aims quite different from Maus. In her persuasive reading of *Lucrece*, MacDonald explores the "varieties of female speech and silence as they help shape Shakespeare's familial Roman ethos" in her analysis of *Lucrece*. For MacDonald, "Lucrece finds her desperate voice only to encounter its limitations in a poem deeply informed by Renaissance assumptions about silence and segregation as indices of chastity; contradictions and oppositions between modes of speech and silence mark the boundaries of her crisis" (MacDonald 1994: 78–9). Lucrece thus becomes doubly marked: a classically derived moral exemplum and an articulation of early modern gender and patriarchal ideologies. Despite its Roman setting, MacDonald finds the narrative depiction of Lucrece's "voice" to be thoroughly informed by the patriarchal ideologies that govern Shakespeare's England.

Similarly, Philippa Berry's insightful essay, "Woman, Language, and History in *The Rape of Lucrece*," contends "that Lucrece is represented in the poem as an important but unorthodox example of Renaissance *virtù*" and "this quality is given most powerful expression in the poem, not through her actions, but through her private use of language – a use which implicitly stresses its performative, even magical powers" (Berry 1991: 34). Like MacDonald, Berry sees Lucrece's "secret and powerful eloquence" as an "indication of republican political ideals in the poem" (Berry 1991: 34), yet Berry differs as to the role this eloquence plays in terms of the overarching signifier of the narrative, the politics of family. It is for Berry, in the end, the dynamic of political "history" and not "social" (and thus, to some degree, the personal) history that allows Lucrece to find a voice (Berry 1991: 34). Berry, like MacDonald and Maus, seeks the key to a feminist reading of Lucrece in terms of rhetoric and the politics of speech. The final essays I wish to highlight pursue a slightly divergent path in their analyses of Shakespeare's poem; a path which redirects attention to questions of space and the female body in Shakespeare's narrative.

In a chapter titled "The Sexual Politics of Subjectivity in *Lucrece*," Coppélia Kahn seeks to balance the seemingly competing, and at times oppositional, issues of language and body. In her discussion, Kahn considers the relationship between the "problematic of rape" of Lucrece through an examination of the "language of power and the power of language with regard to the poem's two main characters, Lucrece and Tarquin" (Kahn 1997: 27). Kahn contends that, in "giving Lucrece a tongue, Shakespeare perforce works *against* the patriarchal codes that, at the same time, he puts into her mouth" (Kahn 1997: 28). What "fascinates and moves" Kahn is that Shakespeare "tries to fashion Lucrece as a subject not totally tuned to the key of Roman chastity and patriarchal marriage and to locate a position in which he as poet might stand apart from those values as well" (Kahn 1997: 82). Yet, according to Kahn, Shakespeare "fails" and "his attempt reveals how narrowly the rhetorical traditions within which he works are bounded by an ideology of gender in which women speak with the voices of men" (Kahn 1997: 82).

Georgianna Ziegler, on the other hand, looks to the "domestic architecture" of Elizabethan and Jacobean England as a way of adumbrating meaning in *Lucrece*. Briefly tracing the emerging sense of "private space," Ziegler outlines the role this concept plays in the cultural discourse on femininity. Women, she argues, become localized in the household and definitions of a woman's "self" were articulated in the rhetoric of inside/outside or, as it has come to be labeled in current critical theories about early modern households, private/public. In an analysis that looks at three Shakespearean female characters, Lucrece, Desdemona, and Imogen, Ziegler writes, "in all of these works the woman's chamber has represented her 'self': both her physical body and mental/spiritual nature" (Ziegler 1991: 87). As Ziegler notes, Lucrece is the only one who does not leave her home, "and, thus, coming out of the genre of classical history, she fits most precisely the ideal of the 'normative Woman', and indeed by Shakespeare's time she had become a type of such women" (Ziegler 1991: 80).

Reading Lucrece's body metaphorically as a "chamber" (which, Ziegler rightly notes, is how Lucrece refers to herself during her attempts to persuade Tarquin not to pursue the rape), Ziegler observes, for Tarquin, "Lucrece is not so much a private chamber to be entered as a public edifice to be stormed" (Ziegler 1991: 80). "Only by making another violent entry into this house or closet [Lucrece's body] and letting the soul go free can Lucrece conceive of redeeming her own honour and that of her husband" (1991: 81), Ziegler argues. In the end, Ziegler concludes, "I think that Shakespeare seems almost to be asking if the patriarchy has not set up this classic, enclosed female icon *because* it is afraid of what it sees as the uncontrollable, unstable functions of the female body and nature. And once having formulated its own ideal, it never quite trusts even the women who seem to fit it" (Ziegler 1991: 87).

Each of these essays plays an important role in shaping the argument that follows. In reading these analyses, I found myself saying, yes *but*. Yes, the poem's narrator is in effect the mediator of Lucrece's voice and thus imposes a "silence" upon her, *but*; yes, her body is mutilated figuratively and literally, first by Shakespeare's use of the blazon (as Nancy Vickers so brilliantly illustrated), and then by Lucrece herself, *but*; and yes, Renaissance patriarchal ideology governs both how Lucrece "sees" herself and how the reader reads/sees that seeing, *but*. I am not entirely certain whether my *but* is a factor of the peculiarities of Shakespeare's narrative poem (which I increasingly suspect is the case), or my belief that female agency manifests itself in a multitude of ways, some not necessarily in accord with a set of feminist prescriptions. Nonetheless, I shall set out to add another feminist voice to the discussion of Shakespeare's *Rape of Lucrece*.

In this essay I will consider the politics of the narrative in light of two concerns: the first is the tradition of reading Lucrece's suicide as a reflection of Christian ideologies on sexuality and on suicide, specifically as articulated in the writing of St. Augustine. Through a reading of Lucrece's actions and speech leading up to and resulting in her death, I will argue that her behavior is consistent with the two competing early modern Christian discourses (Catholic and Protestant) about the nature of "private confession." Thus, unlike other critics of the narrative poem, I read her speeches as reflections of the discourse of the confessional. The second concern that guides this reading is the place of race in Shakespeare's narrative poem. Race, I shall argue, is intertwined with Shakespeare's use of the confessional mode to represent female subjectivity. The conception of race I shall be working with in this discussion is not the current semantics of race, however. Instead, I shall be looking at an earlier notion whereby race signified primarily lineage but, increasingly, was being adapted to new and more geopolitical concerns.

It is my contention that Shakespeare's *The Rape of Lucrece* is an attempt to mediate the tensions (and contradictions) generated by competing discourses of race: race as defined by genealogy or lineage, and race as defined by ethnicity. In this imprecision, as an expression of fundamental distinctions, race's meaning varied depending upon whether a writer wanted to specify difference born of a class-based concept of genealogy, a psychological (and often essentialized) nature, or group typology. In effect,

Shakespeare's narrative reproduction and (re)presentation of the Lucretia myth gives life to a more complex meaning of race, one which defines itself not only in terms of lineage but also in terms of ethnicity.

In my reading of *Lucrece* I make use of Louis Althusser's notion of "interpellation" and Michel Foucault's observations on confession in *The History of Sexuality* to explore what are two of the most effective discourses for constituting subjectivity, and by extension agency – racial identity and religion. Lucrece's confessional moments incorporate, as part of its truth-telling, an early modern racial ideology in the articulation of her subjectivity. My aim in linking the act of confession and the concept of race as features of the narrative representation of Lucrece's subjectivity is to highlight the relationship between speech and a gendered notion of "self" as part of the process of identity-making. And, as I hope to illustrate, confession, gender, and race can work to produce female agency even as they are deployed to prevent it.

The Conduct of Confession

The "confession," Michel Foucault reminds us, is "one of the main rituals [Western societies] rely on for the production of truth. [In effect, confession] came to signify someone's acknowledgment of his own actions and thoughts" (Foucault 1980: 58). What this acknowledgment entails, however, differs according to the political, cultural, gender, and ethnic dictates of subjectivity. Yet, as Foucault argues, confession

> frees, but power reduces one to silence; truth does not belong to the order of power, but shares an original affinity with freedom: traditional themes in philosophy, which a "political history of truth" would have to overturn by showing that truth is not by nature free – nor error servile – but that its production is thoroughly imbued with relations of power. The confession is an example of this. (Foucault 1980: 60)

On the surface, Shakespeare's *Lucrece* might seem an unlikely place to go looking for Shakespeare's possible engagement with the theological controversies surrounding the role of confession within late sixteenth-century Christian practice. Yet, attending carefully to the language Shakespeare uses, we find the exchanges between Lucrece and Tarquin to be replete with the Judeo-Christian language of sin, especially in the extended use of words such as "guilt," "sin," "shame," and "conscience." Moreover, Shakespeare's deployment of less generic terms, such as "convertite," "remission," and "absolution," further localizes the play's depiction of Lucrece's and Tarquin's introspection, respectively, within a clearly delineated Catholic paradigm. As Tarquin declares, "Thoughts are but dreams till their effects be tried; / The blackest sin is cleared with absolution" (354–5).[3] Though these are Tarquin's words, it is Lucrece who becomes the narrative's focus for exploring the implications of this very "Catholic" assumption.

Tarquin's words make reference to two matters of concern in Christian doctrine: the relationship between thought and action or deed, and the possibility of forgiveness or absolution for one's sins.[4] Since the latter constitutes our understanding of the former in *Lucrece*, it will be useful to outline the workings of the pre-Reformation "system of forgiveness of serious sins and reconciliation with the body of the faithful" (Tentler 1977: 4). Thomas Tentler argues that confession is an "ecclesiastical ritual to restore baptized Christians who have committed serious sins, fallen from grace, and forfeited their right to full participation in the body of the faithful." Tentler contends that

> there is . . . a rough continuity between the institutions of forgiveness in the early church and those that were known on the eve of the Reformation. Throughout the history of this ritual of forgiveness four substantive elements persist, even though they receive varying emphasis from century to century. First, to be forgiven, sinners have always been required to feel sorrow at having lapsed. Second, they have consistently made some kind of explicit confession of their sins or sinfulness. Third, they have assumed, or had imposed on them, some kind of penitential exercises. And fourth, they have participated in an ecclesiastical ritual performed with the aid of priests who pronounce penitents absolved from sin or reconciled with the communion of believers. (Tentler 1977: 3)

Succinctly, these elements became manifested in the early Church's canonical process of "penance" whereby the sinner admitted sin (confession) to a member of the clergy (confessor), was ordered to perform public penitential acts (satisfaction) in order to prove "true contrition," and then received absolution for the sin.

In its emergence as part of the early Christian Church's doctrine for governing its members' social and private behavior, penance had a very "public character." According to Tentler, the development of ecclesiastical penitential institutions was to "insure discipline" and "to exercise control" (1977: 13). More explicitly, he contends, "the first function of ecclesiastical penance is discipline, or social control. The penitent was accepted by society and in turn was expected to accept and conform to society's rules"; "the second function is directed more to the individual: it is the cure of a guilty conscience. . . . If the first function is social control, the second is reconciliation with the self and with those social norms that the penitent has internalized. Its purest and simplest formulation is in the language of religion: 'How do I know my sins are forgiven me?'" (Tentler 1977: 13).

The answer to this question was found in the notion of "contrition." According to Tentler, during the twelfth and thirteenth centuries "contrition" became an acceptable and "principal part of the forgiveness of sins," displacing "satisfaction," as a result of the move toward a more private mode of seeking forgiveness. Contrition, it was thought, indicated an "internal sorrow" which stems "from the love of God" (Tentler 1977: 19). "But," as Tentler rightly queries, "if contrition is the principal part of the Sacrament of Penance, is there any need for confession?" (1977: 19). As Tentler illustrates in his study, despite the theological tensions created by this query, the Church's canonical doctrine remains resolute in the necessity of the confession of sins to a priest.

For pre-Reformation Christians, confession was an obligation. It was the priest who stood as the intermediate between the sinner and God in the display of "the remission of guilt" (Tentler 1977: 23). Thus the Church doctrine, following the argument of St. Thomas Aquinas, insisted "that contrition does not produce forgiveness apart from the sacramental absolution of the priest" (Tentler 1977: 25). What is important to note in this doctrinal position is that contrition, or "perfect sorrow," no matter how great, is incapable of generating forgiveness. Only confession can achieve that. The "necessity of confession" became inextricably part of social controls wielded by the pre-Reformation Christian Church. With allusions to specific scriptural sources, Church canons articulated the ecclesiastical laws that required every adult to attend confession and that the jurisdiction for confession belong to the Church. Not until the second half of the sixteenth century did this assumption about confession receive its most rigorous challenge.

Tentler argues that "it is [Martin] Luther, ironically, who must take primary responsibility for the situation in modern Christianity that allows a theologian to assert, by way of definition, 'a Protestant doesn't confess'" (Tentler 1977: 351). Though not opposed to confession *per se*, Luther was opposed to the system of confession. Luther insisted on "the hidden sinfulness of man" and that "only sins that entail full consent to the deed and are universally recognized as serious sins should be confessed; and the examples he gives are murder, lying, stealing, and adultery" (Tentler 1977: 353). Even so, Luther did not advocate the absolute dismantling of the confession; rather, he argued for its modification. It was left to reformers such as Calvin and Zwingli to take Luther's position even further and argue for the complete abolition of the ecclesiastical confession in favor of the more private, individual, and unmediated relationship with God. As Jeremy Tambling suggests, the "Protestant outline certainly does not involve less confession than before: simply the mode alters in which that discourse takes place" (Tambling 1990: 45). Both pre- and post-Reformation doctrine recognized confession as an opportunity to "offer a complete account of the self" (Tambling 1990: 46). The distinction between "Catholic" and "Protestant" modes of confession can be summarized as simply the difference between "a performance confession (Catholic) and the 'real', or interiorized, confession (Protestant)," with "the latter manifesting itself in silence" rather than the public speech of the former (Tambling 1990: 55).

This minor "difference" does not render the Protestant confession any less controlling than its Catholic counterpart, however. On the contrary, in ways not possible within Catholic doctrine, the Protestant confessional interiorizes all four of the elements that Tentler associates with the Christian idea of divine forgiveness and insists on the individual subject as the agent of his own confessional process. Significantly, all four elements, in some manner, can be said to describe the behavior of Lucrece as she responds to Tarquin's rape, despite our "historical" awareness that the events surrounding her suicide reflect a pre-Christian Roman history.[5] In the next section of this essay I wish to explore the possibility and implications of viewing Lucrece as just such a confessing subject.

Lucrece's Confession

One of the subtly provocative issues that Lucrece raises in her voiced and frantic reaction to Tarquin's assault is whether Tarquin's rape has caused her to sin. Specifically, she questions whether, as a result of the sexual act, she has committed adultery and thus sinned. On the surface, the logical answer is no; a perspective reflected in the attitudes of her husband and father: "With this they all at once began to say / Her body's stain her mind untainted clears" (1709–10). While her response, "'No, no,' quoth she, 'no dame hereafter living / By my excuse shall claim excuse's giving'" (1714–15), indicates an awareness of the import of her family's absolution, I want to suggest that the confessional self-examination that Lucrece undertakes prior to her husband's arrival indicates a different assumption on her part; that in fact, she believes her stained body to be a reflection of an inner stain – the sin of adultery.

The question of whether Lucrece commits adultery as a result of Tarquin's actions is one taken up by St. Augustine in his commentary on Lucretia's rape and suicide. Augustine writes:

> What shall we say about her? Must she be judged an adulteress or chaste? Who can think it necessary to ponder over the answer? A certain declaimer develops this theme admirably and accurately: "A wonderful tale! There were two and only one committed adultery." Very striking and very true! For he, taking into consideration this intermingling of two bodies the utterly foul passion on one side and the utterly chaste will of the other, and paying attention, not to the union of the bodies, but to the variance in the souls, says: "There were two and only one committed adultery." (St. Augustine 1957: 85)

Augustine then goes on to suggest that

> perhaps, however, she is not there [in attendance before a tribunal of Roman judges] because she slew herself, not innocently, but conscious of her guilt? What if – but she herself alone could know – she was seduced by her own lust and, though the youth violently attacked her, consented, and in punishing that act of hers was so remorseful that death seemed to be due expiation? (St. Augustine 1957: 85)

Augustine makes these comments as part of a larger exploration of what he considers the true sin committed by Lucretia, her suicide. Yet, in raising the possibility of Lucretia's complicity in her rape, Augustine draws attention to a number of troubling questions that moralists, who offer Lucretia as an icon of chastity, either ignore or overlook: "If she was made an adulteress, why has she been praised; if she was chaste, why was she slain?" (St. Augustine 1957: 89).

It is this point that Augustine sees as the paradox facing those who view Lucretia as an exemplum for Christian women who were raped. Moralists, Augustine observes, give tribute to Lucretia by declaring, "'There were two and only one committed adultery'" (St. Augustine 1957: 89). Augustine counters this argument by stating, "in that case her killing herself, because, though she was not an adulteress, yet she endured the act of an adulterer, proves, not her love of chastity, but her irresolute shame" (St. Augustine 1957: 89). And, he concludes, "for this reason she thought that she must present evidence before men's eyes to show what was in her heart – the evidence of that self-punishment, since she could not exhibit her conscience to them" (St. Augustine 1957: 89).

While we may wish to dismiss Augustine's comments as indicative of a rather severe Christian patriarchal ideology about women and sin, his perspective does provide insight into the problematic that is Shakespeare's representation of Lucrece. In his expanded version of the Lucretia myth, Shakespeare creates a figure far more psychologically complex than his predecessors; and part of this complexity, I would argue, is imbued with the ideological assumptions that Augustine outlines in his commentary on Lucretia. Furthermore, Shakespeare's Lucrece explicitly struggles with the paradox that underscores the complex Christian attitude toward married women's sexuality: *any* sexual relations with a man other than one's husband *de facto* constitutes an act of adultery. The problem with this assumption, of course, is typified by Lucrece's situation. Is this notion to be held true in the case of a woman who is raped? Is adultery to be found only in "consensual" sexual relations between a married woman and someone else? How do we discover the *truth* as to whether a married woman's sexual relation with someone other than her husband is consensual or forced?

There are no clear-cut answers to these questions, especially within the contours of Christian doctrine about the innate sinfulness of women. Augustine's reflections on Lucretia, therefore, cannot help but waver between the two positions articulated in his writings: if she did not commit adultery there was no need for suicide; if in the course of the rape she experienced pleasure in the sexual act then she is an adulteress. Augustine does not believe that Lucretia is an adulteress and thus only condemns her act of suicide (which he views as the greater sin). This moral dilemma informs much of Shakespeare's Lucrece's confessional meditation. In the end, as Shakespeare's representation establishes, it is not what others think but what Lucrece believes herself to be.

When Tarquin's rape of Lucrece comes to an end, the narrator describes the behavior of both characters:

> He like a thievish dog creeps sadly thence;
> She like a wearied lamb lies panting there.
> He scowls, and hates himself for his offence;
> She desperate, with her nails her flesh doth tear.
> He faintly flies, sweating with guilty fear;
> She stays, exclaiming on the direful night.
>
> (736–41)

From this point on, the stage, as it were, belongs to Lucrece. In the speeches that follow, which I call Lucrece's moment of "confession," the raped woman not only resists the silence imposed upon her by Tarquin's threat to proclaim her an adulteress, but also his actual silencing of her voice with "the nightly linen that she" wore (680). These confessional speeches, I would argue, reflect the process of self-examination, contrition, and penance that informs early modern Christian confession in both its Catholic and its Protestant forms.

Immediately after she is raped by Tarquin, Lucrece gives voice to her despair. Shifting between rage, self-pity, shame, and despair, she simultaneously resists and acknowledges the confessional interiority that has come to be associated with "Christian" guilt: "'O unseen shame, invisible disgrace! / O unfelt sore, crest-wounding private scar! / Reproach is stamped in Collatinus' face" (827–9). Railing against Tarquin, "Night," and "time," Lucrece finally abandons her lament and acknowledges that there is a "remedy" for her "foul defilèd blood" (1029). Determined to be "the mistress of my fate," she vows that "with my trespass never will dispense / Till life to death acquit my forced offence" (1070). A few lines later, she declares she will not "fold my fault in cleanly coined excuses. / My sable ground of sin I will not paint / To hide the truth of this false night's abuses" (1074–5). Three points are crucial to Lucrece's thinking here: first, that Tarquin's rape has forced her to commit a sin; second, this sin, whether forced or consensual, and despite a presumption of secrecy, inevitably leaves its surface mark – a mark that can easily be read; and third, that she does have agency.

Interestingly, Lucrece's initial, and almost unconscious, reaction is to view her rape as affecting her familial and marital bonds, especially the latter. Without ever once using the term "race," Shakespeare manages to invest his narrative rendering of Lucretia's rape with all of the semiotic traces of early modern anxiety about defining a concept of race. Race is envisioned as something fundamental, something immutable, knowable and recognizable, yet we only "see" it when its boundaries are violated. It is this "seeing" that Shakespeare's narrative engenders in its rendering of Lucrece's confessional discourse. As the reproductive site for the continuation of Collatine's line race, Lucrece completely understands the immediate and future consequences of Tarquin's action – an accusation that she committed adultery and the possibility of pregnancy. She vows that Collatine "shalt not know the stained taste of violated troth"; that, in a noble gesture, she "will not wrong [his] true affection so, / To flatter thee with an infringed oath" (1058–60). Promising that Tarquin's "bastard graff shall never come to growth," that he "shall not boast who did thy stock pollute / That thou are doting father of his fruit," Lucrece concludes that her only recourse is suicide. As she reasons, death will not only serve to expiate the immediate shame created by Tarquin's rape, but also will extirpate any potential offspring.[6] What is worth noting in Lucrece's words is her belief that Tarquin's rape has left its "racializing mark," on both her and Collatine's bodies.

The ironic paradox, of course, is that this sign is invisible except as it affects the imaginative threads of that locus of racial identity – heraldry. In Lucrece's mind, once the rape has been committed its inscription becomes indelibly etched on her body and by extension on Collatine's lineage. Where this sign becomes visible, as both Lucrece and Tarquin make clear, is in the heraldic depiction of their individual racial history. This illustrative signifier of race is understood to be the site where a noble-man's lineage, honor, and, importantly, acts of dishonor are publicly displayed. Tarquin's complicated self-reflexivity just prior to his rape of Lucrece explicitly draws attention to this belief. In a tense private moment, Tarquin confronts the "public" dimension of his "private" act: "O shame to knighthood and to shining arms! / O foul dishonour to my household's grave!" (197–8). Tarquin is fully aware that should he carry out the rape, and should he die, the "scandal will survive" as "some loathsome dash the herald will contrive / To cipher me how fondly I did dote" (204–6). This concern for family honor will surface once more when Tarquin acknowledges that "he [Collatine] is my kinsman, my dear friend, / The shame and fault finds no excuse nor end" (237–8). Significantly, what Tarquin evokes in his words is his awareness that he should be thinking as a "racial" subject. That is, his consanguinity to Collatine and his own lineage are constitutive of his racial identity and bind him to action that respects those ties. In other words, his place within a race should be a sufficient deterrent to Tarquin's rape of Lucrece. Yet, as both this moment of voiced meditation and his later explanations to Lucrece demonstrate, lust recognizes no racial boundaries.

Though similarly deploying the rhetoric of heraldry in confronting the full impli-cations of Tarquin's crime, Lucrece, in her moment of confession, sets the stage for a redefinition of racial identification. However, I want to argue that not until she acts to interpellate herself as a differently understood racial subject can Lucrece resolve the ideological dilemma created by Tarquin's rape.[7] The narrative mode deployed by Shakespeare in his poem intriguingly positions Tarquin and Lucrece as subjects capable of "hailing" not only each other but also themselves. For Lucrece, an alterna-tive "interpellation" begins when she declares, "Let my good name, that senseless reputation, / Collatine's dear love be kept unspotted" (820). It is her name which enables her to act to expiate the "unseen shame," the "invisible disgrace," that marks both her body and Collatine's race as a result of Tarquin's rape. Lucrece's "hailing," however, is not just an interpellation of herself. This "hailing" also interpellates the readers of Shakespeare's narrative, effectively making them "agents in the reproduc-tion of a violated body" on which a "narrative of liberation"[8] and an ideology of race become simultaneously (re)inscribed in history and, literally, on Lucrece's body, once "white," now marked by Tarquin's "racial stain." Importantly, it is in light of this "racial" marking that Lucrece's "reading" of the tapestry depicting the destruction of Troy can best be understood.

Searching for the face where "all distress is stelled" (1444), Lucrece finds solace in the painter's "anatomized" depiction of Hecuba: "In her the painter had anatomized / Time's ruin, beauty's wreck, and grim care's reign" (1450–1). Hecuba's plight is the catalyst, the analogue, for Lucrece's own grief. Furthermore, her identification with the women of Troy, I would argue, also reminds the narrative's readers of another link between Rome and Troy: the commonplace mythography that the descendants of the Trojan Aeneas found the city of Rome. However historically inaccurate, the lit-erary tradition that linked Rome's genealogy to the fallen city of Troy and Aeneas and the mythography of his grandson Brutus as founder of Britain proved a useful trope for the emerging sense of national and ethnic consciousness in early modern England.

The poem's ekphrasis serves to illuminate not so much a cultural historiography as Lucrece's movement from one form of racial consciousness (and thus subjectivity) to another. While Lucrece condemns the presumed agent of Troy's fall, Helen – "show me the strumpet that began this stir / That with my nails I may tear" (1471–2) – it is clear that Lucrece's condemnation is directed principally at the perpetrator of the heinous crime which directly concerns her. It is Tarquin Lucrece has in mind when she utters the fateful words, "for trespass of thine eye, / The sire, the son, the dame, and daughter die" (1476–7). Yet none of this is evident when she questions, "why should the private pleasure of some one / Become the public plague of many moe? / Let sin, alone committed, light alone / Upon his head that hath transgressed so" (1479–82). Lucrece's words eventually will prove prophetic when, as a result of her suicide, Rome is plunged into civil war.

Though Lucrece has committed no sin, in her despair and shame she finds in the image of the chaos that is the fallen Troy the subjectivity she will need to castigate the potential sin engendered by Tarquin's rape, his "bastard graff." Drawing upon the emotions stirred by the painting of the fallen Troy, Lucrece moves from silence to speech: "And now this pale swan in her wat'ry nest / Begins the sad dirge of her certain ending" (1611–12). Later, in the presence of her husband and her kin, she conducts her own disciplinary ritual of forgiveness: "confessing" the narrative of Tarquin's rape, displaying her contrition by "castigating" the polluted body that continues Collatine's line, and finding "absolution" in the vow sworn by her husband and kin to redress the wrong against her honor. Like the ekphrasis on the destruction of Troy, Lucrece's "confession" renders visible the invisible stain of sin that is her dishonor. Though assured that she is blameless, Lucrece refuses absolution, saying " 'No, no . . . no dame hereafter living / By my excuse shall claim excuse's giving' " (1714–15).

This image is further instantiated when Lucrece sheaths "in her harmless breast / A harmful knife, that thence her soul unsheathed" (1723–4). In her attempt to exorcise Tarquin's violation of her body, Lucrece takes her own life. Yet the use of the word "sheath," with its obvious erotic signification, subtly undermines the high tragedy of this suicide, shadowed by the image of Tarquin's "gaze" which also rendered her breast a site of erotic desires. Lucrece's body, therefore, suffers penetration not once but twice. Once more involving the reader in a prurient gaze, Lucrece's self-inflicted wound is intended to purify, to "tear" away, the flesh that bears not only disgrace but the very real possibility that Tarquin's "momentary joy" might breed "months of pain" (690). Surrounded by her husband, father, and kin, Lucrece elicits from these men a vow to revenge her violated body. What Lucrece's demand entails is more than familial revenge, however; the vow the men make binds them as a "gens" or "ethnos" against Tarquin. Her confession heard and her shame absolved by the men who stand before her, Lucrece's body becomes the figurative and literal site where one meaning of race and racial identity ends and another begins.

Early modern readers of Shakespeare's *Rape of Lucrece* would most likely have been familiar with the ethnic mythology signified in the poem's ekphrasis. Whether or not this audience would have linked the final image of the narrative, where Lucrece's body is "paraded" through Rome as a testament to the tyranny of Tarquin, to an emergent notion of race as constituted in ethnicity is a matter of speculation. This sixteenth-century encounter with the political and ideological semiotics associated with the rape of Lucrece denotes, in a striking and persistent articulation, the necessary engendering of one's ethnicity through violence against the colonized (and generally female) body. What emerges in the aftermath of Lucrece's suicide is the embodiment of the Roman republic and unified ethnos, and ultimately the Roman empire; even as that suicide enacts the deracination of Tarquin's own lineage; what emerges in Shakespeare's retelling of the rape and suicide of Lucrece is the continued necessity to retell the rape to maintain the boundaries of that racial ideology. English imperialism required such a narrative.

Lucrece's Voice

For nearly a thousand years, the culture and politics of the Roman Republic and empire have provided institutions and ideologies for developing nation-states with the "West." The most influential of these phenomena, without doubt, is Christianity (despite its genesis within Judaism, Christianity takes hold in the Roman empire); the other was ethnos.[9] Early Christianity, in turn, set into motion the complex and contradictory, theological and patriarchal ideologies that came to govern societies such as the one Shakespeare inhabited and the empires they set out to create. My reading of Shakespeare's *Rape of Lucrece* through the double lens of confession and race has been an attempt to acknowledge these two powerful institutions as crucial to an understanding of his retelling the Lucretia myth. Though Shakespeare ventriloquizes Lucrece's voice, he offers her a psychological complexity not evident in his source texts. This complexity, in my view, is achieved through the deployment of an interiority that can only be produced within the confessional mode of discourse.

This interiority, in turns, is also instrumental in Lucrece's perception of herself as a racial subject. It is this latter self-awareness that strikes me as potentially useful for recognition of Lucrece's act of resistance. If Tarquin's rape functions to "interpellate" her as an adulterous subject, then her suicide is a refusal to acknowledge that "hailing."[10] This act of agency, therefore, is a feminist one. In this light, Lucrece's suicide, and the rationale behind it, is analogous to the actions of African women slaves who took their own lives rather than allow themselves to be raped or made slaves. As feminists we may deplore such actions, but such dislike should not blind us to the fact that the actions are self-determined acts of power and thus female agency.

Shakespeare's *The Rape of Lucrece* implicitly links the Roman Lucretia to early modern England's conceptualization of its participation in the humanist project, which in turn becomes a central tenet of modern imperialism and colonialism. Recognition of this, and the syncretic ways this tenet continues to require interrogation, must become part of feminist theorizing. The icon of Lucretia serves not just as a strategy of acculturation and assimilation; it equally functions to create a complicated relationship between self-sacrifice and femininity, politics and ethnicity, rape and progress. In what loosely might be termed "border theorizing," postcolonial critics and theorists have isolated a conceptual space where, as Françoise Lionnet argues, "all of our academic preconceptions about cultural, linguistic, or stylistic norms are constantly being put to the test by creative practices that make visible and set off the processes of adaptation, appropriation, and contestation that govern the construction of identity in colonial and postcolonial contexts" (Lionnet 1995: 111).

Lionnet's observation, while made in reference to francophone women writers, has bearing on the issues which concerns feminism in general, and as considerations of race and postcolonialism continue to make in-roads in early modern English, feminist readings of Shakespeare's canon. Feminist considerations of *The Rape of Lucrece* might inquire whether, as part of Shakespeare's importance to English colonialism, especially in Africa and India, his *Rape of Lucrece* played a role in the development of feminist social consciousness among indigenous women, despite the narrative poem's tragic ending. Does the distinction between private and public blur the fact that Lucrece's body is a confessional political body? How did indigenous Western-educated ("subaltern") women "read" Lucrece's rape? Did Lucrece's rape and "confession" become unsettled in the modern colonialist project? Did these indigenous women see Lucrece's suicide as an exemplary model of "feminist" resistance to English hegemony and their own country's liberation? Did these women view the politics of Lucrece's confession and suicide as the female body's literally and/or figuratively (as the idealized mother country or female territory) transformed from victim to political agent in the pursuit of national liberation? Are there postcolonial rewritings of this master narrative of female chastity and sacrifice that challenge not only the humanistic ideology that has kept *The Rape of Lucrece* symptomatically part of cultural capital, but also the imperialist ideology that privileges only one definition of race?

The questions outlined above require more than this brief excursion can allow. Shakespeare's narrative poem, however, does offer feminist scholarship an opportunity to continue to define the terrain of Shakespeare scholarship. And, in taking up the challenges posed by these queries and the problematic Lucrece, feminist critics will once more see that her voice is always political.

NOTES

1   An earlier version of this essay appeared in Orkin and Loomba (1998). I am grateful to Martin and Ania for their judicious interventions and generosity. Dympna Callaghan

is to be lauded for her patience and never-ending support.

2   I do not take up what are probably the two seminal pieces of writing on Shakespeare's

narrative poem, Nancy Vickers's two essays on *Lucrece* (Vickers 1985a, 1985b), as nearly every recent essay on Shakespeare's narrative poem engages Vickers's work and thus it need not be rehearsed here.

3   All references to *The Rape of Lucrece* are from *The Complete Oxford Shakespeare*, edited by Stanley Wells and Gary Taylor (1987).

4   In the discussion that follows, I am heavily indebted to Thomas N. Tentler's study, *Sin and Confession on the Eve of the Reformation* (Tentler 1977), for providing a general history of the system of penance and confession prior to the Reformation. Tentler's work provides a more easily accessible overview than the foundational work of Henry Charles Lea's *A History of Auricular Confession and Indulgences in the Latin Church* (1896).

5   I make this point because of the critical tendency to elide the chronological and historical boundaries that separate Shakespeare's "construction" of his narrative of the rape of Lucretia and those written by Livy and Ovid. This tendency has the effect of generating a problematic essentialism whereby there are no fundamental distinctions, culturally or ideologically, between Roman gender ideologies and those of early modern England.

6   Abercrombie, Hill, and Turner (1980: 90). Abercrombie, Hill, and Turner argue that "the insistence on chastity and virtue for wives as a condition for the economic strength of the feudal family was also closely connected with the ideology of chivalry. Since noble birth was a crucial feature of knighthood, only true-born sons would be brave and worthy of their families. . . . Confusion of blood produced unreliable men."

7   Althusser (1971). According to Althusser, interpellation occurs when "ideology 'acts' or 'functions' in such a way that it 'recruits' subjects among the individuals (it recruits them all), or 'transforms' the individuals into subjects (it transforms them all) by that very precise operation which I have called *interpellation* or hailing, and which can be imagined along the lines of the most commonplace everyday police (or other) hailing: 'Hey, you there!'" When the individual turns to acknowledge the hailing, "he becomes a *subject*. Why? Because he has recognized that the hail was 'really' addressed to him, and that 'it was *really him* who was hailed' (and not someone else)" (Althusser 1971: 174).

8   Jed (1989). Jed observes that "every encounter with a representation of the rape of Lucretia is an encounter with a literary *topos* of Western civilization. And, as a *topos*, the meaning of this rape is constructed as universal, transcending historical conditions: in every age and place, Lucretia had to be raped so that Rome would be liberated from tyranny" (Jed 1989: 49).

9   This statement is not to deny the importance of Greece as the ideological genesis of "ethnos." It is important to recall that Rome, not Greece, has the most influence over Western Europe in the early modern period.

10   See Althusser (1971: 174).

References and Further Reading

Abercrombie, N., Hill, S., and Turner, B. S. 1980: *The Dominant Ideology Thesis*. London: George Allen and Unwin.

Althusser, L. 1971: "Ideology and Ideological State Apparatuses (Notes towards an Investigation)." In *Lenin and Philosophy and Other Essays*. Trans. Ben Brewster. New York: Monthly Review Press.

Berry, P. 1991: "Woman, Language, and History in *The Rape of Lucrece*." *Shakespeare Survey*, 44.

Carter, S. J. 1995: "Lucrece's Gaze." *Shakespeare Studies*, 23.

Foucault, M. 1980: *The History of Sexuality*. Vol. 1. Trans. Robert Hurley. New York: Vintage.

Jed, S. 1989: *Chaste Thinking: The Rape of Lucretia and the Birth of Humanism*. Bloomington: Indiana University Press.

Kahn, C. 1997: *Roman Shakespeare: Warriors, Wounds, and Women*. London and New York: Routledge.

Lea, H. C. 1896: *A History of Auricular Confession and Indulgences in the Latin Church*. 3 vols. Philadelphia.

Lionnet, F. 1995: "'Logiques métisses': Cultural Appropriation and Postcolonial Representations." In Kostas Myrsiades and Jerry McGuire (eds.), *Order and Partialities: Theory, Pedagogy, and The "Postcolonial."* New York: State University of New York Press.

MacDonald, J. G. 1994: "Speech, Silence, and History in *The Rape of Lucrece*." *Shakespeare Studies*, 22, 77–103.

Maus, K. E. 1986: "Taking Tropes Seriously: Language and Violence in Shakespeare's *Rape of Lucrece*." *Shakespeare Quarterly*, 37, 1, 66–82.

Orkin, M. and Loomba, A. (eds.) (1998) *Alternative Shakespeare 2: Postcolonial*. London: Routledge.

St. Augustine 1957: *The City of God Against the Pagans*. 7 vols. Trans. George E. McCracken.

London: William Heinemann, and Cambridge, MA: Harvard University Press.

Shakespeare, W. 1987: *The Complete Oxford Shakespeare*. Ed. Stanley Wells and Gary Taylor. Oxford: Oxford University Press.

Tambling, J. 1990: *Confession: Sexuality, Sin, The Subject*. Manchester and New York: Manchester University Press.

Tentler, T. N. 1977: *Sin and Confession on the Eve of the Reformation*. Princeton: Princeton University Press.

Vickers, N. 1985a: "'The Blazon of Sweet Beauty's Best': Shakespeare's *Lucrece*." In Patricia Parker and Geoffrey Hartman (eds.), *Shakespeare and the Question of Theory*. New York: Methuen, 95–115.

——— 1985b: "'This Heraldry in Lucrece's Face.'" *Poetics Today*, 6, 171–84.

Ziegler, G. 1991: "My Lady's Chamber: Female Space, Female Chastity in Shakespeare." *Textual Practice*, 4, 1, 73–90.

PART THREE
Social Economies

7

Gender, Class, and the Ideology of Comic Form:
Much Ado About Nothing and *Twelfth Night*

Mihoko Suzuki

Elizabeth is said to have regarded the marriages that concluded Shakespeare's comedies to be a reproach to her unmarried state (Marcus 1986: 144). The way in which even a female monarch read the comedies as an attempt to discipline her into a gendered role as wife indicates that her contemporaries also undoubtedly saw represented in the plays their own concerns and preoccupations as gendered and classed members of the social order. Comedies, with their recognizably Elizabethan settings (though many were actually set in Italy), and their focus on establishing social harmony – as emblematized by the marriages that conclude them – would have been especially suitable vehicles through which the audience's concerns with the social order would be dramatized and worked out.

Elizabethan describers of the social order, such as Sir Thomas Smith and William Harrison, remarked upon the volatility of the relations between genders and that among degrees, ranks, or classes. Elizabeth's long reign and her refusal to marry had already called into question – at least at the top – the patriarchal subordination of women. Worries about rebellious wives were represented on stage in anonymous domestic tragedies, such as *Arden of Faversham* and *A Warning for Fair Women*. In these plays, insubordinate wives accomplish the murder of their husbands by allying themselves with ambitious males who refuse to acquiesce to their classed position in the social order. Unlike these tragedies that baldly dramatize the consequences of the rebellion of wives and social upstarts, the comic form of plays such as *Much Ado About Nothing* and *Twelfth Night* enables Shakespeare to manage these disruptions rather than allowing them to be destructive of the social order, as necessitated by the tragic form of *Othello*, a later rewriting of *Much Ado*.

The "Absolute Queene," Companionate Wives,
and the Social Order

It is telling that despite Elizabeth's status as a celebrated and idealized monarch, Sir Thomas Smith, the first Regius Professor of Law at Cambridge and Elizabeth's own ambassador to France, did not consider women to have the ability to rule. Smith wrote his "description of England," *De Republica Anglorum*, in 1565 during his sojourn in France, while he negotiated with Catherine de Medici concerning the possible marriage between Elizabeth and Catherine's son, the Duke of Anjou. Smith's treatise circulated in manuscript until 1583, when it was published six years after the author's death; a third edition was published in 1589 with the addition for the first time of the English title: "The Common-Welth of England, the Maner of Government thereof."

In Chapter 16, the "Division of the Parts and Persons of the Common Wealth," Smith states at the outset that he "reject[s]" women, "as those whom nature hath made to keepe home and to nourish their familie and children, and not to meddle in matters abroad, nor to beare office in a citie or a common wealth no more than children and infantes" (Smith 1982: 64). The only exception is an "absolute Queene, and absolute Dutches or Countesse," such as Elizabeth, who inherits the title in her own right. Such women and children "have the same authoritie . . . as they should have had if they had bin men of full age," but only because they "never lacke the counsell of such grave and discreete men as be able to supplie all other defaultes" (Smith 1982: 65). Even Elizabeth's ambassador felt that she could only rule because of support offered by male counselors. And he was certainly interested in promoting Elizabeth's marriage to Anjou.

Although Smith does not indicate what he meant by the woman ruler's "defaulte" that needed to be supplied by male counselors, popular questioning of Elizabeth's ability was expressed in the malicious gossip that Elizabeth had given birth to illegitimate children (Levin 1994: 66–90). The fact that many of the rumors concerning Elizabeth's liaisons and illegitimate births were told by women indicates that even women felt that Elizabeth was not conforming to gender norms: that her refusal to marry meant her sexuality was not being regulated within patriarchal marriage and that her unruly sexuality made her unfit to rule. The women who circulated these rumors express at once a fantasy of transgressive sexuality and of making Elizabeth sexual, more human, and unexceptional – more like they themselves who did not wield any political power in Elizabethan England. These rumors thus express ordinary women's desire to close the gap between Elizabeth as the exceptional female monarch and themselves. In addition, through these rumors, the women participate, after a fashion, in public and political discourse – and were in fact prosecuted for treason. The accounts of women who were under the delusion that they were queens themselves also indicate that these women's desire to participate in public affairs could only be satisfied by fantasizing themselves as queens, the unique public role that a woman could assume.

These rumors and delusions, then, underscore at once the gap between the female monarch and her female subjects, but also the subjects' consciousness of the sameness of gender they shared with their monarch. It is ironic that Sir Thomas Smith, who in theory allowed a woman to rule, though in practice he limited her power by male counselors, reverses the relationship between theory and practice when discussing the position of ordinary wives in the household. In his chapter "Of Wives and Mariages," Smith states that "wives in England [are] *in potestate maritorum*" (Smith 1982: 130), under the power of their husbands, though not in matters of life and death, *vitae ac necis potestatem*, in the manner of the Romans. He understands marriage to be a homosocial exchange of the woman between the father and the husband: "For the woman at the Church dore was given of the father or some other man next of her kinne into the handes of the husbande, and he layde downe golde and silver for her upon the booke, as though he did buy her" (Smith 1982: 132). Smith sees significant manifestations of the woman's legal disability in her loss, upon marriage, of her own property and her name: "her goods by marriage are streight made her husbandes, and she looseth all administration which she had of them" (Smith 1982: 131); "our daughters so soone as they be maried loose the name of their father, and of the family and stocke whereof they doe come, and take the surname of their husbands, as transplanted from one family to another" (Smith 1982: 131–2). If she brings land to the marriage, however, it "descendeth to her eldest son, or is divided among her daughters, as the manner is of the lande which the husband bringeth to the mariage" (Smith 1982: 133); in this instance, the legal status of a landed woman approaches that of her male counterpart, for the class prerogative of transmitting land trumps her gender disability.

Despite these legal disabilities of wives, Smith remarks that the actual status of women in England may diverge considerably from the theory: "Although the wife be (as I have written before) *in manu & potestate mariti*, by our lawe yet they be not kept so streit as in mew and with a garde as they be in Italy and Spaine, but have almost as much libertie as in Fraunce, and they have for the most part all the charge of the house and houshoulde (as it may appear by *Aristotle* and *Plato* the wives of Greece had in their time), which is in deede the naturall occupation, exercise, office and part of a wife" (Smith 1982: 132–3). Although he confines women to the domestic sphere, Smith nevertheless allows the woman predominance there. While adducing ancient Greece as evidence that the assignment of the domestic sphere to women is "naturall," he nevertheless implicitly acknowledges the constructedness of women's position by noting the differences between contemporary practices in Italy and Spain on the one hand, and France and England on the other. Smith also suggests that actual husbands do not exercise the legal prerogative that they hold over their wives: "although our lawe may seeme somewhat rigorous toward the wives, yet for the most part they can handle their husbandes so well and so doulcely, and specially when their husbands be sicke: that where the lawe gives them nothing, their husbandes at their death of their good will giveth them all. And few there be not made at the death of their husbandes either sole or chiefe executrixes of his last will and testament, and have for the most part the government of the children and their portions" (Smith 1982: 133). While Smith argued that a female monarch needed the advice of male counselors, here he seems to indicate that women are perfectly capable of acting independently and competently while their husbands are sick or after their death.

William Harrison, whose *Description of England* (1587) significantly does *not* include a chapter on women, deplores, with more palpable anxiety, women's various transgressions in attire: chaste and sober matrons are dressing like hussies (a sexual transgression), women are dressing like men (a transgression of the distinction between genders), and younger wives of citizens and burgesses "cannot tell when and how to make an end, as being women indeed in whom all kind of curiosity is to be found and seen, and in far greater measure than in women of higher calling" (Harrison 1968: 147–8) – a transgression of the differences among classes. This moment in Harrison's text exemplifies Lisa Jardine's observation that "patriarchy's unexpressed worry about the great social changes which characterize the period . . . could be made conveniently concrete in the voluminous and endemic debates about 'the woman question'." (Jardine 1983: 6; see also Amussen 1991).

One of the most notable social changes that historians and contemporary observers such as Smith and Harrison describe is the greater social mobility during the late sixteenth and early seventeenth centuries (see Laslett 1984: 36–52; Wrightson 1982: 26–30; Stone 1966; Cressy 1976). During this period of particularly intense economic and demographic change, social movement went in both directions, downwards as well as upwards, leading to unrest and conflict in the social order. Precisely because this movement was particularly apparent and significant between the gentry and the rest of the society, making distinctions between the two became of pressing importance.

Smith divides the commonwealth into "foure sortes" – gentlemen, citizens or burgesses, yeomen, and artificers and laborers. He acknowledges the constructed nature of the divisions in rank – "Knightes therefore be not borne but made" (Smith 1982: 67) – as well as the fluidity of these divisions: the nobility can "decaye" (1982: 66), and then the "prince and the common wealth have the same power that their predecessors had, and as the husbandman hath to plant a new tree where the old fayleth, to honour vertue where he doth find it, to make gentlemen, esquiers, knights, barons, earles, marquises and dukes" (1982: 71). Though in such passages Smith accepts with equanimity as part of the order of things that commonwealths "chaungeth continually" (1982: 67), he also expresses bitterness at what he considers the ease of upward mobility:

> for as for gentlemen, they be made good cheape in England. For whosoever studieth the lawes of the realme, who studieth in the universities, who professeth liberall sciences, and to be shorte, who can live idly and without manuall labour, and will beare the port, charge and countenaunce of a gentleman, he shall be called master, for that is the title which men give to esquires and other gentlemen, and shall be taken for a gentleman . . . (and if neede be) a king of Heraulds shal also give him for mony, armes newly made and invented. (Smith 1982: 71–2)

Harrison echoes Smith, declaring that gentlemen are "made so good cheap" (1968: 114). Just as the upwardly mobile can purchase "arms newly made and invented," so they could literally "fashion" themselves and their social rank by means of apparel officially reserved for the upper classes. The repeated and increasingly elaborate proclamations by Elizabeth concerning sumptuary laws indicate the futility of the government's attempt to police social mobility achieved by means of luxurious clothes; the obsessively detailed distinctions specified in these proclamations unwittingly reveal as well the social construction of distinctions in rank (see Jardine 1983: ch. 3).

Arden of Faversham (1591) and *A Warning for Fair Women* (1599), both anonymous domestic tragedies of the 1590s, and Shakespeare's nearly contemporaneous comedies, *Much Ado About Nothing* (1598) and *Twelfth Night* (1601), dramatize the convergence of an anxiety about shifts in class relations with an anxiety about instability in gender relations. In her study of the tragedies of Shakespeare and Webster, Dympna Callaghan argues that tragedies are the privileged site of the representation of women's subordination (Callaghan 1989: 41). Even the domestic tragedies, though they conspicuously depart from the generic norm of tragedy in taking their material from the everyday life of non-aristocratic characters, still manifest the ideology of tragic form in their representation of gender relations. Perhaps because the hybrid form of domestic tragedies represents a disruptive upward social mobility, they displace blame for social dislocation and disorder from upstart males onto wives. By contrast, in Shakespeare's comedies, the comic form with its attendant marriages reverses this process to scapegoat upstart males in place of transgressive females. Both strategies allow the plays to manage parallel anxieties about gender and class relations by translating one into the other.

The Ideology of Domestic Tragedy: *Arden of Faversham* and *A Warning for Fair Women*

Arden of Faversham and *A Warning for Fair Women* take as their subject the historical murders of Thomas Ardern and George Sanders, murders blamed on their wives, but in fact strongly motivated by tensions resulting from class divisions. The title page of *Arden* baldly states: "[Arden] was most wickedlye murdered, by the meanes of his disloyall and wanton wyfe, who for the loue she bare to one Mosbie, hyred two desperat ruffians Blackwill and Shakbag, to kill him. Wherein is shewed the great mallice of discimulation of a wicked woman, the vnsatiable desire of filthie lust and the shamefull end of all murderers." Alice Arden does indeed plan and participate in her husband's murder; yet her partnership with Mosby, an aspiring servingman, and her ability to recruit Greene, a man dispossessed by her husband, and Michael, Arden's servant, indicate an explosive convergence of instabilities in gender and in class relations. In *A Warning for Fair Women*, Anne Sanders, though she momentarily expresses resentment toward her husband's exercise of authority and, furthermore, is enticed by a fantasy of rising in class, appears to have become caught up in her husband's murder without actively desiring it; the play represents the murderer, George Browne, as a doubly demonized Other, an Irishman posing as an English "gentleman" – a characterization absent from all the historical accounts on which the play is based.

Early in *Arden*, Alice's discontentment with her husband and her rebellious desire find expression in a double transgression: she engages in an adulterous relationship with lower-class Mosby, and plots with her lover to kill her husband. She exalts her extra-marital relationship with Mosby over her marriage to Arden, speaking of how Arden "usurps" the "title" to her heart (i.98–102). Catherine Belsey has argued that *Arden* dramatizes the intensification of a contemporary debate about marriage, at times "present[ing] Alice Arden's challenge to the institution of marriage as an act of heroism" (Belsey 1985: 130; see also Dolan 1994: 51–8). Significantly, Alice expresses her defiance of Arden by subversively asserting the superiority of Mosby's "title," here meaning both the legal right to control property and hereditary rank or status. Alice's challenge to her husband's authority corresponds to the townspeople's questioning of his title to the Abbey lands, from which he derives his preeminence in Faversham.

Through research in the archival record, Lena Cowen Orlin has shown how extensive extra-domestic hostilities worked to bring about the murder of the historical Thomas Ardern (Orlin 1994: 52–53). Although the play elides many of these hostilities, it does feature Greene and Reede, both dispossessed by Arden's acquisition of the Abbey lands through royal grant, which nullifies previous leases on the land. Greene indicts "greedy-gaping" Arden for "wring[ing]" from him the "little land" he has (i.470–7). His desire for revenge quickly finds its counterpart in Alice's already expressed desire to assert her independence from her husband's control: "I shall be the man / Shall set you free from all this discontent. / . . . / I'll pay him home, whatever hap to me" (i.511–15). At least initially, the play takes the perspective of those Arden has dispossessed, even though it repudiates the masterless men, Will and Shakebag, whom Greene hires to murder Arden. The confrontation between Arden and Reede, a sailor, underscores the play's hostility toward Arden as the victimizer and its sympathy with Reede as the victim. Reede pleads with Arden to allow his wife and children the rent from "the plot of ground / Which wrongfully [Arden] detain[s] from [him]" (xiii.12–13). When Arden categorically and abusively refuses him, Reede curses Arden, wishing that the land be "ruinous and fatal" to him, and that he "there be butchered by [his] dearest friends" (xiii.34–5). Although Reede himself does not participate in the murder, the play fulfills Reede's curse and makes clear that Greene's grievance is not an isolated one. The play criticizes Arden's obsession with his own economic advancement, an obsession that supersedes any concern for feudal obligations or relations.

Arden's economic self-advancement contributes to his upward social mobility, for wealth constituted an important index of gentility. He proudly proclaims, "I am by birth a gentleman of blood" (i.36); yet the status he enjoys as the foremost citizen of Faversham cannot be separated from his marriage to Alice, whose superior class Greene remarks upon: "Why Mistress Arden, can the crabbed churl / Use you unkindly? respects he not your birth, / Your honourable friends, nor what you brought? / Why, all Kent knows your parentage and what you are" (i.488–91). Indeed, Alice has brought Arden an alliance with her stepfather, Sir Edward North. Alice's unruliness, partly stemming from her pride in her superior origins, and Arden's own reluctance to chastise the wife who brought him elevation in status, both contribute to the tragedy of Arden, which dramatizes the consequences of his social climbing. Arden expresses disdain for Mosby, the aspiring servingman with whom his wife commits adultery, calling him a "botcher . . . / Who, by base brokage . . . / Crept into service of a nobleman, / And by his servile flattery and fawning / Is now become the steward of his house" (i.25–9). Yet Arden's scorn for Mosby's humble social origin appears stronger than his distress at being cuckolded; his vehemence in describing Mosby's social climbing reveals Arden's desire to repudiate the similarity between Mosby and himself. Indeed, Mosby himself speaks lines that could very well have been spoken by Arden: "My golden time was when I had no gold; / Though then I wanted, yet I slept secure; / . . . / But, since I climbed the top-bough of the tree / . . . / Each gentle stirry gale . . . / . . . makes me dread my downfall to the earth" (viii.11–18). These lines express the play's hostility toward social climbers – Arden and Mosby – and prepare the way for their punishment.

In *A Warning for Fair Women*, "Master" George Sanders – a merchant whose title marks his link to the gentry – focuses his energy, like Arden, on his own economic advancement, spending most of his time at the Royal Exchange. Anne Drury takes advantage of her knowledge that his wife Anne sits at the door, awaiting his return from the Exchange, to advance George Browne's courtship of Anne Sanders. The husband's absence, and specifically his excessive interest in monetary gain, draws his wife out of his house and makes her, and ultimately himself, vulnerable to predators like Browne. Similarly, Arden's proposal to travel to London and stay there "not . . . above a month," "no longer till [his] affairs be done" (i.82–3), allows the conspirators to hatch their plot against him. An undercurrent running through both plays implies that rapaciousness makes these men vulnerable to their murderers, and, in *Arden* especially, that the titular hero to some extent deserves to die. Yet significantly, both plays appear to shift their perspective toward the victims when the murders are about to take place: both Arden and Sanders are repeatedly saved from their murderers. When the murders finally occur, they are marked by supernatural signs: after Arden's death, Alice, Lady Macbeth-like, cannot wash away his blood from the floor ("The more I strive, the more the blood appears!" [xiv.257]), and the outline of his body remains in the grass for over two years after the murder (Epil.12–13); after Sanders's death, the wounds of a witness bleed in the presence of the murderer (1991). Through this shift in perspective that transforms the acquisitiveness of Arden and Sanders into a kind of saintliness, the plays themselves dramatize an ambivalence toward the victims and their social mobility.

If Alice Arden's rebellion against Arden was in part motivated by her consciousness of her superior class origins, Anne Sanders's resentment toward her husband's authority converges with her aspiration to rise in class, and tempts her to exchange her merchant husband for a gentleman. Near the beginning of the play, George Browne approaches the Sanders by falsely claiming to be intimate with "the better sort" (110); he later finds Anne Sanders alone to offer her husband "the favour of some noble personage" (379). When Sanders angers his wife by refusing to pay her milliner and draper so that he can pay his own debt, Anne Drury tempts Anne Sanders by reading on her palm that she will soon become a widow and will marry a "gentleman . . . / A gallant fellow, one that is belov'd / Of great estates" (696–8). Climbing the "Ladder of Promotion" (699) will mean that though her present husband "keeps [her] wel, . . . / Yet better's better" (708–9): her next husband will provide her with a "hood, and gowne of silke," as well as a coach and a "dozen men all in a liverie" (711–13). Here, Drury expresses a prevalent fantasy of class mobility that recalls Harrison's description of burgesses' wives whose lavish dress signals their social aspirations. Significantly, this fantasy of upward class mobility converges with anger at male dominance over women: Anne Sanders bitterly resents her husband for sending his servant to inform her that he is withholding the money promised her. Furthermore, Anne's resentment against her husband expresses itself as anger with his "man," whose homosocial bond with his master takes precedence over the marital bond between husband and wife.

Although the roles of the two women in their husbands' murders clearly differ – Alice Arden, along with Mosby and Shakebag, actually stabs her husband, whereas Anne Sanders is absent from the scene of the crime – both tragedies move to place more blame on the wives than on the other characters. While Alice is only one of many who participate in Arden's murder, it is not entirely clear whether Anne Sanders is even aware of the plan to kill her husband, though the title page unequivocally states that it concerns "the most tragicall and lamentable murther of Master George Sanders . . . consented unto by his owne wife." Unlike Alice, who declares her independence from her husband in taking Mosby as her lover, the more passive and impressionable Anne is manipulated into accepting Browne by Drury – described in the *dramatis personae* as a "surgeon and soothsayer." Unlike Alice Arden, Anne Sanders is represented as a "chaste and honest" (230–1) wife who accepts "God's providence" (718–20) that she must be widowed and must take a second husband. Anne Drury, demonized as a "witch," serves to exonerate her namesake Anne Sanders to some extent and thus partially defuses the anxieties produced by an assertive woman like Alice Arden. Yet such anxieties remain, for the allegorical dumb show represents Anne Sanders as motivated by Lust, a representation at odds with her behavior elsewhere in the play. In fact, Anne expresses great sorrow and regret upon learning of her husband's murder: "Oh my deare husband I wil follow thee: / Give me a knife, a sword, or any thing, / Wherewith I may do justice on my selfe. / Justice for murther, justice for the death / Of my deare husband, my betrothed love" (1542–6). Since Browne vehemently maintains Anne's innocence and she herself denies complicity in the murder until the very end, the degree of her involvement in the murder remains obscure. Nevertheless, the play asserts that she must be punished for having been the occasion for others' transgressions.

When "Lust" – the allegorical figure that represents Anne's guilt – leaves the dumb show and enters the play itself, it becomes a multivalent term not only for transgressive sexual energy but also for other energies and transgressions. One of the officers at Browne's trial remarks, "Oh a lustie youth, / Lustily fed, and lustily appar-elled, / Lustie in looke, in gate, in gallant talke, / Lustie in wooing, in fight and mur-thering, / And lustilie hangd, there's th'end of lustie *Browne*" (2165–9). Like "curiosity" in the passage I quoted earlier from William Harrison, "Lust" here denotes change, transformation, and social mobility. This passage goes further than the one in Harrison, however, in asserting that the refusal to remain satisfied with one's social station leads inevitably to violent social transgression – including murder – which in turn calls for violent punishment. And such transgressive murders are ubiquitous in the world that the play depicts, for it is revealed that Browne has a brother who is about to be executed for a murder he committed in York: "Is there another *Browne* hath kild a *Sanders*? / It is my other selfe hath done the deede, / I am a thousand, every murtherer is my one selfe, / I am at one time in a thousand places, / And I have slaine a thousand *Sanderses*, / In every shire, each cittie, and each towne, / *George Sanders* still is murthered by *George Browne*" (2397–403). These lines represent Browne's murder of Sanders as an exemplary instance of class resentment; by calling attention to the two Georges but not mentioning either Anne, they reveal the women for the pretext (in the case of Anne Sanders) and scapegoat (in the case of Anne Drury) that they are. The introduction of the brother reveals the play's understanding that Browne's murder of Sanders consti-tutes not an isolated or aberrant example; it underscores the prevalence of social disor-der in contemporary England: "Englands two greatest townes, / Both filed with murders done by both the Brownes" (2413–14); "Two lucklesse brothers sent both at one hower, / The one from Newgate, th'other from the Tower" (2427–8). At the same time, the play attempts to displace this threat of social order outward by making Browne (and presumably his brother, too) come from Ireland, where "the inhabitants, / Will not be civill, nor live under law" (115–16).

Although *Arden of Faversham* and *A Warning for Fair Women* appear to focus on dis-contentment within families represented as the murder of the head of the patriarchal family, in fact such an appearance disguises and displaces the anxiety concerning the mobility of the aspiring males in both plays – Arden, Mosby, Sanders, and Browne. As the point of view concerning both the victim and the murderer fluctuates in *Arden* and *Warning*, giving evidence of a strong ambivalence concerning these upwardly mobile males, each play shifts the responsibility for the murder onto the wife, thereby displac-ing the anxiety from the realm of class to the realm of gender relations. The tragedies place the blame on the women, making them scapegoats for the aspiring males.

The Ideology of Shakespearean Comedy:
Much Ado About Nothing and *Twelfth Night*

Shakespeare's nearly contemporaneous comedies, *Much Ado About Nothing* and *Twelfth Night*, do not, of course, represent either the murders of prosperous husbands – the epitome of social disorder as dramatized in *Arden of Faversham* and *A Warning for Fair*

Women – or the apparently inevitable execution of wives blamed for such murders. Yet *Much Ado* and *Twelfth Night*, like the domestic tragedies, negotiate the twin issues of social mobility and volatile gender relations; the comedies, however, reverse the direction of the displacement of categories to translate relations between genders into relations between classes. If some feminist critics such as Linda Bamber have considered comedy to be a feminine form, I will argue that it is because the comic form works to repress anxieties about unruly women to displace them onto male scapegoats: in *Much Ado* the illegitimate and resentful Don John and his subversive retainer Borachio, and in *Twelfth Night* Malvolio, the steward who is represented as harboring unrealistic social aspirations.

The violence represented in Shakespeare's *Much Ado About Nothing* is not the murder of husbands by their wives, but a symbolic murder of a young woman by her betrothed, in unwitting alliance with characters marked as illegitimate and marginal, but also supported by the highest-ranking members of the social order – including the woman's own father. This is a world where those who seek maliciously to disrupt the social order can find a wedge against their betters by exploiting a universal anxiety concerning women's sexuality as an index of her agency and potential unruliness.

Shakespeare's use of and departures from his sources, Bandello and Ariosto, and the recently published *Hero and Leander* by Marlowe and Chapman are, as usual, of significance in assessing the cultural work his comedy performs. For one thing, Shakespeare departs from Bandello in having Hero's own father Leonato readily believe Claudio's accusation of her, even proposing to kill her himself. In Bandello's version, on the other hand, *no one* believes Timbreo's accusation. In Shakespeare, the only characters who believe Hero's innocence are Beatrice, and the Friar, who is outside the network of men exchanging women. Shakespeare presents heterosexual alliances as the only way to bridge the radical fissure in the gendered perspectives when Benedick challenges Claudio to a duel to vindicate the supposedly dead Hero's honor, only because his love for Beatrice compels him to leave the closely knit homosocial circle of Don Pedro and Claudio (see Neely 1985: 53–4). To underscore this alliance, Shakespeare significantly has Beatrice and Benedick together play the role of Ariosto's Rinaldo as the challenger who vindicates the heroine's honor; their actions underscore Claudio's divergence from Ariosto's Ariodante, who also sought to vindicate his beloved.

If Bandello and Ariosto are sources that Shakespeare clearly used, albeit without calling attention to them, then the well-known story of Hero and Leander is one to which he refers explicitly in his choice of the name for his heroine. In fact, Marlowe's unfinished *Hero and Leander*, completed by Chapman, was published in 1598, the year of *Much Ado About Nothing*. These lines make clear that Shakespeare wishes to underscore the deliberateness of his choice and the significance of Hero's name:

> *Claudio.* To make you answer truly to your name.
> *Hero.*   Is it not Hero? Who can blot that name
>   With any just reproach?

Claudio. Marry that can Hero!
          Hero itself can blot out Hero's virtue.

          . . .

          O Hero, what a Hero hadst thou been,
          If half thy outward graces had been plac'd
          About thy thoughts and counsels of thy heart!

                                        (IV.i.78–81, 99–101)

These lines anticipate Troilus's outburst in *Troilus and Cressida* concerning the two Cressidas, one his and true, the other Diomed's and false, and indicate the ubiquitous strategy of Shakespearean heroes to construct women as promiscuous and duplicitous, literally double (Suzuki 1989: 245–50). In fact, Shakespeare indicates the link between the stories of both Troilus and Cressida and Hero and Leander when he has Benedick refer mockingly to "Leander the good swimmer" along with "Troilus the first employer of pandars" as those "whose names yet run smoothly in the even road of a blank verse" (V.ii.30–4). The reappearance of "another Hero" (V.iv.61) at the end of the play reveals, however, that her doubleness does not signify her duplicity, but rather, the violence of patriarchal culture's construction of women as duplicitous, which makes it necessary for Hero to experience a symbolic death in order to reclaim her reputation as a maid.

The ambivalence associated with the name "Hero" in addition derives from its suggestion of trespass across boundaries of gender. The name's masculine connotation of a warrior significantly is underscored only after Hero's apparent death: Leonato constructs a "monument" (V.iii.1) in her honor, and Claudio reads her epitaph, celebrating her "glorious fame" (V.iii.8), and sings of her as "virgin knight" (V.iii.13). This unsettling – if only on the linguistic level – of the strict gender divisions that mark the social order of Messina, where men return from war to court women and marry them, is one that Beatrice more threateningly voices in her exhortation to Benedick to "Kill Claudio" (IV.i.287), wishing that she "were a man" (IV.i.304, 315–16) so that she could challenge him herself.

"Hero" of Hero and Leander even more carries a complex set of traces. Just as Claudio diverges from Leander who swam the Hellespont to join his lover, so Hero, the chaste maid in *Much Ado*, diverges from her namesake. Yet the invocation of her prototype nevertheless brings disquieting associations. In Ovid's *Heroides* XVIII, Leander vividly imagines himself meeting his death at sea, and Hero shedding tears over his broken corpse and admitting her responsibility for her death. In *Heroides* XIX, an eager and passionate Hero impatiently exhorts Leander to overcome his fear of the sea to meet her. Waiting for his arrival, she and her nurse spin threads – an ominous image that likens them to the Fates – and as she falls asleep, letting the shuttle slip from her hands, she, like Leander, has a premonition of his death in a dream of a dolphin washed up on the shore. Both letters bespeak a fear of woman's sexuality as overwhelming, emasculating, and ultimately destroying the male lover, a fear that perhaps underlies Claudio's notable divergence from Leander's example in avoiding Hero.

Marlowe's *Hero and Leander* not only extends Ovid's representation of Hero as destructive, by detailing her "kirtle blue, whereon many a strain / Made with the blood of wretched lovers slain" (I.15–16), but also initiates the characterization of her as a deceitful figure through the description of her veil of "artificial flowers and leaves, / ... [which] both man and beast deceives" (I.19–20). In representing Hero as Venus, with Leander lying Adonis-like before her, Marlowe perhaps alludes to Shakespeare's *Venus and Adonis* (1593), where Venus dominates her younger lover. Moreover, Marlowe represents Leander as a feminine and beautiful young man who is mistaken by Neptune for Ganymede and desired by him. In his continuation, Chapman develops Marlowe's representation of Hero's destructive agency: as Hero embroiders Leander's figure on her scarf, she initially "fear[s] she prick'd Leander as she wrought," but then she seeks to retaliate against him because she fears he "sought her infamy": "as she was working of his eye, / She thought to prick it out to quench her ill" (IV.59, 64–6). Chapman also elaborates Hero's duplicity when she conceals her loss of virginity, as Venus condemns her for her "cunning," "deceit," and "coyness" in appearing "still a maid . . . [to] cozen'd eyes" (IV.250–2, 255). Venus's strong denunciation of her votary culminates in a prophetic statement concerning the duplicity of all women: "But since thy lips (least thought forsworn) forswore, / Be never virgin's vow worth trusting more" (IV.258–9). The flames of Hero's sacrifice become a counterfeit Hero, carrying strong associations with Pandora, Hesiod's originary female, and Spenser's False Florimell, two emblematic figures of female duplicity: Venus "made her architect / Of all dissimulations; and since then / Never was any trust in maids or men" (IV.312–14).

In Shakespeare's version, all these disquieting associations surrounding the character of Hero in the sources are repressed, but never completely. Even before these associations erupt in Borachio's plot to portray Hero as meeting with her lover, as her namesake was famous for doing, Hero belies most critics' assessment of her as a "conventionally feminine; meek, self-effacing, vulnerable, obedient, seen and not heard, . . . a face without a voice" (Cook 1986: 191). In fact, Hero diverges from this prevalent characterization of her and approaches the boldness of Ovid and Marlowe's Hero when she orchestrates the eavesdropping scene to ensnare Beatrice in III.i. Carol Thomas Neely observes that Hero here shows qualities usually associated with Beatrice, "a capacity for aggressiveness, realism, and wit" (1985: 49). If Margaret is guilty of the theatrical impersonation of her mistress, she was only the actress and not the mastermind as is Hero, who scripts and directs this scene. In fact, Hero's stated intention – "I'll devise some honest slanders / To stain my cousin with" (III.i.84–5) – ironically prefigures the "slanders" that will "stain" Hero herself with potentially dire consequences. In this role as theatrical director, she resembles Don Pedro and Borachio, the most resourceful males in the play, as well as Shakespeare himself as the playwright, in this respect recalling Chapman's Hero whose embroidery of Leander – "Her diving needle taught him how to swim / ... / Things senseless live by art" (IV.53, 55) – makes reference to the poet's own activity of representation.

Claudio's strong homosocial bond with Don Pedro – expressed in Don Pedro's surrogate wooing of Hero on his behalf and their palpable relief when Claudio's marriage falls through – recalls the homoerotic bond between the older Neptune and the young Leander in Marlowe. The homoerotic desire *between* men in the Marlovian subtext has been sublimated into a more acceptable, homosocial relationship *among* men, where Benedick serves to defuse the strong bond between Claudio and Don Pedro. (Harry Berger, Jr. calls this notable male bonding the "Men's Club of Messina" [1982: 305]). A similar repression of sexuality motivates the displacement of the nightly assignations between Hero and Leander onto the staged assignation between Margaret – impersonating Hero – and Borachio. What is indicated by these negative and disquieting associations in the sources, and in literary tradition itself – from classical antiquity to contemporary Elizabethan England – is the overdetermined construction of Hero as a duplicitous and sexually experienced woman. Literary tradition here stands for the cultural context in which Shakespeare is writing (McEachern 1988: 269, 272). Just as Hero is defeated by the weight of literary history, so women in Elizabethan England are constructed in accordance with misogynistic assumptions about their "nature" – for example, in the ubiquitous jokes concerning cuckoldry. Even Elizabeth, as we have seen, was not immune to sexual slanders despite – or precisely because of – her self-construction as the Virgin Queen. For Elizabeth, and now Hero, the ascription of female – and disorderly – sexuality works to discipline women who aspire to go beyond their allotted spheres. And in the instance of *Much Ado*, the male characters work together, albeit unwittingly, to bring about the fulfillment of the (negative) promise of Hero's name, just as later in *Othello* and *The Winter's Tale* husbands tailor their perception of reality in order to fulfill the fearful wish that they are cuckolded.

Just as the play's critics as well as its characters attempt to relegate Hero to the role of a passive object of exchange – in keeping with Sir Thomas Smith's characterization of a woman given in marriage – so they make similar efforts to contain the role of Margaret, the "waiting gentlewoman" (II.iii.13–14). When Leonato accuses Margaret of having been an accomplice, "pack'd in all this wrong" (V.i.293), Borachio emphatically refuses to implicate her: "No, by my soul, she was not, / Nor knew not what she did when she spoke to me, / But always hath been just and virtuous / In any thing that I do know by her" (V.i.295–8). Later in Act V, Leonato states ambiguously, "But Margaret was in some fault for this, / Although against her will" (V.iv.4–5). Yet Leonato's contradictory exoneration reveals the general uncertainty about Margaret's guilt. She engages in flirtatious conversation with Balthasar and Benedick (while she is presumably the mistress of Borachio) sprinkled with *double entendres*: in II.i, during the masquerade, Margaret exchanges playful lines with Balthasar, Don Pedro's attendant; and in V.ii, Margaret flirts with Benedick in an exchange that lasts some twenty lines. Her joking request for a "sonnet in praise of [her] beauty" (V.ii.4–5) and her bawdy banter, "To have no man come over me? . . . Give us the swords; we have bucklers of our own" (V.ii.9, 18) continue to cast her in an equivocal light, even though, or especially because, Borachio has just exonerated her as "just and virtuous" in the preceding scene. Her ironic use of military language recalls Beatrice's more serious desire to challenge Claudio. Even though her temporarily successful impersonation of Hero has now been unmasked, her demonstration of the "manly wit" (V.ii.15) that Benedick admires suggests that Margaret can impersonate Beatrice equally well, and that she displays disquieting abilities to transgress gender as well as class divisions.

Yet her disguise as Hero, precisely because it is not represented on stage, and because Shakespeare declines to give Margaret's own perspective on her motivations (as Ariosto gives Dalinda's), becomes an all-purpose index of her duplicity, sexuality, and perhaps even her ambition not to remain always "below stairs" (V.ii.11). Margaret, then, becomes the character that best embodies the anxieties expressed in the ubiquitous jokes about cuckoldry: anxieties about woman's sexuality and her duplicity. Margaret thus functions as a demonized double for Hero, the character who actually embodies the anxiety-producing characteristics repressed from the various versions of the story of Hero and Leander. Yet the play nevertheless attempts to repress this anxiety about Margaret, by repeatedly – if equivocally – exonerating her. At the end of the play, Hero and Beatrice unmask themselves and are about to be married; yet Margaret (and Ursula) remain masked and undomesticated, emblems of the opacity and potential unruliness of women.

If the play attempts to exonerate Margaret, despite residual traces of anxiety concerning her guilt, it blames Borachio, her lover and director, who is her most vocal defender and who accepts the blame. Although Don John has been compared to Edmund in *King Lear* as the illegitimate brother who is resentful of the legitimate one (Berger 1982: 311), it is Borachio who in fact masterminds the plot to slander Hero, and it is also he who faces the consequences of the discovered plot because Don John has absconded from Messina. Don John's absence allows Borachio to assume more prominence – thereby ironically fulfilling his ambition – and his character becomes more complex and interesting than that of Don John, a stereotypical villain and instrument of disorder. Krieger argues that the morally bankrupt aristocracy remains unchallenged because Don John and Dogberry represent inadequate critics (1979: 61); Borachio, though blamed for orchestrating the subversive plot, nevertheless voices reasonable challenges to the insular complacency of the aristocracy.

In his disquisition on "fashion" Borachio indicates his understanding of the social construction of class distinctions, in which clothes function as signifiers of rank. We have already seen that Elizabeth's repeated proclamations concerning sumptuary laws obsessively policed transgressions of social hierarchy, and Anne Sanders's social ambition manifested itself in her desire for finery. From the perspective of the outsider, Borachio demonstrates that "le système de la mode" functions as a system of signifiers, and that fashion is a "deform'd thief" (III.iii.123) because nothing properly belongs to it. Overhearing Borachio, the Second Watch aptly, though unwittingly, says of "Deform'd . . . a vile thief": "'a goes up and down like a gentleman" (III.iii.126). Margaret embodies this aspect of fashion not only in assuming the clothes of Hero, but also in her knowledgeable and detailed comparison of Hero's gown to the Duchess of Milan's: "'s but a night-gown in respect of yours: cloth o' gold, and cuts, and lac'd with silver, set with pearls, down sleeves, side sleeves, and skirts, round underborne with a bluish tinsel. But for a fine, quaint, graceful, and excellent fashion, yours is worth ten on't" (III.iv.17–21). This function of fashion as a means to mark higher social station – or impersonate it – is also evident in Margaret's use of her aristocratic "wit" and her easy ability to converse with her "betters" in order to insinuate herself into their rank.

Borachio's statements concerning "fashion" therefore reveal his use of Margaret-dressed-as-Hero to be a cynical manipulation as well as a trenchant critique of the aristocrats who naively fail to question this arbitrary and constructed system, and who readily are taken in by "fashion" as essential and natural. If Borachio's substitution of an aristocratic woman with her maid is condemned because it disrupts social hierarchy, another apparent substitution – Hero by Leonato's fictitious niece – is tolerated, because it shores up alliances between members of the aristocracy: it accomplishes Leonato's motives to have his heir married to a Count and Claudio's goal to match himself with the heir of the governor of Messina. As Jean Howard argues, the play acknowledges the validity of anti-theatrical tracts by policing women and those who aspire to higher rank, naturalizing the ideology of gender and class difference (1994: 57–8). Similarly, what is at ethical issue is not the use of the woman as an exchangeable commodity, but as in the Duke's substitution of Isabella by Mariana in *Measure for Measure*, the social rank of the agents of such exchanges and substitutions and the ends to which they are put. Don Pedro's sanctioned impersonation of Claudio to woo Hero – "I will assume thy part in some disguise / And tell fair Hero I am Claudio" (I.i.301–2) – nevertheless anticipates Borachio's "lawless" staged wooing of Margaret impersonating Hero. It is Don Pedro's success that prepares the way for Claudio's ready belief in the spectacle of Hero's supposed unfaithfulness.

Yet just as these juxtapositions of Borachio and Leonato as exchangers of women, and of Borachio and Don Pedro as theatrical manipulators, cast an equivocal light on the aristocratic, "legitimate" characters, so Borachio himself with some justice criticizes his "betters," while still asserting his superiority over the lower-class characters: "What your wisdoms could not discover, these shallow fools have brought to light" (V.i.227–9). Here he gives a hint of his own motivation in concocting the plot to dupe his "betters"; like Edmund, he expresses his consciousness of his place in the social order and his sense that it does not answer to his own merits. He speaks contemptuously of his master Don John as a "rich villain" who needs the services of a "poor villain": "for when rich villains have need of poor ones, poor ones may make what price they will" (III.iii.112–14). He also tells Claudio, "you disgraced [Hero] when you should marry her" (V.i.231–2), implicitly contrasting Claudio to himself, who refuses to blame Margaret. Rather, he candidly admits his own guilt and accepts the punishment, unlike his master Don John who escapes to avoid the consequences: "My villainy they have upon record, which I had rather seal with my death than repeat over to my shame. The lady is dead upon mine and my master's false accusation; and, briefly, I desire nothing but the reward of a villain" (V.i.234–8). By contrast with

Claudio and Leonato who barely took notice of Hero's "death," and especially Claudio who in its aftermath continues to engage in banter with Don Pedro, exhorting Benedick to use his wit "to pleasure us" (V.i.130), Borachio expresses his remorse and sorrow. Anticipating Bosola who in *The Duchess of Malfi* repudiates his role as the agent of the duchess's two brothers in disciplining her, and turns against his masters in avenging the duchess, Borachio in the end separates himself from his master and appears to understand his closer affinity with the victim rather than the more powerful victimizer.

At the end, the play remains silent concerning Borachio's fate, refraining from either affirming the punishment which he accepts or pardoning him, as may befit a comic ending. Rather, Don Pedro responds to the revelation that Don John has been captured and will be brought back to Messina by promising to "devise . . . brave punishments for him" (V.iv.125–6); these final lines again shift the responsibility of the disorder – this time from Borachio to Don John. Borachio's uncertain fate confirms his status as an ambivalent figure – responsible for the plot that almost disrupted the social order of Messina, but nevertheless one who demonstrates through that plot his intelligence and ability, and one who expresses, through both his statements and his actions, justified critiques of those placed above him in the social order.

Despite Borachio's critique of the aristocracy, in *Much Ado* the coherence of the aristocracy as a class is never questioned, except in the instance of Don John whose illegitimacy excludes him from enjoying its privileges. By contrast, *Twelfth Night's* representation of the nobility offers a comic and satiric version of Sir Thomas Smith's description of the aristocracy, a representation that deconstructs the coherence of the aristocracy: Count/Duke Orsino whose equivocal title blurs the supposedly clear and definite nature of an aristocratic title; Countess Olivia who inherited her title on the death of her brother; Sir Toby Belch, her uncle, a younger son displaced by primogeniture and so a member of his niece's household; and Sir Andrew Aguecheek, a man whose claim to his title rests on his wealth and who lacks all the traditional qualities associated with the nobility ("O, had I but followed the arts!" [I.iii.92–3], he laments). Thus, all the members of the nobility are represented as anomalous and hence vulnerable in one respect or another. Even Orsino, with the most secure claim to his title – though the title itself may be ambiguous – is represented as a decadent and ineffectual aesthete, whose life centers around courting a distant Olivia whom he has cast in the role of a Petrarchan "cruel fair." Impecunious Toby plots to marry Olivia to his "dear manikin" (III.ii.51), Andrew, in exchange for some of his "three thousand ducats a year" (I.iii.22), and a secure future in his niece's household. If Orsino attempts to deny life's materiality – as expressed in his well-known opening line, "If music be the food of love . . ." (I.i.1) – Toby Belch and Andrew Aguecheek appear bound to the body and its material needs, as evidenced in their preoccupation with "cakes and ale" (II.iii.115). It is fitting, then, that though nominally aristocrats, Toby and Andrew inhabit the "low" plot. Such diversity, indeed polarization, of interests among the aristocrats indicates an uncertainty about the cohesiveness of the nobility.

Citing the example of "the Lady of the Strachy [who] married the yeoman of the wardrobe" (II.v.39–40), Malvolio plots a similar rise, and is satirized for his narcissistic ambition. Recalling Borachio's low opinion of his betters, Malvolio confronts Toby, Maria, and Feste, and chides his "masters" for "gabbl[ing] like tinkers" and "coziers," of "mak[ing] an alehouse of [his] lady's house" (II.iii.87–92). Yet unlike Borachio who from the perspective of the outsider demystifies social hierarchy, Malvolio seeks to better himself within it. Aspiring to gentility, Malvolio is acutely conscious of the "respect of place, persons, [and] time" (II.iii.92–3), and vehemently dissociates his lady from Toby: "though she harbours you as her kinsman, she's nothing allied to your disorders" (II.iii.96–7). Malvolio's fantasies of being "Count Malvolio" (II.v.34) and of having "my kinsman Toby" (II.v.55) curtsey to him recall similar aspirations to social mobility in *Arden* and *Warning*; in fact, Malvolio, in his self-absorption, closely resembles Arden and Sanders in the domestic tragedies.

Those with the most insecure claim to membership in the nobility – Toby, Andrew, and Maria, whose actual marriage to Toby mirrors Malvolio's projected marriage to Olivia – take the greatest pleasure in humiliating him and dissociating themselves from him. Their scapegoating of Malvolio recalls Arden's demonizing of Mosby as an undesirable reflection of his own social mobility. Likening their orchestration of Malvolio's discomfiture to bear-baiting (II.v.8–10), they separate themselves as spectators from Malvolio as object of their entertainment, thereby attempting to affirm the impermeability of the boundary between classes. In fact, all three Malvolio-baiters seek to allay their anxieties about the pervasiveness of social mobility, for they themselves exemplify such mobility. The same characters who trigger Malvolio's ambition by means of the counterfeit letter later plot to imprison him by falsely declaring him mad – "for our pleasure and his penance" (III.iv.138–9). Just as Borachio's villainy was eventually mitigated in *Much Ado*, so the perspective on the initially ridiculous Malvolio and his tormenters shifts as he vainly attempts to convince the Clown that he is being wrongly imprisoned: "Good Sir Topas, do not think I am mad. They have laid me here in hideous darkness" (IV.ii.29–31). Malvolio functions here as a scapegoat for the characters who in fact experience the lack of social coherence as a kind of madness: for example Olivia, who finds herself in love with a reluctant servingman who courts her for his master (III.iv.14–15); and Sebastian, who finds himself suddenly and inexplicably wooed by a powerful lady (IV.iii.10–16).

If Malvolio experiences the ill effects of the "madness" of social dislocation that Sebastian articulates – "I am mad, / Or else the lady's mad" (IV.iii.15–16) – it is Sebastian who succeeds in marrying Olivia, in the place of the aspiring but unsuccessful Malvolio. Like his twin Viola's marriage to Orsino, Sebastian's marriage to Olivia definitely constitutes upward social mobility. Yet unlike Malvolio, who dared to aspire to "greatness," Sebastian has "greatness thrust upon [him]" (II.v.146), because he fulfills Olivia's desire to marry Viola cross-dressed as Cesario. As Olivia's husband, Sebastian satisfies her requirement that "she'll not match above her degree, neither in estate, years, nor wit" (I.iii.106–7). Olivia's refusal to subordinate herself in marriage goes against the grain of Orsino's sweeping dictum: "Let still the woman take / An elder than herself; so wears she to him" (II.iv.29–30); in speaking more specifically of his relation to Olivia, he underscores his superior estate: "Tell her my love, more noble than the world, / Prizes not quantity of dirty lands" (II.iv.82–3). By refusing both Orsino, superior to her in degree, estate, and years, if not necessarily in wit, and Andrew, the suitor approved by her uncle, Olivia jealously guards her independence. By marrying Sebastian, she preserves the anomalous position of independence from patriarchal control which she enjoys through the deaths of her father and brother, the position of "absolute Countesse" described by Sir Thomas Smith. Accordingly, Sebastian remains fittingly inconspicuous and unobtrusive as a character in the play, though his display of swordsmanship shows him more qualified to become Olivia's consort and to enter the ranks of the nobility than his unaccomplished and cowardly aristocratic rival, Andrew.

The difference between *Twelfth Night*'s attitude toward Malvolio and Sebastian stems from Olivia's desire for Sebastian. Although the play satirically represents male desire – in particular Malvolio's and Orsino's courtship of Olivia – as solipsistic and ineffectual, its representation of desiring women is more nuanced and complex. For example, although Maria's position in Olivia's household is analogous to Malvolio's, Maria, unlike Malvolio, succeeds in attaining her desire, and acquires a noble husband in Toby. Moreover, she escapes being punished not only for this ascent, but also for her transgression in impersonating the "character" (V.i.345), or handwriting, of her mistress, Olivia. In *Much Ado About Nothing* where the focus is on male desire, however, such transgressions, most notably Margaret's impersonation of Hero, were condemned. Yet Toby's joking reference to Maria as the Amazon "Penthesilea" (II.iii.177) – recalling the warrior-like resonance of Hero's name and Margaret's joking reference to sword and buckler – barely masks the anxiety about her potentially transgressive intelligence and resourcefulness. For the husband Maria gains in marrying above her class is clearly inferior to her in every *other* way. Viola's marriage to Orsino also conforms to this pattern, though Viola, like Rosalind in *As You Like It*, is given the opportunity to educate her beloved while disguised as a man. She teaches him that women are also desiring subjects, and that "they are as true of heart as we" (II.iv.106). Viola's accomplishments in music and rhetoric support her claim that her parentage is "above [her] fortunes" and that she is a "gentleman" (I.v.281–3). Yet her marriage to Orsino does constitute a definite rise in class, as signaled by Shakespeare's divergence from his source, Barnabe Riche, who makes Viola's prototype, Silla, the daughter of the "duke and governour" of Cyprus. Such marriages, where the woman of inferior class is represented as superior to the man of higher class, interrogate the rationale of hierarchies in class *and* gender.

The women in *Twelfth Night*, Olivia, Maria, and Viola, attain their desires, though the men either are frustrated – in the cases of Malvolio and Orsino (courting Olivia) – or acquiesce to the role of object of female desire – in the cases of Sebastian, Toby, and Orsino (marrying Viola). Yet it is also important to remember that *Twelfth Night* does not allow Olivia's initial desire for Cesario to be fulfilled; her marriage with

Sebastian serves to deflect anxieties concerning not only Olivia's homoerotic attraction for Viola disguised as Cesario, but also Orsino's attraction for Cesario whom he will marry as Viola, and Antonio's for Sebastian (see Traub 1992: 130–9; Howard 1994: 114; Greenblatt 1988: 67–8). In this instance, the crossing of classes defuses what appears to be a more pressing anxiety about homosexuality, which is offered as a less problematic solution to the painful and difficult heterosexual pairings that are shown to involve a sizeable psychic cost. Orsino's closeness with his page Cesario, contrasting starkly with his distant and formal courtship of Olivia, and Olivia's preference of Viola over Orsino demonstrate that sameness in gender here overrides difference in rank: through its repudiation of homosexuality as a utopian but regressive solution, *Twelfth Night* considers the otherness of gender difference to be less surmountable than inequalities in class. In order to satisfy Olivia's desire to marry his twin, Viola, Sebastian separates himself from maternal and protective Antonio, who is marked as "feminine" by his offering of a purse to Sebastian (III.ii.38); Antonio's action reiterates Olivia's offering of a purse to Viola (I.v.287), which signaled her willingness to "pay [the] debt of love" (I.i.34). Sebastian "progresses" from a homosexual relationship with a "feminine" man to a heterosexual one with a powerful, hence "masculine," woman, who "take[s] and give[s] back affairs and their dispatch, / With such a smooth, discreet, and stable bearing" (IV.iii.18–19); the play rewards his acquiescence to her with a rise in class. *Much Ado* more severely represses homosexuality by transforming it into homosociality which nevertheless exerts a competing – and arguably stronger – attraction than heterosexual marriage. The domestic tragedies also present homosocial relations among men – Arden and Franklin, Saunders and Brown or his "man" – as the norm that is disrupted through the agency of women.

Unlike the domestic tragedies and *Much Ado*, which stressed the divisions between both classes and genders, *Twelfth Night* brings about marriages between those of different classes. It allows Maria and Olivia, women who can be nominally contained within the patriarchal family, to cross lines between classes; it even allows Olivia to marry Sebastian, though this marriage constitutes a double transgression in that Olivia will not come under the control of her lower-born husband, who does rise in class by marrying her. The play displaces its disapproval of all the transgressors onto Malvolio, who is punished not only as the obnoxious social climber in the place of more innocuous Sebastian, but also in the place of Olivia, who succeeds in evading patriarchy's control, and of Viola, who transgresses gender divisions through her cross-dressing (see Howard 1994: 115–16; Malcolmson 1991: 39). The play associates Malvolio with Olivia through her own references to being baited like a bear (III.i.120–1) and her acknowledgment that she resembles Malvolio in choosing an unavailable love object: "I am as mad as he" (III.iv.14). Malvolio is linked to Viola through the play's emphasis on the two characters' costumes – Viola's "masculine usurped attire" (V.i.248), which she exchanges for "womens weeds" (V.i.271) in order to marry Orsino, and Malvolio's "yellow stockings" (II.v.153), which do not succeed as well in attaining his desired match (see Callaghan 1993: 433–5). Malvolio's position as steward in charge of the household – the domestic sphere traditionally defined as "feminine" – allows him to be more easily punished in the place of both Olivia and Viola, whose names constitute near-anagrams of his own. Thus *Twelfth Night*'s comic imperative to conclude with marriages entails an accommodation between the genders; the comedy manages residual anxieties about unruly women by displacing them onto the "effeminate" social climber Malvolio, who is excluded from the concluding marriages as a convenient scapegoat – marked as such by the telling prefix "Mal" – for the other offenders.

The chiastic displacement of anxieties concerning the aspiring male onto anxieties concerning the transgressive female and vice versa implies that the two categories – class and gender – were considered analogous; the displacement from one set of categories to another seeks to contain anxieties concerning both. In *Arden of Faversham* and *A Warning for Fair Women*, the displacement proceeds from tensions between classes onto conflicts between genders; in *Much Ado* and *Twelfth Night* the displacement moves in the other direction, from gender to class. One might postulate that tragedy embodies the reality principle in that the terrible or destructive consequences of actions cannot be averted as they invariably are in comedy; indeed, *Arden* and *Warning* are based on well-known contemporary murders. These tragedies appear to regard gender differences as a more stable and manageable category than what they represent as the more unsettling differences in class. The "warning" dramatized in both plays asserts that women should be controlled within the patriarchal family, for aspiring males, triggering disorder in the public sphere, cannot be so easily contained. A similar management of disorderly women marks Jacobean tragedies such as Webster's *The Duchess of Malfi* (1616) and Middleton and Rowley's *The Changeling* (1623): by destroying the Duchess and Beatrice-Joanna, both aristocratic women who elude patriarchal control by joining themselves to servingmen, these tragedies punish women who transgress both class and gender hierarchies. Yet the very ubiquity of the pattern of punishing the woman in these tragedies should cause us to reconsider the view of tragedy as an expression of the reality principle. Instead, in these instances at least, tragedies appear to be expressions of male fantasies that social disorders and contradiction can be assigned to the responsibility of wives, of women. These tragedies punish women whose guilt is at most very dubious – not only for their own discontent and revolt but also for the violence of men against other men who have risen in class.

In transhistorical theories of dramatic form, tragedies are usually considered to represent social tensions in an unmediated form – and I have been arguing that in the case of these domestic tragedies they in fact do not – and conversely, comedies are usually considered a more mediated form in which elements of fantasy and wish-fulfillment play a larger part than in tragedy. The questions that need to be asked of *Much Ado* and *Twelfth Night* are, "whose fantasy?" and "whose wish-fulfillment?" The ubiquitous joke about cuckoldry in Shakespearean comedies expresses the anxious fantasy of male characters about women's sexuality as an index of their agency. In *Much Ado* this fantasy appears to be fulfilled when the majority of the male characters join in denouncing Hero. Claudio and Don Pedro also express the general dread of women when Claudio almost succeeds in avoiding his marriage to Hero, and Don Pedro in fact remains unmarried at the end of the play. Moreover, Claudio's initial motive to marry Hero only because she is the heir of Leonato is underscored when he willingly accepts Leonato's supposed niece – now his heir – as a substitute for the apparently dead Hero. Although in other Shakespeare comedies the cuckolding jokes appear harmless enough, in *Much Ado* Shakespeare not only calls attention to and critiques these male fantasies *as* overdetermined fantasies, but also dramatizes their cost to women – how they serve as instruments of patriarchy to discipline and subjugate women.

Unlike *Much Ado*, which expresses male fantasies if only to critique them, *Twelfth Night* allows all the female characters to obtain the objects of their desires: Maria marries Toby, Viola Orsino, and perhaps most important, Olivia weds Sebastian. Olivia says to Viola disguised as Cesario, "I would you were as I would have you be" (III.ii.142); and in fact, her wish comes true in the person of Sebastian. By contrast, Orsino, despite his superior rank, does not attain Olivia, whom he courts during most of the play, and Malvolio emphatically does not rise into the ranks of the nobility through a match with Olivia. Orsino, Toby, and Sebastian all eventually function as objects of the female characters' desires. In allowing women's fantasies to be fulfilled and having men acquiesce to the roles usually reserved for women as objects of desire, *Twelfth Night* acknowledges the subjecthood of women (a lesson that Orsino learns from Viola), an acknowledgment that constitutes a constraining reality for the male characters. Yet precisely because *Twelfth Night* represses and displaces its anxiety concerning women, its avoidance of blaming or punishing them may even indicate a deeper anxiety toward transgressive women than do the domestic tragedies, which simply designate them murderesses so that they can be unequivocally destroyed. By dramatizing female transgression in its extreme form in order to punish it, the apparently realistic domestic tragedies in fact enact, fulfill, and affirm male fantasies.

Twelfth Night, which may have been performed at Elizabeth's court, needed to be circumspect in the way it presented patriarchy's anxiety about the unruly woman, especially since Elizabeth, like Olivia, came to power through the deaths of both a father and a brother, and was wary, again like Olivia, of coming under the control of a husband as her sister Mary had done. In this case, the comic convention of "woman on top" cannot be dismissed as merely a carnivalesque inversion, because a woman actually occupies the throne (see Davis 1975). If Elizabeth felt that Shakespeare's comedies attempted to discipline her into the position of a wife, her presence in the audience also must have had a shaping effect on the form of Shakespearean comedy. Although Allison Heisch has cautioned that Elizabeth's rule did not improve the general lot of women in England, and some women sought to bring Elizabeth down to their own level by spreading sexual slanders about her, it is nevertheless true that Elizabeth served as a model for those of her countrywomen who aspired to assert themselves against men. Cristina Malcolmson argues that *Twelfth Night* participates in the pamphlet debate on gender, observing similarities (as well as disagreements) between the play and, for example, the 1589 *Jane Anger, Her Protection for Women* (Malcolmson

1991: 41–2). Even Esther Sowernam, another participant in the pamphlet debate who might have been a male author impersonating a woman, significantly cites the example of Elizabeth as "not only the glory of our sex, but a pattern for the best men to imitate" (Henderson and McManus 1985: 231). Lady Anne Clifford began her diary upon the death of Elizabeth and used the monarch as her model in chronicling her determination to contest her uncle's claim to her property – even though her husband and James I allied themselves against her. In light of these examples of the volatility in gender relations in late sixteenth- and early seventeenth-century England, the obviously contrived resolution required by the generic contract of comedy in *Twelfth Night* represents not simply a literary convention but corresponds to and expresses the social and political situation that shaped the play. Despite its subtitle that suggests fantasy and wish-fulfillment – *Or, What You Will* – the comedy *Twelfth Night* acknowledges a constraining reality *for males* through the way it features without chastising a woman dressed as a man, and another woman who refuses to come under patriarchal control. It negotiates the radical instability in the hierarchical differences between genders without blaming or punishing these women for their transgressions against patriarchy, as the domestic tragedies *Arden of Faversham* and *A Warning for Fair Women* were so anxious to do.

REFERENCES AND FURTHER READING

Amussen, S. D. 1991: "Gender, Family, and the Social Order, 1560–1725." In Anthony Fletcher (ed.), *Order and Disorder in Early Modern England*. Cambridge: Cambridge University Press, 196–217.

Bamber, L. 1982: *Comic Men, Tragic Women: A Study of Gender and Genre in Shakespeare*. Stanford: Stanford University Press.

Belsey, C. 1985: *The Subject of Tragedy: Identity and Difference in Renaissance Drama*. New York: Methuen.

Berger, Jr., H. 1982: "Against the Sink-a-Pace: Sexual and Family Politics in *Much Ado About Nothing*." *Shakespeare Quarterly*, 33, 3, 302–13.

Callaghan, D. 1989: *Woman and Gender in Renaissance Tragedy: A Study of King Lear, Othello, The Duchess of Malfi, and The White Devil*. Atlantic Highlands, NJ: Humanities Press International.

—— 1993: "And All Is Semblative to a Woman's Part: Body Politics and *Twelfth Night*." *Textual Practice*, 7, 3, 428–52.

Cook, C. 1986: "'The sign and semblance of her honor': Reading Gender Difference in *Much Ado About Nothing*." *PMLA*, 101, 186–202.

Cressy, D. 1976: "Describing the Social Order of Elizabethan and Stuart England." *Literature and History*, 3, 29–44.

Davis, N. Z. 1975: "Women on Top." In *Society and Culture in Early Modern France*. Stanford: Stanford University Press, 124–51.

Dolan, F. 1994: *Dangerous Familiars: Representations of Domestic Crime in England 1550–1700*. Ithaca: Cornell University Press.

Greenblatt, S. 1988: "Fiction and Friction." In *Shakespearean Negotiations: The Circulation of Social Energy in Renaissance England*. Berkeley: University of California Press, 66–93.

Harrison, W. 1968: *A Description of England*. Ithaca: Cornell University Press. (Original work published 1587.)

Heisch, A. 1980: "Queen Elizabeth and the Persistance of Patriarchy." *Feminist Review*, 4, 45–56.

Henderson, K. U. and McManus, B. F. (eds.) 1985: *Half Humankind: Contexts and Texts of the Controversy about Women in England, 1540–1640*. Urbana: University of Illinois Press.

Howard, J. 1994: *The Stage and Social Struggle in*

Early Modern England. London and New York: Routledge.

Jardine, L. 1983: *Still Harping on Daughters: Women and Drama in the Age of Shakespeare*. Sussex: Harvester.

Krieger, E. 1979: "Social Relations and the Social Order in *Much Ado About Nothing*." *Shakespeare Survey*, 32, 49–61.

Laslett, P. 1984: *The World We Have Lost*. New York: Charles Scribners.

Levin, C. 1994: *The Heart and Stomach of a King: Elizabeth I and the Politics of Sex and Power*. Philadelphia: University of Pennsylvania Press.

McEachern, C. 1988: "Fathering Herself: A Source Study of Shakespeare's Feminism." *Shakespeare Quarterly*, 39, 3, 269–90.

Malcolmson, C. 1991: "'What you will': Social Mobility and Gender in *Twelfth Night*." In V. Wayne (ed.), *The Matter of Difference: Materialist Feminist Criticism of Shakespeare*. Ithaca: Cornell University Press, 29–57.

Marcus, L. 1986: "Shakespeare's Comic Heroines, Elizabeth I, and the Political Uses of Androgyny." In Mary Beth Rose (ed.), *Women and the Middle Ages and the Renaissance*. Syracuse: Syracuse University Press, 135–54.

Neely, C. T. 1985: *Broken Nuptials in Shakespeare's Plays*. New Haven: Yale University Press.

Orlin, L. C. 1994: *Private Matters and Public Culture in Post-Reformation England*. Ithaca: Cornell University Press.

Smith, Sir T. 1982: *De Republica Anglorum*. Ed. Mary Dewar. Cambridge: Cambridge University Press.

Stone, L. 1966: "Social Mobility in England, 1500–1700." *Past and Present*, 33, 15–55 .

Suzuki, M. 1989: *Metamorphoses of Helen: Authority, Difference, and the Epic*. Ithaca: Cornell University Press.

Traub, V. 1992: *Desire and Anxiety: Circulations of Sexuality in Shakespearean Drama*. London: Routledge.

Wrightson, K. 1982: *English Society: 1580–1680*. London: Hutchinson.

8

Gendered "Gifts" in Shakespeare's Belmont: The Economies of Exchange in Early Modern England

Jyotsna G. Singh

I Economies of the Gift

Now the gift, if there is any, would no doubt be related to economy. One cannot treat the gift, this goes without saying, without treating this relation to economy, even to the money economy. But is not the gift, if there is any, also that which interrupts economy? That which, in suspending economic calculation, no longer gives rise to exchange? That which opens the circle so as to defy reciprocity or symmetry, the common measure, and so as to turn aside the return in view of the no-return? If there is a gift, the given of the gift . . . must not come back to the giving.

Derrida (1992)

That Shakespeare's *The Merchant of Venice* is utterly dominated by gift exchange is a critical commonplace. However, an important feature of the play's treatment of this theme is the complicated interplay of connections and displacements between gift exchange and commodity exchange (Sharp 1986: 250–4; Hyde 1983: 4–5). Some critics read these transactions in the play in terms of a specific historical phenomenon, namely, that "Shakespeare was living in an epoch of economic transition, during which the traditional, stable conception of absolute value was yielding ground before a more dynamic and relativistic view according to which the value of an object was to be identified with the price it would fetch on the open market" (Lucking 1989: 356). While the exchanges in *The Merchant of Venice* emphasize the tensions between gifts and commodities – between generosity and expected reciprocity – they do not so much evoke a smooth transition between two periods as they blur the lines between the economic and non-economic or pre-market conditions. Like other cultural texts of the period, Shakespeare's play seems to recognize forms of value or interest other than those produced by early capitalism, yet, repeatedly it reveals the fragile and spurious nostalgia of such invocations of a pre-market world. And as *The Merchant of Venice* reveals the conditions under which objects and bodies circulate in different and unstable regimes of power, one is led to ask: does the gift "interrupt economy" as Derrida suggests, or is it inevitably caught in its circles of exchange, even while defying "reciprocity and symmetry"?

An anecdotal, historical point of entry into this representational and economic whirligig of gifts and commodities in the early modern period can be found in King James's changing role in the new mercantile economy of the early seventeenth century. As the various trading companies of merchant adventurers generated a process of a seemingly boundless circulation of money via the medium of commodities across the globe, an impulse at appropriating and controlling these engulfing market forces is evident in King James's attempt to rhetorically distance his kingship from the vast, decentered network of commodity exchange "out there" by emphasizing his kingly patronage as a *gift*. As for instance, when he wanted the East India Company to present to him and his favorite, Buckingham as Lord Admiral, some monetary compensations as a *gift* (*Calendar of State Papers* 1623: July, IV, 193). While conflicts about the amounts of money led to a blockade of the East India Company ships, and capitulation by the Company, this struggle took an important turn in 1624. The record states that "the king wishes to be an adventurer and his ships go under his royal standard." To this demand, the Company unanimously ruled that they could not "conceive how with his [the king's] honor it may be done, the condition of partnership in trade being a thing too far under the dignity and majesty of the king" (*Calendar of State Papers* 1624).

Issues of reciprocity and profit interact and come into play in this episode, suggesting an ambivalent relationship between a *gift* that is ostensibly given with no assurance of anything in return and a *commodity* that implicitly entails a profit motive. When the king asserts the rituals of his patronage – his "royal standard" – is he trying to conceal his profit motives under the guise of bestowing favors? The merchant adventurers in turn put his rhetoric of kingly beneficence to their own use by keeping separate the monarchy and commerce. This anecdote not so much reveals the complex history of the effects of a mercantile economy on the traditional English social structures and institutions as it captures the anxieties of the dizzying market forces unleashed by England's growing global trade. While the king tries to extend his naturally ordained privilege over these new modes of exchange, the merchants assert a distinction between gifts and commodities, implying that the former belong to a pristine, pre-commercial world from which the monarchy originated and to which it can be relegated.

That the exchange of goods globally, with the accompanying circulation of money, affected all other forms of exchange – social, cultural, political – in seventeenth-century England has been frequently noted, specifically in the case of *The Merchant of Venice* (Chowdhury 1982–3: 34–42). Therefore, when considered *historically*, the concept of the *gift* enters and shapes the cultural dimension of the transition from the feudal/agrarian modes of exchange to mercantile capitalism in its early stages. Yet, since the concept of the *gift* has been an important subject of inquiry in a variety of disciplines – anthropology, sociology, and aesthetics, among others – considering a range of models opens up a further play of possibilities in the complex transition between gifts and commodities.

Marcel Mauss's influential anthropological study, *The Gift*, offers a *complex view of gift giving*; as Mary Douglas explains, according to Mauss:

> each gift is a part of a system of reciprocity in which the honor of giver and recipient are engaged. It is *a total system* (my emphasis) in that every item of status or of spiritual or material possession is implicated for everyone in the whole community. The system is quite simple: just the rule that every gift has to be returned in some specified way sets up a perpetual cycle of exchanges within and between generations. (Mauss 1990: viii)

While Mauss's study also examines relationships within what he considers pre-market social systems, he nonetheless views objects and modes of exchange as *systemic* rather than natural or mysterious. Thus, he does not make sharp distinctions between *gifts* and ostensibly profitable objects. Instead, he describes his *"system of total services,"* as follows:

> In the economic and legal systems that have preceded our own, one hardly ever finds a simple exchange of good, wealth, and products in transactions concluded by individuals . . . Moreover what they exchange is not solely property and wealth, movable and immovable goods, and things economically useful. In particular, such exchanges are acts of politeness: banquets, rituals, military services, women, children, dances, festivals, and fairs in which economic transaction is only one element . . . Finally, these total services and counter-services are committed to in a somewhat voluntary form by presents and gifts, although in the final analysis they are *strictly compulsory* (my emphasis), on pain of private or public welfare. We propose to call all this the *system of total services*. (Mauss 1990: 5)

While Mauss does not offer a materialist analysis, *per se*, of gifts and commodities, he makes important connections between the economic sphere and social institutions and practices. What he implies, then, is that even in most archaic settings, although the gift might appear free and disinterested, it is, in fact, constrained and quite interested. Underlying rules govern the circulation of gifts. Overall, however, he views the market as a human phenomenon and holds the possibility of systems of exchange other than those based on modern notions of money and commodity transaction (Schrift 1997: 4).

In Marshall Sahlins's reading of Mauss entitled "The Spirit of the Gift," he clarifies the political and intellectual imperatives of Mauss, touching upon areas of similarity with Marx. According to Sahlins, Mauss's perspective on "[the] mystic alienation of the donor in primitive reciprocity," – once the gift is given – serves as a useful analogue for the "alienation of human social labor in commodity production" (Sahlins 1997: 94). Thus, according to Sahlins, Mauss's contribution is that while a clear differentiation of spheres into social and economic does not appear, it is because they are not all separated in the first place (Sahlins 1997: 95). In marriage, for example, it is not that commercial operations are applied for social relations within this system of reciprocity, but that the two are never completely separated in the first place. In this context, exchange cannot be understood in its material terms apart from its social dimensions, and vice versa (Sahlins 1997: 95).

Among other things, Mauss's demystification is useful in designating gifts as an integral part of social and economic systems. And yet, as we can note from other models, gifts are too easily mystified and naturalized, though not without some strain. Lewis Hyde, for instance, offers a model of gift-giving distinct from anthropological and sociological perspectives in that he attempts to apply the language and theory of gifts to the life of the artist. Most significantly, he does not "take up the negative side of gift exchange" – gifts that leave an oppressive sense of obligation, gifts that manipulate or humiliate; instead, he aims to "write an economy of the creative spirit: to speak of the inner gift that we accept as the object of our labor, and the outer gift that has become a vehicle of culture" (Hyde 1983: xvi–xvii).

Considering the mainly positive motivations behind gift-giving, Hyde assumes that the gift is offered with no assurance of anything in return. "Partners in barter talk and talk until they strike a balance, but the gift is given in silence" (Hyde 1983: 15). In order to distinguish between gifts and commodities, Hyde draws on distinct yet naturalized distinctions: "It is the cardinal difference between gift and commodity exchange that a gift establishes a bond of feeling between two people, while the sale of a commodity leaves no necessary connection" (Hyde 1983: 56). Thus, "the consumer of commodities is invited to a meal without passion, a consumption that leads to neither satiation or fire" (Hyde 1983: 10). In Hyde's formulation, gifts and commodities do not seem to emerge from economic conditions of production and distribution, but are simply born as given states of being, partaking of two fundamental aspects of human nature: generosity and greed.

In considering these various ramifications of gift exchange, one only has to recall King James I's more vexed struggle with the East India Company in defining gifts and their imperatives. The distinctions are never entirely clear or stable. The concern with the nature of gifts in this episode reflects a common theme in Renaissance literary and cultural texts. Gift exchanges generate a broad range of meanings and associations: frequently, I believe, they are symptomatically related to the early modern economic system in Europe. But in many texts, they complicate this correspondence by gesturing toward modes of exchange other than those based on modern notions of money and commodity exchange. And *often*, one can also note, the *gender* inflections marking multiple, though often overlapping, trajectories of exchange. Thus, in its celebration of *gifts*, Shakespeare's *The Merchant of Venice* signals, on the one hand, a mystification of mercantile surplus extraction with its attendant diffusion of capital. On the other hand, it shows how the economic system involving credit, interest, and profit is closely linked to the social and sexual economies of exchange. Belmont's *gifts* reach far and wide; the circles or cycles of exchange are both propelled and restrained by the calculations of economics and projections of desire. And most notably, it is women and foreigners/or foreign commodities that influence and often destabilize the movements of gifts and money among the Venetian men.

II   Masculine Forms of Desire

"All the world desires her . . ."

How do the rituals of exchange and reciprocity in Belmont interact with the Renaissance economic system within which *The Merchant of Venice* is located? Or, put another way, how does the world of Belmont, with its mythic associations, respond to the commercial imperatives of Venice? According to the conventions of comedy, Belmont is a pastoral retreat, or a green world, where worldly complications may be happily resolved. On this note, critics sometimes view Belmont as antithetical to Venice:

> [The] two plots are aligned with an antithetical series of contrasts between the petti-fogging commercialism of Venice and the leisurely grace of Belmont, between man's justice and woman's mercy, between adversary and amatory relations, hatred versus love (Levin 1989: 14).

In a similar vein, another critic contrasts Portia's generosity to "Shylock's antagonism toward gifts" (Sharp 1986: 252), and goes on to give an elegiac description of Belmont as a natural cornucopia:

> By the end of *The Merchant of Venice* the cumulative power of the gift has become so strong that one has an almost magical sense of riches and bounty. Belmont is trans-formed into the kind of fairyland in which, even at a material level, the more one gives, the more one gets. Vast sums, it seems, are flowing all ways in this cornucopia, whose fertility, fecundity, and sheer joy stand as final emblems for the spirit of the gift, and the world of comic fruition with which it has been identified. (Sharp 1986: 263)

But are the worlds of courtship and extortion so far apart, or, as Kim Hall aptly suggests, the "economic issues which underlie the romantic world of Belmont rise to the surface in Venice, where there appears to be a real cash-flow problem" (1992: 99). "Connections between the romantic and mercantile plots – and between the languages of love and commerce – have often been noted" (Chowdhury 1982–3: 36–42). But perhaps there has not been enough emphasis on the *nature* of Belmont's cornucopia that flows to Venice. Therefore, let us examine the meaning of these gifts as inscribed in their forms, their uses, and their trajectories. If we view this "green world" as embodying the "spirit of the gift," what are the trajectories of exchange between Portia and her desiring suitors? Does Belmont, in the words of Hélène Cixous, embody "a feminine economy" in which women's gifts do not escape the law of the return; but rather "all the difference lies in . . . the values that the gesture of giving affirms, causes to circulate" (Schrift 1997: 11)? Affirming the positive value of plenitude, Cixous describes a "feminine economy" "in which direct profit can be deferred, perhaps infinitely, in exchange for the continued circulation of giving" (Schrift 1997: 12). Portia's giving in Belmont falls short of this plenitude, even though all the pastoral and mythic markers seem to evoke such a world.

Most notably, Portia herself is the gift being offered by her dead father within the terms of a patriarchal sex/gender system. She is being "transacted" within a marriage system, which is represented as a mythical and heroic quest, but which is implicitly exclusionary and coercive – one in which *only* men are the exchange partners (Rubin 1975: 173–5). Scholars have explained this concept of a woman as gift in a variety of ways. For instance, Hyde stresses naturalized distinctions between "male life" and "female life" and argues that a woman given in marriage is "not a commodity," and that gifts presented in marriage are "not a return gift for the bride as much as for her eventual children" (Hyde 1983: 95–6). The premise of Hyde's work is that all human life is a gift, while he strains to separate the largely feminized "gift-labors" which require "emotional or spiritual commitment" from the rewards of the "market place"(Hyde 1983: 107).

Gayle Rubin's feminist analysis views the custom in less blithe and in more systemic terms:

> The exchange of "women" is a seductive and powerful concept. Moreover, it suggests that we look for the ultimate locus of women's oppression within the traffic in women, rather than in traffic in merchandise . . . Women are given in marriage, taken in battle, exchanged for favors, sent as tribute, traded, bought, and sold. (Rubin 1975: 175)

Furthermore, Rubin distinguishes between women and other entities of exchange, explaining that via the "gift of women . . . the relationship thus established is not just one of reciprocity, but one of kinship . . . [and] as in the case of other gift-giving activities, marriages are not always so simply activities to make peace. Marriages may be highly competitive" (Rubin 1975: 173).

Luce Irigaray (1997) states that women are exchanged not as gifts but as commodities. Appealing to Marx's analysis, she discloses the "social status of women as objects of exchange whose value is split between its natural form (as a [re]-productive body) and its social form (as a body possessing value insofar as it can be exchanged)." Thus, confirming homosocial bonds between men, she suggests that "women's role in exchanges manifests and circulates the power of the Phallus as it establishes relationships of men with each other" (Schrift 1997: 12–13). Like Cixous, Irigaray suggests that it is an exclusively masculine form of desire that has enabled "the evolution of a certain social order, from its primitive form, private property, to its developed form, capital." Thus the social order is maintained by "the objectification [of women] within an exchange system that prohibits their occupying position of subject" (Schrift 1997: 13).

Portia's courtship and generosity in *The Merchant of Venice* suggest a telling correlation of the "traffic in women" through marriage in Belmont and the "traffic in merchandise" in Venice. When do gifts and gift-labors begin to partake of the values of market competition in any situation is inevitably a moot point. And in this interplay of forces between the two worlds one can chart not only some of the ideological and cultural displacements of the early modern mercantile economy in England, but also its gendered mobilizations of desire.

Portia exemplifies woman as a sexual gift, given that her person and her considerable fortune are to be bestowed on a husband of her dead father's "choice," implemented via the riddling caskets. Portia acknowledges her father's authority to Nerissa with some frustration:

> But this reasoning is not in the fashion to choose me a husband. O me the word "choose"! I may neither choose who I would nor refuse who I dislike, so is the will of a living daughter curbed by the will of a dead father. Is it not hard, Nerissa, that I cannot choose one, nor refuse none? (I.ii.20–5)

In the critical history of the play, many scholars overlook the gender inflections of the casket "ceremony." Typically, such approaches define Portia's "choice" in terms of a larger social good, which holds the prevailing patriarchy in place. This premise is evident in the following justification:

> what is at stake here is not Portia's happiness alone – in the matter of which she is perhaps entitled to commit her own errors without parental interference – but the future welfare of Belmont itself. For the man who marries Portia will also become master of her realm, and the late Lord of Belmont has therefore contrived the casket test as a procedure for selecting his own successor. The apparently arbitrary and tyrannical decree [of the test of the caskets], so different from the ostensibly rational and liberal statutes of Venice, in fact reveals itself to be a manifestation not only of paternal solicitude, but also of a deeply responsible concern to ensure that political power will remain at the service of what is truly significant in life. (Lucking 1989: 359)

And in a similar unquestioning vein within the play, Bassanio's representation frames the courtship and desired marriage as a universal quest:

> Nor is the wide world ignorant of her worth,
> For the four winds blow in from every coast
> Renownèd suitors, and her sunny locks
> Hang on her temples like a golden fleece,
> Which makes her seat of Belmont Colchos' strond,
> And many Jasons come in quest of her.
> (I.i.167–72)

Both geographically and imaginatively, expanding trade brought numerous non-European races within the range of European social and economic life. Hence, Shakespearean audiences would have been intrigued, though not surprised, by some of Portia's exotic suitors, as for instance, described by the Prince of Morocco:

> . . . All the world desires her;
> From the four corners of the earth they come
> To kiss this shrine, this mortal breathing saint.
> The Hyrcanian deserts and the vasty wilds
> Of wide Arabia are as throughfares now
> For princes to come view fair Portia.
> (II.vii.38–43)

While Europe's "Others" like the Prince of Morocco have access to *compete* for the fair Portia, the cultural conventions of the time must dictate their undesirability to her. Portia makes her cultural position clear when she expresses her relief at the departure of Morocco: "A gentle riddance. Draw the curtains, go / Let all of his complexion choose me so" (II.vii.78–9).

The gift of woman in any sex/gender system not only entails reciprocity, but *kinship*, and hence Morocco, like Caliban, must be prevented from becoming "kin." Moreover, the desirability of a woman as a gift in marriage is inevitably dependent on *competition* as much as on reciprocity and alliances (Rubin 1975: 173). Portia's courtship, despite its culmination in her marriage to the suitor she prefers, is shaped by competitive and distinctly "masculine forms of desire" (Schrift 1997: 13). While she is wooed with fervor and devotion, she is nonetheless part of an exchange system that prohibits her occupying the position of an autonomous, desiring subject. Thus, though the "four winds blow in from every coast / Renowned suitors" (I.i.168–9) to pursue the desired woman, the trajectories of ownership through marriage are blocked off for them by the cultural imperatives of European male exclusivity. The correct suitor, Bassanio, has a familiar, "Venetian" identity. Just after Portia dismisses Aragon, a Messenger declares to her:

> Madam, there is alighted at your gate
> A young Venetian, one that comes before
> To signify th' approaching of his lord,
> From whom he bringeth sensible regreets,
> To wit, besides commends and courteous breath,
> Gifts of rich value.
>
> (II.ix.85–90).

In eager anticipation for this "right" suitor, Portia declares, "Come, come Nerissa, for I long to see / Quick Cupid's post that comes so mannerly" (II.ix.98–9). Given the conventions of comedy, we know that the young woman's longing for Bassanio is sign of the impending union between the worlds of Belmont and Venice. Once the Venetian suitor correctly answers the riddle of the caskets and wins her father's gift, Portia is to leave the green world behind. But to what extent does she take the spirit of the gift into the potentially death-dealing exchanges of goods and bodies that have been initiated in Venice? To answer this, let us further examine the premises which determine Portia's value.

III   Multiplying Gifts

Portia.   *. . . yet for you*
I would be trebled twenty times myself,
A thousand times more fair, ten thousand times more rich,
That only to stand high in your account.

In following the premise that Portia functions as a *gift* within a patriarchal sex/gender system, one can ask: what is her *value* and how is it determined within the moral and sexual economies of the play? The riddle of the caskets establishes a non-commercial value structure, whereas gold and silver have lesser value than the dross metal, lead. Bassanio describes the moral code of this system: "The world is still deceived with ornament." He tells the audience, and then rejects both "gaudy gold, / Hard food for Midas" and silver, "thou pale and common drudge." And instead, he chooses "meagre lead / Which rather threaten'st than dost promise aught, / [while declaring] Thy paleness moves me more than eloquence" (III.ii.74–106). Preparing the audience of his own impending choice, he declares all ornament and beauty as potential sources of deception and evil:

> So may the outward shows be least themselves;
> The world is still deceived with ornament.
> . . . Look on beauty,
> And you shall see 'tis purchased by the weight,
> Which therein works a miracle in nature,
> Making them lightest that wear most of it:
> . . . Thus ornament is but the guilèd shore
> To a most dangerous sea, the beauteous scarf
> Veiling an Indian beauty; in a word,
> The seeming truth which cunning times put on
> To entrap the wisest.
>
> (III.ii.73–101)

In this hyperbolic critique of appearances, Portia's worth and value are established in non-commercial terms. As Portia is "locked in" the casket of lead, Bassanio's correct choice fulfills her expectation that "if you do love me, you will find me out" (III.ii.41). Even earlier, Portia's value is declared in a morally idealistic vein. Bassanio extols her virtue to Antonio by comparing her to the Roman Portia, a paragon of female fidelity. This happens even before the audience has a glimpse of her:

> And she is fair, and fairer than that word,
> Of wondrous virtues . . .
> Her name is Portia, nothing undervalued
> To Cato's daughter, Brutus' Portia,
>
> (I.i.162–6)

If virtue that is more than "ornament" gives Portia value in Bassanio's eyes, then her attraction for him is buttressed by social approval. Overall, the rituals of reciprocity also seem to obfuscate the forces of demand and supply that bring the worlds of Venice and Belmont close together. Portia's value and desirability, for instance, are not intrinsic, but determined by the marketplace of suitors – including foreigners given access to her by European mercantile expansion, as the Prince of Morocco declares: "All the world desires her" (II.vii.38).

One can also explore this courtship by charting the dialectic of giving and receiving central to gift exchange in general – and to the economies of sexual and monetary transactions between Belmont and Venice. In II.ix, the Messenger informs Portia of Bassanio's arrival, bringing "Gifts of rich value" (II.ix.91); yet the audience already knows that Portia is "a lady richly left" with a dowry (I.i.161) and that her Venetian suitor's "chief care" lies in coming "fairly off from the great debts" (I.i.127–8). Portia gives in manifold ways, as the language of commerce is imbricated in her professions of love: before Bassanio makes his choice among the caskets, she objectifies her being and body as a gift and considers her suitor its owner:

> . . . Beshrow your eyes!
> They have o'erlooked me and divided me;
> One half of me is yours, the other half yours –
> Mine own I would say; but if mine then yours,
> And so all yours! O these naughty times
> Puts bars between the owners and their rights!
> And so, though yours, not yours . . .
>
>   (III.ii.14–20)

Once Bassanio chooses the correct casket, Portia's gifts multiply in excess: a cornucopia of hospitality which she later envisages as the necessary capital for the cash-poor merchants of Venice. Here she describes herself as an object of value that might be multiplied:

> I would be trebled twenty times myself,
> A thousand times more fair, ten thousand times more rich,
> That only to stand high in your account,
> I might in virtues, beauties, livings, friends,
> Exceed account. But the full sum of me
> Is sum of something – which, to term in gross,
> Is an unlessoned girl, unschooled, unpractised.
>
>   (III.ii.153–9)

While she deprecates herself for being an "unlessoned girl" in her femininity, she nonetheless recognizes her value, while implicitly revealing the links between the mercantile and sexual transactions of the play. She further reveals her worth as she promises Bassanio the role of the future lord of Belmont.

> As from her lord, her governor, her king.
> Myself and what is mine to you and yours
> Is now converted. But now I was the lord
> Of this fair mansion, master of my servants,
> Queen o'er myself; and even now, but now,
> This house, these servants, and this same myself
> Are yours, my lord's.
>
>   (III.ii.165–71)

Portia's gifts to her husband include a ring, which comes with conditions that block off the further possibility of exchange: "I give them with this ring, / Which when you part from, lose, or give away, / Let it presage the ruin of your love / And be my vantage to exclaim on you" (III.ii.171–4). When Portia sets firm conditions for the ring, she ostensibly interrupts and blocks off the circle of gift-giving. Ironically, however, disguised as Bellario in IV.i, she mocks Bassanio's refusal to pay him for his services with the same ring, while recalling his vow to his wife that he should "neither sell, nor give, nor lose it" (IV.i.441). To which Bellario (Portia) draws on male bonds to mock him:

> That 'scuse serves many men to save their gifts.
> And if your wife be not a madwoman,
> And know how well I have deserved this ring,
> She would not hold out enemy for ever
> For giving it to me . . .
>
> (IV.i.442–6)

This argument works on Bassanio as it is reinforced by Antonio's claims of friendship: "My Lord Bassanio, let him have the ring. / Let his deservings, and my love withal, / Be valued 'gainst your wife's commandement" (IV.i.447–9). The way in which the obligations and burdens of gifts are complicated by gender affiliations here are explicitly revealed in the end of the play, when Portia demands the ring (V.i) – and which I will discuss later.

In Belmont, these gender strains are not yet visible and here we witness a one-way trajectory of generosity. For instance, in III.ii, when Portia hears of Shylock's rigid bond, she reveals both her seemingly unlimited beneficence and wealth:

> Pay him [Shylock] six thousand and deface the bond.
> Double six thousand and then treble that.
> Before a friend of this description
> Shall lose a hair through Bassanio's fault.
> . . . You shall have gold
> To pay the petty debt twenty times over;
>
> (III.ii.299–307)

Yet, this generosity is accompanied by the proviso of marriage: "First go with me to church and call me wife," and based on an awareness of its economic imperative, as she tells Bassanio: "Since you are dear bought, I will love you dear" (III.ii.303, 313). While some critics note the way in which Portia deploys the imagery of market value to describe her love for Bassanio, they nonetheless distinguish between its metaphoric use in Belmont and its literal use in Venice; thus, the former is described as a "transfigured version of the mentality of Venice" (Lucking 1989: 362). Such idealizations of Belmont – whereby we see this "green world" through the prism of romantic/comic conventions – do not hold ground if we consider the economic and social imperatives of the sex/gender system whereby Portia finds the appropriate suitor by excluding Europe's cultural others.

IV   Bonds of Flesh and Blood

Bassanio: *The Jew shall have my flesh, blood, bones, and all*
           Ere thou shalt lose for me one drop of blood.

If foreign trade via the ceaseless and unstable circulation of goods and money complicates issues of reciprocity and profit in Venice, Belmont partakes of the same economy of exchange – with its attendant values of exclusion – though in a more explicitly gendered form. While the Venetians criticize Shylock for enabling the "breeding" of money, yet it is the women characters who play key roles in the circulation of money needed for foreign trade (Hall 1992: 98–9). In this world, non-Europeans/non-Christians are cast as the representatives of the rapaciousness and strangeness of foreign trade; therefore, in this context, Shylock is easily demonized as an embodiment of the seemingly devouring market forces. Yet, it is Shylock who most explicitly articulates the exchange between goods and bodies, complicating and often blurring distinctions between gifts and commodities and between reciprocity and profit. And in his literal insistence on the pound of flesh, Shylock makes visible the material and metaphoric relation between the corporeal and economic body that in turn merges into the body politic.

On several occasions the Jew uses cannibalistic metaphors, vividly evoking both the literal use value and exchange value of goods and bodies. For instance, he rather curiously denies that Antonio's flesh might have commercial value: "A pound of man's flesh taken from a man / Is not so estimable, profitable neither / As flesh of muttons, beefs, or goats" (I.iii.161–3); and declares: "You'll ask me why I rather choose to have / A weight of carrion flesh than to receive / Three thousand ducats. I'll not answer that" (IV.i.41–2). And in imagining his revenge, he wonders how it may be: "I'll go in hate to feed upon / the prodigal Christian" (II.v.14–15). These analogies vividly bring to the fore other characters' reflections on the corporeal, flesh-and-blood body as a site of exchanges and transactions, both as a gift and as a commodity. Bassanio expresses this recognition when he offers his own "flesh, blood, bones" in exchange for his friend's life, as does Antonio when he declares at the end of play, "I once did lend my body for his wealth" (V.i.249). And furthermore, one has to keep in mind that it is Bassanio's acquisition of Portia's person in marriage – inseparable from her worldly goods – that must be paid for by Antonio's "pound of flesh."

Several exchanges between Shylock and Antonio illustrate this complex treatment of issues of reciprocity and profit. Bonds of friendship between the Venetian men are inevitably mediated by the necessary infusions of money and gifts from "outsiders" – from Portia in Belmont and from the Jew of Venice. The term "bond" resonates with multiple meanings in the play, linking abstract concepts of obligation to the literal bodies of the characters, while keeping open the question of whether a body is a gift or a commodity. Portia is "gifted" by her dead father to the suitable Venetian suitor, but during the extended episode of the ring exchange, she ironically reveals the lack of both Bassanio's commitment to and claim on her. Most significantly, she evokes the possibility of making him a cuckold by suggesting that she will be as liberal in her gifts as he by giving herself to the recipient of the ring:

> I will become as liberal as you;
> I'll not deny him anything I have,
> No, not my body nor my husband's bed.
> Know him I shall, I am well sure of it.
> (V.i.226–9)

On the one hand, Portia simply sets the gift into circulation, suggesting the gift passed on is coming to haunt the giver/recipient. On the other hand, she also evokes the exchange of women in a state of constant flux, and subject of interruptions and deflections. Of course, given the corporeal body of the boy actor on stage, one cannot entirely overlook the irony of Portia's assertions of her own agency; the complicated transactions of the ring remain "between men," after all.

Shylock's body is also at stake in the trajectories of exchange that shape the play. At the outset, for instance, he reminds Antonio of the debasement of his body at the hands of the Christian merchants and questions the latter's request for money:

> . . . many a time and oft
> In the Rialto you have rated me
> About my moneys and my usances.
> . . . You call me misbeliever, cutthroat dog,
> And spit upon my Jewish gaberdine,
> And all for use of that which is mine own.
> Well then, it now appears you need my help
> Go to then. You come to me and you say,
> "Shylock, we would have moneys" – you say so,
> You that did void your rheum upon my beard
> And foot me as you spurn a stranger cur
> Over your threshold!
> . . . What should I say to you? Should I not say,
> "Hath a dog money?
> (I.iii.102–17)

Antonio's justification skirts the issue of the mistreatment of the Jew and instead repudiates any implications of gift exchange or generosity.

> If thou wilt lend this money, lend it not
> As to thy friends – for when did friendship take

A breed for barren metal of his friend? –
But lend it rather to thine enemy,
Who if he break, thou mayst with better face
Exact the penalty.

(I.iii.128–33)

Shylock briefly holds out a glimpse of a different relationship between the Christian and Jew:

Why look you, how you storm!
I would be friends with you and have your love,
Forget the shames that you have stained me with,
Supply your present wants, and take no doit
Of usuance for my moneys; and you'll not hear me.
This is kind I offer.

(I.iii.133–8)

These exchanges complicate our understanding of when a gift exchange becomes a commodity transaction. Antonio asks for Shylock's "help," but refuses to consider it as a gift, which does not entail any return or reciprocity. But when he wants Shylock to "lend it [as if] to thine enemy" with a clear "penalty" for non-payment, he is nonetheless flouting the rules of reciprocity, as the Jew reminds him that all he has received from the Christian merchants is abuse and degradation. In a mercantile world dependent on capital – and on the "breeding" of money that the Christians outwardly disdain – profit and generosity are inextricably connected.

Thus, as these financial and personal struggles play out in *The Merchant of Venice*, they both anticipate and participate in the discourse of market forces operating within a culture that still holds a belief in pre-market versions of gift exchange. In these vexed relations of exchange between the Jew and the Christian merchants, one can find, among other cultural traces, a paradigm for King James's conflicts with the East India Company merchants about a share of profits disguised as a *gift*.

V Conclusion: Belmont and Venice

Which is the merchant here? and which is the Jew?

In following the tangled networks of exchange in the play, one is led to reiterate: what is the nature of the connection between the worlds of Belmont and Venice? If, as stated earlier, Belmont's "fertility, fecundity, and sheer joy stand as final emblems for the spirit of the gift" (Sharp 1986: 263), does Portia bring that spirit of largess to Venice? Portia's charitable form of justice in the trial scene certainly represents the ostensible value system of an ideal economy of exchange. Her set piece speech on the "quality of mercy" eloquently articulates the spirit of the gift: "It is twice blest / It blesseth him that gives, and him that takes" (IV.i.182–5). When Shylock is defeated by the very letter of the law he rigidly insists upon, she no longer elicits the values of Belmont – of generosity and charity – in her response to the former:

> One drop of Christian blood, thy lands and goods
> Are by the laws of Venice confiscate
> Unto the state of Venice.
>   (IV.i.308–10)

Shylock's penalty takes the form of coerced "gifts" he must give to the Venetian state and its Christian citizens on whom he initially sought revenge: "The party 'gainst the which he doth contrive / Shall seize one half his goods; the other half / Comes to the privy coffer of the state" (IV.i.350–2).

Thus, ironically, Portia ends not by giving fresh life to the spirit of the gift, but rather, by coercively denying it through the forfeiture of Shylock's wealth. The Venetian Christians' generosity extends to sparing the Jew's life, but not his wealth and goods, and he reminds them of the life-denying consequences of their edict: "you take my life / When you do take the means whereby I live" (IV.i.374–5). Furthermore, Shylock must "record a gift" of all he possesses to his daughter, Jessica, who, unlike Portia, has been "stolen" by the Christian Lorenzo, one who is not her kin. In a patriarchal sex/gender system, Shylock does not participate in the gift exchange of his daughter through her marriage. The Venetians offer a mocking picture of Shylock lamenting his daughter's elopement and theft of his money: " 'My daughter! O my ducats! O my daughter! / Fled with a Christian' " (II.viii.15–16). But does his desire for paternal control over his daughter qualitatively differ from that of Portia's dead father? Dispossessed of everything, Shylock loses his access to all trajectories of exchange, both economic and personal. The most coercive aspects of surplus extraction can be evidenced in the form of Shylock's enforced "gifts" to his daughter and to the Venetian state.

To conclude, while Portia's gifts ensure the circulation of capital to the Christian merchants of cash-poor Venice, the spirit of the gift, I believe, in both Belmont and Venice offers a rhetorical cover or a mystification of the transactions of global capital and trade. The exchange of goods and bodies in Belmont is represented in moral and romantic images: as Jason's quest of the golden fleece, as Bassanio's rejection of the beguilement of ornament, and the flaws of the transaction are displaced onto the Prince of Morocco, whose expulsion mirrors Shylock's. Unlike Prospero in Shakespeare's *The Tempest*, the Christians in *The Merchant of Venice* do not acknowledge the "darkness" of their hearts, nor do they offer forgiveness to Shylock whom they wronged in the past. The gifts of Belmont lack the spirit they profess. Just as Portia ironically points to the Christian merchants' self-righteousness when she wonders about the identity of the "Merchant" and the "Jew," the play ultimately blurs all distinctions between gift-labors and commodity exchanges – and between Belmont and Venice.

REFERENCES AND FURTHER READING

Agnew, J. C. 1980: "The Threshold of Exchange: Speculations on the Market." *Radical History Review*, 21 (March), 119–30.

Calendar of State Papers (Colonial Series) 1513–1624: Vols. 2, 3, and 4.

Chowdhury, B. 1982–3: "*The Merchant of Venice* and the World of Commerce." *The Journal of the Department of English, Calcutta University*, 18, 1, 33–55.

Cixous, H. 1997: "Sorties: Out and Out: Attacks/Ways Out/Forays." In Alan D. Schrift (ed.), *The Logic of the Gift: Toward an Ethic of Generosity*. London: Routledge, 148–73.

Derrida, J. 1992: *Given Time: I. Counterfeit Money*. Trans. Peggy Kamuf. Chicago: University of Chicago Press.

Ferber, M. 1990: "The Ideology of *The Merchant of Venice*." *English Literary Renaissance*, 20, 3 (Autumn), 431–64.

Hall, K. 1992: "Guess Who's Coming to Dinner? Colonization and Miscegenation in *The Merchant of Venice*." *Renaissance Drama*, 23, 87–111.

Hyde, L. 1983: *The Gift: Imagination and the Erotic Life of Property*. New York: Vintage Books.

Irigaray, L. 1997: "Women on the Market." In Alan D. Schrift (ed.), *The Logic of the Gift: Toward an Ethic of Generosity*. London: Routledge, 174–89.

Levin, H. 1989: "The Garden in Belmont: *The Merchant of Venice*, 5.1." In W. R. Elton and William B. Long (eds.), *Shakespeare and Dramatic Tradition: Essays in Honor of S. F. Johnson*. Delaware: University of Delaware Press.

Lucking, D. 1989: "Standing for Sacrifice: The Casket and Trial Scenes in *The Merchant of Venice*." *University of Toronto Quarterly*, 58, 3 (Spring), 355–75.

Mauss, M. 1990: *The Gift: The Form and Reason for Exchange in Archaic Societies*. Trans. W. D. Halls. Foreword by Mary Douglas. New York: W. W. Norton.

Rubin, G. 1975: "The Traffic in Women: Notes on the 'Political Economy' of Sex." In Rayna R. Reiter (ed.), *Toward an Anthropology of Women*. New York: Monthly Review Press, 157–210.

Sahlins, M. 1997: "The Spirit of the Gift." In Alan D. Schrift (ed.), *The Logic of the Gift: Toward an Ethic of Generosity*. London: Routledge, 70–99.

Schrift, A. D. 1997: "Introduction: Why Gift." In Alan D. Schrift (ed.), *The Logic of the Gift: Toward an Ethic of Generosity*. London: Routledge, 1–22.

Shakespeare, W. 1987: *The Merchant of Venice*. Ed. Brents Stirling. New York: Penguin Books.

Sharp, R. A. 1986: "Gift Exchange and the Economies of Spirit in *The Merchant of Venice*." *Modern Philology*, 83, 3 (February), 250–65.

Tovey, B. 1981: "The Golden Casket: An Interpretation of *The Merchant of Venice*." In John Alvis and Thomas G. West (eds.), *Shakespeare as Political Thinker*. Durham, NC: Carolina Academic Press, 215–37.

Zuckert, M. 1996: "The New Medea: On Portia's Comic Triumph in *The Merchant of Venice*." In Joseph Alulis and Vickie Sullivan (eds.), *Shakespeare's Political Pageant: Essays in Literature and Politics*. Lanham, MD: Rowman and Littlefield Publishers, 3–36.

PART FOUR
Race and Colonialism

9

The Great Indian Vanishing Trick – Colonialism, Property, and the Family in *A Midsummer Night's Dream*

Ania Loomba

Containing an element of the forbidden, without its correlate, the abominable, the exotic is that realm of the excluded which is not absolutely prohibited, but merely signposted by danger lights. It has equivalent status in the geo-cultural realm to the day-dream in the psychodynamic. It is marked by frisson more than fear.

Rousseau and Porter (1990: 4)

I

India is only briefly evoked in *A Midsummer Night's Dream*, as the home of the changeling boy over whom Titania and Oberon quarrel, but, as recent criticism of the play has begun to delineate, this evocation is remarkable both for what it articulates and what it obscures. Like a "beauteous scarf veiling an Indian beauty" (*The Merchant of Venice*, II.ii.98–9), the dream-work of the play seems to have worked to deflect critical attention from its ideological investments in, and reshaping of, the discourses of travel, trade, and colonialism. While the play has generated wide-ranging commentaries on the relation between its depiction of erotic and familial tensions and contemporary discourses of gender and sexuality, it is not prominent in analyses of early modern intercontinental and cross-cultural relations.

To some extent, such a critical bias seems warranted by the play itself. Three of its interlinking stories – those of Theseus and Hippolyta, of the Athenian lovers, and of the Fairy world – foreground female rebellion and male dominance. The play opens with Theseus announcing his conquest over an age-old icon of female unruliness – the Queen of the Amazons:

> Hippolyta, I wooed thee with my sword,
> And won thy love doing thee injuries,

> But I will wed thee in another key –
> With pomp, with triumph, and with revelling.
>
> (I.i.16–19)[1]

Marriage is thus an explicit continuation of military domination, a violation of a different kind.[2] However, this proclamation of the triumph of male domination is immediately disturbed by the entry of a disobedient Hermia, who resists the "unwishèd for yoke" of an enforced marriage and challenges what her father calls his "ancient privilege" to "dispose of her" as he wishes. The first scene of the next act depicts yet another act of female defiance: Titania the fairy queen not only refuses to part with a "little changeling boy" that her husband demands of her, but has, we are told, "foresworn" his "bed and company" (II.i.120, 62). By the end of the play, Oberon has mastered Titania and the boy, and the romantic tangles have been sorted out into neat pairings that will complement the Theseus–Hippolyta wedding festivities. The audience is assured that, as Puck says,

> Jack shall have Jill,
> Naught shall go ill,
> The man shall have his mare again,
> And all shall be well.
>
> (III.ii.461–4)

Louis Montrose points out that this ending has long been celebrated as a "paean to 'order'" but also that recent critics of the play widely indicate the "degradation or coercion" of women upon which such an order rests: "the festive conclusion of *A Midsummer Night's Dream* depends upon the success of a process by which the feminine pride and power manifested in Amazon warriors, possessive mothers, unruly wives and willful daughters are brought under control of lords and husbands" (Montrose 1996: 111–12; see also Montrose 1986). Montrose's own influential reading of the play unpacks some of the contemporary resonances of such a process, tracing its contours and contradictions to early modern debates about women and marriage, and especially to the "pervasive cultural presence of the Queen" (1996: 160). The play, he suggests, transforms and "re-mythologizes" Elizabeth by splitting her image between "unattainable virgin" and "intractable *wife* and dominating *mother*" (1996: 176), and its workings "sanction a relation of gender and power that affirms masculine authority in the state, the family and the theater" (1996: 203). Thus, through this play Shakespeare negotiates and indeed shapes what Montrose calls the contemporary "cultural fantasies" of "gender and sexuality."

Since psychoanalysis has provided one of the most influential and seductive analytic vocabularies for the study of both "fantasy" and "gender and sexuality" as well as for the interrelation between them, it is hardly surprising that criticism of *A Midsummer Night's Dream* has repeatedly drawn upon its insights and assumptions. Psychoanalysis traces the webbed, reciprocal, traumatic relations between human development and the formation of gendered identities. Sexual relations within the family are given an explanatory power in relation to both the individual subject and the culture at large. At the same time, most psychoanalytic theories notoriously efface the question of cultural differentiation, or worse, map civilizational "development" onto individual growth, equating non-European subjects with underdeveloped, neur-otic, or infantile Europeans (Sheshadri-Crooks 1994). In one of the few readings which systematically explore the colonial dimensions of *A Midsummer Night's Dream*, Shankar Raman alleges that psychoanalytically inflected interpretations of the play, even the most brilliant ones, have reinforced the invisibility of the play's investments in colonialist discourses and ideologies (Raman forthcoming).

These investments, recent critics are agreed, are best amplified by unraveling the significance of the "lovely" Indian boy, the "changeling" who never appears on the stage but becomes the object of desire for both Titania and Oberon. The dynamic of this struggle lends itself particularly well, it must be said, to a psychoanalytic analy-sis of overbearing mothers, jealous fathers, and male children who need to be torn away from one to the other. Like the play, however, such accounts tend to simply gesture toward the boy as an absent center. Allen Dunn (1988) suggests that the events in the forest are the fantasy of the Indian boy – a response to the trauma of being taken away from his mother. Hence his absence from the play is explained by his cen-trality as the dreamer of the play. James L. Calderwood's reading draws upon Dunn's to suggest that the boy's "particularity" is annulled by his status as a symbol, a sign of Titania's subjection to Oberon (Calderwood 1991). Raman comments that these ingenious readings ignore the Indianness of the boy and hence, "Through the inter-pretative gesture which opens the text to the play of difference – the emphasis on the centrality of the absent Indian boy – these interpretations silently substitute for him a universalised Oedipal subject" (Raman forthcoming: 298). Raman himself suggests, instead, that "Shakespeare's (non) representation of the Indian Boy depends upon the historically specific practices and discourses of colonialism, through which England finally comes into actual contact with 'India'" (Raman forthcoming: 293).

In this essay, I want to probe some aspects of these practices and discourses, and their organic relationship to discourses about gender and the family in Europe. High-lighting gender relations in *A Dream*, I will suggest, need not obscure the colonial theme; we can read the apparent telescoping of the latter into the narrative of patri-archal control to amplify their historic interrelation.

It is now a critical commonplace that discourses, ideologies, and practices about gender cannot be analyzed in isolation from those about "race" and cultural difference because

> there are no unraced gendered persons, nor ungendered raced persons. Racing and gen-dering are social and political processes of consigning bodies to social categories and thus rendering them into political, economic, sexual and residential positions. "Ren-dering" here means both "representing" and "boiling down"; the structures have the effect of radically simplifying identities, of making them comprehensible by selectively identifying certain physical or historical facts about those bodies and making them sig-nificant. (Bradford and Sartwell 1997: 191–2)

A number of critics have analyzed the complex ways in which ideologies of gender during the early modern period were "colored": blackness and whiteness, Kim Hall

(1995) shows, marked deviant or ideal women as much as foreign or domestic peoples. In *A Midsummer Night's Dream*, as in other contemporary plays, the racial inflections of the vocabulary of desire are often most visible in moments of sexual rejection: Lysander, in turning away from Hermia, calls her an "Ethiope" and "tawny Tartar" (III.ii.257, 263) and announces his love for Helena by asking "Who will not change a raven for a dove?" (II.ii.120). What distinguishes the two birds is not just their color but also their temperaments – ravens being quarrelsome and doves meek. Female intractability, foreignness, and rebelliousness are expressed in terms of one another, but they do not betoken simply threatening and undesirable terrains which must be rejected or outlawed. Simultaneously they also provide opportunities for conquest and for the exercise of sexual, colonial, or class power. Danger and desire are thus enmeshed in the discursive overlap of femininity and otherness.

Early modern discourses, it has been often remarked, represent colonial wealth and lands in terms of female bodies and their sexual promise and vice versa. Hence we have the lover of Donne's "Love's Progress" "sailing towards her India" (Donne 1985: 181) and Shakespeare's Troilus becomes "the merchant" yearning for the unattainable Cressida whose "bed is India, and there she lies, a pearl" (*Troilus and Cressida*, I.i.100). Sir Toby compliments Maria by calling her "my metal of India" (*Twelfth Night*, II.v.12) and in *Henry VIII*, the queen is compared to "all the Indies" (IV.i.45). These are but scattered instances of a pattern whose other side is the representation of conquered territories as sexualized women, analyzed in the early modern context by Peter Hulme, and subsequently by Louis Montrose and others (Hulme 1985; Montrose 1993). Guiana, in Ralegh's oft-cited metaphor, "is a countrey that hath yet her Maydenhead," America is a naked woman waiting to be "dis-covered" by Vespucci, and Constantinople is a "Painted Whore" (Ralegh 1904: 428; Hulme 1985: 17; Lithgow 1632: 84). But, as I have argued elsewhere, there are variations within this pattern so that not all alien women are represented as naked, savage, innocent, or rapable: in travel narratives Indian and Turkish women, as opposed to African or American ones, are in fact pictured as veiled, cloistered, luxurious, fecund bodies harboring secrets (Loomba 1996). Of course, these cloistered bodies "invite" penetration and possession as much as do the naked ones, but they generate different discourses about desire and danger. Their possession and conquest involves guile, romance, marriage, and consent rather than force, violence, and rape. Such discursive distinctions are of course never absolute, so that in the theater aspects of both these discourses may feed into the creation of a dark, or alien woman; moreover, their blurring reminds us of the deeper connections between violence and consent, force and seduction.

Given the overlaps between vocabularies of gender, wealth, and colonial conquest, a parental struggle for the control of the Indian boy surely has colonial undertones. Mapping colonial and gender structures onto one another, critics have increasingly interpreted the struggle between Oberon and Titania over the Indian boy as "a gendered contest over the proper control of foreign merchandise," as "a progression both patriarchal and imperial" (Hall 1995: 85; Parker 1996: 65). The patriarchal will is thus also an imperialist will. An oft-cited passage in which Titania explains why she will not relinquish the boy to Oberon certainly marks the boy as the human or material traffic of "India":

> His mother was a vot'ress of my order,
> And in the spicèd Indian air by night
> Full often hath she gossiped by my side,
> And sat with me on Neptune's yellow sands,
> Marking th'embarkèd traders on the flood,
> When we have laughed to see the sails conceive
> And grow big-bellied with the wanton wind,
> Which she with pretty and with swimming gait
> Following, her womb then rich with my young squire,
> Would imitate, and sail upon the land
> To fetch me trifles, and return again
> As from a voyage, rich with merchandise.
> But she, being mortal, of that boy did die;
> And for her sake do I rear up her boy;
> And for her sake I will not part with him.
>
> (II.i.123–37)

In this passage, the Indian woman's pregnant womb is obviously analogous to the fullness of trading ships, the boy and merchandise being the "riches" carried by each of them. Apart from the older fables of Indian riches, more recent accounts such as Richard Eden's *A treatyse of the newe India*, which appeared in 1553 and inaugurated English travel collections, were obsessed with India's "great abundance of gold, precious stones and spices" (Arber 1885: 7). Contemporary travelogues dwelt lovingly on the details of voyages pregnant with Eastern riches and on ships full with merchandise. The Italian traveler Cesare Federici's *Voyage and travaile . . . into the East India*, is awe-struck by the incredible trade at the Indian port of Cambaietta:

for in the time of every new Moone and every full Moone, the small barkes (innumerable) come in and out, for at those times of the Moone the tides and waters are higher than at other times they be. These barkes be laden with all sorts of spices, with silke of China, with Sandols, with Elephants teeth, Velvets of Vercini, great quantities of Pannina, which commeth from Mecca, Chickinos which be pieces of gold worth seven shillings a piece sterling, with money, and with divers sorts of other merchandise. Also these barkes lade out, as it were, an infinite quantitie of cloth made of Bumbast of all sortes, as white stamped and painted, with great quantitie of Indico, dried ginger and conserved, Myrobolans drie and condite, Boraso in paste, great store of Sugar, great quantitie of Cotton, abundance of Opium, Assa Fetida, Puchio, with many other sorts of drugges, Turbants made in Diu, great stones like to Corneolaes, Granats, Agats, Diaspry, Calicidonii, Hematists and some kinde of naturall Diamonds. (Federici 1905: 90)[3]

But how might the transfer of the boy from Titania to Oberon indicate a *colonial* transfer of goods? By what process does Titania become identified with the East and

Oberon with the West? Shakespeare's fairies are, of course, no longer as English as they once appeared. In 1914, in Granville Barker's production of the play, they were dressed in "exotic costumes." At that time, *The Times* wondered, "Is it Titania's Indian Boy that has given Mr. Barker his notion of Orientalizing Shakespeare's fairies?" (quoted in Shakespeare 1994: 26).[4] Recent criticism has established Oberon's literary lineage as vaguely Oriental – in the thirteenth-century *Book of Duke Huon of Bourdeaux* translated by Lord Berners in the sixteenth, Oberon claims to be both the son of Caesar and a brother to the King of Egypt (a combination that hints at Caesar's celebrated liaison with Cleopatra). Margo Hendricks traces his Eastern associations in Spenser's *Fairie Queene* as well as in Robert Greene's *The Scottish Historie of James the Fourth*, concluding that "By the time Shakespeare comes to write *A Midsummer Night's Dream*, images of an Asiatic or 'Indian' Oberon are fairly well established as part of the literary imaginings of the fairy king" (Hendricks 1996: 48). More tangentially, Chaucer's *The Knight's Tale*, from where Shakespeare drew upon elements of the Theseus–Hippolyta pairing, also features the "grete Emetreus, the kynge of Inde," richly clothed and accompanied by "ful many a tame leon and leopart" (Chaucer 1974: 2156–86).

Within *A Dream*, *both* Titania and Oberon are associated with India: she asks him why he has "Come from the farthest step of India" (II.i.69), and in the passage already quoted above, she outlines her own Indian associations. We may be tempted to conclude that Oberon is closer to an Eastern Sultan than a Western patriarch. Contemporary accounts of Oriental Sultans, after all, dwelt upon their jealous power over their wives, but also their distorted paternalism – the despot abandoned his own sons to women and eunuchs, but adopted alien children "either paid in tribute or carried off in war, orphans with no natural or cultural roots, no memory . . . Being nothing to start with, they can become the neutral – but technically qualified – supports of the signifier which will later make them agas, pashas and viziers" (Grosrichard 1998: 132). Montrose rightly points out that Titania's struggle with Oberon has geographical undertones: "The Faery Queen speaks of a mortal mother from the east; the Faery King speaks of an invulnerable virgin from the west. Their memories express two myths of origin: Titania provides a genealogy for the changeling and an explanation of why she will not part with him; Oberon provides an aetiology of the metamorphosed flower that he will use to make her part with him" (Montrose 1996: 170). Titania certainly claims a special bond with "mortal mother from the east," with whom she "gossiped" and "laughed," but does this evocation imply a sisterhood between equals? The dead woman was a "vot'ress of my order," Titania says. "Votaress" implies both a hierarchical relationship of devotee to saint and a sharing, as in a sisterhood of nuns. Kim Hall interprets the Indian woman as Titania's "waiting maid" (1995: 85). Moreover, can we rely on Titania's version of events? After all, Puck tells us that the boy was "stol'n from an Indian king" (II.i.22).

Did Titania steal the boy from a royal Indian father? Did she do so in order to keep faith with the mother, or because (for her as well as Oberon) the child is a prized commodity, the ultimate gift, a culmination of the "trifles" his mother used to "fetch" her? In many contemporary narratives the luxuries of the land become "devilish devices" for Indian women to pamper their own luxuriousness: they consume "Bette-les, Arrequas, and chalk, and . . . handfuls of Cloves, Pepper, Ginger and a baked kind of meat called Chachunde, which is mixed . . . of all kindes of Spices and hearbs and such like meates, all to increase their leachery" (Linschoten 1885: 214). In *A Dream*, however, the Indian mother presents the "trifles" of the land to Titania, thus entitling the latter to the fruits of her womb. Discourses about the New World and Africa rou-tinely portray the natives as unable to comprehend the value of the riches that sur-round them, so they gift these valuables to Europeans, or trade them for worthless baubles. In narratives pertaining to the East, however, the situation was to be reversed: European ambassadors to India and Turkey were frustrated by the fact that *they* had to become gift-givers in order to extract trading privileges, and by the disdain with which their gifts were often received. While on the whole I would agree with Raman that this play evokes India rather than America or Africa (forthcoming: 330), at several crucial points in the play these distinctions cannot be maintained. The Indian boy simultaneously evokes the merchandise of the East, the riches plundered from the Americas, and the human traffic of Africa and the Indies. Although England's involvement in the slave trade was still recent and patchy, dark-skinned slaves had been highly visible in Europe for many decades – as early as 1514, for example, Indian slaves had caused a sensation when they were paraded before the Pope in Rome along with leopards, horses, a panther, parrots, and a trained ele-phant (Lach 1965: 167). Finally, Titania the Fairy Queen also evokes Elizabeth the mortal Queen, in whose name imperial plunder as well as trade was undertaken in both "Indias." Samuel Purchas hails Elizabeth as the "Mother to so many famous Expe-ditions in and about the World and . . . the Mother of Indian Trafficke" (Purchas 1617: Book V, 549). These textual ambiguities and historical complexities make it difficult to read Oberon and Titania's tussle over the Indian boy as one in which the patriarch and the colonialist are straightforwardly or neatly mapped onto each other.

However, Titania's bond with the Indian woman need not be romanticized into an equitable sisterhood in order to draw some distinction between her attitude to the child and that of Oberon. Titania wants to "rear" the "loved boy," not just own him. Puck tells us that she "crowns him with flowers, and makes him all her joy" (a descrip-tion which immediately positions the child as Oberon's rival and anticipates Titania's treatment of Bottom). By contrast, Oberon desires the child in order to make him part of his train, to have as "my henchman." If the boy is colonial property for *both* of them (a reading that would also demand that we read India as the playground of these fairies rather than their native land), Oberon and Titania are positioned differ-ently in relation to this property, although both are possessive about it. In hindsight, we can, if we choose, read into them the different positions occupied by European men and women in the business of empire. The world of women and the colonial world intersect to fragment each other. The crucial point is that Titania must evoke a bond with the Indian mother in order to challenge Oberon, and Oberon must wrest her property, however it was acquired, in order to establish his control. According to Margaret Hunt:

> The classical, Renaissance, and early modern antecedents of what came to constitute a modern "identity" included a self-affirming public voice (often called "citizenship"), an identification with a vocation (e.g., he is a carpenter), personal autonomy, standardly defined in the Renaissance and early modern period as the ability to deploy the labor, reproductive and otherwise, of inferior family members . . . and some measure of bodily self-control, a central attribute of which was the ability to initiate and to definitively refuse sexual intercourse. All these were difficult or impossible to attain for married women, slaves, or servants. (Hunt 1994: 364)

The tussle over the boy demonstrates that, as a married woman, Titania cannot easily assume sovereignty either over her own body or the labor of others.

But why does the tussle over colonial goods have to be represented in terms of a gendered, familial battle? What is at stake in this displacement, and in the invisibility of the Indian boy? The "racial" theme in some of Shakespeare's other plays such as *Othello* or *Antony and Cleopatra* seems plainly visible, even though it had been obscured by a long critical tradition; in the case of *A Dream*, the play seems to generate such obscurity. In the context of *The Tempest*, Thomas Cartelli has suggested the play is "a responsible party to its successive readings and rewritings insofar as it has made seminal contributions to the development of the colonialist ideology through which it is read" (Cartelli 1987: 100–1). Shankar Raman makes an analogous point in relation to *A Dream*, and suggests that "If Shakespeare's play responds so well to psychoanalytic interpretation, this affinity arguably registers the extent to which the theatrical text helped shape those historical conditions underlying the emergence of the psychoanalytic paradigm" (Raman forthcoming: 306). In other words, Shakespeare's play participates in and shapes the emergence of the nuclear family in Europe, and the "normalization" of that historically and culturally specific sex/gender system which psychoanalysis was to later assume as a transhistorical and cross-cultural norm.

Pointing to the simultaneous resonance and dissonance between psychoanalysis and Renaissance culture, Stephen Greenblatt writes that Renaissance images and texts seem "to invite, even to demand, a psychoanalytic approach" and yet turn out "to baffle or elude that approach" (Greenblatt 1990: 131). Exploring this dynamic via the sixteenth-century story of the French peasant Martin Guerre's impersonation by one Arnaud du Tilh and the ensuing trials to determine the "real" Martin, Greenblatt observes that Martin's body figures in the trials, "not as the inalienable phenomenological base of his psychic history," but "rather as a collection of attributes – lines, curves, volumes (that is scars, features, clothing, shoe size, and so on) – that could be held up against anyone who claimed the name and property of Martin Guerre" (Greenblatt 1990: 136–7). The intense exploration, in Shakespeare's work and other dramas of the time, of impersonation and identity revolves around the relationship between property and personhood:

In Renaissance drama, as in the case of Martin Guerre, the traditional linkages between body, property, and name are called into question; looking back upon the theatrical and judicial spectacle, one can glimpse the early stages of the slow, momentous transformation of the middle term from "property" to "psyche." But that transformation had by no means already occurred; it was on the contrary the result (not yet perfectly realized in our own time) of a prolonged series of actions and transactions. The consequence, I think, is that psychoanalytic interpretation seems to follow upon rather than to explain Renaissance texts. If psychoanalysis was, in effect, made possible by (among other things) the legal and literary proceedings of the sixteenth and seventeenth centuries, then its interpretative practice is not irrelevant to those proceedings, nor is it exactly an anachronism. But psychoanalytic interpretation is causally belated, even as it is causally linked: hence the curious effect of a discourse that functions *as if* the psychological categories it invokes were not only simultaneous with but even prior to and themselves the causes of the very phenomena of which in actual fact they were the results. (Greenblatt 1990: 141–2)

Greenblatt's conclusion that "property may be closer to the wellsprings of the Shakespearean conception of identity than we imagine" (1990: 141) helps us unravel what is at stake in the struggle over the Indian boy. The ownership of the boy is crucial to the identities of Oberon and Titania – it makes them who they are. Patriarchal power and female rebellion, matrimonial relations as well as power in the fairy world, will be established through possession of the boy. More recently, Margreta de Grazia has also suggested, via a discussion of *King Lear*, an interrelation between "being and having" in early modern culture (de Grazia 1996: 21). Greenblatt points out that in the discourse of psychoanalysis "property" becomes replaced by the term "psyche" so that identity is understood not as shaped by what one owns, but rather by a prior subjectivity. I will return to the relationship between the discourses of the psyche and of the commodity; for now, I want to point out that the relationship between property and personhood, ownership and identity, is itself intensely gendered. In psychoanalytic discourse, the psyche not only replaces property as the wellspring of identity, but is also understood as simultaneously formed and destabilized in the gendered body and in the power relations of the patriarchal family. Therefore the process Greenblatt discusses is also the one in which the "modern" family is born and retrospectively projected, like the psyche, as the cause rather than the effect of certain historical processes.

The specter of overpowering mothers and wives is not generated by a paranoid or anxious transhistorical male psyche but is, in part, a response to the historical transformation of gender roles during the period. Lisa Jardine (1989) connects patriarchal anxieties in the Renaissance drama and culture to the threat posed by women's bid to own and inherit property. The ideologies of women's subjection fluctuate in tandem with the social transformations and changes ushered in by what is retrospectively understood as the transition from feudalism to capitalism. The new ideal of the companionate, contractual marriage is born in the crucible of the new ideologies of the marketplace. The ideal of the romantic marriage and coupledom was to suggest over the next few centuries that women's increasing isolation from the production process and from the ownership of property was a "willing" retreat, a function of their inner essence as women and their domestic desires, a result of "femininity," rather than the cause. A similar transposition of cause and effect was later visible in psychoanalytic readings of colonialism. Octavio Mannoni (1956) famously appropriated Shakespeare to suggest that colonialism was the result of an unresolved "dependence complex" of "backward" peoples. Frantz Fanon challenged Mannoni by arguing that colonialism *generated* these complexes rather than being produced by them. It is not particular kinds of subjects that produce the hierarchical relations between them; rather social inequalities shape specific kinds of subjectivities and in fact annihilate some subjectivities into "a crushing objecthood" (Fanon 1967: 143). Thus the recovery of both women and colonized people as subjects paradoxically involves highlighting their historical status as objects.

Fanon's critique of colonialism resulted in his rewriting of psychoanalytic paradigms, including its discourse of familial relations. He suggested that the Oedipus complex and the familial structure in which it is housed is incapable of describing the psychic structures of colonized subjects, simply because the larger social structure in which the colonized family is placed warps the gender and other relations within the latter. The power of the father within the colonized family is not amplified and confirmed by society in general, as it is for the white family, but diminished by the colonial hierarchy and the supreme power of the white man. Hence under colonialism the law of the Father becomes the law of the White Man. The colonized subject is condemned by psychoanalysis to be the underdeveloped neurotic, the perpetual "boy" in the saga of human development. Such an insight cautions us against reading the Indian boy of *A Midsummer Night's Dream* as simply the Oedipal child of Oberon and Titania. Their status as parents can only be established by the erasure of another family, here represented in the memory of the boy's mother (the father is in fact erased altogether). The two families are not identical with one another: for the "family" of the colonizer to come into being, the "family" of the colonized must be represented as non-functional or fractured. Indeed, one might argue that Oberon and Titania's "companionate" relation, in which Titania finally (willingly) gives up her prize possession, is a scenario enabled only by the logic of such uneven development of the family. In this play, that is, the ideology of the family smoothes over the extraction of wealth or bodies from the Indies. If there is any discomfort within the play about such extraction of "colonial value," it is assuaged by the resolutions provided by patriarchal, companionate love.

Feminist critics have argued for some time now that early modern English theater, including that of Shakespeare, presents the companionate marriage, the nuclear family, and the heterosexual couple in terms that romanticize as well as normalize them. Others suggest that the drama allows us to glimpse the coercions and inequities of these new families, the violence by which they are legitimized, the fault-lines, or seams of their formations.[5] In either case, the critic must often amplify what the plays seem to relegate to their margins. In order to uncover the discourse of class in *A*

Dream, for example, Patricia Parker traces the "links between the chronic misplacing and misjoining of words or sentences associated with the so-called 'rude mechanicals,' Bottom and his company, and the larger issue of joining in this 'marriage' play, including the proper joining of 'Jack' and 'Jill' that produces its culminating (and consummating) close" (1996: 50). If *A Midsummer Night's Dream*'s participation in an emergent discourse of the patriarchal nuclear family seems to obfuscate its colonial investments, we can examine the terms of this participation by identifying how "India" might have contributed to the emergence of such a family norm in early modern Europe.

II

If for Freud, "the sexual life of grown-up women . . . is still a 'dark continent'" (1947: 34), in *A Midsummer Night's Dream* the dark continents outside Europe shape the play's libidinous and unruly grown-up women, as the representations of Titania, Hippolyta, and Hermia make clear. Titania's intimacy with the Indian boy's mother highlights the contrast between that female-centered world from which fathers are excluded and an Athens in which, as Montrose points out, fathers have absolute right over their daughters and are seen to be the sole creators of their children. Within Athens itself, Hippolyta the Amazonian Queen serves as a reminder of a world where mothers reign supreme and women establish successful communities by banishing men. Athenian patriarchal structures in the play are established in implicit opposition to this specter of female and racial otherness. Laura Brown suggests that "gender represents a category of difference constituted primarily within the geographic purview of the dominant culture, while race in this period remains mainly extrinsic, geographically foreign, a category of difference defined as an external object" (Brown 1994: 118). The figures of unruly women in this play and in the culture at large, and most especially the specter of the Amazon, suggest that the two categories always coalesce, that female unruliness is always another country. Conversely, the very concept of "race," however we may define this term at any given place and time, hinges upon the policing of sexual behavior and gender roles, since sexual contact across its boundaries threatens to "pollute" any community. The more female deviance is constructed as foreign, the greater the fear that it actually lurks at home.

The location of the Amazons constantly shifted in tandem with the horizons of the known world. These "mankynde women" were placed by classical writers "anywhere between Germany and India" (Wright 1940: 434). William Painter's *The Palace of Pleasure* had suggested that they "occupied and enjoyed a great part of Asia" (Painter 1890: 160). Marco Polo located them in Africa, Columbus in the New World, and while these new locales were favored by early modern writers, the earlier Asian tradition did not die out. Several writers continued to place them, *or women like them*, in India. Father Monserrate, a Jesuit priest who visited the court of the Moghul emperor Akbar in 1580, reports a town called Landighana, i.e. the house of women; and stories are told about its ancient inhabitants, resembling those which are told about the Amazons. It is said that the stronghold used to be occupied by women, who waged war on the surrounding tribes. In order to keep up the numbers they attacked and carried off travellers. Boy babies were killed or exposed: girls were brought up and trained to arms. They were finally conquered and driven out, but they have left their name in these ruins. In reality, fables apart, a band of wicked women must have lived there and given their name to the place: as sometimes happens with fugitive slaves. (Monserrate 1922: 146)

Thus, as Monserrate is quick to grasp, Amazonian tales are really stories about female unruliness, an unruliness that is "driven out" to the conceptual and geographic boundaries of the normative community. As Laura Brown puts it, Renaissance chroniclers "availed themselves of a version of the figure that has represented racial difference for over two millennia, locating and shaping that historically efficacious figure according to the new requirements of the expansionist ideology of Western European imperialism" (Brown 1994: 131). Like wild men, however, Amazons do not quietly inhabit their marginalities but threaten to spill out and aggressively overpower the world of (European) men.

Amazons appropriate both the military and the sexual prerogatives of men, warring with as well as seducing them. Amazonian seductions are not, as so many seduction stories are, tales of female surrender; instead they feature a desire to reproduce the Amazonian community, as in the following story narrated by Montaigne:

When Alexander was passing through Hyracania, Thalestris, queen of the Amazons, came to find him with three hundred warriors of her own sex, well mounted and well armed, having left the remainder of a large army that was following her beyond the neighboring mountains; and said to him, *right out loud and in public*, that the fame of his victories and valor had brought her there to see him, to offer him her resources and power in support of his enterprises; and that finding him so handsome, young and vigorous, she, *who was perfect in all his qualities*, advised him that they should lie together, so that of the most valiant woman in the world and the most valiant man who was then alive, there should be born something great and rare for the future. (Montaigne 1965: 675).

Such initiative directly threatens the ideology of feminine passivity, expressed by Helena in *A Midsummer Night's Dream*:

> We cannot fight for love as men may do
> We should be wooed, and were not made to woo.
> (II.i.240)

Amazons, moreover, mock the sexual initiative of men. In his only other reference to Amazons, Montaigne writes:

For the queen of the Amazons replied to the Scythian who was inviting her to make love: *"The lame man does it best!"* In that feminine commonwealth, to escape the domination of the males, they crippled them from childhood – arms, legs, and other parts that gave men an advantage over them – and made use of them only for the purpose for which we make use of women over here. (Montaigne 1965: 791)

Stories of Amazonian cruelty, Montaigne suggests, mirror the real crippling of women in patriarchal Europe. Images of powerful matriarchies are often fantasies produced by patriarchal cultures, a means of containing real-life rebellion by women: an insight Montrose uses to explain the contest of both these visions within *A Midsummer Night's Dream*. Theseus's mastery over Hippolyta not only counters stories of Amazonian power over men, but also inverts and contains popular tales of European women being abducted by foreign tyrants.

The specter of Amazons was, of course, pervasive in misogynist English writings during the early modern period – the title of John Knox's "The First Blast of the Trumpet Against the Monstrous Regiment of Women" echoes descriptions of Amazons as this "monstrous sexe," and Knox describes an England ruled by a Queen as "a worlde . . . transformed into Amazones" (Knox 1966: 375). As several critics have discussed, Elizabeth and her courtiers flirted with descriptions of her as an Amazon, but ultimately adopted a chaster iconography for the Virgin Queen (Schleiner 1978; Montrose 1986: 78–9). Not only was the unbridled sexuality and the foreignness of Amazons difficult to reconcile to the virginity and Englishness of the Queen, but Amazons were entire *communities* of women who formed alternative forms of governance. Hence their iconography was of limited use to a woman who wanted to project herself as an exception to her sex, and as a leader of men. Amazons were not just suffocating mothers who could subvert the patriarchal family, but "foreign" women who had created another kind of family and another kind of nation altogether. As I will show shortly, their representations were not simply fantastic projections of masculine fears, but shaped by early modern European contact with alternative forms of governance and gender roles.

Both rampant female sexuality and formidable but alien social structures were recurrent features of descriptions of foreign, especially Eastern, lands. It has often been noted that non-European women (and men) were routinely described as having uncontrollable sexual appetites, often directed at members of their own sex. But accounts of the East are also obsessed with the minutiae of government and military as well as social organization. The power of the powerful empires in both North and South India, Turkey, and Persia is attributed to their tight and structured hierarchies in public as well as private spheres (Knolles 1610; Roe 1926). The patriarchal organization of these worlds and the absolute power of men over women is castigated as barbaric, but simultaneously both these features are also regarded as admirable and worthy of emulation at home. If the Turkish patriarchal "order were in England, women would be more dutiful and faithful to their husbands than they are," comments one observer, "for there if a man have a hundred women, if any one of them prostitute herself to any man but her own husband, he hath authority to bind her, hands and feet, and cast her unto a river, with a stone about her neck, and drown her" (Biddulph 1745: 792). Similarly, widow immolation (which is commented upon by nearly every visitor to India), arouses a fascinated horror as well as frank admiration: in the mid-seventeenth century, Richard Head was to

> wish for the like custom enjoyn'd on all married English females (for the love I bear to my own Country) which I am confident would prevent the destruction of thousands of well-meaning Christians, which receive a full stop in the full career of their lives, either by corrupting their bodies by venomous medicaments . . . or else his body is poysoned by sucking or drawing contagious fumes which proceed from her contaminated body, occasion'd by using pluralities for her venereal satisfaction. (Head 1666: 92)

The idea that widow immolation was devised to contain deceitful women circulated widely in Europe.

In these narratives, women constantly deceive their husbands to satisfy their sexual appetites, which are often directed at members of their own gender. In Leo Africanus's by now oft-cited tale, women in Fez pretend to be sick so that they can call upon the ostensibly medical but actually sexual services of certain "Witches" (Africanus 1905: 435). In Turkish harems women are "punished for their faults very severely" and their deviousness is anticipated by their keepers:

> Now it is not lawfull for any one to bring ought unto them, with which they may commit the deeds of beastly uncleannesse; so that if they have a will to eat Cucumbers, Gourds, or such like meates, they are sent in unto them sliced, to deprive them of the meanes of playing the wantons; for, they all being young, lustie, and lascivious Wenches, and wanting the societie of Men (which would better instruct them) are doubtlesse of themselves inclined to that which is naught and will be possest with unchast thoughts. (Withers 1905: 347)

Even outside the harem, women are veiled and segregated from men, but take every opportunity to deceive their husbands, even on the pain of being "put away," "being extraordinarily given to the sport, and very dishonest" (Withers 1905: 406). Duplicity is not a prerogative of non-European women, however, but a universal attribute of femininity. In Linschoten's account of Goa, for example, all women, whether they be Portuguese, Mestizo, or "Indian Christian," are closely guarded. The men are "very jealous" because all these women

> are very luxurious and unchaste, for there are verie few among them, although they bee married, but they have besides their husbands one or two of those that are called souldiers, with whom they take their pleasures. . . . They have likewise a herbe called Deutroa, which beareth a seed, whereof bruising out the sap, they . . . give it to their husbands, eythere in meate or drinke, and presently therewith, the man is as though hee were halfe out of his wits, and without feeling, or els drunke, . . . laugh, and

sometimes it taketh him sleeping . . . like a dead man, so that in his presence they may doe what they will, and take their pleasure with their friends, and the husband never know of it. (Linschoten 1885: 208–10)

In *A Midsummer Night's Dream*, the situation is reversed – Oberon uses the juice of "a little western flower" to trick Titania, but he disciplines her by a manipulated arousal of her sexual appetite, so that even her desire is not her own. Europeans were fascinated by stories in which the sexuality of their women was manipulated by Eastern men, such as those of "wife-exchange" or deflowering practices in India and other countries. Such stories were always cited as instances of absolute male control of female sexuality, even when they actually signified the opposite. For example, Ludovico di Varthema (or Lewes Vertomannus/Barthema, as he became in English translations), a Bolognese who wrote one of the earliest accounts of India to circulate in England, mentions the deflowering of the King of Calicut's "wyfe" by one of the priests, who is paid "fiftie pieces of gold" for the purpose, and later a similar deflowering of the Queen in "Tarnassarie."[6] All European accounts of "the land of Malabar" (the same region where Rushdie, four centuries later, opens his *The Moor's Last Sigh*) circulating at that time were fascinated by the fact that royal women were deflowered at the king's command by perfect strangers (white men or priests, according to Varthema).[7] In reality, this deflowering was part of a larger system of matrilineal descent. Women were deflowered by outsiders, who left after the ceremony so that subsequently women could choose their own (usually temporary) mates from their own community. Royal women lived independently, were never in fact married to the king, and were free to take other lovers. The sons did not inherit the father's property or the kingdom; rather the father passed it on to his sister's sons. The practice aroused widespread horror, the royal women were seen as "free and dissolute in their manners, choosing paramours as they please" (Castanheda, quoted in Lach 1965: 355). In another passage, Varthema describes how husbands bring their friends to their wives, saying, "Woman, this man shall hereafter be thy husband," but a few sentences later admits that often "one woman is maryed to seven husbands" (Eden 1577: 390). Thus the specter of female choice was appropriated by European commentators to suggest absolute male dominance.

Of course, Indian matrilineal communities were not free of patriarchal control; nevertheless, Europeans were shocked by them and their narratives attempted to shape them into forms of the nuclear patriarchal structures. Much later, British colonialists were to strenuously interfere with and attempt to "reform" these kinship and inheritance patterns in Malabar, and to domesticate them into patriarchal monogamy (Arunima 1996). On the other hand, European commentators detected a latent matriarchy in the harems of the Mogul or Turkish emperors. The Sultan subjects a hundred women to his will, and yet

All intreagues of State are carry'd on, War and peace are made, Vice-Royships and Governments obtain'd by their Means: In fine, they have the principal distribution of Court

Favors . . . They are properly speaking the Cabinet Council of the Mogol . . . what seems most extraordinary is his always being guarded within the Seraglio by a Company of Tartarian Viragos, consisting of a Hundred in Number, arm'd with Bows and Arrows, a Poynard and a Cimeter. Madam their Captian has the Rank and Pay of an *Ombra* of the Army. (F. F. Catrou, quoted in Teltscher 1995: 45)

Thus the specter of Amazonian power lurks wherever women congregate, even within an institution which locks them from public life. Inside the seraglio, underneath the apparent order and patriarchy,

the difference between the sexes evaporates, . . . the hierarchical relations between them go so far as to be inverted, and . . . the master, far from being the all-powerful male that he seems, is only a name masking a contemptible effeminate creature reduced to nothing at the bosom of his mother, who alone – a dagger at her belt, surrounded by her female janissaries and her eunuchs – holds in her hands all the threads of the Empire. (Grosrichard 1998: 178)

Accounts of Eastern domestic and political organization, then, as much as older tales of Amazons, do not merely develop racial or ethnographic taxonomies but ideologies about gender, sexuality, family as well as the public sphere. Widow immolation, polygamy, matriliny, harems all become ways of negotiating domestic ideologies about gender as well as of course establishing a difference between Europe and non-European worlds. The increasing proliferation of such narratives at a time when the family was being streamlined into its "modern" form in Europe is not accidental. Alain Grosrichard comments that the European ideal of the couple was "invented" by Rousseau against the specter of the seraglio, with its multiple partners, covert homosexuality, and distortions of patriliny (Grosrichard 1998: 179). But, as mentioned earlier, early modern scholars trace the ideology of the couple to an earlier period, and in fact suggest that Shakespeare's plays contributed to its legitimization. By the time of *A Dream*, stories like Africanus's narrative of same-sex eroticism were used by European doctors such as Ambroise Paré to construct and regulate female sexualities and bodies at home – whereas Africanus's homoerotic women did not have any physical irregularity, Paré attributed tribadism to women with an "extremely large monstrous thing that occurs in the labia" and recommended clitoridectomy to keep control of it (Park 1997). Like the Amazons, tribades were routinely banished to the margins of Europe, but then brought home to be controlled and policed, as Valerie Traub (1995) has discussed in some detail. Traub suggests that "the early modern 'tribade' is not a creature of exotic origins imported to Europe by travel writers, but rather is the discursive effect of 1) travel writers' transposition of ancient and medieval categories of intelligibility onto foreign 'matters,' and 2) anatomy's appropriation and refashioning of these 'travel maps.'" (Traub 1995: 97). However, I would like to suggest that accounts of foreign sexual "deviance" were not simply fabrications or refashionings of older European materials. Observations of "the East" are certainly filtered through a Eurocentric lens, but they are also manufactured out of observations of difference that contribute to the making of the lens itself. The relationship between the transformation of domestic ideologies and practices and the distortion of the non-European world is thus a dialectic, symbiotic one.

Critics have pointed out that the heterosexual couplings of *A Midsummer Night's Dream* are achieved by evoking and then containing three images of female bonding and love. The first is that of female communities of the Amazons, the second Titania's shared moments with and loyalty to the Indian mother, and third, most graphic and explicit, Helena's passionate reminder to Hermia about

> . . . all the counsel that we two have shared –
> The sisters' vows, the hours that we have spent
> When we have chid the hasty-footed time
> For parting us – O, is all quite forgot?
> We, Hermia, like two artificial gods
> Have with our needles created both one flower,
> Both on one sampler, sitting on one cushion,
> Both warbling of one song, both in one key,
> As if our hands, our sides, voices, and minds
> Had been incorporate. So we grew together,
> Like to a double cherry: seeming parted,
> But yet an union in partition,
> Two lovely berries moulded on one stem.
> So, with two seeming bodies but one heart,
> Two of the first – like coats in heraldry,
> Due but to one and crownèd with one crest.
> And will you rend our ancient love asunder,
> To join with men in scorning your poor friend?
> (III.ii.198–216)

If, on the one hand, Egeus's "ancient privilege" of patriarchal ownership must be rewritten, then, on the other, this "ancient love" between Hermia and Helena needs also to be set aside to make way for the new coupledom. Both patriarchal coercion and female (always potentially Sapphic) bonding were also, I have suggested, understood to be features of Oriental families, and these families were conjured up within European narratives in part to assist in the formation of an alternative family structure shaped by the ideological imperatives of both mercantilism and colonialism. Thus the "modern" Western family was established by othering, but also appropriating and transforming *both* the dynastic marriages and family structures of a feudal past, and the domestic institutions of the non-Western world.

"At home," writes Montrose, "personal rivalries and political dissent might be sublimated into the strategically neo-feudal chivalric pageantry of courtly culture; abroad, they might be expressed in warfare and colonial enterprise and displaced into the conquest of lands that had yet their maidenheads" (1996: 156). But what of lands that did not have their maidenheads, that were not waiting to be dis-covered by the

English adventurer, and that required not "heroism" but supplication, not gallantry but calculation? In the New World, the violent possession of a naked female body was an apt metaphor for the colonial plunder of the lands, but in Turkey, India, and the Moluccas, I have suggested, colonialism wore a mercantilist garb, and both land and women were often represented in terms of a hidden, veiled, and cloistered fecundity inaccessible to the European traveler-merchant, and to be negotiated through cunning and supplication (Loomba 1996). The relationship between European and native lands and peoples was recast in terms made available from a discourse of trade. As Lewis Roberts's *The Treasure of Trafficke* (1641) was to argue a half-century later:

> It is not our conquests but our commerce, it is not our swords but our sayles that first spread the English name in Barbary, and thence came into Turkey, Armenia, Moscovia, Arabia, Persia, India, China and indeed over and about the world. (Quoted in Ramsay 1957: 1)

In a whole slew of dramatic representations, rich "Indian Queens" willingly enter into romantic liaisons with European merchants and heroes, and submission is coded as love and marriage rather than rape.[8] This is not to suggest that mercantilism is free of violence, or that it does not encode a will to power, only that its ideologies depend far more on the fiction of reciprocity than do those of a colonialism based on settlement. Varthema claims that "the women of Arabia are greatly in loue with whyte men"; in prison, he pretends to be mad and tears off his clothes, and the queen takes great pleasure in seeing him naked, she spends "the whole day in beholding me," and then helps him escape the prison. According to Linschoten, if an Indian woman "chance to have a Portingal or a white man to her lover, she is so proud, that she thinketh no woman comparable unto her" (Linschoten 1885: 212). The organ maker Thomas Dallam, sent to the Turkish court, describes the Sultana's "greate lykinge" for the English Ambassador's secretary, and her soliciting "his private companye" (Dallam 1893: 63). In many English plays, such as Philip Massinger's *The Renegado*, Eastern women fall in love with European men in part to escape the bondage, the "fetters" that their own men have imposed upon them. Sexual and romantic love allows women to cross the boundaries of culture, so that their submission to white men is simply evidence of their free will. The "willing" submission of foreign women to their new husbands and cultures was of course an intrinsic part of the dynastic marriage: royal marriages were also cross-cultural transactions, as we can glimpse from the tensions surrounding the foreign queen in Shakespeare's histories (see Howard and Rackin 1997). Mayoral pageants and royal masques over the next century were to insistently code cross-cultural encounters as well as colonial trade in terms of the power of the British monarch to whiten, or convert, or woo a dark-skinned (and often royal) woman. But it is also productive to place the representations of romantic marriage in English theater including *A Midsummer Night's Dream* against this pattern: Hippolyta, Titania, and Hermia are all "brought under the control of lords and husbands," as Montrose suggests, and this process is indeed a violent one (1996: 161). But it is also represented as involving the complicity of the woman. Hermia, for example, resists the "unwishèd yoke" of an enforced marriage, but freely enters into matrimony with her chosen lover; Titania, in love with Bottom, relinquishes the Indian boy without a murmur, and Hippolyta, however sullen, consents to marriage with Theseus. In all three cases, force and consent are shown to be the two sides of the same coin. The ideology of "willing subjection," I am suggesting, develops simultaneously within the crucible of the family, mercantilism, and colonialism.

A Midsummer Night's Dream was produced five years before the setting up of the East India Company on the last day of 1600, at a time when very few new eye-witness accounts of India were circulating in England, though India was, of course, well represented in older European materials (see Hahn 1978; Lach 1965). The "India" of this play, and more generally the theme of otherness here, is an amalgam of elements drawn from an older exotica as well as newer materials. Some of the accounts I have cited were known to Shakespeare's contemporaries, others had circulated in Europe for a while but were not available in English, and some others were yet to be written. Rather than claim a direct correspondence between them and Shakespeare's play, I have tried to insert another dimension into what Montrose calls "an inter-textual field of representations, resonances and pressures that constitutes an ideological matrix, from which and against which Shakespeare shaped the mythopoeia of *A Midsummer Night's Dream*" (1996: 146). Gender ideologies in the play and in the culture are shaped by fantasies of racial otherness which were molded by contact with worlds outside Europe; in this play, these fantasies and processes can be recovered by tracing their imprint on the relations between men and women. What I have in mind is the kind of "convergence" Judith Butler speaks of:

> And though there are clearly good historical reasons for keeping "race" and "sexuality" and "sexual difference" as separate analytic spheres, there are also quite pressing and significant historical reasons for asking how and where we might read not only their convergence, but the sites at which one cannot be constituted save through the other. This is something other than juxtaposing distinct spheres of power, subordination, agency, historicity, and something other than a list of attributes separated by those proverbial commas (gender, sexuality, race and class), that usually mean that we have not yet figured out how to think the relations we seek to mark. (Butler 1993: 168)

III

Representations of the Orient, it has been widely remarked, are fantastic, often dream-like. In trying to decode them, we may find it useful to recall the Lacanian dictum that one cannot interpret but has to traverse a fantasy. In a play that announces itself to be like a dream, the exotic is even more highly fragmented, "signposted by danger lights" that evoke a range of discontinuous but interrelated aspects of English investments in otherness, and reveal the deep roots of these investments in the discourse of gender as well as class. Slavoj Žižek's analysis of the "fundamental homology between the interpretative procedure of Marx and Freud . . . between their analysis of commodity and of dreams" is provocative for an analysis of the relationship between the Indian boy as a colonial commodity, and the gendered form of A Midsummer Night's Dream:

> The theoretical intelligence of the form of dreams does not consist in penetrating from the manifest content to its "hidden kernel," to the latent dream-thoughts; it consists in the answer to the question: why have the latent dream-thoughts assumed such a form, why were they transposed into the form of a dream? It is the same with commodities: the real problem is not to penetrate to the "hidden kernel" of the commodity – the determination of its value by the quantity of the work consumed in its production – but to explain why work assumed the form of the value of the commodity, why it can affirm its social character only in the commodity-form of its product. (Žižek 1989: 11)

Tracing the process whereby the latent dream-thought is reshaped by the dream, Žižek reminds us that, in Freudian terms, there is nothing unconscious about this thought or signification of a dream, which is entirely "normal," usually non-sexual, and can be articulated in everyday language; however, in specific circumstances it is pushed away into the unconscious, not simply because it is unpleasant, but "because it achieves a kind of 'short circuit' with another desire which is already repressed, located in the unconscious." The latent thought of a dream is submitted to the dream-work "if an unconscious wish, derived from infancy and in a state of repression, has been transferred on to it" (Freud, quoted in Žižek 1989: 13). Hence, Žižek explains,

> The structure is always triple; there are always *three* elements at work: the *manifest dream-text*, the *latent dream-content* or thought and the *unconscious desire* articulated in a dream. Thus desire attaches itself to the dream, it intercalates itself in the interspace between the latent thought and the manifest text; it is not therefore "more concealed, deeper" in relation to the latent thought, it is decidedly more "on the surface," consisting entirely of the signifier's mechanisms, of the treatment to which the latent thought is submitted. . . . This, then, is the basic paradox of the dream: the unconscious desire, that which is supposedly its most hidden kernel, articulates itself precisely through the dissimulation work of the "kernel" of the dream, its latent thought, through the work of disguising this content-kernel by means of its translation into the dream-rebus. (Žižek 1989: 12–13)

A Midsummer Night's Dream cannot, of course, be analyzed as if it were a dream; indeed, dreams cannot be analyzed without historicizing the terms suggested by psychoanalysis. However, the articulation between its "colonial" and its "sex/gender" themes can be fruitfully thought of as a process of "short-circuiting" between them. The telescoping of the colonial theme into a scenario of family politics shapes the form of the play. But this process of short-circuiting should not be seen as the transference of a panhistorical unconscious and sexualized wish, derived from a universalized notion of "infancy," upon a more conscious non-sexual desire, as Freud suggests, but rather as the interrelated and simultaneous development of gendered as well as cultural systems.

The commodity-form, Žižek also suggests, is open to a similar misreading as are dreams: analysts of the commodity are fascinated with trying to identify and detail the "labor" that goes into producing it and which is obscured by it. Instead, it is crucial to analyze "the genesis of the commodity-form itself . . . the process – homologous to the 'dream-work' – by means of which the concealed content assumes such a form" (Žižek 1989: 15). According to Marx's analysis of this genesis, in pre-capitalist societies it is the relations between *people* which is fetishized, not the relations between things: "one man is king only because other men stand in the relation of subjects to him. They, on the contrary, imagine that they are subjects because he is king" (Marx, quoted in Žižek 1989: 25). Thus kingship appears to be a quality possessed by a certain person outside of social relations, subjects think they obey the king because he already is a king, prior to their obedience. Under capitalism, however, the relations between men are not fetishized – people are seen to be constructed not by what they are, but what they own. The two forms of fetishism are incompatible:

> in societies in which commodity fetishism reigns, the "relations between men" are totally defetishized, while in societies in which there is fetishism in "relations between men" – in pre-capitalist societies – commodity fetishism is not yet developed, because it is "natural" production, not production for the market that predominates. (Žižek 1989: 25–6)

As we have already discussed, relations between people in early modern Europe are not now understood as fetishized: on the contrary, property and possessions are seen to crucially shape notions of power, authority, and identity. On the other hand, human relations were not entirely defetishized either, as they would become under capitalism. If the psychoanalytic notion of the "psyche" is not quite appropriate for the early modern period, the same is the case with Marx's notion of the commodity. Commodity fetishism, which for Marx is "a definite social relation between men, that assumes, in their eyes, the fantastic form of a relation between things," is not yet in place (quoted in Žižek 1989: 23). As Peter Stallybrass rightly notes, "the triumph of the commodity betokens the death of the object" in that the commodity is not valued for itself but purely as an object of exchange (Stallybrass 1996: 290). Marx's appropriation of the term "fetishism" from nineteenth-century philosophy and anthropology might confuse this aspect of commodity fetishism because it appears to suggest that under capitalism objects are given a human shape as they are in pre-capitalist tribal societies, whereas what he actually wanted to convey was the idea that they are given magical qualities but actually stripped of all intrinsic qualities other than their exchange value. Stallybrass suggests that in early modern England, things may be fetishes in the anthropological rather than capitalist sense as they take on "a life of their own" (Stallybrass 1996: 291).

But the Indian boy is not a fetish in this sense – if the objects described by Stally-brass take on a life of their own, here is a human subject diminished into a dream of possession, whose only purpose is to confer identity and power upon his owners. He anticipates the power and magic of possessions under capitalism, but is not a full-fledged capitalist commodity either. Although he is a "changeling," he is not prop-erly "exchanged" for anything material, let alone for money – his transfer from his Indian parents to Titania, and from Titania to Oberon, returns nothing material to the previous owner. Thus, as the personification of colonial possessions, the Indian boy is not a fetish in either the pre-capitalist or the capitalist sense, but rather a symptom of the transition into the "Early Colonial" period.[9] After all, colonialism facilitated, even made possible, the transition from feudalism to capitalism and colo-nial possessions were crucial to the reshaping of human relations as well as the com-modity-form itself. Just as colonialism refracted and shaped the form of the gendered unconscious, so also it reshaped the relations between subject and object, not only by objectifying colonized subjects but also by flooding the European market with human and non-human commodities, luxuries as well as necessities. (In the form of slave labor, colonial possessions were also to be fetishized in a very literal sense.) Thus, we might think of the Indian boy as both the commodity-form that enables, and the dream of colonial possession that signposts, the transition from feudalism to capitalism.

If the play's hospitality to psychoanalytic interpretation is a measure of its contri-bution to the development of the ideologies of the patriarchal family, its shadowy evo-cation of "India," I have suggested, allows us to explore the place of colonialism in such a development. If psychoanalysis was to write cultural difference in familial terms and finally to erase it in the name of a universal family, such an erasure is anticipated by the form of the play, and the absorption of the Indian family into the fairy world. Finally, the Indian boy as commodity and child is the symptom of the transitions into capitalism, colonialism, as well as "modern" patriarchy. The poet's pen, says Theseus, "gives to airy nothing / A local habitation and a name" (V.i.16–17). To provide a "local habitation" for the play's "airy" India is to thicken our understanding of the "shaping fantasies" of Shakespeare's own times, but also to consider how these fan-tasies germinated "the forms of things unknown" which were to be consolidated only over the next four centuries.

NOTES

1 All quotations from *A Midsummer Night's Dream* are from Peter Holland's edition (1994). All quotations from other plays by Shakespeare are from *The Riverside Shakespeare* (1974).

2 For a reading of sexual violence in the play, see Levine (1996).

3 Federici's book, published by Thomas Hickock so "that Merchants and other my Cuntrimen may reape by it," appeared in English only in 1588, after *A Dream* (see Parker 1965: 133). Although Shakespeare would not have been familiar with it, the Dutch writer Linschoten's *Itenararío*, pub-

lished in England shortly after *A Dream*, dwells upon Indian women's prowess and joy in water: they are "much used to take their pleasures in bathes, for there are very few of them, but they would easilie swimme over a river of halfe a myle broad" (Linschoten 1885: 215).

4 In Adrian Noble's production at Stratford in 1994, the lovers and Puck also wore "vaguely oriental" costumes (Griffiths 1996: 76).

5 For representative positions in the debate see Jardine (1989), Belsey (1985), Sinfield (1994), Loomba (1989).

6 Ludovico di Varthema, *The Itinerary of Ludovico di Varthema of Bologna from 1502 to 1508*. This was included in Richard Willes's publication of Richard Eden's *The History of Travalyle in the West and East Indies* (London, 1577). The deflowering is described on pages 388 and 399 and is also discussed by

Hendricks (1996: 50), although she erroneously describes Calicut as Calcutta, which was only "founded" in the eighteenth century and is in the Eastern part of the country.

7 See, for example, Duarte Barbosa (1918–21); Lopez de Castanheda in Eden (1582). The commentaries of both Castanheda and Ludovico di Varthema on this practice had been available to English readers in 1582 and 1577 respectively.

8 See my "'Delicious Traffick': Alterity and Exchange on Early Modern Stages" (Loomba forthcoming).

9 In their introduction, de Grazia, Quilligan, and Stallybrass rightly remark that reconceptualizing the "Early Modern" period as "Early Colonial" would help in rethinking the relationship between object and subject at this time (de Grazia, Quilligan, and Stallybrass 1996: 5).

REFERENCES AND FURTHER READING

Leo Africanus 1905: "Navigations, Voyages, and Land-Discoveries, with other Historical Relations of Afrike . . . taken out of John Leo." In Samuel Purchas (ed.), *Hakluytus Posthumus*. Vol. V. Glasgow: James Maclehose and Sons, 307–529.

Arber, E. (ed.) 1885: *The First Three Books on America*. Birmingham.

Arunima, G. 1996: "Multiple Meanings: Changing Conceptions of Matrilineal Kinship in Nineteenth- and Twentieth-Century Malabar." *The Indian Economic and Social History Review*, 33, 3, 283–307.

Barbosa, D. 1918–21: *The Book of Duarte Barbosa Completed about the Year 1518 AD*. Trans. Manuel Longworth Dames. London: Hakluyt Society.

Belsey, C. 1985: "Disrupting Sexual Difference: Meaning and Gender in the Comedies." In John Drakakis (ed.), *Alternative Shakespeares*. London and New York: Methuen, 166–90.

Biddulph, W. and Biddulph, P. 1745: "The Travels of Four Englishmen . . ." (1608). In Thomas Osborne, *A Collection of Voyages and Travels*. Vol. I, no. XII, London 1745, 761–830.

Bradford, J. and Sartwell, C. 1997: "Voiced Bodies/Embodied Voices." In Naomi Zack (ed.), *Race/Sex: Their Sameness, Difference and Interplay*. New York and London: Routledge, 191–204.

Brown, L. 1994: "Amazons and Africans, Gender, Race and Empire in Daniel Defoe." In Margo Hendricks and Patricia Parker (eds.), *Women, "Race" and Writing in the Early Modern Period*. London: Routledge, 118–37.

Butler, J. 1993: *Bodies that Matter: On the Discursive Limits of "Sex."* New York and London: Routledge.

Calderwood, J. L. 1991: "*A Midsummer Night's Dream*: Anamorphism and Theseus' Dream." *Shakespeare Quarterly*, 42, 409–30.

Cartelli, T. 1987: "Prospero in Africa." In Jean E. Howard and Marion F. O'Connor (eds.), *Shakespeare Reproduced: The Text in History and Ideology*. New York and London: Methuen, 99–115.

Chaucer, G. 1974: *The Complete Works of Geoffrey Chaucer*. Ed. F. N. Robinson. London and Oxford: Oxford University Press.

Dallam, T. 1893: "The Diary of Master Thomas Dallam" (1559–1600). In *Early Voyages and*

Travels in The Levant. London: The Hakluyt Society.

Donne, J. 1985: *The Complete English Poems of John Donne*. Ed. C. A. Patrides. London and Melbourne: Dent.

Dunn, A. 1988: "The Indian Boy's Dream Wherein Every Mother's Son Rehearses His Part: Shakespeare's *A Midsummer Night's Dream*." *Shakespeare Studies*, XX, 15–32.

Eden, R. 1577: *The History of Travalyle in the West and East Indies*. London.

——1582: *First Booke of the Historie of the Discoveries and Conquest of the East Indies by the Portingales*. London.

Fanon, F. 1967: *Black Skin, White Masks*. Trans. C. L. Markmann. New York: Grove Press.

Federici, C. 1905: "Extracts of Master Caesar Fredericke his eighteene yeeres Indian Observations." In Samuel Purchas (ed.), *Hakluytus Posthumus*. Vol. X. Glasgow: James Maclehose and Company, 88–143.

Freud, S. 1947: *The Question of Lay Analysis*. Trans. Nancy Proctor-Gregg. London: Imago Publishing Company.

de Grazia, M. 1996: "The Ideology of Superfluous Things: *King Lear* as Period Piece." In Margreta de Grazia, Maureen Quilligan, and Peter Stallybrass (eds.), *Subject and Object in Renaissance Culture*. Cambridge: Cambridge University Press, 17–42.

——, Quilligan, M., and Stallybrass, P. (eds.) 1996: *Subject and Object in Renaissance Culture*. Cambridge: Cambridge University Press.

Greenblatt, S. 1990: *Learning to Curse: Essays in Early Modern Culture*. New York and London: Routledge.

Griffiths, T. (ed.) 1996: *Shakespeare in Production: A Midsummer Night's Dream*. Cambridge: Cambridge University Press.

Grosrichard, A. 1998: *The Sultan's Court: European Fantasies of the East*. London and New York: Verso.

Hahn, T. 1978: "Indians East and West: Primitivism and Savagery in English Discovery Narratives of the Sixteenth Century." *The Journal of Medieval and Renaissance Studies*, 8, 77–114.

Hall, K. 1995: *Things of Darkness: Economies of Race and Gender in Early Modern England*. Ithaca: Cornell University Press.

Head, R. 1666: *The English Rogue*. London.

Hendricks, M. 1996: "'Obscured by Dreams':

Race, Empire and Shakespeare's *A Midsummer Night's Dream*." *Shakespeare Quarterly*, 47, 1 (Spring), 37–60.

Howard, J. E. and Rackin, P. 1997: *Engendering a Nation: A Feminist Account of Shakespeare's English Histories*. London and New York: Routledge.

Hulme, P. 1985: "Polytropic Man: Tropes of Sexuality and Mobility in Early Colonial Discourse." In Frances Barker et al. (eds.), *Europe and its Others*. Vol. 2. Colchester: University of Essex Press, 17–32.

Hunt, M. 1994: "Afterword." In Jonathan Goldberg (ed.), *Queering the Renaissance*. Durham and London: Duke University Press, 395–7.

Jardine, L. 1989: *Still Harping on Daughters*. Second edition. New York: Columbia University Press.

Knolles, R. 1610: *The Generall Historie of the Turkes*. Second edition. London.

Knox, J. 1966: *The Works of John Knox*. Ed. David Laing. Vol. 4. New York: AMS Press.

Lach, D. F. 1965: *Asia in the Making of Europe*. Vol. 1, Book 1. Chicago and London: University of Chicago Press.

Levine, L. 1996: "Rape, Repetition and the Politics of Closure in *A Midsummer Night's Dream*." In Valerie Traub, M. Lindsey and Dympna Callaghan (eds.), *Feminist Readings of Early Modern Culture: Emerging Subjects*. Cambridge: Cambridge University Press, 210–28.

Linschoten, H. van 1885: *The Voyage of Huyghen Van Linschoten* (1598). Ed. A. C. Burnell and P. A. Tiele. London: Hakluyt Society.

Lithgow, W. 1632: *Rare Adventures and Painfull Peregrinations*. London.

Loomba, A. 1989: *Gender, Race, Renaissance Drama*. Manchester: Manchester University Press.

——1996: "Shakespeare and Cultural Difference." In Terence Hawkes (ed.), *Alternative Shakespeares 2*. London and New York: Routledge, 164–91.

——forthcoming: "'Delicious Traffick': Alterity and Exchange on Early Modern Stages." *Shakespeare Survey*, 52.

Mannoni, O. 1956: *Prospero and Caliban: The Psychology of Colonisation*. Trans. P. Powesland. London: Methuen.

Monserrate, A. 1922: *The Commentary of Father Monserrate, S. J. On his Journey to the Court of*

Akbar. Trans. J. S. Hoyland. London: Oxford University Press.

Montaigne, M. E. de 1965: *The Complete Essays of Montaigne*. Trans. Donald M. Frame. Stanford: Stanford University Press.

Montrose, L. 1986: "*A Midsummer Night's Dream* and the Shaping Fantasies of Elizabethan Culture: Gender, Power, Form." In Margaret W. Ferguson, Maureen Quilligan, and Nancy J. Vickers (eds.), *Rewriting the Renaissance*. Chicago and London: University of Chicago Press, 65–87.

——1993: "The Work of Gender in the Discourse of Discovery." In Stephen Greenblatt (ed.), *New World Encounters*. Berkeley and Los Angeles: University of California Press, 177–217.

——1996: *The Purpose of Playing: Shakespeare and the Cultural Politics of the Elizabethan Theater*. Chicago and London: University of Chicago Press.

Painter, W. 1890: *The Palace of Pleasure* (1567). Ed. Joseph Nicoll. London: David Nicoll.

Park, K. 1997: "The 'Rediscovery' of the Clitoris: French Medicine and the Tribade, 1570–1620." In David Hillman and Carla Mazzio (eds.), *The Body in Parts: Fantasies of Corporeality in Early Modern Europe*. New York and London: Routledge, 171–94.

Parker, J. 1965: *Books to Build an Empire*. Amsterdam: N. Israel.

Parker, P. 1996: "'Rude Mechanicals.'" In Margreta de Grazia, Maureen Quilligan, and Peter Stallybrass (eds.), *Subject and Object in Renaissance Culture*. Cambridge: Cambridge University Press, 43–82.

Purchas, S. 1617: *Purchas His Pilgrimage*. London.

——(ed.) 1905–7: *Hakluytus Posthumus*. Glasgow: James Maclehose and Sons.

Ralegh, Sir W. 1904: *The Discoverie of the large, rich and beautifull Empire of Guiana . . .* In Richard Hakluyt, *Principal Navigations*. Vol. X. Glasgow: James Maclehose.

Raman, S. forthcoming: *Framing India: The Colonial Imaginary in Early Modern Culture*.

Ramsay, G. D. 1957: *English Overseas Trade During the Centuries of Emergence*. London: Macmillan.

Roe, T. 1926: *The Embassy of Sir Thomas Roe to India 1615–19*. Ed. William Foster. London: Oxford University Press.

Rousseau, G. S. and Porter, R. 1990: *Exoticism and the Enlightenment*. Manchester: Manchester University Press.

Schleiner, W. 1978: "*Divina virago*: Queen Elizabeth as an Amazon." *Studies in Philology*, LXXV, 2 (Spring), 163–80.

Shakespeare, W. 1974: *The Riverside Shakespeare*. Boston: Houghton Mifflin.

——1994: *A Midsummer Night's Dream*. Ed. Peter Holland. Oxford and New York: Oxford University Press.

Sheshadri-Crooks, K. 1994: "The Primitive as Analyst: Postcolonial Feminism's Access to Psychoanalysis." *Cultural Critique*, 28 (Fall), 175–218.

Sinfield, A. 1994: *Cultural Politics – Queer Reading*. Philadelphia: University of Pennsylvannia Press.

Stallybrass, P. 1996: "Worn Worlds: Cloths and Identity on the Renaissance Stage." In Margreta de Grazia, Maureen Quilligan, and Peter Stallybrass (eds.), *Subject and Object in Renaissance Culture*. Cambridge: Cambridge University Press, 289–320.

Teltscher, K. 1995: *India Inscribed: European and British Writing on India 1600–1800*. Delhi: Oxford University Press.

Traub, V. 1995: "The Psychomorphology of the Clitoris." *GLQ*, 2, 81–113.

Withers, R. 1905: "The Grand Signiors Serraglio: written by Master Robert Withers." In Samuel Purchas (ed.), *Hakluytus Posthumus*. Vol. IX. Glasgow: James Maclehose and Sons, 322–406.

Wright, C. T. 1940: "The Amazons in Elizabethan Literature." *Studies in Philology*, XXXVII, 3 (July), 433–56.

Žižek, S. 1989: *The Sublime Object of Ideology*. London and New York: Verso.

10

Black Ram, White Ewe: Shakespeare, Race, and Women

Joyce Green MacDonald

My title alludes, of course, to Iago's jeering middle-of-the-night warning to Brabantio of his daughter Desdemona's elopement with Othello, the Moor of Venice: "Your heart is burst, you have lost half your soul; / Even now, now, very now, an old black ram / Is tupping your white ewe" (I.i.87–9). Brabantio's response is at first more taken up with the impropriety of being shouted out of his bed – "This is Venice; / My house is not a grange" (105–6) – than with the news Iago and Roderigo are imparting. But when he gathers his wits, his reaction to learning that his daughter has freely yielded herself "To the gross clasps of a lascivious Moor" (126) is everything Iago and Roderigo could have hoped for. He rouses his household, remarking that he has had a disturbing premonitory dream of just such an event, and asks Roderigo whether he thinks Desdemona and Othello are married, and if it's possible that some kind of sinister "charms" designed to exploit Desdemona's "youth and maidhood" (171, 172) have come into play.

This brilliant opening scene works by showing Iago's skillful manipulation of Brabantio's fund of patriarchal and racial anxieties. The facts that Desdemona has both denied her father's authority to choose a husband for her and that she has chosen Othello for herself are otherwise inexplicable to Brabantio except as the possible results of black magic. While he grasps desperately at the possibility that his daughter was not in her right mind when she eloped with her new husband, he nowhere questions Iago and Roderigo's ugly racial characterizations of Othello – "black ram," "lascivious Moor," "the thick-lips" (66) – or of the new marriage as mere animalistic coupling. Desdemona, "cover'd with a Barbary horse," is committing a bestial act which will give Brabantio "coursers for cousins" (111, 113). She has sneaked out of her father's house so that she and Othello can enjoy "making the beast with two backs" (116–17) undisturbed. That his daughter has embraced a relation he can only regard with horror demonstrates for Brabantio, and for that segment of the audience which identifies with the perspective of a beleaguered white father confounded by "his" women's waywardness, the consequences of inadequate gender and racial controls.

This essay's discussion of race and women in Renaissance culture begins with *Othello* because the play seems so central an illustration of how reflexively the period came to entangle racial with gendered identities. But I want to do more here than talk about how the issues raised in the opening scene of *Othello* – paternal authority and obligation, the sexualization of women's self-determination, the preservation of class and cultural distinction – all hinge on ideas about race, although certainly most of my attention will be focused on this provocative play. I also believe that *Othello* points to ways in which fathers, families, and status are racialized elsewhere in the canon. Including *The Rape of Lucrece* and *Titus Andronicus* – two other texts deeply concerned with sex, families, and social and cultural standing – in my analysis reiterates race's multiple manifestations in Shakespeare, a broadness of conception which refutes a narrow modern location of race primarily in skin color (for all that these works do share a strong presumption of a black/white color binary) and transcends differences in genre or artistic "maturity."

Nevertheless: however much I want to argue that racial matters in Shakespeare are not limited to a single text and that race signals an entire set of social, familial, and even economic relationships, the fact remains that it is *Othello*, more than any other Shakespearean text, which has vigorously represented pop culture's sense of the sexualized racial fears of the US in the 1990s. Oliver Parker's successful 1995 film version starred American actor Laurence Fishburne in his first role after his Academy Award-nominated performance as the emotionally needy, drug-addicted, wife-beating Ike Turner in *What's Love Got To Do With It?* One critic judged Fishburne's Othello to be "unusually hot-blooded," and noted that the "hint of Ike Turner" in "this Othello's jealous fury . . . seems to be very much what Mr. Parker had in mind." For many American journalists, *Othello* helped explain why black O. J. Simpson was arrested for the murder of his white ex-wife Nicole Brown Simpson. (Such explanations, of course, had nothing to say about the death of the second victim, Ronald Goldman.) For me, however, *Othello* manifested most notably during the 1991 Senate hearings on Clarence Thomas's nomination to the US Supreme Court. Sen. Alan Simpson of Wyoming, defending Thomas against what he considered an attempt at character assassination by the testimony of Thomas's former employee Anita Hill, directed spectators to the ringing speech on "good name" in III.iii:

> Who steals my purse, steals trash; 'tis something, nothing;
> 'Twas mine, 'tis his, and has been slave to thousands;
> But he that filches from me my good name
> Robs me of that which not enriches him,
> And makes me poor indeed.
>
> (157–61)

What is most striking about Sen. Simpson's use of the passage from *Othello* is that it is so startlingly out of context. Defending Thomas, the senator cites the words of the white arch-deceiver Iago, the one who clarifies the Moor's usefulness as a target for Brabantio's apparently preexistent, free-floating racial loathing. In other words, the senator defends a black man, whom he implies is the victim of a racist attack by a confused and/or malicious black woman, by using the words of a character who announces himself as a proudly deceitful racist misanthrope.

I have no idea whether it occurred to Sen. Simpson that quoting Iago was a peculiar way of defending the contemporary black man whose integrity, he implied, was coming under unfair attack much as Othello's does in the play; so much about Shakespeare is taken out of its textual turn as he is cycled and recycled through popular culture. What is more obvious about the senator's use of *Othello* is the evidence it provides that in the last decade of the twentieth century the play is as powerful an index to the interconnections of raced and gendered identities as it apparently was in the first decade of the seventeenth. It not only tells us what to think about black men, white men, white women (such as Sen. Simpson's friend, Clarence Thomas's loyal wife Virginia), and black women (as Sen. Simpson's citation transmogrified the black woman Anita Hill into the deceitful, manipulative Iago), but it continues to suggest to us how to arrange these thoughts into a coherent world picture.

Feminist readings of *Othello* have powerfully intervened in *Othello*'s production of normative sexual meanings by pointing out how infuriated Brabantio is by Desdemona's daring to deny his right to give her away in marriage, thus situating patriarchal imperatives in Shakespeare's love tragedy. Here, though, I want to press that recognition forward so that this feminist conviction of the significance of the construction of gendered relationships in *Othello* also insists on recognizing how thoroughly race permeates gender and class positions in the play.

An example of a powerful feminist analysis which fails to distinguish how race differentiates the operations of gender in *Othello* can be found in Karen Newman's influential reading of Desdemona's position in her father's household and within Venetian society. Newman has been faulted for forging too hasty an equivalence between Desdemona's subordinate position and that of her husband, as though the racial and sexual differences between them (and between Othello and everyone else) are neutralized by their joint exposure to the corrosive effects of Venetian patriarchy. Hazel Carby is only one black feminist who has argued that an analysis which foregrounds gender above all other sources of social formation for women must inevitably fail to perceive how differently such foundational analytical terms as "family" and "patriarchy" operate within the experiences of white Western women and non-white women from other parts of the world. Following such insistence on historicizing the family as a unit of emotional, as well as sexual, production, I begin my own process of reading for the simultaneous and mutually interpenetrating operations of race and gender in *Othello* by unraveling some of the social meanings assigned to and ideological uses made of "women" and "family" in the developing racial climate of the early modern period. The domestication of women and their sexuality facilitated the accomplishment of explicitly racial goals.

Historians are in increasing agreement about the prohibitions surrounding black women in the colonial societies which were being founded during the early seventeenth century. Legal findings and labor practices busily erected fortresses of distinction between white and black women virtually from the moment of African women's first arrival in British America. Each was, in effect, socially produced in relation to the other, and to white men. The first white women and the first Africans both landed in Virginia in the year 1619, fifteen or sixteen years after *Othello*'s premiere. The white women could be purchased as wives by the white men of the colony in exchange for 120 pounds of tobacco, while the African women could not marry anyone without the permission of their employers. Since African and Indian women quickly came to outnumber white women, interracial marriage soon became common enough that – especially in combination with the increasing substitution of slavery for mere servitude – it became subject to a new tax code in 1643. Under this code, the labor of black women would be taxed at the same rate as that of black men and white men, while the labor of white women was entirely exempt from taxation. A second provision of this law was that white men who married black women would be subject to a new annual tax, while white men who merely cohabited with them would be exempt from taxation. In 1662, the colony reversed centuries of English common law by declaring that all children born there would follow the condition of their mothers rather than of their fathers: white men who fathered children on their black slaves were excused from any legal or moral responsibility, while the children themselves were condemned to a lifetime of slavery.

In Virginia, marriage and the family were early defined as racialized spaces. A white man's entry into any kind of domestic union except an irregular one with a black woman was subject to financial penalty. If he had to pay for the privilege of identifying himself as her husband, he was not legally expected to act as her children's father at all. Later, a 1691 law criminalized sexual contact between whites and members of other races so severely as to suggest a desire on the part of the state to wipe it out entirely. Under this law's provisions, any free Englishwoman who bore an illegitimate child by a black man had to pay a £15 fine or be indentured to the churchwardens, available to be hired out anywhere in the parish, for a period of five years; her child would be indentured until the age of thirty. According to the same law, if a white person, male or female, married a non-white person of any status, the couple would be exiled from the colony. (The punishment Maryland provided for a white woman who married a black slave was even more draconian. There, the woman herself would be sold into slavery for the lifetime of her husband.) Finally, the law forbade any Virginia slaveowner from freeing any slave within the colony, a provision which was not overturned until 1782.

The 1691 legislation racially regulated white people's sexual contacts as much as earlier laws policed the sexuality and labor of black women, and did so by holding their children hostage. A white woman's sexual transgression would be punished by her children's loss of freedom. White men had no legal responsibility for their children by slave mothers, but after 1691 if they wanted to free an enslaved child they had fathered, they would have to forfeit all paternal contact by sending the child to another state. The state's refusal to recognize any family ties but those created within the white race and between men and women of the same status worked to emphasize the colonial family's role as the agent of a stringently racialized public order.

In a colony whose numbers of slaves and indentured workers began growing rapidly in the second half of the seventeenth century, some historians have argued, a race-conscious sexuality became a tool for containing the possibility of social unrest. Virginia's legislators used race as a device for unifying the white population, despite the large numbers and economic importance of non-white workers, and despite the differences in status between free and indentured whites, and between white landowners and white agricultural laborers. The belief in white women's endangered sexual purity and in black women's innate whorishness which came to mark the discourse of US slavery was the social issue of such laws as I discuss here. What is uncanny about *Othello* is the way in which it anticipates such legal codifications of ideologies of race and gender.

Race as it was formulated in British America was relied on to perform social, economic, and sexual work necessary to the interests of state authority. Just as it was (and remains) more than merely a matter of skin color — that the mixed-race and thus potentially light-skinned children of female slaves were also slaves indicates the lack of an even correlation between color, race, and status in our period — it also used, and absorbed, family. Race dictated what could and could not be considered a civically valid relationship between men and women, which children could grow up with their mothers, which children were entitled to their fathers' love.

Othello does not explicitly codify its sense of race's place in the construction and functioning of "family," but this sense is firmly part of the play. Brabantio is perhaps even more distressed that Desdemona has chosen a black man who will degrade his lineage than he is that she has dared to choose for herself. The racial unconscious that Iago and Brabantio share apparently runs deep enough to nullify the class difference which forms part of Iago's animus against Michael Cassio, the "great arithmetician" who has "never set squadron in the field" (I.i.19, 22) and yet has been chosen as Othello's lieutenant. As sensitive as he is to the assault on his social dignity represented by Iago's vulgar shouting at his windows, Brabantio does not rebuke its specifically racist content; indeed, he agrees with the characterization of Othello and the new union so completely as to wish he'd given his daughter to Roderigo when he had the chance. Shared notions of racial standing and identity unite men more intimately than they can be separated by social gradation. Iago bets on the existence of this secret link, and Brabantio's outraged reaction to his news proves him right.

The degree to which gender — both female and male — in the opening scene of *Othello* is constituted within race, and the scene's ideas of how race is crossed by class and sexuality, mark other relations in the play besides those between Desdemona or Iago and Brabantio. Specifically, I am thinking of the surprising connection between aristocratic Cassio and Bianca, the courtesan whom he asks to copy the embroidery on the handkerchief that was Othello's first gift to Desdemona. Just as Brabantio is initially affronted by Iago's daring to disturb his peace by shouting in front of his house, so too does Cassio worry that if he does not soothe Bianca's anger with him by dining at her house, "she'll rail in the streets else" (IV.i.163). It is vitally necessary to

Cassio that Bianca not be provoked into public railing: Othello is standing by, and Cassio obviously does not want his commanding officer to witness a public scene between him and a known prostitute. The fact that he is consorting with her in the first place is a secret he must keep in order to preserve the social credit which may indeed have helped him to his present post.

At least Cassio keeps the relationship with Bianca secret from Othello. Iago knows that Cassio, when he "hears of her, cannot restrain / From the excess of laughter" (IV.i.98–9). Again to Iago, Cassio sneers at Bianca for being so foolish as to love him, for perhaps being as susceptible to his plausible self-presentation as Othello may have been: she "hangs, and lolls, and weeps upon me!" (139). He shares an ugly sexual understanding with Iago as freely as Brabantio partakes of their mutual racism. Iago feels himself to be an abused outsider in Venetian society, but he is surprisingly instrumental to the expression of two highly regarded citizens' racial fear and sexual contempt, fear and contempt which fundamentally shape the ways they see the world and their places in it.

Hypocrite and place-seeker that he is, Cassio's sexual feelings extend beyond his hidden affair with Bianca. He must also sublimate his apparent desire for his commander's wife, a sublimation he will undertake with his mistress's help. The affectionate respect of his greeting to Bianca at her first entrance – he salutes her as "most fair," his "sweet love" (170, 171) – is only the tone he adopts in order to get her to agree to the favor of copying the embroidery on Desdemona's handkerchief, presumably so that he may acquire a likeness of this intimate token to cherish, and fetishize. The handkerchief that passes between them links the virtuous Desdemona and the "huswife" (IV.i.94) Bianca. They are also both brought into the purview of Cassio's masturbatory secrecy, his need to preserve his professional and social standing from public knowledge of his desire.

Although self-absorbed Cassio does not know the handkerchief's significance, we do:

> That handkerchief
> Did an Egyptian to my mother give;
> She was a charmer, and could almost read
> The thoughts of people. She told her, while she kept it,
> 'Twould make her amiable, and subdue my father
> Entirely to her love; but if she lost it,
> Or made a gift of it, my father's eye
> Should hold her loathed, and his spirit should hunt
> After new fancies. She, dying, gave it me,
> And bid me, when my fate would have me wiv'd,
> Give it her.
> . . .
> To lose it or giv't away were such perdition
> As nothing else could match.
>
> (III.iv.55–65, 67–8)

If the public voicing of scandal – once acknowledged, the second time suppressed – appears in the relations between Brabantio, Desdemona, and Iago on the one hand and between Cassio and Bianca on the other, so too does the motif of magic. The "charms" Brabantio fears have been worked on his daughter do in fact exist, and have invested the handkerchief with otherworldly significance – literally "otherworldly," since the handkerchief was given to Othello's mother by an "Egyptian." The "magic in the web" (III.iv.69) of the handkerchief has been associated with, inspired by, non-white women, Othello's mother and the Egyptian "charmer" – figures whose authority, one as queen and the other as enchanter, has been displaced by Venetian and white hegemony in affairs of state and by Iago's love-destroying lies in the domestic arena. The very name of Desdemona's mother's maid "Barbary" also evokes the civic dimension of this displacement: "Barbary" was the English name for the territories of North Africa with which England maintained diplomatic relations at the turn of the seventeenth century, as well as echoing the "Barbary horse" of Iago's hysterical warning in the first act, his racist xenophobia eclipsing sovereign equality. The name also evokes the degree to which this eclipse and displacement is imagined in gendered and sexual terms, since it was Barbary who taught Desdemona the Willow Song. A foreign woman domesticated to the uses of Brabantio's household transmitted to his daughter the song's voicing of feminine mourning for lost love, lost integrity. These three non-white women's association with secret female power – if only the power to grieve – is overwritten within the action of the play by the patriarchal authority on display (in crisis mode) in Brabantio's fear and in the cool adjudication of the elopement by the Venetian signiory.

The handkerchief's hidden feminine history, and his attachment to it, may thus work to feminize and racialize the increasingly distraught Othello in the view of his first presumably all-white audience. A member of a race increasingly relegated to servitude, if not outright slavery, during the period of the play's premiere, Othello's loss of emotional control over the issue of sexual jealousy performs the vivid affirmation of the worst of a set of emerging fears and convictions about his essential racial nature. Significantly, this outburst of barbarism culminating in murder and suicide occurs once he has left the control of the powerful Venetian state and voyaged to the farthest edge of what could be considered "the West." At home, the Duke and Senators are able, in effect, to recognize him as an honorary white man for his services to Venice and excuse his trespass against Brabantio's right to control his daughter's marriage. "I think this tale would win my daughter, too" (I.iii.171), the Duke smiles after Othello's testimony. The trouble only begins once Othello has moved, with Desdemona, beyond their ordering supervision.

If the handkerchief serves as a kind of visual shorthand for the gender and racial significance of Othello's origins, I believe that it also serves some of the same purpose for Bianca. The handkerchief's passage into her hands certainly restates its association with attempts at female assumption of social authority. The sovereignty Othello's mother may have enjoyed as a queen in her own land has been superseded by Venetian authority and her son's subordinate relationship to it, but Bianca attempts

– illegitimately, in Cassio's view – to rise above the social station which is proper to
her. In amused disgust, he reports to Iago that his "bauble" actually dared attempt
to embrace him one day as he stood "talking on the seabank with certain Venetians"
(IV.i.135, 133–4). The idea that they will one day be married comes "out of her own
love and flattery, not out of my promise," he assures Iago (IV.i.128–9).

Whether or not he intends to marry her, however, Cassio does continue to have sex
with her. He discharges onto Bianca the bestial sexuality that he will not allow himself
to impute to Desdemona (the sexual nature, that is, that her father implicitly believes
she has demonstrated in seeking out Othello). That he feels free to express and act on
a fully sexualized contempt for Bianca while putting Desdemona on a pedestal of adoration – to be possessed only secretly, through his copy of her handkerchief – speaks
volumes about the "reputation" whose loss he grieves after being conned into the
drunken brawl on his commander's wedding night. It is not some essential and
immutable inner quality under vicious attack from unprincipled outsiders as a Simp-
sonesque tour of the play might first suggest, or not only that, but a matter of appearance and social plausibility. What he wants to keep is his name for having a good
name, rather than the thing itself. If he can do so by appealing to "virtuous" (III.i.35)
Desdemona's influence by day while continuing to have sex with Bianca at night, he
will. As a courtesan, Bianca is necessary to the attempts of garrison society on Cyprus
to maintain distinctions of gender and sexuality which were first muddled by
Desdemona's openly sexual choice of Othello for a husband; she absorbs the joyless
sex and casual misogyny above which Desdemona is at least publicly elevated.

In addition to a class element, the play's production of Bianca's sexuality may also
bear a certain racial burden. Her very name ("Bianca" means "white") invokes the gendered Petrarchan color symbolism of indifference and distance which her role as courtesan and her association with secret sexual deeds – "And say if I shall see you soon
at night," she implores Cassio (III.iv.198) – immediately contradict. Iago and Desdemona banter about color and women as they wait for Othello's ship to arrive at
Cyprus in Act II. If a woman is both "fair and wise" (129), Iago pronounces, her fairness is "for use" (by men?) while her wit will put her fairness to its own uses, pursuing her own aims within a sexual context. Iago reads conventional languages of color
and beauty so as to project inevitable conflict between men and ("fair") women, a conflict in which men's love may be fated to work at cross-purposes with these women's
manipulative skills. But "If she be black, and thereto have a wit, / She'll find a white
that shall her blackness hit" (132–3), he tells Desdemona. His remark suggests that
women's "blackness" puts them into quite a different relation toward men than does
fairness, foreordaining not only their control by men, but their pursuit of this control,
their self-transformation into sexual targets to be "hit."

Bianca's work as a courtesan reverses the common associations surrounding whiteness or fairness in early modern discourses of beauty and sexual identity. Rather than
disdainfully withholding herself as would some white-skinned and golden-haired
heroine of Petrarchan lyric, thus creating herself in the mind of the frustrated male
lover as an object whose physical unattainability signifies her spiritual integrity,

Bianca sells her body to many men, and pursues one man in particular who insists on denying that their relationship can be anything but exploitatively sexual. For Cassio, the abjected sexuality of "fair Bianca" (III.iv.170) makes her socially invisible and emotionally insignificant, while Iago seizes on her prostitution to implicate her in Cassio's wounding: "This is the fruits of whoring" (V.i.115). The moral guilt these displaced Venetians use to excuse their mistreatment of her and finally to accuse her of a double assault is expressed at the crime scene in terms of skin color: "What, look you pale?," Iago demands of her; and again, "Look you pale, mistress?" (V.i.104, 105).

I do not mean by my attention here to the vocabularies of color and fairness that surround Bianca to suggest that the character is literally dark-skinned. (Trevor Nunn's 1989 *Othello* for the Royal Shakespeare Company did cast a black actress, Marsha Hunt, in the role.) I would say rather that she is racialized as black, assigned a set of negative sexual characteristics associated with Africa and Africans. Telling Iago about Bianca's sexual nature, for example, Cassio calls her a "monkey," a "fitchew" (IV.i.127, 146). Both fitchews – polecats – and monkeys were thought to have particularly strong sex drives. Indeed, many early modern travelers gave credence to the notion that black Africans were the product of cross-species breeding between humans and apes, who were thought to be so lustful that they would even pursue human women. Although by the eighteenth century it was scientifically understood that such breeding had not taken place, the imaginative force of the idea continued to inform conceptions of racial and sexual hierarchy. As Winthrop Jordan notes in *White Over Black* (1968), this imaginary coitus, whether volitional or forced, was always conceived as taking place between African women and male apes. Just as the name "Barbary" summons foreign territories – sexual and sovereign – Cassio's naming his mistress a "monkey" brings to mind discourses of alienness, animality, and unthinking lust. Othello's mother and the Egyptian "charmer" who helped her secure his father's love are absent from the play, but joined to Bianca in this discourse of gender and sexual disorder. Bianca's possession of the handkerchief links this woman figuratively darkened by the weight of the Venetians' need to distinguish between good and bad women – a distinction they declined to make in Desdemona's case because of her rank and especially because of Othello's commodity to them as a great battle commander – to women who are literally dark and contradictory of Venetian notions of sexual and social order. Further, the play also suggests a broadly racialized connection between prostituted Bianca and virtuous Desdemona, because of their mutual association with a bestialized female sexuality.

My analysis of *Othello* develops from a sense of how fluidly and indirectly languages of racial identity can be transmitted in early modern texts, and of how dependent these languages are on gender and sexuality. Obviously, the character of Othello offers a powerful enactment of how mutually constitutive race, gender, and sexuality were felt to be (just as my remarks on contemporary *Othello*s indicate just how formative Shakespeare's play has been to what and how Western societies continue to think about men and women, sex and race). The play's extensive theatrical history calls attention to the multiple interests directors and actors have found in it: the exotic appeal of its ideas of Africa and "Africanness," as was richly acted upon in Ben Jonson's *The Masque of Blacknesse*; the voyeuristic thrill for a white audience of watching a white woman erotically murdered by a black man, as seems to have animated so many eighteenth-century productions; the spectacularization of Othello's savagery, as marked performances by Kean and Salvati; and, in the twentieth century, Paul Robeson's rehabilitation of the hero's African origins, or direct interrogations of the text's racial vocabulary, as in several all-black productions. I would argue that *Othello* has retained its power to reach audiences precisely because it uncannily seems to play out what they think they already know, what they have been taught, about race and sex: about black men's fundamental irreconcilability to the values of civilized society and about what happens to nice young (white) girls who defy their fathers' wishes. Ann duCille has pointed out how much press coverage of O. J. Simpson's murder trial relied on the notions that a savage killer lay somehow just behind his public image as sports hero and affable commercial spokesman, and that Nicole Brown Simpson somehow invited her own violent death by marrying a man who was so "different" from the kind of man she might have been expected to choose. The insidious power of *Othello* stems from the absolute taken-for-grantedness of its racial rhetoric: Brabantio *knows* that his daughter's elopement with a black man is as repulsive as would be a human's mating with an animal.

But for all its frequently uneasy theatrical power, *Othello* is only one place where Shakespeare undertakes the racialization of his characters' identity and relationships. To think about race and women in Shakespeare requires an unraveling of both terms, a recognition that they are relational and internally varied rather than absolute. In *Othello*, for example, race does achieve meaning as a matter of skin color. But lineage, custom, status, geographical origin, and sexuality also figure in what the play means by "race," so that the term's diffuse borders extend far beyond pigment. While, as I have argued, Desdemona and Bianca are both racialized through their sexuality, this crossing of sex and race does not produce consistent or uniform results. Desdemona's death at her husband's hands, despite her father's sense of the transgressiveness of her marriage, ends by confirming her fidelity and bounty: she refuses to name Othello as her murderer. Bianca, while innocent of the violent assault Iago tries to blame on her, is racialized as black because of her sexual activity outside of patriarchal controls over the disposition of her body. The two women's class status also contributes to this racial differentiation, a differentiation which exists despite the fact that Bianca need not necessarily be seen as literally being of a different race – i.e., skin color – than Desdemona.

I have wanted to broaden my field of inquiry into operations of race and sex in *Othello* to include the patriarchal and racial verities whose logic underlies these representations precisely because the verbal and cultural power of the text is such as almost to deflect investigation of just where that power comes from. Certainly, revisers and adapters of the play have implicitly recognized its deep roots in what largely American contemporary race theorists have termed "whiteness," which has been characterized as

> perhaps the primary unmarked and so unexamined – let's say "blank" – category. Like other unmarked categories, it has a touchstone quality of the normal, against which the members of marked categories are measured and, of course, found deviant, that is, wanting. It is thus . . . situated outside the paradigm that it defines. Whiteness is not itself compared with anything, but other things are compared unfavorably with it, and their own comparability with one another derives from their distance from the touchstone. (Chambers 1997: 189)

Analysts of manifestations of this "blank" social category in the US context have drawn attention to its intimate involvement with the performative. It is the master enabler which permits its possessors (or aspirants to its possession) to perform, and thus selectively define, the behavior of its non-white opposites. Since for most of its stage history the title character of *Othello* was played by a white man in some kind of black disguise, the play provides a rich text for studying this indirect production of whiteness, its invocation by the passionate public performance of its racial and sexual opposite.

For example, a climactic moment in William Macready's mid-nineteenth-century performances as the Moor of Venice came in the staging of Desdemona's murder. The actual death struggle was concealed behind the strategically drawn pale draperies of the couple's marriage bed, but the scene climaxed with Macready's thrusting his darkened face out from between the curtains to confront the audience in silent, maddened acknowledgment of the horrible crime. Observers reported that on at least one occasion, a white woman in the audience fainted at the moment of recognition forced by Macready's exposure of his "black" face. The shock of Macready's exposure depended on the audience's racial reaction first to the miscegenous marriage, and then to the savagely sexual overtones of the murder. The staging of the scene, building to the moment when he exposed just his black face between the bed curtains, made what may otherwise have been so ordinary a proposition as not even to require extensive analysis – that black men and their brutal sexuality should be kept safely distant from white girls – seem luridly, demonstrably, true. What Macready's crafty staging exposed was not only the voyeuristic satisfactions available from watching the spectacularization of black men's savagery, but also – and, more perilously, for a spectator viewing the world through a Brabantio's eyes – the fear that that savagery could be unexpectedly unleashed on an unsuspecting white world.

But if, as I have been arguing, all black people in *Othello* are not alike (they are split into the black hero and literally or figuratively "black" women, some of whom exist only in the play's memory), neither are all the white people who have produced the play as the object of a self-affirming racial gaze. Eric Lott has discussed the significance of blackface performance to the construction of a white and masculine working-class consciousness in the United States, arguing that whiteness – so apparently absolute – is actually potently crossed by class and gender. I would suggest that the performances of Othello by blacked-up white actors performed a cognate function on the more culturally elite plane reserved for Shakespeare. Watching the "black" Othello lose control and murder his white wife confirmed white spectators in their own acculturation to structures of racial and gender dominance. Of course, the presence of a black man in the role, instead of a blacked-up white man, can possibly challenge *Othello*'s structuring of racial and sexual feeling, depending on what happens in the rest of the production. Film theorist Manthia Diawara has called for renewed critical attention to black performance as a way out of the circuit of white appropriation, spectacularization, and enactment of dominance that has seemed to mark so much of the representational history of black subjects in the West. But, apart from the dominant role of its tragic hero – who, for more than the first two centuries of the play's theatrical existence, was performed by a disguised white man – *Othello* contains no black characters whose performance can be analyzed. I propose instead that reading for traces of the absent and effaced dark women in *Othello* can begin undermining the great binaries – self and other, public and private, man and woman, black and white, and all their combinations – that organize and enforce the racial and sexual knowledge we keep taking away from the play. These women, who proclaim the primacy of the erotic over the authoritarian, are what must be suppressed and exiled if the play is to fulfill its masculinist and white preconceptions.

Not only is Othello the only non-white person in *Othello*; he is one of the very few characters without white skin in all of Shakespeare. Margo Hendricks has pointed out that Shakespeare's plays rarely even use the word "race," and when it does appear, it has more to do with lineage, region and nationality, or even species than it does with differences in skin color between people. This fullness and indirection require a kind of overreading, a dilation of and investigation into such apparently self-evident terms as "family," "woman," "man," "black," and "white." Such indirection marks *The Rape of Lucrece*, for example, which manifests its sense of race's imaginative utility through the same color-coded references to a Petrarchan femininity that Iago and Desdemona exchange at harborside, and also ultimately links bodily blackness to a woman's sexual nature. Some of the blood that issues from Lucrece's body after she fatally stabs herself "still pure and red remain'd, / And some look'd black, and that false Tarquin stain'd" (1742–3). The black blood is surrounded by "a wat'ry rigol," or border (1745), which separates it from the "untainted" (1749) red blood, but both streams have issued together from Lucrece's body. The poem's patriarchal logic dictates that even though she has been raped, Lucrece's essence has somehow been blackened by non-marital sexual contact.

The emblematic colors of red, black, and clear (white?) are arranged here as a marker of the contamination of her "racial" purity as a Roman wife and mother. The use of these emblematic colors reiterates the color symbolism used to describe Lucrece's first appearance in the poem, her "lily hand," her "rosy cheek," her "hair like golden threads," her breasts as white as "ivory globes" (386, 400, 407). Kim Hall has detailed how sonneteers' employment of this Petrarchan language of color during a period when England was establishing its colonial relations with the New World and Africa can also be seen as projects in aesthetic mastery of gender and racial difference. Shakespeare's "Dark Lady" sonnets exhibit true virtuosity in their reversal of the figure's more usual association of fairness with feminine beauty, so that in them black becomes irresistibly and paradoxically beautiful. *Lucrece*, however, contains no dark ladies. The ugly sexual and familial implications of her rape are literalized by the stream of black blood. She is the "white hind" to Tarquin's "rough beast" (543, 545), so that his intended crime takes on some of that aura of cross-species impropriety Brabantio sees in his daughter's union to Othello. The poem compares her attempts to talk Tarquin out of the rape to what happens when a wind from "earth's dark womb" dissipates a threatening "black-fac'd cloud"; she characterizes his plan as "black payment" for the hospitality she has shown him (549, 547, 576). The natural sovereignty he should possess as a member of a ruling family is instead grotesquely subject to his "[b]lack lust" (654).

Even in the absence of non-white characters, the poem racializes its sense of the horror of Tarquin's crime. The rape darkens or otherwise contaminates Lucrece's purity, a purity which derives from her perfect fulfillment of the roles of Roman wife and mother. As Romans, both Tarquin and Lucrece are formed by the values of *pietas*: of devotion to the good name of her properly patriarchal family and to the welfare of Rome, and submission to the will of the gods. Both of them understand the role sexual knowledge, even forced knowledge as Tarquin proposes, plays in this construction of a Roman identity. If she will not submit, Tarquin tells her, he will rape her anyway, then kill her and one of her male slaves and put their dead bodies together in her bed; he'll give out the story that he came upon the adulterous scene accidentally and, in horrified concern for her family's good name, killed them both. Neither Tarquin nor Lucrece questions his right to commit such an act in the defense of another Roman male's familial and sexual honor. They both know that with an adulterous mother, her children would be forever "blurr'd with nameless bastardy" (522), a "blemish that will never be forgot, / Worse than a slavish wipe, or birth hour's blot" (536–7).

In the poem, marriage is what provides for the continuation of a socially sanctioned family line. The rape compromises the sexual domestication suggested by the poem's comparison of Lucrece to a vulnerable "hind." The disastrousness of losing her "life of purity" (780) is communicated through a strong class consciousness and through a color vocabulary which insistently associates Tarquin with dark evil and Lucrece with fairness. And yet, her ivory and blonde and rosy beauty is more than merely skin-deep. Part of the blood in her body literally becomes black, as though to indicate that every frightening threat Tarquin uses against her is actually true. In the moment of her death, the men of Lucrece's family recognize and claim her: " 'My daughter!' and 'My wife!' with clamors fill'd / The dispers'd air" (1804–5). The conjoined principles of the sanctity of family as an instrument for controlling the social exchange of women, and the undervoiced accompanying fears of the consequences of unregulated exogamy, are ultimately upheld.

The Rape of Lucrece can thus be understood as sharing some of the same fears about women's disruptive power as sexual beings and as mothers as appear in *Othello*. In the narrative poem, however, the specter of this deviant motherhood is not as easily displaced as it is in the tragedy, where the hero is removed from a world ordered by non-white women and placed in one ruled by white men before the action even begins. Lucrece polices the borders of her own Roman womanhood by killing herself once she believes those borders to have been violated; the black blood's exit from her body may offer some hope, on the poem's terms, that her purity and the social and sexual categories on which Romans' self-image is based have been restored.

Like *Lucrece*, Shakespeare's first Roman play *Titus Andronicus* is convinced of patriarchal families' importance as a foundation of the Roman state. But it is far less convinced than *Lucrece* is that patriarchal right will always be done. *Othello* performs the final containment of black masculinity, while *Lucrece* ritually exorcises the suspicion of a sexually communicated blackness. But in *Titus*, race and the language which can racialize moral identity are simultaneously more instrumental to the play's final confirmation of Roman triumph, and less ideologically transparent.

The racial contradictions built into *Titus* stem from the state of the masculine and particularly fatherly dominance which matters so much in the other two works. The play's vision of rule by Roman fathers seems entered upon its senescence: the emperor is chosen by free election, not by inheritance, and the likeliest candidate as the play opens is Titus himself, father of twenty-five sons, twenty-one of whom have died in "the cause of Rome" (I.i.32). It is as though his sons have lived only in order to be sacrificed, to pass into the family tomb which – instead of the body of their absent mother? – is the "sacred receptacle" of his "joys" (92). Instead of a Brabantio's anxious concern for the future generations which will spring from his daughter's marriage, fatherhood in *Titus* seems to be only about death and loss. This denial of the potential which makes children instruments for securing a family's posterity is, of course, strikingly refuted by the black villain Aaron's devotion to his infant son, a scene to which I will return.

The name Shakespeare gives Titus's daughter Lavinia is perhaps the first place where the play begins undoing the connection between the notion of race and its relation to masculine authority. She bears the name of the young girl who is the destined bride of Aeneas, great Trojan ancestor of the Roman race. The *Aeneid* tells how Aeneas and Lavinia's father, Latinus, met and peacefully negotiated Lavinia's passage from her father's house into Aeneas's. This patriarchal exchange which will ultimately enable the foundation of a new civilization is, however, disrupted by Lavinia's mother Amata, in whose heart the goddess Juno has sowed her own endless wrath against the Trojans. Amata inspires her daughter's alternative suitor Turnus into renewed warfare against Aeneas's troops, and the marriage only comes about after a last round of bloody warfare.

Instead of this feminine disruption of the patriarchal processes of dynastic marriage, Shakespeare's Roman patriarch (who compares himself to the Trojan "King Priam," I.i.80) is the one who overturns the prearranged betrothal between his Lavinia and the Roman prince Bassianus. In an excess of zeal to prove his absolute lack of personal ambition, Titus not only refuses the ready offer of the throne, but impulsively offers his daughter to the new emperor Saturninus. When Titus's surviving sons move to defend Bassianus's legitimate prior claim to Lavinia, he deliberately kills his son Mutius: "What villain boy, / Barr'st me my way in Rome?" (290–1). If a Brabantio keenly feels the usurpation of his right to choose his son-in-law, this Roman father in effect usurps the social tradition governing such connections between men and between families. The name "Lavinia" and the comparison Titus makes between himself and Priam, last king of Troy, gesture toward an imperial context for the actions of *Titus*'s opening scene; but if such a context exists, Titus is the one who shatters it.

Race as a matter of lineage and cultural practice is again invoked by the presence of Tamora, the barbarian queen. Her defeat by Titus's Romans allows the play to stage the eclipse of female sovereignty by the rule of civil white fathers which forms such an important part of the context for Othello's racial identity among the Venetians. As a conquered savage queen, her role as Roman slave is explicit and inevitable. (In the 1987 Royal Shakespeare Company production, Estelle Kohler as Tamora came onstage wearing a dog collar around her neck, with Brian Cox's Titus holding the end of the attached leash. When he spoke Titus's sarcastic line at I.i.85, "Here Goths have given me leave to sheathe my sword," he absent-mindedly fondled Tamora's breast.) Again, however, it is a Roman male who disrupts the natural order governing the disposition of women: deprived of a match with Lavinia, who has been spirited away by Bassianus, and already powerfully sexually attracted to the prisoner, Saturninus chooses Tamora for his bride.

Titus, *Othello*, and *The Rape of Lucrece* show us hierarchical societies whose categories of social organization – race, gender, nationhood – are undergoing crisis. Two of these crises are resolved, through the unexpected success of Iago's manipulative intervention and through Lucrece's suicide. The initial categories' serviceability survives, is even proven by, crisis. But in *Titus*, this process of crisis, challenge, and proof is luridly altered. The power of Roman fathers to create and sustain the moral lives of their familial subordinates has been diminished into the mere power to take life away. I would conclude that what is being dramatized is the iron fist beneath the velvet glove of a more socially adept patriarchal dispensation, except that patriarchy does not wear a particularly benign human face in either *Othello* or *The Rape of Lucrece*. *Titus* takes off the gloves altogether.

As the play thus demystifies the authority of white fathers, it presses forward its conviction of a racialized female sexual deviance which justifies masculine control. In II.iii, Tamora's unexpectedly elegant aubade invites her lover to consider the pair of them in the same light as "The wand'ring prince and Dido" (22). Dido, of course, was the queen of Carthage whose love for Aeneas temporarily distracted him from his fated duty to lead the survivors of Troy to a new empire in the West, the founding of Rome. Grief-stricken at his eventual return to his destined path, Dido kills herself.

Tamora's identification of herself and Aaron with Dido and Aeneas strikes at the *Aeneid*'s epic inscription of irrevocable opposition between love and duty, using the master-text of Roman identity to do so. Tamora indeed bears some resemblance to Dido; both are widowed queens, for example, both foreigners to Roman ways who have attempted to elevate love over duty. Unlike Dido, however, Tamora manages to retain both her sovereignty and her lover. If Tamora is a new Dido, her fanciful comparison also revises the ending of the story of Carthage's fateful encounter with Rome: the Goths may have been conquered, but she has not been, and she is laying the groundwork for the ultimate destruction of the Roman empery. Finally, her secret extra-marital attachment to her lover, who is himself an outsider to Rome and Roman ways, refuses the *Aeneid*'s foregrounding of the bonds between men as a foundation of the Roman state. In the poem, Aeneas leaves the burning ruins of Troy carrying his aged father on his back and leading his young son by the hand. Well before the contract with Latinus, the bonds between men – perhaps especially fathers and sons – are held sacred. Rather than homosocial probity, an illicit heterosexual bond will be the shaping relation of the new Roman order Tamora proposes.

Tamora and Aaron's affair is a wildly unRoman scandal, as Bassianus and Lavinia realize, but their understanding of the affair's implications is based on a much narrower vision of what race means than animates Rome's founding legends. It is oddly left to the Goths to acknowledge that the affair has the potential to undermine the patriarchal Roman order. Just as Othello compares his death blow to the way he once killed "a malignant and a turban'd Turk" who "Beat a Venetian and traduc'd the state" (V.ii.353–4) – entirely naturalizing himself to the cultural perspective of the Venice which has disinherited him and whose values have led him to this moment – Tamora is so horrified by the birth of her "blackamoor child" (IV.ii.s.d.) by Aaron that she wants him to kill it. If it became publicly known, the black baby's existence would result in "stately Rome's disgrace" (60). Even the rapists Chiron and Demetrius insist that by the means of the black baby, "our mother is for ever shamed," that "Rome will despise her for this foul escape" (112, 113). After playing so boldly with the familial and marital building blocks of Roman culture, in using the name "Lavinia" and in the Dido comparison, *Titus* suddenly normalizes its view of dynastic marriage. The baby's visible racial difference from Tamora and Saturninus, and his unmistakable resemblance to Aaron, bring the play's delight in showing Romans fall victim to the collapse of their own patriarchal ethos to a screeching halt. On the issue of the miscegenous birth, Goth and Roman speak in a single outraged voice.

Why is the birth of Aaron and Tamora's illegitimate child the occasion of such shock among people who have every reason to hate Rome and Romans? White Tamora has given birth to a child who is as black as the father, as though she herself had no role in his making. One is reminded of the anecdote reported by George Best in 1578 about "an Ethiopian as blacke as a cole" who married an Englishwoman and fathered a child "in all respects as blacke as the father was," despite the fact that the baby was born in England, far away from the possible influence of the hot African sun. Best was certain that this mysterious blackness was a sign of the result of Cham's disobedience to God's order to refrain from sexual intercourse while he and his family were confined in their father Noah's ark. Cham's punishment was that the baby born of this illicit copulation and all its descendants were turned "black and lothsome." Such prohibitions of interracial sex as I noted in colonial Virginia may have been emotionally productive of, and responsive to, just such a sense as Best's of the mysteriousness and irreducibility of blackness, and of white civil society's inability ever to fully master or contain it.

In *Titus*, sex is the crucible, the "dark womb" where racially identifiable bodies are made. The play has worked hard to create a sense of *Romanitas*, with its Latin tags, its interest in Roman history and customs and texts, its framing by the myth of the raped and silenced Philomela. But it has also deliberately muddled the distinction between "Roman" and "barbarian": "Thou art a Roman, be not barbarous" (I.i.378), Marcus Andronicus implores Titus, as he begs permission to have the murdered Mutius buried in the family tomb. The birth of Aaron's and Tamora's baby draws us back from enjoyment of the guilty pleasures provided by the play's cruelty and extravagance, and freshly asserts what Titus's emotional deafness to other parents' suffering and to his son's right to an independent moral existence have obscured: the principle that Roman families are the basis of the Roman state. Finally, truly "incorporate in Rome" (I.i.462), Tamora is as convinced as Titus was when he killed Mutius that evidence of unRoman disobedience to patriarchal control must be stamped out. The baby is living proof of how controlling women is the key to avoiding Roman "disgrace," and of the consequences of weak masculine control over women's sexuality.

Or rather, the baby embodies *white* men's weak control. Lucius only restores order to Rome with the aid of an army of Goths, who have rallied to him out of outrage that "Ingrateful Rome" has heaped "foul contempt" (V.i.12) on a warrior of Titus's stature. The Goth warriors' sympathy for Lucius's and his father's suffering is as strange as Tamora's guilt over the birth of her black baby – why should they care about the anguish of their conquerors?

Here, the play demonstrates Roman masculinity's appropriation of the resources of barbarism. Rome's decaying social and political institutions must be revived, and the barbarians who come to the aid of Rome's disabled leaders furnish the necessary energy. Gender unites men across cultural barriers, as we observed in the case of Cassio's confiding details of his relationship with Bianca to Iago. When it does, even wicked Tamora falls into her proper place. But *Titus*'s sudden decision to reform masculinity and use it to rescue Rome requires the simultaneous rehabilitation of race, or more specifically, of whiteness.

If shared masculine blame of Tamora provides one pole of support for a restored patriarchal order in *Titus Andronicus,* then unanimous white revulsion against Aaron and the fruits of his blackness provides the other. Having stopped toying with a decayed patriarchal rule and decided to restore it, *Titus* must contain the figure of Aaron, whose entirely unexpected devotion to his baby furnishes a potent alternative to Roman fatherhood. In his startling blackness, the baby has reproduced the essence of his father's pride and energy:

> Coal-black is better than another hue,
> In that it scorns to bear another hue;
> For all the water in the ocean
> Can never turn the swan's black legs to white,
> Although she lave them hourly in the flood.
>   (IV.ii.99–103)

It is Aaron who reasserts the father right whose meaning has decayed among the Romans as a principle of social and familial organization. Indeed, he proposes reviving it in a new and more rigorously masculinized form, patriarchy apparently without women. He coos to his baby that he'll raise him in the wild, to "cabin in a cave" and learn "To be a warrior and command a camp" (IV.ii.179, 180). One might expect that this primeval vision of savage fatherhood would appeal to the play's Goths, but – because of race's role in reviving the Rome whose foundations Shakespeare's play with his classical sources has so shaken – one would be wrong.

The world of *Titus Andronicus* is afflicted by categorical disarray. "Roman" and "Goth" have lost their oppositional meaning, foreign women dominate and manipulate Roman men. At the brink of dissolution, *Titus*'s Romans reorganize their categories, opening themselves to the Goths' righteous determination and thereby creating for themselves a hybrid of civility and barbarism which will possess the will and the capacity to build a new kind of state. By absorbing the Goths' moral force, the Romans do not so much end their civilization as prove its adaptability and its power to sustain itself. But if – as in *Othello* and *The Rape of Lucrece* – race and gender work together to define the structures of feeling which allow the state to continue, *Titus*'s version of this compact is a great deal less "natural" than it is made to appear in the other works. The way the Roman tragedy has of looking up from the wreckage of Roman value and seizing on Aaron and Tamora as its true causes points to the constructedness, even arbitrariness, of the norms it has finally decided to defend. Nevertheless, Tamora springs to the defense of these norms, suggesting that male and paternal primacy is the one fiction into which new life must be breathed if *Titus* is to identify itself as a Roman play at all. Aaron's capture and punishment is as much about fatherhood as it is about a simplified notion of race.

The wonderful thing about *Titus* is that its racial simplifications refuse to satisfy the expectation of an audience inculcated in the principles of whiteness of absolute racial closure. Aaron's punishment will be carried out, but that ending is postponed until after the end of the action. (In comparison, *Titus*'s Restoration adaptation burns him alive onstage.) The lack of performance of Aaron's ordained torture and death leaves slightly ajar the racial doors that *Othello*'s and *Lucrece*'s histrionic self-immolations close so firmly. Those works tell us what to think about Lucrece's black blood and Othello's guilt; the characters think it themselves. But the play's final impression of Aaron's voluble pride in his evil is allowed to linger. The Aaron reduced to his physically threatening blackness is somehow more theatrically persistent than the Aaron who was part of a broader conspiracy to erode the paternal basis of Roman authority.

We cannot doubt that the performance of early modern racial identities is frequently about the vindication of white social authority, or that such performance so frequently proceeds through the instrumentality of gender and sexuality. What *Titus* suggests with equal probability, however, is that the performance of racial authority does not always neatly add up to the thing itself. The resolutely "othered" black subjects of imperialist performance sometimes had a way, as is evinced by the Romans' need of barbarism in *Titus*, or by Barbary's passing down of the Willow Song, of escaping firm social binaries and insinuating themselves within the heart of whiteness. Indeed, whiteness without blackness loses much of its ontological point. Studies of race in early modern culture for the twenty-first century might therefore do well to concentrate on the places where the apparently marmoreal surface of whiteness splits to reveal the operating mechanisms just beneath. I am convinced these mechanisms have much to do with suppressing knowledge of the extent of whiteness's reliance on, and concomitant obsession with, the sexual and laboring bodies of black people – perhaps especially of the black women who are so conspicuously rare in the canon of Shakespeare's works, and so essential in the maintenance of colonialist fictions of gender and racial identity.

References and Further Reading

Callaghan, D. 1996: "'Othello was a white man': Properties of Race on Shakespeare's Stage." In Terence Hawkes (ed.), *Alternative Shakespeares 2*. London and New York: Routledge, 192–215.

Carby, H. 1982: "White Woman, Listen! Black Feminism and the Boundaries of Sisterhood." In *The Empire Strikes Back: Race and Racism in Seventies Britain*. London: Hutchinson, 212–35.

Chambers, R. 1997: "The Unexamined." In Mike Hill (ed.), *Whiteness: A Critical Reader*. New York: New York University Press, 187–203.

Diawara, M. 1995: "Cultural Studies/Black Studies." In Mae G. Henderson (ed.), *Borders, Boundaries, and Frames: Cultural Criticism and Cultural Studies*. New York: Routledge, 202–11.

Douglas, M. 1966: *Purity and Danger*. London: Routledge and Kegan Paul.

duCille, A. 1997: "The Unbearable Darkness of Being: 'Fresh' Thoughts on Race, Sex, and the Simpsons." In Toni Morrison and Claudia Brodsky Lacour (eds.), *Birth of a Nation'hood: Gaze, Script, and Spectacle in the O. J. Simpson Case*. New York: Pantheon Books, 293–338.

Finkelman, P. 1997: "Crimes of Love, Misdemeanors of Passion: The Regulation of Race and Sex in the Colonial South." In Catherine Clinton and Michele Gillespie (eds.), *The Devil's Lane: Sex and Race in the Early South*. New York: Oxford University Press, 124–35.

Hall, K. 1995: *Things of Darkness: Economies of Race and Gender in Early Modern England*. Ithaca: Cornell University Press.

Hankey, J. (ed.) 1987: *Othello*. Plays in Performance. Bristol: Bristol Classical Press.

Hendricks, M. 1996: "'Obscured by dreams': Race, Empire, and Shakespeare's *A Midsummer Night's Dream*." *Shakespeare Quarterly*, 47, 37–60.

Hine, D. 1994: "Black Women's History, White Women's History: The Juncture of Race and Class." In *Hine Sight: Black Women and the Re-Construction of American History*. Brooklyn: Carlson Publishing, 49–58.

Jordan, W. 1968: *White Over Black: American Attitudes Toward the Negro, 1550–1812*. Chapel Hill: University of North Carolina Press.

Loomba, A. 1992: *Gender, Race, Renaissance Drama*. New Delhi: Oxford University Press.

——— 1994: "The Color of Patriarchy: Critical Difference, Cultural Difference, and Renaissance Drama." In Margo Hendricks and Patricia

Parker (eds.), *Women, "Race," and Writing in the Early Modern Period*. London: Routledge, 17–34.

Lott, E. 1995: *Love and Theft: Black Face, Minstrelsy, and the American Working Class*. New York: Oxford University Press.

Maslin, J. 1995: Review of *Othello* (dir. Oliver Parker). *New York Times*, December 14, 1995, C11, C20.

Mercer, K. 1994: "Reading Racial Fetishism: The Photographs of Robert Mapplethorpe." In *Welcome to the Jungle: New Positions in Black Cultural Studies*. New York: Routledge, 171–219.

Miola, R. 1983: *Shakespeare's Rome*. Cambridge: Cambridge University Press.

Modleski, T. 1991: "Cinema and the Dark Continent: Race and Gender in Popular Film." In *Feminism Without Women: Culture and Criticism in a "Postfeminist" Age*. New York: Routledge, 115–34.

Morgan, J. L. 1997: "'Some could suckle over their shoulder': Male Travelers, Female Bodies, and the Gendering of Racial Ideology, 1500–1770." *William and Mary Quarterly*, 54, 167–92.

Neill, M. 1989: "Unproper Beds: Race, Adultery and the Hideous in *Othello*." *Shakespeare Quarterly*, 40, 383–412.

Newman, K. 1987: "'And wash the Ethiop white': Femininity and the Monstrous in *Othello*." In Jean Howard and Marion F. O'Connor (eds.), *Shakespeare Reproduced*. New York: Methuen. 141–62.

Parker, P. 1994: "*Othello* and *Hamlet*: Dilation, Spying, and the 'Secret Place' of Women." In Russ McDonald (ed.), *Shakespeare Reread: The Texts in New Contexts*. Ithaca: Cornell University Press, 105–46.

Singh, J. 1994: "Othello's Identity, Postcolonial Theory, and Contemporary African Rewritings of *Othello*." In Margo Hendricks and Patricia Parker (eds.), *Women, "Race," and Writing in the Early Modern Period*. London: Routledge, 287–99.

Stallybrass, P. and White, A. 1986: *The Poetics and Politics of Transgression*. Ithaca: Cornell University Press.

11

Sycorax in Algiers: Cultural Politics and Gynecology in Early Modern England

Rachana Sachdev

Peter Stallybrass, Ann Rosalind Jones, Margo Hendricks, Kim Hall, and Jean Howard, among others, have argued that travelogues provided the early modern European nations not only with a sense of the exotic, but also with a crucial distinction between their citizens and all Others, essential in delineating national identities. In seventeenth-century England, this ideological process was visible in the way the growing field of knowledge, in particular about African and Mediterranean nations and their cultural practices, helped reconfigure the discourse of "Englishness." The knowledge garnered from travel writings had tremendous impact on all aspects of life, including both the visibly cultural categories of race and gender and the more apparently "scientific" fields like medicine. (For analyses of the cultural foundations of medical knowledge, see Thomas Laqueur and Valerie Traub, among others.) The interrelations between the travelogues and the discourses of racial, gendered, and national identities are well charted, but medical knowledge has only recently begun to be analyzed for its connections with travel writings. In order to further the inquiry into the cultural bases of medicine, I explore in this essay the overlaps between the seemingly divergent discourses of medicine, gender, and race in the context of an early modern "travel" text, *The Tempest*.

Sycorax emerges as one of the primary centers of interest when *The Tempest* is examined through the lens of cultural studies. She is completely "Othered" in Prospero's narrative about her – she is a witch from Algiers, lower in status both through her gender and her race, and she is from a distant nation recently rediscovered by English travelers. The primary questions I address in this essay, hence, relate to Sycorax and her location within the text in Algiers. Is it only incidental that Sycorax was identified as originating from Algiers? If not, why was Algiers considered a particularly suitable location for Sycorax? To be more precise, what does the text hope to achieve in Sycorax's characterization through her localization within the Algerian landscape?

Rereading Sycorax through the lens of postcolonialism is an important project, as there are almost no representations of non-white women in Shakespearean drama (except Cleopatra), resulting, until very recently, in a great paucity of simultaneous analyses of race, religion, and gender with reference to Shakespeare in critical studies. Furthermore, the relative antagonism to, or lack of interest in, Islam and Islamic countries within the Western world over the last century made Sycorax doubly inconspicuous to critical eyes. Barbara Fuchs's (1997) article in *Shakespeare Quarterly*, relocating *The Tempest* both within Irish and Mediterranean contexts, has helped in recuperating a Mediterranean/North African past for Sycorax, a past that was manifestly declared as hers in Shakespeare's text. In *The Tempest*, Sycorax is clearly identified as having been a resident of Algiers before her exile thence. Fuchs's article analyzes some of the early modern English cultural paradigms related to the "gendered dynamics of Mediterranean containment in the play" (Fuchs 1997: 61). In this essay, I extend Fuchs's analysis in order to demonstrate that contemporary English attitudes to Mediterranean and North African nations are fundamental in shaping the portrait of this shadowy figure in Shakespeare's text. My reading offers an approach to Sycorax that foregrounds her cultural heritage as understood by early modern English people.

Essentially, my project in this essay is to provide a map for a different reading of Sycorax and *The Tempest* based on the early modern English "discovery" of Africa and of its cultural traditions by the medical and cultural authorities. I examine the ways in which at least one of the cultural traditions of Northern Africa, female circumcision, could be appropriated by the English medical and cultural texts to establish gender and national boundaries within European nations. The gaze outwards to the body parts and cultural habits of women outside England, provided by travel documents and the literary works based on them, is seen, in my argument, to modify the ways in which the English medical authorities understood the English female body. I argue that the medical experts felt compelled not only to use this new knowledge about female circumcision to control gender boundaries, but also to distinguish between English and non-English female bodies. Hence, cultural knowledge of other nations provided the impetus for the medical creation of a specifically "English" female body. On the other hand, medical texts themselves were influential in establishing the contemporary female physiognomy for the travel writers and for the dramatists. It is this congruence of medical and cultural knowledge of Africa that, I contend, leads to the construction of Sycorax in *The Tempest*.

In order to establish that Sycorax represents the threat associated with non-Western cultures and with female circumcision in particular, I first provide a history of early modern English knowledge of and interest in circumcision. There are three related questions arising out of the interesting upheaval in the cultural and medical history of early modern times. To what extent do the English medical treatises of the sixteenth and seventeenth centuries reflect an awareness of the tradition and practice of female circumcision, or clitoridectomy? What conclusions can we draw about the ideological position of the medical profession in England with regard to this practice? And finally, how does this position become evident in popular and literary works, especially works, like *The Tempest*, dealing with a "colonialist" situation?

I

Europeans traveling around the world in early modern times noticed many differences in body parts, skin color, and cultural traditions surrounding the body between the women from their own nations and these "Others." The traditions surrounding the cutting or decorating of the genital organs formed a part of these differences, and many travel writers mention circumcision in particular. Both male and female circumcisions are mentioned overtly in some popular texts circulating widely in early modern England. Leo Africanus's influential history of Africa, translated into English by John Pory in 1600, not only referred to the practice in Egypt and Syria of women being circumcised, but also made English people aware of the role of old women as circumcisers. This text can thus be seen as providing a contemporary validation for fear of older women like Sycorax living in North Africa. Africanus claims: "there goe crying up and downe this Citie *certaine aged women*, who (though that which they say in the streets cannot be understood) are notwithstanding injoyned by their office to circumcise women according to the prescript of Mahumet" (*Pilgrimes*, VI, 27, emphasis added). *A Description of Guinea*, which was written in 1600, made the English public increasingly aware of this cultural tradition by adding another area to the list of nations practicing female circumcision (*Pilgrimes*, VI, 259). In 1602, *A Description of Benin* declared about the inhabitants of the country that "They are circumcised, both Boyes and Girles" (*Pilgrimes*, VI, 359). William Finch, writing in 1607, had asserted about the people of "Sierra Leona" that "howsoever it comes to passe, their children are all circumcised" (*Pilgrimes*, IV, 3). Interestingly, Purchas's *Pilgrimage* (1613) makes circumcision of women a characteristic of both Islam and Africa, while at the same time it makes circumcision accessible to Christians as well. Purchas notes: "They borrowed of the Jewes abstinence from swines-flesh, and circumcision of their males, to which they added *excision of their females*, still observed of the *Christians* in those parts" (577, emphasis added). Indeed, he asserts that both male and female circumcision were practiced even amongst Christian and Gentile peoples in Africa, including the Ethiopians, the Anzichi which "stretch from Zaire to Nubia" (701), "the Cophti and Abassines" (648). The dominions associated with Prester John, in some ways the most sentimentalized African regions because they represented to the Western mind the possibility of the permanent conquest of Africa by the Christians (a possibility also glimpsed at imaginatively in Prospero's rule over the island in *The Tempest*), were also seen to be practicing the circumcision of women (Bulwer, *Man Transform'd*, 380). Even though Leo Africanus cited Egypt and Syria as the only places practicing circumcision of women, the observance of the practice amongst other nations and even amongst non-Islamic people in these nations gave more credence to the belief that non-European nations followed this rite on a regular basis. The reiteration of this topic particularly amongst travel writing from the first two decades of the seventeenth century testifies to the interest of English people in the cultural traditions relating to male and female circumcision. However, despite its growing fascination for European people, female circumcision was still most often seen as being localized in Northern and Central Africa.

In addition to the travel narratives, Europeans in the sixteenth and seventeenth centuries had recourse to the knowledge of female circumcision from another set of sources as well, and these sources helped in the reinforcement of the image of Africa as the land of female circumcision. Most of the standard medical texts used everywhere in Europe from medieval times onwards had included Arabic versions of classical Greek medical texts by Soranus of Ephesus, Aetius of Amida, and Paulus Aeginata who had all recommended "excision of the overgrown clitoris" in their texts. These medical textbooks had Latinized Islamic medical texts, such as Avicenna's *Canon*, the works of Averroës (d. 1198) and Albucasis (d. 1122), and hence standard medical knowledge in early modern Europe was classical medicine filtered through the Islamic world. Albucasis had followed Aeginata to the word, and Avicenna (Ibn Sena 937–1037), the "Prince of Physicians," had recommended using medicines or the knife to excise the clitoris (Adams 1846: 382). From the second century on, knowledge of female circumcision was available to European medical experts since Soranus, Aetius, and Aeginata had all mentioned ways of excising the clitoris in relatively painless procedures.

Most of the classical Greek and Roman texts talked about clitoridectomy only in the context of Northern Africa, and in particular, Egypt, and hence, female circumcision appeared to become more firmly localized in those nations. Aetius, whose works had been widely anthologized in early modern Europe and who was cited by the English medical writer Nicholas Culpeper, calls a large clitoris a "shameful deformity" which could excite a young woman to "venery." To correct this deformity, he recommends excision of the part. Aetius makes this medical practice more acceptable to the practitioners by citing the case of the Egyptians, who regularly practiced female circumcision by "amputating the clitoris" before it grew too large, "chiefly about the time when the girl is marriageable," and by giving detailed "scientific" directions for the procedure:

> The surgeon stands before her and grasps with a forceps the nympha (clitoris) and pulls it by means of his left hand; with the right (hand) he cuts just above the teeth of the forceps . . . only the excess part is amputated. . . . When the surgery is finished, the wound may be wiped with a sponge squeezed in astringent wine or cold water; manna of frankincense is sprinkled, and a liniment is spread moistened with vinegar water. And a sponge squeezed out of vinegar water is placed upon it. (Ricci 1950: 107–8)

The medical solution for the social disease of the excitable clitoris in a marriageable woman is suitably followed by a good "cure" of astringents and dressings. The medical procedure also seems to make the cultural tradition practiced in the Northern African country a little more "civilized" by preventing infections. The practice could be seen as both "savage" and "civilized," depending on the context. In either case, though, whether it was used as a cultural tradition or a medical practice, it could help in the restoration of patriarchal authority by containing licentious women. This ideological agenda makes female circumcision a recurrent topic in the medical texts in both Christian and Islamic worlds.

II

Besides helping patriarchal European societies to control female sexual desire and fix the definitions of gender, circumcision of women can also be seen to be helpful to the English in the mapping of a specific cultural and national identity. The cultural manifestation of the practice of female circumcision, deliberately divorced from its adoption by the medical experts, was seen as heinous and confined to Africa. Africa, appropriately, was the land where Shakespeare imagined Sycorax to have lived. Furthermore, most of the contemporary vernacular medical texts listing excision of the clitoris as a "desirable" surgical procedure were directly implicated in the creation of a specifically English populace. The very use of the English language to spread knowledge about medical matters and about the cultural traditions of other nations, matters until then beyond the scope of knowledge of the general public, testifies to the fact that these texts were deliberately creating a more educated English public. The authors clearly mention this purpose in their prefaces. (See Culpeper and Sharp, in particular.) The dissemination of the knowledge of female circumcision has hence another important cultural dimension: clitoridectomy becomes for the English a useful imaginative tool against women and also one of the ways of building a specifically "English" body.

John Bulwer's *Anthropometamorphosis Or Man Transform'd* (1650) uses circumcision as a marker of difference in exactly this way. Bulwer lists circumcision as well as skin color and breast size as visible signs of cultural and national difference, in this time of increasing uncertainty about what it means to be English during the civil wars. He is at pains to establish an English body and identity by pointing out that all these practices, including the popular practice of face-painting, originated outside England and that they are immoral, heinous, and also non-nationalistic. The section on the "abuses of the privy parts" begins by attributing the blame for these "abuses" upon Satan, "who in the first place hath laid snares for the parts of Generation" (346). Bulwer also indicates the guilt of the participating populations when he specifies that the men and women of these "barbarous nations" decorate and circumcise their genitals for one or more of these reasons: increased pleasure, desire for longevity and youthfulness, cleanliness, or simply superstition. These "barbarous" African nations are hence seen as places where Satan rules. As the Prophet Mahomet was often identified with Satan in early modern European imagination, and Islam was seen as encouraging both circumcision and licentious behavior, Bulwer seems to cement the connection between genital abuses and Islamic and North African nations. The diatribe against nations practicing genital abuses is not totally unambiguous, however. Bulwer notes that castration of women has the potentially desirable effect of controlling lustful desires: *"the end might be the same in spading women as men*, both being thereby made impotent, and so consequently . . . *lesse subject to be corrupted with their passions"* (363–4, emphasis added).

By the time Bulwer gets to the second part of his discussion of the control of female sexuality, when he lists the countries practicing circumcision for women, he begins to equate it with male circumcision, and his last comment on the practice is:

> Many women both here and elsewhere have caused themselves to be cut, as being over-great, and exceeding Nature, but not for any matter of Religion. In all which places it is done by cutting that part which answereth the Prepuce or Foreskin in a man.
>
> Munster (indeed) shewes the originall of this invention, attributing it to the Queen of Sheba, whose proper name was Maqueda, who ordained that women should be circumcised, led to it by this reason, that as men have a Prepuce, so women also after the same manner have a glandulous flesh in their Genitals, which they call Nympha, not unfit to receive the character of circumcision. (381)

The responsibility for these acts is shown to lie on women's shoulders ("women have caused themselves to be cut"). Indeed, this narrative highlights that the practice supposedly originated from a woman's wish to emulate or compete with men, and thus women should be seen as the primary motive forces for the establishment and continuance of the tradition. Bulwer also asserts that circumcision for women is in keeping with Nature because it only excises what "exceeds" Nature. This "tolerant" understanding of women's wish to be circumcised follows an initial seemingly wholesale condemnation of nations that practice female circumcision – "These Abassines have added errour upon errour, and sin upon sin, for they cause their Females to be circumcised" (380). However, as Bulwer slides in the information about the use of circumcision to control sexual desire in women, the cultural invective gets transformed into a demonstration of an effective tool for the containment of women, just as spading was shown to be. If the ancient system of the "castration of women" was the way undertaken by "the jealous Italians" to "secure their wives from the admittance of any Rivall" (366), circumcision of women emerges as a potential new strategy for the maintenance of patrilineal succession, particularly since Bulwer has severed the connection usually maintained between female circumcision and religion. By emptying the cultural act of its religious significance, Bulwer enables the maintenance of the ideologically important dichotomy between the "savage" cultural tradition of female circumcision and the "civilized" medical practice of clitoridectomy.

Even though the accounts of aberrant practices by deviant nations defined the categories of racialized "self" and "other," gender complicated the categories of racial difference, as Englishwomen could be seen both as quintessentially English and at the same time "other" at moments of cultural instability. The same negative descriptions that defined barbarity could also be used as ideological prescriptions for Englishwomen. In Bulwer's description, Englishwomen occupy a liminal space between Englishmen and the monstrous women from other nations. Their bodies could be seen to approximate either to the circumcised bodies of Egyptian women, or with their enlarged clitorises to the male English body. This potential to straddle the difference between male and female, the European and the "heathen," made the position of European women a particularly vexed one. This potential for deviance in women, concretized within the play in the character of Sycorax, can also be seen to guide Prospero's response to Miranda in *The Tempest*. His primary concern as a father is to maintain Miranda's virginity intact at all costs. Only thus can he prevent a dangerous "creolization" of his daughter, and sustain the prize that the desirable groom Ferdinand requires in his wife: "O, if a *virgin*, / And your affection not gone forth, I'll make you / The queen of Naples" (I.ii.450–2, emphasis added).

The lack of proper sexual control could even lead, in extreme circumstances, to accusations of witchcraft: Prospero's naming of Sycorax as a witch derives at least some of its force from her supposedly exuberant sexuality which led her, in Prospero's report, in witch-like form to mate with the Devil. In the middle of the sixteenth century, Johann Weyer (1555–85), in the text that influenced the famous English writer Reginald Scot, *De Praestigiis Daemonum*, had described some women who had been accused of witchcraft for their unnatural sexuality. Weyer, the emancipated physician, used gynecological history to discount witchcraft as the main cause of the sexual appetite. According to him, the organ called the "clitoris by Ruffus of Ephesus . . . gradually increases in bulk and finally rises up into a penis that is fully formed in every respect" (345). Increased sexual desire and sexual intercourse with unnatural partners, like the Devil or same-sex partners, were related to this visible token of deformity – an enlarged clitoris. Clitoridectomy could then make a "witch" into a proper woman.

Early modern French medical experts were seemingly optimistic about the ability of this ideological tool to effect serious change in the contemporary cultural crisis. As Park points out, they started to promote clitoridectomy as a "feasible remedy for clitoral hypertrophy and its inconvenients, not just in far away Africa but in Europe itself" (Park 1997: 183). Jean Riolan, a professor of anatomy and botany at the University of Paris, had suggested the use of this procedure for "*all* contemporary women, as a way of disciplining unbridled female sexuality." He considered the method "not without its utility in this depraved period, when the modesty of virgins is easily overcome by gold, flattery, and licentiousness, and when virgins allow themselves to be conquered by either the weakness of their minds or an almost masculine jealousy" (Park 1997: 184). Clitoridectomy was seen as the cure for everything from prostitution and female rebellion to pre-marital sex. What was appealing to the French about female circumcision convinced the English as well, for exactly the same reasons.

In Helkiah Crooke's widely circulated text *Microcosmographia* (1615), which is amongst the earliest of the English Renaissance medical texts arguing for a necessity for clitoridectomy in some cases, Riolan's "masculine jealousy" is imagined to exist at the physical level as well. His attention is focused on the resemblance of the enlarged clitoris to the "mans member, especially when it [the clitoris] is fretted with the touch of cloaths, and so strutteth and groweth to a rigiditie as doth the yarde of a man." Crooke is quick to mention the practical threats ensuing from this resemblance between male and female sexual parts. Women could use this counterpart of male anatomy to fulfill the role usually played by the male organ in sexual intercourse: "And this part it is which those wicked women doe abuse called Tribades (often mentioned by many authors, and in some states worthily punished) to their mutuall and unnaturall lusts" (238).

Clitoridectomy was useful in European cultures in the early seventeenth century for yet another ideological purpose apart from Bulwer's, as Crooke's narrative outlines. The one-sex model proposed by Aristotle and supported by Galen maintained that there was no essential difference between male and female sexual organs and positioned female as the inferior sex. In the sixteenth and seventeenth centuries in Europe, this model had given rise to interesting tales of gender transformation. Some of these stories are detailed in the works of the famous French gynecologist, Ambroise Paré (see Laqueur 1990: 126–42). Of particular importance is the story of Marie-Germain, who is supposed to have developed male organs during puberty while leaping over a ditch. The anxiety caused by stories of women suddenly producing male genitalia and destroying a credible basis for sexual difference was exacerbated in an age that saw multiple and common violation of the dress codes for men and women (see Henderson and McManus 1995). At such a time, circumcision seemed to be the appropriate remedy to the Dutch judge who had to punish a woman "who dressed as a man, enlisted in the army, and passed in her new role until she was caught taking the man's part in sexual intercourse." When she returned from the wars, she was accused of "immoral lust, for sometimes even exposing her clitoris outside her vulva and trying . . . licentious sport with other women" (Laqueur 1990: 137). The destruction of secure bases for distinguishing between men and women led to the need for external means of control, including circumcision.

As Park has demonstrated, the overt mention of tribadism in medical discourses about hypertrophied clitorises is an early modern invention and refers in particular to the crisis over gender boundaries in which European nations found themselves at the end of the sixteenth century. What is even more striking about early modern and even ancient medical discourses about "hypertrophied" clitorises is that they refer to female circumcision in Egypt, where it is practiced on all women and not just on "unnaturally enlarged" clitorises, to establish the validity of their suggestions. The fear of female–female intercourse drives not only the French Riolan, but also the English Helkiah Crooke to advocate clitoridectomy in a similar manner, though it was usually seen to be practiced only on North African women.

When detailing the need for circumcision amongst Egyptian women, Crooke is careful to maintain a highly scientific tone, even though he points out that Egyptian women need repeated circumcision, once as "Maidens before they grow too long" and then again "before they marry" (237). For him, the reason for the enlargement of the clitoris might be "the affluence of humours" or "attrectation," but the outcome of this enlargement is a feeling of "shame (being in many countryes a notable argument of petulancie and immodesty)." It is for this social imperative to avoid shame that,

Crooke proposes, they "need the Chirurgions helpe to cut them off (although they bleed much and are hardly cicatrised)" (237). As in Bulwer, the burden of "choosing" clitoridectomy is placed on women who seek medical help to overcome their sense of shame over their "deformities." However, the very presence of shame attests to a cultural principle at work underlying the medical necessity for the procedure. Hence, even in the beginning of this process of medicalizing of circumcision, the truth of the ideological agenda behind the practice is clearly evident behind the scientific tone. The practice of circumcision has an ideological significance for the English public and the medical profession that continues throughout the century and becomes increasingly more visible as cultural encounters with other nations gather in force.

Further support for this ideological project could be seen to arrive shortly after Crooke's text was published and republished within a few years in England. Translations of early modern French medical authorities like Paré and Riolan appeared in England starting in 1631. Thomas Johnson's *Workes of that famous Chirurgion Ambrose Parey Translated out of Latine and Compared with the French* appeared in 1634 and made Paré's and Dalechamps's (1570) association of clitoral hypertrophy and female homoeroticism more widely accessible to the English. It is, therefore, no surprise that Nicholas Culpeper and Jane Sharp, two of the most popular writers of handbooks for midwives, both mention and advocate clitoridectomy in their texts.

Nicholas Culpeper's *Directory for Midwives* (first edition 1653) went though several editions in the late seventeenth century itself. In this text, he openly declares that he has no direct knowledge of the profession himself, but that he is making expert medical knowledge available to the midwives who do not have the time or the skills to read foreign and/or difficult medical texts. This act of "quasi-feminism," enabling midwives to take better care of their patients so that they do not have to call in male surgeons for simple procedures, is accompanied by a professional tone that lends credibility to his advice. He is the male medical professional who, despite his lower status in the medical hierarchy which went from physician to barber-surgeons to apothecaries and thence downward to midwives and other unprofessional assistants, has the authority granted by years of experience and the acute lack of good medical professionals to translate, transcribe, and to make available expertise that was not accessible to most people. In this text, Culpeper describes the clitoris thus:

> The clitoris is a sinewy and hard body, full of spungy and black matter within, as the side-ligaments of a yard are, in form it represents the Yard of a man, and suffers erection and falling as that doth; this is that which causeth lust in women and gives delight in copulation, for without this a woman neither desires copulation, or hath any pleasure in it, or conceives by it. . . . The bigger the clitoris is in a woman, the more lustful they are. (22–3)

This ideologically charged scientific description of a body part resonates with Bulwer's accounts of the reasoning of the various cultures that practice female circumcision. The knowledge of the body parts and their function in the sexual acts also descended to the Renaissance through the ancient classical texts which give the anatomical and physiological description of the clitoris along with the ways adopted by ancient cultures to control female sexuality. A conjunction and happy coincidence of ancient medical and neo-colonial knowledge leads Culpeper in this practical guide to advise midwives on how to perform circumcision for women who are too "excessive":

> This part [the wings] sometimes is as big as a mans Yard, and such women were thought to be turned into men. *The causes*: It is from too much nourishment of the part, from the looseness of it by often handling. *The cure*: It is not safe to cut it off presently; but first use Driers and Discussers, with things that a little astringe; then gentle casticks without causing pain, as burnt allum, Aegpyticum. Take Aegpyticum, oyl of Mastick, Roses, wax, each half an ounce. If these will not do, then cut it off, or tie it with a ligature of silk or Horse-hair, till it mortifie. *Aetius teacheth the way of Amputation* he calls it Nympha or Clitoris, between both the wings: but take heed you cause not pain or inflammation. (IV, 3, emphasis added)

The quasi-medical text quotes one of the foremost medical authorities for legitimizing his position, and ends by taking the same position on female sexuality as does the more obviously socially and culturally conditioned text. Masturbation and excessive sexual pleasure in women are both seen as social and medical problems that need a suitable medical cure, and the medical cure is the same as that "abhorrent" practice that Bulwer first castigates in other nations and then recommends. Moreover, both the texts use knowledge from non-English sources to start and legitimize an English practice. In Culpeper's directions to the English midwives for whom this text is ostensibly written, the English "civility" and medical professionalism is visible in the advice not to cause "pain or inflammation."

Jane Sharp's *The Midwives Book* (1671) reproduces most of the medical knowledge and cultural beliefs about the clitoris cited by her male predecessors. However, her discussion of the medical lore and the controversies surrounding the female genitalia is much more extensive than Culpeper's and is also much more aware of the slipperiness of gender difference. Sharp is at pains to establish that the female genitalia are very much like the male, especially in the outer visible parts, except for a difference in size. For her, "The only thing that distinguishes a clitoris from its larger counterpart in the male body, the penis," is the size of the respective organs:

> The head of this counterfeit Yard is called Tentigo . . . ; commonly it is but a small sprout, lying close hid under the wings, and not easily felt, yet sometimes it grows so long that it hangs forth at the slit like a Yard, and will swell and stand stiff if it be provoked, and some lewd women have endeavoured to use it as men do theirs. (44–5)

Hence, with this essential similarity between male and female organs, it is essential that women in England have small clitorises to maintain gender difference.

The construction of Englishness plays a large role in Sharp's medical discussion of female genitalia. Like Crooke, Sharp also attempts to make the English female bodies

naturally "feminine" by noting that it is only women in "the Indies and Egypt" who
have enlarged genitalia. This distinction between Englishwomen and the women from
"the Indies and Egypt" is, however, interestingly grounded in Sharp's text in the
knowledge of ideological pressures. Englishwomen are aware of the construction that
a large clitoris is dangerous and monstrous, and will keep silent about it: "I never
heard but of one in this country, if there be any they will do what they can for shame
to keep it close" (45). The text leaves open the possibility that, like Egyptian women,
Englishwomen have large clitorises, while at the same time it establishes the size of
the female private parts as a measure of national and cultural difference.

Sharp distinguishes between the sizes of the wings as well, and recommends not
only clitoridectomy but also infibulation:

> I told you the clitoris is so long in some women that it is seen to hang forth at their
> Privities and not only the Clitoris that lyeth behind the wings but the wings also . . .
> In some countries they grow so long that the Chirurgion cuts them off to avoid trouble
> and shame, chiefly in Egypt; they will bleed much when they are cut; and the blood is
> hardly stopt wherefore the maids have them cut off betimes, and before they marry, for
> it is a flux of humours to them, and much motion that makes them grow so long. Some
> sea-men say that they have seen Negro women go stark naked, and these wings hanging
> out. (45–7)

The confluence of travel narrative and medical lore in Sharp's text creates a world that
is much harsher than the one created by her predecessors: she describes and recommends excision of the wings as well as the clitoris. The threat of female organs approxi-
mating male genitalia is so great that Sharp forgets that what she is recommending
can possibly be enacted on her own body. The demarcation of gender and sexual difference is important enough to absorb the pain and horror of the mutilation, and since
the procedure is largely seen as beneficial only to women from "the Indies and Egypt,"
the possibility of its enaction is seen as distant enough to make it bearable. To make
this mutilation more acceptable to the medical authorities, Sharp uses a term to
describe the women that is increasingly becoming more pejorative in the seventeenth
century, "Negro," and she also imagines monstrous body parts that grow even after
being cut. The wings in the private parts of the Egyptian and Negro women are seen
to have an enormous potential for increase that needs to be curtailed repeatedly. The
monstrousness of the cut body parts growing again under pressure from the heightened activity and the particular imbalance of humors in the African women makes
Englishwomen appear free from the taint of the enlarged private parts. However, as
in the description of the enlarged clitoris, the difference is superficial and cultural
(dependent on the level of activity) rather than essential. The female quasi-medical
voice can find nothing essential in which to ground gender or cultural difference, even
though she understands the cost of this slipperiness in maintaining boundaries of
gender and sexual difference. She carefully articulates a scientific rhetoric of size and
growth that maintains the bodies of Englishwomen as separate and "proper," at least
for the moment.

The tools for practicing circumcision of women were thus important in this ideological endeavor, and as Callaghan notes, Johannes Scultetus describes one such implement in his catalogue: "pincers to cut off the clitoris both bent and straight" (Callaghan 1996: 337–8). Scultetus had also provided, possibly for the first time, detailed illustrations for "shortening of the clitoris or the woman's yard which had become unprofitably augmented" (Ricci 1949: 127). The presence of the tools and the illustrations point to the readiness with which European medical authorities looked to adapt African cultural norms into a "civilized" European medical procedure while the diatribe against African nations for their "barbaric" traditions remained more or less intact.

III

The English and the Europeans medicalized the ideologically charged practice of female circumcision, ostensibly following the classical Greeks and Romans, in the sixteenth and seventeenth centuries after a hiatus of several centuries. This cultural process can be seen to have significant ramifications for Shakespeare's *The Tempest*, especially as this text carefully and self-consciously locates Sycorax within Algiers, a nation associated in the early modern English mind with the rites of male and female circumcision. As my earlier discussion has shown, circumcision was clearly linked with North Africa in the English popular imagination. The repulsion and fear inspired by the cultural tradition of female circumcision were seriously exacerbated when another factor was added: piracy. The first part of Marlowe's *Tamburlaine* had cried out against "the cruel pirates of Argier / That damned train, the scum of Africa" (III.iii.55–6) and helped to concretize in the English mind an overwhelmingly negative portrait of Algeria. As time went on, and piracy was outlawed by James I, the Algerians were progressively more vilified. Samuel Chew has pointed out that "piracy was at its worst about 1608 at which time John Ward, the most notorious of all the English corsairs, was at the apex of his criminal career" (Chew 1965: 345). The growing fear of African pirates only drove the hatred against Algiers further. Algiers was a particular target for hatred since it alone was supposed to hold some twenty thousand captives (Chew 1965: 378). Some of this hatred is obvious in Robert Knolles's *The Generall History of the Turkes*, which was published in 1603 and republished shortly thereafter in 1610.

The publication of the anonymous *Newes from Sea, Of two notorious Pyrats* in 1609, and of Robert Daborne's *A Christian Turn'd Turk* in 1610, brought both piracy and circumcision within the North African context more in the forefront of English cultural life immediately before Shakespeare's text was written. *A Christian Turn'd Turk*, in particular, highlighted some concerns that had been prevalent in Europe since the middle of the sixteenth century: Christian renegadism and slavery. Forcible or voluntary abnegation of Christianity in favor of Islam often occurred in this time period and was characterized in the popular mind by the circumcised body. Slavery had a similar sexual undertone – female slaves in particular were thought to provide sexual services for the Islamic men. As fears of piracy increased in magnitude, associations of these African shores with slavery and circumcision of both men and women grew as well. Leo Africanus and Purchas provide two famous instances of this trend. Piracy was irrevocably associated with circumcision, since the Europeans captured by the pirates were often forced to undergo conversions, and conversion necessitated circumcision. The circumcised body appeared to the Europeans as a body made irreversibly alien.

The intensity of the fears, produced as a result of the combination of economic and sexual motives, is visible not only in the proliferation of villainous characters from these shores on the English stage, but also in other popular cultural forms. Purchas's famous texts, which were self-consciously instrumental in the creation of a singular English nation, described Algiers as "the Whirle-poole of these Seas, the Throne of Pyracie, the Sinke of Trade and the Stinke of Slavery; the Cage of uncleane Birds of Prey, the Habitation of Sea-Devils, the Receptacle of Renegadoes of God, and Traytors to their Country" (VI, 108). It is within this hated and feared landscape that Shakespeare locates Sycorax, and the appropriateness of this location for Sycorax has been commented on by Samuel Chew in his exhaustive study of Islam and England (1965: 344).

Sycorax's ugly and deformed body can be seen as the quintessential representative of the moral and religious corruption associated with the land, and provides visual contrast between the "civil" Europeans and the "barbaric" Algerians. The creation of this moral binary is most clearly evident in the physical binary provided by the projected bodily differences between Sycorax and Miranda. Miranda appears in the text as an attractive European woman who has all the marks of conventional beauty. All the men she meets on the island refer to her as a "goddess." This beauty is set in visible contrast to Sycorax's physical shape and appearance, as Prospero's, Ariel's, and even Caliban's remarks demonstrate. Interestingly, Sycorax does not appear as a physical presence within the play. However, her body is very important for the establishment of ideological structures. She is described by Prospero as a witch, and as ugly and doubled over with age, and Ariel silently concurs with this description of Sycorax: "The foul witch Sycorax, who with age and envy / Was grown into a hoop" (I.ii.258–9). Prospero's identification of Sycorax with a witch is echoed in this physical description which, as Gareth Roberts points out, originates from the "stereotype of the witch familiar from many renaissance treatises, such as Reginald Scot's, which described witches as 'women which be commonly old, lame, beare-eied, pale, fowle, and full of wrinckles; poore, sullen'" (Roberts 1996: 184). Significantly, this generalized description only describes her ideological status and gives no clues about her skin color, height, breast size, or hair – the most common ways of describing women.

The only other piece of information we have about her physical body is that she was, according to Prospero, a "blue-ey'd hag" (I.ii.269). This lacuna has resulted in some recent speculation on the part of cultural critics about her skin color, as well as about the exact meaning of those words. Unfortunately, there is almost no consensus on the meaning of the words "blue-eyed." In the *OED*, these words carry the primary signification "someone with blue iris," whereas the Arden Shakespeare unquestioningly asserts that "blueness there was regarded as a sign of pregnancy" (27). The Riverside Shakespeare calls it a description of "someone with dark circles around the eyes," preferring not to make judgments about Sycorax's racial identity. The Signet *Tempest* interprets "blue-eyed" as "referring to the livid color of the eyelid, a sign of pregnancy," but gives a more racialized description of the name Sycorax, speculating on its derivation from Greek, sys, "sow," and korax, which means both "raven" and "hook" (51). Stephen Orgel's Oxford edition identifies Sycorax with "Medea, the Scythian raven," basing the interpretation on the roots "Sy" ('Scythia') and "Korax" ('raven') (19–20). Based on these interpretations of the words, Sycorax could either be a white female with blue eyes, a tawny or black female with blue eyes, a pregnant black female, or a woman with no determined skin color who has dark circles around her eyes. Leah Marcus's project of "unediting the Renaissance" leads her to the same conclusion about the indeterminacy of these words. At the end of her chapter on *The Tempest*, she asserts that the "investigation has been inconclusive in that it has not allowed us to settle on any single eye color or condition as properly glossing the phrase, but it has been highly conclusive about the suspect origins of the standard emendation" (Marcus 1996: 16).

The word "hag" linked to "blue-eyed" is equally ambiguous in terms of the physical description of the person. Most of the definitions outlined in the *OED* have to do with moral, ethical, and spiritual concepts rather than with physical ones. However, as the *OED* entry outlines, there are a few more clues embedded within the use of the word "hag": the 1587 *Mirror for Magistrates*, in the line "That hatefull hellish hagge of ugly hue," associates hags with an "ugly hue," or blackness. Spenser thinks of a hag as "loathly, wrinckled" and as "ill favoured and old." Shakespeare in *Macbeth* also links hags with darkness and with the color black by calling the witches "you secret, black, and midnight Hags." The word "hag" seems to go a little further in delimiting the possibilities of skin color for Sycorax, though, of course, the word was often used for white old women as well. Hence, the only clue to Sycorax's physical appearance can be seen to derive from her place of residence: Algeria. She is presumably black because she resided in Africa.

The linguistic uncertainty created in her physical description leads us to look for other sources to establish the ideological import of her role. And she does have a role, even if her role is to be physically absent. Diane Purkiss's discussion of Sycorax reduces her to "a story from the past" (Purkiss 1996: 271), but only because Purkiss sees her location in Algeria as reducible to a reference to Circe or Medea or Dido. Since the only other determinants for Sycorax (besides her worship of the god Setebos) are her nationality and her alleged status as a witch, early modern attitudes to Algeria and witchcraft can be assumed to have a huge part in the determination of Sycorax's role within the play. Other than that, we have very little to go on to decipher the mystery embedded in the following lines:

> This damned witch Sycorax,
> For mischiefs manifold and sorceries terrible
> To enter human hearing, from Algiers
> Thou know'st was banished – for one thing she did
> They would not take her life.
>
> (I.ii.263–7)

What is the one thing that Sycorax did for which they would not take her life? A common hypothesis is that she is pardoned because of her pregnancy, signified by the words "blue-eyed." But as my analysis has shown, no consensus exists about the meaning of that descriptive term. Her "witchcraft" or her worship of Setebos also offers no possible source of mercy for her. By worshipping the god "which Antonio Pigafetta describes as being worshipped by the Patagonian Indians of the storm-beaten wilderness of Tierra del Fuego, Sycorax is identified with the most remote, God-forsaken and degenerate of sixteenth-century Amerindian types" (Gillies 1994: 142–3). Sycorax's worship of an Amerindian god in Algeria does not explain the mercy granted her. However, if we start from Sycorax's identification as a witch and her abode in Algiers before her move to the island, and if we then read African and Mediterranean cultural history back into *The Tempest*, we can significantly enrich our understanding of Sycorax's presence and function within the play.

If piracy was the locus of English mercantile fears and desires, and circumcision and castration embodied the English and European fears of Islamic religion and cultural identity, the identification of Sycorax with Algiers makes her a center of both these fears. Sycorax not only represents a threat to the continued "colonial" presence of future Prosperos and Prester Johns in North African lands, she also symbolizes the threat to the Europeans' own religious identity. It is important to note that even though Algeria was part of the mighty Ottoman empire and was a source of fear for the English, fantasies of the English converting and colonizing the North African natives do not vanish from the cultural imaginary, as the references to Prester John show. These fantasies, indeed, occupy a vital place in keeping the imaginative balance of power in favor of the English. Furthermore, as Prospero's occupation of an island somewhere in the middle of the Mediterranean shows, it was exactly in those lands that were most vulnerable to the Turks and the Moors that the English built their dream empires. (For a history of the legend of Prester John, see Chew 1965: 8n). It was important to see Prospero "legitimately" taking over the island from the hands of Sycorax and her son, Caliban. His role as the liberator of the enslaved Ariel doubles the justification for European rule of the island, as in this act he has broken the spell of the ugly Sycorax and her heathen God, Setebos.

Sycorax had used the power given by this non-Christian deity to threaten Ariel's sense of identity and his peaceful existence on the island with her "earthy and abhorred commands" (I.ii.273), which could range in scope from religious to sexual. Her enforcement of a heathen religion and sexually aberrant practices were both suspicious for a Christian European patriarch, and had to be soundly vilified. Furthermore, given her North African identity, she would be seen by the early modern cultural and medical authorities as unnaturally sexually active and as having "preternaturally large" private parts that needed to be cut. Her "monster" status is exacerbated by the fact that she is both physically monstrous and can make others monstrous through her "earthy and abhorred commands."

Sycorax had one more vital power that made her frightening and repulsive to early modern European eyes. As Leo Africanus had informed the English public through the Pory translation in 1600, circumcision had largely been the work of older women or midwives who had immense power in the society because of their position (see also Lightfoot-Klein 1989: 77). Most of the cultural and medical sources derived from Africanus in early modern times referred to the "old women of Fez" as either circumcisers or as "exorcists" who were primarily interested in deriving pleasure from rubbing their clitorises against the private parts of young women who visited them. Their breaking of the sexual codes was seen in particular to involve young husbands who needed to get wise "and drive the putative spirits out of their wives' bodies with a good clubbing" (Laqueur 1989: 117). The charge that the old women who were supposed to help society in their position as soothsayers and wise women were corrupting the younger married women demonstrates this fear of their power. *The Tempest* makes a similar demonstration of the fear of the power of old women: Sycorax is seen in stereotypically witch-like form as an old hag, associated with social and sexual deviance. Within the text, Sycorax dominates and "emasculates" Ariel by keeping him in servile bondage, and thus can be seen to fit the role of the sexually voracious and dominating older woman, in essence as the circumciser of popular imagination.

In European cultural terms, Sycorax translates into a witch who has overstepped the boundaries prescribed for women and who practices "black magic" and consorts with the Devil. The charges Prospero lays against the absent Sycorax are exactly those that were leveled against most women who were called witches in Europe. The women were accused of sexual activity with the Devil as well as of practicing magic on the unsuspecting population. In *The Tempest*, Prospero accuses Caliban of being the product of Sycorax's sexual union with the Devil, and also refers to Ariel as the hapless victim of Sycorax's lust and abuse of power (I.ii.270–9). Prospero also believes that Sycorax's pregnancy with Caliban at the time of her banishment, a pregnancy at a late stage of her life, combined with her immense power, would certainly evoke a reaction of outrage and horror within her community. Even though the European remedy for women who were powerful enough to deceive or enslave men was death, the knowledge-driven European patriarch envisions another end for the women in non-European lands who are too threatening for their own communities. The power of these alien women can be successfully overcome by the enlightened European men who can thence establish not only their national superiority over the heathenish Algerians, but also seal the victory over the errant female population. Within the text, the moment of recollection of Sycorax's disruptive potential is closely followed by a visible reminder of Prospero's victory: Caliban, Sycorax's son, appears on the stage as rebellious though inescapably enslaved by Prospero. Hence, *The Tempest* provides exile as a solution for these African women who become too powerful ("sorceries manifold") or who misuse their power too openly.

The confluence of all these threats to the social and sexual spheres within the portrait of Sycorax and the negation of those threats by the powerful Prospero give one possible clue into the mystery of her exile from Algiers. As Sycorax becomes identified with these cultural stereotypes of old women from North Africa, her position as a circumciser/witch within her culture explains why she cannot simply be put to death by her own countrymen. As a powerful circumciser within her own culture, she needs to be shown as dominated by Prospero so that "savageness" can be effectively "civilized" by the European. Like the medical authorities who had both rejected circumcision and Europeanized the cultural knowledge of female circumcision into clitoridectomy, Prospero will both castigate Sycorax as the witch and overcome her "black" magic with his own "white" magic. He then becomes the symbolic medical man who has the knowledge and the power to legitimize and perform all "necessary" circumcisions.

If the "necessity" for clitoridectomy in early modern medical texts was provided by the need to control "unnatural" female lust, the fear of this same possibility guides the play as well and provides another "motive" for Sycorax's presence within the play. *The Tempest* presents Sycorax as the deviant, powerful, "monster-like" female, and Miranda as her opposite, a chaste, obedient, and dutiful daughter. However, as Eric Cheyfitz has noted, based on etymological derivatives, Miranda is at least potentially defined as errant and monstrous. Cheyfitz asserts, "At their roots, before the word 'monster' takes on the notion of deformity, both of these words [Miranda and monster] signify something 'marvelous'" (Cheyfitz 1991: 171). This potential for deviance needs to be curtailed, if Miranda has to continue to be the "goddess" to the European visitors and the pawn with which Prospero will win his dukedom back again. Prospero shows his obsession with Miranda's chastity not only in his enslavement of Caliban for the attempted rape on Miranda, but also in his warnings to Miranda and Ferdinand to control their sexual ardor "lest too light winning / Make the prize light" (I.ii.453–4). Prospero's huge ideological and economic investment in Miranda's virginity makes clear the reasons behind the fact that Sycorax is "insistently present in his memory" (Orgel 1987: 19). Sycorax is imagined as the circumcised and circumcising monstrous woman from Algiers who can simultaneously serve as a warning and present the solution, if needed, against Miranda's possible errancy. In *The Winter's Tale*, Antigonus imagines a similar kind of containment for his daughters if the embodiment of female honor and virtue, Hermione, is proved inconstant. As Fletcher points out, Antigonus promises to "have all his three daughters 'gelded' before they reach menarche in case they 'bring false generations'" (Fletcher 1995: 56). In *The Tempest*, the threat of spading or circumcision gets buried within Sycorax, the quintessential other who enables the chaste, virginal self to exist, but who can be herself circumcised/castrated by the powerful Prospero. To maintain Miranda as the image of purity and virginity, the text had to construct Sycorax as monstrous in exactly those ways. To show European culture as superior and being able to transmute heinous African cultural practices into practical knowledge, Sycorax had to be exiled from Algiers so that her power could be visibly negated and transformed by Prospero.

REFERENCES AND FURTHER READING

Adams, F. (ed.) 1846: *The Seven Books of Paulus Aeginata*. Vol. 2. London: The Sydenham Society.

Albanese, D. 1996: *New Science New World*. Durham, NC: Duke University Press.

Bulwer, J. 1650: *Anthropometamorphosis; Or Man Transform'd*.

Callaghan, D. 1996: "The Castrator's Song: Female Impersonation on the English Stage." *Journal of Medieval and Early Modern Studies*, 26, 321–53.

Chew, S. 1965: *The Crescent and the Rose: Islam and England During the Renaissance*. New York: Octagon Books. (Original work published 1937.)

Cheyfitz, E. 1991: *The Poetics of Imperialism: Translation and Colonization from "The Tempest" to "Tarzan."* New York: Oxford University Press.

Crooke, H. 1616: *Microcosmographia: A Description of the Body of Man*. 2nd edition.

Culpeper, N. 1653: *A Directory for Midwives*.

Fletcher, A. 1995: *Gender, Sex, and Subordination in England 1500–1800*. New Haven: Yale University Press.

Fuchs, B. 1997: "Conquering Islands: Contextualizing *The Tempest*." *Shakespeare Quarterly*, 45–62.

Gillies, J. 1994: *Shakespeare and the Geography of Difference*. Cambridge: Cambridge University Press.

Graham, H. [Isaac Harvey Flack] 1950: *Eternal Eve*. London: William Heinemann Medical Books.

Henderson, K. U. and McManus, B. F. 1995: *Half-Humankind: Contexts and Texts of the Controversy About Women in England, 1540–1640*. Urbana: University of Illinois Press.

Laqueur, T. W. 1989: "Amor Veneris, Vel Dulcedo Appeletur." In Michael Feher, Ramona Naddaff, and Nadia Tazi (eds.), *Fragments for a History of the Human Body*. New York: Urzone, Part 3, 90–131.

——1990: *Making Sex: Body and Gender from the Greeks to Freud*. Cambridge, MA: Harvard University Press.

Lightfoot-Klein, H. 1989: *Prisoners of Ritual*. New York: Harrington Park Press.

McKay, W. J. S. 1901: *The History of Ancient Gynaecology*. New York: William Wood and Co.

Marcus, L. 1996: *Unediting the Renaissance: Shakespeare, Marlowe, Milton*. New York: Routledge.

Mora, G. 1991: *Witches, Devils, and Doctors in the Renaissance: Johann Weyer, De praestigiis daemonum*. Trans. John Shea. Binghamton, NY: Medieval and Renaissance Texts and Studies.

Orgel, S. 1987: "Introduction." *The Tempest*. New York: Oxford University Press.

Park, K. 1997: "The 'Rediscovery' of the Clitoris: French Medicine and the Tribade, 1570–1620." In David Hillman and Carla Mazzio (eds.), *The Body in Parts: Fantasies of Corporeality in Early Modern Europe*. New York and London: Routledge, 171–94.

Purchas, S. 1965: *Hakluytus Posthumus, Or Purchas His Pilgrimes*. 12 vols. New York: AMS Press.

Purkiss, D. 1996: "The Witch on the Margins of 'Race': Sycorax and Others." In *The Witch in History: Early Modern and Twentieth-Century Representations*. New York: Routledge, 250–75.

Ricci, J. V. 1949: *The Development of Gynaecological Surgery and Instruments*. Philadelphia: The Blakiston Company.

——(ed.) 1950: *Aetios of Amida: The Gynecology and Obstetrics of Sixth Century A.D.* Philadelphia: The Blakiston Company.

Roberts, G. 1996: "The Descendants of Circe: Witches and Renaissance Fictions." In Jonathan Barry, Marianne Hester, and Gareth Roberts (eds.), *Witchcraft in Early Modern Europe: Studies in Culture and Belief*. New York: Cambridge University Press, 183–206.

Traub, V. 1995: "The Psychomorphology of the Clitoris." *Gay and Lesbian Quarterly*, 2, 81–113.

12

Black and White, and Dread All Over: The Shakespeare Theater's "Photonegative" *Othello* and the Body of Desdemona

Denise Albanese

This essay is sparked by a singular and idiosyncratic staging of *Othello* that resonates beyond its particular theatrical boundaries.[1] Offered by the Washington Shakespeare Theater in the fall of 1997, the production was characterized by those involved in it as "photonegative." Unusually for recent productions, the title role was taken by a white actor; almost every other speaking part, however, featured an actor of African descent, so that the racial dynamics of the script were visually reversed.[2] Although the lead actor, Patrick Stewart, did not modify his appearance to portray Othello, the script's color-coding of the central character as markedly black remained unmodified. For reasons I'll go on to suggest, I consider this production to have been problematic – indeed, unsuccessful, to use the aestheticized and evaluative language of the reviewer. Nevertheless, my aim is less to evaluate it than to consider how director Jude Kelly's realization of "photonegativity," while perhaps a foreseeable consequence of the theater's efforts at color-blind casting, offers a contradictory view of raced masculinity to be read against conflicts about integration and affirmative action in the US at the end of the twentieth century on the one hand, and against the body of a woman on the other.[3]

It has been recognized for some time that *Othello*'s performance history, in which the lead was generally assumed by a white actor wearing blackface make-up, affords ample evidence for racist theatrical practices. Othello has often been played according to dominant and quixotic stereotypes of black deportment (most recently, perhaps, by Laurence Olivier), and the play became, in effect, the elite cultural counterpart of black minstrel shows pervasive in the nineteenth and early twentieth centuries in the US – with which, ironically, many Shakespearean productions might then have shared the bill.[4] In light of the historical affront its production history represents, the title role has in recent decades become the all-but-inalienable province of black actors; indeed, sometimes other parts – notably, Iago – have been given over to actors of

African descent, as well.[5] In attempting to see the play still differently from these corrective productions, the Washington photonegative staging offered a representation of blackness – and, by extension, whiteness, since race properly cannot but be constructed relationally – that was both incoherent and resonant. It proved impossible for many members of the audience to recode raced bodies via the polarities of the photographic image from which the production apparently drew its inspiration; the failure of the conceit, as well as the fact of its having been undertaken, reveal a great deal about the state of race consciousness in the United States at the end of the millennium.

Given the potential box-office appeal of Patrick Stewart, it is likely that the Washington Shakespeare Theater *Othello* represents first and foremost the opportunistic casting of a famous white actor with a production built around him that minimized offensive racial impersonation. Nevertheless, the production's racial reversals seem to imply the prior existence of an extra-theatrical context where race – not simply Othello's race, but all racial identity – can be seen as a performance, a series of discursive positions potentially available to all regardless of birth, rather as gender theorists have already claimed about femininity and masculinity.[6] Yet just as in practice it has gone far harder with women who dare to impersonate maleness than for men who impersonate femininity, what undoes this particular attempt to render race performative is the intransigent asymmetry of overtly raced positions, rather than the particularity of Stewart's "failure" to convince the audience he is a Moor.[7] This asymmetry must be linked not only to minstrel-show practices, but also to dominant casting practices for classical dramatic texts, both in the theater and in Hollywood, that aspire to an enlightened blindness about color. Thus the stage and screen are asked, in effect, to model a utopian space where race doesn't "matter" any more – especially when it comes to Shakespeare, who has long been positioned as the universal property of all humanity. Productions like this one, however, reveal the extent to which the purported insignificance of race is largely a one-sided affair. And perhaps that word "affair" bears more than its usual freight of meaning: as my analysis will reveal, it is often around the problem of cross-racial desire that the return of the racial repressed cannot but force itself on a viewing public otherwise conditioned to look past the overt signs of race in productions of Shakespeare.

I

If viewers were (able) to take Washington Shakespeare Theater production at its word, what could they have been meant to see in a "photonegative" staging of *Othello?* The question concerns whether the production accomplished what the term "photonegative" implies, and whether that term offered the audience a coherent rubric for the experience of spectatorship. Is the demand, as I have argued, that race be seen simply as a form of performance, with an optically sensitive correction reregistering the staged bodies the production arrays to view, which would still leave "blackness" as the term in crisis while visually substituting for "thick lips" Stewart's thin-pursed mouth?[8] Even if so, such a correction would in itself be far from simple, since it depends for its efficacy upon the authority of the text – specifically the *Shakespearean* text – in dominating, overriding, the script provided by Stewart's body, just as it generally does when actors of African descent take part in "color-blind" productions. Kelly needed the audience to recolor the actors as embodied subjects, to accept Shakespeare's words as arbiter of their perception: it, and she, demanded that they read "black" for "white" with Stewart, as well as "white" for "black" for the rest of the cast. To understand the complex negotiation between ideology on the one hand, and perception on the other, involved in this demand, consider what would have happened had Kelly changed some of the more charged descriptions of Othello's appearance to suit Stewart's whiteness (and modifications to the language are sometimes made with other Shakespearean scripts). In that case, Kelly would have been deprived of the graphic qualities of a "photonegative" production – but she also would not have offered a challenge to the audience members to rationalize the discrepancy between what they saw and what they heard, a discrepancy which, as I've argued, pressures the boundaries that separate performance from inalienable somatic identity. Some actors can play "against" their race; others, it seems, cannot.

Kelly's decision to fret the relationship between signs and referents, between words of self-representation and the embodied subject articulating them, manifested at least in part the differential investment between director and audience in the authority of Shakespeare's words. However contingent the occasion, they have long been presumed to put on offer a universalizable tragic experience addressed to a universalized audience: hence the wide acceptance accorded to mixed-race performances. But what happened was far different from a realization of a universalist Shakespeare: Kelly's respectful fidelity to the script was not echoed by the subject position of her audience – at least that segment of the audience which laughed when Stewart pronounced on his blackness.[9] Apparently the visual disparity between Stewart and his proclaimed self-representation broke the fiction of the performance in a way that having black actors in Shakespeare customarily does not, enabling the audience to assert a "commonsense," empirically based response to an apparently absurdist moment. This reaction certainly arose because Stewart's prior reputation might have made it particularly difficult to absorb him into the dramatic fiction, a point to which I'll later return. Nevertheless, it might not have occurred if, as I aver, the audience was united (with Kelly?) in a worshipful dispensation toward Shakespeare. But without the audience's complete surrender to the imaginative and ideological control of *Othello*, the scene became incoherent, risible – and telling.

Much could be said about the evidence of dissent from the reflexive worship of Shakespeare such tendencies to mock betoken.[10] Indeed, even to ask how the production was intended to be viewed is to take its discursive cues to the audience as likely to interpellate them authoritatively, and so to ignore the extent to which Shakespeare, in the theater as in the classroom and the public sphere, represents the contested terrain that elite culture has become at the beginning of the twenty-first century. However tempting it might be to pursue this line of argument, it risks misrecognizing that in the asymmetry of response I've described, the Washington *Othello* might be read as an ideological symptom of something "larger" than a formation around Shakespeare – a symptom, that is, of an underlying shift in the conjuncture around race, specifically concerning affirmative action, at the present moment. Indeed, it is only by virtue of addressing the production as symptomatic that its incoherence about race can be put into an explanatory structure. That structure is bipartite: it involves both understanding how the Shakespearean theatrical practice privileges hegemonic forms of racial identity, and acknowledging that that racial hegemony may be inadvertently denaturalized when the staging of cross-raced heterosexual conduct forces the issue of what performative race represses.

The failure in interchangeability of white for black that rendered the Washington *Othello* flawed reveals the asymmetry underlying the supposedly "color-blind" casting practices that currently obtain whenever elite theatrical texts are reproduced in the United States.[11] In general, convention seems to demand that when non-white actors are cast in Shakespearean roles, their color fades in significance; they are meant to be taken in some sense as indistinguishable from white actors. Indeed, this indistinguishability is not only the result of a classical dramatic training system through which most Shakespearean actors pass; it may also be its point. The disciplinary regime of dramatic training, which manifests itself through a demand for uniformity of voice and bodily decorum, ensures a uniformity of effect among cast members – the better to reproduce what Susan Bennett has called a "monolithic Shakespearean voice," which is only the most privileged marker of an equally monolithic identity as a "Shakespearean actor."[12] While I do not wish to essentialize what are, after all, only conventional markers of racial identity, temporally and geographically contingent, the vocal form of the Shakespearean actor usually naturalized in mainstream theater in the United States, as Bennett's phrase indicates, is informed already by the theatrical values of the dominant – which is, to put it with an undeniable lack of argumentative suppleness, "white," developed in relation to a European, indeed British, acting and elocutionary tradition, Method acting notwithstanding. Even as theatrical practitioners have come to recognize the salutary nature of diversity on stage, there remains a grounding conviction that the universalizing power claimed for Shakespeare's words must be secured by the sacrifice of vocal particularity. Thus the vocal coach Kristin Linklater has claimed that "the actor who allows Shakespeare's text to influence and shape him as any good actor must, will be fulfilling the rich variety of sounds that great poetry demands, and will naturally remove the limiting stamp of regionality" (Linklater, as quoted by Worthen 1997a: 117). As the performance theorist W. B. Worthen has written, "The complicity of actor training in ideological formation is nowhere more visible than at this point: 'Shakespeare' becomes a naturalizing metaphor on the body itself, representing the universal, transcendent, and natural in ways that both legitimate and render unquestionable the dominant discourse of the stage" (Worthen 1997a: 99).

For obvious reasons, such training has not always characterized African American actors who perform Shakespeare. In fact, it was not all that long ago that many were criticized for their perceived verbal and vocal inadequacy to the theatrical task: in

1963 the conservative theater critic John Simon wrote of "the sad fact . . . that, through no fault of their own, Negro [*sic*] actors often lack even the rudiments of Standard American speech."[13] Simon's dated disparagement of alternative vocal models reveals his investment in policing (among other things) the sound of Shakespeare, in keeping the Shakespearean voice monolithic and hegemonic, but it is an investment that goes beyond him and still obtains, albeit in a less fractiously condescending and exclusionary form.[14] For those who have taken the necessity of a "universal" and classic elocutionary tradition as a natural consequence of understanding Shakespearean verse, any difference in articulation is understood pejoratively, as a fall from verbal grace and rectitude.[15] But the training more widely extended to African-American actors (some of it fostered by the Shakespeare Theater) has delegitimated the basis of such criticism, even as it confirms the ideological character of the Shakespearean aesthetic. Indeed, as African-American actors have come under the dispensation of the "naturalized" Shakespeare to which Worthen refers, mixed-race performances have come to seem unremarkable – indeed, natural. This may explain why the analytical problem posed by the *Othello* I'm discussing does not map out onto Ron Canada's Iago, Franchelle Stewart Dorn's Emilia, Teagle F. Bougere's Cassio, or Patrice Johnson's Desdemona, at least not as black actors playing "white" parts.[16] Certainly Washington audiences have been conditioned to seeing these African-American actors, and others, play a variety of Shakespearean roles, even if not within so foregrounded a governing fiction of whiteness. But that foregrounding, as I'll later suggest, raises problems of its own.

If actors of African descent are at this moment readily taken for "white," the situation cannot be symmetrically reversed when white actors are asked to impersonate black characters. Through its reverse casting, the Washington *Othello* denies the material consequences of racial identity, skirts the risk of making race a latter-day minstrel show in its performativity, only lacking the final embarrassment of a blackface fraught with discredited practices. Indeed, so loaded with the possibility for offense is this impersonation that it is not at all clear what it ought to mean for Stewart to indicate that he is "black" – especially within the regime of training I have described and especially for a British actor versed in classical technique. At the same time, the significance of Shakespeare to ideological formations around literature as an imaginative resource for human identity connects Stewart's casting to the larger social fabric that informs, and is informed by, the influential position occupied by *Othello*'s representation of blackness. If the meaning of race is constructed relationally, as I earlier suggested, against what hegemonic practices, what perceived essences was Stewart's Othello to be launched – apart, that is, from the authority of the Shakespearean text and an impugned history of production? When the stage is generally integrated and when actors of African descent are conventionally taken for "white," Stewart's color cannot mean in opposition and as pure figuration. But then what can it mean, given such a production?

The asymmetry of casting practices I have described, in which black can be taken for white but, it seems, not the reverse, reveals a theatrical problem erected on a much larger social fault. "Whiteness," as many critics have suggested, still remains in the US as the invisible, because culturally dominant, state. To take it as under siege while signifying its opposite may demand an act of double vision audiences may not have been prompted to undertake, within the terms the production itself puts on offer – or able to undertake under any circumstances at this particular historical conjuncture. Indeed, as I shall later suggest, the staging of Othello's anger against Desdemona before he murders her introduces a hauntingly (in)apposite juxtaposition of white male body against black female that makes it especially difficult to view Stewart as the racially beleaguered subject of the play.[17]

Critical responses to the immediate challenge of the lines notwithstanding, however, recent legislative and juridical actions indicate that a sizeable portion of the US population feels that whiteness, its own whiteness, is indeed beleaguered, under siege; this is surely one way to read anti-affirmative action measures in California and Texas. Or perhaps more clearly and less tendentiously, reverse-discrimination cases that have been brought in light of Allan Bakke's landmark 1978 Supreme Court victory concerning the University of California Medical School's racially preferential admissions policies, which marked perhaps the first salvo in the battle against the institutional legacy of the civil rights movement. Given the political terrain of the late twentieth century into which Kelly's "photonegative" *Othello* has been inserted (and beyond its own ambiguous/incoherent staging of race), the issue it raises becomes not simply whether white can be read for black, and so the role available again (dare I say rescued?) for a white actor – this time without the unacceptable stigma of blackface. Rather, the production demands we consider whether its spectacular reversal of the play's racial valences becomes potentially symptomatic of the current US conjuncture around black–white relations, particularly concerning affirmative action since *Regents of the University of California v. Bakke*.

Although it is surely obvious that racism is alive and well in many corners of the US, I want to use repudiations of affirmative action policies as my particular focus for two reasons. First, because arguments about the unjust structures of compensation that are its legacy have become an increasingly legitimated aspect of public discourse, and as such are strenuously separated from the more overt forms of white supremacy with which they nevertheless have much in common. The second follows from the first, in that the integration of the Shakespearean stage is itself a legacy of the civil rights era; indeed, Kelly's production can be considered a symptom if not a direct result of the playing out, and subsequent dismantling, of that legacy. If, in the conservative dispensation that permeates public discourse on race, governmental measures designed to compensate for wholesale discrimination in the past have resulted in a hypercorrective set of practices made rigid by force of law, the perceived offense of affirmative action policies lies in having set off a new system of inequity symmetrical with, and complementary to, the old ones, with whiteness now occupying the place of formerly disempowered blackness.[18] Thus what calcified liberal agendas around civil rights have institutionalized is a fetishization of quotas, a knee-jerk privileging of minorities which has, so it is argued, come to displace the receding democratic dream of a nation blind to color and alive only to merit.[19]

Such arguments are, I am sure, highly familiar to most readers, precisely because they have been seen as legitimate and "disinterested" objections to affirmative action (yet for all their exquisite attention to the rights of Asian-Americans, such objections always seem mobilized by the pathos of the white subject who feels discriminated against). Given the absence of a widely attended to counterargument, the claim that affirmative action has "gone too far" constitutes the received wisdom of the day. Even in a world that sees affirmative action as symmetrical discrimination, however, it may yet be "going too far" to consider *Othello* safe again for white actors. Nevertheless, Kelly's production gives us access to a view implicit in such anti-affirmative action movements, albeit not acknowledged, or even necessarily intended, as such. In casting a white man to play a subject increasingly embattled and disempowered by virtue of his race, Kelly summons forth a world where black men have the preferences, the apparently secure hold on "occupations," a world where inertial structures that cannot but favor the status quo, the normative vision, seem to have been obliterated. Left in their wake is Stewart's Othello: not so much the character of the script as the icon of a movement, he offers the spectacle of an aggrieved and displaced white subject, railing against the motivated alienation of a power that he blindly believes is his by merit rather than as an extension of the color of his skin.

That so suggestive and troubling a reading was only intermittently resonant with the experience yielded by the production is undeniable; after all, the script itself militates against too sure a view of Othello's blind privilege. Still, there was an arresting scene, one that does not directly involve Othello, that brought the reverse subtext I have outlined to the threshold of overtness. Shortly after landing on Cyprus, the Venetians – played, as I have indicated, by African-American actors – begin to mingle with, surround, and ultimately menace the Cypriots, who happen to be played by the few white actors other than Stewart in the production. The sense of menace was underscored by the rhythmic stomping of feet which began as the action escalated, and by the rough handling of a female Cyprian soldier. If any scene affected me as spectacle – and I do want to emphasize my position as a white audience member in recording my reaction – it was this one. But at what ideological cost? Why might this scene "work" when, as I have already indicated, those that demand positioning Stewart as disempowered do not? What aspect of the white Imaginary is being engaged in seeing black – their Venetian-ness is forgotten for all intents and purposes – soldiers act out of control?

How the Washington production engaged the white Imaginary that is the legacy of race relations in the United States speaks to the "dread" of my title: the rough handling of a white woman, accompanied by the primitivism of stomping feet, reiterates the staging of a racist nationhood that cannot be meant as interrogative, given the aims of the production. But its echo of an old racial drama, and its engagement with the ideological conditions of its far more suave recrudescence, have the ambiguous virtue of an inadvertent analytic. The phantasmatic spectacle of black men manhandling a white woman Kelly provides is disturbing in itself, given the shopworn fantasies of black male predation it reiterates. But when white Othello's abuse and murder of the black Desdemona is set against the scene in Cyprus, these climactic actions cannot but stand as the historical correction of white mythologies about dark male bodies, sex, and violence with which the production has, whether inadvertently or not, trafficked.

My previous analysis of the homogenizing vocal and bodily decorum of the actor leaves aside the extent to which "blind" casting, at this moment in Shakespearean productions, often reveals a subtext that is not blind at all. Before proceeding to consider how the final moments of the play blow apart the fiction of white beleaguerment, I want to show that this production, which I have already deemed idiosyncratic, actually constitutes part of a terrain: reading it against a selective account of recent color-blind theatrical and cinematic instantiations of Shakespeare makes clear the potentially unintended resonances provided by bodies interacting, put on view, and pressured by the history surrounding the moment of viewing. After all, it is only when race is deployed as though it bore no weight, were yet another neutral variable, like eye or hair color, that it can be flipped, reversed, as well as cast against, indifferently. And that race can be so deployed because systematic discrimination is a thing of the past, and whiteness not the structural basis of privilege, is contiguous with the basis upon which recent challenges to affirmative action have launched themselves.

II

Since the innovative casting work performed by Joseph Papp in New York in the 1960s, it has become an uncontroversial position that actors of other than white skin should and ought to be able to act in productions of Shakespeare.[20] Still, what may be less easy to assume – or more properly, what may be easier to assume than to consider critically and responsibly – is that casting parts without respect to the color of the actors always remains unproblematic as it has become a widely accepted practice. Indeed, even to raise questions about race and casting is to risk being associated with the unpalatable views of such reactionary critics as John Simon, historically antagonistic to Papp's long-standing advocacy of color-blind casting. I have already quoted Simon's disparagement of the speech patterns of African-American actors, but it is worth examining his remarks at greater length, the better to make clear how color-blind casting at the moment of its emergence was understood to reflect political intentions by one of its most virulent opponents:

> Out of a laudable integrationist zeal, Mr. Papp has seen fit to populate his Shakespeare with a high percentage of Negro [*sic*] performers. But the sad fact is that, through no fault of their own, Negro actors often lack even the rudiments of Standard American speech. . . . It is not only aurally that Negro actors present a problem; they do not look right in parts that historically demand white performers. . . .

The critical evaluations of Papp's enterprise have been consistently and thoroughly misleading, whether because of the assumption that something free of charge and for the people must be evaluated along democratic, not dramatic, lines, or simply because of the reviewers' abysmal lack of sophistication, it would be difficult to say.[21]

In deriding the "integrationist" valence of Papp's casting decisions, Simon attempts to separate the stage from the state, and thus to insist on the theater as pure aesthetic practice, to be evaluated on "dramatic" rather than "democratic" criteria. However, the rhetorical framework he establishes for his analysis betrays how theater necessarily serves as a *representative*, as well as representational, cultural practice: looking "right" for the part is inextricably tied to being *seen* on the stage, to participating fully in a dramatic polity that is also a professional workplace from which actors of non-European descent were long debarred, except in the all-black productions that preceded less restrictive mainstream casting.[22] Understood in this way, the stage offers an approximation, however partial and rarefied, of the space of national civic life. Hence Papp's casting decisions in the 1960s could not but be of a piece with the social agendas in which it is enmeshed.

Unlike Simon, I take the political nature of casting as a given within a progressive cultural politics. But I also want to question whether color-blind casting, understood as symbolic practice, achieves what might have been vaunted for it since the breakthrough practices of Papp. Hence I want to consider what happens when Shakespearean plays are cast unreflexively, without a sense of the resonances the extra-theatrical or -diegetic material world, the world of significantly raced bodies, social inequities, and histories of physical and sexual domination and expropriated labor, provides for the space of representation. Productions, of course, are not conceptualized apart from a specific historical moment, so that in speaking about such resonances I am necessarily also inquiring into the way a given production offers itself as an aesthetic artifact mounted within a particular ideological dispensation. Very different questions could be asked regarding Papp's initial practices on New York City stages in the heady aftermath of the civil rights movement, and the way such casting operates in the 1990s, when it has partly become a reflex (if not self-reflexive) practice, and as affirmative action itself has come under criticism – from the standpoint of progressives as well as of conservatives. In the space of this essay, I cannot do justice to the practice of color-blind casting at the moment of emergence; however, given the sketch of context I've provided earlier in the essay, the reason for my interest in productions roughly contemporaneous with the Washington *Othello* is clear.

In general, stage productions of Shakespearean plays, especially productions not constrained by realist settings and mechanisms of verisimilitude, are less vexed with such extra-theatrical and -diegetic resonances. But that theatrical space is not exempt is evinced by a 1997 production of *The Tempest* by the Shakespeare Theater that preceded the *Othello* under discussion, and that offered a white Prospero played against a black Caliban. Although such casting, seemingly anything but "blind," might have opened the play up to a critical encounter with its own significant imbrication in the discourse and material practice of slavery and colonialism – and just as significant, given the venue, with the history of slavery in the US – the fact is that in this production such possibilities went unexplored. The Prospero of Ted van Griethuysen was played as querulous but mostly benign, and the Caliban, Chad L. Coleman, was a physically commanding and attractive man who nevertheless seemed never to speak with politically informed defiance: indeed, the actor was apparently directed never to stand wholly upright. Moreover, with the exception of Ariel, all the island's spirits who appeared in the masque and elsewhere were played, wordlessly, of course, by black actors, who in the event looked to be nothing more than impassive slaves. But given the inscrutable interactions between Prospero and Caliban, to what end were such resonances, such performances of "blackness," invoked? As Barbara Hodgdon has written in another context, production claims that race matters (as the casting choices seem to suggest) "need not automatically correspond with politicization."[23] In this case, the casting of white master and black slaves alludes to a history of racial domination familiar to US audiences. But it only alludes to them, preferring, it appears, not to use the stage to insist on a dialectical relationship between aesthetic artifact and a legacy of material exploitation.

The disturbing set of casting decisions undertaken in Washington could not have been intended as regressive at this late historical moment. In fact, the issue, contrary to Hodgdon's words, is whether race was overtly acknowledged to matter at all here: an actor associated with the Theater, although not part of this production, seemed convinced that the director had intended only to give more up-and-coming black actors theatrical work. Thus he was taken back by the harsh criticism his casting choices received from one DC reviewer – who appeared to have been alone among his colleagues in noting the unreflexively (and, one would have thought, inescapably) racist overtones of the production.[24] However, my own observations, and those of several other attendees, suggest that while the largely white audiences for the Shakespeare Theater were not notably disquieted, the more racially mixed school groups brought to the production manifested discomfort at Caliban's being played as cowering and, indeed, base, especially by an actor whose physical presence suggested the latent possibility of an alternative conception of the character. In the event, the production's resonances generated questions about the politics of casting that had nowhere to go within the production itself. Questions, that is, for selected segments of the audience, who were perhaps never intended as the primary addressees for the production.

Regardless of the director's own possible blindness to the histories his production was invoking and then denying, the fact remains that this *Tempest* (if his colleague's account is correct) provides a clear illustration of the conflicts between a space of imaginative representation, in which color does not "matter" enough to inflect the interpretation, and the space of reception, in which it still cannot but signify, even if recognition of that signification is unevenly distributed among the audience. This uneven distribution suggests that the representation of race is inevitably politicized, to modify Hodgdon's overcompressed statement: the question then becomes whose politics are represented as the neutral state, and whose are marginalized, unacknowledged. Thus the issue raised by the Washington *Tempest* becomes whether the politics it invokes by its racially charged (but color-blind?) casting resist and complicate the history of the text and the moment of production and viewing, or whether they simply refer to history – one safely remote from the dominant audience segment, whose desires (and the Washington Shakespeare Theater's) to disconnect aesthetic experience from historical oppression are represented and ratified in the name of a universalist Shakespeare.

If I turn to more widely available recent Shakespeare films for my texts, some further examples will make clear the potential ideological dissonances of color-blind casting in a representational space defined by the conventions of cinematic verisimilitude.[25] Kenneth Branagh's 1996 *Hamlet* sets the play in a fully realized nineteenth-century court; although certain aspects of the mise-en-scène are principally symbolic, the primary location is the resonant, and quite real and substantial, Blenheim palace. Apparently to signify the Scandinavian ancestry that Hamlet is supposed to have, Branagh bleached his ordinarily red hair quite blond (an admittedly distracting move, which reinforces Branagh's star presence as much as it offers to subsume a distinctive personal attribute under the demands of the role).[26] Moreover, Branagh, who also directed, supplies a bedroom scene between Hamlet and Ophelia, all the better, one presumes, to ground concern about "hot love" in a diegetic reality. What happens, then, given all the efforts to locate this *Hamlet* in a space of textual verisimilitude, when the seamless representation of the nineteenth-century mores and styles is entered by actors of African and Asian descent? A camera pans across the court assembled to hear Claudius's post-nuptial speech; occasionally it records brown and black faces among the courtiers as it records mostly white ones. What nineteenth-century nation could have had so integrated a citizenry, especially at the level of the courtly elite?

For Branagh, the answer lies less with seeing representations as bound to strict historical accuracy than in the film's status as a vehicle for a re-presented past, one which by the dispensation of Shakespeare becomes socially permeable, integrative, and hence utopian.[27] Indeed, an interview he gave shortly after the release of *Hamlet* indicates that the nineteenth-century setting was meant to signify a plausible site of racial and ethnic inclusiveness:

> part of the reason why our setting [is] more impressionistic than specific to a year in the nineteenth century is because I wanted not to worry about casting black actors, or Asian actors, or actors with different accents. We have Russians in there, we have a Pole, we have a Frenchman. I also wanted each of the parts that I had felt over the years were most prone to a clichéd approach, the kind of thing that you fall into – I had seen many heavy-handed versions of the gravedigger scenes, and I wanted actors in the case of say, Billy and Robin, who would be funny but could also be real in the way I felt was necessary. . . .
>
> There would be a price to pay for some people. I'm sure it won't work for everyone, but for me it was a great treat to see all those different approaches come together. I

believe the man belongs to everyone, you know, across the world, and across cultures, across sexes, and so implicitly I wanted to suggest that with the accent-blind, nationality-blind, color-blind casting.[28]

It is, of course, a very different thing to have a Pole or a Frenchman appear in a cinematic representation of a nineteenth-century European court than it is to have an African or an Asian – or, for that matter, an American. Indeed, it seems as if Branagh has allowed the repudiation of slavery that occurred both in Britain and the United States in the nineteenth century to dictate his sense of the representational possibilities inherent in *Hamlet*: for him as for many theatrical practitioners, Shakespeare facilitates access to a utopian vision of the past, where the "openness" of the Shakespearean text to all comers is translated into a corresponding absence of history's material constraints on equal access to state power or even to literacy. Even in light of Branagh's words, however, it may seem that any objection about color-blind casting is based on too literal a reading of the setting, a naive refusal to accept that movies traffic in illusion. Or else a converse refusal to understand the politics of casting, insofar as stars constitute a kind of capital on their own, without which few cinematic endeavors, especially "prestige" projects like Shakespeare that too often lose money for their investors, can hope for funding and distribution.[29]

But my point in the first case concerns production values, and the naturalizing deployment of the camera by Branagh the director, rather than a critique of the restorative function of historicity *per se*. Regardless of the precise date in the 1800s in which his film is set – and regardless of the naive utopianism that constitutes his sense of the Shakespearean past – Branagh seems to have striven to render his setting unproblematic in terms of the conventions of Hollywood realism, and then undone the illusion of verisimilitude by means of casting bodies historically unavailable for the positions they are asked to take. Had Branagh not so relied on the techniques and apparatuses of cinematic verisimilitude, my questions could well substantially vanish, since the issue of their appropriateness is tied specifically to his conflicting desires for the play: both to ground it in a reality-effect concerning the past to which his words about the nineteenth century pay a kind of tribute; and to claim the text, despite its history and the larger histories he invokes, in a phantasmatic space of integration, to add people of color into a history that in general excluded them, and certainly from positions of power and influence in the nineteenth-century European court. A check of the cast reveals the tokenism that pervades many such liberal formations around "nationality-blind, color-blind" Shakespeare. The actors of non-European descent, however much might be claimed for their belonging to the bardolatrous polity, appear only in the background, or in comparatively minor roles: only four speaking parts, all rather incidental, are given over to non-white actors.[30]

As a way to get at the second, converse, point, concerning the politics and economics of casting, perhaps it would do to shift to one of Branagh's other Shakespearean films, *Much Ado About Nothing* (1993), set in a stylized Italian pastoral vaguely redolent of the eighteenth century. It cannot be claimed that this movie relegates non-white actors to vanishingly small roles, since the African-American actor Denzel Washington is cast as the noble Don Pedro of Aragon. Interestingly, however, his bastard brother Don John is played by Keanu Reeves, an actor whose mixed Hawaiian descent still allows him to be read as white. Here, as in *Hamlet*, Branagh is gesturing toward cinematic realism, however uneven its application: although the principals' hair, for instance, is decidedly twentieth century in style, the location shots seem consonant with a bucolic and Italianate pre-industrial languor. Thus there is an element of surprise in making the legitimate offspring black, and the illegitimate one white. (Indeed, such impeccably conscientious casting reads as a symbolic negation of the far more likely possibility that, in the eighteenth century, any black offspring of the aristocracy, should one have existed, was likely to be a bastard.) Given Branagh's penchant, manifested here as well as in *Hamlet*, for casting Hollywood stars in supporting roles, does Washington's status as star outweigh as signifier his raced body to the audiences of the film, given that many of Washington's star roles engage with race?[31] And assuming such circumstances can be rationalized into existence through a liberal suspension of disbelief – it's only a movie, and on some level the pleasure on offer is to see an unlikely star do a star turn – how then to recuperate Beatrice's rejection of Don Pedro's proposal?

As played by Emma Thompson, Beatrice offers a graceful refusal of Don Pedro's offer of marriage, in keeping with the script's characterization of the Prince as "too costly to wear every day," and with her own covert affection for Benedick. Indeed, that the Prince stands mostly as spectator to the various erotic interactions between Beatrice and Benedick, and Hero and Claudio, is a function of the playtext. But it is a function that Branagh's casting and directing, intentionally or not, have exacerbated. Given that Don Pedro's substitute (and suspect) wooing of Hero for Claudio takes place while he is masked – as well as Branagh's lavish climax, which just barely records the Don's isolation from the happy denizens of the villa as the camera cranes over the ever-expanding nuptial festivities – it becomes difficult not to color Beatrice's rejection of the black Don as evidence of the film's covert perception of racial difference and its significance. And it is a perception that runs precisely counter to Branagh's avowed intention to offer an inclusive, all-encompassing instantiation of Shakespeare. While Washington the Hollywood star might appeal erotically to spectators of many races, within the diegesis of Branagh's film its only black actor is repeatedly denied access to amorous subjecthood. That Thompson's reaction *is* graceful occludes the subtext of the moment in which she participates. If she had hesitated, made an obstacle of her repudiation in any way, the film might have offered a more overt purchase on what it stages via Washington – and then appears to look away from; Branagh's *Much Ado* might not then have been "blind" to the restrictive interplay that subtends its mixed-race casting. Because the proposal, shot in close-up, plays off his darker face against her lighter one, contrasts her whiteness with his lack of it, Beatrice's refusal nevertheless makes clear what the other moments to which I've alluded only hint at: *this* Don Pedro, however great his authority, cannot be assimilated to the social realm whose consolidation Shakespearean romantic comedy celebrates – and Branagh's

Hollywood spectacle reiterates.[32] (In this Denzel Washington's Don is, perhaps, luckier than most Othellos: denied the fantasy of romance as unassimilable, he is thereby denied the consequences of domestic tragedy.)

Beatrice's refusal of Don Pedro in Branagh's film of *Much Ado About Nothing* constitutes one of the most interesting moments in the movie, since it reveals that it is often the question of heterosexual desire across differently raced bodies which reasserts the extra-diegetic reality of the moment of viewing.[33] That is, the normative gender roles so important to Shakespearean drama, when played by men and women of different races, make clear that the liberal, utopian, and integrative aspirations of color-blind casting might be canceled out by the pressure to the white Imaginary: hence my reading of the scene in Cyprus. In the wake of the O. J. Simpson trial, which revealed how quickly much of the white population of the US abandoned its ideological commitment to color-blindness when the subject of justice concerns cross-racial desire and a prominent black defendant, that race still matters cannot in general be a surprise. The Simpson trial made abundantly clear that scenes of abstract justice at the turn of the millennium are readily turned into spectacles of embodiment, with the letter of the law – or the text – seemingly secondary to the antique play of black and white, and the haunting specter of miscegenation.

It is not solely because O. J. Simpson was frequently referred to as an Othello figure that he seems apposite to my argument, however.[34] Both the casting of this production and the proceedings in Los Angeles derive their meanings from the failures of color-blindness as project within a society committed to integrationist reforms: indeed, the legal scholar Kimblerlé Williams Crenshaw has suggested that Simpson is himself "the essential symbol of the color-blind ideal" (Crenshaw 1997: 110).[35] Crenshaw's words give us a way to read the white outrage that attended the jury's finding that Simpson was not guilty. Despite the evidence of racism as well as questionable procedures on the part of state agents, the verdict was made apprehensible only when it was deemed that *Simpson*'s lawyer, Johnnie Cochran, was the one who introduced "race" into the proceedings. In acknowledging that race mattered in the case against him – implicit, indeed, in the melancholy comparisons that yoked him with Othello – Simpson was perceived to have violated a tacit contract, an understanding that he was living and operating in a world where color did not matter; at the same time, he was being judged within a system where racial bias was also tacitly normalized.[36] Such a contradiction, by and large invisible to white spectators, suggests that the failures of the color-blind ideal are not operational, a matter of uneven deployment and enforcement; rather, they are conceptual and material. Hence the importance of reading the Washington *Othello* in light of critical race theory, which holds that critical attention to race, and hence skepticism about the discourse of integration and color-blindness, are not incompatible with a progressive racial politics.[37] Thus Crenshaw's characterization of civil rights agendas of the recent past: "the rejection of ideologies of black exclusion and inferiority was not met with any rethinking of the nature and legitimacy of white dominance in American institutions. Racism was framed only in terms of the formal exclusion of nonwhites, not in terms of the privileging of whiteness" (Crenshaw 1997: 106).

It goes without stating that there is much to separate theater as an institution from the legal system, although it is clear that both have notably pursued liberal strategies designed to correct inequities of representation, themselves born out of a history of racist practices. But my abbreviated analysis of the monolithic Shakespearean voice enjoined upon the actor suggests that the implicit "privileging of whiteness" Crenshaw detects as the structural flaw in integrationist projects is not entirely remote from the theatrical mark. Reinforced in varying degrees by the material infrastructure that supports both systems – the juridico-disciplinary apparatus in the case of one, directors, producers, voice and movement coaches, and technical workers in the case of the other – is the *symbolic* persistence of whiteness as the unacknowledged dominant. And nowhere is that made more apparent than in the spectacle of Stewart's "photonegative" Othello.

III

Casting Patrick Stewart in a Shakespearean role is a canny move from a box-office standpoint – perhaps as canny as Branagh's enlisting Billy Crystal as the gravedigger or Robin Williams as Osric. Unlike those actors, however, Stewart combines both the popular name recognition conferred by his seven years playing Captain Jean-Luc Picard on *Star Trek: The Next Generation* with an estimable pedigree as a Shakespearean actor. This pedigree was often alluded to within the science fiction television show; Picard, for instance, keeps a First Folio in his twenty-third-century private quarters, and there are a few episodes in which he helps the android Data perform the discourse of "humanness" by acting in *The Tempest* and *Henry V*.[38] Although such grace notes did not constitute an important thematic of the series, the evidence they provide of Shakespeare's universal pertinence and durability link Stewart imaginatively with a potentially reactionary view of Shakespearean subjecthood.

Stewart's presence, while it guaranteed the staging a great deal of public interest, could not do the same for its conceptual plausibility. As I have already suggested, there were scattered snickers from the audience at Stewart's intoning "Haply for I am black"; yet the reaction, surely unintended on the director's and actor's parts, cannot simply be blamed on the audience's lack of imaginative sophistication. To accept the undeniably pale Stewart as black demands that the power of the script's fiction – what I've already termed the authority of the Shakespearean text – override all the cues to the contrary that the actor playing Othello is *not* black, nor is he making any somatic attempt to impersonate blackness, vexed, indeed, as that possibility would be. Acceptance demands a rarefaction and idealization of the site of viewing perhaps unlikely ever to have been achieved by any audience at any time, but certainly not to be achieved when part of the point of casting Stewart is presumably his fame, either as a mass-culture icon, or as a British Shakespearean actor. The discourse of the star system as elucidated in cinema studies analyzes what is, perhaps, the inevitable case with respect to the theatrical star: that a star is one to the extent that she or he exceeds the role being acted, that she or he is perceived and, indeed, appreciated as *not* wholly absorbed in the role, as signifying beyond it. Thus when Patrick Stewart plays Othello, his characterization as Captain Jean-Luc Picard may constitute an inevitably resonant resource for those segments of the audience that view him as a star. Indeed, given the extent to which Stewart's prior experience as a Shakespearean actor was itself written into *Star Trek: The Next Generation*, it is possible that the boundary between one type of performance and another becomes increasingly hard to chart.

Further complicating the reading of Stewart as Othello are his prestige and cultural capital as a *British* actor and sometime member of the Royal Shakespeare Company. If, via the casting of well-known actors with American accents and less elite training, Branagh models the symbolic diversification of Shakespeare via the discourse of Hollywood, casting Stewart in DC has the reverse effect: rather than making his Britishness a meaningful sign of the exoticism that the part carries along with it, his very presence on a US stage can be read to confer the restrictive legitimacy of Shakespeare's originary culture. Indeed, the effect of casting him is to consolidate many species of institutional power in the person of the actor, and so to turn him – rather than, strictly speaking, Othello – into the center of gravity for the production.[39] And in the space between those two lies the production's main obstacle.

Even for those segments of the audience not particularly conversant with facets of Stewart's prior career, there remains the issue of whiteness as a cultural dominant, given greater effectivity for the problem's not being addressed directly, as a problem of visuality for the theater. In speaking of spectacle over script throughout this essay, I have focused on what may be seen, what is put on display, so as to correlate with the idea of "blindness" with respect to color. Stewart's performance, highly competent as it naturally was within the traditional markers of Shakespearean acting, could not avoid confronting the audience with the brute irreducibility of the articulating subject in collision with a language that would have him be seen as different from what he is, and apart from a theatrical tradition that turns all hues to white. Nor could it avoid having that difference involve a deconstruction of whiteness-as-privilege, a privilege both material and discursive, motivated solely by adherence to the script's letter, insofar as the lead actor is concerned.

At any rate it is not on the level of linguistic signification that the most telling, most chilling instance of the recalcitrance of whiteness – its obstinate resistance to being rendered discursive – occurred. That definitive demonstration was provided by a passing interaction in the final act. Preparatory to Othello's murder of Desdemona, Stewart rages and flings Patrice Johnson about the stage, at one point pushing her up against the wall, speaking at her, as the lines indicate, with a combination of desire and fury. But to be made to see this vulnerable Desdemona as a vulnerable *black* woman, one thus forced and abused by an ineluctably *white* man, is to see the plot's contrary figment of the white racial Imaginary displaced by a primal scene in US history the more disturbing for its failed repression at this critical moment in the production. Instead of the dangerous and desirous black male assaulting a white woman, the play enacts, reiterates, the attacks on powerless black females by masterful white men that constitute the seldom-acknowledged event on which much racial discourse in the US is founded. Throughout the play, Johnson offered a strong and graceful portrayal of Desdemona; her demeanor well suited a young woman of aristocratic privilege. But in the final act, the spectacle of Stewart's white rage, white desire, obliterated whatever sense of privilege might have accrued to her, whatever specificity of class or person Johnson's acting earned in the part. More than abused Venetian wife, the spectacle rendered her emblematic chattel, the objective correlative of a prolonged cultural repression.

As must be clear, such a resonance could precisely not have been intended within the fiction of the photonegative, which asks, however incompletely, that race be taken as performance rather than as endowed with significance because of a material history of dominance and exploitation, because of an uneven distribution of power that persists despite the occasional reverse-discrimination argument to the contrary. Thus in some sense a white Othello's violence toward a black Desdemona responds to, indeed, falsifies, both a textual fantasy and a proximate stage one. Engaged is not only the hoary myth of black male rage and erotic frenzy that *Othello* may well inaugurate, but also the scene of black Venetian menace among the white Cypriots that I have analyzed elsewhere in the essay, which recalls the "rape and rescue" scenario made infamous by *Birth of a Nation*. If that earlier insertion serves as a "guilt-ridden denegation of White man's history of raping Black women," then this scene comes clean about what the production denies as the very fantasy it mobilizes plays itself out, that we are enough "beyond" color to deploy it as a formal property of the stage.[40] Unlike the white Cypriot woman saved from a fate worse than death, an invention, presumably, of the director, Desdemona is inexorably condemned by plot, by a fidelity to script that is unlikely ever to be violated. And since the climax of the play is also the climactic moment of inevitably raced violence in the production, the corrective staging of white laying hands upon black is inserted in the position of revealed psychic truth. What it reveals, however belatedly, is the bad conscience of the production.

IV

In a discussion of "antiliteral" casting practices, Ella Shohat and Robert Stam ask: "What is wrong with non-originary casting? Doesn't acting always involve a ludic play with identity? Should we applaud Blacks playing Hamlet but not Laurence Olivier playing Othello?" (Shohat and Stam 1994: 191). They pose these "irreverent" questions provocatively, the better to argue for a context-sensitive casting practice: "The casting of Blacks to play Hamlet, for example, militates against a traditional discrimination that denied Blacks any role, literally and metaphorically, in both the performing arts and in politics, while the casting of Laurence Olivier as Othello prolongs a venerable history of bypassing Black talent" (Shohat and Stam 1994: 191).

Given the generous amount of work it provided for African-American actors, the Washington *Othello* surely cannot be accused of having perpetuated the material exclusion Shohat and Stam note, and that is part of the history of mainstream Shakespearean production in the United States. But its casting was schematic, symbolic, with fair labor practices onstage an apparent by-product, if a fortunate one, of a "photonegativity" inflected by the casting of Patrick Stewart in the title role. To understand my point, consider the difference between this production and a *Hamlet* with a largely African-American court, one whose production crew was also dominated by African-American personnel.

Looking for new ways to play old texts is part of the business of performance, when it comes to Shakespeare or to other classic dramatists. But there are some texts whose unpalatable propositions mean that any attempt at innovation needs to be taken with a keen eye to the resonances those propositions still retain: *Othello* is surely one, *Taming of the Shrew* is another. Far too seldom, even now, is the symbolic violence of either play addressed in dominant production practice; what obtains instead is a sense that these plays can be rescued from their worst tendencies in the name of preserving an aestheticized and performatively innocuous Shakespeare. So *Shrew* is played as though the brainwashing of Kate might not in fact have defined humor for some audiences, and *Othello* as the tragedy of a distant racism whose continuing truth is belied by the usual presence of non-white actors on the mainstream stage. (The same point might, of course, be made about *The Tempest*.) Hence the casting of Stewart becomes a parody of affirmative action, a parody that befits this dangerous moment in the discourse and material practices of race in the United States, when an ideological clamor suggests racial parity is an accomplished fact, and calls any further attention to race itself a form of racism.

To consider race as a matter for discursive manipulation, of representation and public visibility, is to fall into the limitations of color-blind casting as I have described them. My students' first reading of Desdemona's line in Act I that she "[sees] Othello's visage in his mind" is to suggest that she somehow discerns him truly, which for them signifies seeing beyond his color to the disembodied truth of interiority. But of course at least one other reading is possible: that her love for him is not beyond race but cognizant of it, as Othello is of himself. The former line reading reveals how easy, how "natural" it is, for conscientious post-civil rights subjects to imagine that seeing race means seeing wrong. Instead, I would guess that we have barely begun to perceive it rightly, in theater as everywhere else.

NOTES

1   The essay has benefited from conversations with Devon Hodges, Robert Matz, Zofia Burr, Susan Snyder, and Caleen Jennings.
2   The program notes for *Othello* written by

Miranda Johnson-Haddad refer to the production as "photonegative," as did the actor Ron Canada (who played Iago) on the Diane Rehm Show, broadcast over National Public

Radio ("Reader's Roundtable on *Othello*," November 1997). The part of Bianca (who in the event turned out to be well named) was cast with a white actor, Kate Skinner. According to Ron Canada, the director Jude Kelly was inverting the British theatrical tradition, in which Bianca is cast as a woman of African descent. The other white actors in the production played soldiers from Cyprus.

3 I take as a given that all production decisions, for good or ill, may not be available to analysis in terms of directorial intention. Nor, given the collaborative nature of staging, does it seem wise to hold a director wholly accountable for what is (to be) seen, still less what may be experienced by various segments of the audience.

4 For information on Shakespearean programs that also contained minstrel shows, see Levine (1988: 21–3).

5 A partial bibliography stressing issues of stage and screen performance would include Barnet (1998); Hill (1984b: esp. 7–12); Callaghan (1996); Singh (1994); Hodgdon (1997). While I have restricted my discussion in this essay to the United States, it is surely the case that stagings elsewhere, as my references indicate, are not exempt from the criticism on offer.

6 See, for example, Butler (1990, 1993); Garber (1992); and Bornstein (1994).

7 Here and elsewhere, I do not claim to speak authoritatively about the play's reception. I have tried to be cautious about generalizations, and have based them on discussions and interviews with people who also attended the production.

8 In one sense, this substitution commemorates a long history of the part's being performed by white actors, albeit white actors in blackface. Indeed, given that "the cultural performance of alterity" is a precondition of the Shakespearean stage, there is a sense, as Dympna Callaghan has argued, in which Othello is ineluctably white; see Callaghan (1996: 193).

9 The extent to which a director honors, or not, the text is an aspect of the way in which directors define their practice in relation to the authority of "Shakespeare"; see Worthen (1997b).

10 I do not have time to do justice to the point, but I take the laughter as potentially significant evidence that the cultural formations around Shakespeare variously described by (e.g.) Lawrence Levine and Graham Holderness have begun to recede in influence. For Shakespeare as an elite icon in the United States, see Levine (1988); for "Bardolatry," see Holderness (1988: esp. 2–15).

11 The practice of color-blind casting is not without its own historicity. Since I cannot speak authoritatively about how, for instance, Joseph Papp's breakthrough productions might have disposed and directed integrated casts, I have thought it best to restrict myself to recent productions. However, I'd venture a guess that what might once have been radical theatrical practice has now become the unremarkable demotic of Shakespearean theater – and in that passage from innovation to commonplace lies much of the impetus for my argument.

12 For a brief but suggestive analysis of how conventions of voice in acting are taken to be "natural," see Bennett (1996: 42–3).

13 John Simon in *Commonweal* magazine, 1963; quoted in Epstein (1994: 290–1). Conversely, the possession of such a voice by an actor of brown skin can be viewed as a stupendous achievement: Errol Hill, who is from Trinidad, notes that the principal of the Royal Academy of Dramatic Art assumed he was from "darkest Africa," and considered Hill's "cultivated English accent . . . remarkable"; see Hill (1984a: xix–xx).

14 Errol Hill, in a chapter called "How Relevant Is Race?," notes, and even echoes, the stance of critics who found African-American actors in Shakespearean productions not equal to the task. I take such words as evidence that the display of a particular training is longed for, evidence, that is, of a normativity when it comes to how Shakespeare should be acted; see Hill (1984a: esp. 146–8, 152–3). Indeed, when African-American actresses were praised for their performances, the words can seem suspiciously exoticizing: Walter Kerr refers to Jonelle Allen (in John Guare's 1971 musical *Two Gentlemen of Verona*) as an "untamed enchantress" (quoted in Hill 1984a: 155).

15 Hence even the criticism of Baz Luhrmann's film of *Romeo and Juliet*, for destroying the sound of the verse: the actors speak their lines "prosaically," that is, without an attempt to declaim or sound magniloquent. The resultant performances render Shakespeare both demotic and American.

16 Both Dorn's Emilia and Johnson's Desdemona were particularly impressive performances.

17 Of course, this argument depends to some extent on a normative view of the audience: "whiteness" can have a very different resonance for a largely black audience; for but one illustration, see hooks (1992). Based on my experience over several years of attending Shakespeare productions in Washington, DC, it would be fair to say that adult audiences are mostly white. However, the frequent presence of school groups at productions can change the demographics, and inflect the texture of audience response.

18 I am aware that my summary is far too schematic. For one, it neglects the extent to which current oppositional agendas around affirmative action in the US are not simply conducted along the axis of black–white, but also engage with the very different places and problems of Asian-Americans and Latinos. For another, it is not clear that even places like California, which have been considered the "wave of the future" when it comes to voter-driven challenges to affirmative action programs, offer a coherent depiction of frustration with the "privileges" of minorities.

19 For a provocative and problematic suggestion that affirmative action agendas, by instituting a Foucaultian regime of the statistical normalization of the workplace, have unintentionally offered a blind to racist hiring practices, see Yount (1993).

20 Errol Hill credits Joseph Papp, in his early efforts to bring Shakespeare plays to residents of New York City who were by reason of race or class not seen as target audiences for classic theater, as the first to cast the plays without regard to race of the actors; see Hill (1984a: 143–76, esp. 143–55).

21 John Simon's 1963 piece in *Commonweal*, quoted in Epstein (1994: 290–1, ellipses in original). On Papp's commitment to integrated casting (which went back as far as a 1952 production of a Sean O'Casey play), see Epstein (1994: 77, 92–4, 168–9).

22 A similar objection to interracial casting that offers itself as an attempt to preserve the integrity of Shakespearean drama is cited by Errol Hill: in 1965, Bernard Grebanier wrote that "when the Vivian Beaumont Theater gives me a black Orsino and Maria, I am upset – not out of racial prejudice but out of respect for Shakespeare's plays. After all, a white man doing Othello blackens face, arms, legs, and hands. Is there any reason why a black actor should not whiten his when doing a white role?" (Hill 1984a: 3).

23 Hodgdon's words come out of an essay in which she considers two different televised versions of *Othello* with black actors in the title role; see Hodgdon (1997: 31). This is the place to acknowledge my general indebtedness to Hodgdon's essay: although much of my own essay was conceptualized in advance of my having read hers, we come to many similar conclusions.

24 Edward Gero, in discussion of the production at George Mason University, October, 1997.

25 James L. Loehlin provides a handy characterization of my claim that Branagh's films draw on the conventions of cinematic verisimilitude: "The realist Shakespeare film is characterized by the sort of mid-range naturalistic acting, cinematography and editing that is used in most Hollywood films. The characters are presented as 'real people,' in plausible make-up and costumes, and the film relates the narrative straightforwardly, without calling attention to the medium" (Loehlin 1997: 67).

26 That Laurence Olivier's 1948 filmed version also presented the star with extremely blond hair is also a likely factor in Branagh's tonsorial decision, given that Branagh has seemed to model his film career as a Shakespearean actor in emulation of – and rivalry with – Olivier.

27 My truncated analysis is partly inspired by Susan Bennett's work on Shakespearean productions and their stagings of the past as a form of ideological correction; see Bennett (1996: esp. 1–38).

28 Branagh's words occurred in a public discussion on December 21, 1996, moderated by Susan Stamberg of National Public Radio, and itself a part of the Smithsonian Institution's "Stellar Shakespeare Weekend." I am grateful to Diane Williams for making her transcript of the discussion available to me.

29 In the same discussion, Branagh denies that his casting of Americans has anything to do with box-office considerations – although his desire to make Shakespeare more broadly appealing is surely a matter, if not a purely instrumental one, of expanding audience demographics.

30 During the Royal Shakespeare Company's summer 1998 visit to Washington, DC, two of the productions it offered, *Hamlet* and *Cymbeline*, also cast non-white actors in comparatively minor roles.

31 For instance, Washington has starred in several of Spike Lee's movies, among them the title role in *X*.

32 Of course, neither can Don John – but then he's the bastard.

33 I specify the desire I am concerned with as "heterosexual," in part because I am unsure whether the argument can be extended to same-sex eroticism (and I have not attempted the demonstration), and in part because the historical fears of miscegenation that come into play are specifically engaged with my privileged dynamic.

34 For instance, the poet Anthony Hecht felt impelled to write a letter to the *Washington Post* regarding the notable parallels between the two figures. Such comparisons betray both a suspect desire to ennoble a potential wife-killer (who in this event was deemed guilty before a trial had even occurred), and a limited conceptual repertory for understanding the complexities of race. Playing off this obsession with O. J. as Othello, Ann duCille has analyzed a complementary positioning of Nicole Brown Simpson as the "browned" woman of a captivity narrative; see duCille (1997).

35 The following analysis is much indebted to Crenshaw's essay; see Crenshaw (1997).

36 In reading the case as I have, I do not of course dismiss the evidence of spousal abuse in the case against Simpson – any more than I would the violence against Desdemona in my reading of *Othello*. At the same time, I want to stress that it is precisely because of Simpson's race that the violence against Nicole Brown Simpson mattered as much as it did.

37 For a representative collection, see Crenshaw, Gotanda, Peller, and Thomas (1995).

38 For more on the various connections between Shakespeare and *Star Trek*, see the special issue of the science fiction journal *Extrapolations* for Fall 1995.

39 In an interview conducted during *Othello*'s run with Arch Campbell, the film and drama critic of the local NBC network affiliate WRC, Stewart spoke of his long-standing desire to perform the part, and his fear that it would prove impossible to do so until this production came around. I do not have unequivocal evidence that Stewart was cast first, but in a sense it does not matter: the effect of casting Stewart was to turn him into its focus.

40 The quotation comes from Ella Shohat and Robert Stam's discussion of *Birth of a Nation*; see Shohat and Stam (1994: 159).

References and Further Reading

Barnet, S. 1998: "*Othello* on Stage and Screen." In Alvin Kernan (ed.), *Othello*. New York: Signet.

Bennett, S. 1996: *Performing Nostalgia: Shifting Shakespeare and the Contemporary Past*. New York: Routledge.

Bornstein, K. 1994: *Gender Outlaw: On Men, Women, and the Rest of Us*. New York: Routledge.

Butler, J. 1990: *Gender Trouble: Feminism and the Subversion of Identity*. New York: Routledge.

—— 1993: *Bodies That Matter: On the Discursive Limits of "Sex."* New York: Routledge.

Callaghan, D. 1996: "'Othello was a white man':

Properties of Race on Shakespeare's Stage." In Terence Hawkes (ed.), *Alternative Shakespeares, 2*. New York: Routledge, 192–215.

Crenshaw, K. W. 1997: "Color-Blind Dreams and Racial Nightmares: Reconfiguring Racism in the Post-Civil Rights Era." In Toni Morrison and Claudia Brodsky Lacour (eds.), *Birth of a Nation'Hood: Gaze, Script, and Spectacle in the O. J. Simpson Case*. New York: Pantheon, 97–168.

——Gotanda, N., Peller, G., and Thomas, K. (eds.) 1995: *Critical Race Theory: The Key Writings That Formed the Movement*. New York: Free Press.

duCille, A. 1997: "The Unbearable Darkness of Being: 'Fresh' Thoughts on Race, Sex, and the Simpsons." In Toni Morrison and Claudia Brodsky Lacour (eds.), *Birth of a Nation'Hood: Gaze, Script, and Spectacle in the O. J. Simpson Case*. New York: Pantheon, 293–338.

Epstein, H. 1994: *Joe Papp: An American Life*. Boston: Little, Brown.

Garber, M. 1992: *Vested Interests: Cross-Dressing and Cultural Anxiety*. New York: Routledge.

Hill, E. 1984a: *Shakespeare in Sable: A History of Black Shakespearean Actors*. Amherst: University of Massachusetts Press.

——1984b: "Shakespeare and the Black Actor." In *Shakespeare in Sable: A History of Black Shakespearean Actors*. Amherst: University of Massachusetts Press, 1–16.

Hodgdon, B. 1997: "Race-ing *Othello*, Re-Engendering White-Out." In Lynda E. Boose and Richard Burt (eds.), *Shakespeare, The Movie: Popularizing the Plays on Film, TV, and Video*. New York: Routledge, 23–44.

Holderness, G. (ed.) 1988: *The Shakespeare Myth*. Manchester: Manchester University Press.

hooks, b. 1992: "Representing Whiteness in the Black Imagination." In Lawrence Grossberg, Cary Nelson, and Paula Treichler (eds.), *Cultural Studies*. New York: Routledge, 338–46.

Levine, L. 1988: *Highbrow, Lowbrow: The Emergence of Cultural Hierarchy in America*. Cambridge, MA: Harvard University Press.

Loehlin, J. L. 1997: "'Top of the World, Ma': *Richard III* and Cinematic Convention." In Lynda E. Boose and Richard Burt (eds.), *Shakespeare, The Movie: Popularizing the Plays on Film, TV, and Video*. New York: Routledge, 67–79.

Shohat, E. and Stam, R. 1994: *Unthinking Eurocentrism: Multiculturalism and the Media*. New York: Routledge.

Singh, J. 1994: "Othello's Identity, Postcolonial Theory, and Contemporary African Rewritings of *Othello*." In Margo Hendricks and Patricia Parker (eds.), *Women, "Race" and Writing in the Early Modern Period*. New York: Routledge, 287–99.

Worthen, W. B. 1997a: *Shakespeare and the Authority of Performance*. Cambridge: Cambridge University Press.

——1997b: "Shakespeare's Auteurs: Directing Authority." In *Shakespeare and the Authority of Performance*. Cambridge: Cambridge University Press, 45–94.

Yount, M. 1993: "The Normalizing Powers of Affirmative Actions." In John Caputo and Mark Yount (eds.), *Foucault and the Critique of Institutions*. University Park, PA: University of Pennsylvania Press, 191–229.

PART FIVE
Performing Sexuality

13

Women and Boys Playing Shakespeare

Juliet Dusinberre

In the explosion of interest in Shakespeare's construction of gender and sexuality in his plays, *As You Like It* has received the most intense critical attention, so that to return to the subject yet again seems to risk a response comparable to Touchstone's acid comment on a rather labored joke from Rosalind: "You have said; but whether wisely or no, let the forest judge" (III.ii.117).[1] I trust myself to the judgment of the Forest in the spirit of Erasmus's Stultitia in *The Praise of Folly*, recalling as I do so Touchstone's observation to Audrey and William, that " 'the fool doth think he is wise, but the wise man knows himself to be a fool' " (V.i.30).

Wise man. Yes. But what of the woman? Well, we don't need to mention her because women are always fools. And in any case there weren't any women on Shakespeare's stage. Ay, there's the rub. Were they there or not? Of course, physically they were not there. But to assert that is, in my view, to say nothing. Because none of the shadows on Shakespeare's stage are there. There are no kings, queens, murderers, monsters, fairies, politicians, wise counselors, or even fools. There are only actors. Why should it matter that they are not biologically female, any more than it should matter that they are not royal, Roman, Moors, Egyptian, or Italian? Why should the fact of the male body make it impossible to conceive of a woman on the stage, any more than the fact of the commoner's body might make it impossible to conceive of Richard II's body? Both are figments of the actor's art.

One of the curiosities of criticism of *As You Like It* is that the play contains four women played by boys: Rosalind, Celia, Phoebe, Audrey. Yet in the discussions of gender and sexuality Rosalind stands virtually alone, with a few nods at Celia. Phoebe gets a brief mention as a woman falling in love with Ganymede, whom the audience knows to be a woman, just as Olivia falls in love with Cesario in *Twelfth Night*, whom the audience knows to be Viola. I could pause for a very long time on these matters. But I want to turn my attentions to a silent area. In these discussions, Audrey, also played by a boy, is not mentioned at all. In the case of Phoebe and Audrey it appears that the boy actor's presence is completely subsumed in the "feminine" image of these roles. Phoebe must be all woman to convince the audience of the plausibility of Rosalind's disguise as Ganymede. Audrey is a country bumpkin; she mustn't partake of gender games, because these belong to a world of sophistication, both theatrical and social, court not country. Critics don't talk about Audrey and Phoebe as boys playing women because the boy actor's part is not highlighted for audience inspection in the way that it is for Rosalind, and to a lesser extent, for Celia.

Within the fiction of the play, Audrey is the only one of the women not required to play a part. She is always Audrey. Rosalind plays a boy shepherd, Ganymede. Celia plays her sister, Aliena. Phoebe, a shepherdess, plays at being a cruel court lady to her shepherd lover, Silvius. Only Audrey does not play.

Audrey, bawdry, body. These words go together in this play. The creation of Audrey by Shakespeare marks the biggest difference between Thomas Lodge's romance of *Rosalynde* and Shakespeare's play because her part requires the audience to focus on the body of the character in a way that it does not for anyone else on stage. She is, perhaps, the counterpart to Bottom ensconced in the ass's head, eager to eat hay and have his back scratched. Her physical solidity proclaims that the fiction is not a narrative, not just a poem, "I would the gods had made thee poetical" (III.iii.12), but a play whose life depends on the physical presence of the actor. Audrey offers the audience no metaphors: she simply *is*: "I am not a slut, but I thank the gods I am foul" (III.iii.33). She provides the greatest possible contrast to Touchstone, who is all roleplay, mind and spirit, words and wit. Her natural mate in the play is the tongue-tied William, who admits to a "pretty wit," although the audience is not privileged to see it in action, unless the play itself must stand to witness to the pretty wit of a William also born in the Forest of Arden, the dramatist himself. Even Audrey, however, has a vision of happiness in which she will play a different role. She wants to be a married woman: "I hope it is no dishonest desire to desire to be a woman of the world" (V.iii.3). As the Clown remarks in *All's Well That Ends Well*: "If I may have your ladyship's good will to go to the world, Isbel the woman and I will do as we may" (I.iii.15).[2] Going to the world is embracing the flesh, honest as that may be. It is her last speech and Touchstone does not answer it. In the final scene she is silent, except for body language, for which Touchstone reprimands her: "Bear your body more seeming, Audrey" (V.iv.66).

Audrey can only bear her body one way, a way that is "not seeming," always taken to mean "not seemly" – and often interpreted by the actress as scratching her backside. But this is the only instance in Shakespeare of the word used in this way. In all his other works, dramatic and non-dramatic, it is always used to imply acting, being what one is not. If Shakespeare means "seemly," that is the word he uses. Seeming always means something else. "Seems, madam? nay, it is, I know not 'seems'" (I.ii.76), expostulates Hamlet to Gertrude when criticized for too much outward display of mourning. He disclaims the ostentation and hypocrisy of mourning: "For these are actions which a man might play" (I.ii.84).[3] Touchstone criticizes Audrey for not acting her part well in polite company, not "seeming" to be a lady, as the scene requires. She is among gentlefolk and must behave accordingly. But in not seeming, is she truer to the woman, the bumpkin shepherdess, or to the boy who acts her? The question in Shakespeare's theater might have seemed irrelevant; the boy actor scratching himself in an unseemly manner translates easily into Audrey performing the same action. In fact, as in so many of Shakespeare's best moments, the rebuke from Touchstone might be adopted from a master's reprimand to his boy in rehearsal. In Tom Stoppard's *Rosencrantz and Guildenstern Are Dead*, the Players who will enact "The Murder of Gonzago" before the King proceed to their dress rehearsal, with Alfred, their boy actor, ready to play the Queen. The Player assembles his forces, but turns impatiently to the Player Queen: "Stop picking your nose, Alfred. When Queens have to they do it by a cerebral process passed down in the blood" (Stoppard 1967: 56). In Hamlet Reynaldo prompts Polonius when he forgets the text of his exhortations to be conveyed to his son Laertes:

Pol.   By the mass, I was about to say something.
         Where did I leave?
Rey.   At "closes in the consequence."

                                                              (II.i.50)

In *As You Like It*, written at virtually the same time, I would suggest that "Bear thy body more seeming, Audrey" is a direct instruction from the master actor to the apprentice: "Keep in your part," which Shakespeare uses because it is easily socialized into the part of Audrey, the rustic wench who must play the part of suitable bride for a court jester. Nevertheless, this moment marks a use of the boy actor significantly different from the way Shakespeare exploits his presence in the roles of the court characters, Rosalind and Celia.

In Phoebe's case also, the body of the boy actor becomes a matter of comment, and interrupts the fiction in which Phoebe herself plays, proud shepherdess scorning faithful lover and falling in love with false Ganymede (as Wordsworth calls him in *The Prelude*). Phoebe's interpretation of her role as cruel beautiful lady is curiously literal as well as literary. Like Audrey, she is not poetical, however well she has mastered a literary language. In her unpoetic world eyes are fragile and incapable of murder. Rosalind's rebuke of Silvius for blind adulation exposes Phoebe's physical reality:

>   I saw her hand. She has a leathern hand,
>   A free-stone coloured hand. I verily did think
>   That her old gloves were on; but 'twas her hands.
>   She has a housewife's hand – but that's no matter.
>   (IV.iii.25)

Phoebe's leathern hand can of course exist as much in the realm of dramatic and poetic illusion as the lady of Shakespeare's sonnet 130 whose eyes are nothing like the sun. But part of the joke here might be that the teenage boy actor has much larger and coarser hands than would be appropriate for a lady, and that the dramatist has used this fact and translated it into the "feminine" cultural context of a "housewife's hands," his case, the hands of a shepherdess. For Phoebe, who desires to be not a woman world, like Audrey, but a lady, is ambiguously placed in the pastoral world, where women (like Audrey) kept goats, but men kept sheep. Phoebe is neither house-wife nor shepherdess, but herself a literary creation, a young woman from a pastoral poem, with a good command of fancy language, who is acted by someone with large coarse hands, namely, a boy. Rosalind is not at this point presumably displaying large hands, but it wouldn't matter if she did, because she is now Ganymede, a shepherd-boy. Shepherds, observes Corin to Touchstone, do not kiss hands, because "we are still handling our ewes, and their fells, you know, are greasy" (III.ii.50).

The physical reality of the boy playing Phoebe is used to puncture the fiction of the woman. Yet that puncturing, as in the case of Audrey's scratching, is also fictionalized, because leathern hands belong to the country girl whose working reality contradicts Phoebe's pretensions to gentility. The theatrical origins of both moments lie in the reality of the boy actor, a recalcitrant physical presence which the dramatist exploits for its fictional intransigence, its refusal to be translated into "seeming."

Is there anything of that physical intervention in the way in which Rosalind and Celia are presented? I would like to talk briefly about the tedious jesting of Touchstone on the subject of pancakes and mustard in I.ii, a passage which tests the tolerance of modern actors and audience to the limit for its leathern-handedness. The point of it seems to be that the knight who swore by his honor, although he had none, represents a satirical criticism by Touchstone of Duke Frederick, who in the scene immediately following swears by *his* honor. The palpable hypocrisy of this oath as an accompaniment to the banishment of Rosalind shows an indifference to its meaning comparable to that of Prince John of Lancaster tricking the rebels at Gaultree in *II Henry IV*. Indeed, the dramatist may have intended the audience to remember that notorious betrayal, and conceivably the actor who played the very small part of Prince John in *II Henry IV* at its first performance in 1598 had, by 1599, graduated to the role of Duke Frederick in *As You Like It*. It's as if the dramatist challenged the audience to remember that earlier performance. Would Frederick have been hissed at this moment? He might have been. The conjuring-up of a particular actor at a par-ticular moment has some relevance for the point I want to make about the two boy actors playing Rosalind and Celia while Touchstone delivers his mustard and pancakes joke.

Rosalind recognizes Frederick as the butt of Touchstone's wit in the sharp exchange that follows in which she threatens the Fool with whipping for exceeding his comic license. But there is another aspect of the brief interlude which needs inspection. "Stand you both forth now," orders Touchstone, "Stroke your chins, and swear by your beards that I am a knave." "By our beards – if we had them – thou art," replies Celia, and traditionally both women stroke their chins. "By my knavery – if I had it – then I were," rejoins Touchstone. In the modern theater this interchange is leaden-paced. But in Shakespeare's theater, something else would have been in play.

The prime fear of the boy actor was the advent of a beard: "Nay, faith; let me not play a woman; I have a beard coming," protests Flute in *A Midsummer Night's Dream* (I.ii.47). The beard signals manhood. "Is his chin worth a beard?" demands Rosalind of Orlando, and Celia demurs: "Nay, he hath but a little beard." Rosalind is charitable: "Why, God will send more, if the man will be thankful" (III.ii.199). In the Epilogue the boy actor – simultaneously Rosalind and Ganymede and just himself, an actor – courts the men in the audience: "If I were a woman I would kiss as many of you as had beards that pleased me." The absence of beard proclaims the physical reality of Rosalind and Celia as women. Yet it also draws attention to the opposite potential in the boys who act them. Shakespeare confronts the theatrical fiction that these are women by drawing attention to the absence of the sign of manhood: facial hair. But one longs to know whether there might not have been some comic recognition that the physical reality of the boy actor creates another dimension in the scene. Might not the two boys who play women's parts long for the growth of a beard which would enable them to graduate to male parts, as Flute wants to, hoping vainly that the part of Thisbe will be that of a "wandering knight"? The skilled boy actor could have brought a level of consciousness into the stroking of the chin which would bring into play not only the two ladies without beards, but the two boys for whom beards would spell the end of women's parts.

What would the effect have been of introducing such an awareness into the scene? To shatter the illusion of femininity, or to confirm it? If played as a moment of masculine self-consciousness, this dead passage comes to life as a dress rehearsal for the Forest of Arden: Rosalind reverts to boy actor, and as he strokes his chin, he imagines himself into the role of Rosalind, as Ganymede is later to do. Rosalind, beardless, accommodates to that role her own knowledge of the boy who might, as he stroked his chin, encounter a few bristles. Boy and woman offer the actor a double comic resource which he will exploit in the Forest of Arden. The unfictionalized body of the boy actor obtrudes on the fiction of the play, forcing the play to accommodate it, as it does with Audrey's scratching and Phoebe's hands.

If in the mustard joke the beards which Celia and Rosalind don't possess draw attention to the boy beneath the woman's clothes as much or more than to the biological signs of femininity, what happens when Celia and Rosalind start talking about their disguises? Class is here more important than is usually allowed. If Audrey does not play gender games because she is the thing itself, a rustic keeper of goats, Celia, the court princess, is going to play at being poor: "I'll put myself in poor and mean attire, / And with a kind of umber smirch my face" (I.iii.110). According to this testimony, in Arden Celia will play Audrey not Phoebe, the honest plain woman who does not know what poetry is, rather than the cruel shepherdess who always speaks in blank verse. The boy will stop playing the lady, and play a part where he may scratch his body or wipe his nose on his sleeve, hawk or spit to his heart's content. We never see Celia doing these things. As Duke Frederick's daughter, she is perhaps not a good enough actress, any more than Phoebe is that good at being a proud princess. As a body she resists the disguise of coarse boyhood which for Audrey is not a disguise, and this implies, of course, that far from being a poor actor, the boy who plays Celia is a very accomplished one: he can convince the audience that his most comfortable role is that of a refined court princess. No leathern hands here. In not being very accomplished at playing the hardy rustic girl, Celia testifies to the skill of the boy in transforming his own physical presence. In Arden Celia ceases to be the boy actor who might have a beard coming, who dreams up the whole escape to Arden. She is always Celia, the princess in disguise, just as Audrey is always the country bumpkin.

In this performance the boy playing Celia is much aided by his partnership with Rosalind, eager to transform her outside into that of a man, even though the woman will remain within: "In my heart, / Lie there what hidden woman's fear there will" (I.iii.117). The woman, Rosalind, who has a boy within, will become the boy Ganymede, who has the woman, Rosalind, within. So if the boy actor plays Rosalind, Rosalind also plays a boy, Ganymede. When the two of them arrive in Arden, the woman within wants to weep, as Rosalind did in the scene following her banishment, but Ganymede scorns to do so: "Doublet and hose ought to show itself courageous to petticoat" (II.iv.6).

I don't want to traverse again the well-worn ground of Rosalind's oscillation between boy and woman in Arden; we all know that the boy actor plays Rosalind for the theater audience, Rosalind plays Ganymede for Orlando, Ganymede plays Rosalind for Orlando, and in doing so also plays a boy: Jove's page; a shepherd; a scornful lover of Phoebe; a jester at Jaques; a brother for Celia; and ultimately, himself, a boy actor playing a woman's part. The boy's body is fictionalized by his own performance of it, just as the woman's body is also fictionalized. What is the difference? Not very great, apparently: a moonish effeminate youth and a woman in love are for the most part cattle of the same color (III.ii.394).

Put like this, the processes by which the boy actor undergoes transformation from boy to woman to boy sound pretty complicated, whereas when the audience sees them on stage they acquire simplicity. Shakespeare knew perfectly well that what he was doing was intricate. He sketched it out in *The Two Gentlemen of Verona*, and it is worth noting how fully the dramatic techniques used in *As You Like It* are in place in that very early comedy, considered by the Oxford editors to be the dramatist's first play. When Julia, dressed as Sebastian, the page of her false lover, Proteus, woos Silvia on his behalf, she describes her sorrow in terms that both evoke and fictionalize the body of the boy actor which is, of course, her own body. Proteus's love-making, even by proxy, is as unwelcome to Silvia as it is to Julia, as she is betrothed to Valentine, Proteus's closest friend. Silvia, and the page Sebastian (Julia), talk of Julia, whom the page declares he knows "Almost as well as I do know myself," and describes for Silvia a dramatic production in which he took part while Julia watched. It was a Whitsun performance, and he wore one of Julia's dresses in which to play Ariadne, deserted by Theseus. Julia was moved:

> And at that time I made her weep agood,
> For I did play a lamentable part.
> Madam, 'twas Ariadne passioning
> For Theseus' perjury and unjust flight;
> Which I so lively acted with my tears
> That my poor mistress, moved therewithal,
> Wept bitterly; and would I might be dead
> If I in thought felt not her very sorrow.
> (IV.iv.165)

The boy plays Julia; but Julia plays Sebastian, just as Rosalind plays Ganymede. Sebastian then plays another part, that of Ariadne, lamenting Theseus's desertion of her, with Julia watching, just as Ganymede plays another part, that of Rosalind, responding to Orlando's courtship. But there is another twist to the masquerade because the boy who plays Ariadne is wearing Julia's clothes for the performance, he being the same height as his mistress. He acts Ariadne so movingly that Julia weeps; and seeing her tears, the page Sebastian feels in his heart the same sorrow. He has become Julia, just as Ariadne has also become Julia, both because she is acted by the boy who plays Julia, and because she shares Julia's fate in being deserted by her lover. Ganymede acting Rosalind becomes Rosalind as he plays her for Orlando, just as in order to be eligible to play that part, Rosalind must become Ganymede. The transformation at the end of the play of Ganymede into Rosalind is the culmination of what has been acted out in the Forest of Arden, boy playing woman, but acted out also in Shakespeare's theater. The audience is asked to believe that in the end the boy really is the woman, Rosalind, only to be immediately disabused of that fiction in the Epilogue. Orlando falls in love with a Rosalind projected by the boy Ganymede. Rosalind occupies the position of both Julia watching the performance of the boy playing the woman, and also of the boy actor himself in the Ariadne scene conjured up by Julia, as he experiences the emotions of the woman who watches him perform.

What has happened to the body, male or female, what you will? Under this analysis it totally disappears, has become indeed a fiction. But has it? At the end of Rosalind's wooing scene Celia cries: "You have simply misused our sex in your love-prate. We must have your doublet and hose plucked over your head, and show the world what the bird hath done to her own nest" (IV.i.184). In Shakespeare's theater this is the ultimate act of daring, as risky as the stroking of beards in the second scene of the play. In the only other play where such an unmasking actually takes place, Jonson's *Epicoene*, the body revealed is that of the boy actor, able to refute in one moment the courtiers who claimed to have lain with the silent woman. Perhaps Jonson thought of Celia's threat in *As You Like It* when he devised his own play. When a woman plays Rosalind, Celia's protest verges on being coy and even voyeuristic. When a boy plays Rosalind, the evoking of the body as the test of sexual identity defies that test. Do we believe in the woman's body? I think we do, just as we believe that Malvolio is gulled, despite Fabian's protest: "If this were play'd now upon a stage, I could condemn it as an improbable fiction" (III.iv.127). We believe in it precisely because it is a fiction. Phoebe's leathern hand, Audrey's unseeming bearing of her body, both revert to the physical body of the actor, however clothed that is in fictions of behavior by the women themselves. But Rosalind's body exists only as a constant act of evasion. Is she man without and woman within, or is she woman without and man within? The categories of outer and inner cease at this point to contain any capacity for clarification. The fiction of the play has exploded them.

What happens to this elusive body once the part is played by a woman? Let us return first to Audrey and Phoebe. In the theater these two country girls have become stock figures: Audrey the bumpkin, presenting an image of crude and naive sexuality; Phoebe, refined to the point of tedium – often played by a young actress eager to make the most of her lines. For the boy actor also the part was doubtless a trial-run for larger and more testing roles. Can one see Phoebe progressing to the part of Helena in *All's Well That Ends Well*, the tables rudely turned as the young Count Bertram (played by Silvius?) spurns her for low birth as cruelly as she spurned the shepherd Silvius? Audrey, when played by a man in the Cheek by Jowl production, rose to new levels of hilarity. The male actor relished the female body he had to impersonate. Shakespeare's boy may also have relished not, for once, having to follow the instructions for acting a genteel lady so minutely given by the Lord for the benefit of his Page in the Induction to *The Taming of the Shrew*. This relish can hardly be imitated by a woman because it is rooted in the theatrical reality of cross-dressing.

I want to consider briefly some other aspects of the dynamics of change once the female characters in *As You Like It* are played by women. In the Cheek by Jowl all-male production of *As You Like It*, the early scenes at court between Rosalind and Celia were embarrassingly badly acted. These were two men pretending to be two women expressing intimacy. With boys it might have been different, especially in a theater where children's companies were in currency and the word-play and quick banter of John Lyly's plays are easily annexed to the performance of boys in a predominantly adult company. Adrian Lester's performance as Rosalind came into its own with the arrival in Arden, where the double-take of a man pretending to be a woman pretending to be macho was funnier than anything I have seen a woman do in the part of Rosalind. Nevertheless, it was a curious experience to see a man in a role which has become a star role for actresses, so that one talks of Peggy Ashcroft, Vanessa Redgrave, Juliet Stevenson, and many others, as Rosalind.

In Shakespeare's theater this polarization of the play into a vehicle for a star performance would have been impossible, and to some extent contemporary theater has tried to return the play to a more balanced pattern, evident in the resuscitation of a Celia almost as lively as Rosalind herself, much in evidence when Fiona Shaw played the part opposite Stevenson. This redressing of the balance interestingly took place in the 1970s, with Janet Suzman the first in a line of reinvented Celias, possible in the wake of the women's movement; some of the critical interest in the friendship of the two women is in part the fruit of other aspects of that movement. If Chloë likes

Olivia, said Virginia Woolf in *A Room of One's Own*, a light will be lit in a room which has always been dark.

From the very early days of women's acting Rosalind, the making of the part into a star role has gone hand in hand with the effeminization of Ganymede in Arden, which has brought with it the conviction of the homoerotic aspects of not only Shakespeare's theater, but also of Ganymede's relation with Orlando. It is almost impossible in the modern theater to imagine the boyishness which must have informed the courtship scenes when a boy acted the part of Rosalind/Ganymede, because ever since Sarah Siddons, the point of the disguise has been not to create a fiction which would explore to the full the comic capacities of the theatrical necessity of having boys play women, but instead to exploit the capacity of a male disguise for presenting a particularly alluring aspect of femininity.

The tradition that the actress makes no attempt to disguise femininity is firmly placed with accounts of Sarah Siddons playing Rosalind in the eighteenth century. John Boaden's *Memoirs of Mrs. Siddons* state that "she ventured to appear upon the London stage in a dress which more strongly reminded the spectator of the sex which she had laid down, than that which she had taken up. Even this, which shewed the struggle of modesty to save all unnecessary exposure, was a thousand times more captivating as to female loveliness, than the studious display of all that must have rendered concealment impossible" (Boaden 1827: 166). The actress in fact wore a little skirt over her breeches, and not all her reviewers were as delighted as her biographer.

There is no doubt that dressing as a boy increasingly emphasized womanhood to an audience only too glad to see a decent pair of legs. The femininity of the actress was enhanced by her assumed masculine attire, and this became particularly seductive during the mid-Victorian period of prudishness. When the American actress Ada Rehan played Rosalind in 1897, she also exploited the sexual suggestiveness of her costume as Ganymede. Clement Scott wrote of her London performance: "The great feature of Miss Rehan's Rosalind is that she never for one moment forgets, or allows herself to forget, that she is a woman." Nobody wanted her to look like a boy, let alone be one. The idea that she did look like one was a fiction, just as the pantomime boy in *Cinderella*, or any other pantomime, is a fiction. This situation was first challenged in 1919, with Nigel Playfair's post-First World War production of the play at Stratford, which delighted some by its dispensing with hallowed theatrical traditions, although many people were horrified. The *Manchester Guardian* reported:

> Rosalind has been seen for so many generations in dresses approaching in more or less degree that of the "principal boy" of pantomime that deep disappointment was caused in many quarters by the complete absence of the low-necked tunic, tights, high-heeled boots, and the inevitable pheasant's feather in her cap which have hitherto been regarded as indispensable in her forest dress.[4]

Playfair's production is demonstrably post-war, coming one year after demobilization and at the beginning of the "flappers" period when women finally got the vote. The movement away from pantomime boy mirrored a change in the society that provided the theater audience.

In the stage history of *As You Like It*, Vanessa Redgrave's performance of the role in Stratford in 1961 marked a new attempt to give Rosalind authentic boyishness. A critic from the *Glasgow Herald* wrote that Redgrave "takes her cue from the text and never lets the woman peep out from under the jerkin and top boots," except in her interchanges with Celia. He continues: "She avoids turning the character into a jolly Dick Whittington and she also avoids the pitfall which is so often the rule with showy Rosalinds who make the character so seductively feminine that they reduce Orlando's blindness to the disguise to nonsense."[5] When Juliet Stevenson played the part in Adrian Noble's production of 1985, the whole question of gender had become much more fluid than had been the case in any theater other than Shakespeare's own. Irving Wardle wrote of Adrian Noble's 1985 production with Stevenson that it entered "deeper waters where neither she, her lover, nor the audience can tell truth from masquerade."[6] The play ends in those waters, for the Epilogue defies the audience to distinguish truth from masquerade.

However, I want to talk briefly about one scene which anticipates the Epilogue both in its concentration on the body of the boy actor and in its magical power of transformation; indeed, the two are integrally linked. V.iii is a curious little scene which seems almost like an interpolation from a court performance of the play. Audrey and Touchstone plan their marriage and two pages enter to sing "It was a lover and his lass." The attempts to integrate the pages into the Forest of Arden are minimal: did we know that the Duke was so attended? Are two boys really to walk on in all the Forest scenes? Surely not. Yet here they are, very much boy singers rather than characters in a play: "Shall we clap to it roundly, without hawking and spitting, or saying we are hoarse, which are the only prologues to a bad voice?" (V.iii.10). It's not at all likely that these boys would only have appeared for this scene. They cannot have doubled any of the women, who have to appear immediately in the final scene of the play, yet it is most unlikely that they would have been used without being able to play other parts. It's very unusual also for there to be six boys required to perform in a play. The standard number was four. If they were actors, who did they double? I suggest that they could have played not women, but old men, Corin the shepherd, and Adam, Orlando's faithful servant. Jonson's poem on the death of the boy actor Salamon Pavey claims that he acted old men so well that God mistook him for one. Jaques says in his "ages of man" speech that the "lean and slippered pantaloon" of the sixth age finds "his big, manly voice, / Turning again toward childish treble, pipes / And whistles in his sound" (II.vii.161). If the boys did play Corin and Adam, the scene in Act V with the two pages acquires an altogether new dimension. Corin, whom Silvius complained had forgotten how to love, and Adam, whose age "is as a lusty winter / Frosty but kindly" (II.iii.53), are transformed into boys singing of love and springtime. The order of nature is reversed, where the young grow old, for in this play old men are boys again, in a magical world where Hymen will preside over the marriage of a boy turned into a woman, Ganymede into Rosalind. The body of the boy actor asserts the reality of the fiction by its very refusals: the old are not, after all, old, and they are no longer required to seem so, but only to sing without spitting first.

So what of Rosalind, boy turned to woman? She remains onstage: "It is not the fashion to see the lady the epilogue: but it is no more unhandsome than to see the lord the prologue." It is unhandsome to see the lady the Epilogue because Epilogues are spoken by men. But nor is it polite to see the lord the Prologue, because in polite society the lady should enter first, in front of the gentleman. *As You Like It*, even before the Forest scenes, exposes continuously the complications of etiquette. The fluidity with which the forms of "thou" and "you" are used in the play, with their usual connotations of formality or intimacy, gentility and social inferiority (Calvo 1992), mirrors on a linguistic level the transformations of gender and class in the play. "If I were a woman . . ." Rosalind's masquerade is at an end, and yet she makes boyhood her ultimate masquerade. She takes her leave: "When I make curtsey, bid me farewell." The only way a woman actress could recapture the dizzying illusory quality of this farewell would be to bow as she says the lines, invoking the shepherd-boy she has played, just as the boy actor invokes Rosalind. For if women play boys, they must, to recover the complexities of this play, recover the illusion of the boy's body. If Adrian Lester can play a woman pretending to be the strong man that his physical presence proclaims him to be, while convincing the audience that that physical presence is a charade enacted by a woman, a woman actress can and must also create the illusion that her womanhood is, in the final instance, a charade. Would an audience allow it? Probably not. We are too literal. The only way to do it effectively in the modern theater would be to cross-dress everyone.

NOTES

1 All quotations from *As You Like It* are from Alan Brissenden's edition (1994). Some of the most recent studies which I have used for my thinking on this play are Orgel (1996); Shapiro (1994); Bono (1986); Traub (1992); Butler (1995).

2 Quotations from *All's Well That Ends Well* are from G. K. Hunter's edition (1959).

3 Quotations from *Hamlet* are from *The Riverside Shakespeare* (1974), edited by G. Blakemore Evans. All quotations from Shakespeare's

plays are from this edition unless otherwise specified.

4 H. G., "The Stratford Festival," *Manchester Guardian* (1919), in Theatre Records, 71.2 (c.11), Shakespeare Centre, Stratford-upon-Avon.

5 *Glasgow Herald*, July 7, 1961, in Theatre Records, 71.2 (c.53), Shakespeare Centre, Stratford-upon-Avon.

6 *Sunday Times Magazine*, April 21, 1985.

REFERENCES AND FURTHER READING

Boaden, J. 1827: *Memoirs of Mrs. Siddons*. London: Henry Colburn.

Bono, B. J. 1986: "Mixed Gender, Mixed Genre in

Shakespeare's *As You Like It*." In Barbara Kiefer Lewalski (ed.), *Renaissance Genres*. Cambridge, MA: Harvard University Press, 189–212.

Butler, J. 1995: *Gender Trouble: Feminism and the Subversion of Identity*. New York and London: Routledge.

Calvo, C. 1992: "Pronouns of Address and Social Negotiation in *As You Like It.*" *Language and Literature*, 1, 1, 5–27.

Evans, G. B. (ed.) 1974: *The Riverside Shakespeare*. Boston: Houghton Mifflin.

Orgel, S. 1996: *Impersonations: The Performance of Gender in Shakespeare's England*. Cambridge: Cambridge University Press.

Shakespeare, W. 1959: *All's Well That Ends Well*. Ed. G. K. Hunter. London: Methuen.

——1994: *As You Like It*. Ed. Alan Brissenden. Oxford: Oxford University Press.

Shapiro, M. 1994: *Gender in Play on the Shakespearean Stage*. Ann Arbor: University of Michigan Press.

Stoppard, T. 1967: *Rosencrantz and Guildenstern Are Dead*. London: Faber and Faber.

Traub, V. 1992: *Desire and Anxiety: Circulations of Sexuality in Shakespearean Drama*. London and New York: Routledge.

14

Mutant Scenes and "Minor" Conflicts in *Richard II*

Molly Smith

I The Condition of "Minority"

In a highly charged moment during the Clarence Thomas–Anita Hill hearings, tele-vised live before an intrigued and thoroughly engaged audience, Shakespeare figured prominently in an exchange which swung the emotional momentum decidedly in Thomas's favor. Calling on Thomas to expose his emotional outrage at the slanderous treatment he had received, one senator cited the famous lines from *Othello* where Cassio, speaking to a seemingly sympathetic Iago, bemoans the loss of his reputation; Thomas, the senator pointed out, might feel as Shakespeare did about the importance of reputation and the loss of self and identity that accompanied its tainting. One might raise questions about the appropriateness of such an invocation, the ease with which Cassio's expression glided into Shakespeare's own convictions, the inadvertent irony of citing a passage so charged with ambiguity, etc., but I am less interested in these issues and more so in what followed. As the hearings continued, another invo-cation of Shakespeare occurred, this time by one of the senators more sympathetic to Hill who had raised the specter of sexual misconduct on Thomas's part. As aides hurried to locate the new passage or perhaps to find more passages for others to cite, the emotional balance seemed equally poised between Thomas and Hill, between those who supported the former and those who sympathized with the latter; even Shake-speare, it seemed, confronted with such a difficult situation, might have remained ambivalent and argued passionately for both sides. The decisive moment arrived a few moments later, however, as the first senator (Arlin Specter, I think it was, though the exact identity of the speaker is unimportant to my tale), publicized the error his oppos-ing colleague, in his desperate attempt to match literary quotation with quotation, had so grievously committed. The second passage, the senator very spectacularly announced, had not been from Shakespeare after all but from a minor and later play-wright, William Congreve. How could Congreve, a figure quite on the fringes of dramatic tradition, at least as far as the American general public and political elite were concerned, have said anything more profoundly to the moment than Shakespeare could, the senator seemed to imply. The majority of those watching no doubt agreed, and the momentum, at least it seemed so to me, swung decidedly in Thomas's favor; he did after all have the weight of Shakespeare's support and not even highly trained political aides on Capitol Hill could produce a response to Shakespeare, for the world's literary canon could not yield a greater authority.

I remain intrigued by this moment, half sympathizing with the sentiment being sanctioned (after all, I make my living by teaching Shakespeare not Congreve), and while I could see the logical failure inherent in these invocations of literary authorities, my own choice of literary research and exploration seemed vaguely justified by these public proceedings; as a naturalized American citizen, the moment even testified to the authenticity of my newly nationalized self.

Since then, however, I have become increasingly aware of what I have known but never quite confronted, namely, that while the tenor and flavor of these judicial proceedings might have been American, the sentiments so boldly sanctioned and authorized would find general support elsewhere and there is nothing at all American about the sanctity that surrounds the invocation of Shakespeare's name. Indeed, the battle for priority between Congreve and Shakespeare is being fought even as I speak in the corridors of the English department at Aberdeen as we decide whether Congreve should even be retained on the undergraduate English course in which all potential majors are introduced to drama. Actually, I exaggerate matters by using the word "battle," for there is no real argument to be made; most members of the department would agree that Congreve remains comparatively unimportant in the history of drama and should no doubt be dropped; he is inaccessible to most students anyway, unlike Shakespeare, whose texts continue to speak personally and collectively to otherwise recalcitrant eighteen-year-olds irrespective of whether they come from America or the Continent or the British Isles.

Divested thus of my new-found and tenuous self-identification with the American public and confronted with a growing suspicion about my own conventionality, I find myself pondering the question of "minor" texts anew. I cannot account for the force that enables a sports company to successfully market its products by re-citing Richard III ("now is the discount of our winter tents"), but my own research, so carefully structured around the Shakespeare canon, has taken on a new significance in recent years; I feel compelled to engage with the question of "minor" and "major," to confront my own acquiescence in the creation and reiteration of these categories, and most of all, to come to terms with my very material and permanent investment in Shakespeare. Confronting these issues has sometimes constituted redirecting my energies into other avenues, and I have veered between Shakespeare and Massinger, Heywood and Stubbes, with equal absorption, deriving pleasure from unexpected quarters while still reliving encounters already experienced. My own status on the cultural margins of Western society (I am Indian by birth, American by choice of nationality, Scottish in my choice of academic environments, and committed to teaching early modern

English drama – a more varied collage of dominated and dominant cultures is barely conceivable) has imbued this new engagement with questions of canon and textual significance with a personal tint. But I also remain convinced that "minor" strains and voices (whether among the canon of published texts available to us or within individual texts) speak with a force that demands attention.

Thus, while teaching *Richard II* to undergraduates last year, the voices that made the greatest impression on me were those hitherto regarded as submerged within the text, those supposedly heard in muted strains, those either ignored or designated as farcical by those who engage with the play. In hearing these voices, I remain acutely aware of Annette Kolodny's at once cautionary and liberating account of critical inventiveness: "the only 'perennial feature' to which our ability to read and re-read texts written in previous centuries testifies is our inventiveness – in the sense that all of literary history is a fiction which we daily re-create as we reread it" (Kolodny 1994: 280). My fiction focuses on the insistent appeal of the feminine in a play which many critics describe as staging a masculine, historical world of political strife and national transition. Or maybe it is more useful to think of my fiction as another history, for as Lynn Hunt so convincingly argues, history may be defined as "an ongoing tension between stories that have been told and stories that might be told. In this sense, it is more useful to think of history as an ethical and political practice than as an epistemology with a clear ontological status" (Hunt 1991: 103).

This essay, focusing as it does on the marginal in Shakespeare, exposes my desire to deal at once with the major and the minor, the dominant and the dominated, fiction and history; my critical dilemma and intellectual anguish spring from my developing conviction that trying to distinguish between these polarities is frequently doomed to failure.[1] I will illustrate my point by looking at some so-called "minor" scenes in *Richard II*.

II   Women and the Deterritorialization of Dominant Discourses in *Richard II*

Graham Holderness has recently tried to address the comparative lack of interest in Shakespeare's history plays by feminist critics; even in the work of feminists who have discussed these plays, Holderness detects "an enduring sense of incompatibility between the Renaissance history play and the priorities of feminist analysis," a factor which "has deflected such critics from that dramatic genre" (Holderness 1992: 41).[2] Rescuing these plays from comparative feminist neglect involves, for Holderness, a recourse to new historicist evacuation of the play's active and plural engagement with contexts; thus, "the marginalization of women in a play such as *Richard II* is not simply the symptomatic expression of an unconscious misogyny or a passive reflection of predetermined historical conditions. It is rather a historical reality of the past, grasped by the specific mode of historical consciousness active in the play, a reality which the play in turn foregrounds, interrogates, and criticizes" (Holderness 1992: 76–7). While

Holderness's insistence that "women may not be much in evidence in the play, but femininity is" remains valid, he nevertheless resorts to exploring its presence by tracing charges of femininity between male characters such as Mowbray and Boling-broke in the early scenes, and by seeing femininity in the metaphorical language of figures such as Gaunt. Without challenging his readings of these particular passages, I would nevertheless like to suggest that to read femininity into the language of the text and to see traces of femininity in the vocabulary between males nevertheless commits him to the ideology of equating length of female presence on the stage with textual significance, and to ignoring the emphatic authorization of the feminine which the play stages boldly and crucially in its last scenes after evocatively and consciously dramatizing its erasure and subjection in the first half. If the play can be read as an "intervention" into the Renaissance cultural debate concerning femi-ninity (Holderness 1992: 13), this intervention emerges mainly through the play's female voices, which call attention to such erasure and even proffer a critique of mas-culinist ideologies which they characterize as quite at odds with their own concerns. We encounter similar critiques in other plays, but *Richard II* remains unique in its gesture toward revising dominant masculinist ideologies in accordance with such criticisms.[3]

I want to focus on two characters in particular, the Duchess of Gloucester and the Duchess of York. The early scene involving the Duchess of Gloucester is deliberately placed to interrupt the ceremonious scenes at court involving the conflict between Mowbray and Bolingbroke. Its theatrical position heralds its status as an alternate vision; indeed, the Duchess's and Gaunt's preoccupation throughout the scene with the same issue that has precipitated the court into the present crisis suggests its impor-tance as a parallel scene. The emphasis of the scene, however, remains different; the Duchess sees the death of the Duke of Gloucester as a familial violation demanding revenge from kin. Her pain, expressed through metaphors and images which stress the familial bond, remains unheeded by Gaunt, whose emphasis, like that of most males in the play, focuses on political ideology surrounding the divinity and sanctity of the monarch. The arguments made by the Duchess here will be heard again later in the play:

> Finds brotherhood in thee no sharper spur?
> Hath love in thy old blood no living fire?
>
> . . .
>
> Ah, Gaunt, his [Gloucester's] blood was thine! That bed, that womb
> That mettle, that self, that fashioned thee,
> Made him a man; and though thou liv'st and breath'st,
> Yet art thou slain in him.
>
>   (I.ii.9–25)

Gaunt's response merely reiterates political ideology; Richard may have had a hand in Gloucester's death, Gaunt implies, but the act may have received sanction from above:

> God's is the quarrel; for God's substitute,
> His deputy anointed in his sight,
> Hath caused his death; the which, *if wrongfully*,
> Let heaven revenge, for I may never lift
> An angry arm against his minister.
>
> (I.ii.37–41, emphasis added)

The Duchess recognizes the emphatic nature of Gaunt's refusal to act, and retires, as she suggests, to complete her life in mourning and sorrow. The import of her defeated withdrawal is hard to miss: Richard II's court and courtiers, committed to the ideology of the monarch's divinity, remain oblivious to the competing demands of familial obligation and responsibility. It is precisely this disregard for the bonds of kinship that the play dramatizes so forcefully and repeatedly in the early scenes; Richard and his court are pointedly implicated in this censure.

But what precisely is the Duchess asking from Gaunt in this scene? If, as they both recognize, Richard remains culpable for the conflicts at court and bears responsibility for Gloucester's death, the magnitude of her demand is clear and Gaunt's equal unwillingness to act remains entirely understandable. The Duchess articulates a demand inconceivable to Gaunt; she asks for the enactment of a revenge tragedy, for action to be taken against Richard himself in retaliation for the murder of her husband. Unlike the maneuverings at court, fought behind the facade of allegiance to king and country, the target of her censure is direct and clear. Only to her does Gaunt, who had maintained the veneer of impartiality in the opening scene even as he will again in the scene to follow, express his misgivings about Richard. But despite his emotional sympathy for her arguments, Gaunt in this scene (and Richard's court indirectly) marginalizes her concerns by dismissing them, and the Duchess retires to her country home to pine and die of grief.

But what we as readers and audience cannot forget is that the play itself neither condemns nor trivializes the Duchess's request for a revenge play. Indeed, the actions to follow, Richard's deposition and Bolingbroke's seizure of the throne, enact her will, and Gaunt himself as he lies dying foretells in prophetic fashion the price Richard will eventually pay for his transgressions; his censure of Richard, as if taking its cue from the Duchess's remarks, specifically focuses on his brother Gloucester's death:

> O, spare me not, my brother Edward's son,
> For that I was his father Edward's son;
> That blood already, like the pelican,
> Hast thou tapp'd out and drunkenly carous'd:
> My brother Gloucester, plain well-meaning soul,
> . . .
> May be a president and witness good
> That thou respect'st not spilling Edward's blood.
>
> (II.i.124–31)

His accusation draws its vocabulary from the Duchess's arguments earlier, and he insists as she had that Richard has violated the bonds of kinship. In other words, despite the Duchess of Gloucester's marginal role in the text of the play, her concerns mold our vision of Richard as monarch, and Gaunt's famous censure of Richard draws its force and legitimacy from her earlier grief.[4] Most importantly, the central actions fulfill her desire for a revenge tragedy against Richard by the Lancastrians; it is no accident that she addresses her concerns to Gaunt and not the weak-willed York. What is more, her conviction about the interchangeability of fathers and sons imbues her demands, aware as we are about the historical truth of Henry's succession to the throne even in the opening scenes, with an urgency and immediacy that is hard to miss. If we minimize the Duchess's importance to central actions, we acquiesce in her initial dismissal by Gaunt and Richard's court, forgetting that the play itself both immediately (through Gaunt's obvious recapitulation and our awareness of the historical truth about Henry's succession) and retrospectively (through the elaborate staging of Henry's success) authorizes rather than erases her concerns.

The difference between a culturally absorbed ideological commitment to the monarchy and an inwardly felt commitment to the bonds of kinship receives greater elaboration toward the end of the play as York and his wife tangle over the fate of their son. But unlike the earlier battle, theirs is not fought only in private; brought to court under a new monarch, the newly crowned Henry IV, the Duchess's pleas for her son on the grounds of kinship and family receive a positive hearing from Henry who, perhaps in a politically astute move, pardons Aumerle. The conflict between York and his wife, however, reenacts the earlier argument between Gaunt and the Duchess of Gloucester; in the words of Jean Howard and Phyllis Rackin, "the opposition between masculine political considerations and feminine affective loyalty is reiterated in Act V" (1997: 140).

Unlike Howard and Rackin, however, I am not convinced that a "lowering of the dramatic register" necessarily occurs in these scenes, or if it does, that our contempt or laughter directs itself at the Duchess (Howard and Rackin 1997: 141). A long critical tradition has determined that these scenes involving Aumerle's treachery and forgiveness stage a "comic interlude" (Seelig 1995: 355).[5] While conceding that theatrical enactment could emphasize the comic potential of these scenes, I want to insist that the rehearsal of arguments we have heard before and the different outcome of these scenes impress upon us their importance to central actions; the association of these scenes with the new monarchy in place at the end of the play and with a modified ideology of kingship is hard to miss. The significance of the Aumerle incident looms larger when we remember that the Duchess of York's part in his pardon is an entirely Shakespearean invention. Through the Duchess of York's actions, strategically placed in the concluding act and in Henry's court, Shakespeare deliberately continues and concludes an argument initiated in the opening act of the play by the Duchess of Gloucester.

V.ii, which figures the domestic quarrel, begins, however, with a scene of seeming domestic harmony as the Duke of York recounts Bolingbroke's triumphant procession through the city. Despite York's pity for the humiliated Richard, his allegiance to Henry remains unswerving as he describes the scene. It is the Duchess who registers the greatest sympathy for Richard – "Alack, poor Richard! Where rode he the whilst?" – and she initiates the narrative by stressing her equal emotional loyalty to both her kinsmen: "My lord, you told me you would tell the rest, / . . . / Of our two cousins' coming into London" (V.ii.1–3). York concludes the narrative by explaining his own new allegiance as part of the country's providential movement towards supporting the new king:

> But heaven hath a hand in these events,
> To whose high will we bound our calm contents.
> To Bolingbroke we are sworn subjects now,
> Whose state and honour I for aye allow.
>
> (V.ii.37–40)

The easy recourse to God and providentiality here rings hollow and receives further ironic commentary through Aumerle's similar reliance on it a few lines later. In response to York's insistence that he be present at Oxford to herald the new king, Aumerle's "If God prevent it not, I purpose so" suggests his similar view of possible success in the plots to reinstate Richard. His mother's impassioned plea a few lines later after the treasonous plot is discovered, that York recognize the familial bond – "Is he not like thee? Is he not thine own?" – points to more than a physical resemblance between father and son. Howard and Rackin insist that the Duchess's subsequent "reference to the possibility of her adultery is designed to elicit dismissive laughter" (1997: 139). If the scene provokes comic laughter, York with his new-found energy and commitment to king over kin remains the target of our derision; Halverson's astute comment that Act V sees "the final transformation of York into a comic character" does not necessarily extend to the Duchess (1994: 358). York's condemnation of his wife as "foolish" and "unruly," in other words, his denunciation of her response as hysterical, constitutes what George Rousseau describes as the "negative imaging" of women "necessary in patriarchal cultures that confined power solely in the males to ensure civic cohesion" (1993: 96). The outcome of the following scene, which ends with York silenced and withdrawn, suggests that we are to view his contemptuous dismissal of his wife earlier as hasty, if not misguided. In the later scene before Henry it is she who chastises him in terminology often reserved for deviant or defiant women: "Ah my sour husband, my hard-hearted lord" (V.iii.119).[6]

If we regard the scene of Aumerle's pardon as indecorous and detracting from Henry's royalty, as some critics do, we dismiss the new vision of monarchy that the play so emphatically champions in its concluding scenes. In seeing Henry and York as "diminished by their inability to silence the woman and . . . degraded by their participation in the indecorous scene she stages," Howard and Rackin miss Henry's consummate rehearsal of power. Henry does not capitulate or give in to the Duchess contrary to his natural inclinations. The decision to pardon Aumerle, we might remember, has been made already and directly to Aumerle in the early part of the scene; Aumerle is the first to arrive at court and enacts an insistent drama of repentance elaborated in its mode and content by the Duchess at her appearance later. Refusing to arise from bended knee, Aumerle secures Henry's pardon *before* York enters and *before* being directed to open the door to his mother. Henry's conditioned pardon:

> Intended, or committed, was this fault?
> If on the first, how heinous e'er it be,
> To win thy after-love, I pardon thee.
>   (V.iii.32–4)

reveals an astute grasp of the problem before him. His carefully chosen words suggest that he has anticipated the possibility of treasonous plots against him and perhaps even his cousin's potential part in them; he also attaches a condition of eternal loyalty to his pardon, a condition Aumerle explicitly accepts by reminding Henry of his pardon after York's arrival: "Remember, as thou read'st, thy promise pass'd; / I do repent me" (V.iii.49–50). This vital exchange between Henry and Aumerle, a mini-drama whose full import is surely lost on York and the Duchess, redefines the monarchy as a contractual agreement between king and subjects.[7] While Richard had relied for his authority on his hereditary right to the throne and his sanctity as a monarch, Henry negotiates a series of allegiances through the course of the play, founding his monarchy on a visible contractual agreement between himself and the peers of the realm; Halverson's argument that "the play leaves no doubt that Richard is a bad king, that his conception of kingship is false, and that it is this false conception that causes his downfall" receives visual reinforcement in the last act through the implied contrast with Henry's monarchy (Halverson 1994: 364). Significantly, Henry's contract, rather than Richard's reliance on divine right, receives sanction from the masses.[8]

In other words, Henry exercises his royal authority by careful management of his audience in this scene, by allowing the Duchess to believe that he has acceded to her requests. We thus witness in the concluding scenes of *Richard II* a careful restructuring of the very foundations of royal authority; in Dominique Goy-Blanquet's words, "the stage presents them [Elizabethans] with the end of the magic relationship between king, nature, and divinity and its synthetic reconstruction by a clever governour" (1995: 152).[9] Henry's successful acquisition of the throne has always rested on his ability to convince his subjects of his active interest in their concerns and well-being.[10] As Martha Kurtz argues, "The scenes anchor the new king firmly in . . . popular culture, giving his reign a broad appeal that Richard's sorely lacked" (1996: 595). Contrary to providing a "comic interlude" within an otherwise serious play, Act V dramatizes Henry's ligature rather than fracture of the bonds of kinship and subjecthood. The Duchess's loyalty before this act had divided equally between her two cousins, but her new allegiance to Henry is clear at the end of V.iii as she ushers her son triumphantly from Henry's presence: "Come, my old son, pray God make thee anew" (V.iii.144). And Henry's politic signal that the Duchess's arguments, not York's, have won the day is equally hard to miss: "Uncle, farewell; and cousin too, adieu: / Your mother well hath pray'd, and prove you true" (V.iii.142–3). Henry's view of his potential interaction with the Duchess might have been initially dismissive – "Our scene is alt'red from a serious thing, / And now chang'd to 'The Beggar and the King'" (V.iii.77–8) – but there is little trace of such contempt in his final reminder of loyalty to his cousin and his aunt.

Most importantly, he allows the Duchess to stage a drama of triumph over her husband in which she pointedly emphasizes the difference between culturally acquired political sentiment and heart-felt loyalty born of kinship and love:

> Pleads he in earnest? Look upon his face.
> His eyes do drop no tears, his prayers are in jest,
> His words come from his mouth, ours from our breast;
>
> . . .
>
> We pray with heart and soul, and all beside;
> His prayers are full of false hypocrisy,
> Ours of true zeal and deep integrity;
> Our prayers do outpray his.
>
> (V.iii.98–107)

York's weak attempt at sidestepping the issue through his injunction that Henry speak in French meets with similar dismissal:

> Dost thou teach pardon pardon to destroy?
> Ah, my sour husband, my hard-hearted lord,
> That sets the word itself against the word!
> Speak pardon as 'tis current in our land,
> The chopping French we do not understand.
>
> (V.iii.118–22)

The Duchess's insistence that Henry use the common tongue astutely appeals to those qualities that brought Henry to power and provokes his response: "I pardon him, as God shall pardon me," a statement that also draws attention to his own transgressions with regard to convention and habit. Henry's language yokes Aumerle's transgressions with his own; he implicitly accepts his own culpability for past events and signals retributions yet to unfold, produced in response to the plot opportunely uncovered by Aumerle's indiscretion. Henry's unwillingness to be swayed by York's arguments and his conscious upholding of the Duchess's pleas point to York not the Duchess as a target of derision and comic laughter. Significantly, York is reduced to silence through the latter part of this scene.

Henry's willingness to hear the Duchess's arguments itself signals a difference in the new court's attitude towards its subjects, but in light of Henry's own insistence earlier on the bonds of kinship, it comes as no surprise. The Duchess's mode of operation recalls Henry's own encounter with York earlier after his bold return to England; kneeling before York, Henry expresses sentiments already familiar to us through the Duchess of Gloucester's and Gaunt's arguments in the opening act:

> You are my father, for methinks in you
> I see old Gaunt alive. O then my father,
> Will you permit that I shall stand condemned
>
> . . .
>
> You have a son, Aumerle, my noble cousin;
> Had you first died, and he been trod down,
> He should have found his uncle Gaunt a father
> To rouse his wrongs and chase them to the bay.
>   (II.iii.116–27)

The contrast with Richard, who in the hearing of his courtiers can wish Gaunt a speedy death, could not be more startling; indeed, Richard remains alone in publicly registering contempt for the bonds of kinship. Henry's later desire to be rid of Richard is radically different in scope and import; neither wishful thinking nor a passing hope, his public remark constitutes an order to his subjects and is recognized by Exton as such. Henry's command illustrates Gilles Deleuze and Felix Guattari's point about language acts as acts of power which issue words of order (1987: 95–100); Henry, unlike Richard, recognizes this power and uses language sparingly but with maximum political effect.

The play, in other words, registers two different courtly attitudes: in Richard's court, familial considerations are sidestepped and women's voices, the ones that insist most eloquently on the bonds of kinship, remain muted and marginal; by contrast, Henry's court foregrounds their concerns, allowing them a degree of empowerment even at the expense of silencing proponents of masculinist ideologies such as the loyal York.[11] I am not suggesting that the new court's ideological investment in patriarchy is minimal; on the contrary, Henry's orchestration of affairs in these last scenes testifies to his calculated and meticulous reinvestment in it despite his earlier defiance of these very conventions.[12] Claire McEahern's account of Shakespeare's treatment of patriarchy remains especially applicable to the history of *Richard II*:

> Patriarchy, then, is not seamlessly monolithic . . . but rather is founded in a profound contradiction: it is this contradiction that Shakespeare explores, focussing on the intersection of political and familial loyalties, and examining our attempts to resolve or reject the conflicting demands that patriarchy imposes on us. (McEahern 1988: 273)

Henry may acquire his crown "by the successful performance of masculine virtues," as Howard and Rackin argue, but his performance includes an incorporation, recognition, and even seeming empowerment of oppositional modes of discourse. And one mode of oppositional discourse is located unequivocally in the concerns of female characters in *Richard II*. In ignoring the potency of their voices, we acquiesce in their marginalization and erasure staged ruthlessly and consistently in the early scenes of the play, and ignore the play's and Henry's staged authentication of their concerns in the concluding scenes.

In Deleuze and Guattari's terms, we might regard the Duchesses' voices as constituting "a minor language" emerging from within and without the dominant discourses in the play; minor languages develop as a result of social and artistic marginality but acquire a revolutionary force unavailable to dominant languages. A minor language, as Deleuze and Guattari describe it, undermines the assumptions and systems of a major language, thereby deterritorializing it (1986: 18). Through the voices of the Duchess of Gloucester and the Duchess of York, precisely such a deterritorialization of the basic assumptions which informed court culture occurs in *Richard II*. From one perspective, we might even say that Shakespeare's theatrical contribution to the historical fiction of Richard II's life concentrates on the deterritorialization and undermining of dominant discourses.

NOTES

1   Louis Adrian Montrose's insistence on the ambiguous and ambivalent status of the Elizabethan theater may be of particular relevance in this context; "Shakespeare's professional milieu," he argues, "was a paradoxical phenomenon, at once on the margins and the center of the Elizabethan world" (1996: 210). He attributes theater's engagement with contemporary socio-political issues to its paradoxical status as an emergent popular form of entertainment and a marginal cultural activity: "in a society in which the dominant social institutions were predicated upon an ideology of unchanging order and absolute obedience, an emergent commercial entertainment that was still imbued with the heritage of suppressed popular and religious traditions could address vital collective needs and interests that those dominant institutions and practices had sought to appropriate or to suppress, or had merely ignored" (1996: 39).

2   The view is shared by Jean Howard and Phyllis Rackin who, in their recent study which seeks to rectify the lack, note that "Despite the many achievements of twentieth-century feminist Shakespeare criticism, feminists have devoted much less attention to the history plays than to Shakespeare's comedies, in which women have prominent roles, or to the tragedies" (Howard and Rackin 1997: 21).

3   *Macbeth* provides a case in point. In the scene of her murder, Lady Macduff proffers a stringent critique of masculinist preference for political surety over familial safety. While she enlists our sympathies, her plight foregrounds the play's willingness to stage this opposition while committing itself nevertheless to an emphatic erasure of the feminine; its subsequent authorization of masculinist ideologies in the concluding scenes comes as no surprise. For a fascinating study of the play's spectacular erasure of the feminine, see Karin Coddon's essay (Coddon 1989).

4   Holderness's recognition that "however strenuous Gaunt's efforts to suppress the reality of the feminine, it continues to appear, if only in the interstices of his metaphorical language" presents a partial truth; my reading focuses on Gaunt's initial marginalization and later conscious acknowledgment and legitimation of femininity on his death bed (Holderness 1992: 78).

5   Among these might be listed Phyllis Rackin and Jean Howard, Joan Hartwig, James Black, David Sundelson, and Graham Holderness. For a slightly different emphasis on the importance of these scenes, though within the tradition of parody, see Martha

Kurtz; in a thought-provoking article, John Halverson sees these scenes as further evidence of "absurdity" and "the grotesque," essential aspects of the play as a whole (Halverson 1994: 358).

6 Kate in her notorious speech at the conclusion of *The Taming of the Shrew*, for example, chastises women in these terms. The polemic tracts of the seventeenth century denouncing women's "social transgressions" similarly target their sourness; the pseudonyms attached to these tracts, Joseph Swetnam (sweet name) and Esther Sowernam (sour name), point to the conventional association of sourness with deviant women.

7 Coddon's useful argument about drama's reflection of a movement in early modern England toward "a contractual society rather than one centred on the body and blood of the monarch" is as evident in an early play such as *Richard II* as in the play she analyzes in these terms, *The Duchess of Malfi* (Coddon 1993: 9).

8 Paul Budra's insistence that "history, the broad pattern of events, is something that happens to the great, not the audience watching its representation. . . . The lower classes, because they are unrecorded, do not exist as objects, do not exist as subjects. They do not author themselves, but remain unstable: at best an audience, at worst a mob" seems to me entirely untenable in this play

and indeed, in several other of Shakespeare's plays (Budra 1994: 13–14).

9 Duncan Salkeld makes a similar point when he insists that drama's "critique of sovereignty through staged fictions operated against the codes which guaranteed the monarch's feudal privilege to govern by Divine Right" (1993: 4); the scenes involving the Duchess of York and the Duchess of Gloucester are crucial to our recognition of this critique of sovereignty in *Richard II*.

10 Unlike Richard Helgerson, I am not entirely convinced that "while achieving his obsessive and compelling focus on the ruler, Shakespeare excluded another object of concern, the ruled. Identifying himself, his plays, his company, and his audience with the problematics of early modern kingship, he left out of consideration the no less pressing problematics of subjecthood" (Helgerson 1992: 238–9).

11 I have not discussed Isabella, whose role in the play is inextricably linked to her status as a foreigner. But Richard's parting advice to her, that she spend her remaining years in a cloister remembering him to her friends, reinforces my point.

12 In this sense, Mary Beth Rose's claim about tragedy in general applies especially to *Richard II*: "tragedy functions paradoxically as both a radical and a conservative representation of sexual and cultural change" (1990: 9).

REFERENCES AND FURTHER READING

Bergeron, D. M. 1991: "*Richard II* and Carnival Politics." *Shakespeare Quarterly*, 39, 33–43.

Black, J. 1985: "The Interlude of the Beggar and the King in *Richard II*." In David Bergeron (ed.), *Richard II Pageantry in the Shakesperean Theater*. Athens, GA: University of Georgia Press, 104–11.

Budra, P. 1994: "Writing the Tragic: Richard II's Sad Stories." *Renaissance and Reformation*, 18, 4 (Fall), 5–15.

Coddon, K. 1989: "'Unreal Mockery': Unreason and the Problem of Spectacle in *Macbeth*." *English Literary History* 56, 3 (Fall), 485–501.

——1993: "*The Duchess of Malfi*: Tyranny and

Spectacle in Jacobean Drama." In James Redmond (ed.), *Madness in Drama*. Cambridge: Cambridge University Press, 1–17.

Deleuze, G. and Guattari, F. 1986: *Kafka: Toward a Minor Literature*. Trans. Dana Polan. Minneapolis and London: University of Minnesota Press.

——1987: *A Thousand Plateaus: Capitalism and Schizophrenia*. Trans. Brian Massumi. Minneapolis, MN: University of Minnesota Press.

Goy-Blanquet, D. 1995: "'Sad Stories'." In Jean-Marie Maguin and Michele Willems (eds.), *French Essays in Shakespeare and His Contempor-*

aries: "*What would France with us?*" Newark, DE: University of Delaware Press, 139–52.

Halverson, J. 1994: "The Lamentable Comedy of *Richard II.*" *English Literary Renaissance*, 24, 2 (Spring), 343–69.

Hartwig, J. 1983: "Parody in *Richard II.*" In *Shakespeare's Analogical Scene: Parody as Structural Syntax*. Lincoln, NE: University of Nebraska Press, 113–34.

Helgerson, R. 1992: *Forms of Nationhood: The Elizabethan Writing of England*. Chicago: University of Chicago Press.

Holderness, G. 1992: *Shakespeare Recycled: The Making of Historical Drama*. Sussex: Harvester Wheatsheaf.

Howard, J. E. and Rackin, P. 1997: *Engendering a Nation: A Feminist Account of Shakespeare's English Histories*. London and New York: Routledge.

Hunt, L. 1991: "History as Gesture." In Jonathan Arac and Barbara Johnson (eds.), *Consequences of Theory*. Baltimore, MD: Johns Hopkins University Press, 91–107.

Kolodny, A. 1994: "Dancing Through the Minefield." In David Richter (ed.), *Falling Into Theory*. Boston, MA: Bedford Books of St. Martin's Press, 278–85.

Kurtz, M. 1996: "'Mock Not': The Problem of Laughter in *Richard II.*" *Shakespeare Quarterly*, 65, 4 (Fall), 589–99.

McEahern, C. E. 1988: "Fathering Herself: A Source Study of Shakespeare's Feminism." *Shakespeare Quarterly*, 39, 3 (Fall), 269–90.

—— 1996: *The Poetics of English Nationhood, 1590–1612*. Cambridge, Cambridge University Press.

Montrose, L. A. 1996: *The Purpose of Playing: Shakespeare and the Cultural Poetics of the Elizabethan Theater*. Chicago: University of Chicago Press.

Rose, M. B. 1990: *Renaissance Drama as Cultural History*. Evanston, IL: Northwestern University Press.

Rousseau, G. S. 1993: "'A Strange Pathology': Hysteria in the Early Modern World, 1500–1800." In Sander Gilman, Helen King, Roy Porter, G. S. Rousseau, and Elaine Showalter (eds.), *Hysteria Beyond Freud*. Berkeley, CA: University of California Press, 91–225.

Salkeld, D. 1993: *Madness and Drama in the Age of Shakespeare*. Manchester: Manchester University Press.

Seelig, S. C. 1995: "Loyal Fathers and Treacherous Sons: Familial Politics in *Richard II.*" *Journal of English and Germanic Philology*, 94, 3 (July), 347–64.

Shakespeare, W. 1997: *Richard II*. In Stephen Greenblatt (ed.), *The Norton Shakespeare*. New York and London: W. W. Norton and Company, 943–1014.

Sundelson, D. 1983: *Shakespeare's Restoration of the Father*. New Brunswick, NJ: Rutgers University Press.

Watson, D. G. 1990: *Shakespeare's Early History Plays: Politics at Play on the Elizabethan Stage*. Athens, GA: University of Georgia Press.

15

Lovesickness, Gender, and Subjectivity: *Twelfth Night* and *As You Like It*

Carol Thomas Neely

Love is merely a madness, and, I tell you, deserves as well a dark house and a whip as madmen do; and the reason why they are not so punished and cured is that the lunacy is so ordinary that the whippers are in love too.

(*As You Like It*, III.ii.396–400)

For the past twenty-five years, feminist critics have explored how women's roles and desires are represented, in relation to those of men, in early modern literature and culture. They have documented where and how the ideologies of the state, religion, marriage, and family prescribe women's subordination to men and to male-controlled institutions. But they have also uncovered evidence of women's initiatives, achievements, and disruptions both in Shakespeare's plays and in the culture. We have learned that early modern patriarchy is neither static nor seamless, that ideology is never unified, and that the construction of gender and sexuality is fluid and heterogeneous. This essay participates in this ongoing project by exploring how lovesickness discourse represents and shapes love and transgressive erotic subjects. In this hybrid discourse, love is a romantic fantasy and a somatic disease. Falling in love is both normal and pathological. And desire, however unconventional its objects, demands and deserves satisfaction. Because, in this discourse, desire can strike anyone and fasten on anything, gender roles and erotic object choice are remarkably fluid, and the relationship between gender and sexuality is unstable. Men or women can gain or lose power through erotic momentum or as objects of desire.[1]

Twelfth Night and *As You Like It*, Shakespearean comedies with cross-dressed heroines, play out aspects of this discourse differently. In *Twelfth Night*, eroticism and gender are detached, destabilizing gender formations and releasing ungendered desires. In *As You Like It*, eroticism remains mapped onto gender but gender roles and desires multiply. Attending to lovesickness in the two plays suggests that the concluding marriages may be less a prescriptive imposition of a hierarchical patriarchy than an accommodation to subjects both male and female who negotiate within culture and ideology to attain their compelling desires. These comedies show us that theatrical representations of love can license wayward desires, and that theatrical happy endings do not always reproduce rigid gender hierarchies and normative heterosexual marriages.

Subjectivity, Gender, and Eroticism

Understanding lovesickness provides one way to think about how subjects act both through and against the rules which attempt to govern them. Louis Althusser and Michel Foucault have provided influential accounts of subjects constructed and constrained by ideology and discourse. However, many critics who draw on them find these accounts incomplete. Hugh Grady has usefully summarized such accounts and analyzed the failure of Foucaultian and Althusserian theories to provide sufficiently nuanced conceptions of early modern subjects and their agendas (Grady forthcoming: 2–14). Michel Foucault's theories of subjects constructed through discourse provide little ground for resistance or agency. Gender, race, class, and sexuality, of primary concern to feminist critics, are theorized by him as mere effects of subjectification. Althusser's ideologically hailed subject is likewise conceptualized as male; its gender and sexual differences are elided in a parenthesis (Althusser 1971: 176). Grady proposes that drawing on theorists of the Frankfurt school and on psychoanalytic theories of desire and the unconscious makes it possible to take into account subjects' willfulness, creativity, and difference (Grady forthcoming: 2–23). With Grady, other theorists of the subject in the early modern period persist in discovering or devising theoretical and material sites of agency within subjects and productive contradictions within the ideologies which shape them. Louis Montrose proposes that *subjectification* not only *subjects* individuals to cultural codes, but also endows them with agency and *subjectivity*, making them "loci of consciousness and initiators of action" (Montrose 1989: 21). Catherine Belsey and Jean Howard find possibilities of change in the "contradictions" and "ideological gaps and discontinuities" in ideology – at least for female subjects (Belsey 1985: 8–9, 149–60; Howard 1994: 93ff).

Many such theorists share my interest in desire's ability to instigate agency. With Jonathan Dollimore and Linda Gregerson, I analyze ruptures within subjects which are rooted in their desires. Dollimore insists on "the creative perversity of desire itself" to deconstruct erotic and other binarisms (1990: 484). Gregerson extends Lacan's prescription for specular instability into a catalyst for self- and other-fashioning. The Lacanian subject, she argues, "is one whose foundational instability is itself a form of momentum," whose "ontological precariousness . . . provides the ground for *in*subordination, which is to say for agency and change. . . . [S]ubject formation is a mirror trick. But it is a mirror trick that works" (1995: 93–4). "The same might be said (and often was in sixteenth-century England) of erotic love," Gregerson adds (1995: 94n38). Her primary literary example of specular momentum is Britomart, whose love for Artegall's mirrored image propels her into an epic quest in books Three and Four of *The Faerie Queene*.

In this essay I draw on selectively Gregerson's suggestive analysis of love's ability to promote subjectivity and momentum to explore the dynamics of lovesickness discourse and Shakespeare's comedies. Lovesickness is being refigured in Renaissance medical discourse and theatrical practice as increasingly a disease of women (as well as men) in need of sexual satisfaction. Although the condition subjects humans to painful desires and strange fantasies, it also catalyzes passionate agendas. These can resist or disrupt status roles, rigid gender hierarchies, and binary constructions of sexuality. An examination of lovesickness thus lends additional evidence to the picture of multiple and fluid early modern sexualities uncovered in the work of scholars like Jonathan Goldberg and Valerie Traub.

Like these critics, I will avoid conceptualizing gender or sexuality in terms of simple binary oppositions by employing nuanced and heterogeneous views of their interactions. The early modern discourse of lovesickness is a site that confirms Eve Sedgwick's important claim in *Epistemology of the Closet* (1990: 22–7) that gender and sexuality are not identical, and that many differentiations in desire exceed gender difference and object choice and have "unaccounted-for potential to disrupt many forms of available thinking about sexuality" (1990: 25). The discursive operation of lovesickness in *Twelfth Night* and *As You Like It* elucidates in particular Sedgwick's remark that "Some people, homo-, hetero-, and bisexual, experience their sexuality as deeply embedded in a matrix of gender meanings and gender differentials. Others of each sexuality do not" (1990: 26). Valerie Traub's tripartite definitions of gender and sexuality likewise clarify and can be clarified through lovesickness discourse. She differentiates gender into core gender identity ("the persistent experience of oneself as male, female or ambivalent"), gender role ("the degree to which one complies with societal expectations of 'appropriate' behavior"), and gender style ("the personal choices one makes daily to assert agency within the confines of gender") (Traub 1991: 87). Following and revising Traub, I make a similar tripartite distinction within eroticism, differentiating among erotic identification (e.g., homo-hetero-bi-erotic), erotic role (e.g., aggressive or passive, playful or serious), and erotic style/practice (e.g., particular sex acts or fetishism) (cf. Traub 1991: 88–9). To further defamiliarize early modern concepts and to displace our twenty-first-century assumptions of "heterosexuality" and "homosexuality" as fixed identities rooted in genital relations with gendered objects, I will often use the term "erotic" in place of the term "sexual," and the terms hetero- and homoerotic in place of the terms heterosexual and homosexual. "Erotic" also facilitates a focus on desires rather than on particular sexual acts – which are rarely made explicit in either lovesickness treatises or Shakespearean comedies. Using such articulations, I show that, in the early modern discourse of lovesickness, erotic stances do not always have fixed alignments with gender enactments and that both are multiply nuanced.

Lovesickness

Medical discourses, including the lovesickness treatises that I draw on, are among many texts, laws, and social prescriptions which purvey ideologies of gender, social status, and sexuality. One aim of this essay is to join with other scholars working on the intersections of gender, sexuality, and medicine – for example, Ian Maclean in *The Renaissance Notion of Woman*, Danielle Jacquart and Claude Thomasset in *Sexuality and Medicine in the Middle Ages*, and Mary Wack in *Lovesickness in the Middle Ages* – to challenge the assumption, especially associated with Foucault, that medical discourse is static, unified, and repressive (Maclean 1980: 29–30, 45–6; Wack 1990: 7–8, 66–70; Jacquart and Thomasset 1988: 1–6). Medical discourse in flux encourages theoretical and social change by opening up, outside of the institutions and prescriptions of the Church and the state, a space for inquiry and debate about the body and its erotic demands. In the discourse of lovesickness, gender is less polarized and sexuality less normalized than in many other early modern texts. Because the discourse is concerned primarily with the satisfaction of desires, only secondarily with marriage, and not at all with reproduction, it includes without sharp distinction a wide and weird range of gender behaviors, erotic objects, and amorous styles.

In medical traditions from the second to the seventeenth century, lovesickness is characterized as a disease of the head, heart, imagination, and genitals, and associated with the melancholy humor. Its powerful somatic symptoms, the most agreed-upon aspect of the malady, are summed up in Jacques Ferrand's *Treatise on Lovesickness* (1623, translated 1640): "pale and wan complexion, . . . a slow fever, . . . palpitations of the heart, swelling of the face, depraved appetite, a sense of grief, sighing, causeless tears, insatiable hunger, raging thirst, fainting, oppressions, suffocations, insomnia, headaches, melancholy, epilepsy, madness, uterine fury, satyriasis, and other pernicious symptoms that are, for the most part, without mitigation or cure" (Ferrand 1990: 229). Andre Du Laurens in his rich succinct chapter on the condition, "Of another kinde of melancholie which commeth by the extremitie of love" (1597, translated 1599), further explicates the (for him male) sufferer's maladies, clarifying the connection with melancholy whose main symptoms were fear and sorrow: "feare buffeteth him on the one side, & oftentimes dispayre on the other; he is (as *Plautus* sayth) there where indeede he is not; sometime he is as hot as fire, and upon the sudden he findeth himselfe as colde as ice: his heart doth alwaies quake, and his pulse keepeth no true course, it is little, unequall, and beating thicke, changing it selfe upon the sudden, not onely at the sight, but even at the very name of the object which he affecteth" (Du Laurens 1597: 118). These symptoms, especially the revealing pulse, allow the disease to be diagnosed and brought under the care of doctors – the outcome that lovesickness treatises advocate. Although lovesickness is a pathology, we can see from its symptoms that is also all too normal and that both men and women are at risk.

Although the symptoms of lovesickness were agreed upon by theologians, philosophers, and poets, its exact progression was much debated. Medical treatises, claiming bodily origins to secure their own authority over lovesickness, unfolded a complex somatogenesis, articulating relationships between its disparate sites and symptoms. It might originate in head, heart, imagination, or genitals – or all of the above, as Peter of Spain's 1250 treatise argues: love is "a disease of the testicles . . . a disease of the brain ...a disease of the imaginative faculty" (quoted in Wack 1990: 235, 237,

241; cf. Ferrand 1990: 257, 263–5). In the Renaissance, Du Laurens provides the most logical explanation of how love, after entering through the eyes, becomes an active agent corrupting the body and mind:

> Love therefore having abused the eyes as the proper spyes and porters of the mind, maketh a way for it selfe smoothly to glaunce along through the conducting guides, and passing without any perseverance [*sic*] in this sort through the veines unto the liver, doth suddenly imprint a burning desire to obtaine the thing, which is or seemeth worthie to bee beloved, setteth concupiscence on fire, and beginneth by this desire all the strife and contention: but fearing her selfe too weake to incounter with reason, the principal part of the minde, she posteth in haste to the heart, to surprise and winne the same: whereof when she is once sure, as of the strongest hold, she afterward assaileth and setteth upon reason, and all the other principall powers of the minde so fiercely, as that she subdueth them, and maketh them her vassals and slaves. Then is all spoyled, the man is quite undone and cast away, the senses are wandering to and fro, up and downe, reason is confounded, the imagination corrupted, the talke fond and sencelesse; the sillie loving worme cannot any more look upon any thing but his idol: al the functions of the bodie are likewise perverted, he becommeth pale, lean, souning. (Du Laurens 1597: 118)

Since the primary symptom of lovesickness is unsatisfied desire, and its "immediate cause" for men or women is sperm needing evacuation (Ferrand 1990: 327), the most efficacious cure is therapeutic intercourse, "the injoying of the thing beloved" (Du Laurens 1597: 121). This is ideally to take place within marriage. If not, sex with the loved object or with any available substitutes is traditionally recommended: with prostitutes, slaves, or widows – preferably more than once or with more than one partner so as to evacuate both sperm from the genitals and the beloved's image from the brain. But since this cure may be unobtainable or morally problematic, other methods of prevention or remedy are offered. Friends, doctors, or the beloved may try aversive therapy, or what I call the misogyny cure – which is the first line of prevention for Ferrand (1990: 314). The doctor or a friend is to expose the physical ugliness and moral flaws of the beloved or, more graphically, an old crone is to wave a bloody menstrual rag in the face of the lovesick nobleman, or reveal her own diseased genitals and her cankered breasts to emblematize the repulsiveness of all women (for misogyny cures, see Ferrand 1990: 318; Burton 1994: III, 214; and Wack's discussion, 1990: 70, 103). Physicians' cures in addition focus on ameliorating the body through control of diet or environment; they distract the lover through music, exercise, and travel, or prescribe traditional purges, opiates, and bloodletting (for various cures, see Du Laurens 1597: 123; Ferrand 1990: chs. 30–7; Burton 1994: III, 201–7; and Wack's discussion, 1990: 41–2, 66–70, 103, 142). The discourse manifests the body's susceptibility to desire and offers cures, not condemnation.

As the presence of coital and misogyny therapy suggests, women were traditionally subordinated as subjects in a disease generally construed as male – as in the quotation above from Du Laurens (see Wack 1990: 149–52, 174–6). Although a lovesick woman is the subject of one of Galen's (130–200 AD) rare case histories and her tale circulates through medical history into the late Renaissance (cf. Du Laurens 1597: 119; Ferrand 1990: 266), the physician's skill and not her cure is its point. The diagnosed woman is the wife of Justus, who, unlike the doctor, her husband, and her love object, has no name in the story. Her symptoms are insomnia without fever, a refusal to answer questions about her condition, and the absence of physical disease. Although she keeps her love hidden, Galen diagnoses her condition accurately after discovering that her pulse races when a certain dancer, Pylades, enters the room. No cure, however, is offered because her love is adulterous and crosses class boundaries; therapeutic intercourse is probably unacceptable for one of her gender, station, and marital status. Even when including women, Western medical tradition occluded their satisfaction. In contrast, in Galen's other initiating case history which was likewise cited well into the seventeenth century, when Antiochus falls madly in love with his stepmother, Stratonice, his father willingly gives his wife to his son to prevent the son's demise from lovesickness and is commended for his generosity. Women are, however, more prominent in Arabic treatises which, outside of the restrictive context of Christian theology, promoted an erotics of pleasure which includes detailed instructions for coital cures for sexual frustration, frigidity, impotence, and infertility for men *and* for women. For example, these works are tolerant of women's same-sex liaisons and prescribe masturbation as a reliable cure for excess of uterine blood, sperm, and heat, especially for adolescent girls without sexual partners (Jacquart and Thomasset 1988: 116–38, 152–5).

In the West, however, women do not become prominent subjects in medical discourse on lovesickness and its offshoots until the Renaissance (Wack 1990: 174). There are several reasons for their emergence. The translation of Arabic treatises (though sometimes bowdlerized) and their incorporation into Western medicine encouraged attention to women's pleasures. While literature had represented lovesick women throughout the Middle Ages, more women's stories become available through the Renaissance's rediscovery and translation of ancient literature. These translations circulated female exemplars of the disease, as did the recovery of Galen's works with their initiating case of Justus's wife. Finally, in the Renaissance, as the profession of medicine gained power and authority, treatises increasingly draw on clinical practice, a source for case histories of women and a site of "renewed interest" in the disease of lovesickness as "an issue in practical medicine" (Beecher and Ciavolella 1990: 103).

Renaissance discussions of lovesickness, therefore, increasingly take women into account. They use classical and mythological women as examples; Phaedra, Iphis, Persephone, Dido, Sappho make appearances. Some treatises provide paired male and female exemplars of the disease. This is apparent in the openings of Du Laurens, who names first Antiochus and Justus's wife, and of John Bishop (1577), who begins with a harlot and two men who were sexually promiscuous at early ages (Bishop 1577: 118–19; 50v). Another strategy to include women occurs in Thomas Rogers (1576). Although, like most treatise-writers, he names more male than female victims, he achieves a degree of gender equity by providing paired cases in which Semiramis is exploited as an all-purpose example. First, like Vitellius, she exemplifies a ruined reputation (1576: 20v); then, it is noted, she commits incest with her son as Clodius does with his sister (22r); later, she loves a horse, Persiphaea a bull, Cyparissus a hart, and Aristomachus bees (22v); finally, her love is seen to lead to violence as she murders her friends so they won't talk of her passions as Catiline murders his son to please his new wife (23r).

Women's growing visibility in lovesickness discourse and how this catalyzes rethinking about all aspects of the condition can be best illustrated in Jacques Ferrand's *Of Lovesickness or Erotic Melancholy* (1610, revised and enlarged 1623, translated 1640). This work is the period's most complete compendium of lovesickness, drawing extensively on the traditions, both ancient and modern, while manifesting emerging directions.[2] In it, women's conditions and case histories are central influences on discussions of the symptoms, signs, causes, and cures of lovesickness. The repeated use of Sappho as an exemplum is indicative of Ferrand's (and the age's) new emphases. Ferrand's second chapter, "The Symptoms of Erotic Melancholy," immediately gives women's lovesickness prominence. At the climax of his opening catalogue of those mad for love, he tells us that, "Sappho the poetess, forlorn for her love of Phaon hurled herself from the Leucadian rock into the sea, for women are more frequently and more grievously troubled by these ills than are men" (229).[3] In the rest of this chapter and of the treatise, this new claim is developed and substantiated.

Ferrand's review of the multiple and contradictory causes of the disease accounts for the ubiquitousness of women sufferers by arguing that two causes of erotic melancholy are (male) satyriasis, "an itching or tickling of the private parts," and uterine fury, "a raging or madness that comes from an excessive burning desire in the womb, or from a hot intemperature communicated to the brain and to the rest of the body through the channels in the spine, or from the biting vapors arising from the corrupted seed lying stagnant around the uterus" (263). But the chapter elaborates only on uterine fury. Chapter 14, "Diagnostic signs of love melancholy," continues the emphasis on women by its lengthy testimony to Sappho as a "learned and amorous poet" who both experiences and diagnoses the signs of love. After quoting her in Greek from Longinus, in Latin from Catullus, and in six stanzas from Belleau's translation of Sappho 31 in French ("for those who hate Greek and like Latin no better"), Ferrand asks, "Does it not appear that Sappho was as wise and as experienced in this art as our Greek, Latin, and Arab physicians in light of the fact that they mentioned no indisputable signs that this lady did not already know?" (271–2).

The privileging of women is still more evident in Ferrand's unambiguous new resolution to an old debate concerning who had more pleasure in intercourse, men or women, and hence who was more prone to the disease – women because more irrational or men because hotter. Many treatises compromised, attributing to men more quality of pleasure and to women greater quantity, as does Gregory of Spain (ca. 1250): "pleasure is greater in men than in women. And this is because they emit more and are more consumed in intercourse. But pleasure is double on women's part (in emitting and receiving), yet it is not of such a quality" (quoted in Wack 1990: 247). Ferrand, however, decisively argues that "the woman experiences more violently this brutal desire, and not unreasonably so, since nature owes her some compensating pleasures for the suffering she endures during pregnancy and childbirth" (312). This explanation from nature's justness is seconded by a confusing one from anatomy: women's desires are greater because their reproductive organs are contained inside and curled around each other, not outside and straight as are men's (312). The concealed and self-touching aspect of women's organs causes them to experience greater intensity, quality, and frequency of desire. Ferrand supports his theory by observation: "This opinion is confirmed by daily experience which reveals to us a greater number of women witless, maniacal, and frantic from love than men – for men are far less often reduced to such extremities, unless they are effeminate courtiers, nourished on a life of riot and excess and on the breast of courtesans" (311). Although women's suffering is more somatically rooted, more prevalent, and more extreme, neither misogyny, therapeutic intercourse, nor even marriage can dependably effect a cure (Ferrand 1990: 334–8; Du Laurens 1597: 122–5). Ferrand's response is to stress prevention (chapters 29–32) and cures for married couples (335). Everywhere the treatise, by attending to women's urgent desires, undoes conventional gender roles.

Sexualities

The discourse also overrides distinctions between normative and transgressive desires and between heteroeroticism and homoeroticism. In the second half of Ferrand's ground-laying second chapter, Sappho is the exemplar of homoerotic love. The disease's several effects on women – suicide, organ changes, or tribadism – emphasize the instability of bodies, desires, and love objects. Ferrand disputes the view current in some of his contemporaries that sexually frustrated women may produce penises when, in the heat of passion, their genitals reverse themselves. He argues that what seems to be a penis is a descended uterus or clitoris, enlarged through passion (230). Women need not become men to desire aggressively. He authorizes their own organ of pleasure by providing seven different Latin and Arabic names for it from as many different authorities: *queue, tentiginem, symptoma turpitudinis, nympham, clitorida, amorem et dulcedinem veneris*, and *albatram, id est virgam* (231). The female homoerotic practices which this organ makes possible, identified with Sappho, are represented as widespread. The condition is "known to many other women who unhappily abuse that part, women called *fricatrices* by the Latins, *tribades* by the Greeks and *ribaudes* by the French, among whom Suidas and Muret place the learned Sappho" (231). Women's love for women, usually invisible in early modern legal, theological, and literary discourses (Traub 1994: 62–5), is registered here and in the treatises of Rogers and Burton, although male homoerotic practices are more widely noticed.

Often in the treatises, there is no sharp distinction between homo- and hetero-eroticism. Gendered object choice does not centrally define the boundary between acceptable and unacceptable sexuality for reproductive sexuality is not valorized, or even present. Indeed, the acts which this discourse records are "unstable, resistant to codification, and defiant of limits" (Traub 1994: 64). For men to love men is not represented as much different from their loving prostitutes, sisters, beasts, or disdainful maids. Women loving women, if no better, is also no worse. John Bishop, in his especially moralizing discussion, says that he will show the torments of love "both before, after, and against nature" (1577: 50v), and condemns with equal fervor "heynous incest" (51v) in which a mother sleeps with her son and they beget a daughter, whom he later marries; men who "against nature doe filthily abuse men, and women, women" (51v); and the madness and shame of those who love beloveds they have never seen, beasts, or statues (51v–52r). Tomasso Garzoni's satiric treatise, *The Hospitall of incurable Fooles* (1600), humorously recites the equal folly of those who love concubines, boys, corpses, bulls, and she-goats (85). Robert Burton's *Anatomy of Melancholy* (first edition 1621), not a medical treatise but an encyclopedia of pathology, does indulge in a Latin diatribe which salaciously catalogues the worst excesses of love melancholy and reveals just what an "utterly confused category" sodomy is (Goldberg 1992: 18, following Foucault). Under the notion of sodomy, Burton includes bestiality, sex of "man with man" (651), sex "in the married state, where an opposite part is used from that which is lawful" (652), the "other uncleanness" of "self-defiling monks" (Burton's favorite satiric target 653), and the actions of "wanton-loined womanlings, Tribades, that fret each other by turns, and fulfill Venus even among Eunuchs with their so artful secrets" (Trans. F. D. and P. J.-S. Vol. 2. Kila, MT: Kessinger Publishing Company, 1991: 653). The most transgressive example involves gender and eroticism; it is that of a woman who, disguised as a man, married another woman, hence transgressing simultaneously normative gender roles, conventional eroticism, and, more alarmingly, the institution of patriarchal marriage (653).

Neither particular acts nor human or animal objects, however, constitute the greatest excess to which lovesickness drives its victims; this place is filled by the love of inanimate objects. Such fetishism – the love of statues or pictures – is attributed only to men. This ultimate pathology shows "how love corrupteth the imagination, and may be the cause of melancholy or madness" (Du Laurens 1597: 119). The treatment of these examples suggests it is the most unnatural of loves because it is of the imagination, hence is incapable of satisfaction. Rogers includes it as the "most horrible" of the loves he recites (1576: 23v). A fetishist in love with a statue is the only extended example in Pierre Boaistuau's treatise, *Theatrum Mundi* or *The Theatre or rule of the world* (1581: 199). This primary case history, appearing also in Bishop, Du Laurens, and Ferrand, is that of a noble young man of Athens who falls in love with a marble statue (or picture); frantic with love, he embraces and kisses it, and offers to buy it at any price from the Senate. When refused, he decorates "her" with a robe, binds "her" hair with fillets and garlands, and offers himself up as a suicidal sacrifice to unrequited love (Boaistuau 1581: 199–200). The desire to use a public object for private satisfaction and the sacrifice of his male authority and his life to the statue make the case extreme. In these examples, the gender of the object is of indifference. Men fall in love with a variety of inanimate objects: with a picture of good Fortune (Rogers 1576: 22v), with statues of naked Cupid or naked Venus, or naked boys (Bishop 1577: 52r), with a tree or their own shadows (Ferrand 1990: 260).

Far from being repressive technologies of the self, Renaissance lovesickness discourses and their offshoots partly contest the theological, legal, and moral prescriptions to provide a space in which conventional gender and erotic roles and styles are loosened. Love may make men, like the man of Athens, vulnerable, passive, irrational, and subordinate – that is, more like normative women. Or it can render men insatiable tyrants. Love can banish women's modesty and turn their bodies hotter and their actions more aggressive; making them, like Semiramis, more like normative men. Or love can silence them as it does the wife of Justus. Love can give and take away power. Since lovesickness, the inability to satisfy desires, springs invariably from the love of inappropriate or unobtainable objects, whether these objects are homoerotic or heteroerotic is not of great importance. These discourses display a mixture of pity, tolerance, and appalled amazement at the "strange capers" that lovers indulge in (*As You Like It*, II.iv.52), partially licensing desire and privileging satisfaction.

Lovesickness in Shakespeare's Comedies

The conflicts and shifts which mark the textual history of lovesickness in medical discourse insist that desiring bodies, increasingly including women's, must be reckoned with. We would expect this to be true in early modern culture and drama as well. In fact, in Shakespeare's plays, women's love is routinely represented as urgent, aggressive, and acted on. In contrast, men's love is more often passive, subordinating, or fetishistic. To be sure the comedies are tamer than the treatises, for there, love objects are humans, not beasts or trees. But in them too the gender of love objects may be less important than their age, class, or erotic roles or styles – which can shift. Or it may be central. As in the non-dramatic works, desire gives characters both male and female momentum and agency. The connection is manifested especially in ubiquitous puns on "will" meaning genital organs (male or female), desire (especially sexual), but also purpose, intention, determination, resistance.

Some contemporary feminist criticism holds that the purposeful activities of desiring women in Shakespeare's comedies are vitiated by leading to marriages that (allegedly) reproduce patriarchy and secure normative gender hierarchy. I reject this claim. Action in the body of these plays both outweighs and complicates the concluding moment of marriage or the promise of it (Traub 1992: 120). It seems likely that early modern audiences, like our own audiences for popular films, found much more to turn them on in the body of the plays than in their predictable outcomes. Furthermore, comic endings and happy marriages, like unhappy families, are not all alike; they are not all equally conventional, hegemonic, or subordinating of women and erotic possibility. Every Shakespearean comedy arrives at marriage by different routes and performs it differently. Many Renaissance comedies, and especially the two Shakespeare plays I will discuss, care more about individual satisfaction and less about social reconciliation than Northrop Frye's and C. L. Barber's influential interpretations of comic form and festive comedy have led us to believe. Finally marriage, as the lovesickness discourse insists and the plays hint, assures *neither* permanent satisfaction *nor* social harmony.

Examining *Twelfth Night* and *As You Like It* through the lens of lovesickness discourse reveals how love can catalyze subjectivity and overturn normative gender and erotic roles. It encourages attention to aspects of the plays other than the cross-dressed heroines. The plays intersect with many themes of the treatises. They represent the somatogenesis of love through eyes, heart, imagination, and liver and its conventional symptoms. They include debate about who loves most, men or women, and seem to agree with the treatises that women do – at least by portraying them as pursuing love more aggressively. They explicitly seek cures for the condition. Most tellingly, the plays intensify the treatises' attitude of amusement, titillation, and sympathy for the lovesick. Because these are romantic stage comedies that unfold extended characterizations instead of citing brief examples, they elicit identification with lovers and considerable investment in their satisfaction.

But the two plays use this discourse in opposite ways. The contexts in which love explodes are different: in a utopian world without rulers, fathers, or reproductive politics in *Twelfth Night*, in a patriarchy governed by all three in *As You Like It*. The role of the cross-dressed heroines functions differently. Viola/Cesario blends gender roles, Rosalind as Ganymede enacts them sequentially. The first mirrors others' ungendered desires back to them, while the second elicits desire by representing several gendered stereotypes of it. Hence the relationship between gender and erotic desire is loosened in *Twelfth Night* and cemented in *As You Like It*. The marriages at which the two plays arrive underline their differences; the ending of *Twelfth Night* keeps triangular circulations of desire open and subordinates gender differences, whereas the ending of *As You Like it* eliminates triangles of desire and proliferates a variety of gendered heterosexual couples.

Twelfth Night

I begin with *Twelfth Night* because its subtitle "What you Will" and its three symbolically named willful characters, Viola, Olivia, and Malvolio (their names all anagrams of their "volition"), make it a likely site of unruly desires. Yet recent discussions by Jean Howard, Cristina Malcolmson, Valerie Traub, and Dympna Callaghan qualify earlier claims for the liberating potential of comedies with cross-dressed heroines by arguing that *Twelfth Night* subordinates women and erotic possibility. Jean Howard, focusing on the implications of cross-dressing, argues that Viola's "properly feminine subjectivity" (1994: 113) makes her masculine attire non-threatening while the genuinely unruly woman, Olivia, is humiliated and punished by "being made to fall in love with the cross-dressed Viola" (1994: 114), resulting in the play's "containment of gender and class insurgency" (1994: 112). Cristina Malcolmson suggests that the play displaces class anxieties and struggles onto marriage and then reestablishes gender hierarchies underwritten by loving female service and subordination (1991: 50–1). Valerie Traub, finding, as I do, circulations of homoerotic desire in *Twelfth Night* both through and outside of cross-dressing figures, argues that these are displaced onto Antonio and decisively suppressed (1992: 123). Dympna Callaghan analyzes *Twelfth Night* as curtailing women's power by circulating denigrating representations of their bodies and desires, most prominently through Malvolio's references to Olivia's C's, U's, and T's, and great P's (1993: 436–40).

Although indebted to all of these critics, I find less suppression of erotic and gender irregularity in *Twelfth Night* than they do. Cesario's role and the shifting triangular identifications of lovers tease apart gender and eroticism. Rather than class anxiety being displaced onto gender as Malcolmson suggests, status, not gender, is the primary modality which incites and circulates unruly desires. Erotic momentum is a function of age, status, and body type more than of gendered objects. Viola/Cesario, the cross-dressed character at the center of the triangles, is not adequately defined by a polarized "feminine" inside and external male dress and role (Howard 1994: 113). Because her disguise as Cesario is sustained throughout most of the play, her "masculinity" and "femininity" are simultaneous and inseparable.

The character's gender and erotic identifications, roles, and styles are nuanced but sustained. She identifies as a woman in love in brief soliloquies but plays the role of a boy in company; her "masculine" gender style oscillates between wistfully adolescent (with Orsino) and cheekily adolescent (with most others) – between passive resignation and assertive wit. These qualities are apparent out of disguise as in it. Her erotic identification is female, her/his erotic (and bi-gendered) role is service, and his/her erotic style is to express desires covertly and elicit them from others through specularity. Hence she/he can elicit by mirroring (in cross-gendered fashion) different modalities of desire from differently gendered lovers/love objects whom she similarly serves self-interestedly. The servant's subordinate position mobilizes erotic power.

Cesario/Viola uses her own desires to specularize those of others as she travels back and forth between Olivia's and Orsino's households. She engenders Olivia's desires (for him/her) by anticipating their urgency in the promise to act and speak – to "Make me a willow cabin at your gate. . . . Write loyal cantons of contemned love. . . . Hallo your name to the reverberate hills" (I.v.266–72). Here Cesario ventriloquizes Orsino's desires for Olivia so Viola can speak her own for Orsino. These reverberations catalyze Olivia's desires as she responds immediately, "You might do much. What is your parentage?" (I.v.275). Later, Viola/Cesario mirrors and elicits Orsino's more fantasy-driven desires by speaking her own for him, relayed through those of an imaginary lovesick sister: "She pined in thought; / And, with a green and yellow melancholy, / She sat like Patience on a monument, / Smiling at grief" (II.iv.112–15). This self-projection represents Orsino's and her own passivity, whereas the willow cabin builder represents Olivia's and her initiative-taking. Jonathan Crewe analyzes the effects of those two scenes to show how the desire released in them is neither "definitively homosexual or heterosexual. . . . Its relays are complex, its circulation endless, its field practically boundless" (1995: 111).

Most characteristically, Cesario enacts Viola's desire to serve forcefully. On first hearing of the Duke's love for Olivia, her response is to "serve" one or the other (I.ii.41, 55) and she becomes page to Orsino. Later, in Act III, Cesario is "votre serviteur" to Andrew, vows "most humble service" to Olivia, and is said to be "servant" to the Count Orsino: "Your servant's servant is your servant," quips Cesario/Viola (III.i.73, 97, 99, 101, 103–4). "Service" here connotes a status, a bi-gendered role, and an erotic style, one which perhaps is an incentive to disguise and which the disguise facilitates. The reverberations of desire that Viola exudes and elicits undo polarized gender roles, represent permeable subjectivities, and loosen boundaries between homoerotic and heteroerotic desires.

Gendered object choice likewise seems to play only a small part in Orsino's and Olivia's attachments. Their wealth, aristocratic status, and power as head of household give both a similar habit of command and love for servants, although their erotic styles are differently expressed. Olivia likes to "command" (II.v.103) and is drawn to youthful subordinates of either gender. Sir Toby tells us that she won't marry the Count because she has sworn not to "match above her degree, neither in estate, years, nor wit" (I.iii.105–6). She admits Cesario/Viola to her only on learning that he is "Not yet old enough for a man nor young enough for a boy" (I.v.155–6). She is attracted to his poor but gentlemanly state ("'Above my fortunes, yet my state is well,'" she quotes, I.v.288) and to attributes which are not gender specific: "thy tongue, thy face, thy limbs, actions, and spirit" (I.v.290). She "catch(s) the plague" conventionally when she feels "this youth's perfections / With an invisible and subtle stealth / To creep in at mine eyes" (I.v.293–6). Since Sebastian has the same adolescent attributes, the same face and limbs, more pliability and less money, he is an equally apt object of Olivia's desires.

Sebastian like Olivia seems more turned on by age and economic markers than by gendered attributes. What he wants is to be kept and is perhaps willing to sleep with anyone who is willing to do so.[4] Like his twin, Viola, he finds protective possessiveness in older men and in rich women especially attractive. So he easily slides from dependence on Antonio's power and purse to dependence on Olivia, who has more rank and money and is equally dominating. She runs her household and Sebastian with a firm hand. "Would thou'dst be ruled by me!" Olivia demands. "Madam, I will," replies Sebastian. "O, say so, and so be," she replies (IV.i.65–6), completing a traditional spousal which reverses prescribed gender hierarchies.

Orsino, even more than Olivia, likes giving orders to servants (see especially I.iv and II.iv). In Viola/Cesario, Orsino is attracted to the same adolescent and subordinate qualities as Olivia is; indeed, it is his awareness of the potential appeal of Cesario's "youth" to Olivia (I.iv.27) that triggers his own eroticized perception: "Diana's lip / Is not more smooth and rubious; thy small pipe / Is *as* the maiden's organ, shrill and sound, / And all is semblative a woman's part" (I.iv.31–4). As my italics suggest, Orsino is attracted to Cesario because he is appealingly *like* a woman but not a woman – that is, not like imperious Olivia. Although the tender "part" Cesario plays for and with Orsino is less witty than the one he plays for and with Olivia, it is equally obstinate and not necessarily more "feminine." He responds to his master's and his mistress's needs differently, just as he reverberates differently to each the shapes of their own desires.

Orsino's love for Olivia, in contrast to his intimate exchanges with Cesario, partakes of the fetishism and narcissism, the love for an idealized, unobtainable object that, in the treatises, only men exhibit. His opening speeches document, as critics have long noted, his absurd fixation on his own desires and his lack of interest in contact with the disdainful Olivia. They also delineate all the symptoms of lovesickness which he fantasizes Olivia catching. Love fills his "liver, brain, and heart" (I.i.38) as it may hers. His "fancy" or imagination is "full of shapes"; his "desires" "pursue" him (I.i.14, 23–4), and the solitude and music, recommended as cures in treatises, only exacerbate them. Proud of his grandiose love, he argues, as do some treatises, that men's capacity for love is greater than women's – because women's hearts are too small and their palates only, not their livers, are infected. He also claims they "lack retention" – both the physical capacity for love and the ability to remain constant – responding to an old debate about genital pleasure with a new argument for male psychosomatic capacity (II.iv.93–103). But Viola, who earlier claimed that women's "waxen hearts" and "frailty" make them more susceptible to love than men (II.ii.30–1), articulates and acts out in the play, as does Olivia, the culture's growing belief that women's lovesickness is greater than men's.

It is Antonio, however, who is the play's most passionate, expressive, and constant lover; his beloved object, Sebastian, is unconventional only in his gender. Their intimacy is well established, and Antonio's passion is both romantic and erotic. His gender and erotic roles are complex. He is a sea captain and a pirate, a romantic hero who will brave anything for love, declaring his "devotion" and "sanctity of love" to his beloved's "image" (III.iv.364–6). He is physically passionate: "My desire / (More sharp than filèd steel) did spur me forth" (III.iii.4–5). He is older and richer than Sebastian, yet he also begs to be his beloved's "servant" – (II.i.36) – an erotic stance consonant with his lower-status role. His scenes (II.i, III.iii, and III.iv) provoke relief through their directness and poignancy, a sharp contrast to the romantic fancy and triangular suggestiveness of adjacent parallel love scenes between others. Like Olivia who is his surrogate and whose erotic roles are comparable, his passion is represented sympathetically, as confirmed by Laurie Osborne's discussion of cuts and rearrangements of his role which nineteenth-century performance editions effected to suppress this passion (1996: 80–9). He is baffled by confusing the identical twins, but is not rendered absurd or humiliated by either the characters or the play itself.

At the play's ending, Antonio's relationship with Sebastian (whatever its precise nature) must now be shared; but it is not decisively ended by the youth's marriage and he is not excluded from the ending (Pequigney 1992: 206). After his first encounter with Olivia, Sebastian immediately seeks out Antonio: "His counsel now might do me golden service" (IV.iii.8). His exclamation when they are reunited after his marriage is passionate; "Antonio, O my dear Antonio, / How have the hours racked and tortured me / Since I have lost thee!" (V.i.217–19). Although Sebastian's reunion with Antonio is displaced by his longer one with Viola, he exchanges no more words with Olivia – and has exchanged none as passionate as these. The ending leaves open the possibility that patriarchal marriage and homoerotic attachments can coexist (Bray 1995: 58–70; Goldberg 1992: 17–20).

The "specific anxiety about reproduction" which Valerie Traub "hypothesize(s) as a *structuring* principle" for these comedies (1992: 139) is, as she is aware, virtually unacknowledged in them. Indeed, in *Twelfth Night* it is absent altogether – which is the norm in lovesickness discourse, but is uncharacteristic of Shakespearean comedy. There is no older generation, no emphasis on lineage, indeed no represented family or political order at all. Unlike the conclusions of a majority of Shakespeare's comedies, including *Midsummer Night's Dream*, *Much Ado About Nothing*, *Merchant of Venice*, and *As You Like It*, *Twelfth Night* contains no anticipation of reproduction or of the accompanying fear of cuckoldry. These are missing even from Feste's final disillusioned song which narrates a man's progression through life – although his protagonist does "wive" (V.i.398). The lack of projection of a social order or of a reproductive or political future allows the circuits of desire to remain open at the ending of the play. *Twelfth Night*'s irregular matches are further made acceptable – structurally, thematically, and ideologically – by the humiliation of Malvolio for desires which, like those of the others, are incited by status markers; but his are more self-interested and less erotic, and hence more unacceptable than any others in the play (Howard 1994: 115–16; Neely forthcoming: ch. 5).

The marriages which the play anticipates or completes don't reestablish conventional erotic pairings or gender hierarchies. Instead the fluidity of desire and gender is reemphasized at the conclusion by the "large residue of bigendered and bisexual subjectivity" which remains (Crewe 1995: 112). As we have seen, Sebastian remains loved by Antonio and Olivia and Viola and loves all three. Although Cesario is revealed as Viola, the twins share "one face, one voice, one habit" (V.i.215). Their many similarities of looks, desires, and roles make their nominally different genders of scant importance. Orsino's affections easily enlarge to embrace Viola along with Cesario. He effortlessly moves Viola into the place formerly held by Olivia as "Orsino's mistress and his fancy's queen" (V.i.389). At the same time he offers his "boy" and "lamb" his hand for service already tendered, continues to call him Cesario, as she/he continues to "over swear" the "sayings" Cesario formerly swore (V.i.266–73). She/he remains in male dress and the retrieval of her "other (female) habits" is deferred (V.i.272–7, 388), as is her movement into a normative gender role. Like the Duke, Olivia is "betrothed both to a maid and man" (V.i.262). Olivia likewise embraces her surrogate love object with equanimity since he has all the qualities she desired in Cesario. Her affection for the Viola in Cesario easily takes a new path: "a sister; you are she" (V.i.326). The play begins in the household of Orsino but ends at Olivia's, for she has displaced the Duke as the authority figure in Illyria. His marriage will take place at her house and at her cost (V.i.316–20). Neither marriage is represented as quite conventionally gendered or even exclusively heterosexual, as bonds other than marital ones persist and are acknowledged.[5]

As You Like It

As You Like It also circulates desire through a cross-dressed heroine and draws on the discourse of lovesickness still more directly than does *Twelfth Night* – but with very different effects. Some critics have found the play more transgressive than *Twelfth Night* in its representations of gender and sexuality. Jean Howard, for example, argues that the Epilogue reopens and makes visible "the contamination of sexual kinds and the multiplication of erotic possibility" the play has intimated (1994: 121). Valerie Traub shows how the performance of the mock marriage of Rosalind/Ganymede/Rosalind with Orlando has the effect of "appropriating the meaning of matrimony for deviant desires" and "exposing the heterosexual imperative of matrimony as a reduction of the plurality of desire into the singularity of monogamy" (1992: 127). I argue that the play represents eroticism as more deeply "embedded in a matrix of gender meanings and gender differentials" (Sedgwick 1990: 26) than does *Twelfth Night*, and circulates more stereotyped representations of gender and eroticism and their connections with each other and with reproductive sexuality than does that play. But the proliferation in *As You Like It* of stereotypes of desire, gender, and marriage and the abruptness with which the characters shift their roles or their love objects ultimately call into question the possibility of normative desire, fixed gender roles, or stable marriages.

The genre of pastoral romance itself conventionally employs a shift in locale from court to pastoral world to precipitate changes in character and role and to mock or undo conventions. The most famous example, Jaques's seven ages of man speech, satirizes a series of pathetic male roles but has its representations challenged by the entrance of compassionate Orlando carrying lusty old Adam. Touchstone's and Corin's dialogue about courtier's and shepherd's roles comically reveals their lack of differentiation and fixity (III.i.11–87). The same unmooring occurs as stereotypes of gender relations and lovesickness multiply in the play.

Shifts of character and allegiance are the rule. The usurping Duke Frederick, an irascible textbook villain, converts to meditative pleasures. The bad older brother, Oliver, turns filial when Orlando saves his life. Desire, as in lovesickness discourse, causes equally sudden transformations. Touchstone, a mocker of love's conventions, desires the "poor thing" Audrey, enough to marry her. Audrey abandons her swain William for Touchstone and the prospect of becoming a courtier's wife. Phebe veers from disdain for Silvius to love of Ganymede to a resigned marriage to Silvius; Orlando from a heroic wrestler to a pupil of love. Rosalind and Celia give up their affection for each other to become lovers of men.

The character of Rosalind/Ganymede, of course, undergoes the most changes of role and desire; she also precipitates changes in others by putting into circulation multiple stereotypes of masculinity and femininity, of love and marriage. As these are ventriloquized through Rosalind, they are rendered comic and unstable. Her quadruple role of the boy actor (or "ganymede") playing Rosalind playing Ganymede playing Rosalind is sequentially unfolded rather than layered like that of Viola/Cesario – because Rosalind has a confidante in Arden, whereas "Viola" exists throughout most of *Twelfth Night* only under and through her Cesario role. This sequential role-playing makes it difficult to conceptualize for the central character a sustained and unified identity or a stable "femininity" or "masculinity." The play unfolds a series of "Rosalinds" and "Ganymedes" and there is no incorporation of them at the conclusion. And these shes and hes generate instability in others.

The first act of *As You Like It* unfolds a representation of the romantic (and in performance potentially homoerotic) love of Celia and Rosalind, which is more extended than any cited in lovesickness discourse or performed elsewhere in Shakespearean comedy, and which is vowed permanent. It is more fully represented than that of Antonio and Sebastian in *Twelfth Night* although not, in the text, specifically eroticized as theirs is. Before we meet the cousins we learn that "never two ladies loved as they do" and that Rosalind remains at court after her father's banishment because Celia (like Antonio) "would have died to stay behind her" (I.i.105–10). To each other they are, "my sweet Rose, my dear Rose" (I.ii.21–2) and "Dear Celia" (I.ii.2). Celia's greater resources and greater affection make her Rosalind's protector: "Rosalind lacks then the love / Which teacheth thee that thou and I am one. / Shall we be sund'red, shall we part, sweet girl? / No, let my father seek another heir" (I.iii.95–8), and she resists other loves. She possessively spurns Rosalind's suggestion that they play at the sport of "falling in love" (I.ii.24); although equally taken with Orlando's youthful charm, she never falls for him as Rosalind does. The trip to the forest with Rosalind as Celia's protector continues the intimacy while reversing the power dynamics; Rosalind, whether because of her disguise, her lovesickness, or the change in venue and status, now takes the lead. Celia, abandoning endearments, is increasingly subordinated; she is reduced to watching, mocking, and eventually mimicking Rosalind. Both the Celia represented in Act I and the love between women gradually evaporate from the play (DiGangi 1997: 52–3).

Love overtakes Rosalind and Orlando simultaneously as both "fall" romantically in love at first sight (I.ii.245–51). Neither, however, acknowledges physical desire or acts on it until Rosalind plays Ganymede playing, sometimes, "Rosalind." Rosalind exploits the conventions of the discourse of lovesickness to draw Orlando's attention away from trees and his fetishized poems: "From the east to western Ind, / No jewel is like Rosalind. / Her worth being mounted on the wind, / Through all the world bears Rosalind" (III.ii.87–90), and to incite his desires. Pretending a cure for love, Ganymede induces lovesickness by modeling for Orlando the symptoms of desire: a "lean cheek," a "blue eye and sunken," and a "beard neglected," and a "careless desolation" of dress (III.ii.371–9). Next she incites Orlando to a rehearsal of wooing, a desire for kissing, and a walk through the marriage ceremony. The "cure" (III.ii.400, 401, 415, 419, 420) she undertakes is precisely the standard misogynistic denigration of women recommended in the treatises. Du Laurens, for example, advises accusing the lover's mistress of being "light, inconstant, foolish, devoted to varietie, mocking and laughing to scorne this his griefe and corrasive, disdainful as not acknowledging his deserts" (1597: 122–3). Ganymede improvises on this scheme by performing the stereotypical woman's role the misogynists construct; she will, she says, "grieve, be effeminate, changeable, longing and liking, proud, fantastical, apish, shallow, inconstant . . . now like him, now loathe him, then entertain him, then forswear him" (III.ii.405–11). By playing these roles, he/she takes some of the sting out of misogynist claims.

Rosalind, playing Ganymede playing "Rosalind," subordinates Orlando. To catalyze his desires, she replaces the unthreateningly static, asexual object, "Rosalind," of his poems with another "Rosalind," a specularized image of a powerful, sexually promiscuous woman and wife. In doing so Ganymede/Rosalind perhaps imagines herself into the role of this "Rosalind," in order to alleviate her own anxieties about being subordinated to a lover or husband. To cure love (or romance), she maps out for Orlando (and herself) the oft-cited dangers of marriage. The "Rosalind" that Ganymede performs will be a wife, "more clamorous than a parrot against rain, more newfangled than an ape, more giddy in my desires than a monkey" (IV.i.147–9). Marriage demands economic arrangements, she warns penniless Orlando: a snail is an apt wooer because he "carries his house on his head; a better jointure, I think, than you make a woman" (IV.i.52–3). It leads to childbearing: "let her never nurse her child herself, for she will breed it like a fool" (IV.i.171–2). And it presages the cuckold's horns. "Rosalind's" italicized commonplaces remind both the couple and the play's audience that marriage does not necessarily provide a cure for love, produce a stable gender hierarchy, or lead to a happy ending.

"Rosalind's" ventriloquizing of the discourse of misogyny reveals that it is the discourse in which the Renaissance most fully acknowledges women's power, voice, and eroticism (Neely 1993: xiii). "Rosalind" especially represents to Orlando her uncontainable wit, a metonymy for her "will," sexual and otherwise: "the wiser, the waywarder. Make the doors upon a woman's wit, and it will out at the casement; shut that, and 'twill out at the keyhole; stop that, 'twill fly with the smoke out the chimney." If a husband were to meet "your wife's wit going to your neighbor's bed," she'd say: "She came to seek you there" (IV.i.157–60, 164–8). Rosalind here attributes aggressive sexual promiscuity to herself and, perhaps, homoeroticism to herself or her future husband – depending on who is imagined with whom in that neighbor's bed (DiGangi 1997: 58). No wonder Orlando flees: "for these two hours, Rosalind, I will leave thee" (IV.i.174). Meanwhile, Celia executes a much milder version of the same debunking strategy, calling into question Orlando's looks, his kisses, his fidelity for Rosalind's benefit (III.iv).

Rosalind's appropriation of misogyny does not eliminate desire but induces it. Talking about sex is titillating for the couple, as perhaps reading lovesickness discourse or misogyny tracts was for early modern audiences. For Rosalind as for Orlando, acting out marriage and talking bawdy about sexual organs and going to bed gives body to romantic imaginings and arouses desire. Since Ganymede/Rosalind's mockery is playful and italicized, it promotes interchange and intimacy with Orlando. Such witty exchanges, Stephen Greenblatt shows, generate erotic friction (1988: 88–90). Celia accurately recognizes Rosalind's mockery as a "love-prate" that exposes female genitalia/desires: "We must have your doublet and hose plucked over your head, and show the world what the bird hath done to her own nest" (IV.i.200–2). Rosalind, in response to the couple's extended witty intercourse, passionately expresses the emotional and erotic depth of her love. "O coz, coz, coz, my pretty little coz, that thou didst know how many fathom deep I am in love! But it cannot be sounded. My affection hath an unknown bottom, like the Bay of Portugal" (203–6). I read this acknowledgment of her insatiable desires not as an expression of "properly feminine subjectivity" as Jean Howard does (1994: 118), but as an assertion of what might be called *improperly* feminine subjectivity, akin to that circulated by misogyny.

Ganymede/Rosalind's passion and witty role-playing likewise induce erotic desires in others by example and design. Her angry denunciation of the static Petrarchan affair of Phebe and Silvius again counters one set of gender stereotypes with another, denouncing Phebe and praising Silvius to reverse the Petrarchan power dynamics of the relationship. Her attack on Phebe's ugliness ("inky brows," "black silk hair," "bugle eyeballs," III.v.46–7) and low value ("Sell when you can, you are not for all markets," III.v.60), and her challenge to Silvius's subordination ("You are a thousand times a properer man / Than she a woman," III.v.51–2) are conventionally recommended cures. Her attack jolts both, but in fact deepens Silvius's desires and attracts Phebe's to Ganymede. Here again, a dose of misogyny serves to empower Phebe – in the short run. Celia and Oliver, who must both endure the love-prates of their "sister" and brother, mimic their siblings and plunge into love with textbook regularity: in the space of a single sentence they "looked," "loved," "sighed," diagnosed their condition, and "sought the remedy" – immediate marriage to avoid being "incontinent" before (V.ii.33–9). In turn, the recital of Celia's and Oliver's movement toward satisfaction, made first by Orlando and then by Rosalind (V.ii.1–4, 30–41), reverberates back on them. Their mirrored narrations precipitate Orlando's comment that he "can live no longer by thinking" (V.ii.50) and Ganymede/Rosalind's yearning beyond roleplay and foreplay: "I will satisfy you if ever I satisfied man" (V.ii.114).

While all the erotic styles and gender roles circulated in the play through characters and text are conventional, their multiplicity is unsettling. The changes in gender roles, erotic styles, and power inflections which mark Rosalind's role, although each one is explicitly stereotypical, deconstruct any simple notions of gender and desire. The character plays: the dependent adolescent girlfriend with Celia in Act I, "coupled and inseparable" (I.iii.75); the protective young man, Ganymede, who parodies the self-importance adolescent boys project, hopefully, around girls: "I must comfort the weaker vessel, as doublet and hose ought to show itself courageous to petticoat" (II.iv.5–7); another Ganymede with Orlando, the youthful misogynist, wise in the ways of women and love; the aggressively promiscuous wife, Rosalind; the woman in love who weeps and faints (III.iv; IV.iii); the self-subordinating daughter and wife who recites "To you I give myself, for I am yours" to father and husband in the last scene (V.iv.116–17). Even apart from the homoerotic vibrations potentially aroused by the name "Ganymede," that of Jove's page and the standard slang term for a youthful homoerotic object of desire (especially a boy actor), and the fact of the quadruple bi-gendered role-playing, a topic extensively treated elsewhere (Hobby 1991; Howard 1994; Traub 1992), the play disperses multiple images of gender and eroticism, as do the lovesickness treatises.

As the treatises sometimes advocate, the play's multiple desires are channeled by Rosalind, Hymen, and the play into a highly ritualized and apparently conventional set of marriages. These are explicitly situated within a social context emphatically marked as patriarchal, in which economic and political and marital power is expressly controlled by men (Montrose 1981: 51–4). The hymn of the male god Hymen imposes the social, community-building, and reproductive functions of marriage, absent from *Twelfth Night*: "'Tis Hymen peoples every town" (V.iv.143). Hymen's blessings on "you and you," perhaps introduce some mutuality into these marriages. But while, in the body of the play, the women characters established positions of power over their lovers – Phebe by disdain, Audrey by resolute chastity, Rosalind by role-playing deferral, and Celia as heir to the ruling Duke – this power is eliminated in the last scene through the performance of the marriages and the Duke's abdication. Whereas bonds between Antonio and Sebastian, Orsino and Cesario, Viola and Olivia were reasserted at the moment of marriage, those of Celia and Rosalind, Phebe and Ganymede, Orlando and Ganymede are altogether suppressed from the text of the last scene. When, in *Twelfth Night*, Viola emerges out of her Cesario role, she retains aspects of it, as Orsino acknowledges. But the decorous and nearly silent bride who appears in the final scene of *As You Like It* contains no traces of former Ganymedes or former Rosalinds.

What is powerfully represented here, unlike in *Twelfth Night*, are conventionally gendered heterosexual unions enunciated in Jaques's concluding blessings. These assert the political and economic along with the sexual functions of marriage; their ordering delineates a hierarchical society from Duke down to fool. They emphatically position the four husbands as subjects, relegating their unnamed wives to possessed objects:

> [*To Orlando.*]   You to a love that your true faith doth merit;
> [*To Oliver.*]   You to your land and love and great allies;
> [*To Silvius.*]   You to a long and well-deservèd bed;
> [*To Touchstone.*]   And you to wrangling, for thy loving voyage
>   Is but for two months victualled.
>
> (V.iv.188–92)

But viewed in the light of the play as a whole, the ending may be interpreted as less than perfectly hegemonic and normative. The highly formalized and ritualized enactment of the weddings suggests that this is just one more moment of roles performed.

They may be no more permanent than any of the others we have seen enacted or circulated. Rosalind's stereotypes of powerful wives remain salient, challenging the view that marriage permanently subordinates women. The lack of acknowledged affection between Celia and Rosalind in the last act reminds us that love can disappear. Jaques's precisely differentiated blessings make clear that the four marriages serve different functions and that Touchstone's will not last forever. The same may be true for the rest. Like Shakespeare's audience, we know from lovesickness discourse and experience that marriage, while one strategy for satisfying inordinate desires, does not always work.

The Epilogue encourages this view by reopening erotic possibility and circulating it to the audience, married or unmarried. The actor playing Rosalind claims, while still in his female costume, that if he were a woman he would kiss men, and if a man would kiss women. The Epilogue, like the play, continues to suture eroticism to gender by making the play's success depend upon "the love (women) bear to men" and "the love (men) bear to women" (Epil.12, 14). The boy actor's female role-playing, however, renders even this mapping less secure and reminds us of the multiple possibilities for "masculinity" and "femininity" and "marriage" that the play has put into circulation. In the examples of the lovesickness treatises, in the eroticized intercourse between performers on the stage, in the charged exchanges between performers and audiences, and in the exchanges within the audience which continue after the play is over, a heterogeneous, volatilely erotic and gendered subject with unpredictable momentum emerges from both these Shakespeare comedies. And lovesickness discourse teaches us to hope for satisfaction of subjects' desires, however untoward.

NOTES

1 I want to acknowledge useful contributions to an early draft of this essay by students in my 1996 graduate seminar on "Shakespearean Subjectivities" at the University of Illinois, Urbana-Champaign, and by members of the seminar on "Reconsidering Subjectivity" chaired by Valerie Wayne and Akiko Kusunoki at the 1996 International Shakespeare Congress in Los Angeles. Subsequent commentary by my colleagues Jan Hinely, Lori Newcomb, Michael Shapiro, and Dick Wheeler was, as always, invaluable. An expanded version of the essay is chapter 4 of my nearly completed book manuscript, *Distracted Subjects: Madness, Gender, and Confinement in Shakespeare and Early Modern Culture*.

2 Ferrand's treatise, not translated into English until 1640 (by Edmund Chilmead), does not directly influence medical discourse or drama

in England until then. But it is a remarkably complete record of developments in lovesickness discourse in the late sixteenth and early seventeenth centuries. It was published in its first version in 1610, seven years after Ferrand started practicing medicine; a second edition, doubled in size, appeared in 1623. Its main influence, Du Laurens's succinct chapter on lovesickness, part of a longer treatise on melancholy, was published in Paris in 1597 and translated into English in 1599, making available in England the basic material on which Ferrand elaborated. Ferrand's debt to Du Laurens, Beecher and Ciavolella show, was "global in nature." Du Laurens's treatise was for Ferrand, "matter entirely digested, memorized, and absorbed," which affected his structure, emphases, and arguments (Ferrand 1990: 104). Similar ideas were available in the

English discussions I cite, including Burton's Third Partition, "Love Melancholy," in the *Anatomy of Melancholy*, which first cites Ferrand in its fourth edition (1632). Since direct influence is not at issue, I quote from the indispensable modern translation of Ferrand's 1623 treatise by Donald Beecher and Massimo Ciavolella.

3 In the six references to Sappho in his treatise (229, 231, 250, 270–1, 337, 347), Ferrand draws on both classical (Ovid, Suidas) and Renaissance (Belleau, Muret) sources to circulate several of the "fictions" of Sappho that Joan DeJean identifies as prominent in France in the sixteenth and seventeenth centuries. In Ferrand's treatise, as elsewhere in sixteenth-century France, her homoeroticism is acknowledged and she is figured as a writer ("poetess" 229) and an authoritative figure ("learned" 231, 270). She is also represented as the suicidal victim of het-eroerotic love for Phaon – which DeJean finds to be the primary representation of Sappho in

the first half of the seventeenth century (DeJean 1989: 29–42). See also Harriette Andreadis (1996) on Sappho's reputation in England.

4 Pequigney (1992: 205). He makes a plausible case that Sebastian and Antonio, during their three months together when Sebastian assumes the name Roderigo, have been engag-ing in sexual relations which Sebastian now tries to terminate; hence his resumption of his own name and dismissal of Antonio (1992: 204–5).

5 A Chicago Repertory Theater production of *Twelfth Night*, directed by Michael Pennington in 1996, concluded with Olivia and Orsino exiting arm in arm, dressed in matching upper-class whites, followed by Cesario and Sebastian, still in identical pages' garb and embracing. This graphic signal that Olivia and Orsino remain twinned, as do Viola and Sebastian, kept the circuits of desire open within and between the marriages.

References and Further Reading

Althusser, L. 1971: "Ideology and Ideological State Apparatuses (Notes Towards an Investi-gation)." In *Lenin and Philosophy and Other Essays*. Trans. Ben Brewster. New York: Monthly Review Press, 127–86.

Andreadis, H. 1996: "Sappho in Early Modern England: A Study in Sexual Reputation." In Ellen Greene (ed.), *Re-Reading Sappho: Reception and Transmission*. Berkeley: University of California Press, 105–21.

Barber, C. L. 1959: *Shakespeare's Festive Comedy: A Study of Dramatic Form and its Relation to Social Custom*. Princeton: Princeton University Press.

Beecher, D. A. and Ciavolella, M. 1990: Intro-duction. In Jacques Ferrand, *A Treatise on Lovesickness* (1623). Ed. and trans. Donald A. Beecher and Massimo Ciavolella. Syracuse: Syracuse University Press.

Belsey, C. 1985: *The Subject of Tragedy*. London: Methuen.

Bishop, J. 1577: *Beautifull Blossomes, gathered by John Bishop. . . .* London: Henrie Cockyn.

Boaistuau, P. 1581: *Theatrum Mundi, the Theatre or rule of the world. . . .* Trans. J. Alday. London: J. Wyght.

Bray, A. 1995: *Homosexuality in Renaissance England*. Second edition. New York: Columbia University Press.

Burton, R. 1994: *The Anatomy of Melancholy* (1632 edition). Ed. Thomas C. Faulkner, Nicolas K. Kiessling, and Rhonda L. Blair. Vol. 3. Oxford: Clarendon Press.

Callaghan, D. 1993: "'And all is semblative a woman's part': Body Politics and *Twelfth Night*." *Textual Practice*, 7, 3, 428–52.

Crewe, J. 1995: "In the Field of Dreams: Trans-vestism in *Twelfth Night* and *The Crying Game*." *Representations*, 50, 101–21.

DeJean, J. 1989: *Fictions of Sappho: 1546–1937*. Chicago: University of Chicago Press.

DiGangi, M. 1997: *The Homoerotics of Early Modern Drama*. Cambridge: Cambridge University Press.

Dollimore, J. 1990: "Shakespeare, Cultural Ma-terialism, Feminism, and Marxist Humanism." *New Literary History*, 21, 471–91.

Du Laurens, A. 1597: Chapter X, "Of another kinde of melancholie which commeth by the extremitie of love." In *A Discourse of the Preservation of the Sight: Of Melancholike Diseases.* Trans. R. Surphlet (1599). London: F. Kingston for R. Jacson, 117–24.

Ferrand, J. 1990: *A Treatise on Lovesickness* (1623). Ed. and trans. Donald A. Beecher and Massimo Ciavolella. Syracuse: Syracuse University Press.

Foucault, M. 1980: *The History of Sexuality.* Vol. I. Trans. Robert Hurley. New York: Random House.

—— 1982: "The Subject and Power." *Critical Inquiry*, 8, 777–95.

Frye, N. 1949: "The Argument of Comedy." In D. A. Robertson (ed.), *English Institute Essays 1948.* New York: Columbia University Press, 58–73.

Garzoni, T. 1600: *The Hospitall of incurable Fooles: erected in English as neer the first italian modell and platforme. . . .* Trans. E. Blout. London: Edm. Bollifant for Edward Blout.

Goldberg, J. 1992: *Sodometries: Renaissance Texts, Modern Sexualities.* Stanford: Stanford University Press.

Grady, H. forthcoming: "On the Need for a Differentiated Theory of (Early) Modern Subjects." Manuscript. To appear in John Joughin (ed.), *Philosophical Shakespeare.* London: Routledge.

Greenblatt, S. 1988: "Fiction and Friction." In *Shakespearean Negotiations: The Circulation of Social Energy in Renaissance England.* Berkeley: University of California Press, 66–93.

Gregerson, L. 1995: *The Reformation of the Subject: Spenser, Milton, and the English Protestant Epic.* Cambridge: Cambridge University Press.

Hobby, E. 1991: "'My affection hath an unknown bottom': Homosexuality and the Teaching of *As You Like It.*" In Lesley Aers and Nigel Wheale (eds.), *Shakespeare in the Changing Curriculum.* London: Routledge, 125–42.

Howard, J. E. 1994: "Power and Eros: Cross-dressing in Dramatic Representation and Theatrical Practice." In *The Stage and Social Struggle.* London: Routledge, 93–128.

Jacquart, D. and Thomasset, C. 1988: *Sexuality and Medicine in the Middle Ages.* Trans. Matthew Adamson. Princeton: Princeton University Press.

Maclean, I. 1980: *The Renaissance Notion of Woman.* Cambridge: Cambridge University Press.

Malcolmson, C. 1991: "'What You Will': Social Mobility and Gender in *Twelfth Night.*" In Valerie Wayne (ed.), *The Matter of Difference: Materialist Feminist Criticism of Shakespeare.* Ithaca: Cornell University Press, 29–57.

Montrose, L. A. 1981: "'The place of a brother' in *As You Like It*: Social Process and Comic Form." *Shakespeare Quarterly*, 32, 28–54.

—— 1989: "Professing the Renaissance: The Poetics and Politics of Culture." In H. Aram Veeser (ed.), *The New Historicism.* London: Routledge, 15–36.

Neely, C. T. 1993: *Broken Nuptials in Shakespeare's Plays.* Urbana: University of Illinois Press.

—— forthcoming: *Distracted Subjects: Madness, Gender, and Confinement in Shakespeare and Early Modern Culture.* Book manuscript.

Osborne, L. E. 1996: *The Trick of Singularity: Twelfth Night and the Performance Editions.* Iowa City: University of Iowa Press.

Pequigney, J. 1992: "The Two Antonios and Same-Sex Love in *Twelfth Night* and *The Merchant of Venice.*" *ELR*, 22, 201–21.

Rogers, T. 1576: *A philosophical discourse entitled, The Anatomie of the Minde.* London: I. C. for Andrew Maunsell.

Sedgwick, E. K. 1990: *Epistemology of the Closet.* Berkeley: University of California Press.

Shakespeare, W. 1972: *The Complete Signet Classic Shakespeare.* Ed. Sylvan Barnet. New York: Harcourt Brace Jovanovich.

Traub, V. 1991: "Desire and the Differences it Makes." In Valerie Wayne (ed.), *The Matter of Difference: Materialist Feminist Criticism of Shakespeare.* Ithaca: Cornell University Press, 81–114.

—— 1992: *Desire and Anxiety: Circulations of Sexuality in Shakespearean Drama.* London: Routledge.

—— 1994: "The (In)Significance of 'Lesbian' Desire in Early Modern England." In Jonathan Goldberg (ed.), *Queering the Renaissance.* Durham, NC: Duke University Press, 62–83.

Wack, M. F. 1990: *Lovesickness in the Middle Ages: The Viaticum and its Commentaries.* Philadelphia: University of Pennsylvania Press.

16

. . . in the Lesbian Void: Woman–Woman Eroticism in Shakespeare's Plays

Theodora A. Jankowski

Hermione dies in III.ii of *The Winter's Tale*. Hauled out of jail shortly after having given birth, she is forced to stand trial for adultery – a trial that literally proves fatal to her. Thus Act III of this play ends tragically with the loss of a mother and a daughter – the mother to actual death, the daughter to abandonment. Yet the swift and auspicious discovery of Perdita (IV.ii) virtually in the teeth of death – her mother, her brother, Antigonus – serves to cast into relief the culture of death from which she sprang. Her life reinforces the fact of her mother's death. Thus it is quite surprising to discover, two acts later (V.iii), a revivified Hermione ready to embrace her now grown daughter and her penitent husband. Hermione's reappearance causes much confusion not simply because a "dead" Shakespearean character miraculously comes to "life" – after all, the canon provides us with many such amphibious characters: Hero, Egeon, an Antipholus and a Dromio, Sebastian, Thaisa, Marina, Innogen, Postumus, etc. – but because a character the audience *knows* to be dead comes back to life. All other revived characters are *known* by the audience to be alive. In no other instance has Shakespeare so tricked his audience. Hermione's resurrection, therefore, causes students no end of problems. While they are not easy considering Hermione's rebirth to be "magical" – that is, a real statue turns into a real human – they are equally uneasy being *tricked* by the playwright, especially when they realize that they did *not* misread, or skip over, some important line that would let them in on the *truth* about Hermione. While such student questioning of the "facts" of Hermione's existence may seem either daft, perversely tangential – along the lines of "how many children did Lady Macbeth have?" – or merely uncooperative, these kinds of resistance to an "easy" answer do pressure our readings of plays, forcing us to consider interpretations we might not normally entertain. This is what I want to do as regards Hermione's disappearance. I want to consider just how the lack of textual evidence regarding Hermione's location forces us to put a certain kind of pressure upon the text in an attempt to find an explanation for what seems to be an anomalous situation in a Shakespeare play.

Hermione's "resurrection" does not occur until sixteen years after her death. If we are, indeed, to accept this revived Hermione as the *real* Hermione of Acts I–III – as I believe the text means us to do – the important question of where Hermione has been remains. Paulina states that she has kept her "Lonely, apart" (V.iii.18)[1] until Leontes has enacted sufficient penance to deserve his exemplary wife or Perdita has returned home. But given the logistics of the early modern aristocratic household, the presence of servants, and the effectually "public" character of even the most private of spaces, where was Hermione kept so secretly for sixteen years that no hint of her presence was revealed? Did Paulina pay all of her servants to be silent? Are we to believe that no one noticed food or clothing going into – and waste products being removed from – some "secret" place in Paulina's house? Did Hermione remain totally silent during this period? Did she not make contact with anyone but Paulina? Was Paulina able, secretly, to take care of *all* of Hermione's needs? What did Giulio Romano do while he supposedly worked on a statue? And, for sixteen years, did Leontes, dense though we know him to be, never have *any* suspicion that his wife was living at Paulina's?

The questions I have raised are clearly not answered in *The Winter's Tale*. At least they are not answered in what we might consider the "traditional" way of answering "plot" questions about a Shakespearean play. I suggest that part of the reason that we do not have any "critical" answers to these questions, answers that have a history of scholarly debate, is because both questions and answers involve issues of various kinds of invisibility. My answers, therefore, will not be presented in a "traditional" scholarly way. I have raised the above questions because I believe that *asking* them, as well as trying to figure out *how* to answer them, allows me to challenge both modern and early modern assumptions regarding the position and extent of woman–woman eroticism in early modern texts. I want to begin by looking at that anomalous "space" in *The Winter's Tale*, the space that allows Hermione to be both dead and yet available for resurrection, seemingly at a moment's notice.

This void space of invisibility exists both within Shakespeare's play and seemingly also within the early modern aristocratic residence. I see this space as coinciding metaphorically with the even greater void space of invisibility within early modern society and early modern literary texts, the space occupied by the "lesbian." Now while there were quite literally no "lesbians" in the early modern period – the word "lesbian" not achieving current usage until the nineteenth century – there quite obviously *must* have been women who desired other women and had erotic and/or sexual relations with them.[2] But to look superficially at literary texts of the early modern period, we might suspect otherwise. We might suspect that early modern "lesbians" – if they existed at all – did so in that same invisible, inconceivable place Hermione existed for sixteen years until revived by Paulina. But does being so completely hidden, so "closeted," mean that one is, *indeed*, a "lesbian?" Can we apply such an identification to Paulina and Hermione, or to other seemingly "hidden" women pairs? Before I attempt to answer these last two questions, I want to consider in some detail the metaphorical space I will call "the lesbian void."

The subject of this essay is the virtual invisibility of woman–woman eroticism not only in Shakespeare's plays but in almost all plays of the early modern period. In his early study of male–male eroticism, Alan Bray questioned whether "female homosexuality . . . was recognised at all" (1982: 17). Such a comment could only have been made by a man who was raised in a patriarchal culture that was concerned exclusively with male-authored texts.[3] If twenty-first-century women – lesbian or straight – are routinely ignored by actual men, whether or not they are authors, it is not surprising that actual early modern women, as well as literary characters, would be equally ignored. Indeed, one of the projects of twenty-first-century academic feminism has been to make actual and literary early modern women *visible*. I propose to do the same for "lesbians." In recent and forthcoming publications, I have examined the condition of virginity as a "space" which both challenged the early modern sex/gender system's prevailing belief that all women were destined for marriage and which allowed the existence of erotic relationships between women.[4] In this essay I want to look at two different "spaces," each a kind of "female realm," where erotic relationships between women could occur: within the newly created private spaces of the early modern aristocratic home and within the mistress–servant relationship. These two "spaces" are not mutually exclusive, for I will also suggest that the development of the geographical private space allowed for the fuller development of woman–woman eroticism between various kinds of partners, servants, and other close household members as well as friends.

Let me return to Paulina's house, where Hermione has lived hidden for sixteen years, and again ask the question: where could Hermione have been kept all this time and *not* excited any sort of suspicion? To answer this question I want to consider two things: the development of early modern notions of privacy and the concomitant changes in the early modern upper-class home based upon such developments. I want to consider two new geographical "spaces" within the early modern house, the closet and the banquet. The first was an inner room, initially called a "withdrawing chamber" (Girouard 1978: 94), which was entered through the, somewhat public at this time, bedchamber (Thompson 1979: 293). Although this chamber became a combined private sitting, dining, and reception room for the bedchamber's occupant, it "continued to be slept in by his [*sic*] servants until at least the end of the sixteenth century" (Girouard 1978: 94). The servants who slept in these withdrawing chambers did so on pallets that were hidden during the day (Girouard 1978: 94). Thompson refers to the withdrawing chamber located beyond the bedchamber as a "closet" (or "*cabinet*" in French) and defines this space as

> a room to which the occupant of the bedchamber could retire and where he or she could normally expect to enjoy *complete* privacy to rest, read, study, write letters, or entertain intimate friends. . . . [C]losets . . . formed the innermost and therefore most secluded room of the apartment concerned . . . [C]losets by their nature were separate and therefore freed from the conventions that governed the principal rooms. One could . . . behave in them in a more relaxed manner, . . . All formality was thrown to the winds. (Thompson 1979: 296)

The room was private in the sense that it was out of the way of the flow of business of the house and could be locked by its primary occupant (Alberti 1971: 78 and Day 1592: 83, both cited in Stewart 1995).[5] Since a noblewoman would not normally carry refreshments to whatever guests she was entertaining in her private space, I imagine that *some* servants would have had *some* access to this room at *some* time(s).

I want to raise the possibility that the privacy of the mistress's closet meant both that things, as well as people, could be hidden in it and that the woman of the house controlled access to it. The (virtually proverbial) jealousy of husbands like Leontes as well as the very real problems a woman faced if she provided a husband with too many children who were not his own might make her wary of entertaining male lovers in the "complete privacy" (Thompson 1979: 296) of her closet. But house servants would be less apt to remark upon the entrance of woman visitors into this space. I suggest that the closet represented a secure, private place where a woman could engage in erotic interludes with another woman without arousing suspicion. I would go even further and suggest that an upper-class woman could also use her closet as a space in which to engage in erotic interludes with a lady-in-waiting or a servant. Entrance into the closet by a servant would be even less remarked, and the widespread practice of early modern men being erotically involved with their (male and female) servants (see Bray, Smith, Orgel, DiGangi, Stewart, etc.) suggests that such a possibility existed for women as well.[6] It would be especially possible given the fact that a woman servant often lived in the same house as her mistress for many years – hence allowing long-term relationships, perhaps ones in which the older of the two women initiated the younger into woman–woman sex.[7]

Sleeping arrangements for servants provided a way in which erotic encounters could even occur at night. Mark Girouard points out that a servant often slept in the closet adjacent to the main bedchamber (1978: 94). Peter Thompson indicates that servants "often slept by the door to their master's or mistress's apartment" (1979: 169) within easy call to render whatever "services" – and I will consider the full implications of this term later – might be required during the night. Alternatively, a "trundle-bed-stead" or "truckle bed," which "was mounted on wheels and could be stowed under the main bed in the room" (1979: 151), allowed personal servants to "sleep close to their masters" (1979: 153) or mistresses (Orlin 1994: 185). Servants probably also slept in the same bed with their mistresses. In the case of *The Winter's Tale*, I want to suggest that, as Hermione's servant but also her protector, Paulina is in the position similarly to serve her mistress while she perhaps keeps her safely in her closet.[8]

Another place where Hermione could have been hidden is in the "banquet."[9] This word does not describe the sumptuous feast that we would understand today by the term but an intimate and important *part* of that feast. During the medieval period, feasts were held in the hall, later in the great chamber, which was also the location of the dancing that usually followed the feast. Guests stood and consumed wine and various kinds of sweetmeats while the hall was "voided" – emptied – of dinner tables and food. By the early modern period, this course had become the "void" – later to be called "dessert" – and, as a result of increasing notions of privacy, these expensive and elaborately constructed confections of sugar and candied fruit[10] were usually only partaken of by the hosts and the most important guests at the feast. These people usually "withdrew" from the hall to take the "void" in a room set apart for the purpose, initially, a small chamber off of the great hall, called the "banquet." For Patricia Fumerton, as well as for my argument,

> the critical point in the history [of the banquet] is when the void more decisively withdrew: when it split off from the trajectory of decreasingly public rooms and . . . [became] a special room set apart in immaculate privacy. (1991: 114)

Lacock Abbey, in Wiltshire, is an example of such an arrangement. It had two banquets; one was entered through the house, the other, directly above it, "was only approachable by an external walk across the leads" of the roof (Girouard 1978: 106). Longleat had several small banquets on the roof, while some houses, like Callowden House in Warwickshire, situated their banquets in retired spots in the gardens (Girouard 1978: 104–6). Some banquets grew large and turned into "lodges" which

> were often built in secluded or remote situations, and were as a result, lonely and romantic places . . . Their seclusion and separation from the coming and going of the big house made them useful places for private meetings. (Girouard 1978: 108)

The isolation of the banquet – tower or detached house or lodge – would mean that it would be rarely visited when feasts were not in progress. It would, therefore, be an ideal place to hide someone, especially someone who was supposed to be dead, supposed to have "voided" this life exactly as guests voided the great hall when the meal was over. In this void space one can also locate the invisible experience of woman–woman desire.

Let me return to the Sicilia of *The Winter's Tale*. Even though Leontes's charge of jealousy as regards Hermione is ludicrous, the staging of the play could be taken to suggest the possible truth of the accusation, since the character usually only appears with men, her husband, or Polixenes. While Shakespeare's other falsely slandered woman, Desdemona, is as often seen with Emilia as she is with Cassio, Hermione is rarely seen with women. In fact, her only appearance with her champion, Paulina, occurs briefly in Act III, before she "dies." But Hermione's one appearance with other women, the First and Second Lady (II.i), reveals some very interesting language. While the First Lady amuses Mamillius, she reminds the young prince that

> The Queen your mother rounds apace. We shall
> Present our services to a fine new prince
> One of these days
>
> (II.i.17–19)

I would like to pause here to focus on the word "services" and the action of "presenting our services." The *OED* defines "service" in several ways:

I. The condition of being a servant; the fact of serving a master. . . . II. The work or duty of a servant; the action of serving a master. . . . 6a. Performance of the duties of a servant; work done in obedience to and for the benefit of a master.

In a related sense, in feudal usage, the word could be defined as: "8a. Feudal allegiance, fealty; profession of allegiance, homage." Thus the First Lady's speech can refer to two potential kinds of service she and her companion will provide for Hermione's unborn child: they will serve the child as a servant serves her master or as a vassal serves her feudal overlord. Either definition makes sense in this context, since the child of Sicilia's ruler would be in the position of a feudal overlord to a member of the minor nobility, and such members of the minor nobility as ladies-in-waiting would serve their master/mistress as servants. But this is all quite ordinary. What is somewhat out of the ordinary are other uses of the word "service." The word may also refer to "6c. the flesh's service, sexual intercourse. Also the service of Venus, . . . 10. The devotion or suit of a lover; professed love." (In the sense of 6c is also the, perhaps later, usage of "the action of covering a female animal.") The word may also define "19a. The action of serving, helping or benefitting; conduct tending to the welfare or advantage of another. Chiefly in *to do, render service.* . . . 23. Supply the need *of* (persons, occasionally of things)."

The use of "service" to refer to amatory or sexual service is not a far reach from the servantly definitions, especially if we consider the conventions of the Courtly Love tradition, in which the male lover strove to *serve* his beloved in whatever way(s) he could. By moving into these definitions of sexual service or love, I do not want to imply that the First Lady had some kind of deviant pederastic service in mind as regards Hermione's unborn child. But I *do* want to take these various definitions of "service," combine them, and use them as a means of understanding not only the character Paulina, but her relationship to Hermione.

Paulina does not appear in the play until II.ii, yet once she does, her role is central to the action in Sicilia. And it is important to remember that *all* of her actions are consistently directed toward *serving* Hermione in whatever way(s) she can. Paulina initially appears at the jail, a "gentle visitor" (II.ii.12) come to find out how the queen is faring. Once Hermione's child is born, Paulina assumes the job of trying to reconcile the king both to his new daughter and to his wife. Given Leontes's overweening jealousy, such a task would be better suited to a person with years of experience in the diplomatic corps. Paulina is hardly diplomatic. Instead of trying to persuade Leontes to reconsider his opinions of his wife – or using the infant Perdita as a tool to plead for her mother's release: few people are so hardened as to resist the gurgly appeals of a newborn! – Paulina appears as an avenging angel to demand Leontes's immediate repentance. Her behavior is totally out of character for a virtuous woman. Even though she professes to be Leontes's "loyal servant, . . . physician, . . . most obedient counsellor" (II.iii.54, 55), her refusal to be "ruled" by her husband (49) in appearing before the king precipitates his condemnation of her. He not only deems her "audacious" (42), but she is named "a mankind witch" (68), "a most intelligencing bawd" (69), and "a callat / Of boundless tongue" who "hath beat her husband" (91–2).

This collection of images that paint Paulina as a completely unruly woman, excessively verbal, a witch, and a husband-beater, has received much critical commentary. The names and images Leontes uses are proverbial, and the picture of Paulina is thus stereotypically anti-feminist in the worst traditions of early modern misogynist literature. Yet the character is also seen as justified in her actions, since she is not acting as a shrew simply to disrupt the existing gender order. She is "allowed" this verbal outrage because she is acting for the greater good: clearing the names of both Hermione and her "bastard" child. I want to argue, however, that Paulina behaves in this transgressive way for a much more transgressive reason. True, she may owe Hermione "service" as her "overlady," the wife of Leontes, Antigonus's overlord. And she may be one of Hermione's "servants," a lady-in-waiting who owes her service in this context as well. But I want to consider another way in which Paulina feels she owes Hermione "service." In the midst of her tirade against Leontes, Paulina exasperatedly threatens:

> Good queen, my lord, good queen, I say good queen,
> And would by combat make her good, so were I
> A man, the worst about you.
> (II.iii.60–2)

In one sense this speech recalls Beatrice's wish to cut out and eat Claudio's heart in the marketplace (*Much Ado About Nothing*, IV.ii.303–4). Both speeches reveal the frustration a woman feels when she *knows* something is wrong but, because she is a woman and therefore powerless in patriarchal society, *does not* have her word accepted and *cannot* engage in any physical action to rectify the situation. I want to focus here not on the emotion of Paulina's speech – clearly indicated by the repetition of "good queen" – but on certain aspects of its wording. Paulina says that she "would by combat make [Hermione's reputation] good" if she were a man. This wording shows her speech to be radically different from Beatrice's, for it moves beyond the emotional desire to inflict pain or exact revenge to a ritualized means of exacting justice: trial by combat. Now, such a trial could refer to the fact that early modern monarchs still had "champions" who took their places should such medieval methods of problem solving become necessary. The female Hermione might thus conceivably be represented by a female champion, the knight Paulina. Another possibility is suggested, however, by two of the *OED* definitions of "service": "10. The devotion or suit of a lover" and "19a. The action of serving, helping, or benefitting; conduct tending to the welfare or advantage of another." While engaging in combat to prove Hermione's innocence certainly is an action that "tends toward the advantage of another," I want also to suggest that Paulina's wish simultaneously indicates "the devotion or suit of a lover." Thus, like the knight in the Courtly Love romances, Paulina is willing to protect the honor of her Lady by combat, no matter who the adversary. That the adversary is the husband stresses the "adulterous" quality of Paulina and Hermione's love, which was a characteristic of all love relationships within the Courtly Love tradition.

Even though Paulina may not have been successful in convincing Leontes of Hermione's innocence – indeed, Divine retribution resulting in the death of his only son is the only thing that *does* convince him – she does manage to secrete and protect her lady until she can finally clear her name. For sixteen years Hermione lives secure with Paulina. Perceived to have entered the void of death, she may indeed only have entered the void location of Paulina's banquet. Or, to push definitions and metaphors still further, she may have entered the "void" of early modern "lesbian" activity: unseen, unknown, unacknowledged. *The Winter's Tale* provides us with no details of where Hermione has been for those sixteen years beyond "lonely, [and] apart" (V.iii.18). Yet if we think back to V.ii, where various gentlemen catch Autolycus up on what has happened before he arrived, there is a small remark that gives a clue to Hermione's location. In relating the history of the statue, the Second Gentleman indicates that he "thought [Paulina] had some great matter there in hand, for she hath privately twice or thrice a day, ever since the death of Hermione, visited that removed house" (V.ii.94–6). Only when we learn in V.iii that Hermione is alive can we reflect back upon Paulina's "removed house" and suspect that was where Hermione resided for sixteen years. The fact that the *Norton Shakespeare* glosses "removed" as "distant, hidden" (2947, l.96n) suggests that Paulina's house was, indeed, a banquet or a lodge. However, the only thing we know definitely about what has gone on during that time is that Hermione has aged and developed wrinkles. But in describing the "statue" she displays to Leontes and Polixenes, Paulina may be revealing *something* of what has transpired during those lost years. She describes the "statue" as "my poor image . . . for the stone is mine" (58, 59), suggesting that in some way she either "owns" Hermione or has taken control of her. This control is reinforced by her claim that she can "make the statue move indeed" (88) and by the orders she gives "it":

> Descend. Be stone no more. Approach.
> Strike all that look upon with marvel. Come,
>   . . . Nay, come away.
> Bequeath to death your numbness
>   (99–100, 101–2)

In one sense it seems as though Hermione and Paulina have reversed roles and Hermione is now the servant subject to Paulina's commands. Possibly, but I want to raise another possibility. Early modern marriage theory claimed that, once married, a husband and wife became "one flesh." Theoretically, then, one should not know where the wife ended and the husband began since they were, in a kind of mystical way, coterminous.[11] Thus I want to suggest that Paulina "owns" Hermione in the way that any lover might claim to "own" her beloved and can thus "command" her as Paulina does Hermione. I want to consider the invisible void years of Hermione's sojourn with

Paulina as a time when she was served and serviced – in both ordinary and erotic ways – by a woman whom she, then, similarly served and serviced as she does now by obeying her commands to return to the "life" of a wife and mother. The strange and unprepared-for pairing of Paulina with Camillo reinforces the removal of Hermione from the "lesbian" void, stresses the violent severing of her relationship with Paulina, and signals the recuperation of the missing queen back into the patriarchal sexual economy.

Some twenty-first-century lesbian theorists suggest that woman–woman erotic relationships are preferable to man–woman ones because they are, necessarily, more egalitarian. Others suggest that a power differential (of whatever kind) is necessary to pique erotic interest.[12] I do not necessarily want to argue for or against egalitarian erotic relationships between women in the early modern period but simply call attention to the fact that, while some women might want lovers of their own rank and personality type, other women might want to dominate their lovers, and still others to be dominated by them. The inequality in relative power – indeed, a vexed term at a time when whatever actual power women had was highly mediated – between women may occur in various ways, though my focus here is on the differential that occurs within the mistress–servant relationship. Yet such a differential cannot be considered without also considering the way age complicates the arrangement. Paulina seems to be somewhat older than Hermione. Antigonus claims their three daughters are aged eleven, nine, and five (II.i.146–7), thus the eldest would be no more than five or six years older than Mamillius. This would suggest that the two women are fairly close in age, though staging and certainly her extreme self-possession in II.iii suggest that Paulina is a good deal older – more of a mother-figure, perhaps? – than the often quiet Hermione. Yet this "feeling" that Paulina is older may arise simply because she so completely manages Hermione's affairs once the queen is imprisoned. This power, added to her slightly lower rank, may "raise" Paulina to Hermione's "level." But maybe Hermione *enjoys* being controlled and managed. Catherine of France certainly enjoys Alice's English lesson (*Henry V*, III.iv), and the older woman's forthright "translations" of the Princess's remarks to Henry (V.ii) indicate that she holds a certain amount of power as regards her charge.[13]

The fairy queen Titania's relationship with her votress is one that contains women obviously different in rank or class. The votress seems to be a much lower-class servant than Paulina or Alice, for she "sail[s] upon the land / To fetch . . . trifles" (*A Midsummer Night's Dream*, II.i.132–3) for her royal mistress. Yet even though she clearly serves her mistress in a more menial way than Paulina, or even the First Lady, the women's relationship is quite close. They behave almost as though they were relatives, a situation reinforced by the description of what they so often did together: gossip (125). The twenty-first-century understanding of "gossip" as catty, malicious, or meaningless chat forgets that the word originally meant "godparent." Godparents were often related in some way to their godchildren, though being godparents actually *creates* a relationship to the child and the child's family as well as *between* the godparents. Thus speech between godparents – "gossip" – takes on the connotation of intimate speech between family members. That early modern social conditions usually meant that women godparents more often gathered together than men for occasions like births meant that *their* speech, intimate female speech suitable to a "family" context, became defined as "gossip." An example of how women gossips can create a female-only world within a patriarchal society is the christening scene (III.ii) in Thomas Middleton's *A Chaste Maid in Cheapside* (ca. 1613). Here the women's affectionate conversation, eating, drinking – and the resultant peeing – creates an intimate and communal space where the male guests feel decidedly less "at home."[14] I would argue that Shakespeare's use of "gossip" to describe what Titania and her votress do together recalls the female communal spaces that grow up around births, christenings, wedding preparations, etc. and suggests yet another "space" where women might easily be able to show affection for one another. Thus Titania's feelings for her servant can be regarded as close, "familial" feelings that certainly can move into eroticism.

Portia and Nerissa's relationship similarly occurs within an essentially woman-only space. While there are some male servants in Belmont, their roles are small and their lines few. In fact, it is the spirit of Portia's father and not any "real" man who represents the most consistent male presence. Thus the quick turnover of suitors combined with the virtually invisible servants make it easy to accept Belmont as a space whose beauty results from the lack of male challenge to the female autonomy of Portia and her companion Nerissa. But how are we to define Nerissa? Like Alice, Paulina, Charmian, or Iras, she seems to be a woman of virtually the same class as Portia – in fact, she marries Bassanio's friend Graziano – perhaps technically a lady-in-waiting, though actually a friend. That the depth of these characters' affection may go deeper than simply friendship is borne out by their jokes at the expense of the suitors, Nerissa's accompanying "the lawyer" Portia to Venice as her clerk, and their dual participation in the ring-trick.

If we suspect or accept that Portia stages the casket test in such a way as to ensure Bassanio's success (Howard 1994: 117), we could also suspect that, as Nerissa implies, they have similarly ensured the failure of undesirable suitors. But if the relationship between Portia and Nerissa is an erotic one, then why does the latter so easily accede to Portia's plans to marry? There are two possible answers which perhaps are both operative: Nerissa may feel that Portia's affection for the remarkably inept Bassanio may be no threat to the feelings the two women have for each other; and/or Nerissa may assume that she will continue as Portia's servant and that her position – both geographical and emotional – transcends and remains unaffected by marriage.

Portia and Bassanio marry with little evidence of real love on either side. Portia apparently has a passing acquaintance with Bassanio (*The Merchant of Venice*, I.ii.94–101), and he makes no secret of the fact that he is hanging out for a rich wife (I.i.161). The strangely fairy-tale aspect of the casket lottery seems the only reason they marry. It is almost as though the lottery becomes a metaphor of the arranged marriages necessary to keep early modern society in motion. As Jean Howard has said of Beatrice and Benedick (1994: 65–6, 68, 71), Portia and Bassanio marry because they must. And, not surprisingly and with a similar lack of previous affection, Nerissa and Graziano also marry. Their union seems to be simply a parody of Portia and Bassanio's. While these matches are conveniently made, there are few Shakespearean couples who marry with less of a history of love or previous courtship. Thus it is not surprising that the women go off to help Antonio without telling their husbands of their plan. Used to plotting and acting together, Portia and Nerissa are as much a "unit" as Bassanio and Graziano or Bassanio and Antonio. Thus the trial scene can be considered not so much a dramatization of Portia's bravura skills in the courtroom as an example of Portia's alliance with *Nerissa* to solve whatever problems arise. Just as she plotted with her servant to reject or accept suitors, Portia similarly plots with her – *not her husband* – to save Antonio. And the fact that Antonio is Bassanio's friend/lover has no effect on her disinclination to include Bassanio in the plan.

Portia's success in court can, of course, be read as a means by which she binds Bassanio to her by saving Antonio. I do not necessarily want to challenge that reading – because I do agree with it – but I want to expand it somewhat to include Nerissa's presence. Portia could just as easily have gone off alone – or with a male groom for protection – to plead Antonio's case. But she does not; she chooses to go with Nerissa. The pattern of working with, or counting on, Nerissa is reinforced in the ring-trick. Portia may have instigated it, but Nerissa doubles it by demanding Graziano's ring for the lawyer's servant. Thus the women become mirror images of each other here, duplicating each other's actions for the sole purpose of gaining control over their husbands.

Even the rhetoric of describing how each woman lost the ring in bed is similar (V.i.257–61). We know, of course, that the women did not sleep with *actual* men. The question remains, though: did the women sleep with each other as men? Did Nerissa sleep with the lawyer, or Portia with the clerk? Perhaps they did. Does this mean, then, that they are unfaithful to their husbands, or simply unfaithful to themselves? Like many early modern women, Portia could have been in the habit of sleeping with her servant. Will, or how will, these sleeping arrangements change once Bassanio and Graziano move in? Interestingly, though, the almost communal living arrangements modeled in Belmont at the end of *The Merchant of Venice* suggest that Nerissa and Graziano will continue to live in close proximity to Portia and Bassanio. Such living arrangements will certainly allow Portia and Nerissa to continue their mistress–servant relationship, but might they not sever that between Bassanio and Antonio? Early modern marriage usually meant that the wife traveled away from her family and the friends of her childhood to reside with her husband and his family. Such a dislocation would destroy any pre-marital erotic relationships a woman had with another woman whose marriage would similarly uproot her. A woman servant, however, might well move with her mistress and continue to serve her throughout her marriage and in her new location. *The Merchant of Venice* rings a change on this theme by uprooting Bassanio from Venice and perhaps destroying his relationship with Antonio. There seems to be no danger that Portia and Nerissa will be separated.

This perhaps temporary, though highly portable, female space is also present in *Antony and Cleopatra*. The Egypt of the woman ruler Cleopatra is remarkably different in character, tone, and realpolitik from the male-dominated Rome of Octavius. Yet even within that more "effeminate" realm lies the still more female space occupied by Cleopatra and her women, Iras and Charmian.[15] The only consistent "male" presence in these scenes is that of the eunuch, Mardian, whose testicular/phallic lack serves to render him female.[16] Within the female space occupied by Cleopatra, Charmian, Iras, and Mardian, conversation revolves around sex, erotic relationships, reminiscent nostalgia for both, and speculation on Antony's sexual doings in Rome. Mardian's contributions to these topics of conversation reinforce his "womanliness."

I want to consider this female-only space of Egypt as similar in kind both to the female space occupied by Titania and her votress and to the "lesbian" void. I do not deny that there is more textual evidence to suggest an erotic relationship between Titania and the votress – (II.i.124–37) plus Titania's desire to hold onto the Indian boy for his mother's sake – than between Cleopatra and Charmian and Iras, but this is not to imply that *no* evidence of woman–woman eroticism occurs in *Antony and Cleopatra*. Cleopatra's fixation on Antony may seem to reify heterosexist interpretations of the play that deny the queen any "lesbian" outlet for her libido.[17] I would argue otherwise. The extremely high level of erotic rhetoric when the three women are together – which often includes their wishes for multiple lovers and sexual encounters (I.ii) or reflections upon Mardian's inability to satisfy them phallically (I.v, II.v) – suggests that they are ripe for *any* kind of sexual activity with *any* kind of (perhaps even multiple) partners. In fact, in the scene with the Soothsayer (I.ii), Iras reveals that she and Charmian share the same bed: (to Charmian) "Go, you wild bedfellow, you cannot soothsay" (44). The term "bedfellow" seems currently to hold a somewhat vexed position in terms of Shake-spearean glosses. Some editors see the word as having no sexual connotations, defining it as "close friend" (Gurr, II.ii.8n), or stating merely "it was common for men to share a bed" (Shakespeare 1997: 1467, II.ii, n1) during the early modern period. Gordon Williams, however, defines the word as "sexual partner" (1997: 41), while one *OED* def-inition identifies a bedfellow as "a husband or wife; [or] a concubine."[18] It is interest-ing to note that Iras calls Charmian a "wild bedfellow," an adjective Walter Cohen glosses as "licentious" (Shakespeare 1997: 2631). Now, Iras's use of "wild" could refer to Charmian's behavior with male lovers. But the line could equally refer to Iras's analy-sis of Charmian's erotic behavior as *her* bedfellow, behavior quite consistent with the heady erotic atmosphere of the female space within Cleopatra's court. In this scene Charmian also agrees that she "love[s] long life better than figs" (28). Cohen glosses the word as "genitalia" generally (Shakespeare 1997: 2631, n4), though Williams specifically identifies "fig" with vagina by indicating that, in Italian, *ficone* means both a lover of figs and of women.[19] Charmian could, of course, be referring to an affection for her own genitalia, and the pleasure they bring her, but the line could equally refer to the figs/vaginas of her female lovers. What I want to suggest here is that, even if there are no incontrovertible descriptions of woman–woman eroticism in this play, the highly charged erotic space of Cleopatra's court strongly suggests such eroticism. And if Cleopatra's servants/ladies-in-waiting engage in erotic encounters with each other, it is quite possible that, in a space where these servants dress their mistress (V.ii) and perform many intimate duties for her, erotic encounters may develop with the queen of Egypt as well.

The question of what exactly Iras and Charmian do together in the bed they share as "fellows" brings us again to early modern sleeping arrangements. I want to look at perhaps the most well-known use of the word in a Shakespeare play: Exeter's condemnation of Lord Scrope in the "traitor scene" (II.ii) of *Henry V*. The three lords who begin the scene are upset by discovery of the treason, but Exeter is particularly concerned about

> the man that was his [Henry's] bedfellow,
> Whom he hath dulled and cloyed with gracious favours –
> That he should for a foreign purse so sell
> His sovereign's life to death and treachery
>
> (II.ii.8–11)

This indignant speech may simply refer to the fact that a courtier, a "lord-in-waiting," was intimate enough with the king to share his bed – a common fact in the early modern period. Yet if the word is to be taken here as simply referring to a close friend or companion, how can we explain Henry's excessive condemnation of Scrope in a speech that runs 48 lines (II.ii.90–139), as compared to the six lines employed to condemn Cambridge, and the two and a half lines that condemn Grey? Henry's exasperation and hyperbole – he likens Scrope's fall from grace to Adam and Eve's (138–9) – suggest an emotion stronger than mere anger at the discovery of treason in his midst, or why not expend a similar amount of lines and emotion on Cambridge and Grey? The use of "bedfellow" in this context, I would argue, implies an erotic relationship between Henry and Scrope.[20]

If we can, in this case, allow "bedfellow" as a term that can mean something like the twenty-first-century term "lover" as well as "intimate friend" or "companion," then we need to allow the same definitional expansion as regards application of the term to women. Thus Benedick's question to Beatrice after Hero "dies" in the chapel – "Lady, were you her bedfellow last night?" (IV.i.146) – should cause us to wonder about the extent of the relationship between the two cousins, especially in light of Beatrice's response to Benedick: "No, truly not, although until last night / I have this twelvemonth been her bedfellow" (IV.i.147–8). Leonato's response to this declaration – "Confirmed, confirmed" (149) – is usually read as confirmation of "the fact" that, if Beatrice were not in Hero's bed the previous night, her empty place could easily have been taken by a man. But I want to suggest that it is possible to read Leonato's response somewhat differently. Even though it may have been common practice for people to share beds, the accusation of Hero as a "strumpet" may be "confirmed" because she has shared a bed for a year with Beatrice. What might, previously, have been assumed to be "innocent" – in the sense of non-erotic – sharing, might now need to be reconsidered as erotic, non-chaste behavior. In other words, if Hero could have been unchaste with a strange man the night before her wedding, then it is entirely possible that she has been unchaste with her cousin – a notorious opponent of marriage – for at least a year previously. Thus an accused unchastity with a man allows Leonato to review a previously unconsidered – or innocently considered – bed-sharing and pronounce it equally unchaste. Presumed sexual activity with a man has now cast the "lesbian" void into relief and made it visible.

A similar relationship between woman–man and woman–woman eroticism can be observed in the diary of Lady Anne Clifford. In one of the entries for 1603, before she was married, she writes,

> my Mother and I, my Aunt of Bath, and my Cozen Fraunces, went to North-hall (my Mother being extreame angrie wth me for rideinge before wth Mr. Meuerell), wher my Mother in hir anger comaunded yt I should Lie in a chamber alone, wch I could not endure; but my Cozen Fraunces got the key of my chamber, and lay wth me, wch was the first tyme I loved hir so verie well. (Nichols 1828: I, 196, cited in Mallin unpublished).

While the text is not as clear as we might wish, it seems that Lady Anne's behavior in "rideinge before" – ahead of her mother? before Meverell in the saddle on the same horse? – was considered transgressive and worthy of the punishment of sleeping alone. Interestingly, this is something Lady Anne "could not endure," perhaps because she has been used to sharing her bed. Cousin Fraunces, though, comes to the rescue by getting hold of the key and spending the night with Lady Anne. The climax of this revelation is that the incident represented "the first tyme I loved hir [Fraunces] so verie well." Lady Anne, denied a bedfellow – and we might ask whether she had a "usual" one? who it was? or whether she shared her bed with various companions depending upon preference or geography? – is bereft. Fraunces arrives with a key to lock the two women into a secure bedchamber – a "lesbian" void – and Lady Anne proceeds, for the first time, to love Fraunces "so verie well." The rhetoric of this entry suggests that erotic activity occurred between the cousins, though for the first time. However, the entry also shows that Lady Anne was not a stranger to a shared bed, though there is no way of telling from this entry who her previous companions were, whether she loved them, or to what degree she loved them in relation to Cousin Fraunces.[21] That Fraunces is so willing to come to her cousin's rescue and that the cousins create a loving and void space for themselves serve as interesting glosses to the action that occurs in *Much Ado About Nothing*. Also, the "heterosexual" flirtation with Mr. Meverell has no effect on the relationship between the cousins or the affection they show each other. In fact, it might be said that the woman–man flirtation "provokes" the woman–woman erotic encounter, since it causes Lady Anne's mother to lock up her daughter, thus "creating" the "lesbian" void space that Fraunces exploits once she has obtained the key. We might thus read the incident with Mr. Meverell in the same way that Leonato seems to read Hero's supposed encounter with the stranger at her window: as evidence that confirms a much stronger, more important "lesbian" bond.

Accepting the erotic relationship between Beatrice and Hero – hidden though it may be in the "lesbian" void – reveals a way of dealing with a persistent problem in *Much Ado About Nothing* criticism: why has Margaret agreed to the plot to condemn Hero? The text is not very clear on the reason. When accusing Borachio, Leonato vows he

> Shall face to face be brought to Margaret,
> Who I believe was packed in all this wrong,
> Hired to it by your brother
>
> (V.i.282–4)

The old governor's assessment of the situation makes sense. Underpaid servants could always be bribed ("hired") to act against their mistresses or masters. Yet for some odd reason – his response is certainly out of character – Borachio protects Margaret from Leonato's charge:

> No, by my soul, she was not,
> Nor knew not what she did when she spoke to me,
> But always hath been just and virtuous
> In anything I do know by her.
>
> (V.i.284–7)

But his protestations of Margaret's innocence make no sense. Borachio absolves Margaret of guilt by stating she "knew not what she did" when she spoke to him. Yet the deception would have been impossible were Margaret totally guiltless. Her conversation with Borachio occurred "betwixt twelve and one" (IV.i.83) at Hero's chamber window (83, 90). Granted the readiness with which Claudio and Don Pedro believe in Hero's unchastity is determined by their own male insecurities and fears of having their honors contaminated through alliance with a known slut. Yet for the deception to work, it must be believable. Since it is quite dark in Sicily between midnight and 1 a.m., measures must have been taken first, to ensure that the woman who played Hero was accepted *as* Hero and, second, to ensure that the woman was *not* thought to be anyone else. Stationing Don Pedro and Claudio some distance from the house so they could not make out voices distinctly and having Margaret appear backlit at Hero's real bedroom window would go far to advancing the deception. Yet while such a "staging" could convince the watchers that Margaret could be Hero, nothing except the specific room definitely identifies the woman as Hero. Only by wearing Hero's actual clothes (Howard 1994: 62) or answering to "Hero!" could Margaret completely deceive Don Pedro and Claudio. But by doing either she is hardly the "just and virtuous" woman Borachio claims. Even if we eliminate responding to the name "Hero" as so overt an attempt at deception that Margaret could not have avoided knowing about it, then we are still left with trying to explain why she is blameless even though she wears Hero's clothes and appears at her window.

I do not believe the character Margaret is blameless. The *dramatis personae* identify both her and Ursula as "waiting-gentlewomen attendant on Hero" (Shakespeare 1997: 1389), and Margaret is further identified in the text by Borachio as "the Lady Hero's gentlewoman" (III.iii.127), and by Leonato as a gentlewoman (V.iv.10). Margaret is not a lower-class servant and is thus less apt to betray Hero for money as Leonato suggests (V.i.284). But as a waiting-gentlewoman, a lady-in-waiting, Margaret would have had access to Hero's chamber, to her clothes, and to her body. Like Alice, Iras, and Charmian, and perhaps Paulina, Margaret would have been intimate with Hero's wardrobe and with her body. Ladies-in-waiting and ladies of the chamber dressed their mistresses.[22] They were also responsible for other duties perhaps not so elegant, such as dealing with waste products. The most famous holder of such a post was the king's Groom of the Stool, a post which manifested an "exquisite combination of intimacy, degradation, and privilege" (Paster 1993: 32).[23] Yet such a post, especially under Henry VIII, was desired for, as Peter Stallybrass has pointed out in conversation, the Groom of the Stool was *always* granted some totally private time with the king each day. His lips were always guaranteed proximity to the royal ear, even if such occurred only when he was in the act of wiping the royal bottom.

I do not necessarily want to claim that Margaret was Hero's "Groom" of the Stool. I do, however, want to point out that, like Iras and Charmian, she could have been virtually as close and intimate with Hero as was her bedfellow Beatrice. Margaret's intimate encounters with Hero in their own private female space could have become erotic or erotically charged. Or they could not. Hero *could* have rebuffed Margaret's erotic overtures, preferring those of her bedfellow. A rejected Margaret, a jealous Margaret, or simply an unfulfilled Margaret could have "gotten back" at Hero by participating in Don John's plot. She had access to the clothing and location that would "guarantee" her audience's perception of her as her mistress. Borachio's belief in Margaret's virtue and justice could simply be the result of his inability to conceive of any motive she might have for harming Hero. And if Margaret succeeded in eliminating Claudio and getting Hero branded a strumpet, there might be further opportunities for erotic encounters with her mistress once she – like Hermione – entered the void space of her "death."

Early modern "lesbians" are hard to pin down. Sometimes they are ghostly – or "apparitional" (cf. Castle 1993) – appearing at the extreme margins of our field of vision of the early modern period. Sometimes they are "elegaic" (cf. Holstun 1987), appearing only to die – literally, or metaphorically in marriage. Few *obvious* "lesbian" characters appear in early modern texts. But perhaps the reason there are so few is that we do not know exactly where to look for them. And this is my point. Early modern "lesbians" may be invisible simply because we have not yet become competently trained observers. My exploration of the "lesbian void" has been a conscious effort to push the boundaries of our early modern field of vision, to try to "see" the previously invisible, to consider where "lesbians" have been hidden and how we might draw them out of the – consciously or unconsciously constructed – early modern "closet" into which they have been relegated. Part of this closeting has come about as a result of the fears of modern critics – those who want bedfellows to be non-sexual friends and figs to remain solely fruit. Part has resulted simply from a lack of knowledge about where to go to *find* early modern "lesbians." What I have done in this essay is to try to find "lesbians" by broadening my early modern field of vision in two ways: looking more deeply into the semiotics of some words whose definitions have shifted or been modified over time; looking for literal and metaphoric spaces where women who enjoyed erotic encounters with other women could go to experience them. What I have discovered is not so much a "closet" as a "void," but a void that is, paradoxically, full of possibilities.

Notes

1 All references to Shakespeare's plays will be to the Norton edition (1997) and will appear, parenthetically, in the text.

2 Given the fact that "lesbian" does not have an early modern definition that refers to a self-conscious sexuality or sexual identity, I will only employ it with quotation marks and use the term "woman–woman eroticism" to refer to sexual activity between two women.

3 Bray indicates that the history of female homosexuality is "best to be understood as part of the developing recognition of a specifically female sexuality" (1982: 17). Some male authors who explore male–male eroticism in the early modern period do not work with woman–woman desire: Bredbeck (1991); Orgel (1996); Smith (1994). Other male authors – Goldberg (1992); Masten (1997); DiGangi (1997) – raise issues regarding woman–woman desire, though it is not the primary focus of their work. Holstun (1987) and Fisher (unpublished) are the only male authors I know who have written entire essays on woman–woman desire in the English literature of this period.

4 Jankowski (1993, 1996, 1998, 2000). Traub (1992) considers a different kind of "lesbian" invisibility.

5 Both Orlin and Stewart discuss the locks – and their keys – attached to closet doors as a means of ensuring the privacy of the chamber's occupant(s). Orlin indicates that

the presence in the master's closet of the strongbox and money necessitated a lock on the door (1994: 185). Although the mistress's closet would usually not have contained money, it could contain stuffs that were equally valuable, though in a different way: knives, shears, glasses, bottles, conserve jars, sweetmeat barrels, and later sugar, an expensive commodity (Stewart 1995: 82; Fumerton 1991: 125). So, even though both master's and mistress's closets were rooms that could be locked, the gendered nature of their contents meant they were locked for different reasons. In the following discussion I will be concerned primarily with the mistress's closet.

6 Girouard – from the autobiography of Thomas Whythorne (1978: 83) – Stewart (1995: 87–8), and DiGangi (1997: 71, 85) give examples of "heterosexual" mistress–servant relationships. Given evidence of all the various possibilities of master/mistress–servant erotic exchanges, mistress–woman servant erotic exchanges *must* have occurred. I will have more to say about actual erotic relationships between upper-class women later.

7 I am considering the possibility that the older woman could be either mistress *or* servant. Lawrence Stone documents the case of women servants introducing the very young Louis XIII to various kinds of erotic encounters.

8   Calling Paulina a "servant" runs the risk of
    suggesting that the duties a lady-in-waiting
    performs are similar to those of a lower-class
    servant. While I do not in any way want to
    erase the relatively small class distinction
    that existed between Paulina and Hermione
    or Paulina and the First Lady, I also do not
    want to erase the comparatively huge dis-
    tinctions that existed between a character
    like Paulina and one like Nell/Luce (*The
    Comedy of Errors*). Shakespeare's plays provide
    us with *many* kinds of servants occupying
    many class positions. Nell/Luce would prob-
    ably wind up at the bottom of anyone's
    Shakespearean class hierarchy list, but where
    would we rank such "servants" as Maria
    (*Twelfth Night*) or Nerissa (*The Merchant of
    Venice*)? What *is* the difference in rank
    between Titania and her votress or that
    between Cleopatra and Iras and Charmian?
    We *might* be tempted to say that the differ-
    ence in rank between Cleopatra and Iras is *less*
    than that between Hero and Margaret (*Much
    Ado About Nothing*), but there is no clear evi-
    dence to support such a hypothesis beyond a
    feeling that we "know more" about early
    modern "Italian" social formations than we
    do about Ptolemaic Egyptian ones. I do not
    raise this "problem" to suggest that we elim-
    inate all considerations of class when dis-
    cussing women in Shakespeare – because I do
    not think such a stand to be fruitful or useful
    – but simply to point out that, in many cases,
    it is extremely difficult to determine just
    exactly what the relative class positions of
    many Shakespearean mistress–servant pairs
    are. Consequently, questions of whether a
    mistress runs the risk of "debasing" herself by
    having a sexual encounter with a servant are
    often terribly moot. Thus I want to focus not
    so much on what the *exact* class distinction is
    between the members of a mistress–servant
    pair, but rather more on the erotic potential
    that may reside within a relationship that
    may not be completely egalitarian.

9   Fumerton's fascinating analysis of the
    "banquet" and the "void" (1991: esp. ch. 4)
    has sparked my own work in this area, even
    though our foci are somewhat different. She
    is concerned with how the retreat from the
    hall to increasingly more "private" spaces,
    like the "banquet," led to the development
    of early modern subjectivity (esp. 122, 136).
    I am interested in the development of these
    "private" spaces as a means for explaining
    why certain aspects of early modern sexual-
    ity – namely woman–woman eroticism –
    have remained both critically and literarily
    invisible for so long. My brief history of both
    the banquet and the void derives both from
    Fumerton (1991) and her main source,
    Girouard (1978).

10 Hall (1996) brilliantly considers how the
    trade in and use of sugar caused (mostly)
    upper-class women to become complicitous
    in both empire building and the slave trade.

11 Halkett quotes Erasmus, John Dod and
    Robert Cleaver, Henry Smith, and William
    Perkins, who all indicate that marriage is a
    joining of two people into "one flesh" (1970:
    10–11). See also *The Comedy of Errors*,
    II.ii.119–46.

12 Englebrecht's theorization of the lesbian
    self/other-self is one argument in favor of
    "egalitarian" lesbian relationships (Engle-
    brecht 1990). The twentieth-century lesbian
    S-M debates (cf. the essays in Vance 1992 as
    representative) were an example of lesbian
    relationships based upon an unequal power
    relationship.

13 What Olivia (*Twelfth Night*) seems to *enjoy*
    about Viola/Cesario – and later Sebastian –
    may simply be the fact that she/he is con-
    trollable, easily able to be dominated,
    willing to subjugate him/herself to Olivia's
    superior class, age, and wealth.

14 See Paster (1993: ch. 1, esp. 52–63) on how
    this female space in *A Chaste Maid in Cheap-
    side* threatens the male characters.

15 Whether Antony is in Rome or in Egypt,
    many Egyptian scenes consist primarily
    of Cleopatra and her women with the occa-
    sional presence of soothsayers or messengers:
    I.ii, I.iii, I.v, II.v, III.iii, IV.xiv, V.ii. Even
    when Antony is present, there are occasions
    – like III.xi and IV.xvi – when Cleopatra and
    her women still may be considered as a
    "unit."

16 Italian *castrati* had their testicles removed. A man could also be rendered a eunuch by "complete" castration – having both the testicles *and* the penis removed – as were many eunuchs in Byzantium and China. Lack of a penis, or the inability of the organ to achieve an erection once the testicles were removed, would render a man "woman." See Callaghan (1996).

17 As Sinfield (1996) argues, a similar kind of heterosexist bias denies the male–male eroticism and the traffic in boys present in *The Merchant of Venice*.

18 Gurr's gloss comes from the New Cambridge edition of *King Henry V* (1992), while Maus's comes from the Norton edition of the same play. The *OED* definition quoted is number 2 for "bedfellow." Number 1 defines the word as "one who shares a bed with another." Bray points out that lack of privacy in the early modern period "usually made who shared a bed with whom a public fact" (1994: 42).

19 Williams indicates that the "obscene" gesture of thrusting the thumb between two of the closed fingers is called a "fig." *Fico* (fig) in Italian is similar to *fica* (vagina), and the thumb and finger gesture "has a genital symbolism" (1997: 124). He sees the fig as described in Charmian's line as a definite vaginal emblem (1997: 124).

20 Branagh makes this situation explicit in his film of *Henry V* (1989). Henry removes his gauntlet to stroke Scrope's cheek with his bare hand and delivers his long speech nose to nose with Scrope while the accused is lying with his back forced down upon a table. Thus the close-up of Henry's face above Scrope's – which obliterates the table and the gathered nobles – parodies a lovers' quarrel in bed with Henry being "top" to Scrope's "bottom." Exeter reinforces Scrope's personal betrayal of Henry by slapping him after he pronounces his arrest (II.ii.143–4), an action not inflicted on the other men.

21 Mallin's paper posits a complex and far-reaching set of woman–woman erotic bonds involving not only Lady Anne but Queen Anne and Lady Hertford, all of which occur within what can only be considered a "lesbian" void surrounding the queen's court (Mallin unpublished).

22 Those of us who are twenty-first-century non-aristocrats can have no idea of what it would have been like to be dressed by an army of servants. Some sense of what might have occurred can be glimpsed in the opening scenes of Stephen Frears's film *Dangerous Liaisons*, in which two aristocrats, the Marquise de Merteuil and the Vicomte de Valmont, are being dressed. I want to look at the Marquise. We see her hair being combed, her face being made up, earrings being placed into her ears, her bodice being sewn to her corset, the back of her dress being laced up. During this time the Marquise does nothing actively to dress herself or to aid in the process beyond standing up for the lacing. She, and her body, are passively acted upon by a corps of maids engaged in the production of a clothed, aristocratic masterpiece. The Marquise rarely responds at all to the activity around her, with the one exception of a deep smile of pleasure when her dress is sewn to her corset aside her full breasts. What are we to make of both the smile and the army of servants, one of whom must have produced that smile?

This scene contrasts completely to any experience I – or anyone I know personally – has ever had. Yet it was a common situation for any aristocratic woman in mid-eighteenth-century France – when the film is set – or, indeed, in late sixteenth–early seventeenth-century England, when all of Shakespeare's plays were written. What we do not see in the scenes from *Dangerous Liaisons* I alluded to are other, more intimate moments when the servant women make even closer contact with the Marquise's naked body while washing her or aiding her at the water closet.

23 See Paster (1993: ch. 1) on Grooms of the Stool. Paster points out that, unlike her father, Elizabeth I did not have a specific person assigned to this office (1993: 32).

REFERENCES AND FURTHER READING

Alberti, L. B. 1971: *The Albertis of Florence. Leon Battista Alberti's "Della Familigia."* Trans. Guido A. Guarino. Lewisburg, PA: Bucknell University Press.

Branagh, K. (dir.) 1989: *Henry V.* With Kenneth Branagh. CBS/Fox.

Bray, A. 1982: *Homosexuality in Renaissance England.* London: Gay Men's Press.

—— 1994: "Homosexuality and the Signs of Male Friendship in Elizabethan England." In J. Goldberg (ed.), *Queering the Renaissance.* Durham, NC, and London: Duke University Press, 40–61.

Bredbeck, G. W. 1991: *Sodomy and Interpretation: Marlowe to Milton.* Ithaca and London: Cornell University Press.

Callaghan, D. 1996: "The Castrator's Song: Female Impersonation on the Early Modern Stage." *Journal of Medieval and Early Modern Studies,* 26, 2, 322–52.

Castle, T. 1993: *The Apparitional Lesbian: Female Homosexuality and Modern Culture.* New York: Columbia University Press.

Day, A. 1592: *The English Secretorie.* London.

DiGangi, M. 1997: *The Homoerotics of Early Modern Drama.* Cambridge: Cambridge University Press.

Englebrecht, P. J. 1990: "'Lifting belly is a language': The Postmodern Lesbian Subject," *Feminist Studies,* 16, 85–114.

Fisher, W. unpublished: "Home Alone: Placing Women's Homoerotic Desire in the Social Order." Unpublished paper.

Frears, S. (dir.) 1988: *Dangerous Liaisons.* With Glenn Close and John Malkovich. Warner Bros.

Fumerton, P. 1991: *Cultural Aesthetics: Renaissance Literature and the Practice of Social Ornament.* Chicago and London: University of Chicago Press.

Girouard, M. 1978: *Life in the English Country House: A Social and Architectural History.* New Haven and London: Yale University Press.

Goldberg, J. 1992: *Sodometries: Renaissance Texts, Modern Sexualities.* Stanford: Stanford University Press.

Halkett, J. 1970: *Milton and the Idea of Matrimony.* New Haven and London: Yale University Press.

Hall, K. 1996: "Culinary Spaces, Colonial Spaces: The Gendering of Sugar in the Seventeenth Century." In V. Traub, M. L. Kaplan, and D. Callaghan (eds.), *Feminist Readings of Early Modern Culture: Emerging Subjects.* Cambridge: Cambridge University Press, 168–90.

Holstun, J. 1987: "'Will you rent our ancient love asunder?': Lesbian Elegy in Donne, Marvell, and Milton." *English Literary History,* 54, 835–67.

Howard, J. E. 1994: *The Stage and Social Struggle.* London and New York: Routledge.

Jankowski, T. A. 1993: "'The scorne of savage people': Virginity as Forbidden Sexuality in John Lyly's *Love's Metamorphosis.*" *Renaissance Drama,* 24, 123–53.

—— 1996: "'Where there can be no cause of affection': Redefining Virgins, Their Desires, and Their Pleasures." In V. Traub, M. Lindsay Kaplan, D. Callaghan (eds.), *Feminist Readings of Early Modern Culture: Emerging Subjects.* Cambridge: Cambridge University Press, 253–74.

—— 1998: "Pure Resistance: Queer(y)ing Virginity in William Shakespeare's *Measure for Measure* and Margaret Cavendish's *The Convent of Pleasure.*" *Shakespeare Studies,* 26, 218–55.

—— 2000: *Pure Resistance: Queer Virginity in Early Modern English Drama.* Philadelphia: University of Pennsylvania Press.

Mallin, E. unpublished: "'I loved hir so verie well': Lady Anne Clifford's Lesbian Adolescence." Unpublished paper.

Masten, J. 1997: *Textual Intercourse: Collaboration, Authorship, and Sexualities in Renaissance Drama.* Cambridge: Cambridge University Press.

Nichols, J. (ed.) 1828: *The Progresses, Processions, and Magnificent Festivities of King James the First.* 5 vols. London; rptd. New York: Burt Franklin, n.d.

Orgel, S. 1996: *Impersonations: The Performance of Gender in Shakespeare's England.* Cambridge: Cambridge University Press.

Orlin, L. C. 1994: *Private Matters and Public Culture in Post-Reformation England.* Ithaca and London: Cornell University Press.

Paster, G. K. 1993: *The Body Embarrassed: Drama*

and the Disciplines of Shame in Early Modern England. Ithaca: Cornell University Press.

Shakespeare, W. 1997: *The Norton Shakespeare.* Ed. S. Greenblatt, W. Cohen, J. E. Howard, and K. E. Maus. New York and London: W. W. Norton.

Sinfield, A. 1996: "How to Read *The Merchant of Venice* Without Being Heterosexist." In T. Hawkes (ed.), *Alternative Shakespeares, 2.* London and New York: Routledge, 122–39.

Smith, B. R. 1994: *Homosexual Desire in Shakespeare's England: A Cultural Poetics.* Chicago and London: University of Chicago Press.

Stewart, A. 1995: "The Early Modern Closet Discovered." *Representations*, 50, 76–100.

Stone, L. 1977: *The Family, Sex, and Marriage in England, 1500–1800.* New York: Harper and Row.

Thompson, P. 1979: *Seventeenth-Century Interior Decoration in England, France, and Holland.* New Haven and London: Yale University Press. (Work originally published 1978.)

Traub, V. 1992: "The (In)significance of 'Lesbian' Desire in Early Modern England." In Susan Zimmerman (ed.), *Erotic Politics: Desire on the Renaissance Stage.* New York and London: Routledge, 150–69.

Vance, C. S. (ed.) 1992: *Pleasure and Danger: Exploring Female Sexuality.* London: Pandora. (Work originally published by Routledge and Kegan Paul 1989.)

Williams, G. 1997: *A Glossary of Shakespeare's Sexual Language.* London and Atlantic Highlands, NJ: Athlone.

17

Duncan's Corpse

Susan Zimmerman

I

In the hallucinatory realm of Shakespeare's *Macbeth*, sex, violence, and blood are inextricably meshed in a tragic mode that represents the netherside of civilized order. If signification is structured by means of concepts that safely situate phenomena in categories – male/female, sacramental/diabolic, familiar/alien, living/dead – then *Macbeth* is about the tenuousness of these distinctions and the psychic and social horror that ensues when they collapse. As several scholars have noted (see especially Garber 1987; and Willbern 1986), the text is pervaded – one might say obsessed – with the *un*categorizable, the marginal, the in-between: androgynous witches who disappear into the air, "sightless couriers" who ride the winds, nightmarish ghosts, dreams, and illusions that blanket over the reassuring tangibleness of stones, sounds, and corporeal life. In effect, *Macbeth* represents a realm that is worse than death because – at least in the imagination of its protagonist – nothing is totally obliterated, nothing is final.

It will be the argument of this essay that Duncan's corpse emblematizes and reinforces the indeterminacy of Macbeth's own horrific vision, and that this corpse functions in addition as a composite image for the representation of gender indeterminacy in both Macbeth and Lady Macbeth. In unpacking the multiple meanings of Duncan's corpse in Shakespeare's text, my primary focus will be on its connections with early modern attitudes toward the dead, as seen, specifically, in funerary practices and in the new public practice of anatomical dissection. However, I would like to begin my analysis ahistorically, with an anthropological perspective on the significance of the corpse as the foremost emblem of the primal violence of nature.[1]

In the memorable phrase of the anthropologist Georges Bataille, nature functions as an "orgy of annihilation" (1986: 61); it is a relentless killing machine that orgiastically reproduces as part of the killing process. The "natural" cycle of death and reproduction is, in fact, violent, terrifying, a "virulent activity of corruption" (1986: 56) that the human subject would hold at bay. Paradoxically, however, the generative power of corruption and decay, as signified preeminently in the corpse, also exerts a strong attraction for the human subject. This erotic dimension in the subject's apprehension of putrefaction may resonate with the "unmistakable links between excreta, decay, and sexuality" (1986: 58) in the channels of the living human body; but Bataille also locates eroticism in the subject's fascination with the corpse's indeterminate status, its absence of definable form, of identity. In her own anthropological theory, which has many affinities with that of Bataille, Mary Douglas coins the word "dirt" to designate all such marginal being (including the corpse) which escapes logical categorization, and which exerts an attraction/repulsion by virtue of its indeterminacy (1991: 160–1, *passim*). Douglas contends further that "dirt" is often associated ritualistically with the creative potency and menstrual blood of the female (1991: 96); these female attributes point back, in turn, to the violent power that inheres in the cosmos, beyond human control, and ultimately beyond human signification.[2]

In this theoretical framework, then, "nature" signifies a violent, generative power, mindless and undifferentiated, that kills and reproduces simultaneously: not only is this power uncontrollable, but insofar as it operates so as to erase difference – to reproduce without reference to gender, to blur the distinction between living and dead – it is literally indescribable. Thus the corpse's emblematic significance in the cultural matrix of most societies not only testifies to the universal experience of death, but also to the subject's ambivalent recognition of, and attraction to, the annihilative/generative properties that constitute "nature." To *categorize* such power is to partially displace its fearsomeness, which in patriarchal societies is usually effected through the demonization of the reproductive female.

These anthropological concepts would seem to intersect usefully with the ideological inscription of the corpse in the cultural matrix of early modern England. Post-Reformation England was, in fact, profoundly invested in reformulating the signification of the corpse in theologically specific ways. The distinction between "living" and "dead" took on new urgency in the Protestant attack on idolatry, an issue that quickly became the lightning rod in the Reformist effort to usurp Catholic ritual and practice. As described in Protestant religious discourse, idolatry, or the human construction and institution of false gods, was thought to originate in man's perverse desire to demystify the deity, and signified the failure to distinguish between spheres of being – the dead, or inanimate image was mistaken for the living spirit. The Protestant destruction of images and relics (which of course were parts of dead bodies) was thus symptomatic of a more far-reaching effort to eradicate an institutionally inscribed and enforced mode of perception. In effect, Protestantism undertook an ideological transformation in which the flesh and the spirit would be demarcated as separate – even opposed – categories.[3]

In this portentous context, the newly dead posed a virtually intractable problem. Unamenable to physical destruction like the statues and artifacts of Catholic ritual, the corpse foregrounded the flesh/spirit dilemma in a way that was at once universal and intensely personal. Thus the attempt by the Tudors to supersede the Sarum Manual by prescribing new funerary practices (disseminated in successive editions of the Book of Common Prayer) was not wholly successful. The more elaborate rituals of the Manual had been an integral part of communal life for over a century (Litten 1991: 148–55), and these rituals acknowledged and sought to contain the power of the corpse. Fear of this power was ubiquitous, as witnessed in techniques for dressing the dead, in folk customs surrounding the burial process, in the grotesque sculptures of the northern European transi tombs, and in the still-pervasive, erotic iconography of the *danse macabre*. Despite the efforts of the Reformist movement to quell it, the quasi-sentient corpse of English popular culture remained a powerful presence in the communal imagination.[4]

In addition, the emblematic power of the corpse took on new life, as it were, in the socially divisive controversy over the practice of anatomical dissection, recently established in the European arena of the so-called theaters of anatomy.[5] If Protestant religious discourse was compelled to reconceptualize the relationship between body and spirit in opposition to long-standing ritual and belief, so also was medical science, and in the face of similar resistance. The suspicion that in probing the internal secrets of the corpse the new "high priests" of the theaters of anatomy were violating fundamental prohibitions was manifest in both learned and popular culture (Sawday 1995: esp. 54–84). By exploring the boundaries between living and dead, the anatomist presumed to interrogate the mystery of what cannot (or should not) be seen, to challenge divinely ordained orders of being. Significantly, the corpse at the center of the frontispiece of Andreas Vesalius's *De Humani Corporis Fabrica* (published in England in 1545) is that of a woman, and it is literally her womb – the mystery of reproduction itself – which Vesalius the anatomist opens for display. The legitimation of such questionable public practices – like the demystification of idolatry – ultimately depended on establishing the dead as detritus, devoid of informing spirit.

Despite new pressures from religion and science, however, the mysterious power of the corpse, long connected in the popular imagination to the notion of a kind of smothered sentience, or animation, was not easily extinguished. The ensuing tensions between new ideologies and outmoded practices were inevitably exploited by the public theater, and not only because it was the business of this theater to keep its finger on the pulse of the time. Visitations from revenants were the stuff of spectacle and melodrama, both popular fashions in early modern drama, and as a consequence the stage was crowded with corpses, ghosts, and spirits. These representations had literary antecedents to be sure, including Seneca's tragedies, but undoubtedly they also articulated contemporary anxieties, anxieties which may in fact have been partially deflected for the early modern audience (and for us as well?) by the frequently sensationalist style of popular tragedy.

In Shakespeare's *Macbeth*, however, the full, undeflected significance of Duncan's corpse is wholly, horrifically realized, and by means of a dramaturgical mode that is distinctively Shakespeare's own. Undoubtedly, the power of this representation derives in large part from the play's exploitation of the early modern milieu – here, in particular, the popular discomfort with official agendas for neutralizing the power of the corpse. But Shakespeare's tragedy seems deliberately to tap these tensions in order to enlarge them, to suggest a more fearsome, elemental power (like Bataille's "nature") that is undifferentiated (beyond individuality and gender), and undefined (beyond signification). Thus in *Macbeth*, the most horrific aspect of Duncan's corpse is the indeterminacy of its representation. It is an absent corpse, never visible on the stage, amplified symbolically by its very invisibility, and by its assimilation of both "male" and "female" principles. The pervasive power of Duncan's corpse is fully and finally invested only in the "fatal vision" of Macbeth himself – a vision which obliterates life because it obliterates difference.

II

If *Macbeth* dramatizes "a series of taboo border crossings" (Garber 1987: 91), a phantasmagorical realm of witches, nightmarish apparitions, cannibalism, and thickening light, it is Duncan's corpse more than any other interstitial emblem in the play that both defines the border between the licit and the taboo and simultaneously destroys this border, drowns it, in "the multitudinous seas" of his unstaunchable blood. In a kind of ironic inversion, the play takes its metaphoric life chiefly from the blood of Duncan's dead body. The power of this blood, as Shakespeare constructs it, is on one hand its amplitude, its capacity to engross so much meaning; and on the other its precision in emblematizing the complementary nightmares of Macbeth and Lady Macbeth. But as we shall see, the paradoxical potency of Duncan's corpse and Duncan's blood was in a fundamental sense already deeply inscribed in the cultural consciousness of Shakespeare's England.

In her study of the development of the corpse-related practices of embalming, postmortem examination, and anatomical dissection in early modern Europe, Katherine Park distinguishes between the customs of Italy and those of the northern countries, including England. According to Park, both the private, diagnostic postmortem and the public, illustrative dissection met little resistance in late medieval Italy because of the Italian belief in "a quick and radical separation of body and soul" at death: as a shell or memorial to the living person, the body could be put to practical or scientific use without violating the "personhood" of the deceased.[6] In the north, on the other hand, death was envisaged "as an extended and gradual process," more or less concomitant with putrefaction. It could take up to a year for the corpse to decompose, to become a skeleton, during which time it was perceived as "active, sensitive, or semi-animate, [and] possessed of a gradually fading life" or "personhood" (Park 1994b: 115).[7] In this interim, the corpse had the power to pollute and also to torment the living (as did vampires, for example), but the "vital spirits" of the recently dead could also produce an elixir for life, the so-called *mummia* (Park 1994b: 116). The corpse was therefore an object of both fear and reverence in northern Europe, and it inspired what Philippe Ariès calls "an iconography of the macabre" (1981: 110) in the late medieval period.

This iconography of the north demonstrates a preoccupation with putrefaction, very possibly exacerbated by outbreaks of the plague and the accompanying proliferation of rotting corpses (Cohen 1973: 27–9; Neill 1997: 19–22). It is readily apparent in the graphic imagery of the popular sermon, and in other religious literature, but is perhaps most dramatically manifested in the bizarre sculptures of the transi tombs, and in the disturbing eroticism of the *danse macabre*. The transi sculptures, which date from the late fourteenth century and first appear in England in 1425, represent decaying corpses with protruding intestines in the process of being consumed by snakes, worms (these were thought to generate spontaneously from the body's "manure"), lizards, and frogs. In order to emphasize the inextricability of life and death, the sculptor often provided two figures situated above and below the coffin, one depicting the decomposing body of the deceased and the other his/her fully clothed figure; alternatively, a single sculpture was sometimes divided so that the putrefying half was juxtaposed to the intact and living form (Cohen 1973: esp. 38–47).

The violent and voyeuristic imagery of the transi tombs – particularly the horrific detailing of vermiculation[8] – had a ghoulish counterpart in the "grim coupling," the "shaking of the sheets" of the *danse macabre* (Neill 1997: 75). In the erotic iconography of the Basel *Totentanz*, for example, the multiple figures of the skeleton-lover Death – a series of "prancing cadavers" (Neill 1997: 74), including one that is partially fleshed – seek to copulate with victims of both genders. Death's "absent genitalia" are rendered variously, at times "chastely" concealed, at other times revealed as "stripped" by "worms of corruption," and in one instance Death's loins are adorned with the "obscene simulacra . . . [of] shin-bone and skull" (Neill 1997: 76). As "a revel of monstrous uncreation," a copulation that generates food for worms, the death-dance, like the vermiculation of the transi tombs, graphically identified "the vicious place of begetting as the fountainhead of death" (Neill 1997: 77).

This iconographic blurring of the boundaries between putrefaction and reproduction underscores Park's contention that the corpse in northern Europe was not viewed as wholly dead: to be rendered fleshless, beyond the process of consumption and generation, took time. Accordingly, the preparation of the corpse for burial functioned as a kind of containment: "in the north . . . the dead body was tightly sewed into a cloth shroud . . . and, increasingly, beginning in the fourteenth century, shut up in a wooden coffin" (Park 1994b: 118), as opposed to its sometimes sumptuous display in Italy. Ironically, embalming, which was limited to persons of importance, was an effort to *prolong* the physical integrity of the deceased (usually for practical reasons, as, for example, a state funeral),[9] but in effect, the temporary staunching of the process of putrefaction succeeded only in extending the liminal power of the corpse (Park 1994a: 6). In general, northern European burial customs, especially those deriving from popular tradition, were designed to immobilize and demystify the corpse, and to prevent its remigration. Thus it was common practice to ring bells and make other kinds of noise; to stop clocks and cover mirrors; to tie the feet of the shroud and sprinkle the corpse with salt to prevent it from walking; and to assume the sins of the deceased through the ritual of "sin-eating" – that is, the consumption (usually by a poor person) of bread and beer that had been in direct contact with corpse or coffin (Richardson 1963: 9, 26–7; Gittings 1984: 135–56; Cressy 1997: 421–5).

This wrapping up and shutting down of the corpse was complicated, however, both literally and metaphorically, by the difficulty of containing its great quantity of fluids, especially its blood. The foul liquids produced by moldering bodies (partially absorbed through sawdust and bran in the case of coffined corpses [Litten 1991: 92]), were partly composed of "dead" blood, but the oxymoronic concept of blood divested of its vivifying power was difficult to grasp, at least by the popular imagination. Thus the beliefs in *mummia*, in the notion of the corpse as contagious, that is, able to transmit death, and the expectation that the corpse of a murder victim would start to bleed again if the murderer touched it (Gittings 1984: 108–9; see also Muir's edition of *Macbeth* [Shakespeare 1957: 100, n25]). Such notions were at least indirectly reinforced by Galenic medical theory, which privileged blood as the primary bodily concoction resulting from the transmutation of food and drink, a concoction that not only stimulated the production of other life-sustaining bodily fluids but also enabled the body's reproductive agency (Laqueur 1990: 38–42, *passim*; Paster 1993: 68–84, *passim*). Blood was, then, the primary symbol of a nourishing, *generative* "nature," but the corpse served as reminder that "nature" also figured as cannibal, converting, in a further transformative process, the "dead" blood of the deceased into the life-sustaining fluids of other creatures. Paradoxically, then, the blood of the corpse signified past and future potencies – vivifying fluid as it was and as it would be, mysteriously shifting between temporal states of being.

Blood as elemental nutrient also figured of course in the Christian feast of the Eucharist, a ritual which in effect raised the paradox of natural process to the level of the sacerdotal and invested it with redemptive power. In the "symbolic cannibalism" (Bynum 1991: 185) of the Eucharist, made possible by the mystery of transubstantiation – or the phenomenon by which Christ was materially present in the substances of bread and wine – the faithful consumed and ingested the incarnated deity. Thus the Christian religion appropriated corporeal process in a sacramental system that theoretically transcended it: at the center of the religion was a deity who was at once fully human and material (subject to death), and fully divine and immaterial (not subject to death, or incorruptible); further, in an act which served as an analogue to Christ's Incarnation, the ordinary Christian in-corporated (or fused with) the body and the blood of the man/God, and was thereby redeemed, that is, immortalized. Given this theological underpinning, Christian ritual consistently foregrounded metaphors of bodily process, especially cannibalistic feasting, which helped to displace anxieties in the faithful about the ultimate consumption of their own bodies. The elaborate eating and drinking (by rich and poor alike) that Gittings identifies as the central event in the early modern funeral (1984: 154–9), especially, perhaps, the "sin-eating" of debased forms of bread and "wine," thus reinforced the formalized ritual of the sacramental feast. Presumably, by communally *celebrating* the process of consumption, both within liturgical ritual and outside it, mourners sought to disempower the fearsome feeding taking place concomitantly in the corpse.

Christian iconography also foregrounded blood as reproductive agent by collapsing gender boundaries in its depiction of Christ the savior. Thus the crucified body of Christ gave birth through the bloody wound in his side to the Church (Adam and Eve were frequently depicted beneath the cross, receiving the stream of redemptive fluid). This "delivery" was prefigured by Christ's own birth, and further in the cutting and bleeding of his foreskin at the circumcision (Steinberg 1983); and it anticipated the reenactment of Christ's sacrifice in the sacrament of the Eucharist. Such linkages in sacramental symbolism imbued Christ's blood with a double efficacy: not only did this blood blur the boundaries between the material and the spiritual, as in the Eucharist, but between male and female as well: blood as nurture ("mother's milk") and blood as power (potency inherent in the product of the cut foreskin) were inextricable. Moreover, representations of "Jesus as Mother" frequently featured bleeding breasts which fed the Christian subject – like Adam and Eve at the foot of the cross – with the blood of life (Bynum 1982: *passim*; 1991: 79–118).

With respect to the reproductive agency of blood, Galenic medical theory once again provided secular reinforcement for Christian paradox. Because body fluids in Galen's system (blood, semen, milk, sweat, etc.), were produced by the body's transmutation of food, they were porous, fungible, and not wholly sex-specific (Laqueur 1990: 35). As a consequence, distinctions between male and female blood and their reproductive potentialities depended on degrees of heat and of refinement that were not always readily determinable. Moreover, the transformative agency of blood made its functions difficult to categorize: for example, "breast milk was the purified form of menstrual blood" since both derived from "the same essential substance" (Paster 1993: 39–40). Thus the multiple functions of blood contributed to the breakdown of borders between blood and other fluids, and between the bloods of imperfectly differentiated sexes.[10]

The blood of the *corpse*, however – sustaining agent of the "body-rot" or detritus of both genders – served as the ultimate, encompassing emblem for the mysterious relationships of death to life, killing to giving birth, and male to female. Certainly, as we have seen, funerary practices in early modern England, both liturgical and secular, attempted to "de-animate" the corpse during its period of putrefaction, to disempower its fetishistic presence in the cultural consciousness. But the fear of the corpse's undefinable influence – especially the fear of its indeterminate yet material blood – seems to have been deeply inscribed in the popular imagination, and it is of course probable that the social practices I have outlined here, aimed at defusing this fear, served equally to reinforce it. In any event, it would seem that the pre-Reformation culture of the dead in early modern England is relevant to the theatrical representation of a post-Reformation corpse – Duncan's corpse – because of the tenacity with which popular beliefs about the dead resisted erasure.

But Duncan's corpse is not, after all, the product of a Catholic culture, and Reformation pressures for change in the society's most fundamental systems of belief –

religion and science – were formidable. As I suggested earlier, both these intersecting spheres of early modern society were attempting, at the same historical moment, to reformulate the popular conception of what constituted the "dead." On one hand, Protestant Reformers attacked the idolatrous worship of painted images and relics through state-sanctioned homilies, issued new regulations for the decorations of churches, homes, and tombstones, and, as we have seen, attempted to overhaul "superstitious" attitudes toward the corpse as manifested in Catholic burial and funerary practices. Concurrently, English practitioners of the new anatomy, following the example of Vesalius, whose *Fabrica* was hugely influential, were conducting public anatomies modeled after Italian practices in which anatomical and physiological principles were demonstrated through the dissection and dismembering of corpses. The corpse was thus situated at the center of ideological strife in early modern England, particularly with respect to the furor over the new anatomy.

According to Park, the difference between English and Italian responses to Vesalius and his methods can once again be attributed to the northern European belief in the corpse's liminality. In both countries, the *public* display of an anatomized body was viewed as a violation of personal identity, but in England, where resistance to the new practice was far stronger, "the complete or near-complete disaggregation of the body including the face" (1994a: 8) also violated the invisible, liminal principle that was still believed to animate the corpse.[11] Thus public execution of treasonous felons in England by means of drawing and quartering was deliberately punitive: dismembering the body was meant to symbolize the complete disintegration – physical and spiritual – of the criminal.[12] But the new practice of anatomy, even when restricted to the bodies of criminals (which, of course, was rarely feasible), presupposed that the materiality of *any* corpse was open to empirical investigation because *all* corpses were devoid of animation. This objectification of the "specimen" helped anatomists to justify (at least to themselves) such scandalous practices as procuring bodies by means of grave-robbing, or ghoulishly monitoring the deaths of gibbeted felons, which in the public imagination had a decidedly sacrilegious resonance.[13]

To be sure, the iconography of the frontispiece of the *Fabrica* and of other illustrations of anatomical theaters (Sawday 1995: 68–78, *passim*), attempted to confer a magisterial dignity onto the new profession, presumably as part of a larger effort to contravene public skepticism. Thus the anatomist, invariably situated in these illustrations at or near the central axis of a circular, basilica-like structure, suggested a kind of physician/sovereign/priest – privileged to "open to our gaze . . . the principle of life" concealed within the corpse (Sawday 1995: 70), and to explore the principles of "divine craftsmanship" (Park 1994a: 16). This reinscription of the new science as a quest for mysteries of the body that "were not merely physiological, but moral-ontological" (Neill 1997: 123) was, in fact, largely adopted by members of the English intelligentsia, writing in genres ranging from *belles lettres* to pseudo-scientific treatises, and including such notable figures as Sir Thomas Browne, Helkiah Crooke, Phineas Fletcher, and of course Robert Burton.[14] Collectively, the texts of these writers represent a somewhat awkward effort to accommodate empirical method while simultaneously insisting on "occluded meanings" that lay "deep within the fabric of the body" (Neill 1997: 125). Such a measured, if qualified, assessment of anatomical practice by influential thinkers would seem to have little in common with popular outrage over the medical violation of the corpse.

But the insistence in these writings on the body's *occluded* meanings – meanings not visible to the ocular investigative techniques of the new science, but secret, hidden, mystifyingly intangible – had, on the contrary, much in common with the popular notion of the semi-animate corpse, and even with the popular fear of the corpse's power. The antithetical relationship between "occluded" and "ocular" suggests that there is perhaps much that *should* not be seen, that is deliberately proscribed from view, that will, in fact, destroy the viewer.[15] One of the mythological formulations for this taboo is, of course, the story of Medusa, the female Gorgon who turned to stone anyone who dared to look on her, and Sawday invokes this myth to identify the early modern concept of petrifying vision as the view of the "interiority" of the corpse – that is, the body in dissolution, its status indeterminate (Sawday 1995: 6–15). Anatomy purported to disempower such vision: its precision instruments, its ordered and sequential methodology, its names and categories would harness the horror associated with the corpse, or even deny its existence. But in the early modern theater of the imagination, in Shakespeare's *Macbeth*, Medusa cannot be denied. Duncan's corpse is "a new Gorgon" (II.iii.73) – a corpse deeply inscribed by preceding traditions, but newly inflected with the discomfiting ideological tensions of Shakespeare's time.

III

Perhaps more than any other play of Shakespeare, *Macbeth* conveys the enormous power of the human nightmare: a slippery state in which there is no surety, no anchorage, no dependable structures of any kind. The compact design of the play concentrates a variety of images suggesting preternatural intrusions into ordinary life, including witches, ghosts, monstrous shapes and creatures, and an infernally enveloping darkness. But the heart of the horror in *Macbeth* derives from the inversion of the ordinary itself in the lives of the protagonists, their recognition of the thin line that separates the reassuring structures of everyday existence from the chaos they mask. Sleep – "Chief nourisher in life's feast . . . that knits up the raveled sleave of care" (II.ii.39, 36) – is "murdered," revealing the hallucinatory underside of the unrelenting dream; feasting, the communal ritual with "troops of friends" (V.iii.25), becomes horrifically bound up with another kind of "supping," with "magot-pies" and bloodied ghosts. As a consequence of their sacrilege in killing Duncan, Macbeth and Lady Macbeth find themselves negotiating these interstitial spaces; exiled from the protective framework of human society, they are suspended in a kind of no-(wo)man's land. They seek Duncan's power as king, but discover instead Duncan's power as corpse.

Macduff's description of Duncan's corpse as "the new Gorgon" – the Medusa head that petrifies the viewer – foregrounds its sacramental dimension: Duncan's hacked-up, bloodied body – unthinkable and unviewable – is hypostatized as sacred.[16] The Eucharistic imagery that precedes the murder conflates the murder of Duncan as "the Lord's anointed temple" (II.iii.69) with the sacrifice of Christ (both Duncan and Jesus have "almost supped"; Jesus tells his betrayer "That thou doest, doe quickly"; Macbeth refers to "our poison'd chalice" [I.vii.11; see also John 13: 27, as cited by Muir in Shakespeare 1957: 37, n2]). Later in the play, a second inversion of the Eucharistic feast invests Banquo's ghost with a similar sacramental signification. As Garber has pointed out, Banquo's Medusa-like "gory locks" replicate Duncan's Gorgon (1987: 108–90, 115–16), so that the terrible sacrilege of Duncan's murder bleeds afresh, as it were, in the "twenty mortal murthers" of the "blood-bolter'd Banquo" (III.iv.80; IV.i.123).

It is of course Duncan's sacramental blood, flowing from multiple wounds, like stigmata, that seems to animate his corpse with a fearsome power transcending death. Macbeth's hope that "the spring, the head, the fountain of [Duncan's] blood / Is stopp'd; the very source of it is stopp'd" (II.iii.98–9) proves hopelessly wrong. After the murder of Banquo, Macbeth alludes to "the time has been, / That, when the brains were out, the man would die, / And there an end" (III.iv.77–9), but he has already recognized that *his* times are saturated in a blood so potent it can "incarnadine" "the multitudinous seas" (II.ii.61). To the Scotsmen who hope to reclaim their country, Duncan's blood is generative; it will mingle with "Each drop of us" (V.ii.29) in "our country's purge" (28), "Or so much as it needs / To dew the sovereign flower, and drown the weeds" (29–30). But to Macbeth and Lady Macbeth, the murderers, Duncan's blood is a deadly contagion; like the knife in Duncan's wound, it sticks deep, an unexpungable mark of death.

Prior to the murder the Macbeths do not, of course, anticipate the "uncanny retaliatory power" (Willis 1994: 7) of Duncan's corpse. On the contrary, they construct individual fantasies of regicide in which the appropriation of Duncan's sovereign power depends on their own superior strength: thus the double action of hyperbolizing their own potency in overtly sexual terms, and of diminishing Duncan's. Lady Macbeth's scenario would reduce Duncan to the status of an old man, sleeping, unguarded, not unlike the image of her own nursing babe, dashed to death at a moment of intimate trust (Adelman 1987: 112; Willbern 1986: 525); Macbeth, as Tarquin, would descend upon his unsuspecting victim "with ravishing strides" (II.i.55). Significantly, both fantasies depend upon the confusion of gender identities in the Macbeths themselves, but also in Duncan. By infantilizing and feminizing Duncan, the Macbeths rob him (at least for the duration of the murder) of the patriarchal power they seek to procure; by denying their own procreant, nurturing qualities (which, of course, are qualities greatly admired in the "gracious" Duncan), they idealize a delusional notion of masculinity. The dreadful consequences of these sexually inflected fantasies of power are inscribed in the play's representation of the bi-gendered agency of Duncan's blood – its excessive, generative flow, and its power to kill.

That Lady Macbeth constructs Duncan-as-victim as disabled, and therefore not to be feared, is consistent with the play's representation of her mode of apprehending and categorizing "reality." Initially, Lady Macbeth would herself be the murderer, but in her curious invocation to the furies, she seems to express opposing desires: to be unsexed, stripped of all feminizing weaknesses ("Come you Spirits / . . . unsex me here, / . . . make thick my blood" [I.v.40–1, 43]), and yet to avoid the sight of the very act that would empower her as a kind of super-male ("Come, thick Night, / . . . / That my keen knife see not the wound it makes" [50, 52]). This tension in Lady Macbeth between unnatural aggression and a habit of dissociation is apparent elsewhere as well – for example, in her conflation of the images of sleep and death during her castiga-tion of Macbeth's reluctance to kill Duncan ("The sleeping, and the dead, / Are but as pictures" [II.ii.52–3]), and in her related insistence that pictures, painted images and air-drawn daggers, as products of the imagination, are unreal. To dare to be a man is to eschew such "foolish thought" (21), but the success of Lady Macbeth's system for denying psychic phenomena seems to depend on keeping her distance from the act of violence itself, despite her rhetoric to the contrary. Accordingly, after Lady Macbeth is forced to dip her hands in Duncan's blood and to "gild" the grooms with it, the sensory properties of this blood – its stickiness, its smell – become ineradic-able images in her mind, although even in her madness she instantiates this illusion as a visible stain on her hands.

Lady Macbeth's pathetic query, "Yet who would have thought the old man to have had so much blood in him?" (V.i.38–9), resonates with her earlier excuse for failing as executioner: "Had he not resembled / My father as he slept, I had done't" (II.ii.12–13). Presumably, it is the horror of parricide that unhinges Lady Macbeth, that *un*stops "th' access and passage to remorse" (I.v.44), and eventually prompts the obsessive reenactment of the aftermath of the murder. But Duncan's corpse as Gorgon is more than an image of Lady Macbeth's father: as a male Medusa, it is unnatural, terrifying, incorporating "both the femaleness [Lady Macbeth] sought to escape and the supermasculinity she aspired to attain" (Willis 1994: 8). In a sense, the power of this Gorgon's blood is beyond anything Lady Macbeth dares to imagine, and her obses-sive fixation suggests a final, extreme act of dissociation from the full recognition of Duncan's insensible power. Significantly, Lady Macbeth would not hesitate to con-front the furies on their own turf, in "the dunnest smoke of Hell" (I.v.52), because these monsters have a place in what might be termed her ontological universe. But the Gorgon that is Duncan's corpse does not: as a sleepwalker, Lady Macbeth fears to shut her eyes, to surrender herself to the dark; she "has light by her continually" (V.i.21–2).

Like his wife, Macbeth also invokes a fantasy of male potency as an incitement to murder, but in Tarquin Macbeth would identify as well with a heroic persona whose warrior reputation resembles his own. As "Bellona's bridegroom, lapp'd in proof [gore]" (I.ii.55), Macbeth is famed among the Scots for his "bloody execution" (18) on the battlefield ("he unseam'd him from the nave to th' chops" [22]). But the image of Bellona's bridegroom, "paradoxical because the goddess of war was a fierce unyield-ing virgin" (Berger 1997: 81), connects disturbingly with the surprise assault of Tarquin the rapist on another chaste woman, and also with the iconographic figure of death-as-lover in the *danse macabre*. In Macbeth's fantasy, the figure of Tarquin is overlaid with that of "wither'd Murther" (II.i.52), so that Tarquin's "ravishing strides" (55) are at the same time "stealthy" (54) – he "Moves like a ghost" (56). Thus the composite metaphor figures Tarquin/Death/Macbeth advancing inexorably to inflict the "deep wound" with the "keen knife" on Duncan, the fierce and innocent Bellona/Lucrece. Macbeth vanquishes Duncan, but not, of course, in the violent throes of battle, as would befit the bridegroom of Bellona; instead, the bloody violation of Duncan's privacy and person is a shamefully secret act. The cumulative effect, then, of Macbeth's fantasy of regicide is an alienation from his own public persona. After Duncan's death, Macbeth becomes "the *secret'st* man of blood" (III.iv.125, my emphasis); he can never return to a battlefield in which his adversaries, however terrifying, are tangible – "the rugged Russian bear, / The arm'd rhinoceros, or th' Hyrcanean tiger" (99–100).

The destabilizing of Macbeth's familiar persona is proleptically suggested by the "dagger of the mind" (II.i.38) that Macbeth sees but cannot grasp on his way to murder Duncan, a floating signifier that does and does not correspond to the palpable dagger in Macbeth's hand. The imagined dagger, a "false creation," "marshal'st me the way that I was going" (38, 42), suggesting an eerie agency that is not included in the signified of its corporeal referent. Macbeth recognizes a breach between his two modes of seeing ("Mine eyes are made the fools o' th' other senses, / Or else worth all the rest" [44–5]), but his attempt to retain an empirical test for reality ("There's no such thing" [47]) ironically locates the crux of his dilemma. There is no such *thing* as the imagined dagger, but it exists nonetheless in some frame of vision, and to the degree that it does not correspond to the dagger "which now I draw" (41), its signification no longer belongs to the symbolic system that orders Macbeth's world.

As Macbeth's "horrible imaginings" worsen immediately after the murder (he is fixated on the prayers of the grooms, and on the ghostly voice that denounced him), Lady Macbeth counters with her own insistently reductive theory of perception: "Consider it not so deeply . . . The sleeping, and the dead, / Are but as pictures; 'tis the eye of childhood / That fears a painted devil" (II.ii.29, 52–4). The confusions of this metaphor, as I have already suggested, function for Lady Macbeth as a mode of denial, but they also foreground a larger problem in signification. The metaphor conflates the painted artifact, falsely animated, with the semi-conscious sleeper, and the de-animated dead – leveling the playing field, as it were, so that at least for Lady Macbeth Duncan's corpse is as dead as the painted image. Ironically, however, after Macbeth has seen the ghost of Banquo, Lady Macbeth invokes the same metaphor, but changes its terms so as to ascribe agency to Macbeth's insensible fear: "This is the very painting of your fear: / This is the air-drawn dagger" (III.iv.60–1). By mid-play, of course, Lady Macbeth's shaming tactics strike a hollow note, since Macbeth is already "cabin'd, cribb'd, confin'd" (23) in a private universe in which the distinctions between painted images and horrible imaginings have all but collapsed. Thus his scornful castigation of his servant shortly before his death ("Go, prick thy face, and over-red thy fear, / Thou lily-liver'd boy . . . Take thy face hence" [V.iii.14–15, 19]) represents an almost comic degradation of Lady Macbeth's injunctions, as well as of Macbeth's own early efforts to objectify his fear.

Indeed, after the regicide, Macbeth's alienation from the signifying structures that once comprised "reality" is apparent in his precipitous decline from the status of "warrior" to that of "hangman" and "butcher," all of whom (together, of course, with the early modern anatomist) know how to unseam a person from the nave to the chops. "Now does he feel / His secret murthers sticking on his hands" (V.ii.16–17), observes Angus near the end of the play, referring not only to the sacrilegious stamp of Duncan's blood, but also to the plague-like pile of corpses Macbeth has left in his wake – a virtual sea of blood that Macbeth must "wade." For Angus and the other Scots, the gore-soaked Macbeth, "lapp'd" in a "proof" that befits Hecate far better than Bellona, has become a monster, no longer recognizable as a "natural" man. In fact, by demonizing Macbeth as *un*natural, the Scots are able to isolate him as sole agent of the transformation of Scotland into a nether-kingdom, an "Acheron," rife with cannibalistic creatures of death both in the air and under the ground (including the worms and serpents who eat the dead, as in the transi sculptures). If the "Beauteous and swift" horses of the king, "the minions of their race" (II.iv.15), now eat each other, like the infanticidal sow in the witches' brew, it is because the butcher-fiend Macbeth, in transgressing a divide between human and inhuman, has inverted the natural order.

Macbeth himself acknowledges this transgression ("Returning were as tedious as go o'er" [III.iv.137]) and is not insensible to his own transformation; his bitter irony with Banquo's murderers, for example, suggests that he, as well as they, belong in the catalogue of dogs and not of men (III.i). But Macbeth's "fatal vision" encompasses far more than an awareness of himself as monster; it is the vision *of* the monster, in which ordinary distinctions, including the demarcation of the "natural" from the "unnatural," have blurred. The Scots, as "natural" men, would appropriate Duncan's corpse so as to strengthen, not loosen, these distinctions. To them, Duncan as Gorgon bears witness to the horror of transgressing the sacred law against regicide, as does the terrible transformation of their country. In this context, the nightmarish imagery of their speech functions as a correlative to their sacramentalizing of the Gorgon's blood. When appropriated as sacrifice (like the Eucharistic feast), the horrible and holy murder of Duncan reinvigorates the Scots, refortifies the taboo against regicide, and obliterates Acheron.

But for Macbeth, "blood will have blood" (III.iv.121) in a never-ending generation of death, so that the "wild and violent sea" (IV.ii.21) of blood which he cannot ford ultimately seems to engulf both the sacred and the profane, the living and the dead. "If charnel-houses and our graves must send / Those that we bury back" (III.iv.70–1), if "Stones have been known to move, and trees to speak" (122), then "nothing is, but what is not" (I.iii.142). "Nature *seems* dead" (II.i.50, my emphasis), but so do "the surfeited grooms" (II.ii.5) before he kills them, whereas the murdered Banquo does not. Macbeth would fix Banquo among the dead ("Thy bones are marrowless, thy blood is cold; / Thou hast no speculation in those eyes / Which thou dost glare with" [III.iv.93–4]), but the "bloody business" of slaughter "informs" Macbeth's own eyes (II.i.48), infects them, so that ultimately Macbeth's "speculation" inhabits the hallucinatory gaps in signification. In these unfixed spaces, Macbeth's "deep desire" is imbricated in an "orgy of annihilation" (to quote Bataille once again) that erases even the distinctions between the sacramental and the sacrilegious, god and devil, Duncan's blood and Macbeth's own.

At the conclusion of *Macbeth*, the Scots restore the metaphysical framework that they purport to represent: when Macbeth's demonic agency is destroyed, the walking dead return to their graves. In this respect, the play functions in much the same way as English rituals of the dead did, by simultaneously exploiting and defusing fear of the semi-animate agency of the corpse. But for most of the play, the dead Duncan is a fetishistic presence, foregrounded by direct and oblique references to the iconography of the nether-world, to the annihilative/generative properties of the bi-gendered blood of the corpse, and to the function of the Eucharistic feast in transforming and sacramentalizing the cannibalism of nature; and the transgressive Macbeth, who sees much that he should not, evokes the popular association of hangman ("butcher") with anatomist. The play is thus saturated with an unsettling ambience of the dead that is not wholly dispelled by the recuperation of hegemonic ideology.

Significantly, it is the Medusa symbolism that intersects the transgressive and recuperative visions of the play and that strikes a particularly disturbing note at the end. As Garber points out, Macbeth's decapitated head is itself a Medusa image, appropriated atropaically by the Scots (as was Medusa's on the shield of Athena) to ward off future evil (Garber 1987: 114–15); for similar purposes, his image as "rarer monster" will be "Painted upon a pole" and displayed publicly (V.viii.25, 26). On one level, the communal demonization of Macbeth bears witness to the restoration of the natural order: for the Scots, the function of his head as trophy inverts the power of his monstrousness; and the painted image, in a return to Lady Macbeth's categorical conflations, attests to the insentience of his corpse. But the play has already dramatized the failure of Lady Macbeth's mode of apprehension, and Macbeth's Gorgon – however symbolically isolated from humankind – nonetheless resonates uneasily with its sacramentalized counterpart in Duncan/Banquo. In the end, the play's attempt to differentiate Gorgons seems undermined by its powerful representation of Macbeth's own deconstructive vision: such sights as none should behold cannot so easily be laid to rest.

IV

To argue that *Macbeth* is about the representation of a "deconstructive vision" is to recognize that it is about the nature of representation itself, particularly as it pertains to the performative conventions of the early modern theater. Strictly speaking, of course, there is no way to represent a vision that derives from the collapse of the discursive structures that themselves comprise signification. What *Macbeth* enacts instead is the consequences of such a collapse, and by means of a representational mode that itself functioned (like Macbeth's hallucinations) so as to destabilize distinctions.

The blurring of categorical divides was of course integral to early modern theater *as* theater: impersonation obscured the differences between actor/fictional figure, disguise/identity; and spectators were invited to imagine the staged fiction, at least to some degree, as an extension of extra-theatrical experience. But the historically distinctive conventions of this theater (for example, natural lighting, unlocalized settings, anachronistic costumes, the mixture of dramaturgical modes) consistently foregrounded the *artifice* of theatrical illusion – the inner workings, as it were, of the fantasy machine. Thus the theater's representational process created a tension between the dramatic fiction and its illusionary apparatus, and overtly so, so that the possibilities of spectator response were shaped by the metatheatricality of performance.

Within this context, the representation of the corpse demarcated the limits of theatrical signification. As Elisabeth Bronfen has argued, every image of death is fetishistic in that it represents "a severing of the body from its real materiality" (1992: 44), but in the theater, it is the material body itself that represents the image: theater is "illusory *embodiment*" (Greenblatt 1993: 122, my emphasis). Thus the representation of the corpse on the early modern stage entailed not only the foregrounding, but in effect the collapse of illusion: a material, sentient body was supposed to signify an insentient one, severed from "its real materiality" – a *dis*embodied body.

Further, any representation of a *female* corpse in this theater was significantly complicated by the centuries-old tradition of transvestite acting, or the impersonation of women by boy actors. Because transvestism foreclosed the possibility of representing women apart from the agency of male bodies, the "female" on the early modern stage was axiomatically an illusion. But as a metatheatrical convention, transvestism also worked to expose the illusion of the "real," enabling the theater to interrogate the viability of hegemonic gender distinctions, and inviting the audience to explore fluid and shifting erotic possibilities. The female *corpse* was thus a conundrum, doubly compounded: the boy actor was sentient, rather than dead; and he was also a male impersonator, inevitably inscribing his/her corpse with complicated erotic valences.

Given these dramaturgical complexities, it seems significant that many early modern dramatists (including, on occasion, Shakespeare) chose to blatantly showcase the female corpse – to defy the representational odds, so to speak – especially when the corpse served as erotic idol in the dramatic fiction.[17] For example, in at least three non-Shakespearean plays (*Monsieur D'Olive* [1604–5], *The Second Maiden's Tragedy* [1611–12], and *The Duke of Milan* [1621–2]), a boy actor impersonating a dead woman was propped in a chair, cosmeticized, and worshipped. Moreover, *The Revenger's Tragedy* (1607–8) featured two eroticized corpses – the fully fleshed body of the dead wife of Antonio, centerpiece of a wake in which her public rape was verbally reenacted; and the skull of Gloriana, dressed up and prosthetically extended (again, in a chair) so as to seduce the Duke with a kiss and poison him. In all these instances, the concept of the "dead" and the concept of the "female" were simultaneously hyperbolized, evoking the Reformist proscription against idols/whores and the "rot," spiritual and material, that underlay their painted/cosmeticized exteriors. But although the complexities of staging corpse infatuation in such sensationalist modes should not be underestimated, these plays nonetheless serve collectively to demonstrate what does *not* happen in *Macbeth*.

To be sure, the play is not without hyperbolic modes of dramatizing its sexual issues. Most obviously, the impersonation of the "unsexed" Lady Macbeth by a boy actor exploits the ambiguities of the transvestite convention almost to the point of parody. The monstrousness of Lady Macbeth would seem incompatible not only with her fictional persona as Macbeth's wife, but also with the customary interpretive range of the boy actor, who in this role was called upon to impersonate a female who herself would impersonate a super-male. On one level of the action, then, the sexual issues of the play are laid out with a quasi-parodic explicitness, but always in contradistinction to the subtle and implicit unfolding of the symbolism of Duncan's corpse.

As do other plays, *Macbeth* foregrounds a corpse as erotic idol, but the singularity of Duncan's corpse is that it never materializes. Instead, Shakespeare renders the dead body of Duncan as an invisible presence throughout the play, thereby amplifying and extending its erotic dimensions. As I suggested earlier, Duncan's corpse is initially inflected by the confused fantasies that Macbeth and Lady Macbeth have constructed around Duncan himself: both desire the superpower of the patriarchal king, but in order to wrest this power unto themselves, they imagine their victim as feminized, enfeebled, vulnerable to rape/violation. The bi-gendered Duncan is thus established as the focal point for the play's interrogation of gender indeterminacy, but unlike the transvestite actor "playing dead," the offstage corpse does not visibly contravene the symbolic import of its representation.

What *Macbeth* does materialize, in a move that comes brilliantly close to representing the unrepresentable, is Duncan's blood – a substance whose *physical* properties, as we have seen, were firmly inscribed in the cultural consciousness as fundamentally indeterminate. Thus the blood on the hands of the Macbeths has deconstructive power both as sign and as substance, and this disturbing conflation serves as ideal analogue to Macbeth's "fatal vision," in which the relationship of signifier to signified is in jeopardy, as is the principle of differentiation in signification itself – male/female, life/death. In contrast to the torments of this "speculation," the sexually inflected fantasies of Macbeth and his wife prior to the murder seem almost naively simplistic. By the end of the play, Macbeth's cosmos has been horrifically enlarged by the encompassing sea of Duncan's blood – a sea in which materiality provides no anchor and sexuality itself is inextricably bound up with death. By generating the possibilities of this vision, Duncan's absent corpse signifies as the play's most powerful presence.

NOTES

1 Despite the dangers of such a methodology, I believe it can be useful to read historical evidence against a transhistorical paradigm, provided that the paradigm is not superimposed on the historical evidence. Admittedly, purity in such an enterprise is impossible, but the *Macbeth* criticism demonstrates well the impossibility of wholly synchronic

critical analysis: virtually no contemporary scholar discusses *Macbeth* without reference (silent or explicit) to concepts of fantasy, dissociation, repression, etc., which inevitably carry modern and postmodern inflections. The criticism thus demonstrates the need to distinguish the methodological aims of history and of psychoanalysis/anthropology, but also to clarify their connections.

2   For a fuller explication of these concepts, and an attempt to relate Bataille's theory of desire to that of Jacques Lacan, see Zimmerman (1998).

3   These categories were, of course, already established as opposites in medieval exegetical tradition, which customarily identified the contaminating flesh with the female gender and the purifying spirit with the male. Lust was, in fact, thought to be at the heart of idolatry, and the woman (especially when artificially cosmeticized) functioned as stimulus for both sins. But the doctrinaire insistence of Reformers on the principle of categorical division – apparent, for example, in the homily on idolatry – revised the emphasis of the earlier theology.

4   According to Gittings's study of English funerary practices from 1580 to 1660, "religious and doctrinal changes [had] little actual effect" on attitudes toward death and burial (Gittings 1984: 59; see also 39–58). Cressy (1997: 396–411) also acknowledges that rituals of birth, marriage, and death customarily undergo gradual rather than radical transformation, however thoroughly the official prescriptions for such rituals may be reformulated.

5   In England, as elsewhere, the practice of anatomical dissection had of course preceded its public demonstration in amphitheaters. For a description of dissections in the mid-sixteenth century by practitioners at Oxford and Cambridge, by members of the Companies of Barbers and Surgeons (united by the Act of 1540), and by the College of Physicians in London, see Sawday (1995: 4, 56–7).

6   Park states that "the first unambiguous record of an Italian autopsy dates from 1286," and that by the fourteenth century, postmortems and anatomical dissections also were being performed in Italy; however, "there are few known references to autopsies and only one to a dissection in Germany, England, or France before the late fifteenth century" (Park 1994b: 114). There was, nonetheless, serious resistance in Italy to the northern practice of dividing the body in order to bury its parts in different places (expressly forbidden in 1299 by Pope Boniface VIII in his bull *Detestande feritatis*). In this connection, Park contends that "Italians treated the body as an object of memory and commemoration," whereas believers in the "liminal" corpse assumed that this liminality "could inhere in its scattered parts as easily as in the whole" (1994b: 113, 119). For a further development of these distinctions, see Park (1994a); and Brown (1981).

7   Interestingly, Georges Bataille distinguishes the semi-animate corpse from the desiccated skeleton in much the same terms. Bataille contends that "decomposing human flesh serves as anguishing reminder of the sickening primary condition of life," whereas "whitened bones . . . draw the first veil of decency and solemnity over death" (1986: 56).

8   Such detailing is also apparent in late medieval literature, for example the anonymous 31-stanza poem entitled *Disputacioun Betwyx the Body and Wormes*, 1435/40 (London, BL, Add. ms. 37049, fols. 33ff). The poem stages a debate between the corpse of a Lady and the worms who are preparing to eat her; the Lady ultimately submits to her own ravishment/consumption. See Cohen (1973: 29–30).

9   The embalming of Henry VIII (which involved surgeons, apothecaries, and wax chandlers) may be taken as representative of the process at its most elaborate, and involved spurging, or the washing and spicing of the body; cleansing, or the emptying of the bowels and the plugging of the rectum; boweling, or the removal of the soft organs by means of a cut from the bottom of the rib cage to the pelvis; searing, or the cauterizing of the blood vessels after boweling; embalming, or the purification of the inner cavity; dressing, or the application of balms

and oils on the outer body; and furnishing, or the positioning of the sudarium, or linen square covering the face, and the wrapping of the corpse in cerecloth and waxed twine. See Litten (1991: 39–40). As Park points out (1994a: esp. 4–8), techniques of embalming and autopsy were very similar.

10 Despite the flattening out of gender differentiation in certain Christian and Galenic concepts, the sexuality and reproductive agency of woman was nonetheless perceived as a serious threat in both systems. Thus, for example, the necessity in Christianity to establish the mother of the bi-gendered Christ as a virgin; and in Galen, to explain the female anatomy as an anatomically incomplete version of the male.

11 Park notes that "the continuing and widespread popular resistance" to the practice of anatomical dissection in England and other northern European countries "culminated in the Tyburn riots of the mid-eighteenth century, in which Londoners protested violently at the gallows to deny surgeons access to the bodies of the hanged" (1994b: 130). See also Linebaugh (1975).

12 In Christian hagiography, on the other hand, the death of the martyr by some mutilating means, such as being torn by animals, was considered a sign of special holiness. Park discusses the often contradictory linkages between the martyr, the criminal, and the anatomist's corpse in Park (1994a: esp. 23–9).

13 Many reports of such practices in Italy and elsewhere originated with Vesalius himself, who, in the first edition of the *Fabrica*, "recounts with evident relish and amusement" the illegal lengths to which he and his students were willing to go to obtain cadav-

ers (and if necessary to obscure their identities by flaying). Not surprisingly, fear of vivisection was also common among opponents of anatomical dissection. See Park (1994a: 18–20).

14 For discussion of Browne's *Religio Medici* (1642), see Neill (1997: 125–6); for Crooke's *Microcosmographia* (1618), see Sawday (1995: 167–9) and Neill (1997: 130–3); for Fletcher's *The Purple Island; or The Isle of Man* (1633), see Sawday (1995: 170–82) and Neill (1997: 130–3); for Burton's *The Anatomy of Melancholy* (1621), see Sawday (1995: 2–3, *passim*).

15 In her seminal essay on *Othello* and *Hamlet*, Patricia Parker explores the tension between images of discovery, of opening up, and images of the hidden, secret, and frequently monstrous, especially as they delineate concepts of the female (Parker 1996: 229–72).

16 This is not to say that Duncan merits sanctification, either as an individual or as a king. Harry Berger, Jr. has persuasively demonstrated Duncan's complicity in the machismo warrior ethic that has ravaged Scotland, as well as the ironies implicit in the play's seeming opposition of Duncan and Macbeth (1997: 70–97). But in the context of my argument, as we shall see, the social destabilization effected by Macbeth's violation of taboo necessitates Duncan's idealization as King and Macbeth's demonization as Murderer.

17 Shakespeare's most elaborate experiment with this mode was *Romeo and Juliet*, repeated later in a different key in *Antony and Cleopatra*. The resurrected Hermione in *The Winter's Tale* may also be viewed as a kind of showcased "corpse."

REFERENCES AND FURTHER READING

Adelman, J. 1987: "Fantasies of Maternal Power in *Macbeth*." In Marjorie Garber (ed.), *Cannibals, Witches, and Divorce: Estranging the Renaissance*. Baltimore and London: Johns Hopkins University Press, 90–121.

Ariès, P. 1981: *The Hour of Our Death*. Trans. Helen Weaver. London: Allen Lane.

Bataille, G. 1986: *Eroticism: Death and Sensuality*. Trans. Mary Dalwood. San Francisco, CA: City Lights.

Berger, Jr., H. 1997: "The Early Scenes of *Macbeth*: Preface to a New Interpretation." In Peter Erickson (ed.), *Making Trifles of Terrors: Redistributing Complicities in Shakespeare*.

Stanford, CA: Stanford University Press, 6–97.

Bronfen, E. 1992: *Over Her Dead Body: Death, Femininity and the Aesthetic.* New York: Routledge; Manchester: Manchester University Press.

Brown, E. A. R. 1981: "Death and the Human Body in the Later Middle Ages: The Legislation of Boniface VIII on the Division of the Corpse." *Viator*, 12, 226–41.

Bynum, C. W. 1982: *Jesus as Mother: Studies in the Spirituality of the High Middle Ages.* Berkeley, Los Angeles, and London: University of California Press.

——1991: "The Body of Christ in the Later Middle Ages: A Reply to Leo Steinberg." In *Fragmentation and Redemption: Essays on Gender and the Human Body in Medieval Religion.* New York: Zone Books; Cambridge, MA: distributed by MIT Press, 79–117.

Cohen, K. 1973: *Metamorphosis of a Death Symbol: The Transi Tomb in the Late Middle Ages and the Renaissance.* Berkeley, Los Angeles, and London: University of California Press.

Cressy, D. 1997: *Birth, Marriage, and Death: Ritual, Religion, and the Life-Cycle in Tudor and Stuart England.* New York: Oxford University Press.

Douglas, M. 1991: *Purity and Danger: An Analysis of the Concepts of Pollution and Taboo.* London and New York: Routledge.

Garber, M. 1987: "Macbeth: The Male Medusa." In *Shakespeare's Ghost Writers: Literature as Uncanny Causality.* New York and London: Methuen, 87–123.

Gittings, C. 1984: *Death, Burial, and the Individual in Early Modern England.* London and Sydney: Croom Helm.

Greenblatt, S. 1993: "Shakespeare Bewitched." In Jeffrey N. Cox and Larry Reynolds (eds.), *New Historical Literary Study: Essays on Reproducing Texts, Representing History.* Princeton, NJ: Princeton University Press, 108–35.

Laqueur, T. W. 1990: *Making Sex: Body and Gender from the Greeks to Freud.* Cambridge, MA: Harvard University Press.

Linebaugh, P. 1975: "The Tyburn Riot against the Surgeons." In Douglas Hay, Peter Linebaugh, John Rule, and E. P. Thompson (eds.), *Albion's Fatal Tree: Crime and Society in Eighteenth-Century England.* Harmondsworth: Penguin Books, 65–117.

Litten, J. 1991: *The English Way of Death: The Common Funeral Since 1450.* London: Robert Hale.

Neill, M. 1997: *Issues of Death: Mortality and Identity in English Renaissance Tragedy.* Oxford: Clarendon Press; New York: Oxford University Press.

Park, K. 1994a: "The Criminal and the Saintly Body: Autopsy and Dissection in Renaissance Italy." *Renaissance Quarterly*, 47, 1, 1–33.

——1994b: "The Life of the Corpse: Division and Dissection in Later Medieval Europe." *Journal of the History of Medicine and Allied Sciences*, 50, 1, 111–32.

Parker, P. 1996: *Shakespeare from the Margins: Language, Culture, Context.* Chicago and London: University of Chicago Press.

Paster, G. K. 1993: *The Body Embarrassed: Drama and the Disciplines of Shame in Early Modern England.* Ithaca and New York: Cornell University Press.

Richardson, R. 1963: *Death, Dissection, and the Destitute.* New York: Penguin Books.

Sawday, J. 1995: *The Body Emblazoned: Dissection and the Human Body in Renaissance Culture.* New York and London: Routledge.

Shakespeare, W. 1957: *Macbeth.* The Arden Shakespeare. Ed. Kenneth Muir. Cambridge, MA: Harvard University Press.

Steinberg, L. S. 1983: *The Sexuality of Christ in Renaissance Art and in Modern Oblivion.* New York: Pantheon.

Willbern, D. 1986: "Phantasmagoric Macbeth." *English Literary Renaissance*, 16, 520–49.

Willis, D. 1994: "A New Gorgon: Engendering Horror in *Macbeth* and Contemporary Film." Unpublished paper submitted to seminar at The Shakespeare Association of America. Quoted with permission of author.

Zimmerman, S. 1998: "Marginal Man: The Representation of Horror in Jacobean Tragedy." In Viviana Comensoli and Paul Stevens (eds.), *Discontinuities: New Essays on Renaissance Criticism.* Toronto: University of Toronto Press, 159–78.

PART SIX
Religion

18

Others and Lovers in *The Merchant of Venice*

M. Lindsay Kaplan

The Merchant of Venice explores the tension between same and other in several contexts, as a number of critics have noted (Auden 1962; Hall 1992; Shapiro 1996; Shell 1979); this essay will attend particularly to the ways in which one strand of the play's Christian ideology attempts to subsume and incorporate Jews and women into a social hierarchy. The historical concerns of the status of Jews in Reformation thought as well as the status of married women in English common law will provide our context for reading the play. Additionally, I would like to consider the problem of difference staged by the play in terms of Emmanuel Levinas's work on alterity, or otherness, in his philosophical treatise *Totality and Infinity*.

Ambivalence about Judaism's relation to Christianity dates back to the origin of the latter: while Christianity is a continuation of Judaism, it also constitutes a break from it; the Hebrew Bible is a source of Christian doctrine, but is also in part antithetical to that doctrine. Judaism's refusal to accept Jesus as the Messiah could be perceived as a challenge to Christianity itself. Hence Jewish separateness may be read not as a neutral decision to believe differently, but as an act of intolerance or blasphemy. These issues achieve a new level of interest in the early modern period with the advent of the Reformation. In their rejection of Catholic traditions and authority, Protestants turned to the Scriptures to develop a new definition of Christianity and its origins that was more "authentic" than Catholicism, and yet remained distinct from Judaism.

> The sixteenth-century Reformation was a movement led by Martin Luther and reformers who appealed to Scripture as the norm of Christian faith and life. With the Reformation, therefore, came a keen interest in the Hebrew Scriptures, the Old Testament, and in Judaism. When confronting Jews, most reformers adhered to the early but enduring and decisive notion that God's Old Testament covenant with Israel had been abrogated, or superseded, by a new covenant grounded in Jesus which thus created the Christian Church, a "new Israel." (Gritsch 1994: 197)

The doctrine of supersession did not nullify the value of even post-biblical Jewish texts for the reformers: "Luther and the German Humanist John Reuchlin defended the use of the Talmud in Hebrew to interpret the Bible," the latter contending "that scholarly dialogue with Jews, based on authentic literary sources such as cabala [Jewish mysticism], would open the way for the Jews to accept Jesus as the Messiah" (Gritsch 1994: 198). Clearly, this desire to use Jewish texts to support Christian aims did not amount to an acceptance for Judaism *per se*. As Reuchlin argues in 1504:

> The misery of the Jews is not the consequence of man-made injustice but of God-willed punishment, to be escaped only through conversion. He concludes by pointing to the Good Friday prayer for the *perfidi Iudaei* [faithless Jews]: "I pray God that He will illumine and convert them to the right faith so that they are liberated from captivity by the Devil. . . . Once they acknowledge Jesus as the true Messiah everything will turn to their good in this world and in the world to come." (Oberman 1983: 333)

Although the reformers came under attack for allegedly supporting the Jews, their ultimate goal was the eradication of Jews and Judaism through mass conversion.

While the status of women in the early modern period would seem to be quite different from that of the Jews, the former also suffers from a theological impediment. As in the case of the Jews, women are also seen as guilty of committing a terrible sin and as being punished by subjection. The Church Fathers are quite articulate on this point in their discussion of original sin. St. John Chrysostom (ca. 347–407) discusses the origins of female inferiority in his *Homily IX on St. Paul's Epistle to Timothy*:

> Man was formed first; and elsewhere Paul shows man's superiority: "Neither was the man created for the woman, but the woman for the man." Why does he say this? He wishes for the man to have the pre-eminence in every way; let man take precedence, he means, both for the reason already given [man's prior creation] and because of what happened afterwards. The woman taught the man once and made him guilty of disobedience, and ruined everything. Therefore, because she made bad use of her power over the man, or rather her equality with him, God made her subject to her husband. "Your desire shall be for your husband [and he shall rule over you]." (Blamires 1992: 59)

St. John first suggests that male superiority comes from his earlier creation. However, he also implies that woman had power over man, or, backing off from this disturbing thought, at least equality with him, and exercised it to both their detriments. Her subjection to him hence results from the sin of eating of the forbidden fruit, and encouraging her husband to do the same, rather than some preexisting hierarchy. St. Augustine considers the same problem in his exegesis, *The Literal Meaning of Genesis*, and his account is similarly contradictory:

> We must give consideration to the statement, "And you shall be subject to your husband, and he shall rule over you", to see how it can be understood in the proper

sense. For we must believe that even before her sin woman had been made to be ruled by her husband and to be submissive and subject to him. But we can with reason understand that the servitude meant in these words is that in which there is a condition similar to that of slavery rather than a bond of love (so that the servitude by which men later began to be slaves to other men obviously has its origin in punishment for sin). St. Paul says, "Through love serve one another." But by no means would he say, "Have dominion over one another." Hence married persons through love can serve one another, but St. Paul does not permit a woman to rule over a man [1 Tim. 2: 12]. The sentence pronounced by God gave this power rather to man; and it is not by her nature but rather by her sin that woman deserved to have her husband for a master. But if this order is not maintained, nature will be corrupted still more, and sin will be increased. (Blamires 1992: 79–80)

Augustine seems to assert that female inferiority existed before her sin, but then pronounces that her sin, not her nature, determined her subjection. Perhaps Augustine understands her initial inferiority as somehow prefiguring her sin, and hence is fulfilled in her disobedience. At any rate, he clearly identifies sin as the source of her servitude and uses her example as the model for slavery. Here, the bond of love between husband and wife merely cloaks her status as his bond-woman, or slave, and the maintenance of this hierarchy is necessary for the right ordering of the world.

These theological opinions had legal and economic implications for women in the early modern period, as *The Lawes Resolutions of Women's Rights* makes explicit. Though not published until 1632, *The Lawes Resolutions* only cites laws up to the year 1597/8; hence it adequately reflects the state of women's law for the late sixteenth century (Klein 1992: 27). The anonymous author gives two reasons for the inferior status of women in early modern common law:

Now because Adam hath so pronounced that man and wife shall be but one flesh, and our law is that if a feofment [grant of property] be made jointly to John at Stile and to Thomas Noke and his wife, of three acres of land, that Thomas and his wife get no more but one acre and a half, *quia una persona* [because they are one person], . . . and by this a married woman perhaps may either doubt whether she be either none or no more than half a person. But let her be of good cheer, though, for the near conjunction which is between man and wife and to tie them to a perfect love . . . they be by intent and wise fiction of the law, one person, yet in nature and in some other cases by the law of God and man, they remain diverse.

. . . Return a little to Genesis, in the third chapter whereof is declared our first parents' transgression in eating the forbidden fruit. . . . Eve because she had helped seduce her husband hath inflicted on her a special bane. *In sorrow shalt thou bring forth thy children, thy desires shall be subject to thy husband, and he shall rule over thee.* See here the reason of that which I touched before, that women have no voice in parliament. They make no laws, they consent to none, they abrogate none. All of them are understood either married or to be married and their desires are subject to their husband. I know no remedy, though some women can shift it well enough. (Klein 1992: 32)

The doctrine of unity of person, which the author expounds upon here, held that a woman's legal persona "is suspended during the marriage, or at least is incorporated and consolidated into that of the husband" (Baker 1990: 551). While not universally applicable, this concept officially nullified a woman's capacity to make contracts or hold property in marriage, though some legal instruments were available to alleviate this latter impediment (Erickson 1993: 129–51, *passim*). Our text here makes clear that this doctrine has its roots in Genesis: because man and woman "shall be but one flesh," they constitute only one person in the eyes of the law. However, the reason for this person being the husband, rather than the wife, is given implicitly in the discussion of the consequences of Eve's sin. Again, we see that her subordination to her husband is due to her transgression and results in the virtual disappearance of her legal rights; she neither makes, nor consents to, nor abrogates law. Not only does she lose power to hold land while in marriage, but is always seen in some relation to marriage, and therefore in perpetual subjection to an actual or potential husband. (How the author dealt with the fact of Queen Elizabeth, many of whose statutes he quotes in this text, is entirely mysterious to me.)

Of particular interest to me in the cases of women and of Jews is the effort to erase them, via justification of the Scriptures, in subsuming them into some "superior" entity. The doctrines of supersession and unity of person function much in the same way the idea of the universal or totality operates in the philosophy of Emmanuel Levinas. In *Totality and Infinity*, Levinas defines a concept of difference which cannot be assimilated or subordinated into another entity, which remains radically other:

> The absolutely other is the Other. He and I do not form a number. The collectivity in which I say "you" or "we" is not a plural of the "I." I, you – these are not individuals of a common concept. Neither possession nor the unity of number nor the unity of concepts link me to the Stranger, the Stranger who disturbs the being at home with oneself. But Stranger also means the free one. Over him I have no power. He escapes my grasp by an essential dimension, even if I have him at my disposal. (Levinas 1969: 39)

The relationship between the self and the other does not constitute a collectivity in which I can subsume the other to myself. In fact, by virtue of her or his absolute difference from me, the other disturbs my own sense of self precisely by not being within my power. "The strangeness of the Other, his irreducibility to the I, to my thoughts and my possessions, is precisely accomplished as a calling into question of . . . [the exercise of the same], as ethics" (Levinas 1969: 43). The acknowledgment of otherness that unsettles the self prevents totality and establishes the ethical relationship between two independent entities. Levinas sees a totalizing effort in the tradition of Western philosophy of defining the essences of things, or ontology, which he defines as "a reduction of the other to the same by interposition of a middle and neutral term that ensures the comprehension of being" (1969: 43). This accomplishes an appropriation of the other by defining him or her in one's own terms, hence in determining and delimiting the other by one's thoughts.

Thematization and conceptualization, which moreover are inseparable, are not at peace with the other but [with] suppression or possession of the other. For possession affirms the other, but within a negation of its independence. "I think" comes down to "I can" – to an appropriation of what is, to an exploitation of reality. Ontology as first philosophy is a philosophy of power. It issues in the State and in the non-violence of the totality, without securing itself against the violence from which this non-violence lives, and which appears in the tyranny of the State. Truth, which should reconcile persons, here exists anonymously. Universality presents itself as impersonal; and this is another inhumanity. (Levinas 1969: 46)

The possession of the other is accomplished by means of a stereotype, in effect, which represents itself as universal truth but is in fact a subjective definition. While this process is not in and of itself violent, it precludes the ethical relation which would recognize the other, and opens up the possibility for violence. Against the threat of totality, Levinas posits the "infinity" of the other, that is, the quality which makes it effectively impossible for one to define, contain, or possess another (1969: 48–52).

The Merchant of Venice presents otherness or separateness as an ostensibly negative Jewish value; alterity would seem to create the central conflict of the play, however it also provides a way of solving it. In this essay, I will examine the ways in which maintaining difference provides for the autonomy of women and Jews. Through their use of the law, both Shylock and Portia attempt to protect their independence from forces which would work to nullify it. Although Portia is ultimately more successful than Shylock, she fails to pursue the ethic of alterity to its logical conclusion and thus fails to break open the play's totalizing forces. Without establishing difference as a consistent principle insuring ethical relations, the danger that the powerful will work to subordinate the other remains at the play's conclusion.

Shylock introduces the distinction between Jews and Christians in his first scene in the play when he vehemently refuses Bassanio's cordial dinner invitation:

> Yes, to smell pork, to eat of the habitation which your
> prophet the Nazarite conjured the devil into: I will
> buy with you, sell with you, talk with you, walk with
> you, and so following: but I will not eat with you,
> drink with you, nor pray with you.
>
> (I.iii.29–33)

Shylock's initial response concerns the Jewish dietary laws, or *kashrut*, which determine what is or is not appropriate for food. However, rather than citing a Jewish source for his practice, Shylock demonstrates his knowledge of Christian Scripture by referring to an episode in the Gospels in which Jesus casts a host of demons into a herd of swine (Matt. 8: 30, Mark 5: 13, Luke 8: 33). In so doing, he offers a reason from a Christian perspective why one might not eat pork, which in effect attempts to view and justify the practice as a Christian might. This could be seen as a positive acknowledgment of difference, though in referring to Jesus as "your prophet the Nazarite," he clearly distinguishes himself from the Christian community in a way which could seem blasphemous to a believer. Nevertheless, the speech could represent a neutral way of balancing differences: here is where we can relate – in commerce, walking, and talking – and here is where we cannot – eating, drinking, and praying. It is an argument for coexistence which does not require either side to submit to the other.

However, Shylock also describes a much more hateful relationship once Antonio appears which seems entirely intolerant of difference. The multiple reasons for this antagonism bear some consideration:

> I hate him for he is a Christian:
> But more, for that in low simplicity
> He lends out money gratis, and brings down
> The rate of usance here with us in Venice.
> If I can catch him once upon the hip,
> I will feed fat the ancient grudge I bear him.
> He hates our sacred nation, and he rails
> (Even there where merchants most do congregate)
> On me, my bargains, and my well-won thrift,
> Which he calls interest: cursed be my tribe
> If I forgive him!
>
> (I.iii.37–47)

In interpreting these lines we must decide whether Shylock is offering separate reasons for his rancor or if these reasons are related or even causal. The first reason seems the most bigoted and when read by itself indicates that Shylock only registers difference in order to reject it. However, he follows with what might be an amplification or recasting of the first point; more important is the fact that Antonio lends money interest-free, which reduces Shylock's profit. The money-lender bears the merchant "an ancient grudge," which may simply be a result of their differing lending practices or may arise from the fact that the latter "hates our sacred nation." Its longevity could refer to a long-standing feud between Shylock and Antonio, or the historical conflict between Jews and Christians. The odd point here is that Shylock's practice of usury is bound up with this theological enmity. Shylock's hatred of Antonio seems to be something he owes the Jewish people as a whole, yet it is unclear why usury should be such a tribal sore point.

The biblical laws of usury form the basis of the prohibition on taking interest which fuels early modern debates on the subject. In the book of Exodus, the children of Israel are commanded: "If thou lend money to any of my people that is poor by thee, thou shalt not be to him as an usurer, neither shall thou lay upon him usury" (22: 25). This law is quite clear here and similarly in Leviticus 25: 35–7, which also suggests that one refrain from practicing usury with a poor stranger as well as "thy brother." However, Deuteronomy allows the lending upon usury, though here kinship, not poverty, is the issue: "Unto a stranger thou mayest lend upon usury; but unto thy brother thou shalt not lend upon usury" (23: 20). While the distinction is prejudicial to strangers, it also makes sense on a practical level. Presumably, one knows what type of credit risk a "brother" or community member might be; charging usury might be a means of compensating for a risk one takes with a stranger. Hence, it provides for commerce between two people who might not otherwise interact; it can be understood as a type of contract establishing relations between two strangers.

When Antonio explains that he wants to borrow money on interest even though it is not his custom, Shylock does not cite the law of Deuteronomy as his justification, but a pastoral episode in Genesis. The story tells of Jacob's attempt to gain his wages from his unreliable uncle Laban (here more a stranger than a relative) by requesting only the spotted sheep and goats as his payment. Laban agrees, but takes all the spotted livestock and gives it to his sons, then separates himself from Jacob. By means of a savvy method, Jacob causes the strongest animals in the herd to bear spotted offspring, and hence increases his share of the flock (30: 27ff). Negotiating difference lies at the heart of this narrative, from the fact that Jacob selects wages that would be visibly distinct from his uncle's property (and hence avoids charges of theft) to the challenge of getting his fair pay from a hostile and unwilling employer. Jacob is at a disadvantage with regard to his uncle, but cuts a deal with him which takes the risk involved into account and still allows a profit. Like usury, his strategy is a model for establishing business with a potentially or actively hostile other. Shylock responds to Antonio by employing a biblical text as a parable or allegory, as opposed to a legal justification. As in his earlier use of the Gospels to justify his refusal to eat pork, Shylock here offers an answer which might be more familiar to and consonant with a Christian perspective without, however, altering his views about the validity of his own Jewish practice; his account proposes a type of difference which allows for coexistence.

Antonio's reaction to Shylock's explanation is almost allergic in its vehemence. He rejects Shylock's reasoning and demonizes the Jew's interpretation of the Bible: "The devil can cite Scripture for his purpose" (I.iii.93). Curiously, his response is theological rather than rational or economic in nature. In Levinas's terms, he has defined Shylock's essence as diabolical in order to avoid facing the Jew on his own terms. He assumes that Shylock has no authentic understanding of, or right to interpret his own Scripture; implicit is the belief that Antonio's own view of Genesis is superior. We recognize the outline of a supersessionist argument here, but it is not immediately clear why usury should elicit such a response. Shylock initially tries to ignore his attacker, but finally confronts him and reveals the core of their conflict:

> In the Rialto you have rated me
> About my moneys and my usances:
> . . . You call me misbeliever, cut-throat dog,
> And spet upon my Jewish gaberdine,
> And all for use of that which is mine own.
> (I.iii.102–8)

Shylock makes explicit the connection between the merchant's rejection of usury and his attack on Judaism. It is apparent now that in his angry speech discussed earlier Shylock was only reacting to Antonio's concern. The question still remains why Antonio should relate usury to Judaism and condemn both.

An examination of Antonio's views of money-lending will help clarify our discussion. In responding to Shylock's complaint of his treatment, Antonio justifies his actions and offers an explanation of his own philosophy of loans:

> If thou wilt lend this money, lend it not
> As to thy friends, for when did friendship take
> A breed for barren metal of his friend?
> But lend it rather to thine enemy . . .
>   (I.iii.127–30)

Antonio does not charge interest because he believes it is wrong to make money from one's friends. In so doing, his behavior is consonant with the opinions expressed in the biblical texts which prohibit taking interest from one's "brothers." However, the corollary to this view is that Antonio only lends money to his friends. In rejecting usury, he is in effect rejecting the toleration of difference, since usury may only be charged of "others." This poses a paradox for Shylock insofar as Antonio clearly sees him as a stranger, which should justify the employment of usury, while he simultaneously insists the practice is illegitimate.

Difference, in and of itself, constitutes enmity for Antonio; his impulse is to reject and obliterate it. Usury is permitted only when difference exists; and in this case Judaism is the constituting factor of that divergence. The merchant's desire to eradicate usury reveals that he wishes strangers, that is to say, Jews, to be eradicated as well. This is why Shylock understands Antonio's attack on usury as an attack on his "sacred nation." The merchant's view becomes clear in his final thoughts about Shylock after the latter offered to lend the money without interest: "Hie thee gentle Jew. / The Hebrew will turn Christian, he grows kind" (I.iii.173–4). The terms of approbation are clearly theologically loaded. As other critics have noted, the Jew is only "gentle" to the extent that he can be "gentile"; Antonio takes Shylock's actions here as predictive of conversion. "Kind" not only means benevolent here, but "related," as in "humankind." Shylock can only be perceived as good to the extent that he is willing to become Christian; Antonio has no positive category for the Jew as Jew (see Shell 1979: 65–70 and 1991: *passim* for related analyses).

Ultimately, the conflict between Antonio and Shylock centers on the doctrine of supersession and the Jew's resistance of its totalizing stance. While Shylock does not like the Christians, his interactions with them suggest that he is willing to tolerate them; Antonio, on the other hand, while preaching friendship, wants to exclude all who are not Christian from his society. Shylock's commitment to difference preserves his own existence in Venice; why then does he propose the murderous "merry bond," which, even if not intended to be enforced at this point, certainly has the potential of killing his adversary? Shylock is fully aware of the implications of Antonio's hatred of difference as manifested in the linking of usury and Judaism. His bond proposes a comparison to Antonio meant to "call into question . . . [his exercise of the same]" (Levinas 1969: 43). Is usury worse than murder, or to rephrase the question, is the toleration of difference as represented in usury law worse than the totalizing obliteration of difference? While many Reformation theologians believed that conversion to Christianity was the Jews' only hope for salvation, from a Jewish perspective, conversion is a kind of self-destruction, a death; the term for conversion in Hebrew, שמד (*shamad*), also means to destroy or annihilate. Shylock sets up for Antonio the same specter of death that conversion poses for him as a Jew: it is equivalent to having your heart cut out. Antonio's commitment to his universal vision precludes him from even perceiving Shylock's question. He only notices the gesture toward the same, which he reads as a step toward conversion, and he happily accepts the terms of the bond.

Portia, as a woman, would seem to be at a similar disadvantage owing to her gender difference. Although she is unmarried, she cannot exercise her will because she is constrained by her father's will, that is, his testament, which prevents her from marrying or not marrying as she desires. The lottery which promises her and her wealth to the suitor who chooses the correct casket effectively puts her in a state of perpetual courtship. It does not seem to allow Portia the ability to refuse marriage and do as she pleases with her inheritance. However, as a white, aristocratic Christian, Portia also participates in the dominant culture of the play which is intolerant of difference. She is introduced in I.ii as witty and prejudiced, cavalierly dismissing potential suitors on the basis of mean-spirited stereotypes. While a contemporary English audience might easily have laughed along with her petty sniping at the Neopolitan prince and the French lord, they might have found her jokes about Falconbridge, the young baron of England, a little unsettling. Although this moment passes quickly in the play, it does communicate the unhappy experience of difference when one becomes the excluded or diminished other. Nevertheless, I would like to argue that Portia understands the value of difference that Shylock attempts to exercise; while she employs a method similar to his, she is ultimately more successful in her achieving a status of difference which is not subordinated to the dominant other.

The structure of the usury agreement is essentially that of a contract: I agree to lend you a certain sum of money and you agree to pay me back that sum plus interest given the risk I take in lending to a stranger. The bond into which Shylock enters with Antonio is obviously another contract and the Jew is the character most associated with this type of legal relation in the play. It in fact is taken as an aspect of his intolerant Jewish legalism that he insists on pursuing the cruel bond. However, the contract has the same valuable function as usury insofar as it allows the establishment of safeguarded relationships between strangers who would otherwise not be able or willing to interact. Portia is also associated with the law and the protection of difference in a number of contexts, although, unlike Shylock, she always manages to turn the law to her favor while appearing to uphold it. The lottery, which appears to be a neutral contract regulating all wooers by the same standard, treats white suitors differently from dark ones (Shell 1979: 72) and is susceptible to manipulation, as is evident in Bassanio's trial where the rhyme and meaning of the song performed before his choice point to the lead casket (III.ii.63–72; see also I.ii.91–5 for a different example of deviousness). Her marriage provides another example of the contract and it is one that should be considered in more detail.

Early modern conceptions of marriage were undergoing redefinition as a result of the Reformation. While marriage had always been understood in canon law as a contract requiring the consent of both parties (Witte 1988: 62–5), Protestant doctrine deemphasized its sacramental nature and focused more on the relationship: "the primacy of mutual help in marriage is tied to [the Puritans'] conception of marriage as based on an essentially covenantal model" (Johnson 1971: 109). When understood as a sacrament, marriage was seen as indissoluble; however, in a covenantal model both parties are expected to perform their duties or be punished for non-performance (Johnson 1971: 115–16). Portia clearly understands marriage in its contractual aspect and turns it to her own advantage. She appears to acknowledge her subordination to her husband when she gives herself and her possessions to Bassanio after he has "won" the casket lottery:

> Myself and what is mine, to you and yours
> Is now converted. But now I was the lord
> Of this fair mansion, master of my servants,
> Queen o'er myself: and even now, but now.
> This house, these servants, and this same myself
> Are yours, – my lord's – I give them with this ring,
> Which when you part from, lose, or give away,
> Let it presage the ruin of your love,
> And be my vantage to exclaim on you.
>
> (III.ii.166–74)

The humble and self-deprecating tone of her lines which precede this passage is strikingly unlike Portia's assertive and sharp-witted persona exhibited elsewhere in the play; it suggests we look carefully at her speech to understand why she would present such a subservient and helpless account of herself. Portia does give everything to Bassanio here, but she gives it conditionally *with the ring*. She and all she has is his as long as he keeps the ring; implicit in this contract is the condition that she regain all she has given if he should lose possession of the ring. Portia's intention to maintain control over her property is signaled by her continued use of the singular possessive pronoun in referring to the house and servants she has presumably just given to Bassanio (III.iv.25, V.i.89, 119, 273). When he gives the ring away to the disguised Portia, he breaks the contract and, in effect, returns his control over her and her property back to his wife (see Karen Newman [1987] for a different account of Portia's triumph at the play's conclusion).

In her insistence on Bassanio adhering to the bond, Portia greatly resembles Shylock and differs from most of the other Christian characters in the play who break their bonds: Launcelot who leaves his master, Jessica who leaves her father and her faith, Antonio who forfeits his bond to Shylock, and Bassanio. This in some measure parallels the difference in the ways Jews and early modern Christians viewed God's covenant with the children of Israel; while the Jews maintained that their covenant with God held, Christians argued that the covenant had been broken or superseded by their new relationship with God. The Christians in the play demonstrate a particularly cavalier attitude about the importance of the marital bond, especially regarding their wives' individual autonomy. Bassanio refuses at first to give his ring to Balthazar (his disguised wife), but is won over by Antonio's argument that his "love whithal / Be valued 'gainst your wife's commandement" (IV.i.446–7); here we have a doctrine of love superseding a doctrine of law, with Portia associated with Judaism in contrast to Christianity. Earlier in the court scene, both Bassanio and Gratiano essentially wish their wives dead in order to save Antonio from Shylock (IV.i.278ff). While their disguised wives are humorously trenchant in their responses, Shylock also comments on the husbands' lack of fidelity to their spouses: "These be the Christian husbands! I have a daughter – / Would any of the stock of Barrabas / Had been her husband, rather than a Christian" (IV.i.291–3). We do have doubts about the ability of Christian husbands in the play to see their wives as distinct others, in a positive sense, rather than sources of wealth or extensions of themselves. Lorenzo gains a great deal of money from his marriage, as does Bassanio, however, both reveal ambivalence in their feelings about their wives; the latter, as discussed above, and the former in his lateness when eloping with Jessica (which is seen as a sign of waning love) and in his bantering with her in V.i, when they place themselves in the roles of other mostly exogamous relationships which end tragically. Jessica, now a Christian, clearly disregards her parents' own marital bond, and particularly her mother's role in forming it, by selling the betrothal ring Leah gave to Shylock. However, Shylock accords the ring an affective value beyond any monetary worth, suggesting his wife was not a possession but a person whose agency he respected by guarding the ring she gave him (III.i.108–13). In her insistence on the immeasurable worth of her betrothal ring, Portia again echoes Shylock (V.i.199).

Given their similarities, it is therefore interesting that Portia appears as an adversary to Shylock in the play's climactic court scene. This is especially true insofar as, disguised as the lawyer Balthazar, she exhibits an adherence to the law that even supersedes that of Shylock: "This bond doth give thee here no jot of blood, / The words expressly are 'a pound of flesh'" (IV.i.302–3). Although Portia advocates mercy to Shylock, she wins her case by reading the bond with Talmudic closeness and establishes the impossibility of its fulfillment (Isaac 1992: 354). In so doing, Portia also protects the integrity of Venetian law through interpretation rather than undermines it with mercy. As it turns out, the state of Venice, like Portia, has an interest in preserving difference which requires them to honor contracts made between strangers. As Antonio points out in response to Solanio's hope that the Duke will nullify the bond:

> The duke cannot deny the course of law:
> For the commodity that strangers have
> With us in Venice, if it be denied,
> Will much impeach the justice of the state,
> Since that the trade and profit of the city
> Consisteth of all nations.
>
> (III.iii.26–31)

Contracts are necessary for Venetians to establish profitable relations with others; if strangers felt that the law did not offer them impartial protection, this would not only call into question "the justice of the state" but, more importantly, jeopardize its commerce.

This law protecting contracts with strangers appears to preserve the very difference that Antonio was so eager to obliterate in his stand against usury and Judaism. Yet the Venetians seem no more tolerant of Shylock than the merchant. We see the Duke privately conferring with Antonio before the trial and clearly stating his prejudice against Shylock, whom he defines as "A stony adversary, an inhuman wretch, / Uncapable of pity, void, and empty / From any dram of mercy" (IV.i.3–5). Of course the Duke has cause to condemn here, as Shylock has decided to insist on the fulfill-ment of his bond, yet the state's neutrality in the matter is suspect. The Duke's assess-ment also raises the question: how can they demand mercy from the Jew when they think him incapable of it? When Shylock enters the court, the Duke asks for mercy, but again in such a way that would make the plaintiff's compliance impossible. The Duke expects Shylock to act according to "human gentleness" by releasing the for-feiture and forgiving part of the debt, arguing that Antonio's case is pitiable enough to elicit a kind response "From brassy bosoms and rough hearts of flint, / From stub-born Turks, and Tartars never train'd / To offices of tender courtesy" (IV.i.31–3). Other kinds of hard-case "infidels" are cited here as capable of mercy in this instance; if they can be compassionate, surely the Jew can. However, it is not clear that they really do believe him capable of mercy. The Duke's concluding statement: "We all expect a gentle answer Jew!" (34) indicates that he expects Shylock to give a gentile, that is, a Christian answer. As Antonio makes clear a few lines later, the Venetians believe the Jew to be like a force of nature who, by definition, cannot behave mercifully:

> I pray you think you question with the Jew,
> You may as well go stand upon the beach
> And bid the main flood bate his usual height,
>
> . . .
>
> You may as well do any thing most hard
> As seek to soften that – than which what's harder? –
> His Jewish heart!
>
> (70–2, 78–80)

As a Jew, Shylock is constitutionally unable to act benevolently; behavior is defined by religious group and not by one's actions. Levinas's discussion of conceptualization as suppression of the other is pertinent here; we can see how the apparent non-violence of totality (goodness can only be defined in terms of sameness, that is, Christianity) can appear in the tyranny of the state (Levinas 1969: 46). To assume that Shylock can only be good as a Christian is to insist that he cease to exist. While Shylock's pursuit of the bond is cruel and vengeful, it may be read as a reaction against the Venetian desire to annihilate him.

While there is an apparent interest in preserving difference in Venice, it is only tolerated to the extent that it works to the benefit of the state. The laws regarding commerce are impartial insofar as they protect the contracts of both natives and strangers, but foreigners are not accorded the same status that Christian Venetians enjoy in the law. While Portia is able to get the better of Shylock by reading the bond more literally than he, her real advantage lies in a series of laws that are prejudicial to non-Christian aliens. On closer consideration, the problem for Shylock begins not with the shedding of mere blood, but of Christian blood: "if thou does shed / One drop of Christian blood, thy lands and goods / Are (by the laws of Venice) confiscate / Unto the state of Venice" (IV.i.305–8). Shylock asks if this is indeed the law, and Portia assures him he "shalt see the act" (310). While we are never given the contents of this law, it seems clear that Christian blood has greater value in Venice and that the spilling of it, presumably by a non-Christian, results in the confiscation of his or her property (see Schotz 1991 for a different explanation). It seems unlikely that Venetian law protects non-Christian blood to the same extent. When Shylock declines to break this law and suffer the consequence, Portia insists that he stand by his word and fulfill it: "The Jew shall have all justice" (IV.i.317). She, in effect, forces him to violate this statute, and adduces another crime in his fulfillment of the forfeiture:

> Therefore prepare thee to cut off the flesh, –
>
> . . .
>
> . . . if thou tak'st more
> Or less than a just pound, be it but so much
> As makes it light or heavy in the substance,
> Or the division of the twentieth part
> Of one poor scruple, nay if the scale do turn
> But in the estimation of a hair,
> Thou diest, and all thy goods are confiscate.
>
> (IV.i.320, 322–8)

It is not clear if this regulation is related to the law about shedding Christian blood or not (see Shapiro 1996: 133ff). Here Portia focuses on what appears to be a different issue, the exact fulfillment of the bond. If Shylock does not fulfill the terms of the bond *exactly*, an impossible task as defined by Portia, his property will be confiscated, which the first law already stipulated, and he will be liable for death. Difference does not seem to be the issue in this instance, but rather the state's power to employ the harshest measures possible to punish a party for non-fulfillment of a bond. It is odd that Portia directs this penalty against the creditor rather than the debtor, who is logically responsible for the forfeiture. However, although this law ostensibly protects the conditions of a contract, and hence preserves Venetian commerce, its arbitrary application here suggests that it can be held in reserve and applied in such a way to protect friends of the state from their obligations to others.

The third law cited by Portia clearly articulates the bias in Venetian laws against strangers:

> It is enacted in the laws of Venice,
> If it be proved against an alien,
> That by direct, or indirect attempts
> He seek the life of any citizen,
> The party 'gainst the which he doth contrive,
> Shall seize one half his goods, the other half
> Comes to the privy coffer of the state,
> And the offender's life lies in the mercy
> Of the Duke only, 'gainst all other voice.
>
> (IV.i.344–52)

The partiality of the law raises disturbing questions. While no one would deny the seriousness of attempted murder or dispute that the state and the victim are both interested parties in this crime, nevertheless it seems sufficient to prohibit any perpetrator from seeking the life of another. By focusing on the citizen as victim and the alien as felon, other important categories of wrongdoing are ignored. For example, can a citizen seek the life of an alien with impunity? What is the penalty for a citizen seeking the life of another citizen? What or who determines the criteria for Venetian citizenship, and why, finally, is Shylock not a citizen of Venice, since he clearly lives and works there? Ultimately, Venetian law only preserves difference positively when this serves the interest of the state, as in the protection of contract law. There is no legal commitment to the disinterested protection of difference; on the contrary, difference is more likely to hold a negative charge in Venice.

Portia commands Shylock to beg for mercy, which he does not do. The Christians of Venice offer Shylock mercy: the Duke pardons his life and offers to reduce the half of his property Shylock owes the state to a fine; Antonio asks to hold his half of the property in use (hence Shylock retains nominal ownership) if Shylock convert and leave all his property to Jessica and Lorenzo in his will. From the perspective of the Christians, their offers, though conditional, are merciful, insofar as they do not choose to enforce the full extent of the law against the guilty party. From Shylock's perspective, he can only choose between two kinds of death and must be content to do so. Although Shylock complains about losing so much property when the sentence is first given, "you take my life / When you do take the means whereby I live" (IV.i.372–3), he still has enough sense of self at this point to struggle against his punishment. However, when Antonio stipulates that Shylock convert to Christianity, and the Duke makes his own pardon of the Jew's life conditional on his acceptance, he is effectively annihilated either way. His acquiescence "I am content" and its attendant illness indicate the obliteration of his will as he is subsumed into Christian culture. Antonio has finally triumphed in his desire to eradicate Jewish distinctiveness from his community; Shylock's difference has been destroyed, and he disappears from the action. Nevertheless, the play's refusal to display a successfully converted Shylock testifies to its uneasiness over this forced dissolution of difference.

Although she acts as the crucial catalyst in Shylock's destruction, Portia appears to be successful at the conclusion of the play in maintaining her own difference and independence as Bassanio's wife through her calculated use of contract. What finally is the nature of Portia's relation to the law and hence her dedication to difference as an ethical category? In Alice Bentson's consideration of the first part of this question, she pauses to distinguish between commercial contracts and marriages: "The difference between the two kinds of contracts is that the first makes possible the interaction among strangers, even enemies, as Antonio observes, while the second requires love. The haunting irony underlying this scene [V.i] is that no contract will secure love. Love, like mercy, will not be yielded on compulsion" (1991: 193, n15). I would argue that Portia understood this when she made the contract with Bassanio. She did not rely on marital love, which can be mystified to serve the ends of totality; we should remember that St. Augustine thought that the bonds of love and female servitude coexisted naturally in marriage (Blamires 1992: 79–80). Rather, she used the conditions of the contract to secure her personal autonomy, and did so successfully. However, the accomplishment of her own liberty does not signal a consistent commitment to difference. Portia, like the Venetians, protects difference when it serves her own ends.

Jessica provides a strong counter-example to her father and Portia insofar as she chooses totality; her fate demonstrates the dangers of seeking the dissolution of the self into the other. Whereas Portia devises a plan to maintain control over her property at the moment of her betrothal, Jessica throws caution to the wind when she throws her dowry out the window to her fiancé, Lorenzo. Jessica believes that by marrying a Christian and converting she will achieve a measure of autonomy she lacks as a Jewish woman. However, her position appears to decline rather than improve after her marriage. Launcelot, formerly her cordial subordinate, is condescending and cruel after her conversion (Gaudet 1991: 364). Rather than welcoming her to the faith, he views Jessica as "damn'd" whether she is the legitimate offspring of a Jew or not; he is doubtful that she is fully Christian. When Jessica insists that she "shall be sav'd by [her] husband . . . [who] made [her] / a Christian!" (III.v.17–18), Launcelot replies uncharitably that "we were Christians / enow before" (19–20), again ostracizing and demeaning her rather than offering respect and acceptance. Jessica's cool reception in the Christian community after her elopement also reinforces the inferiority of her position (Gaudet 1991: 366–8). Even more disheartening is her relationship with Lorenzo. As noted earlier, Lorenzo misses the appointed time of their elopement, signaling, in his friends' estimation, a certain lack of ardor (II.vi.2ff). After they are married and have taken refuge in Belmont, Lorenzo asks his wife for her estimation of Portia

(III.v.67–77). When Jessica implicitly deprecates herself in giving a glowing account of their hostess, Lorenzo does not immediately respond with words of loving assurance as a besotted new husband should do; rather, he takes the opportunity to praise himself, which emphasizes her indebtedness and subordination to him: "Even such a husband / Hast thou of me, as [Portia] is for a wife" (77–8). In their final conversation they playfully list a number of couples, including themselves, whose relationships end unhappily. Although Jessica seeks conversion while her father shuns it, both end silenced and subordinated at the play's conclusion.

Unlike Shylock who is forced to convert to Christianity, and Jessica who willingly chooses it and a conventional marriage, Portia only appears to "convert" (III.ii.167) to a subordinate wife while protecting herself by making use of the law. She would then seem to be the only character of the three who successfully preserves her alterity. Yet it is disturbing that she alone enjoys her autonomy (none of the other women in the play attain this relation with their husbands), and it is bought at the expense of Bassanio's independence. In fact, at the play's conclusion, most, if not all of the characters present are in some sense beholden to or dependent upon Portia's power, and therefore lacking full self-determination. While she effectively subsumes everyone to her control, she has not broken out of the totalizing world which threatened her earlier in the play. The strength of Portia's position is undermined by the final lines of Gratiano, the voice of aggression in the play: "Well, while I live, I'll fear no other thing / So sore, as keeping safe Nerissa's ring" (V.i.306–7). The crude joke that Gratiano makes here is that a husband must be vigilant in policing his wife's "ring" or genitalia by keeping his finger in it; in other words, her sexuality is in his power. Here the ring loses the significance of female integrity and agency that Portia and Shylock accorded it; instead, the woman's sexuality is commodified into an object that her husband controls, and her identity is subsumed to his. As long as alterity is not respected in and of itself, only power will determine who remains free.

REFERENCES AND FURTHER READING

Auden, W. H. 1962: "Brothers and Others." In *The Dyer's Hand and Other Essays*. New York: Random House, 218–37.

Baker, J. H. 1990: *An Introduction to English Legal History*. London: Butterworth.

Bentson, A. N. 1991: "Portia, the Law and the Tripartite Structure of *The Merchant of Venice*." In Thomas Wheeler (ed.), *The Merchant of Venice: Critical Essays*. New York and London: Garland Publishing, 163–94.

The Bible. King James Version.

Blamires, A. 1992: *Woman Defamed and Woman Defended: An Anthology of Medieval Texts*. Oxford: Clarendon Press.

Erickson, A. L. 1993: *Women and Property in Early Modern England*. London: Routledge.

Gaudet, P. 1991: "Lorenzo's 'Infidel': The Staging of Difference in *The Merchant of Venice*." In Thomas Wheeler (ed.), *The Merchant of Venice: Critical Essays*. New York and London: Garland Publishing, 351–77.

Gritsch, E. W. 1994: "The Jews in Reformation Theology." In Marvin Perry and Frederick M. Schweitzer (eds.), *Jewish–Christian Encounters over the Centuries*. New York: Peter Lang, 197–213.

Hall, K. F. 1992: "Guess Who's Coming to Dinner? Colonization and Miscegenation in

The Merchant of Venice." Renaissance Drama, 23, 87–111.

Isaac, D. 1992: "The Worth of a Jew's Eye: Reflections of the Talmud in *The Merchant of Venice." Maarav*, 8, 349–74.

Johnson, J. T. 1971: "The Covenant Idea and the Puritan View of Marriage." *Journal of the History of Ideas*, 32, 1, 107–18.

Klein, J. L. 1992: *Daughters, Wives, and Widows: Writings by Men about Women and Marriage in England, 1500–1640*. Urbana and Chicago: University of Illinois Press.

Levinas, E. 1969: *Totality and Infinity: An Essay on Exteriority*. Pittsburgh, PA: Duquesne University Press.

Newman, K. 1987: "Portia's Ring: Unruly Women and Structures of Exchange in *The Merchant of Venice." Shakespeare Quarterly*, 38, 1, 19–33.

Oberman, H. 1983: "Three Sixteenth-Century Attitudes to Judaism: Reuchlin, Erasmus and Luther." In Bernard Dov Cooperman (ed.),

Jewish Thought in the Sixteenth Century. Cambridge, MA, and London: Harvard University Press, 326–64.

Schotz, A. 1991: "The Law That Never Was: A Note on *The Merchant of Venice." Theatre Research International*, 16, 3, 249–52.

Shakespeare, W. 1985: *The Merchant of Venice*. Ed. John Russell Brown. London and New York: Methuen.

Shapiro, J. 1996: *Shakespeare and the Jews*. New York: Columbia University Press.

Shell, M. 1979: "The Wether and the Ewe: Verbal Usury in *The Merchant of Venice." Kenyon Review*, n.s., 1, 65–92.

——1991: "Marranos (Pigs), Or From Coexistence to Toleration." *Critical Inquiry*, 17, 306–35.

Witte, Jr., J. 1988: "The Transformation of Marriage Law in the Lutheran Reformation." In J. Witte, Jr. and F. Alexander (eds.), *The Weightier Matters of the Law: Essays on Law and Religion*. Atlanta, GA: Scholars Press, 57–97.

19

Between Idolatry and Astrology:
Modes of Temporal Repetition
in *Romeo and Juliet*
Philippa Berry

In her study of Shakespeare's histories, Phyllis Rackin (1990: ix) observes that "the practice of historiography has become a subject of intense controversy and radical transformation" within the academy, and certainly it seems that the thorny question of the relationship between text and history still haunts literary studies of the Renaissance.[1] Although implicitly problematized by new historicism, in fact this issue has seldom been directly addressed by new historicist critics, who, as Steven Mullaney points out, have "primarily focussed on discrete historical moments and [been] silent about processes of historical change." In its use of the historical fragment or anecdote, new historicism has elegantly introduced a postmodern awareness of temporal relativism or "randomization" into the field of Renaissance studies; however, new speculations about the relationship between textuality and temporality have recently begun to emerge in Shakespeare studies.[2] What may be a new intellectual trend is less indebted to quasi-Foucaultian considerations of history as a conflict-ridden site of subversion and containment than to a postmodern suspicion of history – that is, of time conceived of as linear and teleological or end-driven. In this respect the emergent set of concerns affords some interesting parallels to the speculations on time of postmodern thinkers such as Nietzsche, Heidegger, Kristeva, and above all Derrida, and is sometimes explicitly influenced by this intellectual tradition.

Two important texts in this connection are Patricia Parker's *Shakespeare from the Margins* (1996) and Ned Lukacher's *Time Fetishes* (1998). Both these authors – albeit in very different ways – identify a textual differing of the diachronic ordering of time and history as a recurring effect within the Shakespearean corpus. Parker's book reads the Shakespearean reconfiguring of temporality primarily as a literary device, in a brilliant analysis of Shakespeare's fondness for the rhetorical trope of the preposterous; she defines this trope as performing "a reversal of priority, precedence and ordered sequence which also disrupts the linear orders of succession and following" (1996: 21). Lukacher's book, on the other hand, offers an explicitly deconstructive reading of Shakespearean and other texts which stresses Shakespeare's philosophical indebtedness to classical models of cyclical time, which he argues resemble what Nietzsche called eternal recurrence. These two studies serve to remind us of the fundamental ambivalence at the heart of Renaissance ideas of temporality, whereby its Christian view of time (as linear history versus unmoving eternity) was entwined or crossed with a circular, repetitive timing which had agricultural and astrological as well as philosophical dimensions. Similar themes have been explored in works by Renaissance critics such as Francis Barker and Michel Jeanneret, while historians such as D. R. Woolf and Nicholas Campion have reemphasized the extent to which many Renaissance thinkers rediscovered the ancients' cyclical and repetitive version of time in works by classical writers such as Plato and Polybius.[3]

What I want to suggest in this essay is some of the ways in which *Romeo and Juliet* puts the putative singularity and linearity of time and history into question. In its combination of frantic temporal acceleration with what might be described as a turning backwards of time (in the form of the repetitive and cyclical timing of calendrical and festive modes of memorialization), this play's imagery encapsulates the perceived multifaceted character of time in the late sixteenth century. For as both historical allusion and temporality in general are "textualized" within the "short time" of the tragedy, so these elements are also differed, doubled and extended, in a way which requires us to expand both our critical and our temporal perceptions.

I read Shakespeare's Juliet as the textual site through which this late Renaissance inconsistency about time – which is also an awareness of an inconsistency or rift within time itself – becomes manifest. I owe a debt, in this formulation, to Julia Kristeva's important but controversial essay, "Women's Time," in which she allies female subjectivity, and a feminine *jouissance* in particular, with two modes of time – repetitive or cyclical, and monumental (or eternal) – in opposition to the linearity of historical time. Kristeva notes that: "female subjectivity as it gives itself up to intuition becomes a problem with respect to a certain conception of time: time as project, teleology, linear and prospective unfolding: time as departure, progression and arrival – in other words, the time of history" (Kristeva 1986b: 192). What I shall suggest here, however, is that not only does Juliet peculiarly encompass or attract to herself the "feminine" aspects of temporality identified by Kristeva; she also has an important connection with two apparently contrasting aspects of time that have a historical or teleological as well as a cyclical or repetitive significance. These different timings briefly cohere in the play's focus upon a particular calendrical moment that, while it is highly specific, is also embedded in an ambivalent festive tradition encompassing both celebration and destruction. Yet as the play ends we are implicitly reminded that these contrasting temporalities also cross or converge, equally briefly, in all acts of remembrance, whether these assume religious or aesthetic form.

Juliet's multifaceted significance in respect of time is adumbrated on her first appearance, in I.iii, when the Nurse's tedious narrative of her weaning splits her name into two suggestive syllables – as the "Jule" who is also, since she always responds thus, "ay," or continuous: "'Yea,' quoth my husband, 'fall'st upon thy face? / Thou wilt fall backward when thou comest to age, / Wilt thou not Jule?' It stinted, and said 'Ay'" (I.iii.47–8).[4] While this nominal splitting appears to equate Juliet, on the one hand, with the devouring mouth as *gula* or *gueule* (in Latin and French) – a conventional figure for forward-moving time – it implies that she also has a mysterious affinity with time's mysterious non-linear existence, as eternity, or "ay." Yet if we recombine them, these two syllables metamorphose Juliet into "July," configuring her as a feminine personification of her birth month, and hence as a figure whose highly individual fate is peculiarly embedded in a calendrical cycle of temporal repetition. We are told by the Nurse and her mother, of course, that Juliet's birthday will be on the night of July 31 or Lammas-eve, a "fortnight and odd days" after the Capulet ball.

The July setting of Shakespeare's play contrasts strikingly with that of his main source, Arthur Brooke's *Romeus and Juliet*, where the lovers first meet at a Christmas feast, and their tragedy does not escalate until Easter. One effect of the late summer dating of the tragedy is to reinvest late July with a carnival significance comparable to that which it seems to have formerly enjoyed, in pre-Reformation culture. This time of the year was still distinguished by some important forms of popular festivity, most notably pageants and fairs; before the Reformation, however, it had been full of important holy or saints' days. And at the same time, it also had enormous importance in the astrological time-reckonings of antiquity – an importance still recognized not only in the popular Elizabethan almanac, but even in the almanac or liturgical calendar used by the Church of England in the Book of Common Prayer. In the calendar which prefaces Cranmer's 1559 prayer book, in fact, while the only saint's day which has been retained for veneration in the month of July is that of the apostle St. James (on July 25), the calendar notes the passage of the sun into the astrological sign of Leo (it gives no details about the moon) and also records the date of the beginning of the dog days – a detail to which I will return. These astrological details are retained in late sixteenth-century editions of the prayer book, while several saints' days are also restored.[5]

Shakespeare is thought by a number of critics to have written *Romeo and Juliet* around the same time as *A Midsummer Night's Dream*, possibly in late 1595 or 1596, and certainly it seems that the "finding out" or consultation of an almanac is just as relevant to the concerns of this play as it is to the rehearsals of the mechanicals in *A Dream*, where Bottom calls for "A calendar, a calendar – look in the almanac, find out moonshine, find out moonshine" (III.i.45–6). But while, in the comedy, the mechanicals need an almanac in order to know whether the moon will shine during their production of Pyramus and Thisbe (as indeed it does, in the form of the new moon which has been awaited so eagerly by Theseus and Hippolyta as the signal for their wedding); in the tragedy, the play's implicit concern is rather with plotting the sun's passage in late July – together with the peculiar effects of the doubling of its heat at this time, which was termed the "canicular" or dog days. In the late sixteenth century, the dog days were calculated as extending from mid-July to mid-August, since this was the time of the heliacal rising of the brightest star in the sky, when it was once more visible on the horizon just before dawn. The star in question was Sirius, the dog-star, chief star of the constellation Canis Major, and regarded by the ancients as the near double of the sun. In the prayer book of 1559, the dog days are listed as beginning on July 7 and ending on August 17, but the dates progressed forwards due to the phenomenon of equinoctial procession.

This astrological context has a particular relevance to the lovers' definition, in the play's opening chorus, as "star-crossed," as I will show. But while its several references to the "fateful" influences of the stars emphasize a pagan alternative – if also a partial analogue – to the Calvinist doctrine of predestination, like the Elizabethan almanac, *Romeo and Juliet* interweaves this remnant of pagan astrological lore with traces of another model of temporal repetition, in the form of a pre-Reformation (and possibly also a recusant) calendrical piety. My contention, however, is that none of these temporal allusions has a simple or singular meaning, but serves rather to illuminate the tragedy's significance through a complex process of semiotic differentiation and even negation, as the combination of piety and festivity associated with major saints' days *before* the Reformation is replaced by the paradoxical piety of the lovers' extreme passion, whereby sexual desire is troped both as pilgrimage and as image-worship. One implication seems to be that, far from being either careful readers of almanacs or observant Catholics, the lovers fail to observe a range of different calendrical signals which might conceivably have altered their fates. Another, however, is that their tragedy cannot be made sense of according to a singular time scheme, but instead requires us to combine different versions of time, and specifically, different types of information about late July – calendrical and religious as well as astrological and folkloric – in order to account for it.

In accounts of the Christian liturgical calendar, the month of July is sometimes characterized as marking the beginning of the half-year of "secular time"; however, Eamon Duffy has reemphasized the importance of this month in the context of pre-Reformation popular piety in England:

> A major feast of England's most important saint, Thomas Becket, the translation of his relics, fell on 7 July . . . In the same month there were . . . the feasts of St Mary Magdalene [22], St Margaret [20], St James the Apostle [25], and St Anne [26] . . . all were immensely popular and very widely kept. (Duffy 1992: 47)

Duffy observes also that before the Reformation the great civic festivities of the year (which had a strong religious dimension usually expressed in pageant or play) were often held at the end of July or on the first day of August (Lammas):

> At Lincoln the greatest convergence of civic and sacred ceremonial came on Saint Anne's day, at the end of July, when the city gilds organized an elaborate series of pageants. Even at York, where the most famous Corpus Christi cycle in England was normally played on the feast day itself, the Creed play and the Paternoster plays which sometimes replaced the Corpus Christi plays were performed in Lammastide. (Duffy 1992: 48)

Many of the most popular saints' days of this period had been excised from the liturgical calendar in 1536 at the Reformation, partly to increase the time available for agricultural labor; all feast days falling in harvest, from July 1 to September 29, were abolished, excepting only feasts of the Apostles, the Blessed Virgin, and St. George. In July, therefore, only the feast day of St. James the Apostle, the patron saint of pilgrims, which was on July 25, was initially retained, in quite splendid isolation. (Before the Reformation even this date had enjoyed an additional significance, because it was then shared by St. James with the gigantic Christ-bearer – or light-bearer – St. Christopher.) Yet what is often overlooked in accounts of the Reformers' attacks on the cults of the saints is that it was not until 1547–8 that the images of saints were ordered to be removed from churches, or defaced (Duffy 1992: 394). Indeed, both the slowness and the uncertainty of the process of iconoclastic reform was attested to on the accession of Elizabeth I in 1559: on the one hand, there was another wave of image destruction; on the other, many saints' days were reintroduced into the prayer book, although not as red letter or full holy days. (This process of partial reintroduction continued through Elizabeth's reign and into that of James I.) A 1563 Convocation voiced the dissatisfaction of many clergy at the continued existence of saints' days; but it seems that purging the calendar was easier to proclaim than enforce. David Cressy (1989) points out that law terms were still marked by the ancient religious festival days, as were the legal calendars of all courts operating by civil rather than common law, while popular almanacs (which listed far more saints' days than the prayer book calendar) likewise kept in mind memories of holy days that the Reformers wanted to be forgotten. Amidst this uneven process of cultic extirpation, the end of July and the beginning of August seem to have retained a symbolic significance, primarily as marking the official end of summer, the first fruits of the harvest and (specifically on August 1, or Lammas), the time of a quarterly payment of rents and the opening of common lands for pastures. A catalogue of fairs in 1661 showed that fifty-eight towns had fairs on St. James's Day, twenty-eight on Lammas; it was probably no coincidence, also, that James I and his queen, Anna, were crowned on July 25, the date of St. James's Day and the eve of St. Anne's Day (Cressy 1989).

Thus although officially abolished by Protestantism, it seems clear that the pre-Reformation calendar of holy days (with its attendant connotations of idolatry or image-worship) must have continued to exert a strong imaginative and memorial influence on middle-of-the-road Protestants. And in areas with a developed culture of recusancy, such as Lancashire and Warwickshire, this memorial survival would presumably have been far more complete. As a young man growing up in Warwickshire (where there were two churches of St. James the Great in his immediate vicinity: one in Stratford-upon-Avon itself, and another in his grandfather's village of Snitterfield), Shakespeare would have been especially aware of this festive calendar. The memorial importance of the abolished holy days would naturally have been augmented for the son of a (belatedly) recusant father, most of whose mother's family, the Ardens, also retained their Catholic faith. Yet (as we know from both Hamlet and Jacques Derrida) remembrance is never a simple act of repetition, since the memory which remains will always differ from the remembered object, name, or event, typically expanding its significance through diverse metonymic or metaphoric associations. Before the Reformation, this process of memorial accretion had already built complex imaginative and aesthetic structures around the cults of individual saints which Reformers would see as a dangerous supplement to their original religious function. And in Shakespeare's post-Reformation play, while the traces of these cults, where discernible, may have reminded some theatergoers of Catholic piety, the dramatic and secular context of these signs suggests that their emblematic function once again exceeds any dogmatic system of interpretation.

A saint's holy day equates his or her presumed date of death with a *dies natalis* or birthday in heaven, as a saint. And in *Romeo and Juliet*, the close temporal connection between Juliet's birthdate and her death configures the lovers' double death (which occurs, on the evidence of the play, some ten days before the anniversary of her birth) as the site or occasion for another quasi-festive memorialization. So we are told at the end of the play: "That whiles Verona by that name is known, / There shall no figure at such rate be set / As that of true and faithful Juliet" (V.iii.299–301). This conclusion gives material (albeit secular) form to Romeo's inaugural perception of Juliet, at the Capulet ball, as a "dear saint" to whose (bodily) shrine he must make pilgrimage as a *romero* or pilgrim; in John Florio's *A New World of Words* (1598), he notes "Romeo, as Romitággio, *a roamer, a wanderer, a Palmer for devotion sake.*"[6] But in their two families' choice of the striking memorial device of two golden statues, the play's conclusion is also acutely problematic from a Reformation perspective. Indeed, it can be interpreted in several different ways. Is it a mistaken act of idolatry paralleling and reminding us of the lovers' own transference of the language of worship from divine to mutable objects of adoration? *The Second Tome of Homelyes*, published in 1563, condemns "the glorious gylte images and ydolles [of the saints], all shynynge and glytterying with metall and stone, and covered with precious vestures," reminding us that it was just such *rich* images of the saints – presumably the gifts of wealthy donors who also signaled their social status through such acts – that were especially reviled by the Reformers.[7] Or alternatively, the families' decision could serve as an oblique reminder to those in the audience who, like and yet unlike Juliet, were "true and faithful" in their veneration of forgotten saints, and perhaps especially those of late July and early August: saints whom Claude Gaignebet, for reasons which will become apparent below, describes as the "canicular" saints (1986: *passim*).[8]

Only Saints Francis and Peter are specifically mentioned (as saints) in this play. Yet the names of two Capulet servants evoke those of saints who were directly connected with this period. The name of St. Peter, with its Roman connotations, is both repeated and diminished in that of the Capulet servingman, Peter. This saint to whose church Juliet is to be dragged by Capulet in order to marry Paris, "on a hurdle," like a condemned traitor or recusant priest going to his death, formerly had August 1 or Lammas as one of his (now excised) feast days, when his miraculous liberation from prison was commemorated by the feast of St. Peter-in-Chains. And the name of another Capulet servant, Samson, may echo as well as differ from not only the memory of the biblical Samson, but also that of another saint associated with this calendrical period: St. Samson, whose feast was formerly held on July 28.[9] (The name of Verona's "holy" Friar Lawrence also evokes the feast day of Romeo's most famous post-apostolic martyr, St. Lawrence, held a few days later on August 10.) Yet it is the name of the other Capulet servant which begins I.i of the play: "Gregory." This too was a familiar saint's name, including St. Gregory the Great (sometimes called the apostle of the English), who had famously affirmed the legitimate use of icons. But it may also allude to Pope Gregory XIII, references to whose reformation of the calendar, in 1582, Steve Sohmer (1999) has deciphered in *Julius Caesar*. Friar Lawrence comments to Paris on the abbreviated temporal perspective of the play: "the time is very short." In a manner both like and unlike the hasty lovers and their equally hasty families, Gregory had shortened time; in his case, because he had to jump over or omit ten days – a figurative bank of time – in order to correct the faulty Julian calendar. This faulty calendar had been created, of course, by Julius Caesar, the man who gave his name to the month of July.

The events of *Romeo and Juliet* appear to unfold in the third week of July. Yet because of the ten-day gap between the old Julian calendar (still observed in England in the late sixteenth century) and the newly corrected Gregorian calendar, as pointed out by Sohmer, any spectator who recognized the validity of the new calendar might well have mentally adjusted the play's date-scheme: that is, moved it forward by ten days. And given the imagery used by the lovers, a Catholic member of Shakespeare's audience might well have inferred that Capulet's "old accustomed feast," held "a fortnight and odd days" before Juliet's anticipated fourteenth birthday (which according to the Julian calendar seems therefore to be sometime around July 14 or 15), is being held on what in the newly corrected Gregorian calendar was in fact the eve or feast day of St. James and St. Christopher, July 24 or 25. Certainly this was the only feast day in the latter part of July that was still observed by Reformed as well as Catholic countries. It is as a "pilgrim" and "palmer" that Romeo presents himself at Juliet's "shrine" – and finally, by implication, at her tomb, while the consummation of his marriage to this earthly saint is assisted by the use of another attribute of St. James – cords or ropes; the saint's traditional ability to untie the bonds of souls extended to a patronage of ropemakers. But James also has a biblical association with the motif of fire from heaven, since he shared with his brother John, Christ's most beloved disciple, the title of "Boanerges," son of thunder; in the Gospel of St. Luke, the brothers ask Jesus if they should command fire to come down from heaven and consume the Samaritans who have refused to receive him (Luke 9: 51–6). And within the play, the motif of an uncanny fire with a specific temporality has an important resonance. But in the decision of Romeo, on his way to the Capulet ball, to be a light-bearer there seems also to be an oblique allusion to James's companion saint, St. Christopher, who shared the same feast day: "Give me a torch, I am not for this ambling; / Being but heavy, I will bear the light" (I.iv.11–12). This saint, traditionally held to have been a giant from Canaan, owed his name to the story of his carrying the Christ-child (the light of the world) over a river or sea. In the medieval hagiographic imagination, this evidently fictional narrative concerning the giant's assistance of a holy traveler allied him, like St. James, with pilgrimage to the shrines of saints. Although St. Christopher's legend and cult was singled out for attack by both Erasmus and Luther, his association with the protection of travelers and pilgrims ensured him an especial veneration which survives to this day.[10]

If there is also an allusion to St. Christopher in the play's references to bearing a light, it seems in one sense extremely ironic, since one of this saint's additional but very important functions was to protect his devotees against a sudden death or *mors improvisa*. Nonetheless, the motif of carrying or bearing an uncanny light or fire that is also a burden is a central figurative element in *Romeo and Juliet*'s representation of death's strange duality, as the site of a mysterious chiasmus or reversal of meanings and perceptions which also appears to involve a disordering or crossing over of conventional temporality. In a multifaceted and encrypted trope, Macbeth would image his own tragic transgression both as crossing a river and as leaping over time, as he appears to reject a linear model of time encompassing both history (the present) and eternal judgment (the life to come): "here, upon this bank and shoal of time / We'd jump the life to come" (I.vii.6–7). In *Romeo and Juliet*, however, this act has a calendrical specificity that is not only festive, but also astrological.

For while the festive calendar of late July may plausibly have elicited "rites of memory" on the part of Elizabethan Catholics as well as half-hearted Protestants, it does not fully explain why that particular month was chosen as the setting for what Friar Lawrence calls the lovers' "violent delights." And here it is the residual trace, within Elizabethan calendrical culture, of classical astrological lore and timing that accounts for their conversion of orderly festivity – in the form of Capulet's "old accustomed feast" – into an extremity of sexual heat or mutually devouring *jouissance*: a *jouissance* of which *Ju*liet is, unconventionally, the most passionate advocate. "Starcrossed" by a "consequence yet hanging in the stars," the lovers seem to have fallen under the ambivalent influence of another, stellar mode of timing, and specifically that of the dog days, which the imagery of the play implies to have recently commenced. So the nurse tells Romeo that the letter which begins his name is "the dog's name, 'R' is for the –" (II.iv.205), as she inadvertently connects the growling "ar" of the dog with the arse, while Benvolio observes "Now these hot days is the mad blood stirring" (III.i.4).

Associated visually with the "enormous gaping jaws" of Leo, the chief star of the greater dog constellation, Sirius, was described by classical astronomers and astrologers as positioned in its mouth, like a fiery torch: "The tip of his [Canis Major's] terrible jaw is marked by a star that keenest of all blazes with a searing flame and him men call Serius" (Aratus 1969: 326–36). Traditionally, the dog days were a time of dramatic climactic extremes, which the ancients often figured by the fiery devouring mouth of the "thirsty" greater dog. As the burning heat of the sun was "doubled" in this period, it was sometimes compared to the phenomenon of *ekpyrosis*: this was the final conflagration in which, according to the Stoics, both linear time and the world were to end – only to be renewed, in a repeating cycle of fiery death and rebirth. Manilius observes that:

When the lion of Nemea [the constellation of Leo] lifts into view his enormous gaping
jaws, the brilliant constellation of the Dog appears: it barks forth flame, raves with its
fire, and doubles the burning heat of the sun. When it puts its torch to the earth and
discharges its rays, the earth foresees its conflagration, and tastes its ultimate fate . . .
the world looks for another world to repair it. (Manilius 1977: V, 206–14)

This ancient association of Sirius with a seasonal extreme that could be fatal to crops
extended both to humans and animals; in *The Gardens of Adonis*, his discussion of the
agricultural associations of this period in antiquity, Marcel Detienne concludes that
the appearance of the dog-star was believed to inaugurate a period of exaggerated
imbalance in humans, animals, and plants, involving a switching between opposite
extremes that included a kind of sexual role reversal (Detienne 1977: 120–2). It was
thought to be then that dogs were most prone to rabies, yet the dangers of the period
reputedly came from women as much as from dogs. The ancients had bizarrely opined
that the menstrual blood of virgins, which they believed was incompletely purged
because of their unbroken hymens, could become a dangerous poison in this period;
Pliny even went so far as to posit a sympathetic affinity between the two "poisons"
(of the rabid dog, and unpurged menstrual blood).[11] But Hesiod had famously
described women in general as having "a doglike spirit," and as "a flaming fire" that
burns a man alive by consuming his sexual strength.[12] It is in the dog days, according to Hesiod, that "women are most wanton, but men are feeblest, because Sirius
parches head and knees, and the skin is dry through heat."[13] Versions of these ancient
superstitions survived in Europe, in popular contexts such as the almanac, until the
seventeenth century; incredibly, it seems to have been quite widely believed that to
have sexual intercourse or to take medicine during the dog days was dangerous.[14]

Something of the peculiar intensity of the dog days is communicated in the
play's comical yet also enigmatic first scene, where the quibbles of Sampson and his
fellow servant Gregory on *coal-collar-choler* and *maidenhead* anticipate some of the play's
recurring motifs, as they figuratively elide darkness with light/heat and
mouths/necks/throats with the genitals:

Sampson.	Gregory, on my word, we'll not carry coals.
Gregory.	No, for then we should be colliers.
Samp.	I mean, and we be in choler, we'll draw.
Greg.	Ay, while you live, draw your neck out of collar. . . .
Samp.	I will show myself a tyrant, when I have fought with the men, I will be civil with the maids; I will cut off their heads.
Greg.	The heads of the maids?
Samp.	Ay, the heads of the maids, or their maidenheads, take it in what sense thou wilt.
Greg.	They must take it in sense that feel it.

(I.i.1–26)

To "carry coals" was a colloquialism for accepting an insult; however, the additional
sense here is of an inert matter suddenly becoming inflamed, producing a "choler" or

rage (the hottest humor) that may lead either to literal death (the "collar" of the hangman's noose) or to a sexual dying (the lost maidenheads).[15] The seasonal, or canicular, character of this rage is implied not just through Sampson's implied and clearly ironical association with the valor of his biblical namesake Samson, himself a famous riddle-teller, who had wrestled with the solar beast the lion, and was compared by St. Jerome to the sun (whose astrological sign was Leo); but also in his attribution of choler to "a dog of the house of Montague."[16] At the same time, the servants' riddling exchanges introduce the crucial question of what "sense" to make of such jests; the physical sense is clear enough, and may encompass an unspoken play on "coal" and *cul*, French for the backside or arse. Yet given the biblical and religious associations of their names, the servants' quibbling may hint at another level of meaning, fusing their imagery of a seasonal – canicular – choler and desire with allusions to an iconoclastic repetition of martyrdom, in order to extirpate the cults of the saints (from the Latin *colere*, to venerate). Much iconoclasm, of course, simply involved cutting off the heads of saints' statues, and Huston Diehl has recently drawn attention to the way in which Protestant iconoclasts tended to trope saints' images as both sexualized and feminized (Diehl 1998: 170–1).

Later in the first act, the ambivalent throat/mouth imagery which seems to evoke the fiery mouth of the dog-star as well as a fiery sexuality is associated with Juliet herself. In fact, the Nurse remembers Juliet's weaning "aleven years" ago through its metonymic association with an earthquake, in a troubling anticipation of that subterranean opening or "maw" of the tomb in which the lovers will literally die. The devouring as well as the nurturing associations of the mouth are likewise implied in the lovers' first meetings; at the feast, Romeo tropes Juliet's mouth as "saint's lips," while in Act V he reports a dream in which, as he imagines himself to be dead, she "breath'd such life with kisses in my lips / That I reviv'd, and was an emperor" (V.i.8–9). But in the balcony scene their love is figuratively allied with the predatory mouths of hawks (the "tassel-gentle" and the "niesse"), and on her wedding-night, Juliet asks Night to "Hood my unmanned blood, bating in my cheeks, / With thy black mantle" (III.ii.14–15).[17] Through these avian tropes, the familiar trope of a sexual dying is expanded to encompass physical death as a mutual feasting, in which an important part of the erotic pleasure seems to be that time is itself consumed as it consumes the lovers; as Mercutio comments to Romeo on their way to the Capulet ball: "we burn daylight" (I.iv.43).

Yet the ancient astrologers had also agreed that, while the canicular days brought to most of the world a doubling of solar heat which could have *disastrous* consequences (connoting injuries resulting from the stars), it could nonetheless confer exceptional blessings. It was because of the extreme heat of this time, Detienne points out, that the most precious spices – frankincense, myrrh, and balsam – could be harvested, and in Egyptian antiquity, the heliacal rising of Sirius had marked a time of renewed fertility by heralding the annual flooding of the Nile, which simultaneously inaugurated the Egyptian new year. Roman astrologers consequently stressed the perplexing duality of Sirius' effects. So Manilius observed:

No star comes on mankind more violently or causes more trouble when it departs. Now it rises shivering with cold, now it leaves a radiant world open to the heat of the Sun: thus it moves the world to either extreme and brings opposite effects. Those who . . . observe it ascending when it returns at its first rising learn of the various outcomes of harvest and seasons, what state of health lies in store, and what measure of harmony. It stirs up war and restores peace, and returning in different guise affects the world with the glance it gives it and governs with its mien. Sure proof that the star has this power are its colour and the quivering of the fire that sparkles in its face. Hardly is it inferior to the Sun . . . In splendour it surpasses all other constellations. (Manilius 1977: I, 396–417)

Certainly this play is full of ambivalent feasts – feasts whose festive or memorial function is always disturbingly altered. And it concludes with "the feasting presence" of Juliet's body in the tomb, as that "dearest morsel of the earth" upon which death's "detestable maw" has "gorg'd" itself. The imagery is consistent with Juliet's natal association with the Lammas festival of the first fruits of the harvest, yet her status as food seems also to have a sacrificial, quasi-Eucharistic dimension.

In conclusion, then, my argument is that the calendrical subtext of this play invites us to reconsider late July – together with its momentary presiding deity or "saint," Juliet – through several different temporal lenses, as it draws both on the perceived duality of Sirius' effects during the dog days and on the divided attitude of late Elizabethan society toward idolatry and the cults of the saints. The play seems to foreground both the disastrous and the benefic aspects of this month, which in a neglected crux from the last scene of the play is described by Escalus as "the moneth of out-rage"; in Quarto 1, he asks that Verona "Seal up the month of outrage for a while," although all later texts of the play replace "month" with "mouth" (V.iii.215).

By interweaving images of festivity and death with a calendrical specificity, the play identifies this fiery devouring mouth-like month with a familiar aspect of time – as devouring time – but it also suggests that, in the moment of heightened festive as well as erotic intensity, time briefly devours itself. The "candle-holder" or torch-bearer Romeo declares on first seeing Juliet that "she doth teach the torches to burn bright" (I.v.43), and the subsequent intensity of the lovers' torch-like passion is seemingly so great that it can briefly illuminate the Capulet funeral vault – as well as interrupting the hostility which has formerly characterized Veronese society.

But what Romeo's torch finally and most specifically illuminates, in a suggestive elision of the astrological motif of the dog days (the devouring mouth represented by Sirius) with the religious theme of the saints' conversion of human suffering into sacred festivity, is Juliet as an uncanny feast. It seems, however, that this feast which is not a feast – just as Juliet is and is not a corpse – requires a final garnish, in the form of Romeo's death on the body of his beloved. The Nurse has previously compared Romeo to rosemary – the herb that, as Ophelia reminds us, is "for remembrance" – and it is indeed the same herb which has already been "stuck" on Juliet's "fair corse" by her mourning relatives. Strewn at both weddings and funerals, rosemary's most common culinary usage was as an aid to taste and digestion, when it was "stuck" in an incision made by a knife in a joint of meat. This emblematic aspect of the tragic catastrophe appears to problematize the desire which informs all attempts at memory or remembrance, as it reminds us of memory's eventual consumption or death along with the temporal event – or feast – upon which it briefly "sticks."

Thus even as the plot interpellates the lovers and their fate in a calendrical cycle of seasonal repetition and cultural memorialization, their sudden deaths (*mortes improvisae*) appear to reveal a momentary rift, not simply in the calendar, but also in our very natural desire to shape and order temporality, through memory, into coherent historical forms. Derrida has described the instantaneous decision to make a gift of death as:

> irreducible to presence or to presentation, it demands a temporality of the instant without ever constituting a present . . . it belongs to an atemporal temporality, to a duration that cannot be grasped: something one can neither stabilize, establish, grasp, apprehend, comprehend. Understanding, common sense, and reason cannot seize, conceive, understand, or mediate it. (Derrida 1995: 65)

The *jouissance* which distinguishes the deaths of Romeo and Juliet resembles Derrida's description of an "atemporal temporality." Yet an important aspect of this quasi-sacrificial ecstasy is its suggestive transfiguration of remembrance. Like Romeo, remembrance is consumed along with the intensity of the moment or event – Juliet as feast – which it has both venerated and desired; nonetheless, it seems that, like a festive torch, this state of consciousness can briefly illuminate a momentary temporal fusion, as tragedy's historical singularity is interfused with the strangely recurrent patterns of a different timing.

NOTES

1 For several historians' views of this debate, see Ankersmit and Kellner (1995), where the "historical" is accepted as a rhetorical practice, a form of discourse, which can consequently produce "congeries of incompatible historical worlds" (Ankersmit and Kellner 1995: 18). See also recent issues of the journal *History and Theory*.

2 The term is Perry Anderson's, who reads poststructuralism as "the randomization of history." See Bennington, Attridge, and Young (1987: 4).

3 See for example Jeanneret (1998: ch. 7);

Barker (1993); Howard (1991); Baldo (1996); Berry (1999: ch. 5); Woolf (1990); Campion (1994).

4 Marie-Dominique Garnier (forthcoming) observes that "Juliet's solar name shifts throughout the play in a mobile, paronomastic fashion, from associations to *July* to *Jewel* and *Jule, Ay*, a configuration which displaces her towards another mobile character in the canon, Julius Caesar. Julius's own patronym is derived, according to Littré, from the Greek *youlos*, 'curly' – a loop-line, a loop-hole, a figure of deviance." Citations

from *Romeo and Juliet* are from the Arden edition, edited by Brian Gibbons (1988); all others from Shakespearean texts are from *The Norton Shakespeare*, edited by Stephen Greenblatt et al. (1997).

5 See *The Book of Common Prayer 1559*, edited by John E. Booty (1976). Booty comments: "The book is a product of the sixteenth century . . . Nothing is more striking in this regard than the appearance in the Almanac of the signs of the zodiac . . . It would be quite surprising to find these signs included in the Prayer Book, particularly in such a book as that prepared by Thomas Cranmer, a person who along with many other Reformers condemned the use of astrology, if we did not remember that Elizabeth not only had an Archbishop but also had her Dr Dee, and that John Jewel, Bishop of Salisbury, while arguing against soothsayers and the like, admitted their power. The presence of the signs in the Prayer Book should be understood against the background of the times and in relation to other writings, such as the *Preces privatae* (1564), wherein the zodiac is included in the calendar, presented in special tables, and explained for the common reader" (381–2).

6 See McAlindon (1991: 66) on Romeo as *romero*, a pilgrim. I am also indebted to Katherine Duncan-Jones for sharing with me her unpublished essay on *Romeo and Juliet*, "Star-Crossed and Double-Crossed," where she mentions this passage in Florio.

7 *The Second Tome of Homelyes* (1563: 2), "Agaynste parell of Idolatry and superfluous decking of churches," sigs. Dd4 ff.

8 I am grateful to François Laroque for directing me to this encyclopedic work.

9 The biblical Samson, taming the lion which was his most notable solar attribute, is carved over the gateway of Hoghton Towers in Lancashire, where Shakespeare is thought by some scholars to have spent part of his lost years in the service of a recusant Catholic household.

10 Embedded in these oblique and partially ironic allusions to this "canicular" saint (as Claude Gaignebet has described him) there may also be references to a holy traveler who was a much more immediate object of recusant piety and regret, and whose impetuous Counter-Reformation zeal seems similarly to have lacked the protection of St. Christopher: this is the Jesuit priest and martyr Edmund Campion. It may not be wholly coincidental, in this connection, that the "fearful date" of the lovers' first meeting, and the beginning of their tragedy, appears to be the eve or day of July 16. For this was the date of an event which had sent shock waves through the entire recusant community in the Midlands and North of England. On that day in 1581, some *fourteen years* before Shakespeare's presumed composition of his play, Campion was finally arrested, while saying mass at a house outside Oxford. (An additional coincidence is that the date chosen by Shakespeare for Juliet's anticipated fourteenth birthday, "a fortnight and odd days" later, July 31, was the day on which Campion was first put to the rack. July 31 was also the date of death in 1556 of the founder of the Jesuits, Ignatius Loyola; when Loyola was canonized in the seventeenth century, it became his feast day.)

11 For summaries of these arguments, see Gaignebet (1986: 271–3); and Vernant (1989: 21–86).

12 Hesiod, "Works and Days," ll. 67, 185, in Hesiod (1967). *The Homeric Hymns and Homerica*, trans. Hugh G. Evelyn White (London: Heinemann, 1967).

13 Ibid., 586–88.

14 See Capp (1979).

15 François Laroque notes that there is a possible (second meaning) Latin pun in this exchange, on head/*caput*, "that refers us directly to the name Capulet, so that the word 'maidenhead' could already be an indirect allusion to the play's heroine – Juliet Capulet" (Laroque 1995: 22).

16 St. Jerome thought that the name Samson was etymologically derived from *shemesh*, the Hebrew word for sun. See Gaignebet (1986: 343–6).

17 The solar association of these birds in Egyptian antiquity is noted in *The Hieroglyphics of Horapollo* (1993: I, 6–7).

REFERENCES AND FURTHER READING

Ankersmit, F. and Kellner, H. (eds.) 1995: *A New Philosophy of History*. London: Reaktion.

Aratus 1969: *Phaenomena*. Trans. G. R. Mair. London: Heinemann.

Baldo, J. 1996: "The Politics of Aloofness in *Macbeth*." *English Literary Renaissance*, 26, 3 (Autumn), 531–60.

Barker, F. 1993: *The Culture of Violence: Tragedy and History*. Manchester: Manchester University Press.

Bennington, G., Attridge, D., and Young, R. 1987: *Poststructuralism and the Question of History*. Cambridge: Cambridge University Press.

Berry, P. 1999: *Shakespeare's Feminine Endings: Disfiguring Death in the Tragedies*. London: Routledge.

The Book of Common Prayer (1559) 1976: Ed. John E. Booty. Charlottesville: University of Virginia Press.

Campion, N. 1994: *The Great Year: Astrology, Millenarianism and History in the Western Tradition*. Harmondsworth: Penguin.

Capp, B. 1979: *English Almanacs 1500–1800: Astrology and the Popular Press*. Ithaca: Cornell University Press.

Cressy, D. 1989: *Bonfires and Bells: National Memory and the Protestant Calendar in Elizabethan and Stuart England*. London: Weidenfeld and Nicolson.

Derrida, J. 1995: *The Gift of Death*. Trans. David Wills. Chicago: University of Chicago Press.

Detienne, M. 1977: *The Gardens of Adonis: Spices in Greek Mythology*. Trans. Janet Lloyd. New Jersey: Humanities Press.

Diehl, H. 1998: *Staging Reform, Reforming the Stage: Protestantism and Popular Theater in Early Modern England*. Ithaca: Cornell University Press.

Duffy, E. 1992: *The Stripping of the Altars: Traditional Religion in England 1400–1580*. New Haven: Yale University Press.

Gaignebet, C. 1986: *Au plus haut sens: L'Ésoterisme spirituel et charnel de Rabelais*. 2 vols. Paris: Maisonneuve et Larose.

Garnier, M.-D. forthcoming: "Philosophy and the Fairy, Madness and *The Method*." In Philippa Berry and Margaret Tudeau Clayton (eds.), *The Texture of Renaissance Knowledge*.

Hesiod 1967: *The Homeric Hymns and Homerica*. Trans. Hugh G. Evelyn White. London: Heinemann.

The Hieroglyphics of Horapollo 1993: Trans. George Boas. Princeton: Princeton University Press.

Howard, J. 1991: "Towards a Postmodern, Politically Committed, Historical Practice." In F. Barker et al. (eds.), *The Uses of History: Marxism, Postmodernisn and the Renaissance*. Manchester: Manchester University Press, 101–22.

Jeanneret, M. 1998: *Perpetuum Mobile: Métamorphoses des corps et des œuvres de Vinci à Montaigne*. Paris: Macula.

Kristeva, J. 1986a: *The Kristeva Reader*. Ed. Toril Moi. Oxford: Blackwell.

——1986b: "Women's Time." In *The Kristeva Reader*. Ed. Toril Moi. Oxford: Blackwell, 187–213.

Laroque, F. 1995: "Tradition and Subversion in *Romeo and Juliet*." In Jay L. Halio (ed.), *Shakespeare's "Romeo and Juliet": Texts, Contexts and Interpretations*. Newark, DE: University of Delaware Press, 18–36.

Lukacher, N. 1998: *Time Fetishes: The Secret History of Eternal Recurrence*. Durham, NC: Duke University Press.

McAlindon, T. 1991: *Shakespeare's Tragic Cosmos*. Cambridge: Cambridge University Press.

Manilius 1977: *Astronomica*. Trans. G. P. Gould. London: Heinemann.

Parker, P. 1996: *Shakespeare from the Margins: Language, Culture, Context*. Chicago and London: University of Chicago Press.

Rackin, P. 1990: *Stages of History: Shakespeare's English Chronicles*. London: Routledge.

The Second Tome of Homelyes 1563: London.

Shakespeare, W. 1988: *Romeo and Juliet*. The Arden edition. Ed. Brian Gibbons. London: Routledge.

——1997: *The Norton Shakespeare*. Ed. S. Greenblatt, W. Cohen, J. E. Howard, and K. E. Maus. New York and London: W. W. Norton.

Sohmer, S. 1999: *Shakespeare's Mystery Play: The*

Opening of the Globe Theatre, 1599. Manchester: Manchester University Press.

Vernant, J.-P. 1989: "At Man's Table: Hesiod's Foundation Myth of Sacrifice." In Marcel Detienne and J.-P. Vernant, *The Cuisine of Sac-* *rifice among the Greeks*. Trans. Paula Wissy. Chicago: University of Chicago Press.

Woolf, D. R. 1990: *The Idea of History in Early Stuart England*. Toronto: University of Toronto Press.

Index

absolutism, 28–9, 32–9
Adams, F., 211
Adelman, J., 329
Aetius of Amida, 211
affirmative action, 231–2
Africa, 210–12, 213, 215, 218–19
Alberti, L. B., 302
Albucasis, 211
Algiers, 219, 220
Alley, Hugh, 51
All's Well That Ends Well: class distinctions in, 255; *dramatis personae* in, 73; Helena's virtues, 45; marriage in, 252; misogyny in, 68; tears in, 65
Althusser, L., 107, 117, 277
Amazons, 163–4, 173–5, 178
American Shakespeare Magazine, 5, 21
Amussen, S. D., 124
Andreadis, H., 297
Angelou, Maya, 18
Ankersmit, F. and Kellner, H., 369
Anne, Queen, 53
annotation: background, 63–4; of bawdiness, 68–71; and different belief systems, 66–7; and editorial glosses, 65, 66–8, 310; linguistic sensitivity, 67–8; misogynist, 63–8; and racism, 64; and sexual slang, 64, 69–70; use of notes, 64; and women's tears, 64–5; *see also* feminist editing
Antony and Cleopatra: female relationships in, 310–11; queen as object of pollution, 44–5; use of "whore" in, 90
Arber, E., 166

Arden of Faversham: rebellious wives in, 121, 125, 126–9
Arden Shakespeare, 62; bawdiness in, 69; on blueness, 221; tears in, 65
Ariès, P., 324
Aristophanes, 59
Aristotle, 215
Arunima, G., 177
As You Like It: address to female playgoers, 53; Audrey in, 251–3, 258; boys as women as boys in, 252–8; Celia in, 254–7, 258; containment of Rosalind in, 46–7; and female-headed households, 50; as gender-sensitive, 61–3; lovesickness in, 285, 291–6; Phoebe in, 253–4, 258; Rosalind in, 254–7, 258–61; women as boys as women in, 258–61
Astell, Mary, 23
attainment of desires, 138
Auden, W. H., 341
Augustine, St., 103, 110–11, 342–3
Averroës, 211
Avicenna (Ibn Sena), 211

Bacon, Delia, 18–19
Bacon, Lady, 18
Bacon, Sir Francis, 18–19
Baker, J. H., 344
Bakke, A., 231
Baldo, J., 369
Balfour, Lord, 3, 17
Ballaster, R., 29
banquet, 302–3, 306